# Lecture Notes in Computer Science 11771

More information about this series at http://www.springer.com/series/7408

Manuel Mazzara · Jean-Michel Bruel ·
Bertrand Meyer · Alexander Petrenko (Eds.)

# Software Technology: Methods and Tools

51st International Conference, TOOLS 2019
Innopolis, Russia, October 15–17, 2019
Proceedings

Springer

*Editors*
Manuel Mazzara ⓘ
Innopolis University
Innopolis, Russia

Jean-Michel Bruel ⓘ
IUT de Blagnac
Blagnac, France

Bertrand Meyer ⓘ
Innopolis University
Innopolis, Russia

Alexander Petrenko ⓘ
Ivannikov Institute for System Programming
Russian Academy of Sciences
Moscow, Russia

ISSN 0302-9743          ISSN 1611-3349   (electronic)
Lecture Notes in Computer Science
ISBN 978-3-030-29851-7          ISBN 978-3-030-29852-4   (eBook)
https://doi.org/10.1007/978-3-030-29852-4

LNCS Sublibrary: SL2 – Programming and Software Engineering

This Springer imprint is published by the registered company Springer Nature Switzerland AG
The registered company address is: Gewerbestrasse 11, 6330 Cham, Switzerland

# Preface

Started in 1989, the TOOLS conference series has played a major role in the development of object technology and has contributed in making it popular, mainstream, and ubiquitous. The 50th edition of the series "The Triumph of Objects," was held in Prague in 2012 and was meant to be the closing edition for a conference that had brought, to a large audience, ideas originally shared only by a niche. After an interruption of seven years, TOOLS now starts again with a scope extended to software technologies and applications and all the modern approaches to software engineering, robotics, and machine learning.

The edition 50th+1 was held at Innopolis University, the educational center of the techno-city of Tatarstan, Russia. The numbering (50+1) is to emphasize the reopening of the series and celebrate it. The venue, being one of the most recently established universities in the world (2012), seemed to be the right place to celebrate a synergy between tradition and future. This volume contains the papers presented at TOOLS 50 +1 during the period October 15–17, 2019. There were 62 submissions. Each submission was reviewed by at least three Program Committee members. The committee decided to accept 32 papers, including long and short contributions. The program also includes four invited talks.

The conference was made possible by the joint effort of several colleagues and departments. We would like to thank Bertrand Meyer and Alexandr Tormasov in their role as general chairs, as well as Inna Baskakova, Oksana Zhirosh, Sergey Masyagin, Giancarlo Succi, Alberto Sillitti, Andrey Sadovykh, Mansur Khazeev, and Alexandr Naumchev for supporting the creation and organization of the event. JooYoung Lee, Adil Adelshin, and Sophie Ebersold were instrumental in promoting the conference in Russia and abroad. Last but not least the Program Committee that operated effectively in defining the program (a full list of names of additional reviewers is included in this volume). The process of volume preparation was enabled and simplified by a fundamental tool like EasyChair. Financially, we have also received the support of Eiffel Software, SOFTEAM, and Springer, which funded the Best Paper Awards.

July 2019

Manuel Mazzara
Jean-Michel Bruel
Bertrand Meyer
Alexander Petrenko

# Organization

## Program Committee

| | |
|---|---|
| Muhammad Ahmad | Messina University, Italy |
| Danilo Ardagna | Politecnico di Milano, Italy |
| Marco Autili | Università dell'Aquila, Italy |
| Sergey Avdoshin | National Research University Higher School of Economics, Russia |
| Luciano Baresi | Politecnico di Milano, Italy |
| Alexandre Bergel | University of Chile, Chile |
| Jean Bezivin | Software Consultant, France |
| Judith Bishop | University of Stellenbosch, South Africa |
| Jean-Michel Bruel | IRIT, France |
| Antonio Bucchiarone | FBK-IRST, Italy |
| Paolo Ciancarini | University of Bologna, Italy |
| Salvatore Distefano | Messina University, Italy |
| Nicola Dragoni | Technical University of Denmark, Denmark |
| Catherine Dubois | ENSIIE-Samovar, France |
| Schahram Dustdar | Vienna University of Technology, Austria |
| Angelo Gargantini | University of Bergamo, Italy |
| Adil Khan | Innopolis University, Russia |
| Victor Kuliamin | Institute for System Programming, Russian Academy of Sciences, Russia |
| Cosimo Laneve | University of Bologna, Italy |
| Jooyoung Lee | Innopolis University, Russia |
| Manuel Mazzara | Innopolis University, Russia |
| Hernan Melgratti | Universidad de Buenos Aires, Argentina |
| Bertrand Meyer | ETH Zurich, Switzerland |
| Raffaela Mirandola | Politecnico di Milano, Italy |
| James Noble | Victoria University of Wellington, New Zealand |
| Manuel Oriol | ABB Corporate Research, Sweden |
| Richard Paige | University of York, UK |
| Alexander K. Petrenko | ISP RAS, Russia |
| Mauro Pezzè | University of Lugano, Switzerland |
| Victor Rivera | Australian National University, Australia |
| Andrey Sadovykh | Softeam, France |
| Ebersold Sophie | IRIT, France |
| Jan Vitek | Northeastern University, USA |
| Jim Woodcock | University of York, UK |
| Gianluigi Zavattaro | University of Bologna, Italy |

## Additional Reviewers

Ali, Mohsin
De Sanctis, Martina
Giaretta, Alberto
Ivanov, Vladimir
Kumar, Devender
Ligozat, Anne-Laure
Missiroli, Marcello
Nibouche, Omar
Strugar, Dragos
Veschetti, Adele

# Abstracts of Invited Talks

# Science of Computing: From Functions and Sequentiality to Processes and Concurrency

Davide Sangiorgi

Focus Team, University of Bologna and Inria

**Abstract.** The first part of the talk will be about history: I will discuss the origins of a few important concepts of concurrency theory, and how these concepts have changed the meaning of 'Science of Computing'.

The second part of the talk will focus on one of such concepts, namely coinduction. Coinduction is the dual of induction – a pervasive tool in Computer Science and Mathematics for defining objects and proving properties on them. Today coinduction is widely used in Computer Science, but also in other fields, including Artificial Intelligence, Cognitive Science, Mathematics, Modal Logics, Philosophy, particularly for reasoning about objects that may be potentially infinite or circular. If time permits I will show examples in which coinductive techniques are combined with other techniques, such as inductive techniques or type-based techniques or techniques based on unique-solution of equations [1–3].

# References

1. Durier, A., Hirschkoff, D., Sangiorgi, D.: Eager functions as processes. In: 33nd Annual ACM/IEEE Symposium on Logic in Computer Science. LICS 2018. IEEE Computer Society (2018)
2. Pous, D., Sangiorgi, D.: Enhancements of the bisimulation proof method. In: Sangiorgi, D., Rutten, J. (eds.) Advanced Topics in Bisimulation and Coinduction. Cambridge University Press (2012)
3. Sangiorgi, D.: Typed $\pi$-calculus at work: a correctness proof of Jones's parallelisation transformation on concurrent objects. Theory Pract. Object Syst. **5**(1), 25–34 (1999)

# Design and Assurance Methods for Dependable Cyber Physical Systems

Sergey Tverdyshev

sergey.tverdyshev@sysgo.com

**Abstract.** Cyber-Physical Systems (CPS) control modern critical infrastructures such as connected cars, train networks, airplanes. Nowadays these systems are functioning in complex environments with mixed safety and security criticalities. The design of these systems is the first important step to enable a trustworthy and affordable assurance for safety and security. We stress the word "affordable", in the both senses time and needed human resources, as one of the ways for adoption and achieving impact. We cover the state of the art for deployments for critical infrastructures and we present how a typical CPS is built. To illustrate the nitty-gritty details, we show how a CPS can be attacked. The main design challenges are introduced separately for safety and security properties. We present a MILS framework for designing safety/security critical systems with composable assurance. We discuss different types of assurances: what has to be achieved and what are the challenges to solve.

**Keywords:** Cyber-physical-systems · Mixed-criticality · Safety · Security · Assurance · Certification · MILS.

# Kent Beck or Pablo Picasso? Speculations of the Relationships Between Artists in Software and Painting

Sergey Masyagin, Milana Nurgalieva, and Giancarlo Succi

Innopolis University, Innopolis, Russia
{s.masyagin,m.nurgalieva}@innopolis.ru
giancarlo.succi@gmail.com

**Abstract.** The way software is created is somehow similar to the process of creating pieces of artwork. To consider this issue further we have considered the similarities between the software development process and painting in the quest for artistic practices that are transferable to software.

# Towards an Anatomy of Software Requirements

Bertrand Meyer[1,2,3], Jean-Michel Bruel[2], Sophie Ebersold[2],
Florian Galinier[2], and Alexandr Naumchev[1,2]

[1] Innopolis University, Innopolis, Russia
[2] University of Toulouse/IRIT, Blagnac Cedex, France
bruel@irit.fr
[3] Schaffhausen Institute of Technology, Schaffhausen, Switzerland

**Abstract.** Requirements engineering is crucial to software development but lacks a precise definition of its fundamental concepts. Even the basic definitions in the literature and in industry standards are often vague and verbose. To remedy this situation and provide a solid basis for discussions of requirements, this work provides precise definitions of the fundamental requirements concepts and two systematic classifications: a taxonomy of requirement elements (such as components, goals, constraints...); and a taxonomy of possible relations between these elements (such as "extends", "excepts", "belongs"...). The discussion evaluates the taxonomies on published requirements documents; readers can test the concepts in two online quizzes. The intended result of this work is to spur new advances in the study and practice of software requirements by clarifying the fundamental concepts.

# Contents

## Machine Learning

## Internet of Things

# Invited Talks and Papers

# Kent Beck or Pablo Picasso?
# Speculations of the Relationships Between
# Artists in Software and Painting

Sergey Masyagin, Milana Nurgalieva, and Giancarlo Succi[✉]

Innopolis University, Innopolis, Russia
{s.masyagin,m.nurgalieva}@innopolis.ru, giancarlo.succi@gmail.com

**Abstract.** The way software is created is somehow similar to the process of creating pieces of artwork. To consider this issue further we have considered the similarities between the software development process and painting in the quest for artistic practices that are transferable to software.

**Keywords:** Software development · Painting · Agile methods

## 1 Software and Art

We can have the fortune of seeing Kent Beck coding, unfortunately we cannot any more see Pablo Picasso painting. Still, looking at the two there could be some striking similarity, and this beyond the inevitable fashion that surround them. This lead us to think that software is not only engineering but it has components of art and craft. There are many reasons supporting this claim.

For instance, as in any artwork, at the very beginning, it is hard to say exactly, what the final product will be, as aspects influencing development software changes fluently. Hence, it is difficult to plan everything in advance or even if any plan exists - it is always hard to follow. These circumstances make the result of developing software application unpredictable and unique (which is characteristic of artwork) and, of course, raise an issue of project management.

As another example, there is a similar step at the beginning of work for both artists and software engineers: artists do a sketch before writing a picture and developers do the design of the application before development is started. Also, both painters and programmers often use an iterative and incremental approach in their work: breaking down work into smaller chunks, work on them and only after the main part complete do gradual refinement.

Existed approaches to manage software processes have almost never discussed how to manage creative people, hence the question is whether we can find useful approaches present in art that can be applied to software development.

Indeed, we need a starting point, so we focuses our attention to painting.

M. Mazzara et al. (Eds.): TOOLS 2019, LNCS 11771, pp. 3–9, 2019.
https://doi.org/10.1007/978-3-030-29852-4_1

## 2   Background

The idea of linking software development and art has been already explored in the past, though mostly superficially. In 1962 Donald Knuth started a series of volumes titles "The Art of Computer Programming," which started to be printed from 1968 and which is mostly incomplete [11]. In the 80's Sterling and Shapiro wrote a book titled "The Art of Prolog" using the term "art" as a metaphor for software development [18]. More recently Herlihy and Shavit published "The Art of Multiprocessor Programming" [9].

There is also a book named "Hackers[1] and Painters" written by Graham [8], where the author considers some similarities between developers and visual artists. He also suggests lessons, that software developers can learn from artists (these lessons are presented below).

## 3   How We Are Progressing

Our work now focuses on investigating the similarities between software development and painting, to verify that these areas have something in common, and to support the hypothesis that software engineers really have something to learn from artists.

To this end we care considering specific situations, like how artists create paintings in pairs and explore other artistic practices to identify whether artistic methods can be transferred into software. Doing this it is expected to select appropriate techniques and determine how it could be applicable to software development.

A similar approach is then linked to how art work is being licensed in comparison to software [6,12,15,16,19] or the overall ideas of transforming selfies and images made from mobile devices forms of art [3–5].

Eventually expected to come out with methods that could be useful for software developers to improve the process of creating an application.

Our idea is both to work at two levels:

1. studying the existing works via reading the literature, visiting exhibitions, etc, and then formulating hypothesis and theses,
2. interviewing existing artists, also trying to verify our hypotheses and validate our theses.

## 4   Early Results

At the moment intermediate results have been obtained, specifically: revealed some similarities between software development and drawing, the literature review has been conducted and several artists have been interviewed.

As mentioned, the starting point for the research was the ideas presented in the mentioned book "Hackers and Painters" [8], namely:

---

[1] by "hackers" the author refers to developers.

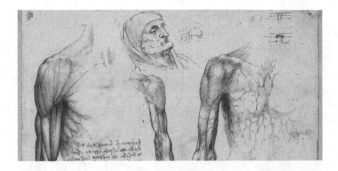

**Fig. 1.** Various sketches of Leonardo with his comments

**Fig. 2.** A sketch by the Russian painter Repin to the Italian singer Eleonora Duse

- Painters and software developers "... are both makers"
- Painters and software developers both try to make good things.
- Painters and software developers in the course of trying to make good things discover new techniques.
- "In hacking (programming), like painting, work comes in cycles."
- Software like painting is intended for a human audience.

These findings support the hypothesis that developers have something to learn from artists.

This can be elaborated further analyzing [13], where it is evidenced that the way a painting is conceived and created is not simple, as it might seem. Each painting requires a particular, individual approach, therefore, special methods and techniques are required for its solution. There are no exact recipes for creating pictures. This is also true for software development.

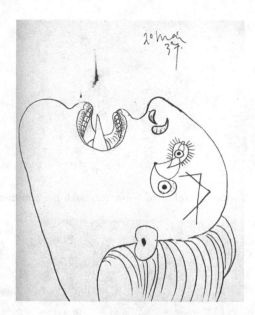

**Fig. 3.** A sketch of Picasso of his famous painting "Guernica"

Another similarity lies in the creation cycle of a picture: painters of most styles of art have performed sketches, from Leonardo (Fig. 1), to Repin (Fig. 2), to Picasso (Fig. 3), etc. Then, they divide the work in self-contained parts, like in a spiral or agile approach, and then operate, and, when needed, they performs changes [7,10]. This is really like software and if the reader had the privilege of seeing Kent Beck at work, s/he would find a stunning similarity!

Another notable point is that other painters, like Serov, approach very systematically their work, fully involving prototyping and interaction with customers, as it is evident in his masterpiece "Girl with Peaches" (see Fig. 4), coming out of an intense interaction with the subject, ad discussed in wikipedia[2]. This principle is especially familiar to agile software developers ("Customer collaboration over contract negotiation" [2]) and to people employing domain analysis techniques or software measurement approaches [17,20,21].

Also, there is a genre in painting, which is similar to what developers call a technical assignments or software requirement specification. This genre is named "Art by instruction" [1,22], it is characterized by the creation of a work of art with the help of instructions written by the artist. The main objective of which is to create an open work with a variable end with the possibility of different interpretations of the author's text-instructions.

Another analogy existed between painters and developers is that their work is supported by best practices, rather than by formal methods, or how the learning process occurs [7,14].

---

[2] See URL https://en.wikipedia.org/wiki/Girl_with_Peaches, visited on May 20, 2019.

**Fig. 4.** The "Girl with Peaches" by Serov

## 4.1 Lessons

Literature review brings ideas about what artistic techniques could be applied to software engineering and what lessons developers could learn from artists. For example, P. Graham relying on observation on artists suggests the following lessons [8]:

- Developers need to program to learn.
- Regularly start from scratch, instead of working on one project for years.
- Developers need to learn from the source code of good programs.
- Developers need to write programs in a way that allows specifications to change on the fly.
- Right model for collaboration: "... when painters worked together on a painting, they never worked on the same parts. It was common for the master to paint the principal figures and for assistants to paint the others and the background. But you never had one guy painting over the work of another."

To this end it is interesting to consider the work of Yakovleva [23], where she analyses best practices for the success of the joint work of the two artists Alexander Yakovlev and Vasily Shukhaev:

- Division of work and doing your job in your own temp (the division of work allows Shuhaev to accomplish picture 52 years later after Yakovlev finish his part)
- Both painters studied in one academy of arts and had the same level of training.
- The artists had a common vision and common methods of work.

This information is valuable and even could be projected onto the software development domain.

## 5   Conclusion

In this document we have presented preliminary considerations on the similarities between software development and painting. We have identified a high level of congruence and claimed that specific methodologies coming from painting can also be applied to software.

Our next step would be to move forward with this idea, exploring more in deep the analogies and the differences and elaborating a pervasive and convincing set of ideas and practices that could be beneficial for software.

**Acknowledgments.** The work presented in this paper was supported by the grant of Russian Science Foundation №19-19-00623.

## References

1. Altshuler, B.: Art by instruction and the pre-history of do it
2. Beck, K., et al.: Manifesto for agile software development (2001)
3. Corral, L., Georgiev, A.B., Sillitti, A., Succi, G.: A method for characterizing energy consumption in Android smartphones. In: 2nd International Workshop on Green and Sustainable Software (GREENS 2013), pp. 38–45. IEEE, May 2013
4. Corral, L., Sillitti, A., Succi, G.: Software development processes for mobile systems: is agile really taking over the business? In: 2013 1st International Workshop on the Engineering of Mobile-Enabled Systems (MOBS), pp. 19–24, May 2013
5. Corral, L., Sillitti, A., Succi, G., Garibbo, A., Ramella, P.: Evolution of mobile software development from platform-specific to web-based multiplatform paradigm. In: Proceedings of the 10th SIGPLAN Symposium on New Ideas, New Paradigms, and Reflections on Programming and Software, Onward! 2011, pp. 181–183. ACM, New York (2011)
6. Di Bella, E., Sillitti, A., Succi, G.: A multivariate classification of open source developers. Inf. Sci. **221**, 72–83 (2013)
7. Fronza, I., Sillitti, A., Succi, G.: An interpretation of the results of the analysis of pair programming during novices integration in a team. In: Proceedings of the 2009 3rd International Symposium on Empirical Software Engineering and Measurement, ESEM 2009, pp. 225–235. IEEE Computer Society (2009)
8. Graham, P.: Hackers & Painters: Big Ideas from the Computer Age. O'Reilly Media, Newton (2004)

9. Herlihy, M., Shavit, N.: The Art of Multiprocessor Programming. Morgan Kaufmann Publishers Inc., San Francisco (2008)
10. Kivi, J., Haydon, D., Hayes, J., Schneider, R., Succi, G.: Extreme programming: a university team design experience. In: 2000 Canadian Conference on Electrical and Computer Engineering. Conference Proceedings. Navigating to a New Era (Cat. No.00TH8492), vol. 2, pp. 816–820, May 2000
11. Knuth, D.E.: The Art of Computer Programming. Addison-Wesley Professional, Boston (2011)
12. Kovács, G.L., Drozdik, S., Zuliani, P., Succi, G.: Open source software for the public administration. In: Proceedings of the 6th International Workshop on Computer Science and Information Technologies, October 2004
13. Ostrovskij, G.: In Russian: Kak sozdayetsya kartina. In English: How the picture is created. Gosudarstvennaya Akademiya Hudozhestvennyh nauk (1962)
14. Pedrycz, W., Russo, B., Succi, G.: Knowledge transfer in system modeling and its realization through an optimal allocation of information granularity. Appl. Soft Comput. **12**(8), 1985–1995 (2012)
15. Petrinja, E., Sillitti, A., Succi, G.: Comparing OpenBRR, QSOS, and OMM assessment models. In: Ågerfalk, P., Boldyreff, C., González-Barahona, J.M., Madey, G.R., Noll, J. (eds.) OSS 2010. IAICT, vol. 319, pp. 224–238. Springer, Heidelberg (2010). https://doi.org/10.1007/978-3-642-13244-5_18
16. Rossi, B., Russo, B., Succi, G.: Adoption of free/libre open source software in public organizations: factors of impact. Inf. Technol. People **25**(2), 156–187 (2012)
17. Sillitti, A., Janes, A., Succi, G., Vernazza, T.: Measures for mobile users: an architecture. J. Syst. Architect. **50**(7), 393–405 (2004)
18. Sterling, L., Shapiro, E.: The Art of Prolog. MIT Press, Cambridge (1986)
19. Succi, G., Paulson, J., Eberlein, A.: Preliminary results from an empirical study on the growth of open source and commercial software products. In: EDSER-3 Workshop, pp. 14–15 (2001)
20. Valerio, A., Succi, G., Fenaroli, M.: Domain analysis and framework-based software development. SIGAPP Appl. Comput. Rev. **5**(2), 4–15 (1997)
21. Vernazza, T., Granatella, G., Succi, G., Benedicenti, L., Mintchev, M.: Defining metrics for software components. In: Proceedings of the World Multiconference on Systemics, Cybernetics and Informatics, vol. XI, pp. 16–23, July 2000
22. Vladislava, R.: In Russian: Stanovleniye kontseptsii "iskusstva po-instruktsii". In English: Formation of the concept of "art on-instructions". Art & Cult, pp. 72–77 (2017)
23. Yakovleva, E.: Russian: Eto bylo schastliveysheye vremya...(a.ye. yakovlev, v.i. shukhayev i v.e. meyyerkhol'd. k istorii sozdaniya dvoynogo avtoportreta a. yakovleva i v. shukhayeva arlekin i p'yero) english: It was the happiest time...(a.e. yakovlev, v.i. shuhaev i v.eh. mejerhol'd. to the history of the creation of a double self-portrait of a. yakovlev and v. shukhaev "harlequin and pierrot"), Neva, pp. 171–176 (1987)

# Towards an Anatomy of Software Requirements

Bertrand Meyer[1,2,3], Jean-Michel Bruel[2(✉)], Sophie Ebersold[2],
Florian Galinier[2], and Alexandr Naumchev[1,2]

[1] Innopolis University, Innopolis, Russia
[2] University of Toulouse/IRIT, Blagnac Cedex, France
bruel@irit.fr
[3] Schaffhausen Institute of Technology, Schaffhausen, Switzerland

**Abstract.** Requirements engineering is crucial to software development
but lacks a precise definition of its fundamental concepts. Even the basic
definitions in the literature and in industry standards are often vague
and verbose. To remedy this situation and provide a solid basis for discussions of requirements, this work provides precise definitions of the
fundamental requirements concepts and two systematic classifications:
a taxonomy of requirement elements (such as components, goals, constraints...); and a taxonomy of possible relations between these elements
(such as "extends", "excepts", "belongs" ...). The discussion evaluates
the taxonomies on published requirements documents; readers can test
the concepts in two online quizzes. The intended result of this work is
to spur new advances in the study and practice of software requirements
by clarifying the fundamental concepts.

## 1 Introduction

A software system, like any other engineering construction, exists to satisfy certain human objectives, known as its requirements. The evolution of software
engineering has produced ample evidence that the quality of systems fundamentally depends on the quality of their requirements.

It has also led to the realization that *requirements are software*: like code,
tests and other products of the software process, requirements for today's ambi-
tious systems are software artifacts, susceptible to some of the same practices
(such as configuration management), and in need of theoretical studies. The
present discussion defines a standard framework for such studies.

Section 2 explains the scope of the discussion. Section 3 defines basic terminology. The next two sections provide the principal contribution of this work in
the form of two taxonomies: a taxonomy of requirement elements themselves in
Sect. 4; and a taxonomy of relations between requirements in Sect. 5. The rest
of the discussion explores the application of these concepts: Sect. 6 applies the
taxonomies to analyze an extract from a representative requirements document;
Sect. 7 examines popular approaches to requirements engineering in light of the

© Springer Nature Switzerland AG 2019
M. Mazzara et al. (Eds.): TOOLS 2019, LNCS 11771, pp. 10–40, 2019.
https://doi.org/10.1007/978-3-030-29852-4_2

taxonomies; after a discussion of related work in Sect. 8, Sect. 9 assesses the applicability of the approach and prospects for future work, including automatic analysis.

Two online quizzes [9,10] enable readers to test anonymously their understanding of the taxonomies of requirements and relations.

## 2 Scope

This presentation is *descriptive* rather than prescriptive. Textbooks are an example of prescriptive presentation, stating how one should write requirements. Here the intent is to study requirements as they are, which in the industry's practice does not always mean as they should be. For example, the relationship taxonomy (Sect. 5) has a category for requirements that contradict each other, a case that is obviously not desirable but occurs in practice. Prescriptive discussions will benefit from the analysis, since they should be rooted in a precise understanding of the concepts. Occasionally, as in Sect. 9, the discussion veers into prescriptive territory.

The presentation is, however, *normative*, since it proposes standard definitions and classifications of requirement concepts and terminology relevant to requirements authors regardless of which methodology they follow.

Its ambition is also *universal*: we have tried to cover all possible properties of requirements, with the understanding that this work should be revised if we missed any. In this spirit, enumerations (see for example the list of activities in the definition of "project" in Sect. 3.1) never end with such phrases as "*etc.*", useful to protect authors but detrimental to the quality of definitions. Here there is no such protection; any omission is a mistake and will have to be corrected.

While Sect. 9 is the place for a more detailed analysis of the applicability of this work, it is legitimate to ask at the outset for a general justification: why is it worthwhile to engage in such an effort at precision (at the risk of pedantry) to define and classify concepts that are widely used in practice with their intuitive meaning?

The general justification is that requirements are a difficult concept to apprehend because they straddle the border between the formal and the informal, the exact and the approximate, the technical and the human. Some software engineering concepts are formal, exact and technical: programming languages, for example, have precise definitions, and any single detail of a million-line program may critically affect its correctness. At the other end of the spectrum, equally important concepts of software engineering, such as methods of project management, are informal, approximate and human.

Requirements bridge these two worlds. To be effective, they must cover the needs of both. Insufficient rigor in the handling of requirements concepts hampers this goal. As an example, there is wide disagreement in the field as to what constitutes the difference between "functional" and "non-functional" requirements, to the point that some authors even reject this distinction altogether. The rest of the literature treats it as a given, but without a generally agreed precise definition.

A software system is often just one part of a larger system whose other elements may be people and organizations, as in enterprise systems, or physical devices, as in cyber-physical systems. While the authors' primary interest and the examples in this article are software-related, the intent of the definitions and taxonomies is to encompass systems of any kind.

# 3   Underlying Concepts

To discuss requirements we need a set of basic concepts and their precise definition. This section introduces the terminology that serves as a basis for the rest of the discussion. It does not intentionally introduce any novel concept, but gives precise definitions of known concepts. These definitions are not the most general possible ones for the corresponding English words as used in an arbitrary context; rather, they are tailored to the needs of this discussion of requirements.

## 3.1   General Concepts

**Universe of Discourse.** The assumed context for the present discussion is a *project* to develop a *system* in a certain *environment*.

*Comment*: the definitions of project, system and environment follow.

**Definition.** A *system* is a set of related artifacts.

*Comment*: In the case of pure software systems, the artifacts are virtual: programs, databases, design diagrams, test cases... In line with the goals stated in Sect. 2, the definition is more general, encompassing enterprise and cyber-physical systems. Even if the system involves only software, the project and the environment may include material and human elements.

**Definition.** A *project* is the set of human processes involved in the planning, construction, revision and operation of a system.

*Comments*:

- A project is, per this definition, applied to one system. While a project can in practice involve the development of several systems, the definition loses no generality since we can consider them, for the purpose of the definition, to be subsystems of one larger system.
- A particular project may involve only some of the activities mentioned (planning, construction, revision, operation). In particular, the revision of a system (which may also be called maintenance, reconstruction, redesign, evolution and "brownfield development") can be an extension of a previous project for this system, or a new project.

**Definition.** An *environment* for a project or system is the set of entities (people, organizations, regulations, devices and other material objects, other systems) external to the project or system but with the potential to affect it or be affected by it.

*Comments*: the environment is also called, in classic Jackson-Zave terminology [12], the "domain". It includes all external elements constraining the project or the system; "external" in the sense that unlike features of the system and project they are imposed from the outside and not susceptible to decisions by the project. As an example of the difference, *"all accounts must maintain a non-negative balance at all times"* is an environment property (affecting the system); *"a withdrawal request for an amount greater than the balance shall produce an error message and leave the balance unchanged"* is a system property, devised to enforce the preceding environment property. Similarly, *"at least 50% of the code shall be developed in-house"* is an environment property (affecting the project); *"the implementation of the user interface module shall be outsourced to company X"* is a project property, which should comply with the environment property.

Environment properties in requirements will be called *constraints* (Sect. 4.1.F).

## 3.2  Properties and Their Statements

The definition of "requirement" will use the auxiliary concept of "statement", itself relying on the notion of "property" (a term already used informally). These are general term, not specific to software or requirements; although they essentially retain their ordinary meaning, it is useful for the purposes of the present work to give them precise, slightly more restricted definitions.

**Definition.** A *property* is a boolean predicate.

*Comments*: an example of property is that today is Sunday, a predicate (true or false in a given context). The properties of interest for this discussion will apply to a project, system or environment. A system example is the property that response time for a certain kind of query must not exceed one second. A project example is the property that the project uses sprints (iterations) of one month each. An environment example is the property that no more than 50 vehicles at a time are permitted in a tunnel.

**Definition.** A *statement* is a human-readable expression of a property.
  *Comments*:

- Discussions of programming languages use the term "statement" to mean "instruction", a command to be executed by a computer (prescriptive). Instead "statement" as used here retains the same connotation as in ordinary English: a phrasing that "states" a property (descriptive).
- *"Today is Sunday"* and *"query response time shall not exceed one second"* are statements. The difference between a property and a statement is that the

property is the abstract predicate and a statement its expression in a certain notation. Different statements can express the same property; for example the statement *"c'est aujourd'hui dimanche"* is a different statement (in French) of the first example's property.

- A statement, however, specifies just one property. This convention causes no loss of generality since a property, being a predicate, can be built out of logical combinators such as "and" and "or", and hence arbitrarily complex. The next definition will reflect this observation.
- Not all statements have to be expressed, like the preceding examples, in natural language: a statement could be a UML diagram specifying a system property, a mathematical formula describing a constraint property, a PERT diagram or (in agile development) a burndown chart specifying a task property. For any statement, it should be clear what underlying notation it uses (see the notion of "requirement type" in Sect. 3.5).

**Definition.** A property, and a statement expressing it, are ***composite*** if the property is a logical combination of simpler properties, and ***elementary*** otherwise.

*Comments*: since a property is a boolean predicate, it may result from applying boolean operators to one or more simpler properties, in which case we call it composite.

**Definition.** A composite property, and a composite statement expressing it, are ***homogeneous*** if the property combines properties of a similar nature, and ***heterogeneous*** otherwise.

*Examples*: *"customers will have access to customer functions, and employees to both customer and flight management functions"* (from [4]) is homogeneous. *"Error messages shall be recorded in a log"* specifies both the presence of a system component (if the log is not defined elsewhere) and a system behavior, and hence heterogeneous.

*Comments*: from a prescriptive viewpoint (as discussed in Sect. 2), it is good practice for requirements documents to avoid heterogeneous statements. The second example would be better expressed, in a requirements document, by two distinct requirements: one specifying the need for a log; the other stating that error messages must be recorded in that log.

### 3.3   Relevant Properties

The definitions of "property" and "statement", when applied to projects and the associated system and environment, underlie the definition of "requirement". But many properties are not of interest as requirements, for example the system property that the executable has a "load" instruction at offset 3FD04, or the project property that no code was committed past 11:30 PM on December 31st. We are interested in properties that are relevant to some stakeholder.

**Definition.** A *stakeholder* for a project is a person who may affect or be affected by the project or its associated system.

*Comments*:

- This definition is a considerably simplified version of the one on the IEEE systems and software terminology standard [1]. The IEEE version talks of a person or organization, but organizations can only be involved through their (human) members. It specifies *"individual or organization having a right, share, claim, or interest in a system or in its possession of characteristics that meet their needs and expectations"*, *"individual, group or organization that can affect, be affected by, or perceive itself to be affected by, a risk"* etc., all possibly interesting but only adding musings to the simple definition above. (The mention of perceiving to be affected is correct but not necessary: if you believe you are affected by the system you are affected by it, if only through the effect on your mindset.) There seems to be no need for such a bloated definition for a clear and simple concept.
- Concretely, stakeholders may include users of the system, people responsible for commissioning and accepting the system (such as "product owners" in agile methods), developers, testers and many others as discussed in detail in the software engineering literature, e.g. [13].
- The definition only mentions the project and system. Affecting or being affected by the environment is not enough to make you a stakeholder. As a taxpayer you are affected by the tax rules, but that does not make you a stakeholder of a tax-related project if the resulting system does not apply to your category of taxpayer.

**Definition.** A property of a project, system or environment, is *relevant* if it is of interest to a stakeholder.

*Comments*: we saw above examples of non-relevant project and system properties. As an example of an environment property, knowing that the system might be deployed in Costa Rica is relevant for a payroll system which must take local regulations into account, but probably not for a computer game.

## 3.4   Requirement

**Definition.** A *requirement* is a statement of a relevant project, system or environment property.

*Comments*:

- This definition introduces the central concept of the present discussion. From the definition of "statement", a requirement is a specification of a property of a project, system or environment. (For simplicity we limit ourselves to requirements characterizing only one of the three dimensions.)
- The classification of Sect. 4 defines what kinds of property are pertinent for software requirements.

- Software engineering discussions often use the plural "requirements" as a collective, as in "the requirements of a system", a phrase that denotes a whole (the specification of the system) beyond just the collection of its parts (the individual requirements). To avoid any ambiguity, the present discussion only uses "requirements" as the plural of "requirement", as in "four requirements", meaning four statements of project, system or environment properties. For the collective we can always use a more elaborate phrase such as (depending on the exact meaning sought) "the requirements document" or "the overall requirements for the system", or "the Software Requirement Specification", often abbreviated SRS.
- The definition only says that a requirement specifies a property, and does not specify a level of granularity for that property: it could characterize the entire project, system or environment, one of its major components, or just an elementary component. At one extreme, the entire SRS is "a requirement"; so is, at the other extreme, the statement of a single elementary property, such as "*Clicking Exit shall result in termination of the session*". The next definition addresses this variety.
- By specifying a boolean property, a requirement defines a criterion which an actual environment, project or system either confirms or refutes. "*Have the test plan ready for next Monday!*" is not boolean and hence not a requirement. ("*The testing team shall produce the test plan in at most a week*" is a requirement.) When teaching requirements engineering we go further, telling students that requirements must be verifiable: "*the query shall be processed in real time*" is not good enough, "query response time shall be one millisecond or less" is better (see e.g. [19] for such advice). Here again, the present document is descriptive and taxonomic, not normative. Except in Sect. 9 it does not discuss what makes requirements "good", only what makes them requirements.

## 3.5  Characterizing Requirements

**Definition.** A requirement is *composite* if it includes other requirements (its *sub-requirements*) and *elementary* otherwise.

*Comments*: the distinction is the same as for "statements" in general (Sect. 3.2) but introduces the notion of sub-requirement, which will become more precise through the definitions of "component", "sub-goal" etc. in Sect. 4.

**Definition.** The *type* of a requirement is the notation in which it states its associated property.

*Comments*: the term "notation" is taken here in its ordinary meaning. Examples of notation are English text, a UML diagram type, a tabular format, a particular programming language, a (well-defined) mathematical notation. Since requirements can be composite, the notion of "notation" must support the possibility of a combination of notations, as in the example of a requirements document that contains both English text and graphical illustrations.

**Definition.** A requirement R *specifies* a property P if P follows from the property stated by R or a sub- requirement of R.

    *Comments*: this definition is a bit of hair-splitting but reflects the different nature of statements and properties. A property is just a predicate: the border of a certain control on the screen is (or is not) black. A statement is an expression of that property in some notation, for example "*The border shall be black*" or "*La bordure doit être noire*", both of which express the same property although in different notations (types). Yet another way to specify that property would be a figure, or an entry in a table listing attributes of UI elements. The definition uses the informal term "follows from" since it cannot use "R implies P" unless requirements are expressed in a formal mathematical notation.

## 4    Classification of Requirements

This section introduces the first of the two fundamental taxonomies proposed by this article: the taxonomy of requirements themselves. Section 4.1 defines the fundamental categories, disjoint from each other. Section 4.2 introduces other categories, important in practice but defined as subcategories of the fundamental ones.

### 4.1    Requirements Classification: Basic Categories

**Classification.** Every requirement states a property of one of the following categories. Section 4.2 will introduce more categories as special cases of the fundamental ones given here.

A. **Component:** the property that the system, project or environment includes a certain part.

    *Comments*: a component can be material, virtual or human. A human component can be a single person, group of persons, organization or category of persons involved in the system, project or environment. A component of the environment can be another system with which the given system must be interfaced.

    *Examples*: "the operating system is designed to run on the iPhone 8 and later models" (system component, material); "database operations shall run in a separate process" (system component, virtual); company CEO (if referenced explicitly in the requirements, single person); reservation agents (category of persons).

B. **Goal:** an objective of the project or system, in terms of their desired effect on the environment.

    *Comments*: Requirements documents often present goals at the beginning of the text. The external entity could be a company (enterprise goals) or a physical device such as a phone (cyber-physical goals). Having an effect on the environment means having an effect on an external entity, such as a company (enterprise goals, as in this example) or a physical device (cyber-physical goals).

*Example*: "One of the advantages expected from the system is to reduce the amount of fraudulent invoices".

C. **Behavior:** a property of the results or effects of the operation of the system or some of its components.

*Comments*: requirements in this category often get the most attention since they describe elements of what the system will do. A behavior can characterize the system as a whole or a specific component. Section 4.2 introduces the classic distinctions of behaviors into functional and non-functional.

*Example*: "Display the list of available elements."

D. **Task:** the property that the project includes a certain activity.

*Examples*: program coding, stakeholder interview, daily meeting.

E. **Product:** the property that a task uses or produces a material or virtual object.

*Examples*: a test plan, a user story, a design document, a program module.

F. **Constrain:** an environment property that may affect components, goals, behaviors, tasks or products.

*Comments*: it would seem enough to say "an environment property", since by definition the environment is (Sect. 3.1) the set of external entities that have the potential to affect or be affected by the project (and hence the system and the environment). But this does not work, since those entities have other properties with no relation to the project. Hence the restrictive formulation. Section 4.2 will distinguish between *obligation* and *assumption* constraints.

*Examples*: "every transfer over EUR 10,000 requires authorization" (behavior constraint); "testing shall use the JUnit framework" (task constraint).

G. **Role:** the property that a component carries some or all of the responsibility for a behavior or task.

*Example*: "the Bangalore subsidiary shall be responsible for the implementation of the user interface subsystem" (task role, human component of the project); "the reservation system's UI shall be designed for operation by railway-station booking agents" (behavior role, human component); "smart contract computations shall be executed on the GPU" (behavior role, material component).

H. **Limit:** the property that the project, system or environment does not include a requirement of one of the preceding kinds.

*Example*: "Providing a interface to SAP accounting falls outside of the scope of the present system" (component limit); Integration testing will be performed in a follow-up project (project limit).

I. **Lack:** a property that should have a requirement, but does not.

*Comments*: this category is different from the others, and paradoxical since it characterizes what is not in the requirements. Our discussions with requirements practitioners indicate that they spend a considerable part of their efforts uncovering lacks. Human scrutiny is indeed usually required to find lacks, although some automatic analysis is possible; for example, a term that appears repeatedly in an SRS but not as an entry in the glossary (a list of definitions of project, system and environment concepts, which any SRS should include) may signal that the requirements are missing the specification of an important property.

J. **Meta-requirement:** a property of requirements themselves (not the system, project or environment).

*Example*: a section title in the requirements document (which does not express any new property but helps structure and understand the actual, non-meta properties); more generally, any observation intended to facilitate the reading of an SRS, such as "the details will appear in Sect. 7"; a statement of priority between requirements, such as a classification of components into "critical", "necessary" and "nice to have"; an explanation, such as "the behavior in this case is specified by table 7.1" or "figure 7.2 illustrates the concept".

*Comments*: large composite requirements, for example an entire SRS, will contain requirements in several of these categories. The classification is, however, designed with the intent that in practical usage it will be possible without much hesitation to classify any elementary requirement (or small composite requirement) into just one category.

The classification makes it possible to be more precise about the elements of a composite requirement (a requirement made of other requirements):

**Definition.** A *sub-goal*, *sub-component*, *sub-behavior* etc. is a sub-requirement of respectively a goal, component, behavior etc.

And consequently:

**Definition.** A goal, component, behavior etc. is *elementary* (non-composite) if it has no sub-goal, sub-component, sub-behavior etc.

*Comments*: in principle, the definition of sub-requirement allows arbitrary mixing of categories, for example a task as a sub-requirement of a goal. The above definitions only cover sub-requirements that are of the same category as the enclosing requirements.

## 4.2   Some Derived Categories

The following kinds of requirement are special cases, important in practice, of the categories of Sect. 4.1.

An **actor** is a human component. Examples include the stakeholders of a project as defined in Sect. 3.3 (project actors); and people involved in the operation of the system, such as an end-user or a system administrator (system actors).

A **justification** is a meta-requirement explaining the rationale for a requirement (of any kind) in terms of a goal. As an example, if an SRS for a software system does not specify Android among the platforms to be supported, it might include the justification that the company has made the strategic decision to equip its sales agents with iPhones.

A **responsibility** is a human role. (In the general case, roles can be defined for components other than humans, e.g. software components.) The first two examples in the above definition of "role" (Sect. 4.1.H) are responsibilities.

An **obstacle** is a goal defined as the need to overcome a negative property of the environment, as in "with the current system, too many enquiries that could lead to sales are missed". KAOS [18] has a closely related definition.

A widely established terminology for behavior distinguishes between statements of "what" and "how" properties:

- A **functional behavior** specifies results or effects of the system.
- A **non-functional behavior** specifies a property of how these results or effects are to be achieved. Classical examples are timing limits and security conditions.

The following subcategories exist for constraints (environment properties):

- A **business rule** is a constraint resulting from organizational practices. Examples are the rules on bank accounts from Sect. 3.1 and Sect. 4.1.F. Another is "delivery of phosgene [a chemical] requires that the recipient have taken a refresher course in handling hazardous chemicals in the past twelve months". This example appears in [19], as the background for a system property: the software must reject a request for chemical if the requester does not meet the criterion.
- A **physical rule** is a constraint resulting from laws of nature. A typical example is the application of the laws of mechanics to a satellite launching system.
- An **engineering decision** is a constraint resulting from human choices. Examples are the minimum and maximum bandwidths for a networking system.

A separate classification of constraints is between:

- An obligation, describing a property that the environment is known to possess. Examples: the rules on bank transfer in Sect. 4.1.E; in a cyber-physical system, limits (such as signal transmission speed, laws of mechanics, bandwidth) imposed by physics and engineering.
- An assumption, describing a property that the environment may or may not possess but which the project may assume to hold for the development of the system. *Example* (in a system to control a railroad crossing): "cars travel at no more than 200 km/h and trains at no more than 400 km/h". Unlike the absolute limits imposed by the laws of nature or by a choice of technology, an assumption is the result of an explicit human decision, and might conceivably not hold, but may be needed for the requirements to guarantee certain properties. In the example, it may be possible to make trains run faster than 400 km/h, but no railroad-crossing system can guarantee the avoidance of collisions without assuming some upper limit on the speed of trains.

– An invariant, describing a property that is both as an assumption and as a behavior. *Example* (in a factory control system): "the system shall operate between $-30$ and $+50\,°C$", which means both that the system's operations may assume they start within this temperature range and that they must refrain from causing overheating or over-cooling.

While requirements of all three kinds cover properties of the environment, the difference is important in practice since obligations make the work of system developers harder and assumptions make it easier. (Invariants do both. To keep the three categories disjoint we classify a constraint as an obligation if it is not also an assumption, and conversely.)

The two classifications are orthogonal: for example, a business rule can be an obligation (as the bank transfer example rule) or an assumption (the New York Stock Exchange is closed on Labor Day). The same observation holds for engineering decisions, which gave us an example of obligation (car and train speeds) and an example of invariant (temperature limits).

The following table, intended for reference, includes all the categories in alphabetical order, and their subcategories. Every requirement should fit into exactly one category and at most one subcategory (except for constraints which may belong to elements of the two orthogonal classifications) (Table 1).

**Table 1.** Categories and subcategories of requirements

| Basic categories | Subcategories | | Short definition (for full definition see text) |
|---|---|---|---|
| Behavior | | | Property of an operation's effects |
| Component | | | Part of the project, environment or system |
| | *Special case:* **Actor** | | Human component |
| Constraint | | | Environment property |
| | *Classification by nature* | **Assumption** | Assumed constraint |
| | | **Obligation** | Imposed constraint |
| | | **Invariant** | Both assumption and obligation |
| | *Classification by source* | **Business rule** | Constraint due to organizational practices |
| | | **Engineering decision** | Constraint due to human choices |
| | | **Physical rule** | Constraint due to laws of nature |
| Goal | | | Intended effect of project or system on environment |
| Lack | | | Missing requirement |
| Limit | | | Property beyond scope of project/system/environment |
| Meta-requirement | | | Property of requirements but not of project, system or environment |
| | *Special case:* **Justification** | | Rationale expressed in terms of a *goal* |
| Product | | | Material or virtual object used or produced by a task |
| Role | | | Component's responsibility for behavior or task |
| Task | | | Project activity |

An anonymous online quiz [9] invites readers to test the practicality of the requirements classification and their understanding of it by classifying requirements elements from a sample requirements document [3], which also provides the background for the discussion in Sect. 6.

## 5  Taxonomy of Inter-requirements Relations

With requirement elements sorted into categories, we proceed to a classification of the relations that may hold between them.

**Classification.** A requirement Y may depend on another X in one of the following ways, each given with: a name in upper case (a verb, such as "REPEATS", whereas names of requirement categories were nouns); a symbol (generally borrowed from mathematics, for its mnemonic value only); a definition of its meaning; a comment if necessary.

DISJOINS $X \parallel Y$ Y and X are unrelated.
*Comment*: In this case, the most common for two randomly selected statements in a requirements document, there is no relation between the properties they specify.

BELONGS $X \subseteq Y$ X is a sub-requirement of Y.
*Comment*: this case corresponds to textual inclusion (sub-section, sub-figure etc.), unlike inclusion of properties as in EXTENDS below.

REPEATS $X \Leftrightarrow Y$ X specifies the same property as Y.
*Comment*: this case is identity of the properties although not necessarily of their statements (since they might use different notations). See below for variants: EXPLAINS (different notations), DUPLICATES (same notation).

CONTRADICTS $X \oplus Y$ X specifies a property in a way not compatible with Y.
*Comment*: remember that this discussion is descriptive, not prescriptive. No one would recommend writing contradictory requirements. But existing SRS, especially large ones, may contain contradictions; in some contexts it might be crucial to detect them.

FOLLOWS $X \dashv Y$ The property specified by X is a consequence of the property specified by Y.
*Comment*: interesting in particular if Y is a goal and X a behavior or task.

EXTENDS $X > Y$ X assumes Y and specifies a property not specified by Y.
*Comment*: also called "refines".

EXCEPTS $X \setminus\setminus Y$ X changes or removes, for a specified case, a property specified by Y.
*Comment*: this case is not the same as CONTRADICTS. It is the explicit and often legitimate introduction of an exception to a general property.

CONSTRAINS $X \triangleright Y$ X specifies a constraint on a property specified by Y.
CHARACTERIZES $X \rightarrow Y$ X is a meta-requirement involving Y.

The following derived cases are useful in practice:

DETAILS $X \gg Y$ X adds detail to a property specified by Y.

> *Comment*: this is a case of $X > Y$ (EXTENDS). The nuance is that in this case there is no fundamentally new property, just more detail about an already specified property.

SHARES $X \cap Y$ $X' \Leftrightarrow Y'$ for some sub-requirements X' and Y' of X and Y.

DUPLICATES $X \equiv Y$ $X \Leftrightarrow Y$, and X has the same type as Y.

> *Comment*: also a case of REPEATS. This is the true redundancy case. From a prescriptive viewpoint, it usually reflects a deficiency in an SRS; compare with the next case.

EXPLAINS $X \cong Y$ $X \Leftrightarrow Y$, and X has a different type from Y.

> *Comment*: again a case of REPEATS, but not necessarily bad. Y introduces no new property but helps understand Y. For example Y may describe a property textually, and X may be a graphical illustration of that property.

*Comments*:

- As with the taxonomy of requirements, the intent is to ensure that given two arbitrary requirement elements their relationship can be classified in at most one of the primary relations and at most one of the derived ones. If two or more categories appear to apply, one should clearly be more relevant than the others.
- The mathematical symbols informally suggest the relations' meaning, but do not imply theproperties, such as associativity or commutativity, of their ordinary mathematical counterparts. Further research should indeed study (in the style of [15]) the mathematical properties of these relations.
- The relations may hold between requirements of any complexity. In practice, one should first look for their occurrences between elementary requirements.
- SHARES is an example of a relation on composite requirements derived from another (DUPLICATES) on their sub-requirements. It is possible to generalize some of the other relations in the same way, or simply to accept, as a small abuse of language, that for example $Y > X$ holds if $Y' > X'$ holds for sub-requirements. Except for SHARES, we ignore this issue in light of the preceding comment.
- An analysis examining how two given requirements are connected may in principle identify more than one of the relations. For simplicity, it is advisable to choose only one (from the complete list including derived relations); just pick the relation that comes out as most relevant.

Like its counterpart for the first taxonomy, the following table provides a list of all the categories and subcategories of the relation taxonomy (Table 2).

**Table 2.** List of all the categories and subcategories of the relation taxonomy

| Basic categories | Subcategories | Symbol | Short definition (for full definition see text) – X is first operand, Y second operand |
|---|---|---|---|
| Belongs | | ⊆ | X textually included in Y |
| Characterizes | | → | Meta-requirement X applies to Y |
| Constrains | | ▶ | Constraint X applies to Y |
| Contradicts | | ⊕ | X Properties specified by X and Y cannot both hold |
| Disjoins | | ‖ | Y and X are unrelated |
| Excepts | | \\ | X specifies an exception to the property specified by Y |
| Extends | | > | X adds to properties of Y |
| | *Special case:* **Details** | ≫ | X adds detail to properties of Y |
| Follows | | ⊣ | X is a consequence of Y |
| Repeats | | ⇔ | X specifies the same property as Y |
| | **Shares** | ∩ | Some subrequirements are common |
| | **Duplicates** | ≡ | Same properties, same type (notation) |
| | **Explains** | ≅ | Same property, different type |

As with the previous taxonomy, an anonymous online quiz [10] invites readers to test the practicality of the requirements-relations classification and their understanding of it by classifying requirements relations from a sample requirements document [3], which also provides the background for the discussion in Sect. 6.

## 6  Dissecting an Example

[3] is an example requirements document, obviously inspired by industrial practice but devised for a course at Ohio State University. It provides a good testbed for the concepts of this article since it is small enough to lend itself to analysis yet large and realistic enough to be representative of the contents of requirements for actual industry projects.

We analyzed the entire text and found that the taxonomies cover both all requirements and all the relations we considered. Here we only show a few representative samples of the analysis. The entire analysis is available as an online complement to this article [8].

First, examples of classifying requirements according to the first taxonomy:

| Section 1. Introduction | Meta-requirement |
|---|---|
| 1.1 Purpose of Document | Meta-requirement |
| This is a Requirements Specification document for a new web-based sales system for Solar Based Energy, Inc. (SBE) | Goal |
| 1.2 Project Summary | Meta-requirement |
| Project Name: SBE Sales System | Component |

...

1.4 Project Scope

| The scope of this project is a web-based system that supports the marketing of SBE products directly to customers as well as through the existing sales agent network. | Goal |
|---|---|
| Advertising of products, inventory control, and account billing are not part of this project. | Limit |
| In addition, changes to the logical and physical design of the current databases are expected. | Obstacle |
| The primary responsibilities of the new system: | Meta-requirement |
| provide customers direct access to up-to-date, accurate product information on which they can make a decision to buy | Behavior |

...

Section 2. Functional Objectives

| 2.1. High Priority | Meta-requirement |
|---|---|
| "The system shall allow for on-line product ordering by either the customer or the sales agent" | Behavior |
| "For customers, this will eliminate the current delay between their decision to buy and the placement of the order" | Goal |
| "This will reduce the time a sales agent spends on an order by x%. The cost to process an order will be reduced to $y" | Goal |
| "The system shall display information that is customized based on the user's company, job function, application and locale" | Behavior |
| 2.2 Medium Priority | Meta-requirement |
| The system shall provide a search facility that will allow full-text searching of all web pages that the user is permitted to access. | Goal |
| The system must support the following searches:<br><br>- find all words specified<br>- find any word specified<br>- find the exact phrase<br>- Boolean search | Behavior |

...

Section 3: Non-Functional Objectives

| 3.1" Reliability" | Meta-requirement |
|---|---|
| * "The system shall be completely operational at least x | Constraint |
| * "Down time after a failure shall not exceed x hours" | Constraint |

. . .

Section 4: The Context Model

| | |
|---|---|
| 4.1 "Goal Statement" | Meta-requirement |
| "The goal of the system is to allow SBE to increase sales revenue by x% over the next y years with only a z% increase in sales and customer service staff by" | Goal |
| "allowing complete and accurate customer and order information to be captured directly from the customer as well as from sales agents" | Goal |
| 4.2 "Context Diagram" | Meta-requirement |
| | Behavior |
| 4.3 "System Externals" | Meta-requirement |
| "Customer" | Actor |
| "A customer is any user of the system that has not identified himself as an SBE employee" | Actor |
| "A customer may search for public product information by keyword, access white papers for a particular product, order a product or request assistance from a sales agent" | Role |
| "A customer who provides personal information will get search and query results customized to his preferences" | Behavior |

. . .

5.2 Use Case Descriptions (for selected cases)

| | |
|---|---|
| "For all use cases, the user can cancel the use case at any step that requires user input. This action ends the use case. Any data collected during that use case is lost" | Behavior |
| "For all use cases that require a logged in user, the current login session is updated during the use case to reflect the navigation paths through the use case" | Behavior |
| Use Case Name: Login User | Meta-requirement |
| Summary: In order to get personalized or restricted information, place orders or do other specialized transactions a user must login so that the system can determine his access level | Goal |
| Basic Flow | Meta-requirement |
| 1. The use case starts when a user indicates that he wants to login. | Constraint |
| 2. The system requests the username and password. | Behavior |
| 3. The user enters his username and password. | Role |
| 4. The system verifies the username and password against all registered users. | Behavior |
| Alternative Flows | Meta-requirement |
| Step 4: if username is invalid, the use case goes back to step 2. | Behavior |
| Extension Points: none | Component |
| Preconditions: The user is registered. | Constraint |
| Postconditions: The user can now obtain data and perform functions according to his registered access level. | Behavior |
| Business Rules: Some data and functions are restricted to certain types of users or users with a particular access level" | Constraint |

Now, some examples of requirements relationships per the second taxonomy.

CONSTRAINS:

| | |
|---|---|
| "Preconditions: The user is registered." | "Postconditions: The user can now obtain data and perform functions according to his registered access level." |

EXCEPTS:

| | |
|---|---|
| "if the password is invalid the system requests that the user re-enter the password. When the user enters another password the use case continues with step 4 using the original username and new password." | "4. The system verifies the username and password against all registered users". |

BELONGS:

| | |
|---|---|
| "A customer is any user of the system that has not identified himself as an SBE employee." | "4.3 System Externals Customer A customer is any user of the system that has not identified himself as an SBE employee. A customer may search for public product information by keyword, access whitepapers for a particular product, order a product or request assistance from a sales agent. A customer who provides personal information will get search and query results customized to his preferences. Sales Agent A sales agent is a user who has been verified as an SBE employee. A sales agent may access all available product information and whitepapers, including the product owner. A sales agent may place an order on behalf of a customer. He will be informed by the system of any customers in his region who have requested assistance. Product Owner The product owner is a user who has been verified as an SBE employee. The product owner may update product information and whitepapers for those products for which he is responsible. Accounting The Accounting department is responsible for all SBE financial transactions. The Accounting department is informed of all purchases and is responsible for later collection of accounts receivable. Shipping The Shipping department is informed of purchases so that it can process the order and update inventory. Marketing The Marketing department is responsible for creating demand for SBE products. It will receive website navigation data to use in planning marketing strategies." |

DETAILS:

| | |
|---|---|
| "The system shall be completely operational at least x% of the time" | "Down time after a failure shall not exceed x hours" |

CHARACTERIZES:

| | |
|---|---|
| "2.1 High Priority" | "The system shall allow for on-line product ordering by either the customer or the sales agent." |

DISJOINS:

| | |
|---|---|
| "A sales agent may access all available product information and whitepapers, including the product owner. A sales agent may place an order on behalf of a customer" | "if the password is invalid the system requests that the user re-enter the password. When the user enters another password the use case continues with step 4 using the original username and new password." |

EXPLAINS:

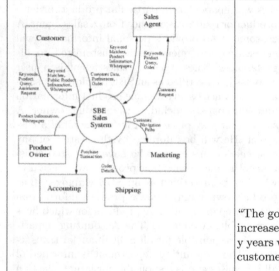

"The goal of the system is to allow SBE to increase sales revenue by x% over the next y years with only a z% increase in sales and customer service staff by

  – - allowing complete and accurate customer and order information to be captured directly from the customer as well as from sales agents
  – - providing customers and sales agents fast access to up-to-date and accurate product information and whitepapers."

# 7   Analyzing Available Requirements Methodologies

This section surveys a few important requirements methodologies, selected from those covered in a recent survey involving some of the authors [6]. At this stage we only consider the classification of requirements in well-known requirements textbooks.

## 7.1   Wiegers-Beatty

Wiegers and Beatty ("WB"), include in [19], page 7, a table of requirements categories, with the following figure (page 8) illustrating their connections (Fig. 1):

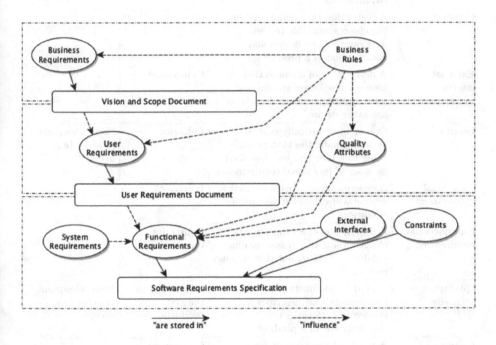

**Fig. 1.** Categories and relationships (from [19])

The first two columns in the following table are reproduced from Wiegers and Beatty; the third column gives in each case the corresponding category in the present classification.

The classification of this article appears to cover the Wiegers-Beatty categories.

| WB category | WB definition | Category from the present discussion | Comment |
|---|---|---|---|
| Business requirement | A high-level business objective of the organization that builds a product or of a customer who procures it | Goal | Can also include limits |
| Business rule | A policy, guideline, standard, or regulation that defines or constrains some aspect of the business. Not a software requirement in itself, but the origin of several types of software requirements | Constraint | See also business rule subcategory (Sect. 4.2) |
| Constraint | A restriction that is imposed on the choices available to the developer for the design and construction of a product | | |
| External interface requirement | A description of a connection between a software system and a user, another software system, or a hardware device | Component | |
| Feature | One or more logically related system capabilities that provide value to a user and are described by a set of functional requirements | Behavior | From viewpoint of actor (e.g. user) |
| Functional requirement | A description of a behavior that a system will exhibit under specific conditions | Behavior | |
| Nonfunctional requirement | A description of a property or characteristic that a system must exhibit or a constraint that it must respect | Constraint on the system | |
| Quality attribute | A kind of nonfunctional requirement that describes a service or performance characteristic of a product | Constraint on the system or products | From viewpoint of actor (e.g. user) |
| System requirement | A top-level requirement for a product that contains multiple subsystems, which could be all software or software and hardware | Component | |
| User requirement | A goal or task that specific classes of users must be able to perform with a system, or a desired product attribute | Goal | |

## 7.2   Van Lamsweerde

In the same style as Sect. 7.1, the following table considers the classification by [17] ("AVL") from which the first two columns are reproduced verbatim.

| AVL category | AVL definition | Category from the present discussion | Comment |
|---|---|---|---|
| Functional requirements | Functional effects that the software-to-be is required to have on its environment | Constraint or Behavior | |
| Non-functional requirements | Constraints on the way the software-to-be should satisfy its functional requirements or on the way it should be developed | Task | Can also be product |
| Quality requirements | Additional, quality-related properties that the functional effects of the software-to-be should have | Constraint | Usually engineering decisions |
| Compliance requirements | Prescribed software effects on the environment to conform to national laws, international regulations, etc | Constraint | Usually business rule |
| Architectural requirements | Imposed structural constraints on the software to fit its environment | Component | |
| Development requirements | Non-functional requirements on the way the software-to-be should be developed | Task | Can also be product |

The following artifacts are not defined as requirements categories in [17], but are important enough for inclusion here:

| Goals | Prescriptive statements of intent that the system should satisfy through the cooperation of its agents (active system components) | Goal | |
|---|---|---|---|
| Expectations | CPrescriptive statements of intent that the system should satisfy through the cooperation of its agents (active system components) | Goal | |
| Domain properties | NDescriptive statement about the environment, expected to hold invariably regardless of how the system behaves | Constraint | Or Component if the property holds on a structural description |

Coverage again appears good.

# 8    Normative Work

This section considers some existing normative work on requirements.

## 8.1    IEEE Definition

The current version of the IEEE standard for software terminology [1], released in 2010, offers a definition of "requirement", retained and confirmed from a 1990 version. Under that definition, a requirement is:

1. *A condition or capability needed by a user to solve a problem or achieve an objective.*
2. *A condition or capability that must be met or possessed by a system, system component, product, or service to satisfy an agreement, standard, specification, or other formally imposed documents.*
3. *A documented representation of a condition or capability as in (1) or (2).*
4. *A condition or capability that must be met or possessed by a system, product, service, result, or component to satisfy a contract, standard, specification, or other formally imposed document. Requirements include the quantified and documented needs, wants, and expectations of the sponsor, customer, and other stakeholders.*

That definition cannot be right. Its very length is just a symptom of the problem: "requirement", either in ordinary usage or as applied to software, is a simple concept which merits a simple definition.

In clause 1, a requirement is a "condition or capability", but it is not clear what these terms mean and how the meanings differ; "capability" is not defined in the standard, and "condition" is defined as "a description of a contingency to be considered in the representation of a problem, or a reference to other procedures to be considered as part of the condition", where "contingency" is not defined. This definition of "condition" is indefensible: it is again far too complex and mysterious, especially in light of the ordinary- language meaning of the term (as everyone knows, a condition is simply, a property that can be true or false). That ordinary meaning would seem just right in a systems/software context too. Coming back to the definition of "requirement", the distinction between "solve a problem" or "achieve an objective" seems spurious (solving a problem is an objective, and reaching an objective raises problems).

The distinction between clause 2 and clause 1 is equally uninteresting, since the definition of "user" in the standard, too long (18 lines!) to be reproduced here, is broad enough to encompass anyone having an interest in an agreement, standard etc. Worse, clause 2 makes the definition circular, since a "specification" (defined as "a detailed formulation, in document form, which provides a definitive description of a system for the purpose of developing or validating the system") certainly includes the description of all "conditions" and "contingencies" of the system, whatever those may be; so a requirement is defined as a condition that must be met to satisfy a specification of conditions!

Viewed in light of the distinction between a property and a statement of that property (Sect. 3.2), clause 3 commingles these two notions under the term "requirement", a source of confusion: a property is not the same thing as one representation of that property in some notation such as English, UML or Telugu.

Clause 4 is entirely mystifying, since it is almost identical to clause 2 but not quite, raising issues of consistency; in addition, the commingling of property and statement of clause 3 does not apply to clause 4, leaving the reader wondering.

As to the last sentence, it is not in the form of a definition like the preceding ones, but comments on what requirements may "include"; such sentences, inappropriate in a definition since they can only serve to confuse the reader further (if the first four clauses, already lengthy and redundant, are supposed to define requirements, what else is needed?); it sounds more like a "remorse", a typical flaw of definitions [14], trying to make up for an unsatisfactory definition by adding a broad net of precautionary qualifications at the end.

Insistent as it is on including irrelevant and redundant details, the definition manages to miss crucial aspects of requirements: it focuses on system requirements, but does not cover properties of the project, and may cover environment properties only by a stretch of the imagination.

This addled attempt at a definition, which sounds like an attempt to integrate the comments of everyone in a committee, is unlikely ever to have helped a software practitioner. One should note here that such self-defeating pomposity is inevitable neither for standards in general nor for IEEE standards. The 1998 IEEE requirements standard [2], long marked as obsolete but still widely used in the industry (which prefers it to its successors, an understandable attitude in light of the present discussion's example), is a short, clear, no-frills standard, and as a result remarkably useful in practice.

The IEEE-2010 definition does have one redeeming feature: its restriction to properties *"needed by a user"*. Through this clause, the definition expresses that not all properties (of a project, system or environment) are interesting as requirements only if they are of interest to someone. That someone should be defined not as *"a user"* but as a stakeholder. (Many legitimate requirements are intended for stakeholders other than users, for example to company management in the case of requirements that the present discussion classifies as goals. A goal such as "take market share away from competitor X" is relevant as a requirement, but hardly *"needed by a user"*. It is needed by a stakeholder. This sloppiness in terminology is all the more surprising that the standard does define "stakeholder".) Still, the underlying idea is correct: a requirement is not just any property of the system (or project, or environment) but one that some stakeholder (e.g. a user) finds important. The present article's definition of requirement recognizes that idea by defining the concept of a relevant property (Sect. 3.3) and including it in the definition of "requirement" (Sect. 3.4).

## 8.2   SWEBOK

SWEBOK, the IEEE-originated Software Engineering Body of Knowledge [5], is an effort to classify existing knowledge in software engineering, with numerous elements in common with the IEEE standard discussed above.

SWEBOK defines a "requirement" as "*a property that must be exhibited by something in order to solve some problem in the real world*". This definition is in part useless and in part wrong:

– It is grammatically challenged. As written, it implies that it is the "property" that must "solve some problem". Since properties do not solve problems, the most reasonable interpretation, which we will assume, is that the definition is incorrect English for "*. . . in order for someone to solve some problem*". This point of pure form is not just quibbling since a definition, particularly in a document attempting to define best practices, is only useful if it is clear.
– On the substance: why the "real" world? What would be a "problem" in an unreal world? "Real world" is informal language, not a concept for a standard of industrial practice. SWEBOK uses it more than a dozen times but does not define it. The intention seems to be that software should not exist just for itself, and instead should be related to some issue in the non-software world, like banks or airplanes. But this view, while common in simplistic discussions of software engineering, is incorrect: requirements are defined and necessary for systems that are entirely virtual and not part of the physical world, like a compiler, an operating system, a Web browser...
– While too restrictive in its focus on the "real world", the definition is too general in other ways. "In order to solve" the "problem" of building a software system, a "property" that must be "exhibited by" the building hosting the team ("something") is that it should not be on fire, and a property of the team members (another "something") is that they should be awake. Those are hardly requirements in any meaning pertaining to software engineering.

After this useless definition, SWEBOK introduces some more relevant concepts, such as "product requirement" and "process requirement" which, tellingly, are defined without reference to it: respectively, "*need or constraint on the software to be developed*" and "*essentially*" (?) "*a constraint on the development of the software*". The first of these definitions seems to confuse behaviors and constraints, since it is illustrated by the example "*The software shall verify that a student meets all prerequisites before he or she registers for a course*". Such a property is not "a need or constraint *on* the software" (which would be something like "registration to a course is conditional on satisfying the prerequisites", an environment property) but a property *of* the software (a behavior in the terminology of the present work). The fundamental distinction between properties of the environment and properties of the system is one of the insights gained in the progress of software engineering over the past two decades, but SWEBOK is not aware of it, other than in a brief mention of "business rules" in the section on requirements elicitation.

As these samples illustrate, SWEBOKS's strength is not in definitions of software engineering concepts, or more generally in precision and clarity (all the more regrettable that many textbooks reverently cite SWEBOK as a font of software engineering wisdom). It naturally tends to the prescriptive mode and includes (aside from such time-wasting platitudes as requirements elicitation being "*fundamentally a human activity*") some reasonable advice, such as ensuring "*effective communication between the stakeholders*" to guarantee good requirements elicitation.

The aspect of SWEBOK most relevant to the present effort at taxonomy is the attempt at requirements classification along "a number of dimensions": functional vs nonfunctional, single versus emergent, product versus process, higher or lower priority, scope, volatility versus stability.

## 8.3   Essence

Essence [11], by the Semat consortium under the leadership of Ivar Jacobson, is an effort to develop a systematic understanding of software engineering concepts and best practices. Requirements appear as one of seven "alphas" (key elements) of Essence, along with Software System, Team, Work, Way of Working, Opportunity (*"The set of circumstances that makes it appropriate to develop or change a software system"*) and Stakeholders. Essence defines the role of requirements as "*what the software system must do to address the opportunity and satisfy the stakeholders*". This definition is indefensible since it covers only one of the three relevant aspects, the system (Sect. 3.4), missing the project and the environment. (It fails to cover such typical requirement examples "version 1 shall be operational no later than September 2023" and "the social security number uniquely identifies a person", respectively project and environment properties.)

Like many software engineering discussions, Essence does not devote much effort to defining basic concepts and instead veers quickly into prescriptive mode. In fact, immediately after the preceding definition comes the prescriptive observation that "*It is important to discover what is needed from the software system, share this understanding among the stakeholders and the team members, and use it to drive the development and testing of the new system.*" The main contribution of the Essence discussion of requirements is indeed prescriptive: defining a sequence of states through which requirements progressively become more mature, including successively:

– Four states relative to the requirements just by themselves: Conceived (need for a new system agreed), Bounded (purpose is clear), Coherent (consistent description of system essentials), Acceptable (requirements are satisfactory for stakeholders).
– Two states that also involve the implementation: Addressed (enough to satisfy the need for a new system); Fulfilled (fully satisfies stakeholders).

Could Essence contribute to the present effort at taxonomy? Unfortunately (and surprisingly for such a recent effort) Essence suffers from the same dated view of requirements as SWEBOK, not integrating the progress of its understanding over the last two decades. The basic definition, as noted above, covers only the system part. Interestingly, the notion of environment does appear, but only twice and without explanation, in the description of the Bounded state (*"constraints are identified and considered"* and *"assumptions are clearly stated"*). There is no mention of project aspects, other than a condition in the Conceived state that *"the stakeholders that will fund the initial work on the new system are identified"*. The early section on *"Justification: Why requirements?"* starts: *"the requirements capture what the stakeholders want from the system"*; this view is naïve since the requirements for a practical system requirements cannot just consider what the stakeholders want but also what is possible. In fact, out of the nine basic categories of requirements from Sect. 4.1 (ignoring meta-requirements), an SRS capturing only "what the stakeholders want" would only cover one, goals, and possibly part of another, behaviors.

Essence does introduce a concept useful to the discussion of requirements: one of the alphas, "opportunity" defined (as noted) as *"the set of circumstances that makes it appropriate to develop or change a software system"*. In relation to the present work's terminology, an opportunity is the basic reason behind a goal. For example, if one of the goals of a project (back in the late 1990s) was "make our billing system ready for the transition to the Euro", that goal only made sense because of the opportunity, in the Essence meaning, that some European countries are replacing their separate currencies by a common one. For the discussion of requirements, this notion is one level too far from software development: a software system does not directly *"address the opportunity"*, as the Essence definition of requirements (cited above) says: it addresses a goal. Between the switch to the euro, an opportunity in Essence terms, and the software update, a system effort, stands a goal: adapt the software to be ready for the switch. The goal addresses the opportunity; the requirements address the goal. Still, by highlighting the concept of opportunity Essence reminds us that in the broader context of software engineering behind every goal stands an opportunity.

The six stages in the Essence progression of requirements are also an interesting contribution, but they belong to the prescriptive realm beyond the scope of the present work.

The other way around in the relationship, we suggest that future versions of Essence could take advantage of the present work. Essence is a commendable effort to establish software engineering on a more solid basis, but cannot reach this goal without precise definitions (which, as we saw, industry standards do not provide) of the core concepts. In the case of requirements it needs to be brought in line with the modern understanding of these concepts.

# 9 Assessment and Future Work

The expected contributions of this work include providing a basis for:

1. Clarifying requirements concepts, through precise, non-bureaucratic, non-pompous but effectively usable definitions.
2. Requirements methodology ("prescriptive" discussions of requirements).
3. The critical analysis of requirements documents, as part of a quality assurance and improvement process.
4. Automatic processing of natural-language requirements documents.
5. Formal approaches to requirements (as discussed in a survey [6]).

On point 2, we may note that much of the existing literature on requirements is prescriptive: textbooks tell students what distinguishes good requirements from bad, and research articles propose new requirements methods meant to improve on existing practices. This focus is understandable, particularly since it is a widely shared assessment that the quality of requirements as actually written in industry is overall not very good. The present work is at a different, more basic level: providing fundamental definitions and taxonomies to enable better understanding and discussions of requirements. As one of its applications, it can help inform prescriptive discussions, and make them more effective, by defining the framework precisely. We saw some examples of possible prescriptive consequences of the descriptive approach of this work:

– The distinction between homogeneous and heterogeneous composite requirements (Sect. 3.2) leads to the observation that the second kind is to be avoided. If a requirement is composite, it should bind together sub-requirements of a similar nature and not, for example, a component and a behavior, or a behavior (applying to the system) and a constraint (characterizing the environment).
– The notion of component is closely connected to the advice (present in all good requirements methods, going back to the venerable IEEE standard on requirements [2]) to list and define all relevant concepts in a glossary. All important components should appear in the glossary.
– The notion of lack directs requirements engineers and quality assurance teams to look for requirement elements that have been overlooked. An example of lack is a component that does not appear in the glossary.
– The notion of contradiction again provides guidelines for quality assurance on requirements. Practical requirements document often contain a surprising number of contradictions, arising in particular from long periods of requirements development and the intervention of many different people in the process.
– The notion of repetition (REPEATS relation) is also important, in particular when distinguishing between two of the relation's variants: EXPLAINS is legitimate (provide different views of the same property, in different notations), although it is important to ensure consistency as in the "multirequirements" approach [16]; DUPLICATES, on the other hand, is in our view always bad. (One could state that repeating the same information in different ways but in the same notation can be harmless, but it is not: the duplication contributes to requirements document bloat; it wastes the reader's time; it can confuse the reader who does not know which of different explanations of

the same property to believe; and it fares poorly in the context of software evolution since it is easy to update one variant and forget the others.)

– The important recurring debate between traditional ("waterfall") and agile approaches to requirements can benefit from the precise analyses of the present work.

On points 3 and 4 (analysis of SRS), the precision that we have tried to apply to the definitions and taxonomies should help efforts to perform automatic NLP (Natural-Language-Processing) analysis of requirements document. There has been considerable research interest in this topic. NLP and more generally AI techniques have made astounding advances, but they are better at inferring a good-enough approximation of a considerable amount of information than at inferring precise information. An example (hijacked from a discussion of agile methods in [7]) is, in a requirements specification for a seminar scheduling system, the property that "the hotel is booked": it could mean that we have just succeeded in booking the hotel, or that it was already booked by someone else and hence that we have to look for another. While humans can handle this kind of subtlety, it seems beyond the reach of algorithms. But automatic analysis does not raise that level of difficulty if it focuses on structure rather than deep semantics. Its goal then is to organize the requirements, decode ("parse") the structure of the project, system and environment, and identify relations. Such an analysis could yield a first level of formalization of informal requirements, useful by itself (and also as a starting point for finer semantic analysis, automatic or partly manual). Building the corresponding tools, by relying on the concepts developed in this article, seems a promising avenue of research with achievable goals.

Such NLP processing based on the taxonomies of this article is part of our current work. Other efforts in progress include:

– Exploring properties of requirements in relation to other software artifacts, such as code, whereas the present discussion mostly considers requirements by themselves.
– Validating the approach on many further examples, academic and industrial.
– Assessing its teachability, by using it in courses on software engineering and requirements.
– Using it as a basis for a formal specification of requirements concepts. There have been various attempts to describe software engineering concepts in formal frameworks. (An early example was [15] which provides a mathematical model for binary relations between program elements such a modules, expressing formal properties of these relations.) The present discussion provides a solid basis for discussing requirements concepts, but it is still expressed in natural language rather than mathematics. We believe it provides an excellent starting point for mathematical modeling of the concepts under discussion and hope to develop the corresponding formal specifications, with a view to uncovering laws of software engineering that admit rigorous mathematical statements.

Even without these further developments, we hope to have provided a clearly defined framework that can serve as a reference for future work on requirements, and help improve the state of the art in this critical area of software engineering.

**Acknowledgements.** We are grateful to Dr. Bettina Bair from Ohio State University for writing the original (2006) version of the course project document [3] and providing us with a more recent version.

Attendees of talks given on this work by some of the authors provided particularly relevant feedback: at Politecnico di Milano (Meyer, March 2019), Elisabetta Di Nitto, Carlo Ghezzi, Dino Mandrioli and Maurizio Patriarca; at the University of Toulouse (Meyer, March 2019), Mamoun Filali Amine, whose comments led to a revision of the classification of constraints; at Innopolis University (Meyer, March 2019); at the GDR meeting, Génie de la Programmation et du Logiciel, also in Toulouse (Bruel, June 2019).

We are further indebted to Joëlle Guion for important comments on the concerns of practicing requirements engineers.

# References

1. IEEE 24765-2010. ISO/IEC/IEEE International Standard - Systems and software engineering - Vocabulary (2010). https://standards.ieee.org/standard/24765-2010.html
2. IEEE 830-1998. IEEE Recommended Practice for Software Requirements Specifications (1998). https://standards.ieee.org/standard/830-1998.html
3. Bair, B.: SBE Sales System (2006). Example requirements document for a course at Ohio State University. http://bit.ly/2OsNdmN
4. Bandakkanavar, R.: Software Requirements Specification document with example (2017). Technical paper. http://bit.ly/2XTSjOs
5. Bourque, P., Fairley, R.E., et al.: Guide to the Software Engineering Body of Knowledge (SWEBOK (R)): Version 3.0. IEEE Computer Society Press (2014)
6. Bruel, J.-M., Ebersold, S., Galinier, F., Naumchev, A., Mazzara, M., Meyer, B.: Formality in Software Requirements (2019, to appear)
7. Cohn, M.: Succeeding with Agile: Software Development Using Scrum. Pearson Education, London (2010)
8. Galinier, F., Ebersold, S., Bruel, J.-M., Meyer, B., Naumchev, A.: Detailed analysis and classification of a requirements document, September 2010. http://bit.ly/2F8NY2I
9. Galinier, F., Ebersold, S., Bruel, J.-M., Meyer, B., Naumchev, A.: Online quiz on taxonomy of requirements, September 2010. http://bit.ly/2Ww1vYk
10. Galinier, F., Ebersold, S., Bruel, J.-M., Meyer, B., Naumchev, A.: Online quiz on taxonomy of requirements relations, September 2010. http://bit.ly/2Ww7fBl
11. Object Management Group. Essence - Kernel and Language for Software Engineering Methods, October 2018. http://semat.org/essence-1.2
12. Jackson, M., Zave, P.: Deriving specifications from requirements: an example. In: 1995 17th International Conference on Software Engineering, p. 15. IEEE (1995)
13. Laplante, P.A.: Requirements Engineering for Software and Systems, 3rd edn. Auerbach Publications (2017)
14. Meyer, B.: On formalism in specifications. IEEE Softw. **3**(1), 6–25 (1985)

15. Meyer, B.: The software knowledge base. In: Proceedings of the 8th International Conference on Software Engineering, pp. 158–165. IEEE Computer Society Press, August 1985
16. Meyer, B.: Multirequirements. Modelling and Quality in Requirements Engineering (Martin Glinz Festscrhift) (2013)
17. Van Lamsweerde, A.: Requirements Engineering: From System Goals to UML Models to Software, vol. 10. Wiley, Chichester (2009)
18. Van Lamsweerde, A., Letier, E.: Handling obstacles in goal-oriented requirements engineering. IEEE Trans. Softw. Eng. **26**(10), 978–1005 (2000)
19. Wiegers, K., Beatty, J.: Software Requirements, 3rd edn. Microsoft Press (2014)

# Software Engineering and Programming Languages

# Preferred Tools for Agile Development: A Sociocultural Perspective

Paolo Ciancarini[1,2], Marcello Missiroli[1]([✉]), and Alberto Sillitti[2]

[1] DISI, University of Bologna, Bologna, Italy
{paolo.ciancarini,marcello.missiroli}@unibo.it
[2] Innopolis University, Innopolis, Russian Federation
a.sillitti@innopolis.ru

**Abstract.** Tools are of paramount importance in supporting software development methods, Agile ones included. In this paper, we aim to identify the most popular tools used by the Agile developers community, studying whether there are shared opinions or there are discrepancies, that could be related to cultural or geographical differences. The study is based on the DESMET approach, enhanced with some additional considerations.

Results show that Agilists are well integrated and tend to use the same tools even if some regional differences exist. Moreover, they prefer well-known and established products; interestingly, planning tools are generally regarded as unsatisfactory. We list, classify, and discuss the most popular tools.

## 1 Introduction

Every software development method carries its own set of tools. Traditional, plan-based development approaches (e.g., Waterfall, V-shape, etc.) have established the importance of project management tools (e.g., GANTT, PERT, etc.), software estimation techniques (e.g., CoCoMo, function points, etc.), and testing approaches (e.g., white, gray, and black box). Some of them have become part of the standard set of tools that support and automate programmers' tasks: IDEs, build automation, testing frameworks, and more. Collectively named Computer-Aided Software Engineering (CASE) tools, they encompass the entire production cycle and have been in use for several decades.

When the Agile manifesto was published in 2001 [9], it proposed a radically different approach to software development that included and combined several practices and concepts developed and applied with success by some professional developers of the time.

Beck, one of the signers of the Manifesto, for instance, claimed that contemporary tools were not suited for the Agile approach [8]. Therefore, developers were urged to modify and adapt existing tools or to create their own to fit their needs. As a result, the use of low-tech tools began to spread and become a synonym of Agile development. To avoid the problems and distractions introduced

© Springer Nature Switzerland AG 2019
M. Mazzara et al. (Eds.): TOOLS 2019, LNCS 11771, pp. 43–58, 2019.
https://doi.org/10.1007/978-3-030-29852-4_3

by tools and to focus on the new approach, the preferred way to spread the agile principles and practices was to use cheap low-tech solutions – pens, paper, and sticky notes [27]. While being instrumental in teaching the new method and having obvious relations with the Manifesto's philosophy, such an approach was also a response to the excessive use of *cold* tools and procedures which de-humanized the coding practices over time.

Indeed, several professionals believe that physical tools are adequate for all uses and disdain digital tools[1] in all cases except for automating certain tasks (e.g., continuous integrations and version control).

Limiting a team to just low-tech tools does not work, particularly when scaling [26,32]. The Agile revolution calls for a different set of powerful tools that either substitute or work alongside paper-and-pencil ones. We are aware that analyzing and/or recommending tools is difficult, especially in this area: methodologies change rapidly [13], tool are frequently updated [29], developer are always looking for new solutions [12], etc. However, we think that, for this very reason, it is important to analyze the current situation to understand the limitations and the advantages of the current tools. Moreover, it will be interesting to monitor their evolution and relate them to the technological and methodological changes.

This work compares the software tools that are currently the most popular and related to Agile development and classify them according to several user categories, also highlighting differences due to employers, culture, and location.

The rest of this paper is organized as follows: Sect. 2 investigates related research; Sect. 3 describes the overall structure of our investigation; Sect. 4 performs a first screening survey based on publicly available information and focus group reports; Sect. 5 refines results by performing a feature analysis survey on the Agile Community; Sect. 6 analyzes the threats to validity; Sect. 7 discusses the final results; finally, Sect. 8 draws the conclusions.

## 2   Related Work

Some investigations on agile tool usage are found in [14,19]. The most complete report available is *Forrester Wave*, a comprehensive review of the Agile development landscape [34], which includes some considerations on software tools.

There are two papers investigating a closely-related area: the reviews by Azizyan *et al.* [5] and Gottstein *et al.* [16]; the latter notable for its rigorous approach. These are both quite obsolete in the fast-changing world of software development. Almost every product reviewed has virtually disappeared and the tools used today did not even exist at that time.

Wang [33] reviews tools specifically aimed at distributed projects. This report is outdated as well. The annual State of Agile report[2] offers a listing of the most used and recommended tool, but its findings may be biased due to the involvement of VersionOne. The most recent independent work is [22] providing some regional and qualitative data.

---

[1] https://pragprog.com/magazines/2011-09/the-only-agile-tools-youll-ever-need.
[2] https://stateofagile.versionone.com/.

There are also some studies on specific tools such as the ones on Atlassian Jira [15] and Confluence [11]; a specific work directly compares JIRA and Redmine [28]. Finally, even if systematic reviews exist, such as [24], they do not focus specifically on Agile tools.

Moreover, while there are some works linking Agile success to cultural aspects in companies [20], we found no works linking Agile tools usage and national and/or language factors (with the possible exception of [1]).

## 3  Research Design

Our research is based on the Kitchenham's DESMET *Method for evaluating Software Engineering Methods and Tools* [21], providing software development organizations with a flexible research framework, also used in academic research [4,18]. The main deviation we applied to the original method is in its application to a self-defined community (the *Agile Community*) instead of a formal organization or company.

The Agile movement began officially in 2001. Its practitioners started from the very beginning to share ideas and information using the opportunity provided by the Internet. As a result, with respect to traditional programmers, Agilists tend to be more sociable, communicative, and united [35].

Unsurprisingly, in just a few years, a global Agile Community emerged. Though not formally defined, it presents itself as a myriad of local user groups, conferences, and very active online groups. In this perspective, we assume that the Agile Community fits the general definition of an organization used in DESMET [21]. Of course, a community lacks the internal structure and reliability of a normal organization. However, Agile developers share the same vision on practical problems, and this alleviates the differences, at least partially.

In this study we target the global Agile Community. This gave us the opportunity to compare some local communities identifying similarities and differences due to cultural and linguistic differences.

We can now formalize the research goals as follows:

- RQ1: Which are the best and most widespread computer-based tools for the Agile lifecycle (ASDLC [2]) used by the Agile Community?
- RQ2: Are there differences based on cultural or geographic location?
- RQ3: In this context, which are the common and different aspects of the Agile Communities participating in this study?

To reach our goal, the instrument we chose is a Feature Analysis, which is an "attempt to put a rationale on the gut feeling for the right product" [21]. We follow the DESMET methodology rather closely but using in a two-step approach:

- First, we performed a *Screening Survey* based on available information, creating a shortlist of the most used tools.
- Then, using the information obtained, we performed a *Feature Analysis Survey* which produced the final results.

### 3.1   User Groups

Since the community is vast and diverse, it is important to identify a more specific user group, as stated in [21]; each group can have a different perception of the concept of "best tool". In this work, we consider two broad groups of users: *professional* and *education*. The first includes people employed in the software development industry, the latter people involved in learning and teaching software development. Moreover, according to both our experience and available research [23], the company size affects the Agile projects success, far more than domain or location. Therefore, we divided the professional group according to the size of their companies. The cultural aspect, mainly defined by the mother tongue language used, is used to partition answers and identify possible trends. There are many other possible discriminating factors such as experience, level of implementation of the agile practices, team size, etc. Therefore, we included them in the questionnaire. To summarize, the identified groups are as follows: Micro enterprises (MiE), Small businesses (SB), Medium enterprises (MeE), Large enterprises (LE), CS-oriented Educational Institutions (CSEI).

### 3.2   User Groups by Culture

Another important factor is the cultural-linguistic context of developers. It is conceivable that results vary considerably in relation to location, language, and cultural background. As a result, we prepared several localized versions of the survey, to understand whether our intuition was correct. Localized version include vehicular languages (English, French, Spanish, Arabic), widely spoken but highly localized communities (Russian, Chinese) and middle-sized uniform cultural environments (Italian, Japanese, Iranian).

### 3.3   Scope

According to the DESMET methodology, we performed comparative evaluation of tools to understand how well they fit the need and culture of users group within the target organization. Please note that DESMET only evaluates specific methods and not their interaction. In case of tools providing multiple features or even fully integrated system, they are rated separately. This is a well known threat to validity of DESMET and it needs be taken into account.

### 3.4   Methodology

To correctly perform a review of the tools, it is necessary to identify which categories of tools are used in an Agile development environment. As a starting point, we used the list of Agile programming practices [7]. Taking the whole lifecycle into account, we identified three main areas in which Agile practices and values can benefit from software tools, namely (a) **Project Management & Strategic Planning**, (b) **Coding, Tactical Planning & Deployment** and (c) **Communication & Collaboration**:

In our work, we considered only tools that fulfill the following conditions:

1. They significantly impact one or more of these areas of interest.
2. They are targeted at the Agile Community, thus excluding IDEs, classic project management tools (e.g., Microsoft Project); some general-purpose tool that have large user base among Agilists were included as exceptions.
3. They have a sizable user base; we excluded niche, abandoned, or beta-quality tools.

### 3.5   Assumptions and Confidence in Results

A major problem we have is the tool granularity. Some tools are vertical products (or tightly integrated components) aiming to address all development needs. Other tools focus on one or two aspects of the development cycle. For example, Jira and the Microsoft suite belong to the first kind, while Toggl to the second one. We considered the impact of each tool on the most relevant area (as defined in Sect. 3.4), taking into account the ease of interaction with third party tools. We evaluated only tools that have been available for at least two years. This time is sufficient for the community to acquire experience and evaluate a tool in production and not only in test projects.

## 4   Screening Survey

We can formalize the research question of this step as a sub-question of RQ1:

– RQ1.1 Currently, which are the most popular tools related to the Agile development?

   There is a large number of computer-based tools that are related to the Agile development, so many that it is impossible to examine them all in a reasonable amount of time. Therefore, the initial part of the work consisted in identifying *the most used tools by the Agile community*. Though, this is different from finding the best ones, we assume that the wisdom of the crowds principle [31] holds, allowing us to include the best tools in the most used ones.
   The evaluation method used is a Screening Survey, as defined by DESMET [21]. It is used when "various tools have been used in a group organization" and executed by collecting information from a number of users.

### 4.1   Initial Product Selection

To build the initial list of tools, we analyzed a set of websites specialized in software reviews. They included TrustRadius, Software Advice, BestVendor, FindTheBest, AppAppeal, Cloudswave, GetApp, Serchen, Alternativeto, SocialCompare, Credii, IT Central Station, G2 Crowd, TopAlternatives, DiscoverCloud, Project Management Zone. We also considered Wikipedia, looking for products labeled as "Agile". We built a list of all products that were mentioned or reviewed at least twice.
   Then, we created the list applying the following criteria [21]:

- Support of at least one of the following development areas: planning, communication, coding (Mandatory).
  Since we are considering very diverse tools, building and ranking a feature list would be both impossible and pointless. Rather, we grouped tools into the three mentioned areas of interest and considered tools that could be applied to at least one of them.
- Established user base and support (Mandatory).
  This excludes *abandonware* (defined in this context as software with no updates in the last 24 months), beta-quality software, and products without available support (either paid or community-based).
- Conceived for Agile development (Highly Desirable).
  When starting to embrace Agile, many companies decided to adapt existing tools to the new methods instead of acquiring new ones. In fact, some reviews [14] show that one of the most used Agile tools are spreadsheets as Microsoft Excel. Since it is difficult to discriminate their use for common tasks, plan-driven development and agile development, we decide to favor Agile-specific tools, though not exclusively.
- Free/Open source software (Desirable).
  This criteria is motivated by the fact that most top FLOSS developer-oriented tools are high-quality, reliable, and long-lived. Moreover, their adoption has frequently lower barriers since developers can often use them bypassing their purchasing offices.

Before applying our criteria, we removed tools related to development in general, such as IDEs, Version Control Systems (e.g., Subversion, Git, etc.) and testing frameworks, since they are are ubiquitous, regardless the development methodology adopted.

Applying such criteria, we built a list of 80 tools, partitioned in the three areas defined in Sect. 3.4.

## 4.2 Popularity Filter

We had to narrow down the list according to popularity, an indication of market share, renown and appreciation. Popularity is important for various reasons, such as ease of personnel recruitment, continued and reliable support, and available knowledge base in the community.

There is limited reliable information available on this matter, such as sale figures, download data, user-based reviews. In many cases, software companies are not interested in publishing such data. Since a worldwide survey is impossible in a reasonable timescale, we defined a popularity index that allowed us to rank and identify the most popular products based on several information sources available on the Internet and the information provided by a focus group.

More specifically, the index was built by joining information from four different sources:

1. **Google Trends**
   This tool is often used as a reliable source of information in academic research [10], even in the software engineering field [25]. Google Trends gives

us an idea of the overall popularity of the product. Then, we ranked the results and assigned points according to the following scale: 20 points for the first place, 17 for the second, then 13, 10, 8, 6, 5, 4, 3, 2. Thereafter, 1 was awarded if the result was at least 1, 0 otherwise. This sublinear scale was devised after experimenting with linear and Fibonacci successions; it was the best suited to achieve the following goals: (a) assign an equal weight to all factors, since we did not have any *a priori* knowledge of relative reliability and (b) give ranking leaders a substantial, but not overwhelming advantage over the next in rank.

2. **Stack Overflow**
   Stack Overflow is arguably the most popular Q&A website for developers. It provides practical advice and can be used as an information source in research [3,6]. We counted the number of questions tagged to specific products, as an indication of the interest within the programmers' community. Results were ranked and points assigned using the same scale as above.

3. **Agile-oriented reviews websites**
   The importance of word-of-mouth has not been widely used in Computer Science, though it has in other contexts [17]. We re-examined the reviews of the websites used in Sect. 4.1, and we noted that only a fraction of them has a significant presence of Agile-specific software reviews. In practice, only two sites were considered as significant: *Software Insider* and *G2crowds*.
   As the review quality is very different and sometimes of dubious reliability, we used the number of reviews as a measure of the interest of the community. Therefore, our metric was calculated by adding the numbers of reviews of a given product from the two websites, then ranking results and assigning points as above, assigning the same weight to both websites.

4. **Agile expert group**
   We convened an expert group of about 20 developers and entrepreneurs with a solid experience of Agile practices belonging to companies of various size. They were asked to cite the most useful tools they actively use. Then, we counted the number of occurrences that a product was listed and added the number of times that a given product was cited in the following discussion. Final results were also discussed online in specialized international mailing lists, sometimes adding products that were not cited during the meeting. Again, results were ranked and points assigned as above. In case of a tie, we summed and averaged the points awarded rounding down. Note that neither Microsoft Excel nor Project were ever mentioned by the expert group, supporting our intuition to exclude them in the early stages.

Table 1 shows the results of our popularity investigation. Since, some products are related to more areas and we are interested in identifying the most popular tools overall, the table shows such products only once, in the best-ranking area.

The overall popularity score is the sum of the four scores, ±5% in case of rising or falling Google Trend.

**Table 1.** Popularity evaluation: (1) Jira Agile results could be affected by the possible overlapping searches of JIRA, Atlassian Jira, Agile Jira and Grasshopper, its previous name. (2) Slack result do not include data from Screenhero, a Pair Programming tool acquired. (3) Most of the results about Skype for Business were based on the program's former name, Lync. In addition, though slightly below the Confluence score, we took into account the positive trend (in contrast to the Confluence's negative one) and awarded a better ranking. (4) Gitlab includes Gitlab and Gitlab-CI.

| Program Mangement & Strategic Planning | Overall | Google Trends | Points | G2crowd & Software Insider | Points | Stack Overflow | Points | Expert Group | Points |
|---|---|---|---|---|---|---|---|---|---|
| Jira Agile (1) | 67 | 1 | 20 | 794, 64 | 20 | 3817 | 17 | 3 | 10 |
| Redmine | 59 | 3 | 13 | 63, 96 | 8 | 1572 | 20 | 4 | 18 |
| Trello | 50 | 2 | 17 | 595, 59 | 13 | 315 | 10 | 3 | 10 |
| Pivotal Tracker | 41 | 4 | 10 | 69, 7 | 10 | 58 | 3 | 4 | 18 |
| Trac | 30 | 7 | 5 | 7 | 2 | 674 | 13 | 3 | 10 |
| Wrike | 23 | 6 | 6 | 661, 17 | 17 | 0 | 0 | 0 | 0 |
| Toggl | 19 | 5 | 8 | 37 | 6 | 0 | 0 | 2 | 5 |
| Mylyn | 18 | 12 | 1 | 17 | 4 | 204 | 8 | 2 | 5 |
| Visual Paradigm | 13 | 8 | 4 | 0 | 0 | 80 | 9 | 0 | 0 |
| VersionOne | 11 | 10 | 2 | 35, 48 | 5 | 130 | 4 | 0 | 0 |
| Youtrack | 10 | 11 | 1 | 9 | 3 | 193 | 6 | 1 | 0 |
| IBM Jazz | 9 | 9 | 3 | 1 | 1 | 149 | 5 | 0 | 0 |
| Target Process | 5 | 13 | 1 | 0 | 0 | 0 | 0 | 1 | 4 |
| Coding & Tactical Planning | | | | | | | | | |
| Github | 80 | 1 | 20 | 311 | 20 | 20700 | 20 | 8 | 20 |
| Jenkins | 66 | 2 | 17 | 121 | 17 | 18358 | 17 | 6 | 15 |
| Bitbucket | 49 | 3 | 13 | 83 | 13 | 3210 | 8 | 6 | 15 |
| Team Foundation Server | 35 | 4 | 10 | 42 | 6 | 13881 | 13 | 1 | 6 |
| Gitlab (4) | 27 | 5 | 8 | 13 | 3 | 2667 | 6 | 3 | 10 |
| Teamcity | 27 | 6 | 6 | 39 | 5 | 4190 | 10 | 1 | 6 |
| Travis CI | 24 | 7 | 5 | 56 | 8 | 1923 | 5 | 1 | 6 |
| Codeship | 15 | 10 | 2 | 79 | 10 | 124 | 3 | 0 | |
| Bamboo | 15 | 11 | 1 | 30 | 4 | 867 | 4 | 1 | 6 |
| Concourse | 6 | 8 | 4 | 0 | 0 | 18 | 2 | 0 | |
| Circle CI | 3 | 9 | 3 | 0 | 0 | 0 | | 0 | |
| Node-CI | 1 | 12 | 1 | 0 | 0 | 0 | 0 | 0 | |
| Communication | | | | | | | | | |
| Slack (2) | 66 | 3 | 13 | 912 | 20 | 337 | 13 | 5 | 20 |
| Skype 4 business (3) | 57 | 4 | 10 | 432 | 17 | 502 | 17 | 2 | 13 |
| Confluence | 51 | 5 | 8 | 180 | 10 | 677 | 20 | 2 | 13 |
| Google hangout | 48 | 2 | 17 | 166 | 13 | 297 | 10 | 1 | 8 |
| Teamviewer | 46 | 1 | 20 | 98 | 13 | 0 | 0 | 2 | 13 |
| Rational Jazz | 21 | 7 | 5 | 4 | 8 | 149 | 8 | 0 | 0 |
| Zoom.us | 14 | 6 | 6 | 0 | 0 | 0 | 0 | 1 | 8 |
| Hackpad | 10 | 8 | 4 | 3 | 6 | 0 | 0 | 0 | 0 |
| Floobits | 3 | 9 | 3 | 0 | 0 | 0 | 0 | 0 | 0 |
| Ideaboardz | 2 | 10 | 2 | 0 | 0 | 0 | 0 | 0 | 0 |
| Stormboard | 1 | 11 | 1 | 0 | 0 | 0 | 0 | 0 | 0 |
| Retrium | 1 | 12 | 1 | 0 | 0 | 0 | 0 | 0 | 0 |

### 4.3   Analysis of the Results

In all areas, the five best ranked tools are the same, regardless of the inquiry method. This indicates that the Community has a shared opinion on the subject. After the top ones, things start to diverge. For example, Wrike has an excellent score in reviews, but is ignored by experts and programmers. In the communication area, experts seem to rely on established, general-purpose tools instead of specialized ones.

Said that, we consider the first ten products in each category to be included in the subsequent section of our analysis. Programs appearing in more than a category (such as Team Services and Github) were assigned to the best ranking one.

## 5   Feature Analysis Survey

The screening survey provided us with a list of target tools, which we used to prepare the survey targeted at the worldwide Agile Community.

Performing such a large-scale survey provided us a good opportunity to investigate something more about the Agile Community as a whole. For example, whether their tools preferences are influenced by other factors, such as cultural heritage and experience. We are aware that other similar surveys exists but they only provide aggregated data.

### 5.1   Survey Distribution and Turnout

The survey was mainly performed via Google Forms. The link was distributed on several social media. As we wanted to maximize the number of answers and at the same time investigate on cultural differences, we prepared several localized versions of the survey. The main rationale was that filling a form in one's own mother tongue language is easier that in any other one, even if used often. This also allowed a conscious partition of the respondents according to their cultural attachment. All links were provided via bit.ly, to obtain additional data about the participants.

We addressed several LinkedIn, Google, and Yahoo groups as well as several local Agile groups, but the response was limited. Unfortunately, a centralized information hub does not really exist in this field. *Scrum Alliance* and *Agile Alliance* do provide some pointers to groups and lists, but most information is US-centric and/or outdated. Therefore, we had to perform a manual search, addressing private mailing lists, Facebook pages, Twitter accounts, and in some cases even emails of individuals.

We had a significant number of respondents, but their distribution was uneven, as shown in Sect. 5.2. While a majority of Italian and Russian responses was to be expected, due to our strong ties to these communities, we did not expect such a low response from large communities such as: Chinese, Arabic, and Japanese. Since we used the same communication channels, there are three possible (non-exclusive) explanations of the phenomenon:

1. **Different channels**. These communities, due to cultural or political factors, do not use the same social media used in the Western social landscape (Iran-farsi would however be a notable exception).
2. **Limited size**. The Agile Community is not as large as expected in these countries or cultural areas, severely limiting responses.
3. **Reputation**. The authors are relatively well-known in the Western Agile Community, being active participants for more than 15 years. Reputation and personal relations can have influenced the response rate.

The questionnaire was distributed as a standard Google Form link. Participation was anonymous and entirely voluntary.

From now on, we group results in three main categories: "Italy" (IT), "Russia & Ukraine" (RU-UA), and "Rest of the World" (ROW). About the ROW, please note that the majority of responses come from the western cultural environment (Iran being the only exception).

## 5.2   Results

We are well aware that our analysis does not have the strength of a full statistical and parametric analysis. However, opinion surveys used in DESMET, in general, and Likert scale analysis, in particular, do not fit well a deep statistical analysis [30]. Therefore, simple descriptive statistics is used to reveal trends and overall attitudes. Our idea is reinforced by the fact that responses are clustered along cultural differences.

Figure 1 shows the geographic location of the respondents (which might differ form the language used to perform the survey).

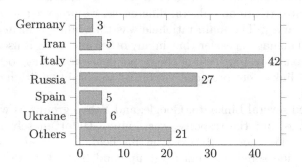

**Fig. 1.** Respondents location distribution

**Tools Known and Used:** Table 2 refers to the current use of tools in various areas. "Current use" is the answer to the question: *"Does your company use computer-based tools that relate to PLANNING/CODING/ COMMUNICATION?"*. "Need more" is the answer to the question: *"Do*

**Table 2.** Current tools use in organization

**ITALY**

| Area | PLANNING | | CODING | | COMMUNICATION | |
|---|---|---|---|---|---|---|
| Question | CURRENT | MORE | CURRENT | MORE | CURRENT | MORE |
| Mean | 3.31 | 2.74 | 3.89 | 3.63 | 3.00 | 3.26 |
| Std. Dev. | 1.35 | 1.58 | 1.28 | 1.31 | 1.28 | 1.09 |

**RUSSIA & UKRAINE**

| Area | PLANNING | | CODING | | COMMUNICATION | |
|---|---|---|---|---|---|---|
| Question | CURRENT | MORE | CURRENT | MORE | CURRENT | MORE |
| Mean | 3.56 | 2.53 | 4.06 | 3.65 | 4.35 | 2.71 |
| Std. Dev. | 1.21 | 1.28 | 0.95 | 1.37 | 1.07 | 1.62 |

**REST OF THE WORLD**

| Area | PLANNING | | CODING | | COMMUNICATION | |
|---|---|---|---|---|---|---|
| Question | CURRENT | MORE | CURRENT | MORE | CURRENT | MORE |
| Mean | 3.38 | 3.25 | 3.88 | 4.83 | 3.42 | 3.33 |
| Std. Dev. | 1.21 | 1.45 | 1.03 | 0.82 | 1.25 | 2.01 |

*you think your company would work better, if tool usage in the PLAN-NING/CODING/COMMUNICATION area increases?"*. In all cases, we used a standard 5-point Likert scale (1 = Strongly disagree; 5 = Strongly Agree). We report here the mean and standard deviation for each category.

Results show that there is a significant tool use in the Agile Community, especially in the coding area, and the general consensus is that more tool usage would be beneficial. Italian and especially Russian respondents are less fond of tools in the PLANNING section, but use tool more intensively in the CODING area. Russians also seem to have more than enough tools related to COMMUNI-CATION – though, in this area, results are more defined, especially considering ROW developers.

**Tool Evaluation Analysis:** We can now consider the evaluation of tools.

The overall appreciation of tools is very low in the PLANNING section, with only one product scoring above average (3.00). This is a clear indication that the "killer application" in this field is yet to be discovered. It seems that the most loved (or less hated) tools are **Trello** and **Jira Agile**. Trello has also a good rating for a very specialized task. A slight positive difference in the Italian ratings is to be noted. If we consider the company size, Micro Enterprises assigned lower than average to almost all products, except Trello and Trac. Medium and Large Enterprises prefer Wrike, Visual Paradigm, and Version One. In the case of Education, there is almost no difference, except a marked negative score for Trello.

CODING tools fare much better. **Github, Jenkins, Gitlab** and **Bitbucket** – in this order – all score well above average. Both Italian and Russian Agilists' opinions are very similar to their colleagues abroad, showing enthusiasm for several tools, Gitlab and Teamcity in particular. Micro Enterprises seem to appreciate the above products more, whereas educational institutions seem to have difficulties with Github. Small and Large enterprises show particular interest for Bamboo.

Several COMMUNICATION tools also have good average scores, in particular **Slack**, **Teamviewer** (Russia's favorite), **Skype for Business**, and even **Confluence**—almost. Again Italians and Russian speakers show more enthusiasm for these tools, especially for Zoom.it and Hackpad (not even mentioned by ROW Agilists). Floobits and Ideaboardz have better scores in a corporate environment, though they reach a sufficient score only among ROW respondents.

## 6  Validity

We evaluate the overall confidence in the results according to DESMET [21]. A Feature Analysis is associated with very high risk of incorrect conclusions. However, Feature Analysis Surveys only have a Medium Risk. Since we combine the results of the two methods, we assume that the overall risk of incorrect results is Medium.

In the feature survey, we are aware that the limited size of the sample does not allow a meaningful statistical analysis. However, this is counterbalanced by the uniformity of the answers and the large amount of data provided by Google Trends that provide the base of our analysis.

Threats to external validity are mainly due both due to the limited amount of samples and their geographical distribution – specifically, the limited response of North-Americans, that comprise a large percentage of the worldwide Agile developer community. Given that, we can only assume that results apply to the European community, and extension of validity is demanded to future work in this area.

## 7  Results

### 7.1  RQ1: The Best and Widespread Tools

We provide the main research question by dividing results into three quality tiers, regardless of cultural or language differences. This classification can orient organizations and individuals in finding the most suited tools for their business.

**Tier 1**: these are products that combine a large user base in the Community and positive overall reviews. They are to be considered a "safe choice" for everyone, especially newcomers in the Agile field. The exact choice of tool (or their combination) depends on the individual needs of the company or institution and cannot be examined in detail. Tools in this category are: **Atlassian**

**Jira, Trello, Toggl** for PLANNING; **Github, Jenkins, Gitlab,** for CODING; **Slack, Skype for Business, Teamviewer** for COMMUNICATION.

**Tier 2**: these products have either a limited diffusion or are more appreciated in specific contexts. These are **Redmine** and **Trac** for MiE, **Bitbucket** for Education, **Bamboo, Confluence, Wrike, Visual Paradigm** and **VersionOne** for Medium to Large Enterprises.

**Tier 3**: these products do not have a particular brilliant score or enjoy much popularity but might be of interest in specific environments. For example, Team Foundation Services could be a sound choice if the development of the company is strongly Microsoft-oriented. These include: **Confluence, Team Foundation Services, Floobits, Ideabordz, Teamcity**.

## 7.2 RQ2 Demographic Differences

According to our survey, the opinions of the overall Agile Community on tools are rather similar. We can even use the demographic data acquired to define the "Average Agilist" (or, better still, "EuroAgilist", given the geographical distribution of respondents). The average respondent is male (90%), generally works in a country speaking his mother-tongue language (85%) and has and university degree (70%) (mostly Bachelor in case of English and Spanish speaking countries, Master in the other cases). He works for several types of companies and customers, with a slight preference for middle-sized enterprises (ME - 35%). When coding, generally prefers a complete IDE (75%). He has about 3 years of Agile experience (Scrum - 80%, Kanban - 50%). However, the practices used vary considerably from country to country. The lack of responses from a very large population of programmers (Asian and most Arabic countries) does not allow us to determine if the Agile Community is really "global" or rater limited to the Western world - with some exceptions, such as Iran and Russia.

Almost everyone (95%) has some experience with Scrum; the second-favorite method is more localized as Russians, Italians, and Spaniards tend to use Kanban, whereas the rest of the world prefer hybrid methods. The practices used are different. German, Farsi, and English-speaking Agilists tend to use many of the recommended practices (even all of them), but Russians and Iranians tend to be more selective, cherry-picking the ones that best suits them. Italians do not show any particular tendency. The most used practices overall are Pair Programming, TDD, and Small Releases; least used ones are On-site customer, Continuous Integration, and System metaphor.

## 7.3 RQ3: Italian and Russian Communities

According to our survey, both the Italian and Russian-Ukranian Agile Communities are very similar to the ROW community, possibly more enthusiastic in tool usage. In the case of Italy, considering all possible answers only in 8 cases the difference with the ROW responses exceeds 0.5 in the Likert scale (either way). Moreover, 5 of such cases are related to the Planning section. In the second case, difference are definitely more relevant—Russian Agilists tend to be more extreme in their evaluation but still following the ROW trends. Therefore, the Italian and Russian-speaking Agile Communities can be considered well integrated in the global Agile Community.

# 8   Conclusions

In this work, we examined the attitude of the Agile Community (in particular of the Italian and Russian ones) towards Agile tools using the DESMET methodology. We found out that most of the opinions of these two localized Agile Communities are in line with those of the global Agile Community. We provide a ranked list of the current tools most favored by the Community, giving indication on possible cases that might favor a tool over another. We also plan to repeat the survey in the future to identify market trends, community needs and focus on the US-Canada community.

**Acknowledgements.** We thank for the support from CINI/MANTIS and from CNR-ISTC.

# References

1. Stankovic, D., Nikolic, V., Djordjevic, M., Cao, D.B.: A survey study of critical success factors in agile software projects in former Yugoslavia IT companies. J. Syst. Soft. **86**(6), 1663–1678 (2013)
2. Ambler, S.W., et al.: The agile system development life cycle (2010). http://www.ambysoft.com/essays/agileLifecycle.html. Accessed 14 Aug 2019
3. Anderson, A., Huttenlocher, D., Kleinberg, J., Leskovec, J.: Discovering value from community activity on focused question answering sites: a case study of stack overflow. In: Proceedings of the 18th ACM SIGKDD International Conference on Knowledge Discovery and Data Mining, pp. 850–858. ACM (2012)
4. Aversano, L., Canfora, G., De Lucia, A., Gallucci, P.: Integrating document and workflow management tools using xml and web technologies: a case study. In: Proceedings of the 6th European Conference on Software Maintenance and Reengineering, pp. 24–33. IEEE (2002)
5. Azizyan, G., Magarian, M.K., Kajko-Matsson, M.: Survey of agile tool usage and needs. In: 2011 Agile Conference (AGILE), pp. 29–38. IEEE (2011)
6. Barua, A., Thomas, S.W., Hassan, A.E.: What are developers talking about? An analysis of topics and trends in stack overflow. Empir. Softw. Eng. **19**(3), 619–654 (2014)
7. Beck, K.: Extreme Programming Explained: Embrace Change. Addison-Wesley Professional, Boston (2000)
8. Beck, K.: Tools for agility. Microsoft White Papers, pp. 1–12 (2008)
9. Beck, K., et al.: Manifesto for agile software development (2001)
10. Choi, H., Varian, H.: Predicting the present with google trends. Econ. Rec. **88**(s1), 2–9 (2012)
11. Clarke, R.: Collaborative authorship with Atlassian confluence. GLiNTECH White Paper, p. 10 (2007)

12. Coman, I.D., Sillitti, A., Succi, G.: Investigating the usefulness of pair-programming in a mature agile team. In: Abrahamsson, P., Baskerville, R., Conboy, K., Fitzgerald, B., Morgan, L., Wang, X. (eds.) XP 2008. LNBIP, vol. 9, pp. 127–136. Springer, Heidelberg (2008). https://doi.org/10.1007/978-3-540-68255-4_13
13. Corral, L., Sillitti, A., Succi, G.: Software development processes for mobile systems: is agile really taking over the business? In: International Workshop on the Engineering of Mobile-Enabled Systems (MOBS 2013) (2013)
14. Dubakov, M., Stevens, P.: Agile Tools: The Good, the Bad and the Ugly. Report, TargetProcess, Inc. (2008)
15. Fisher, J., Koning, D., Ludwigsen, A.: Utilizing Atlassian JIRA for large-scale software development management. In: 14th International Conference on Accelerator and Large Experimental Physics Control Systems (ICALEPCS) (2013)
16. Gottstein, D., Renè, A., Fechner, T.: Vergleich verschiedener Softwarewerkzeuge zur agilen Softwareentwicklung (2011). http://winfwiki.wi-fom.de/index.php/Vergleich_verschiedener_Softwarewerkzeuge_zur_agilen_Softwareentwicklung
17. Gretzel, U., Yoo, K.H., Purifoy, M.: Online travel review study: role and impact of online travel reviews (2007)
18. Hedberg, H., Lappalainen, J.: A preliminary evaluation of software inspection tools, with the DESMET method. In: Fifth International Conference on Quality Software (QSIC 2005), pp. 45–52. IEEE (2005)
19. Hunt, J.: Tools to help with agile development. Agile Software Construction, pp. 217–237 (2006)
20. Iivari, J., Iivari, N.: The relationship between organizational culture and the deployment of agile methods. Inf. Softw. Technol. **53**(5), 509–520 (2011)
21. Kitchenham, B., Linkman, S., Law, D.: DESMET: a methodology for evaluating software engineering methods and tools. Comput. Control Eng. J. **8**(3), 120–126 (1997)
22. Kropp, M., Maier, A.: Swiss Agile Study (2014). http://www.swissagilestudy.ch/files/2015/05/SwissAgileStudy2014.pdf
23. Kruchten, P.: Scaling down large projects to meet the agile sweet spot. IBM developerWorks 13 (2004)
24. Portillo-Rodríguez, J., Vizcaíno, A., Piattini, M., Beecham, S.: Tools used in global software engineering: a systematic mapping review. Inf. Softw. Technol. **54**(7), 663–685 (2012)
25. Rech, J.: Podcasts about software engineering. ACM SIGSOFT Softw. Eng. Notes **32**(2), 1–2 (2007)
26. Reifer, D.J., Maurer, F., Erdogmus, H.: Scaling agile methods. IEEE Softw. **20**(4), 12–14 (2003)
27. Rubin, K.S.: Essential Scrum: A Practical Guide to the Most Popular Agile Process. Addison-Wesley, Boston (2012)
28. Sarkan, H.M., Ahmad, T.P.S., Bakar, A.A.: Using JIRA and Redmine in requirement development for agile methodology. In: 5th Malaysian Conference on Software Engineering (MySEC), pp. 408–413. IEEE (2011)
29. Sillitti, A., Succi, G., Vlasenko, J.: Toward a better understanding of tool usage. In: International Conference on Software Engineering (ICSE 2011) (2011)
30. Sullivan, G.M., Artino Jr., A.R.: Analyzing and interpreting data from likert-type scales. J. Grad. Med. Educ. **5**(4), 541–542 (2013)

31. Surowiecki, J.: The Wisdom of Crowds. Anchor, Norwell (2005)
32. Tell, P., Babar, M.A.: Requirements for an infrastructure to support activity-based computing in global software development. In: Proceedings of the 6th IEEE International Conference on Global Software Engineering Workshop (ICGSEW), pp. 62–69. IEEE (2011)
33. Wang, X., Maurer, F., Morgan, R., Oliveira, J.: Tools for supporting distributed agile project planning. In: Šmite, D., Moe, N., Ågerfalk, P. (eds.) Agility Across Time and Space, pp. 183–199. Springer, Heidelberg (2010). https://doi.org/10.1007/978-3-642-12442-6_13
34. West, D., Hammond, J.S.: The Forrester Wave: Agile Development Management Tools. Forrester Research (2010)
35. Whitworth, E., Biddle, R.: The social nature of agile teams. In: Agile, vol. 7, pp. 26–36 (2007)

# Interpretizer: A Compiler-Independent Conversion of Switch-Based Dispatch into Threaded Code

Yauhen Klimiankou[✉]

Belarusian State University of Informatics and Radioelectronics,
6 P. Brovki Street, 220013 Minsk, Belarus
klimenkov@bsuir.by

**Abstract.** Performance of program bytecode interpretation depends significantly from instruction dispatch technique implemented in the virtual machine. Threaded code is a well-known approach of instruction dispatch implementation of efficient interpreters. However, the plurality of current high-level programming languages and popular compilers are limited in support of threaded code and enforce designers of interpreters to either stick to GCC compiler which supports "Labels as Values" custom C extension or to resort to the implementation of a dispatch loop in assembler. In this work, we present the Interpretizer, a standalone tool which can be integrated into arbitrary interpreter build toolchain readily and transparently and which effectively converts switch-based dispatch loops into efficient threaded code. Therefore, Interpretizer reverts to the virtual machine designers flexibility of choice of programming language and compiler while it preserves the efficiency of the produced interpreter.

**Keywords:** Threaded code · Switch-based dispatch · Dispatch loop · Object file

## 1 Introduction

Interpretation is one of the fundamental ways for implementation of programming languages, as well as for the execution of programs. Bytecode interpreters take a significant position between classical AST interpreters and compilers while attempting to inherit the main benefits of both. On the one hand, like AST interpreters, bytecode interpreters provide a secure and portable environment for programs execution. On the other hand, bytecode interpretation is much more efficient than AST interpretation (however, still much less efficient than compiled code execution). Furthermore, bytecode interpreter is more suitable for Just-In-Time compilation which can be seamlessly integrated into the interpreter, if the additional boost in program execution would outweigh the cost of JIT-compiler implementation. Additionally, the efforts required for interpreter design and implementation are significantly smaller than in the case of compiler

© Springer Nature Switzerland AG 2019
M. Mazzara et al. (Eds.): TOOLS 2019, LNCS 11771, pp. 59–72, 2019.
https://doi.org/10.1007/978-3-030-29852-4_4

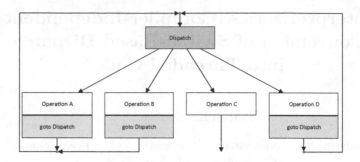

**Fig. 1.** Switch-based dispatch.

development. Due to this, interpretation is especially attractive for programming language prototyping and in the case of small-scale domain-specific applications.

Instruction dispatch technique employed by the virtual machine is one of the principal sources into the interpretation overhead. Furthermore, the type of employed dispatch technique affects maintainability and portability of the interpreter. There is two main instruction dispatch approach used in modern bytecode interpreters: switch-based dispatch and threaded code.

In the case of switch-based dispatch, the dispatch loop of the interpreter is a loop containing one huge switch statement that maps virtual instruction opcode onto the defined behavior of virtual machine. Switch-based dispatch (Fig. 1) can be implemented using standard primitives of high-level programming languages, and due to this is language- and compiler-independent and hence is portable and maintainable. However, switch-based dispatch is well-known for its inefficiency appearing from the increased level of branching in the interpreter code and from related branch misprediction performance penalty.

Threaded code (Fig. 2) is a well-known programming technique [3]. Switch-based dispatch separates the instruction dispatch from the instruction implementation. In contrast, in threaded code, the instruction dispatch is embedded into the end of each VM instruction implementation and thus replicated into them all. Therefore it tends to be larger than the equivalent switch-based code. However, at the same time, it tends to be more efficient due to the reduced number of branchings performed during bytecode interpretation (1 and 2+ branchings for threaded and for switch-based codes respectively) and produces fewer mispredictions in Branch Target Buffers of CPU [6]. The reported benchmarking results show that for some architectures the performance difference between switch-based code and threaded code can reach up to 2.02 times in favor of the last one [10]. Due to such significant difference in the performance, VM developers focusing interpretation efficiency tend to favor threaded code instead of switch-based dispatch.

Unfortunately, current high-level programming languages do not provide constructions which allow native implementation of the threaded code. The notable exception is GCC compiler which provides custom "Labels as Values" extension

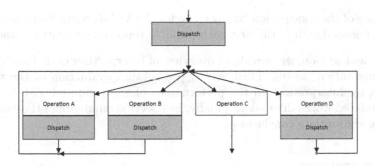

**Fig. 2.** Threaded code.

to the C programming language [1]. This extension provides a means which allow implementation of threaded code without resorting to assembler language. Therefore, at present, VM developers striving for the efficiency of interpretation, are forced to adhere not only to the C programming language, but also to the GCC compiler, or implement a dispatching loop and VM instructions with extensive assembly language involvement. The second way is not only expensive in terms of developer efforts but also seems to be limited in efficiency, because modern compilers are much more efficient in optimization than humans especially in the case of such massive functions as dispatcher loops.

In this paper, we present an approach that solves the current limitations on toolchains available for developers of threaded code based interpreters. We present Interpretizer, a standalone tool that converts the switch-based dispatch loop into the threaded code and does it transparently for the main toolchain used for VM development. Interpretizer gives VM developers the freedom to choose not only the programming language in general but also any compiler in particular, as well as entire build toolchain, and allows to inherit almost all optimizations made by the chosen compiler for dispatcher loop. Therefore, Interpretizer can be considered to be an external compiler-independent VM-specific binary code optimizer.

In summary, our contribution presented in this paper is the following:

- We propose a new approach to the development of efficient bytecode interpreters, which provides freedom of programming language and compiler choices for the developers, while preserves the original optimizations performed by a compiler and allows to produce an efficient threaded code based bytecode interpreters.
- We present Interpretizer, a standalone tool for automatic conversion of switch-based dispatch loops into the threaded code with an application of VM-specific optimizations. Interpretizer transparently and straightforwardly integrates into existing build toolchains.
- We provide results of Interpretizer evaluation from the viewpoint of implication on the interpretation performance of the produced virtual machine. We report the comparison of different compilers from the viewpoint of the

efficiency of the code generating by them for the VM dispatch loop. According to our knowledge, it is the first such publicly reported comparison results.

In the next section, we provide an overview of Interpretizer design and discuss its implementation details. Then Sect. 3 presents an evaluation of the impact producing by Interpretizer on the performance of the produced VM. Section 4 contains related works discussion. Finally, last section summarizes the work and draws out appropriate conclusions.

## 2   Interpretizer

This section discusses the principal design of Interpretizer by illustrating its architecture and role in the VM build toolchain as well as the expected way of its usage. The general idea behind Interpretizer is to apply VM-specific optimizations directly to the dispatch loop on the level of compiled binary code. Due to this, Interpretizer can be integrated into any build toolchain, placing itself in the workflow between compiler and linker and modifying the dispatch loop function on the level of the object file. The successfully modified object file is passed to the linker continuing a regular VM build-flow of the original toolchain.

Interpretizer accepts a set of the command-line arguments: paths to the source and target object files, the symbolic name of the dispatch loop function and the set of optimizations requested.

Interpretizer consists of three principal components:

- Object File Composer
- The Instructions Decoder
- Optimizer

Using Object File Composer, Interpretizer disassembles the source object file and extracts specified function which contains dispatch loop. The extracted code section is passing to Optimizer. In its turn, Optimizer, using the Instruction Decoder constructs the control flow graph of the function. Then, on the control flow graph, it looks up for a basic block (or group of basic blocks) which implements VM instructions dispatch. Using the knowledge about that basic block and having a function control graph, Optimizer can apply three optimizations:

- Range Control Elimination
- Code Straightening
- Code Threading

The resulted control flow graph is serialized back into function code which Object File Composer inserts back into the object file. The symbols and relocations in the object file are fixed to adjust them to the updated function code. Finally, resulted object file is assembled and stored into a file system.

## 2.1   Object File Composer

Interpretizer currently supports only Common Object File Format (COFF) object files.

COFF files contain three components: *sections, relocations,* and *symbols.* The COFF *section* is continuous binary blob containing a single compiled code object with explicitly defined dependencies and export points. Each section wires with a variable-length set of *relocations,* each of which represents a dependency to external compiled object and points to appropriate symbol. *Symbols* represent the export points of the sections. They assign a symbolic name from the string table to the export point of the section (in the form section:offset).

Interpretizer accepts through the command line arguments path to the source object file and symbolic name of the method containing the dispatch loop. Using them, Object File Composer disassembles the source file and finds the respective symbol and hence object address in the form *section:offset* to which it points. Knowing the location of dispatch loop function, Object File Composer extracts the body of the function. Finally, the intra-function linkage is performed using a list of relocations of the section to resolve absolute references in the body and thus fill the dispatch table by relative addresses of the VM instruction handlers. Linked function code is passed to Optimizer.

After accomplished optimization Object File Composer receives the modified body of function and translation map generated by Optimizer. Translation map maps the instruction offsets from the modified function body to the offsets of the same instructions in the original function body. This map is needed to fix symbols and relocations of the object file. While optimization does not generate new symbols and only shifts already existing ones, it can massively create new relocations due to the possible replication of instruction dispatch block. These new relocations need to be added to the relocations list of the section to allow the linker correctly assemble the final executable binary using optimized object file. The corrected object file is reassembled and finally stored in the file system.

## 2.2   Instructions Decoder

Interpretizer employs Instruction Decoder mainly for control flow graph construction. Due to this, the slightly extended version of the instruction length decoder is enough for Interpretizer purposes. The required extension is the ability to decode control transfer, *test* and *cmp* instructions. Interpretizer needs detection of *test* and *cmp* for Range Control Elimination optimization.

## 2.3   Optimizer

The Optimizer is a core of Interpretizer. Its purpose is to analyze input function code and generate at the output the optimized version of the code as well as the translation map which describes how the instructions from the original function map to their equivalents in the modified version. Optimizer performs its work in six steps:

1. Build Control Flow Graph of the function
2. Find Dispatch Basic Block
3. Apply Range Control Elimination
4. Apply Code Straightening
5. Apply Code Threading
6. Serialize Control Flow Graph to the plain binary code

Control Flow Graph construction is based on Instruction Decoder and in general, uses the well-known techniques. During this process, Optimizer parses the binary code, assembles basic blocks and establishes linkage between them. For each basic block, it remembers the original address and size of each instruction but ignores its semantics. The only significant difference between the regular assembling of Control Flow Graph and the implemented in Optimizer is a special care about table-based dispatch instructions.

All optimizations applied by Interpretizer require knowledge about Dispatch Block. Dispatch Block is a basic block (or a group of blocks) which exit point is a table-based jump instruction (*jmp dword ptr [imm + 4 · eax]*). The entry point to the Dispatch Block is the address to which the handlers listed in the table pass control at their exit points. The correct dispatch loop function contains exactly one table-based jump instruction. If no table-based jumps are present in the code, then this is a regular function without a dispatch loop. If more than one of them is present, then the dispatch loop is probably already threaded. In both cases, Interpretizer discards further optimizations as inapplicable and potentially unsafe.

**Range Control Elimination.** When a compiler translates *switch* statements of a high-level programming language into machine code, it inserts range control instructions in front of the table-based jump to handle the cases when the table index goes out of table lengths. It is correct from the language semantics viewpoint. However, in the case of interpreter dispatch loop, the instructions stream is trusted in most cases, either due to the trusted code generator or due to the verification of the code performed before its execution. Programming languages provide no means to give the compiler a hint that the dispatch table index value is guaranteed to be in the range of dispatch table length and hence the compiler should not generate redundant range control instructions.

Range Control Elimination removes redundant dispatch table index control. Knowing the dispatch block, and its exit point Optimizer looks at the instructions preceding table-based jump and checks for *jcc* instruction targeting the entry point of dispatch block. Then it analyzes a few more previous commands looking for *cmp* or *test*. In the case when both instructions are present, Optimizer removes them and merges the basic block containing table-based jump into its parent as depicted in Fig. 3.

**Code Straightening.** Modern compilers tries to generate compact code. In the case of dispatch loop, this means that compiler can partially merge different

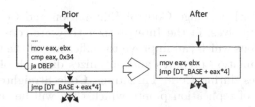

**Fig. 3.** Range control elimination

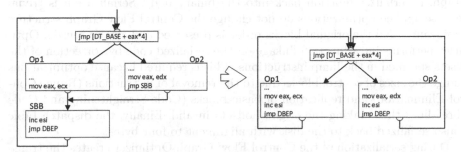

**Fig. 4.** Code straightening

instruction handlers into a single basic block. In this scenario, compiler replaces all replicated blocks of instructions by jump to a single instance of shared block of instructions. While such optimization reduces the footprint of the generated code, it introduces additional branching into intensively executed short instruction handlers, increases pressure on Branch Prediction Buffer and hence can finally lead to increased overhead.

The aim of code straightening is the elimination of all unnecessary branching by replication of shared basic blocks of the instruction handler bodies. To achieve this goal optimizer, guided by found dispatch table, goes down for each instruction handler through its default path and replaces each unconditional branch instruction found by basic block to which branch instruction points. Therefore, the default control flow of the instruction handler becomes straight and finishes by a jump to the dispatch block. Figure 4 demonstrates the effects of Code Straightening optimization.

**Code Threading.** Code threading is the central optimization applied by Interpretizer and at the same time is the simplest in implementation.

To convert switch-based dispatch into threaded code, Optimizer locates the dispatch block in the control flow graph. Then it iterates through all basic blocks in the control flow graph and replaces jumps to dispatch block found in the code by dispatch block body as depicted in Figs. 1 and 2. As a result, all instruction handlers finish by direct dispatch to the next instruction instead of loop-based iteration over the single shared dispatch block.

Despite the fact, that Range Control Elimination and Code Straightening are valuable by themselves, in the Interpretizer they are considered mainly as auxiliary optimizations which can improve the efficiency of the Code Threading. Range Control Elimination prepares and optimizes dispatch block which Optimizer then replicates during Code Threading. Code Straightening in its turn increases the count of replication points which then will be replaced by Optimizer during Code Threading.

Finally, once Optimizer has applied all optimizations on the Control Flow Graph, it serializes function back into the binary body. Serialization is trivial because applied optimizations do not change the Control Flow Graph structure significantly and the original blocks order is preserved and can be reused. Optimizer performs intra-function linkage on the serialized code by correction of the offsets specified in the jump instructions. This is required because optimizations change the sizes of control blocks due to the removal of instructions (Range Control Elimination) and replication of basic blocks (Code Straightening and Code Threading) thus making the original offsets invalid. Finally, the dispatch table is also serialized back to the disk with alignment to four bytes.

During serialization of the Control Flow Graph Optimizer creates the translation map which contains mappings between original instruction addresses and their addresses in the optimized code. Take note, that due to the massive code replication the single instruction from the original function can have multiple counterparts in the optimized version of function.

All optimizations performed by Optimizer are not universal and strictly interpreter-specific. In the general case, they either degrade the performance and increase the footprint of the generated code (Code Straightening and Code Threading) or break the semantics of the overlaying high-level programming language (Range Control Elimination). However, they can significantly increase throughput in the case of interpreters.

## 3   Evaluation

In this section, we evaluate the influence created by Interpretizer on the performance of bytecode interpreter. In addition, we compare the level of impact in dependence on the host CPU architecture. Finally, we evaluate and compare multiple C++ compilers on their efficiency of interpreter code generation.

Figures 5, 6, 7 and 8 demonstrate execution time for benchmark applications in dependency on the compiler and on set of optimizations applied by Interpretizer integrated into bytecode interpreter build toolchain. We have used two different benchmark applications, both based on the processing of typical data structures like binary trees and linked lists. Both benchmarks was built on the basis of real industrial-quality code extracted from the Linux kernel and converted into KA-32 bytecode. Each evaluation was performed 10000 times and the average result is reported in Figs. 5, 6, 7 and 8. Furthermore, we have run the same set of evaluations on two different hardware platforms. One of them is a computer system based on the AMD FX-8350 CPU. The second one is a

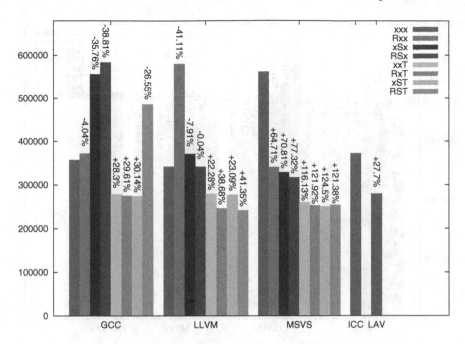

**Fig. 5.** Benchmark A. AMD FX-8350.

laptop based on Intel i7-4600U CPU. In Figs. 5, 6, 7 and 8, the bar labeled as "xxx" shows baseline execution time for low-level JVM-like bytecode interpreter (KA-32 VM) compiled without Interpretizer usage. Other bars represent execution time of benchmark applications on the same interpreter compiled with various sets of optimizations applied by Interpretizer. In the bar labels, R means Range Control Elimination enabled, S – Code Straightening enabled, T – Code Threading enabled, x means that respective optimization is disabled. Thus, bar label "xSx" should be read as "Code Straightening enabled while Range Control Elimination and Code Threading disabled". Bar "ICC" shows the performance produced by Intel C++ compiler and bar "LAV" – the performance of interpreter compiled by GCC with usage "Labels As Values" C language extension. Interpretizer is incompatible with ICC, because Intel compiler produces non-trivial instruction dispatching code with dispatch table compaction and multi-stage calculation of target jump address. We have compiled all variants of interpreters with maximal optimization level provided by host compiler.

As can be seen from Figs. 5, 6, 7 and 8, the performance of bytecode interpretation significantly depends on all components of the system: CPU microarchitecture, compiler, workload and on the set of optimizations applied by Interpretizer. Note that on more ILP-efficient processors the performance difference produced by different instruction dispatch techniques becomes smaller. For example, while the highest speedup achieved on the AMD platform lies in the range of 19.54–124.5%, on the Intel platform it falls into the range 5.21–20.07%.

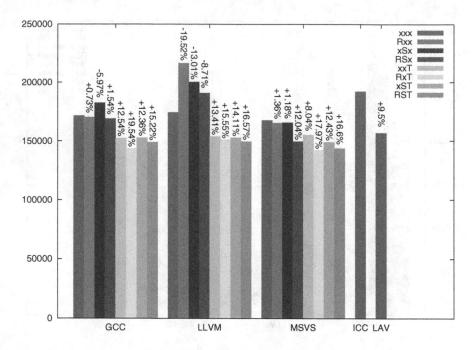

**Fig. 6.** Benchmark A. Intel i7-4600U.

These results agree with observations highlighted in [9]. GCC (v.8.2.0) and LLVM (v.7.0.1) have proven to be efficient interpreter code generators. Microsoft C++ (v.16.00.30319.01) has produced interpreter which is most efficient on Intel platform and at the same time least efficient on AMD platform. Intel C++ compiler (v.19.0.0.117) according to the evaluation results is the wrong choice for interpreters creation even for Intel platform. In general, the right choice of the baseline compiler can lead to 19.97–64.41% speedup of the compiled interpreter. Usage of "Labels As Values" extension of C language implemented in GCC can produce speedup in the range from 0.29% and up to 27.7%. Finally, experiments have demonstrated that integration of Interpretizer into bytecode interpreter build toolchain not only provides freedom in choice of programming language and compiler but also generates a significant speedup of produced code: 5.21–30.14% for GCC, 1.67–41.35% for LLVM and 3.42–124.5% for MSVS. It is interesting to note that interpreters produced by GCC with Interpretizer are 1.91–9.17% more efficient than they analogs produced with the use of custom "Labels As Values" extension of C programming language. On the other hand, the set of applied optimizations leading to maximal efficiency of the produced interpreter is not universal and should be carefully chosen with taking into account the compiler used, the target hardware platform and typical workload expected. Application of inappropriate set of optimizations can significantly degrade the performance of the produced bytecode interpreter.

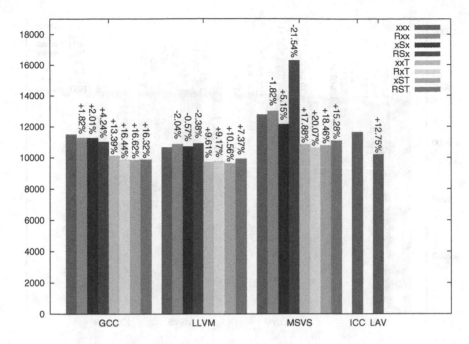

**Fig. 7.** Benchmark B. AMD FX-8350.

In our experiments, the most efficient versions of the interpreter for both platforms were built using Interpretizer. For AMD platform using LLVM compiler with a full set of optimizations enabled (15.68% more efficient than GCC with LAV and 41.35% more efficient than LLVM-compiled VM without Interpretizer involvement). For Intel platform using Microsoft C++ compiler with Code Straightening disabled (10.35% more efficient than GCC with LAV and 17.97% more efficient than MSVS-compiled VM without Interpretizer involvement).

## 4  Related Work

Most of the published works on the bytecode interpretation efficiency are either describes design and implementation of a particular virtual machine [2,14] or consider various optimization techniques which improve interpretation efficiency [4,11,12]. A. Ertl in 2002 made the first proposal for instrumental support of the development of virtual machines [7]. He proposed a "vmgen" generator of efficient virtual machines. Vmgen transforms specification of bytecode passed to its input into the C source code implementing interpreter engine which then compiled by GCC compiler. In contrast, Interpretizer works on the level of already compiled but not yet linked binary code to apply interpretation-specific optimizations. Thus, it allows developers to be stuck neither to C programming language nor to GCC compiler.

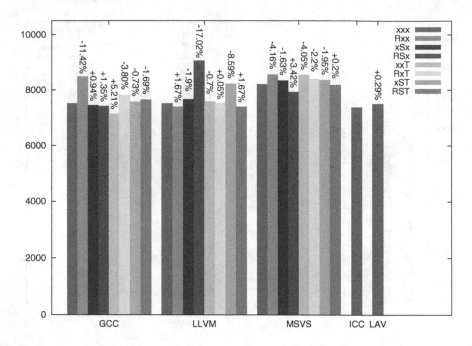

**Fig. 8.** Benchmark B. Intel i7-4600U.

RPython [5] is a translation and support framework for producing implementations of dynamic languages. It can automatically generate a Just-in-Time compiler. RPython toolchain takes an interpreter implemented in a high-level domain-specific language and creates efficient VM for it using a tracing JIT technique. RPython focuses on high-level virtual machines and forces developer to describe (implement) the bytecode interpreter in domain-specific RPython language, which then compiles into efficient VM. Interpretizer works as an optimizer performing its job transparently to the target interpreter build toolchain and can optimize low-level virtual machines.

Truffle [13] is another framework designed for the implementation of efficient interpreters. In contrast to Interpretizer, which optimizes bytecode interpreters, Truffle performs optimization of AST interpreters and thus dynamic languages [15]. Furthermore, Truffle targets JVM.

Levis has proposed an Application Specific Virtual Machines, an architecture which allows the user to tailor the VM to specific application domain [8]. Proposed Mate framework allows building VM extensions in conjunction with application compilation and customizes the host VM on the fly. While Interpretizer aims the maximization of VM throughput, the Mate framework aims mainly bytecode compactness and relies on the specifics of the sensor networks.

# 5   Conclusions

Bytecode interpreters continue to play an important role in application development, distribution, and execution. In this paper, we have proposed an approach of the interpreter-specific and compiler-independent optimization of dispatch loop on the level of binary code. We have presented an Interpretizer, a command line tool which can be transparently integrated into any interpreter build toolchain and perform selective interpreter specific optimizations on the level of binary code. Interpretizer is capable apply to the interpreter dispatch loop three optimizations: range control elimination, code straightening, and code threading, and therefore converts inefficient switch-based instruction dispatch into efficient threaded code. Interpretizer gives developers the freedom to use the programming languages and compilers of their choice to develop performant bytecode interpreters, breaking the long-term dependency on the GCC with its "Labels As Values" C language extension. We have demonstrated that Interpretizer can improve the efficiency of bytecode execution on the VM up to 124.5% and outperform GCC with "Labels As Values" enabled and used. Furthermore, we have compared GCC, LLVM, MSVS, and ICC compilers, from the viewpoint of the efficiency of bytecode interpretation on produced VMs. Finally, we have considered bytecode interpretation on processors with different microarchitectures and have shown that for maximal efficiency the compiler, optimizations, and target hardware architecture should be chosen in conjunction with each other.

# References

1. Using the GNU Compiler Collection (GCC): Labels as Values. https://gcc.gnu.org/onlinedocs/gcc/Labels-as-Values.html. Accessed 26 Feb 2019
2. Adams, K., et al.: The HipHop virtual machine. In: Proceedings of the 2014 ACM International Conference on Object Oriented Programming Systems Languages and Applications, OOPSLA 2014, pp. 777–790. ACM, New York (2014)
3. Bell, J.: Threaded code. Commun. ACM **16**(6), 370–372 (1973)
4. Berndl, M., Vitale, B., Zaleski, M., Brown, A.: Context threading: a flexible and efficient dispatch technique for virtual machine interpreters. In: Proceedings of the International Symposium on Code Generation and Optimization, CGO 2005, pp. 15–26. IEEE Computer Society, Washington, DC (2005)
5. Bolz, C., Cuni, A., Fijalkowski, M., Rigo, A.: Tracing the meta-level: PyPy's tracing JIT compiler. In: Proceedings of the 4th Workshop on the Implementation, Compilation, Optimization of Object-Oriented Languages and Programming Systems, ICOOOLPS 2009, pp. 18–25. ACM, New York (2009)
6. Ertl, A., Gregg, D.: Optimizing indirect branch prediction accuracy in virtual machine interpreters. SIGPLAN Not. **38**(5), 278–288 (2003)
7. Ertl, A., Gregg, D., Krall, A., Paysan, B.: Vmgen: a generator of efficient virtual machine interpreters. Softw. Pract. Exper. **32**(3), 265–294 (2002). https://doi.org/10.1002/spe.434
8. Levis, P., Gay, D., Culler, D.: Bridging the gap: programming sensor networks with application specific virtual machines. In: Submitted to Proceedings 6th Symposium on Operating Systems Design and Implementation, OSDI 2004 (2004)

9. Rohou, E., Swamy, B., Seznec, A.: Branch prediction and the performance of interpreters: don't trust folklore. In: Proceedings of the 13th Annual IEEE/ACM International Symposium on Code Generation and Optimization, pp. 103–114, CGO 2015. IEEE Computer Society, Washington, DC, USA (2015)
10. Romer, T., et al.: The structure and performance of interpreters. SIGOPS Oper. Syst. Rev. **30**(5), 150–159 (1996)
11. Savrun-Yeniçeri, G., et al.: Efficient interpreter optimizations for the JVM. In: Proceedings of the 2013 International Conference on Principles and Practices of Programming on the Java Platform: Virtual Machines, Languages, and Tools, PPPJ 2013, pp. 113–123. ACM, New York (2013)
12. Shi, Y., Casey, K., Ertl, A., Gregg, D.: Virtual machine showdown: stack versus registers. ACM Trans. Archit. Code Optim. **4**(4), 2:1–2:36 (2008)
13. Würthinger, T., Wöß, A., Stadler, L., Duboscq, G., Simon, D., Wimmer, C.: Self-optimizing AST interpreters. In: Proceedings of the 8th Symposium on Dynamic Languages, DLS 2012, pp. 73–82. ACM, New York (2012)
14. Zaleski, M.: YETI: a gradually extensible trace interpreter. Ph.D. thesis, University of Toronto, Toronto, Ont., Canada, Canada (2008). aAINR57946
15. Zhang, W.: Efficient hosted interpreter for dynamic languages. Ph.D. thesis, University of California, Irvine, Irvine, California, U.S. (2015)

# Towards Static Verification of Clojure Contract-Based Programs

Gheorghe Pinzaru and Victor Rivera[✉]

Innopolis University, Innopolis, Russia
{g.pinzaru,v.rivera}@innopolis.ru

**Abstract.** Detecting possible weaknesses in a dynamically typed functional programming language at compile time plays an important role in the development of correct Software. Unfortunately, this is still an open problem for some functional programming languages. This paper proposes a translation of Clojure programs into Boogie. Thus, users can write formal specifications of Clojure programs, using pre- and post-conditions that are supported by the language, translate the code to Boogie, and use Boogie's automated theorem provers to formally check the correctness of the code w.r.t. its specifications. This enables users to formally prove Clojure programs enriched with pre- and post-conditions. This paper shows the translation rules, its implementation and discusses some of the challenges faced due to differences between the source and the target languages.

## 1 Introduction

The correctness of a program is the ability of the program to run without errors and to do as it is specified. One approach to specify programs is *Design by contract* (DbC) which was initially introduced by Bertrand Meyer as a methodology to ensure correctness and robustness of Object-Oriented programs [8]. Design by contract relies on assigning contracts (in the form of pre- and postconditions) to routines to ensure that all specifications are met: a *precondition* expresses how a client should call a routine. A call without meeting the precondition makes the program stops and arise an assertion; a *postcondition* expresses the semantics of the routine (what the routine is supposed to do) if the precondition is met. While a precondition is an obligation to the client caller, the postcondition is its benefit. The main purpose of DbC is to help software developers to write correct systems as it goes.

There exist several ways to make use of contracts. On one hand, contracts can be checked during run-time, called *Dynamic Checking*. One can run the program with specific inputs and check whether pre- or postconditions are violated. On the other hand, contracts can be used to statically verify code, called *Static Checking*. One can use different tools to translate the source code, along with its specification, to an automatic theorem prover which is in charge to prove that the code meets the specification.

© Springer Nature Switzerland AG 2019
M. Mazzara et al. (Eds.): TOOLS 2019, LNCS 11771, pp. 73–80, 2019.
https://doi.org/10.1007/978-3-030-29852-4_5

Clojure [5] is a dynamic, general-purpose programming language. Clojure supports Design by Contract through pre- and post-conditions. Contracts in Clojure are checked at runtime and when they are not met an AssertionError is thrown. While it is true that this approach plays a crucial role in development of correct software, it is also true that it is too limited, we need to run the program on specific inputs to catch errors. Proving ahead errors for some mission-critical programs is very important. This paper, proposes a way to statically analyse Clojure programs, equipped with pre- and postconditions, in order to find possible errors in the code at compilation time. The analysis is done by automatically translating Clojure code to Boogie [6], and use Boogie's theorems provers to prove the correctness of the code.

This paper is organised as follows: Sect. 2 presents the translation rules from Clojure programs to Boogie. Its implementation, the Speculator tool, is presented in Sect. 3. Section 4 discusses the related work and Sect. 5 is devoted to conclusions and future work.

## 2   Translation Rules

The translation starts with a contracted Clojure program, a program with annotated pre- and postconditions. The Clojure program is translated to the Boogie (using the Speculator tool – implementation in Sect. 3). To help in the specification and verification process, an additional mathematical model library (MM.bpl) has been implemented in Boogie as a prelude. The generated Boogie code along with the mathematical model is fed into Boogie. Boogie automatically translates the code to a Satisfiability Module Theories (SMT) prover for verification. Finally, the output of the solver is fed-back to the Clojure program so users can either continue with their implementation or correct the problems.

### 2.1   Rules

The translation is done with the aid $\delta$ : Clojure $\rightarrow$ Boogie. $\delta$ is defined as a total function that maps contracted Clojure programs to Boogie implementations. $\delta$ uses three helper functions: $\alpha$ translates arguments in Clojure to arguments in Boogie; $\tau$ infers the type of Clojure variables and functions and translate them into the corresponding Boogie type. No all types in Clojure has a corresponding type in Boogie, see Sect. 3; and $\beta$ translates Clojure expressions to their counterpart in Boogie.

In Clojure, functions are defined using **defn** keyword. They are first-class objects. Rule **func**, depicted in Fig. 1, shows the translation rule of Clojure functions into Boogie procedures. We are not translating to Boogie's functions since they are side-effects free, so no change in the state is allowed. The name of the function in Clojure is used as the name of the procedure in Boogie. In case of name clashing, the implementation will add a unique identifier to the name. Name clashing might happen in Boogie since Boogie does not allow users to define procedures with the same name and different signature. This is possible in Clojure. For instance, in Clojure, function (**defn** $foo$ $[a](\ldots)$) might have a different execution than function (**defn** $foo$ $[a\ b](\ldots)$), even though the names are the same. In Boogie, it is recommendable to list all locations that the procedure is allowed to modify. For this, rule func lists all variables in the **modifies** clause. The operator Mod takes as input the body of the function and infers all locations that are being modified. This operator, not implemented yet, could be implemented using [16]. Pre- and postconditions in Clojure, if any, are translated into Boogie using the clauses **requires** and **ensures**, accordingly. Both define the same semantics as in Clojure.

$$
\frac{\tau(foo) = \mathsf{T} \quad \beta(exp1) = \mathsf{pre\text{-}exp} \quad \beta(exp2) = \mathsf{post\text{-}exp}}{\substack{\alpha(args) = \mathsf{A} \quad \delta(body) = \mathsf{B} \quad \mathrm{Mod}(body) = \mathsf{lst}}} \text{(func)}
$$

$\delta((\textbf{defn}\ foo\ args$
$\quad \{: pre\ [exp1]$
$\quad\quad : post\ [exp2]\}$
$\quad body)) =$
**procedure** $foo$ ( A ) **returns** (r: T)
$\quad$ **modifies** lst;
$\quad$ **requires** pre-exp;
$\quad$ **ensures** post-exp;
{
$\quad$ B
}

**Fig. 1.** Translation rule for functions.

Procedures in Boogie define a return local variable. This is done after the keyword **returns**. In the func rule, the return local variable is r (that stands for return) and has the type of the function in Clojure (in this case T, as given by the operator $\tau$). $\delta(body)$, as shown by the rule body in Fig. 2, takes each instruction defined in the body of the Clojure function and returns the counter part in Boogie. For the last instruction in Boogie (represented in Fig. 2 as $(expn)$), the translation is assigned to the local variable return, r.

Arguments in Clojure can be defined as shown in rule **n-arguments** (Fig. 3). The operator $\tau$ infers the type of each argument (attached information of the argument – we assumed such an information). In Clojure, users can pass any number of arguments to a function. In the body of the Clojure function, these arguments can be referred using a vector of arguments. This is translated as a Map of arguments in Boogie. Argument-less functions are also possible in Clojure. They are translated as argument-less procedures in Boogie (the rule is trivial, so we omit it).

**do**, in Clojure, evaluates the expressions in order and returns the value of the last. This is translated in Boogie by unfolding the sequence of expressions and assigning the result of the last element to return variable, as shown in rule do in Fig. 4.

$$\frac{\delta(exp1) = \mathsf{Exp}_1 \quad \delta(exp2) = \mathsf{Exp}_2 \quad \delta(expn) = \mathsf{Exp}_n}{\begin{array}{l}\delta\ ( \\ \quad (exp1) \\ \quad (exp2) \\ \quad \ldots \\ \quad (expn)) = \\ \mathsf{Exp}_1; \\ \mathsf{Exp}_2; \\ \ldots \\ \mathtt{r}\ \mathtt{:=}\ \mathsf{Exp}_n;\end{array}} \ \texttt{(body)}$$

**Fig. 2.** Translation of the body function.

$$\frac{\tau(x) = \mathsf{T}_1 \quad \tau(y) = \mathsf{T}_2 \quad \tau(args) = \mathsf{T}}{\delta(([x\ y\ \&\ args])) = x : \mathsf{T}_1,\ y : \mathsf{T}_2,\ args : Map\langle\mathsf{T}\rangle} \ \texttt{(n-arguments)}$$

**Fig. 3.** $n$ argument-passed definition rule.

$$\frac{\begin{array}{l}\delta(A) = \mathsf{A} \\ \delta(B) = \mathsf{B}\end{array}}{\begin{array}{l}\delta((\textbf{do}\ A\ B)) = \\ \mathsf{A}; \\ \mathsf{B};\end{array}} \ \texttt{(do)}$$

**Fig. 4.** Translation rule for **do** evaluation.

### 2.2 Translation Issues

One of the main challenges of the translation is to cope with the different paradigm that both the source and the target languages have: Clojure is a functional programming language whereas Boogie is an imperative language.

In Clojure, everything is a s-expression, Symbolic Expression. All code is written as an expression and when it is evaluated it returns a value which is passed as an argument to parent node expression. Boogie does not allow such behaviour, and each expression should be assigned to a variable. Furthermore, only values can be passed as an argument to a procedure or function, since functions in Boogie are not first-class citizens.

Another challenge is variadic functions. Variadic functions are functions that take a varying number of arguments, some arguments are required and the others are optional. A variadic argument can be a *map* or a *vector*, depending on structure of the argument in the function definition. One approach to this problem is to store globally all variadic functions definitions and check for that on every function call. The variadic argument can be replaced with a polymorphic map in Boogie.

Functions in Clojure are multi-arity. This raises a problem when translating to Boogie since Boogie does not allow users to define same name functions with different signature. To solve this problem, the implementation generates a procedure with different name for each arity. This way all procedures should be outputted in a reversed order, so the scope of bigger arity is available for the call inside procedure with smaller arities.

Local scoped functions are not allowed in Boogie. This, naturally, arises a problem as nested functions can be defined in Clojure. To cope with the problem, the implementation transverses the source code twice: in the first pass, the implementation stored all nested function definitions in the scope (the same for variables); during the second pass, the implementation outputs all the inner functions before the current function, thus, all scoped functions are available to the translated function. For anonymous functions, a random global name is generated.

## 3   Implementation

This section shows the implementation of the tool Speculator, a tool that implements the rules presented in Sect. 2.1. The translator takes as input Clojure contracted programs and produces Boogie programs.

The translation is in its early stages, it is a proof of concept. Hence, there are some limitations: the implementation takes into consideration the core part of the source language, Clojure. The translation implements the fundamental library of the Clojure language i.e., clojure.core; the implementation does not assume multi-threading; finally, the translation does not assume any Java interoperability. Clojure was designed to directly interoperates with the Java Virtual Machine (JVM), for instance, for method calls on Java objects. The translation assumes that no method calls on Java objects are being performed.

The translation starts by analysing Clojure code and generating the Abstract Syntax Tree (AST). We use the Analyzer library in [9]. The implementation covers 66% of them. Most of the remaining nodes are used to access platform specific code, which is outside our scope. The implementation transverses the tree using multi-methods which are dispatched based on the type of the node. The tool is publicly available at [10], It is fully written in Clojure and contains four main namespaces, namely *speculator.core*, *speculator.types*, *speculator.utils* and *speculator.flow*. *speculator.core* contains the implementation of the translation rules presented in Sect. 2.1. Traversing the tree is implemented using a multimethod with dispatch on node type. The nodes that are not implemented will fallback to a default method where the node will be outputted in a raw form; *speculator.types* contains all methods in charge of types translations; *speculator.utils* contains utility functions.

In order to assist the verification process, we have implemented a library in Boogie that implements Clojure types, as data structures. We have also implemented a mathematical model, along with its axioms and theorems (not yet proven). These data types (along with the axioms and theorems) can be used by the provers to verify the corresponding conditions. The implementation of the library can be found in the namespace *speculator.flow* in [10].

The mathematical model is an implementation of structures such as sets, relations, sequences, bags (multisets), and maps. It is implemented in Boogie as a prelude library. The initial version is taken from Dafny [7] and modified in a way to support Clojure data structures. A part of the Clojure core functions are implemented and all axioms for them are provided.

Most of the Clojure datatypes can be mapped to Boogie using polymorphic maps. Some basic data types like `integer` and `boolean` are directly mapped to Boogie's `int` and `bool`. The rest of the data types implementation was taken from Joogie [1], a translation from Java to Boogie. It uses polymorphic maps from a reference to values.

Boogie type system includes only primitive types, instantiated type constructors, and map. Primitive types are `integers`, `reals`, `booleans` and `bit-vectors`. Type constructors are used to add parametric types. `Map` type is polymorphic map which maps keys to values. Clojure offers a wide variety of built-in types: `Integers`, `Floating Point`, `Boolean`, `Char`, `String`, `Nil`, `Atom`. In addition, Clojure has all Java native types (Clojure inherits from Java type system). These types are implemented in Boogie to ease the translation.

## 4  Related Work

An intermediate verification language embodies the subject of translation from some high-level languages to logic which can be understood by SMT solvers. Boogie and WhyML [4] are two of those languages that have gained popularity in recent years. Dafny [7] is a programming language that uses Boogie as a verifier. It is used to provide an interface for proving different programs and algorithms. It is an imperative, class-based language which is directly encoded into Boogie. Spec# [2] is a formal language which extends Microsoft C# program language. It provides a sound programming methodology that allows writing specifications. Thus, they want to provide a tool for a more cost-effective way to develop and maintain high-quality software. Joogie [1] is a tool that aims to detect unfeasible code in Java programs at the bytecode level. It is used to detect problems in real-world Java applications.

On the other hand, there are tools that take advantage of Design by Contract (DbC) methodologies (advocated by Boogie). The Eiffel programming language, the pioneered in DbC, comes with Autoproof [18], an automatic verifier for Eiffel code. It uses built-in DbC in Eiffel to provide a mechanism for reasoning about code functional correctness. It allows developers to prove existing code without extra annotations and work from developers. With the same spirit of taking advantage of Design by Contract, [13,14] present a translation from Event-B to Java (and its implementation [3,12]), annotating the code with JML (Java Modelling Language) specifications (a way to encode Design by Contract in Java), and [11,15] present a translation from Event-B to Eiffel.

All these tools aim at providing functional-correctness in an automatic form which will be also easily used by end programmers: programmers will have no interaction with the solver but requires a more complete specification on the language level. Our work is similar, however, the source language is different. we translate Clojure annotated programs and use Boogie to take full advantage of Design by Contract.

*Spectrum* [17] is a library for doing static analysis of Clojure code. It does not prove the full correctness of programs. *Spectrum* is a tool which sacrifices the full proof by giving an easy tool which finds just a big subset of errors. It uses Clojure Spec to define specifications which will be checked on compile time. It uses a different approach to code checking. The checking is based on Symbolic Analysis and multiple optimisation and type checking strategies of the source code.

## 5   Conclusion and Future Work

This paper presents a series of rules to transform a contracted Clojure program to Boogie. The main idea of such a translation is to take full advantage of contracts by verifying the code against them. It is important to perform this step statically as one could discover errors at compilation time. We also presented Speculator, a tool implemented in Clojure that implements the translation rules.

In order to be able to fully automate the translation, *(i)* the full syntax of the language needs to be implemented. Speculator currently implements 66% of the core functionality of Clojure. There is 33% remaining and all other libraries attached to the language. *(ii)* Type inference needs to be implemented. Clojure is a dynamically typed language in contrast to Boogie that needs types to be specified. The current work assumes users to put type information, however, this can be inferred automatically. *(iii)* The implementation needs to support concurrency. For instance, the current implementation of Speculator treats *Atom* type variables as regular variables due to the fact that it cannot deal with concurrency. *(iv)* Finally, there is a need to provide a proof of soundness of the translation.

Using Boogie as a tool for the static analysis of Clojure programs provides an opportunity to have a mathematical proof by using SMT solvers. The automation of the process allows users to use these solvers without (or little) intervention (users still need to provide the semantics of the program – pre- and postconditions), reducing the cost of development. The work presented here is still in the initial stages of development, but it does give several steps towards the static verification of Clojure contract-based programs.

## References

1. Arlt, S., Rümmer, P., Schäf, M.: Joogie: from Java through Jimple to Boogie. In: SOAP@PLDI, pp. 3–8. ACM (2013)
2. Barnett, M., Leino, K.R.M., Schulte, W.: The Spec# programming system: an overview. In: Barthe, G., Burdy, L., Huisman, M., Lanet, J.-L., Muntean, T. (eds.) CASSIS 2004. LNCS, vol. 3362, pp. 49–69. Springer, Heidelberg (2005). https://doi.org/10.1007/978-3-540-30569-9_3

3. Cataño, N., Rivera, V.: EventB2Java: a code generator for event-B. In: Rayadurgam, S., Tkachuk, O. (eds.) NFM 2016. LNCS, vol. 9690, pp. 166–171. Springer, Cham (2016). https://doi.org/10.1007/978-3-319-40648-0_13

4. Filliâtre, J.-C., Paskevich, A.: Why3—where programs meet provers. In: Felleisen, M., Gardner, P. (eds.) ESOP 2013. LNCS, vol. 7792, pp. 125–128. Springer, Heidelberg (2013). https://doi.org/10.1007/978-3-642-37036-6_8

5. Hickey, R.: The Clojure programming language. In: Proceedings of the 2008 Symposium on Dynamic Languages, DLS 2008, p. 1:1. ACM, New York (2008)

6. Rustan, K., Leino, M.: This is Boogie 2 (2008)

7. Leino, K.R.M.: Dafny: an automatic program verifier for functional correctness. In: Clarke, E.M., Voronkov, A. (eds.) LPAR 2010. LNCS (LNAI), vol. 6355, pp. 348–370. Springer, Heidelberg (2010). https://doi.org/10.1007/978-3-642-17511-4_20

8. Meyer, B.: Applying "design by contract". Computer 25(10), 40–51 (1992)

9. Hickey, R., Mometto, N.: clojure.tools.analyzer - analyzer for clojure code (2013). https://github.com/clojure/tools.analyzer

10. Pinzaru, G.: Speculator (2019). https://github.com/Ferossgp/speculator

11. Reznikova, S., Rivera, V., Lee, J., Mazzara, M.: Translation from event-B into Eiffel. MAIS 25(6), 623–636 (2018)

12. Rivera, V., Bhattacharya, S., Cataño, N.: Undertaking the tokeneer challenge in event-B. In 2016 IEEE/ACM 4th FME Workshop on Formal Methods in Software Engineering (FormaliSE), pp. 8–14, May 2016

13. Rivera, V., Cataño, N.: Translating event-B to JML-specified java programs. In: Proceedings of the 29th Annual ACM Symposium on Applied Computing, SAC 2014, pp. 1264–1271. ACM, New York (2014)

14. Rivera, V., Cataño, N., Wahls, T., Rueda, C.: Code generation for event-B. Int. J. Softw. Tools Technol. Transf. 19(1), 31–52 (2017)

15. Rivera, V., Lee, J.Y., Mazzara, M.: Mapping event-B machines into Eiffel programming language. In: Ciancarini, P., Mazzara, M., Messina, A., Sillitti, A., Succi, G. (eds.) SEDA 2018. AISC, vol. 925, pp. 255–264. Springer, Cham (2020). https://doi.org/10.1007/978-3-030-14687-0_23

16. Rivera, V., Meyer, B.: Autoframe: automatic frame inference for object-oriented languages. Under submission (2019). https://arxiv.org/pdf/1808.08751.pdf

17. Rohner, A.: Spectrum (2019). https://github.com/arohner/spectrum

18. Tschannen, J., Furia, C.A., Nordio, M., Polikarpova, N.: AutoProof: auto-active functional verification of object-oriented programs. In: Baier, C., Tinelli, C. (eds.) TACAS 2015. LNCS, vol. 9035, pp. 566–580. Springer, Heidelberg (2015). https://doi.org/10.1007/978-3-662-46681-0_53

# Problems in Experiment with Biological Signals in Software Engineering: The Case of the EEG

Herman Tarasau, Ananga Thapaliya[✉], and Oydinoy Zufarova

Innopolis University, 1 Universitetskaya, Innopolis 420500, Russia
{h.tarasau,a.thapaliya,o.zufarova}@innopolis.ru

**Abstract.** The electroencephalograph (EEG) signal is one of the most widely used signal in the field of computer science to analyze the electrical brain waves from software developers and students. In this paper we present initial research results of an empirical study related to application of EEG in measurement of software development activities. We discuss existing methods and problems of running such experiments in future. In particular, we focus on the different kinds of limitations implied by modern EEG devices as well as the issues related to evaluation of the collected data set.

**Keywords:** Empirical methods · Software experimentation

## 1 Introduction

Software developers have worked in multiple environment over the years and these environments have different effect on their brain behaviour relations. As an outcome, the perspective of developers assume a focal job in the quality and the productivity of the produced software. Researchers have various methodologies available for the study of effect of environment external conditions in brain-behaviour relations. The electroencephalogram (EEG) is considered by numerous individuals to be a standout amongst the most proficient and moderately inexpensive methodologies for analyzing these effects [2]. We prefer the EEG since it additionally permits an examination of formative changes without emotional impedance on typical progressing behaviours.

EEG estimates the electrical potential between two electrodes on the scalp, with proof that the origin of this electrical signals is in the brain [1]. The EEG signal is unconstrained however setting related; EEG produced amid calm rest is quantitatively not the same as that created amid intellectual handling. The EEG signal has temporal resolution on the order of milliseconds. Along these lines, post-synaptic changes are promptly reflected in the EEG, making this strategy remarkable for following quick moves in the functioning of brain "test subject" or simply "subject", so it should not be confused with any other meaning. We explore whether the given different conditions (in this case: pair programming

M. Mazzara et al. (Eds.): TOOLS 2019, LNCS 11771, pp. 81–88, 2019.
https://doi.org/10.1007/978-3-030-29852-4_6

and programming with (without music)) has an effect on the programming expertise and the productivity of output. Also we will see that on a basic level of the
explained case, it must be underlined that brain wave measurements are firmly
influenced by an assortment of unspecific factors, for example, the thickness of
the skull or the volume of cerebrospinal liquid, by methodological and specialized factors(for instance interelectrode separation) yet additionally by increasing explicit factors, for example, age, experience and the sort of psychological
requests amid actual task execution [4,5,15,17].

In a nutshell, our goal is first to assemble a superior comprehension of the
chances by examining how the given conditions and external factors affect the
productivity and quality of the software and then to understand the issues emerging when gathering and examining students and developers data utilizing EEG
in the desire for supporting and encouraging future research. In general, the
data accumulation process was time consuming and effort intensive. A few times
after running an experiment it was unrealistic to utilize the collected data, for a
number of factors, including the way that at first we needed to characterize our
very own test convention, since this is among the main investigations of this sort
and the current collection of knowledge in the literature is very constrained, as
examined underneath.

## 2  Methodologies

As it was mentioned earlier, there are several methodologies used in brain behavioral study. We conducted experiments using two Mitsar SMART-BCI Bluetooth
devices. Test subjects involved in experiments belong mainly to three groups of
undergraduate students, graduate students and professional software developers.
They were assigned various tasks based on their experience and skills. Different
type of tasks, different participants and the required infrastructure for the experiment is described as follows:

### 2.1  Test Subjects and Assigned Tasks

Several participants (subject) were involved in experiments using their own programming language as desired [8,20]. Four types of experiments were held on
each participants as solo programmer (with and without music) and as pair
programmers (driver and navigator).

While programming, each undergraduate participant was assigned a simple
(according to the rating from the users) task from *Codeforces*. Graduate students
and software developers were implementing their ongoing projects (own industry
projects). As for the choice of music, participants has free will for their choice
of music while programming their respective tasks [19].

### 2.2  EEG and the Process

We utilized remote 24 channel Mitsar SMART-BCI flexible top for our experiments. The arrangement of electrodes was based on standard 10–20 plot. One

of the significant steps of EEG recording is the readiness of the EEG cap. We utilized the authoritative sort of cleaning before the trial which is cleaning with spirit (mixture of ethyl alcohol and water).

The EEG device was used with more than one channel and the channels that were chosen are the center of the processing. From one perspective, numerous channels give a wide scope of data from the entire scalp. Then again, this data can be excess [13]. We discovered that a signal from the frontal electrodes can't be cleaned with EEG inclining procedures like individual component analysis and manual process of filtering. Therefore, we chose to investigate just focal electrodes (**Fz, F4, F3, Cz, C4, C3, Pz, P4, P3**) since they give legitimate quality information which can be utilized in further examination.

We were unable to collect clean data as the signals were disturbed by different metal devices, the EEG device itself being old and imperfect, wireless networks, the subjects themselves not being able to be still for a longer amount of time, blinking of eyes and different noise from surroundings or the place where the experiment was held [18].

There are many factors to consider, similar to the age, the gender, and other physiological factors of the subject. So after the selection of proper electrodes and channels, cleaning of data was done with the use of filters which are **notch filter** used for removing noise, **high and low pass filters** used for filtering range according to alpha and theta waves and **amplitude filtering** was used to filter artifacts, the signals that were not in range [6,12].

## 2.3 Processing Tools

We chose to utilize just clean channels. The decision of clean channels was contemplated by EEG artifacts that are difficult to be recouped to the original data. Additionally, we used the tools such EEG official software tools and python MNE library version 0.16.1 with libraries NumPy and SciPy.

## 2.4 Experiment Steps and Formula

### Pair Programming

- Subject one and Subject two calibration: The calibration part comprises of two sections. Initial one is when subjects sit with shut eyes before the computer in a relaxing state and the second one is the equivalent however with opened eyes. The required step is to quantify alpha and theta synchronizations amid quiet state.
- Subject one and subject two get started with solo programming with the specific task assigned to them which ends after one hour.
- Now after finishing the solo mode, they get started with pair programming in which subject one being the driver and subject two being the navigator.
- Break. In this state, subjects are not involved in any type of activities, they are in relaxed and calm state.
- Again the pair programming starts, just with the reversed role of subject one with subject two and vice versa.

**Programming with (Without) Music**

- Subject one calibration: The calibration part comprises of two sections. Initial one is when subjects sit with shut eyes before the computer in a relaxing state and the second one is the equivalent however with opened eyes. As said before, the required step is to quantify alpha and theta synchronizations amid quiet state.
- Subject one gets started with programming with the specific task assigned to them which ends after one hour, without music which ends after one hour.
- Break. In this state, the subject is not involved in any type of activities, subject is in relaxed and calm state.
- Now the same subject starts programming with music, with the individual choice of music. It also ends after one hour.

ERD is calculated with the given formula:

$$ERD = \frac{(amplitude)_{rest} - (amplitude)_{programming}}{(amplitude)_{rest}} \times 100\%$$

Fast Fourier Transformation (FFT) is used for ERD calculation of 2000 ms window of signal. Therefore, we get a period arrangement or circulation of ERD for each sub-band for each programming movement difference.

## 3   Analysis

For our experiments we chose two popular software developing techniques: pair programming (PP) and programming while listening to music (PM). We ran several experiments and collected a dataset of 11 graduated students for PP analysis, 3 undergraduate students for PM and 3 software developers from industry.

Pair programming is an agile software development technique in which two programmers work together at one workstation. There are two roles in PP. Driver is the one who writes code while navigator coordinates the process and reviews each type of code as it is typed in. PP has been picked for this experiment due to it's popularity among different studies. In our work we present two ways of PP analysis and their results.

Software development while listening to music is very popular among programmers but very rarely investigated technique. During our experiments the students were able to listen to music of their choice and the same as for PP, we applied two ways of analysis for PM.

### 3.1   ERD (Event Related Desynchronization) Analysis

During the analysis we compared different values according to our dataset. For this work we compared among each other, two groups of software developing techniques. After that we checked the difference between the values using **Mann-Whitney** test and determine the significance of the difference. We pay more attention on theta waves as consider them to be connected to higher memory load and on alpha waves as they have a strong dependence with attention level and semantic memory processing. Using this information gives us an understanding of how to compare sub-bands values.

### 3.2 Correlation Analysis

The correlation analysis was not applied for EEG data before, which means that we applied this technique in order to understand if it might be used for future research. Using correlation we compare Pearson's correlation coefficients between programming with (without) music and all the roles of PP. We consider the difference between waves as the increment of neurons synchronization which implies the increasing of attention and memory load processes. Using this information we can calculate the correlation on some sub-bands and compare the results with ERD analysis.

## 4    Results

The analysis shows us that in case of **pair programming** the ERD is higher for pair-navigator mode and the values are equivalent for the other mode due to the asynchronous lower alpha band. It might imply that pair programming in navigator mode requires more consideration, and this mirrors the instinct that the navigator part requires assessing and controlling the improvement, which in turn instinctively requires a huge exertion of consideration, additionally due to the fact that the navigator isn't engaged with a physical contact with the input device. As for the theta value, solo programming, navigator, and driver have values in the descending order respectively. Thus we found out that theta and alpha waves are inversely proportional to each other. In case of **music programming**, we could not find out the specific patterns and result due to lower number of participants (test subjects).

The investigation of the relationship for pair programming shows up some way or another to help the cases made with the examination of ERD. In fact, the small dataset isn't indisputable, as yet observing a second analysis led with an alternate methodology alluding to a similar pattern as the first which gives some observational affirmation of the explanation that the navigator in pair programming has more concentration. The investigation of correlation with music is once more not indisputable, and again we can recreate the points of confinement of the small set of data.

## 5    Limitations and Problems

As the objective of this paper is basically to give a reference to future encounters in utilizing biological sensors to recognize the conditions of brains of software developers, it is imperative to underline the distinctive difficulties that rose before the experiment, amid the experiment and after the experiment, with the goal that future researchers can apply necessary precautions to attenuate the problems or even remove them.

## 5.1   Before the Experiment

- Regardless of the design of study utilized, researchers should design both the acquisition of data and analysis of procedures totally at individual experiment and different group of individuals before beginning the actual experiment [11].
- These analysis contemplation can possibly change how the stimuli really should be conveyed or how troublesome the initiation task might be, e.g., to guarantee that there are sufficient preliminaries and ratio of signal to noise in right conduct preliminaries [10].
- As this was significantly a new experiment in the field of software engineering, there was an absence of different literature works due to which we had some trouble for setting up our whole experiment which required an impressive exertion to characterize a strong experiment convention.
- It required a significant amount of time to begin the experiment as the device required an intricate arrangements of numerous electrodes around the head with the utilization of various gels.

## 5.2   During the Physical Experiment (Data Collection)

- A lot of muscle movement was picked up during the data collection which clouded our data. So subjects needed to remain as still as would be possible and squint as least as would be possible [9].
- The skull carries on like a low-pass channel and misshapes the underlying brain electrical action over an extensive zone of the scalp. Moreover, possibilities recorded at the scalp are likely created by numerous groupings of cortical and sub cortical generators spread over a moderately wide zone.
- Even the addition of extra gel, it was impossible to collect data from subjects with thick hair.
- Substantial number of subjects were required and a tremendous number of analyses were directed for extraction of useful data and information from the device in light of the fact that the device had poor signal to noise ratio, therefore, this approach is very time consuming and exhaustive.

## 5.3   After the Experiment (Phase of Analysis)

- A significant amount of time is required to process the EEG data and should understand that it is a complex data analysis because of poor signal to noise ratio.
- In the analyzing process we found out that EEG experiment was highly impacted by environment conditions (for instance noises, squeaks) which lead us to perform a lot of filtering to our data.
- It is troublesome to dispense with bits of the EEG record that are debased by gross motor movements or eye blinks preceding to analysis of data as the EEG signal is of very small amplitude due to which these gross motor movements tend to suppress the EEG signal.
- EEG requires intense interpretation just to conjecture what areas are enacted by a specific reaction as EEG shows very low spatial resolution on the scalp.

# 6    Conclusion

The objective of our work is to give a new commitment to individuals keen on performing investigation of software development utilizing biological signals, hence finding a totally different comprehension of the perspective of developers, who are the fundamental asset in the field of software production. Although there were some problems as discussed in Sect. 5, the methodology seems to work. For the experiment including 10 subjects, we obtained some observational ends affirming past proof that pair programming builds the dimension of consideration from a reasonable biological viewpoint. We feel that this outcome is astounding. As for the instance of programming with music, we did not accomplish any huge outcome. We are not debilitated by this – it is an impact of the noteworthy measure of work required to run such test and we believe that a bigger trial may prompt progressively indisputable explanations.

# 7    Future Scope

There are a lot more acquisition techniques that are for the most part utilized these days: (f)NIRS, (f)MRI, ECoG, PET and MEG [16]. These devices can have less restrictions and issues making the research less tedious and less effort intensive with increasingly solid outcomes. Our research will be based on progressively focused experimentation with EEG as well as other accessible devices mentioned above on explicit programming circumstances utilizing bigger datasets of students and after that, without a doubt, attempting to move our investigation to the industry in a bigger premise [14]. Thus with the concrete results, one can apply this research to find out the better environment conditions that can be used for software developers to get quality products and software.

# References

1. Pizzagalli, D.A.: Electroencephalography and high-density electrophysiological source localization. Handb. Psychophysiol. **3**, 56–84 (2007)
2. Klimesch, W.: Memory processes, brain oscillations and EEG synchronization. Int. J. Psychophysiol. **24**(1–2), 61–100 (1996)
3. Sillitti, A., Succi, G., Vlasenko, J.: Understanding the impact of pair programming on developers attention: a case study on a large industrial experimentation. In: 2012 34th International Conference on Software Engineering (ICSE), pp. 1094–1101. IEEE, June 2012
4. Raziq, A., Maulabakhsh, R.: Impact of working environment on job satisfaction. Proc. Econ. Finance **23**, 717–725 (2015)
5. Doborjeh, Z.G., Kasabov, N., Doborjeh, M.G., Sumich, A.: Modelling peri-perceptual brain processes in a deep learning spiking neural network architecture. Sci. Rep. **8**(1), 8912 (2018)
6. Keil, A., et al.: Committee report: publication guidelines and recommendations for studies using electroencephalography and magnetoencephalography. Psychophysiology **51**(1), 1–21 (2014)

7. Xu, J., Mitra, S., Van Hoof, C., Yazicioglu, R.F., Makinwa, K.A.: Active electrodes for wearable EEG acquisition: review and electronics design methodology. IEEE Rev. Biomed. Eng. **10**, 187–198 (2017)
8. Delorey, D.P., Knutson, C.D., Chun, S.: Do programming languages affect productivity? A case study using data from open source projects. In: First International Workshop on Emerging Trends in FLOSS Research and Development (FLOSS 2007: ICSE Workshops 2007), p. 8. IEEE, May 2007
9. Bell, M.A., Cuevas, K.: Using EEG to study cognitive development: issues and practices. J. Cogn. Dev. **13**(3), 281–294 (2012)
10. Wendel, K., et al.: EEG/MEG source imaging: methods, challenges, and open issues. Comput. Intell. Neurosci. **2009**, 13 (2009)
11. Puce, A., Hämäläinen, M.: A review of issues related to data acquisition and analysis in EEG/MEG studies. Brain Sci. **7**(6), 58 (2017)
12. Jiang, X., Bian, G.B., Tian, Z.: Removal of artifacts from EEG signals: a review. Sensors **19**(5), 987 (2019)
13. Das, S., Tripathy, D., Raheja, J.L.: An insight to the human brain and EEG. In: Real-Time BCI System Design to Control Arduino Based Speed Controllable Robot Using EEG. BRIEFSAPPLSCIENCES, pp. 13–24. Springer, Singapore (2019). https://doi.org/10.1007/978-981-13-3098-8_2
14. Bigdely-Shamlo, N., et al.: Hierarchical Event Descriptors (HED): semi-structured tagging for real-world events in large-scale EEG. Front. Neuroinform. **10**, 42 (2016)
15. Züger, M., Fritz, T.: Interruptibility of software developers and its prediction using psycho-physiological sensors. In: Proceedings of the 33rd Annual ACM Conference on Human Factors in Computing Systems, pp. 2981–2990. ACM, April 2015
16. Kosmyna, N., Lécuyer, A.: A conceptual space for EEG-based brain-computer interfaces. PLoS ONE **14**(1), e0210145 (2019)
17. Müller, S.C., Fritz, T.: Stuck and frustrated or in flow and happy: sensing developers' emotions and progress. In: 2015 IEEE/ACM 37th IEEE International Conference on Software Engineering, vol. 1, pp. 688–699. IEEE, May 2015
18. Chaparro, E.A., Yuksel, A., Romero, P., Bryant, S.: Factors affecting the perceived effectiveness of pair programming in higher education. In: PPIG, p. 2, June 2005
19. Lesiuk, T.: The effect of music listening on work performance. Psychol. Music **33**(2), 173–191 (2005)
20. Nanz, S., Furia, C.A.: A comparative study of programming languages in Rosetta code. In: 2015 IEEE/ACM 37th IEEE International Conference on Software Engineering, vol. 1, pp. 778–788. IEEE, May 2015

# Developing Medical Devices from Abstract State Machines to Embedded Systems: A Smart Pill Box Case Study

Andrea Bombarda, Silvia Bonfanti, and Angelo Gargantini$^{(\boxtimes)}$

Department of Economics and Technology Management,
Information Technology and Production, University of Bergamo, Bergamo, Italy
{andrea.bombarda,silvia.bonfanti,angelo.gargantini}@unibg.it

**Abstract.** The development of medical devices is a safety-critical process, because a failure or a malfunction of the device can cause serious injuries to the patients whom use it. The application of a rigorous process for their development reduces the risk of failures since validation and verification activities can be performed in a objective, reproducible, and documentable manner. In this paper we present an approach based on the Abstract State Machine (ASM) formal method. Starting from the model, validation and verification (V&V) techniques can be applied. Furthermore, by step-wise refinement, a final model can be obtained, which can be automatically translated to C++ code. The process is applied to the smart pill box case study. Starting from the ASM model, we generate C++ code for the Arduino platform after the application of V&V activities. Furthermore, we introduce regulation (IEC62304) and guidelines (FDA General Principles of Software Validation) that support the developer in medical software development. In particular, we explain how ASMs formal process can be compliant with them.

## 1 Introduction

Software is becoming an essential part of medical devices, so it is very important that its development process adheres to certification standards. All the standards available provide only general description of common software engineering activities, but nothing is said about the techniques that have to be used to guarantee the safety of the devices and the correctness of their software. The main references concerning the regulation of medical software are the standard IEC 62304 (International Electrotechnical Commission) [12] (see Sect. 6.1) and the FDA guidelines [15] in which several concepts that can be used as guidance for software validation and verification are defined (see Sect. 6.2). The regulation and the guideline aim for more rigorous approaches for software development and validation, but neither of them recommend a particular method or technique.

In this paper we propose a formal approach that can be used to develop and validate the software of an embedded medical device, in compliance with the IEC regulation and FDA guidance for software validation as shown in Sect. 6.

© Springer Nature Switzerland AG 2019
M. Mazzara et al. (Eds.): TOOLS 2019, LNCS 11771, pp. 89–103, 2019.
https://doi.org/10.1007/978-3-030-29852-4_7

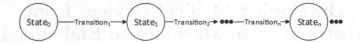

**Fig. 1.** An ASM run with a sequences of states and state-transitions (steps)

Our formal approach is studied over a simple example of a smart portable pill box, called e-Pix (electronic PIll boX), modelled with Abstract State Machines (ASM) by using the `Asmeta` framework. We have applied several validation and verification (V&V) techniques [13], such as model simulation (see Sect. 4.3), scenario-based testing (see Sect. 4.4) using the `Avalla` language, and property verification (see Sect. 4.5). As final step, we have used `Asm2C++` to generate the C++ code to be executed by Arduino.

The paper is organized as follows. Section 2 introduces the ASMs and all the tools provided by the `Asmeta` framework. In Sect. 3 we explain the e-Pix case study. Section 4 presents modelling by refinement, validation, testing and verification procedures applied to the case study. Section 5 explains how we have built the prototype of e-Pix and generated C++ code. Section 6 gives a comprehensive review about how our approach can be used to comply the main regulations concerning the development of medical software. Section 7 presents works related to the use of rigorous approaches in medical software development, and Sect. 8 concludes the paper.

## 2   Abstract State Machines and `Asmeta` Framework

Abstract State Machines (ASMs) [7] are an extension of Finite State Machines (FSMs), where unstructured control states are replaced by states with arbitrarily complex data. ASM *states* are mathematical structures, i.e., domains of objects with functions and predicates defined on them. An ASM *location* - defined as the pair (*function-name*, *list-of-parameter-values*) - represents the abstract ASM concept of basic objects container. The ordered pair (*location*, *value*) represents a machine memory unit.

Location values are changed by firing *transition rules*. They express the modification of functions interpretation from one state to the next one. Note that the algebra signature is fixed and that functions are total (by interpreting undefined locations $f(x)$ with value *undef*). Location *updates* are given as assignments of the form $loc := v$, where $loc$ is a location and $v$ is its new value. They are the basic units of rule construction. There is a limited but powerful set of *rule constructors* to express: guarded actions, simultaneous parallel actions, sequential actions, nondeterminism, and unrestricted synchronous parallelism.

An ASM *computation* or *run* is, therefore, defined as a finite or infinite sequence of states $s_1, s_2, \ldots, s_n, \ldots$ of the machine. $s_1$ is an initial state and each $s_{i+1}$ is obtained from $s_i$ by firing the unique *main rule*, which could fire other transitions rules (see Fig. 1).

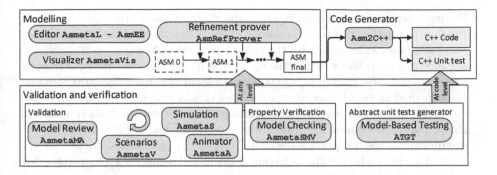

**Fig. 2.** The ASM development process powered by the `Asmeta` framework

During a machine computation, not all the locations can be updated. Functions are classified as *static* (never change during any run of the machine) or *dynamic* (may change as a consequence of agent actions or *updates*). Dynamic functions are distinguished between *monitored* (only read by the machine and modified by the environment) and *controlled* (read in the current state and updated by the machine in the next state). A further classification is between *basic* and *derived* functions, i.e., those coming with a specification or computation mechanism given in terms of other functions.

An ASM can be *nondeterministic* due to the presence of monitored functions (*external* nondeterminism) and of choose rules (*internal* nondeterminism).

**Asmeta framework.** The ASM method can facilitate the entire life cycle of software development, i.e., from modeling to code generation. Figure 2 shows the development process based on ASMs. The process is supported by the `Asmeta` (ASM mETAmodeling) framework[1] [4] which provides a set of tools to help the developer in various activities:

- **modeling:** the system is modeled using the language `AsmetaL`. The user is supported by the editor `AsmEE` and by `AsmetaVis`, the ASMs visualizer which transforms the textual model into a graphical representation. The user can directly define the last ASM model or s/he can reach it through refinement. The refinement process is adopted in case the model is complex. In this case, the designer can start from the first model (also called the ground model) and can refine it through the refinement steps by adding details to the behavior of the ASM. The `AsmRefProver` tool ensures whether the current ASM model is a correct refinement of the previous ASM model.
- **validation:** the process is supported by the model simulator `AsmetaS`, the animator `AsmetaA`, the scenarios executor `AsmetaV`, and the model reviewer `AsmetaMA`. The simulator `AsmetaS` allows to perform two types of simulation: interactive simulation and random simulation. The difference between the two types of simulation is the way in which the monitored functions are chosen.

---

[1] http://asmeta.sourceforge.net/.

During interactive simulation the user inserts the value of functions, while in random simulation the tool randomly chooses the value of functions among those available. `AsmetaA` allows the same operation of `AsmetaS`, but the states are shown using tables which make the readability of the state easier. `AsmetaV` executes scenarios written using the `Avalla` language. Each scenario contains the expected system behavior and the tool checks whether the machine runs correctly. The model reviewer `AsmetaMA` performs static analysis in order to check quality attributes like minimality, completeness, and consistency.

- **verification:** the properties derived from the requirements document are verified to check whether the behavior of the model complies with the intended behavior. The `AsmetaSMV` tool supports this process.
- **testing:** the tool `ATGT` generates abstract unit tests starting from the ASM specification by exploiting the counterexamples generation of a model checker.
- **code generation:** given the final ASM specification, the `Asm2C++` automatically translates it into C++ code. Moreover, the abstract tests, generated by the `ATGT` tool, are translated to C++ unit tests.

## 3    The e-Pix Case Study

Adherence to pharmacological therapy [8] is one of the most well-known problem in medical field. Sometimes it happens that the patient is not adherent to the therapy because he does not remember to take the medicine or he does not remember if he has already taken it. For this reason the patients have the need to adopt a system that can help them to follow the therapy. The device introduced in the market is the pill box, where pills are inserted based on the scheduled doses of medications. The first pill boxes were simply multicompartment boxes where each compartment was filled with the corresponding medicine. The simplest boxes have one section for each day, while the most complicated have multiple sections corresponding to different times of the day. The box helps the user to prevent/reduce medication errors because once the pills are in the correct section the user has only to remember to take it at the right time. With the introduction of technology in the medical field, even the pill boxes have evolved. They are integrated with electronic components that provide alerts to patients when the time of medicine comes. Usually the pill box is provided with a memory where the list of pills with the therapy time are saved and at the right time the box notifies to the user. The notifications can take place with a sound/light signal or, for smarter pill boxes, they can be displayed on the smartphone. In this paper, we consider a pill box developed using Arduino[2], an open-source electronic prototyping platform. We were asked by a local company to re-engineer the software of an existing pocket portable pillbox called e-Pix, following the guidelines discussed in Sect. 6. In particular, the company wants to certify its product w.r.t. the FDA guidelines and IEC regulation and, because of that, needs to be sure it works properly. Furthermore, they have provided some functional

---

[2] https://www.arduino.cc/.

requirements which the prototype has to satisfy, e.g. if the patient does not take the pill in time the red light of the corresponding compartment has to blink.

*Requirements.* The existing e-Pix has an array of *compartments* each containing an unique type of unpackaged pills and having a sensor able to signal the opening of the related window. Each compartment is provided with a red led, used as output to indicate which pill has to be taken (red led turns on until the patient opens the compartment) and if the pill has been taken. When the pill time has passed and the set timeout expires the red led starts to blink for a certain period of time to attract patient's attention because he forgot the pill.

After that the red led is turned off and a message is shown on the e-Pix display. In case the patient takes the pill but he forgot closing the compartment window, the red led starts to blink for a certain period of time. The prescription file is generated by the user by interacting with some buttons on the e-Pix and stored inside e-Pix as JSON file (see Code 1). It contains for each pill the compartment in which it is contained, the name of the pill and the time at which the pill has to be taken (expressed as

```
{ "patient" : "patient_name",
  "pills" : [
    { "compartment" : "
        compartment_number",
      "name" : "pillName",
      "time_consumption" :
          ["t1", "t2", ...],
    },
    {...}
  ]
}
```

**Code 1.** Example of the JSON file containing the prescriptions

the number of seconds passed since 01/01/1970). e-Pix loads the JSON file containing the times at which the pills have to be taken during the initialization phase and, following the schedule, indicates when the patient has to take the pill from the compartment.

## 4   Modeling and V&V

Starting from the informal requirements of the e-Pix, we have applied the process described in Fig. 2. Using the editor AsmEE we have implemented the AsmetaL specifications[3] with different refinement levels. Then validation and verification tools have been used to validate and to verify the model.

**Table 1.** Refinement levels of e-Pix (0 compartments means only one type of pills).

| Refinement | Time management | # compartments | # controlled functions | # monitored functions |
|---|---|---|---|---|
| Level 0 | Monitored boolean function that indicates the overpassing of the time threshold | 0 | 4 | 3 |
| Level 1 | Controlled by the system | 0 | 8 | 1 |
| Level 2 | Controlled by the system | 3 | 9 | 1 |
| Level 3 | Monitored function | 3 | 8 | 2 |

---

[3] The specifications are available at https://foselab.unibg.it/asmeta/PillboxASM.zip.

## 4.1   Modeling by Refinement

We have modeled e-Pix starting from a simple model and then applying step-wise refinement. At each refinement step we have introduced some controlled and monitored functions, we have gradually added compartments, and we have managed the time differently - using some abstractions at level 0, having a controlled time at levels 1 and 2, and as monitored value at the final level (see Table 1).

In the following paragraphs we explain the main characteristics of each refinement level and we analyze how we have modeled the switching on of the red led when the time of a pill comes.

**Level 0.** In the first model, i.e. the *ground model*, we have considered only one pill and no compartments. Instead of using an actual timer, a boolean monitored function `takeThePill` reports when the pill has to be taken. Similarly, the overpassing of all the timeouts (used to switch from a state of the LED to another state) is indicated by the boolean function `timeDiffOver600`. The red led is switched on when a pill has to be taken and it is managed by the following AsmetaL rules:

```
main rule r_Main =                          rule r_pillToBeTaken =
    [...]                                       par
    if redLed = OFF and takeThePill then            redLed := ON
        r_pillToBeTaken[] endif                     outMess := TAKE_PILL
    if redLed = ON and not timeDiffOver600 and  endpar
    opened and not openSwitch then          rule r_pillTaken_compartmentOpened =
        r_pillTaken_compartmentOpened[] endif   par
    [...]                                           redLed := OFF
                                                    outMess := NONE
                                            endpar
```

**Level 1.** At this refinement level, we have continued considering only one pill and no compartments. The time management has been realized using the function `systemTime` as `Natural`, controlled by the system and increased at each machine step. Also at this refinement level we have not considered the list of prescriptions, but only a single deadline for the contemplated pill: we have used a boolean function, `requestSatisfied` to check whether the pill has already been taken or not. The possible output and log messages are taken from an enumerative domain `OutMessages`. The condition according to which the red led is switched on checks the value of the actual timer of e-Pix, whose value is controlled by the system:

```
main rule r_Main =                          rule r_pillToBeTaken =
    [...]                                       par
    if redLed = OFF and (time_consumption<=     if redLed != ON then
        systemTime and not requestSatisfied)    compartmentTimer := systemTime endif
    then r_pillToBeTaken[]                       redLed := ON
    endif                                       outMess := TAKE_PILL
    [...]                                       endpar
```

**Level 2.** The second refinement level introduces three compartments, each with a single type of pill. Other features are similar to the previous level: we have used a single deadline for each pill, the output and log messages come from the enumerative domain OutMessages, the timer systemTime is managed by the system and takes value in a bounded range. Compared to the previous refinements, the red led switch on condition is checked for each single compartment as follows:

```
main rule r_Main =
[...]
if redLed($compartment) = OFF and
    (time_consumption($compartment)<=systemTime and not requestSatisfied($compartment)) then
        r_pillToBeTaken[$compartment]
endif
[...]

rule r_pillToBeTaken($compartment in Compartment) =
par
    if redLed($compartment) != ON then compartmentTimer($compartment) := systemTime endif
    redLed($compartment) := ON
    if ($compartment=compartment1) then
        outMess($compartment) := TAKE_TYLENOL
    else if ($compartment=compartment2) then
        outMess($compartment) := TAKE_ASPIRINE
    else
        outMess($compartment) := TAKE_MOMENT
    endif endif
endpar
```

**Level 3.** The 3rd model we have considered has three compartments and we have included all the features of the system:

- The systemTime is monitored from the machine and updated by the environment.
- Every string can be used as output and log message.
- It is possible to assign a list of time prescriptions for each compartment, stored in the function time_consumption.

The guard that makes the red led switch on, when it is time to take the pill, has been modified with respect to the previous levels, because we have to manage more prescriptions for each pill. The correct item in the sequence containing the prescription times, i.e. the current time threshold to be considered, is selected by the function drugIndex. Therefore, for the compartment $d$, when systemTime passes time_consumption($d$) at position drugIndex($d$), then the pill in $d$ should be taken.

```
main rule r_Main =
[...]
    if redLed($compartment) = OFF and
    (at(time_consumption($compartment),drugIndex($compartment))<systemTime) then
            r_pillToBeTaken[$compartment]
endif
[...]

rule r_pillToBeTaken($compartment in Compartment) =
par
    if redLed($compartment) != ON then
        compartmentTimer($compartment) := systemTime endif
    redLed($compartment) := ON
    outMess($compartment) := "Take " + name($compartment)
endpar
```

| | Type | Functions | State 0 | State 1 | State 2 | State 3 | State 4 | State 5 |
|---|---|---|---|---|---|---|---|---|
| ☑ ∨ | M | openSwitch(drawer1) | false | false | false | true | false | |
| ☑ ∨ | C | time_consumption(drawer1) | 1 | 1 | 1 | 1 | 1 | 1 |
| ☑ ∨ | C | redLed(drawer1) | OFF | OFF | ON | BLINKING | BLINKING | OFF |
| ☑ ∨ | C | systemTime | 0 | 1 | 2 | 3 | 4 | 5 |
| ☑ ∨ | C | outMess(drawer1) | | | TAKE_TYLENOL | TAKE_TYLENOL_IN_10_MIN | CLOSE_TYLENOL_DRAWER_IN_10_MIN | NONE |

**Fig. 3.** Simulation steps with the animator `AsmetaA` at the last refinement level

## 4.2  Automatic Refinement Proof

To automatically prove the correctness of the model refinement process, used in our ASM formal approach, we have employed the tool `AsmRefProver`, which is based over the Satisfiability Modulo Theories (SMT). With the execution of this software, presented in [3], one can specify two refinement levels and ensure that an ASM specification is a correct refinement of a more abstract one.

In our case study we have proven the correctness of the refinement process. To make this possible, since `AsmRefProver` maps refined functions to abstract ones with the same name, we had to introduce in the refined level, some `derived` functions representing predicates over the abstract or refined states. For example, in the first refinement level, to prove the correctness of the refinement process, we have added two derived functions: `takeThePill` that indicates if the patient has to take the pill and `timeDiffOver600` to represent if the patient has forgot taking the pill within a certain time.

```
function takeThePill = (time_consumption<=systemTime)
function timeDiffOver600 = (systemTime−compartmentTimer>tenMinutes)
```

## 4.3  Validation

Validation activity consists in the execution of different tools. Initially we have validated the specification using the simulator `AsmetaS` and the animator `AsmetaA`. In particular we have intensively used the animator because it provides a graphical interface which is more readable for the user during the model execution.

In Fig. 3 we have reported some simulation steps using the animator `AsmetaA`. Specifically, after the system initialization, we have simulated the scenario in which the time is controlled by the ASM and we have only a pill in the first compartment. The red led goes `ON` when it is time to assume the pill (`systemTime > time_consumption`) and turns to `BLINKING` when the timeout has passed. When the compartment is closed the red led turns `OFF`. Also the display message (`outMess`) changes according to the state of e-Pix.

## 4.4  Scenario-Based Testing

In the scenario-based testing activity we have checked the behaviour of e-Pix against the expected one by simulating all the possible states, and transitions between them.

We have written our scenarios using the Avalla language [9] and tested each scenario with the validator AsmetaV, which checks if the machine runs as expected. We have also checked, with the coverage evaluation tool included into AsmetaV, that our scenarios execute all the rules of the ASM model. An example of the tested scenarios is shown in Code 2. Initially all the compartments are closed and after the ASM step the red led is off and no messages are shown. When the time to take the pill is reached (step until command) the state changes, the red led turns on and the message shows which pill the patient has to take.

```
// Setting-up the initial state
set openSwitch(comp1) := false;
set openSwitch(comp2) := false;
set openSwitch(comp3) := false;

step

check redLed(comp1) = OFF;
check outMess(comp1) = NONE;
check logMess(comp1) = NONE;

// Time to take the pill in comp1
step until systemTime = 2;

check redLed(comp1) = ON;
check outMess(comp1) =
      TAKE_TYLENOL;
check logMess(comp1) = NONE;
```

Code 2. Example of an Avalla scenario for the e-Pix

### 4.5 Property Verification: AsmetaSMV

Once the modeler is confident enough that the model correctly reflects the intended requirements, heavier techniques can be used for property verification. In the proposed case study we have identified four CTL (*Computational Tree Logic*) properties that we have tested in the refined models:

**P1.** If the pill has to be taken, red led must lights up.
**P2.** If the patient does not take the pill or the compartment has to be closed, the red light has to blink.
**P3.** The red light has to change value after 10 min if the patient does not take the pill.
**P4.** If the patient takes the pill and closes the compartment, red light becomes off.

We have generated SMV models from the ASM specification using AsmetaSMV and we have verified the properties by means of the model checker NuSMV[4]. Table 2 reports the first property **P1** verified in the models, all the others are available online.

The property is different from one model to the other because we have managed the time differently (initially it was a monitored function, then we have used the function systemTime controlled by the system and increased at each machine step). Furthermore, in the last case we have added more than one compartment, for this reason the property has been verified over each compartment. It is not possible to test the property on *Level 3* because the model contains unlimited domains (like natural numbers and strings) which are not supported by our model checker.

---

[4] http://nusmv.fbk.eu/.

**Table 2.** The property P1 in different refinement levels

| Level | CTLSPEC |
|-------|---------|
| 0 | **ag**((takeThePill and redLed = OFF)**implies** ax(redLed = ON)) |
| 1 | **ag**((takeThePill and not requestSatisfied and redLed = OFF)**implies** ax(redLed = ON)) |
| 2 | (**forall** \$d **in** Compartment **with ag**((time_consumption(\$d)<systemTime and not requestSatisfied (\$d)and opened(\$d)and not(openSwitch(\$d))and not(redLed(\$d)= OFF)and not(systemTime− compartmentTimer(\$d)>=tenMinutes))**implies** ax(redLed(\$d)= OFF))) |

## 5    From Asmeta Specification to C++ Code for Arduino

In addition to the validation and verification activities, we have created an hardware prototype of e-Pix and we have automatically generated the C++ code. The hardware used in our implementation is:

- Arduino Mega 2560
- 3 reed switches, used to signal the opening of each compartment
- 3 red LEDs to signal the state of each compartment
- 1 LCD (Liquid Crystal Display) to interact with the user
- 1 DS3231 module to get the current time
- Arduino SD card reader module, used to store the JSON prescription file and the log ones
- Potentiometers and resistors.

Using the `Asm2C++` tool, we have generated from the last ASM refinement level the following files: the `ino`, which contains the execution policy to run an ASM on Arduino (see Code 3), the `a2c` and the `hw.cpp` files that contain hardware information, the `.h` and `.cpp` files, which contain the translation of the ASM model into C++ code.

The `a2c` configuration file is automatically generated by the `Asm2C++` tool to bind each ASM function to an Arduino physical pin. The file must be completed by the user who has to insert the correspondence between Arduino physical pins and functions defined in the ASM model (see Code 4). Then the `hw.cpp` file, which contains C++ code to load the inputs and set the outputs, is automatically produced (see Code 5) to allow the interaction between the software and Arduino physical pins.

```
#include"pillbox.h"
void setup(){
}

pillbox pillbox;

void loop(){
  pillbox.getInputs();
  pillbox.r_Main();
  pillbox.fireUpdateSet();
  pillbox.setOutputs();
}
```

**Code 3.** Example of the ino file containing the implementation of the ASM execution

## 6    IEC Regulation and FDA Guidance Application

As reported in Sect. 1, the main references concerning the development of medical software are the IEC 62304 regulation [12] and the FDA General Principles of Software Validation [15]. Afterwards, we map the two documents in the ASM process using the `Asmeta` framework.

```
{
    "arduinoVersion": "
         MEGA2560",
    "stepTime": 0,
    "bindings": [
        { "mode": "DIGITAL",
          "function": "redLed(
              comp1)",
          "pin" : "D1"
        },
        { "mode": "DIGITAL",
          "function": "redLed(
              comp2)",
          "pin" : "D2"
        },
        [...]
    ]
}
```

**Code 4.** Example of the a2c configuration file

```
#include "pillbox.h"
#include <Arduino.h>
void pillbox::getInputs(){
    openSwitch[comp1] = (digitalRead(7) == HIGH);
    [...]
    systemTime = analogRead(A1)*(double)(1.0/1024.0);
}
void pillbox::setOutputs(){
    if(redLed[1][comp1] == OFF)
        digitalWrite(1, LOW);
    else
        digitalWrite(1, HIGH);
    if(redLed[2][comp1] == OFF)
        digitalWrite(2, LOW);
    else
        digitalWrite(2, HIGH);
    [...]
}
```

**Code 5.** Example of the hw.cpp file

| 5.1 Software development planning | 5.2 Software requirements analysis | 5.3 Software architectural design | 5.4 Software detailed design | 5.5 Software unit implementation and verification | 5.6 Software integration and integration testing | 5.7 Software system testing | 5.8 Software release |
| --- | --- | --- | --- | --- | --- | --- | --- |

**Fig. 4.** IEC 62304 development process

## 6.1   IEC 62304 Standard

The standard IEC 62304 [12] does not prescribe a specific life cycle model, it defines process, activities and tasks that the life cycle model has to follow. In particular, we will focus on the characteristics of the software development process (Fig. 4) described in Section 5 of the standard. We have identified how ASMs can be used to satisfy the process.

– *Step (5.1) consists in defining a life cycle model and planning all procedures.* ASMs can supply a precise iterative and incremental life cycle model, based on model refinement. With the ASMs, the developers can perform modeling, validation, verification and conformance checking, which we have performed in Sect. 4 for the e-Pix.
– *Step (5.2) consists in defining and documenting functional and non-functional software requirements.* ASMs can be used to define the system requirements with a mathematical model that can be also analyzed and checked before the implementation development. Informal requirements, which are the results of the requirements gathering activity, are out of the scope of the ASM method. ASMs do not deal natively with non-functional requirements like performance, fault tolerance and reliability either. Thus complementary techniques should be used for these purposes.
– *Step (5.3) regards the specification of the software architecture from the software requirements.* In the e-Pix, the verification of software requirements is executed along all the ASM development process using the property verification tool AsmetaSMV (see Sect. 4.5). Risk control can be performed also

during this phase, by verifying the required functional safety properties and executing critical scenario-based testing written in `Avalla` (see Sect. 4.4).

- *Step (5.4) regards the refinement of the software architecture into software units.* The software refinement can be obtained by means of the model refinement mechanism, typical of our ASM approach. We have applied the software refinement to the e-Pix and we have checked the correctness of refinement using the `AsmRefProver` tool (see Sect. 4.2).
- *Steps (5.5)–(5.7) regard the refinement of the software architecture into software units, software implementation and testing at unit, integration, and system levels.* With our ASM-based development process, the actual code can be obtained by the automatic translator `Asm2C++` as last model refinement step, so if the model has been correctly tested, the developers can be sure about the correctness of the C++ code. However the developer can change something in the generated code, so the ASM process cannot fully cover these development steps. For the e-Pix, in Sect. 5 we have automatically generated the Arduino code that we have deployed on the real system.
- *Step (5.8) includes the demonstration, by a device manufacturer, that software has been validated and verified.* If the development process adopts the ASM process, demonstration that the software has been validated and verified is straightforward, since V&V are continuous activities during all the process.

### 6.2   FDA General Principles of Software Validation

FDA accepts the standard IEC 62304 and pushes for an integration of software life cycle management and risk management activities. The organization promotes the use of formal approaches for software validation and verification, by defining in [15] the list of general principles. For each FDA principle we have identified how ASMs can be used to satisfy the requests.

- *A documented software requirements specification should provide a baseline for both V&V*: in ASM it is provided by means of a chain of models (or single model in case of simple specifications). The models are written using `AsmetaL` language as partially reported in Sect. 4 for the e-Pix models.
- *Developers should use a mixture of methods and techniques to prevent and to detect software errors*: in ASM safety properties are proved on models at each modeling level. In particular `Asmeta` framework provides the `AsmetaSMV` tool that verifies the properties defined by the developer showing if they are satisfied or not. We have applied the property verification to the e-Pix models as reported in Sect. 4.5.
- *Software V&V should be planned early and conducted during all the software life cycle; software V&V should take place within the environment of an established software life cycle; software V&V process should be defined and controlled through the use of a plan*: as shown in Fig. 2 the V&V process can be applied at each model. V&V activities can be integrated in the V model of software development. In particular it is possible to insert them in the module design, coding and unit testing phases.

- *Software V&V process should be executed through the use of procedures*: V&V are supported by precise procedures defined for each tool which have been followed during the application to the e-Pix.
- *Software V&V should be re-established upon any software change*: if software changes do not affect the model, it is required to re-run unit tests on the changed software and verify if the behavior has been modified or not. In case the software changes have effects on the model V&V activities must be re-executed.
- *Validation coverage should be based on the software complexity and safety risks*: during validation activity of an ASM model, it is possible to provide the coverage report in terms of rules, which points out how many lines of code have been covered. It can be used by the designer to estimate if the validation activity is commensurate with the risk associated with the use of the software. The coverage of e-Pix models was 100%, all rules have been covered using the validation activity, in particular the scenario-based testing, as reported in Sect. 4.4.
- *V&V activities should be conducted using the quality assurance precept of "independence of review"*: this can be obtained because V&V are performed by exploiting unambiguous mathematical based techniques.
- *Device manufacturer has flexibility in choosing how to apply these V&V principles*: all the presented V&V activities can be executed at the discretion of the manufacturer because they can be executed independently of each other. Even if the software has been developed by an external developer, the manufacturer can apply the activities presented to guarantee the correctness w.r.t. the verified model.

# 7 Related Work

As shown by [6], formal methods are increasingly used in the development of medical software and devices because human safety depends upon the correct operation of the product. Even automatic code generation is already available into commercial solutions (such as MATLAB/Simulink[5]) or UML-based solutions but none of them is based on the ASM method and permits the verification and validation of the written models. In [2], the ASM method has been used to show how an hemodialysis machine can be designed providing a rigorous approach for medical software validation and verification. Despite this, the code to be executed by the final embedded system has not been produced.

The process that allows the automatic code generation has been described into [5] where the car panel case study is analyzed.

Most of the other works related to the approach used into this paper are based on Event-B [1]. These solutions use a multi-formal development paradigm: the requirements are modeled by using UML-B [16] and then the verification is executed into the framework of Event-B using theorems proving the model checking or using model animation. This framework is used into [14] where a hemodialysis

---

[5] https://it.mathworks.com/products/simulink.html.

machine is developed by specifying the requirements using a refinement-based modeling approach. Subsequently model checking and animation techniques are applied to check the consistency and the conformance to the formal requirements. A code generator produces, at the end, the code from the model. The major cons of this solution are that the tool is able to translate only a limited set of the B syntax and it lacks of a formal proof that the produced code maintains all the safety properties of the initial requirements.

There are several papers presenting the design and development of pill box or smart pill dispenser for individual use. Some of them, such as [10], are also Arduino-based. However, no one at the best of our knowledge has adopted a rigorous approach like ours. In [17], the authors present the architecture and the implementation of an automatic medication dispenser. Part of the system is actually generated from models that define user behavior. They have tackled the problem of validating such models mainly by simulation. During simulation, events in interactions of the user, controller and scheduler are registered in a database. They then check the correctness by processing and analyzing the logged events to find errors. A formal modeling has been applied to the design of a mobile prescription application [11]. However, the author has used only UML for modeling of the mobile application.

## 8  Conclusion

The development of a safe and reliable medical device can be very challenging because it is a safety-critical process. To address the software development in a safer manner, different regulations have been released. However, all these documents are limited to describe only general software engineering activities that have to be executed but they do not require the use of specific method or technique.

In this paper, we have applied the ASM based development process to the smart pill box e-Pix case study. The approach consists in an iterative life cycle model realized by model refinement: starting from a ground model, which considers only the simplest features of the system, the developer can release many incremental models, considering step by step all the characteristics. Along this process, different validation and verification activities (such as model animation, scenario-based validation and property verification) can be performed over each refinement step, to prove the correctness of each produced model compared to the requirements. The final model of the system can be seen as the last refinement step, from which one can obtain the C++ code to be used in the embedded system, thanks to Asm2C++ tool. In addition, we have developed a simple hardware prototype using Arduino on which we have loaded the generated C++ code, the hardware configuration file and the main Arduino file (all of them automatically generated using the Asm2C++ tool).

Finally, we have shown how the proposed process aims to guarantee safety and reliability of the final product by remaining compliant with the IEC 62304 regulation and FDA General Principle of Software Validation guidelines.

# References

1. Abrial, J.-R.: Modeling in Event-B: System and Software Engineering. Cambridge University Press, Cambridge (2010)
2. Arcaini, P., Bonfanti, S., Gargantini, A., Mashkoor, A., Riccobene, E.: Integrating formal methods into medical software development: the ASM approach. Sci. Comput. Program. **158**, 148–167 (2018)
3. Arcaini, P., Gargantini, A., Riccobene, E.: SMT-based automatic proof of ASM model refinement. In: De Nicola, R., Kühn, E. (eds.) SEFM 2016. LNCS, vol. 9763, pp. 253–269. Springer, Cham (2016). https://doi.org/10.1007/978-3-319-41591-8_17
4. Arcaini, P., Gargantini, A., Riccobene, E., Scandurra, P.: A model-driven process for engineering a toolset for a formal method. Softw. Pract. Exp. **41**, 155–166 (2011)
5. Bonfanti, S., Carissoni, M., Gargantini, A., Mashkoor, A.: Asm2C++: a tool for code generation from abstract state machines to Arduino. In: Barrett, C., Davies, M., Kahsai, T. (eds.) NFM 2017. LNCS, vol. 10227, pp. 295–301. Springer, Cham (2017). https://doi.org/10.1007/978-3-319-57288-8_21
6. Bonfanti, S., Gargantini, A., Mashkoor, A.: A systematic literature review of the use of formal methods in medical software systems. J. Softw. Evol. Process **30**(5), e1943 (2018)
7. Börger, E., Stark, R.F.: Abstract State Machines: A Method for High-Level System Design and Analysis. Springer, New York (2003). https://doi.org/10.1007/978-3-642-18216-7
8. Brown, M.T., Bussell, J.K.: Medication adherence: WHO cares? Mayo Clin. Proc. **86**(4), 304–314 (2011)
9. Carioni, A., Gargantini, A., Riccobene, E., Scandurra, P.: A scenario-based validation language for ASMs. In: Börger, E., Butler, M., Bowen, J.P., Boca, P. (eds.) ABZ 2008. LNCS, vol. 5238, pp. 71–84. Springer, Heidelberg (2008). https://doi.org/10.1007/978-3-540-87603-8_7
10. Huang, S.-C., Chang, H.-Y., Jhu, Y.-C., Chen, G.-Y.: The intelligent pill box - design and implementation. In: 2014 IEEE International Conference on Consumer Electronics - Taiwan. IEEE, May 2014
11. Ikhu-Omoregbe, N.: Formal modelling and design of mobile prescription applications. J. Health Inform. Dev. Countries **2**(2), 6–9 (2008)
12. Jordan, P.: Standard IEC 62304 - medical device software - software lifecycle processes. In: 2006 IET Seminar on Software for Medical devices, pp. 41–47, November 2006
13. Kemmerer, R.A.: Testing formal specifications to detect design errors. IEEE Trans. Softw. Eng. **SE-11**(1), 32–43 (1985)
14. Mashkoor, A., Biro, M.: Towards the trustworthy development of active medical devices: a hemodialysis case study. IEEE Embed. Syst. Lett. **8**(1), 14–17 (2016)
15. A. Ohne Autor Fd.: General Principles of Software Validation; Final Guidance for Industry and FDA Staff, Version 2.0. FDA document formal, January 2002
16. Snook, C., Butler, M.: UML-B: Formal modeling and design aided by UML. ACM Trans. Softw. Eng. Methodol. **15**(1), 92–122 (2006)
17. Tsai, P.-H., Chen, T.-Y., Yu, C.-R., Shih, C.-S., Liu, J.W.S.: Smart medication dispenser: design, architecture and implementation. IEEE Syst. J. **5**(1), 99–110 (2011)

# The Impact of Dance Sport on Software Development

Irina Erofeeva[(✉)]

Innopolis University, Innopolis, Russia
i.erofeeva@innopolis.ru

**Abstract.** There are two general questions that the study follows: Can a parallel be drawn between dance as a sport and software development? And can the IT sphere borrow something from dance sports to improve performance? But IT, indeed, is a broad area, to narrow down the scope of study two more concrete paths were chosen: software development methodologies and educational approach in IT.

**Keywords:** Software development · Development methodologies · Dancesport · Ballroom dancing

## 1 Introduction

Software development is one of the youngest scope of human activity, that was built by people from elements of other spheres, it was noticed that it has features that are similar to other, much older, disciplines practices by humans [7]. Currently the most popular software development methodology, Agile [17], actually also inspired by approaches originated outside IT [16]. The first time it was used by the physicist and statistician Shewhart as the Plan-Do-Study-Act cycles to improve products and processes, then his student Deming made it popular this method during the reconstruction of Japan after the Second World War, and finally transferred this method to the industry, which led to the creation of the famous Toyota Production System, the primary source of modern lean manufacturing.

Being a dancer and programmer, I conducted a study to find out if there is a connection between areas of dancing and computer science and how this connection could be useful. I selected dancesport because it gives a broader landscape for discussion, as it includes both the sport industry and art [25].

From a sport perspective, it is possible to gain productivity, motivation and passion, perseverance and ability to overcome fears, to expand barriers. From art perspective also motivation, inspiration and creativity can be considered as a source of innovative ideas for improving software development [14].

M. Mazzara et al. (Eds.): TOOLS 2019, LNCS 11771, pp. 104–112, 2019.
https://doi.org/10.1007/978-3-030-29852-4_8

## 2    Necessary Background Information

Ballroom dancing is a set of partner dances that are performed both socially and competitively around the world. While dancesport is more narrow and refers to the five International Standard and five International Latin style dances.

The purpose of this work is to apply the theory of a conceptual blending, that is according to Gilles Fauconnier and Mark Turner a deep cognitive activity that "makes new meanings out of old." [13], in comparison of software development and dancing spheres and analyse how techniques coming from dancesport can be used effectively in software development.

The example of this approach is present by Brenda Laurel "Computers as Theatre" [19]. Based on the analysis of the form and structure of the drama of Aristotle the author shows how similar principles can help to understand what people experience when interfacing with computers.

While authority of facts in computer sciences is evidence based and research, the dancing authority is performance based. People who work in dance, and in performance art, understand that authority comes from being able to do the performance. That is why some journalistic and informal sources are also included as a literature background for the study.

During the process of reviewing of existing scopes on interests in this direction within the academia, three of the most popular topics were defined: IT education, software development methodologies and human computer interaction. Being a part of a IT University community, I have chosen two of these fields - IT education and software development methodologies.

### IT Education

Dancing along with the visual arts and literature is a more high-level and abstract level of information transfer comparing to a programming, and therefore more comprehensible to a wider audience. Therefore, such abstractions are often used in preschool and school education. There a number of courses that have been created, in which programming concepts are explained through dance.

There are courses for K-12 students with names like "Coding Choreography" that offer learning programming using dancing. Abstracting to dance, students study concepts such as algorithms, conditionals, functions, loops, patterns and so on. "The students in this class move and create pieces for their virtual characters to perform, bringing about connections between computational thinking and what their bodies are doing" [4].

Daily et al. (2014) found that dancing helps to promote learning software development in students of grades 5 and 6. They designed a special software for ladies, which allowed them to sync their body movements with the computer. Fifth- and sixth-grade girls were tested with the novel technology that required them to create a virtual character in a three-dimensional environment. The girls were required to think up new computer strategies to improve their dance choreography, evaluate new animation algorithms, and align them with their own body movements. "We want to understand how body syntonicity might enable young learners to bootstrap their intuitive knowledge in order to program a three-dimensional character to perform movements," the study's coauthor Leonard said in a press release. "Executing one bit of code or movement one after the other exists in both programming and choreography. Likewise, loops or repeating a set of steps, also occur in both contexts" [10].

The course "Dancing computer" by Dillon et al. [12] was prepared to teach elementary school students both dance terminology and concepts of coding such as sequencing and conditionals. One of the main goals of this course is to teach children to read code before writing it.

Such courses exist not only for children, but for students, teams of students. Faculty members from Clemson University also designed a program called VEnvI (Virtual Environment Interactions) [26] that combines basic concepts of computational thinking and basic concepts from dance, so students can dance and pick up key computational skills at the same time. Using VEnvI, students can learn programming concepts like sequencing, looping and conditionals.

In addition to face-to-face courses, there are several online courses that also turn to the dance field in order to simplify the learning process with the help of visual dance examples. "Made with Code" is specially prepared for teaching middle and high school girls programming skills. Among the projects presented there you can find a section "Dance visualization" [2], which uses a simple gamified, block-like interface to create a part of the program that will make a dancer move. A similar approach is used in a lesson titled "Dance Moves" [1], which introduces Python language course on the website Codesters, but instead of block interface students have to write a real code.

## Software Development Methodologies

This is not the first work on this subject. The author of "Agile dancing. Scrum training. Is it even possible?" (2017) has already drawn a parallelism between dancing and software development. In particular, she has analysed how to apply the Agile methodology to her training process, considering time between competitions as sprints, coach as a product owner, "who will know exactly what is the main priority and he will also be able to tell if the sprint is finished with success" [5].

Lee presented similar results in her work [20] - also being a dancer in the past and a developer in the present, she drew several parallels between these areas, here are the main points she highlighted as similarities between learning how to code and learning how to dance:

1. Focus on the basics
2. Strive to be well-rounded
3. Collaboration is crucial for improvement
4. Step back and look at the Big Picture

Some new parallels were drawn at a seminar at Bilkent University in 2013 [3]. They looked at the methods and processes of software engineering by relating it to the systematic structure of dance. Some common features were highlighted:

- Processes employed in software engineering, such as analysis, design, implementation and testing were associated with the rules of professional dancing
- The Waterfall model examined the steps and the structure that dancers use while preparing a dance performance as if they were a part of engineering.
- Importance of teamwork and professionalism was considered.

Perez superficially makes a reference a crucial reference to ballroom dancing talking about interaction between team members. "Much like a ballroom dance, the art of collaborative software development requires that the partners work together for the harmony to come alive" [23]. The author compares the result of this cohesive and harmonious work with a smooth dance.

Oliver expressed the idea of parallelism between dancing and computer science through comparing modern dancing styles in terms of their movements, music and composition to agile methodology, because of their freedom. He compared on the other hand classical ballet to formal methods: "Formal methods are computer science's version of ballet: strict rules and technique and hard to master but forming the basis for the rest of the subject, especially software engineering [21]." This author admits that he was inspired by the work of Baez [6] that contains evidence of interdisciplinary communication between various scientific disciplines - Physics, Topology and Logic through category theory.

## 3 Methods and Data Collection

The collection of the relevant information from dancesport is organized in three parts:

1. Review of the relevant literature on dancesport, on its regulations, on the training processes, etc
2. Interviews with experts to identify aspects not (well) covered in the literature
3. Personal observation and experience§§§§§§§§

On the survey stage one of the main tasks was to develop a questionnaire. The questions were divided into four sections according to their aims:

- Questions to analyse professional's level
- Goals and challenges
- Relationships in a team
- Productivity and self-development

In order to motivate the respondents and direct the reasoning in the right way for developers the goal of the survey was explained as an attempt to find weaknesses and gaps in the current popular methods of development with further attempts to introduce new strategies to eliminate these gaps. For dancers - as an attempt to collect, analyze the best practices from their sphere.

The interviewees are 10 professional dancers and 10 developers from local companies. The sample among dancers was very diverse: from the lowest class (hobby) to the dancers of the highest class (M), performing for competitions from city to international level. Some had behind their back more than 10 years of experience, some have already completed their careers and became coaches.

The programmers who participated in the survey also covered a wide range of professions in this field, such as chief technical officer, tester, senior web-developer, backend developer, team leader, analyst. All of them had an experience from 1 to more than 10 years.

The plan is to interview developers from the local companies for the validation of new techniques. Among them there are several startups created by students that are looking for new methodologies that can be more convenient and accurate, than already existing. Also there are a lot of developers working for many years in different companies, so it will be also useful to hear the criticism from such experienced professionals.

## 4 Collected Evidence

This section includes preliminary results of interviews, that are not categorised by chosen direction. These are only some similarities that were discovered based of literature review and specific interviews with professionals.

When you first and naively look at these two concepts - dancing and programming - you can immediately notice that the dance, like the program, is nothing more than an algorithm, a sequence of actions performed by the dancer in dependence on various conditions such as rhythm, tempo, style of music, personal experience and experience of the partner, the presence of each of the dancing couples on the floor.

In dancing, people are organized based on their level, experience and achievements. The more advanced have the possibility to include some harder figures and poses in their performance, and also to add new dances. A similar practice is present in the software industry, where specialists are divided into "junior", "intermediate", and "senior" developers, with different sets of tasks and responsibilities.

For those who start to dance and want to develop faster there is a chance to practice with more experienced partner. There is a special category called Pro-Am (Professional-Amateur), where the professionals dance with novices or with much less experienced dancers. In this situation both, beginner and professional dancer, gain something useful for their dancesport career: beginner gets a quick start, professional gets a chance to consolidate his knowledge and understand the material deeper during the explanation. In software development it is present as one variation of pair programming, where a beginner and a more experienced developer are working together. Beginner adopts the knowledge, experience and habits of a more experienced specialist, which helps him to learn faster [15,31].

The leading role in the dance pair is always taken by the man, that is, he is responsible for the safety of the pair on the dance floor and for the correct execution of composition. If there is an obstacle in the way of the pair, the partner can change the direction of the movement or dance a more convenient and appropriate movement for this situation, and the girl must follow it. The appointment of a leader in a pair, who chooses strategy in a difficult situation, helps prevent errors on the dance floor. Error prevention in the way of choosing a leader in a team is present in software development in a role of team leader and also project manager.

The most common practice in ballroom dancing is recording performances for analyzing the mistakes and revealing the work front for the following workouts. In software development it is called retrospective [27]. Not every team runs retrospective sessions, but every team should, because this is the way to find out what we can do to be better.

The software development methodology called Lean concentrates on minimizing the waste and autonomation of the process and widely used in companies in form of Agile [16] also using significantly domain-centered approaches and metrics [28–30]. Its concept of elimination of waste appears in dancesport - after a specific point in sportsman's career, it is obligatory to choose only one program, Standard or Latin, to develop only in one direction. It was noticed, that dancers, who choose two programs are less successful, than those who were concentrated on one goal.

During group practises, where participants have different levels and experience, the coach can mix partners to try different techniques with other partner, this practice help to improve leading and following skills, and identify mistakes that was not obvious with your own partner. In software development there are equivalent situations, especially considering joint pair programming sessions, as evidenced by the work of Succi and colleagues [15, 22].

**Table 1.** Table of results

| Software development | Dancesport |
|---|---|
| Pair programming | Pro-Am category |
| Project manager or team leader | Man as a leader |
| Software design patters | Books with steps and compositions |
| Testing with different inputs | Exchanging partners during trainings to find gaps in knowledge |
| Retrospective sessions | Reviewing the tape |
| Elimination of waste | Choosing and concentrating on one program |
| **Gap** | Warm-up before each activity to perform better |
| **Gap** | Constant work on basic movements, since they represent the foundation of any composition |
| **Gap** | Proper nutrition, so your main instrument - you body works properly |
| **Gap** | Proficiency in foundations of the classical dance as the basis for the proper operation of all the muscles of the body |

For now we saw a lot of similarities between spheres of dancing and software development, but what are features, that take place in dancing and can be useful in software, but not yet represented? There are also concepts commonly used in the sphere of ballroom dancing, such as warm-up, constant work on basic movements, proper nutrition, proficiency in foundations of the classical dance. And these ideas will be the central for the further study. The preliminary results of comparison is present in Table 1.

## 5   Conclusion

After analysing the similarities between dancing and software development we will move on with the proposed plan - to analyse in deep features from dancesport that are applied or applicable in software development and to see the extent to which they can be concretely used, with the help and validation of interviews with professionals. We are going to present several variations of adaptations of new features borrowed from dancesport, validate and choose the most promising and suitable ones with the help of software specialists from local companies.

Furthermore, in exploring this study further, it would be important to go deeper into the analysis of the brain. For example, compare impulses during dance classes, perform a learned composition and implement the algorithm just explained. Give the past experience it is likely that a significant amount of responses will be collected, so that suitable statistics could be built.

It would also be interesting to compare open performances with Open Source approaches to software development [11,18,24] and to the fast-paced development of apps for mobile systems [8,9]

## References

1. Dance moves. Accessed 28 Oct 2018
2. Made with code. Accessed 28 Oct 2018
3. The meeting of software engineering and dancing, January 2012
4. Glowing coding and choreography (2013). Accessed 27 June 2018
5. Agile dancing: Scrum training. Is it even possible? December 2017. Accessed 28 June 2018
6. Baez, J., Stay, M.: Physics, topology, logic and computation: a rosetta stone. In: Coecke, B. (ed.) New Structures for Physics. LNP, vol. 813, pp. 95–172. Springer, Berlin (2010). https://doi.org/10.1007/978-3-642-12821-9_2
7. Baragry, J.: Understanding software engineering: from analogies with other disciplines to philosophical foundations, July 2000. Accessed 27 June 2018
8. Corral, L., Georgiev, A.B., Sillitti, A., Succi, G.: A method for characterizing energy consumption in Android smartphones. In: 2nd International Workshop on Green and Sustainable Software (GREENS 2013), pp. 38–45. IEEE, May 2013

9. Corral, L., Sillitti, A., Succi, G.: Software development processes for mobile systems: is agile really taking over the business? In: 2013 1st International Workshop on the Engineering of Mobile-Enabled Systems (MOBS), pp. 19–24, May 2013
10. Daily, S.B., Leonard, A.E., Jörg, S., Babu, S., Gundersen, K., Parmar, D.: Embodying computational thinking: initial design of an emerging technological learning tool. Technol. Knowl. Learn. **20**(1), 79–84 (2014)
11. Di Bella, E., Sillitti, A., Succi, G.: A multivariate classification of open source developers. Inf. Sci. **221**, 72–83 (2013)
12. D. C. O. M. E. D. K. D. W. S. B. W., Dillon, L.K., Dobbins, A.: Dancing computer (2015). Accessed 28 Oct 2018
13. Fauconnier, G., Turner, M.: The way we think: conceptual blending and the mind's hidden complexities, May 2003. Accessed 28 June 2018
14. Fronza, I., Sillitti, A., Succi. G.: An interpretation of the results of the analysis of pair programming during novices integration in a team. In: Proceedings of the 2009 3rd International Symposium on Empirical Software Engineering and Measurement, ESEM 2009, pp. 225–235. IEEE Computer Society (2009)
15. Fronza, I., Sillitti, A., Succi, G.: An interpretation of the results of the analysis of pair programming during novices integration in a team. In: Proceedings of the 2009 3rd International Symposium on Empirical Software Engineering and Measurement, ESEM 2009, pp. 225–235. IEEE Computer Society (2009)
16. Janes, A., Succi, G.: Lean Software Development in Action. Springer, Heidelberg (2014). https://doi.org/10.1007/978-3-642-00503-9
17. Kivi, J., Haydon, D., Hayes, J., Schneider, R., Succi, G.: Extreme programming: a university team design experience. In: 2000 Canadian Conference on Electrical and Computer Engineering. Conference Proceedings. Navigating to a New Era (Cat. No. 00TH8492), vol. 2, pp. 816–820, May 2000
18. Kovács, G.L., Drozdik, S., Zuliani, P., Succi, G.: Open source software for the public administration. In: Proceedings of the 6th International Workshop on Computer Science and Information Technologies, October 2004
19. Laurel, B.: Computers as theatre, September 2014
20. Lee, C.: Learning to code is just like learning to dance, May 2018. Accessed 28 Oct 2018
21. Oliver, I.: The ballet-software engineering "isomorphism", March 2012. Accessed 11 Nov 2018
22. Pedrycz, W., Russo, B., Succi, G.: Knowledge transfer in system modeling and its realization through an optimal allocation of information granularity. Appl. Soft Comput. **12**(8), 1985–1995 (2012)
23. Perez, J.C.: Collaboration and software development, September 2015. Accessed 20 Nov 2018
24. Petrinja, E., Sillitti, A., Succi, G.: Comparing OpenBRR, QSOS, and OMM assessment models. In: Ågerfalk, P., Boldyreff, C., González-Barahona, J.M., Madey, G.R., Noll, J. (eds.) OSS 2010. IFIPAICT, vol. 319, pp. 224–238. Springer, Heidelberg (2010). https://doi.org/10.1007/978-3-642-13244-5_18
25. Predonzani, P., Succi, G., Vernazza, T.: Strategic Software Production with Domain-Oriented Reuse. Artech House Inc., Norwood (2000)
26. Ravipati, S.: Students learn computer programming skills through dance, February 2016
27. Rubin, K.S.: Essential scrum: a practical guide to the most popular agile process (2012). Accessed 27 June 2018
28. Sillitti, A., Janes, A., Succi, G., Vernazza, T.: Measures for mobile users: an architecture. J. Syst. Architect. **50**(7), 393–405 (2004)

29. Valerio, A., Succi, G., Fenaroli, M.: Domain analysis and framework-based software development. SIGAPP Appl. Comput. Rev. **5**(2), 4–15 (1997)
30. Vernazza, T., Granatella, G., Succi, G., Benedicenti, L., Mintchev, M.: Defining metrics for software components. In: Proceedings of the World Multiconference on Systemics, Cybernetics and Informatics, vol. XI, pp. 16–23, July 2000
31. Coman, I.D., Sillitti, A., Succi, G.: Investigating the usefulness of pair-programming in a mature agile team. In: Abrahamsson, P., Baskerville, R., Conboy, K., Fitzgerald, B., Morgan, L., Wang, X. (eds.) XP 2008. LNBIP, vol. 9, pp. 127–136. Springer, Heidelberg (2008). https://doi.org/10.1007/978-3-540-68255-4_13

# Proof Strategy for Automated Sisal Program Verification

Dmitry Kondratyev[✉] and Alexei Promsky

A.P. Ershov Institute of Informatics Systems, 630090 Novosibirsk, Russia
apple-66@mail.ru, promsky@iis.nsk.su

**Abstract.** The Sisal programming environment which is being developed in IIS also includes a verification module. The previously developed C-light verification system serves as its base, since the C language representations of Sisal programs are actually processed. At the moment we concentrate our efforts on verification of Sisal loop expressions which are translated into the C for-loops. Trying to avoid the well-known problem of the loop invariants we apply a symbolic method of definite iterations. This technique expresses the loop effect in symbolic form. However, the Sisal loop expressions sometimes lead to peculiar C loops. The symbolic forms of such loops in verification conditions are too complex to be proved automatically. In this paper we represent a proof strategy for such formulas. Our strategy introduces logical formula transformations which, in general, do not maintain equivalence. However, the truth of resulting formula guarantees truth of the original one. We proved the soundness of this strategy. We also describe here a verification example.

**Keywords:** Automated theorem proof · Deductive verification · Sisal · C-light · C-lightVer · Definite iteration

## 1 Introduction

Programming environment for the Sisal language [7] is one of the urgent projects in IIS. It aims mainly at efficiency, so the input program is translated into an intermediate form which, in turn, can be aggressively optimized [7]. In addition, intermediate form can be translated into the C language [6].

A more recent feature of the project relates to deductive program verification, which traditionally rests on axiomatic semantics and verification condition (VC) generation. However, at the moment we do not have a Hoare's logics for Sisal. And this is where translation into the C comes in handy. Another actual project of IIS is the C-lightVer system for deductive verification of C-light programs. Despite its name, the C-light is a quite representative subset of the Standard C with a full operational semantics [13]. This project also involves a

This work was carried out with a grant from the Russian Science Foundation (project 18-11-00118).

M. Mazzara et al. (Eds.): TOOLS 2019, LNCS 11771, pp. 113–120, 2019.
https://doi.org/10.1007/978-3-030-29852-4_9

two-stage scheme, thus introducing a special core, the C-kernel language, which possesses a sound axiomatic semantics. Another example of intermediate verification language is WhyML [10]. But the translation to subset (from C-light to C-kernel) allows us to easily prove the preservation of semantics unlike the translation from C to WhyML. Trying to mechanize the verification proofs we experiment with popular tools. In this paper we address the interactive theorem prover ACL2 [8].

Another approach to formal verification is the use of Constraint Logic Programming [2,4]. It is based on modeling program by logic constructs. But it is necessary to use special strategies for processing such model.

Among traditional woes of deductive verification, loop invariants begin to play a crucial role here. Invariants are provided by user prior to verification process. But the loop expressions of Sisal are translated on the fly into the C for-loops, thus requiring automatic generation of appropriate invariants. This is a very complex task, though some successes were demonstrated by researchers [3]. To avoid it we actually apply to the third actively developing project of our institute. The symbolic method of verification of definite iterations over altered data structures introduces a special replacement operation rep [9,12]. As name suggests the idea is to represent the loop action in some symbolic form. The well-known system for C program verification is the Frama-C. Its plugin Agen provides loop invariant generation based on predicate abstraction [5]. But the user should define these predicates in some cases using the construct for agen.

The recursive nature of rep requires induction over iteration numbers. Our initial attempts to validate such induction in ACL2 were unsuccessful. So we need to develop automatic proof strategies. Some of them were invented in adjacent experiments. For example, a strategy from [11] defines lemmas satisfying certain restrictions which, in turn, depend on VC structure. Unfortunately, that strategy is only interactive. In this paper we represent a more recent strategy which allows a fully automated proof in ACL2.

## 2    Preliminary Information

### 2.1    Symbolic Method of Verification of Definite Iterations

The general representation of definite iteration over data structure takes the form **for x in S do v := body(v, x) end**. Here $S$ is a data structure, $x$ is a variable of type *element of* $S$, $v$ is a tuple of loop variables (excluding $x$) and *body* represents calculations within the loop which do not alter $x$. The loop body only allows assignments, if statements (including nested ones) and break statements. Only expressions without side-effects are allowed at right hand sides of assignments and in conditions of ifs. Then the loop body consecutively iterates in such manner that $x$ equates to $s_1, s_2, \ldots, s_n$ and $body(v, s_j)$ can modify $s_1, s_2, \ldots, s_{j-1}$. Thus, $v$ is a tuple of all objects that can be altered in loop body. Suppose $v_0$ is a value of $v$ before the loop and $v_i$ denotes the value of $v$ after $i$th iteration. Then $v_i = body(v_{i-1}, s_i)$ for $i = 1, ..., n$. The main advantage of this approach reveals itself in the proof of Hoare triples. It does not require loop invariant and does not split the proof tree. It simply introduces a linear replacement operation $rep(v, s, body)$ which expresses the value of $v$ after iteration.

Let $rep(0, v_0) = v_0$ and $rep(i, v_0) = body(rep(i - 1, v_0), s_i)$. Thus, the main property of this operation is $rep(i, v_0) = v_i$. The recursive definition of $rep$ is built automatically by analysis of $body$ [11]. If break was executed during iteration $j$ ($0 < j \leq n$) we model it as if iterations still go on, but the value of $v$ does not change. I.e. for all $k$ such that $j \leq k \leq n$ $rep(j, v_0) = rep(k, v_0)$. So the inference rule for definite iteration takes the following form:

$$\frac{\{P\} \, \mathbf{A}; \{Q(v \leftarrow rep(n, v_0))\}}{\{P\} \, \mathbf{A}; \ \mathbf{for} \ (\mathbf{i} = 0; \mathbf{i} < \mathbf{n}; \mathbf{i}++) \ \mathbf{v} := \mathbf{body(v, i)} \ \mathbf{end}\{Q\}}$$

Here $\mathbf{A}$ is a context (i.e. all statements preceding iteration), $\leftarrow$ denotes substitution. Since the replacement operation returns vector $v$ of length $m$, it may be appropriate to define $m$ replacement operations for each variable of vector $v$.

## 2.2    The Sisal Language and ACL2

The data structure handling in Sisal is based on loop expressions [7]. The loop expression combines three parts: loop control, loop body and returns clause. The heading loop control (denoted by keyword for) declares variables and their ranges during iterations. Loop body consists of expressions modifying loop variables. The operator old returns argument value from the previous iteration. The control expressions (the keyword while) can also take place. The falsity of such expression results in abrupt termination. The returns clause is a list of reductions. Every loop variable is associated with a reducible sequence of values corresponding to iterations. Reductions allow us to apply certain operations to those sequences. For example, reduction value produced the last value of a reducible sequence. This list of reduction itself is a value of whole loop.

On the contrary ACL2 prefers recursion to manipulate data structures. The type checks in our examples will use special predicates. For instance, integerp tests whether its argument is an integer, zp match its argument against zero and integer-listp is satisfiable only by lists of integers. We use lists to model Sisal arrays as well as intermediate C arrays. The function nth accesses list elements while length returns the number of list elements.

## 2.3    Study Case

Consider the following Sisal program counting occurrences of some key in array:

```
function search_count (a: array of integer,
                    n, entr, key: integer returns integer)
    for count := 0, result := 0; i in 1..n
    while !(count = entr) do
        count := if a[i]=key then old count + 1;
        result := if count=entr then 1;
    returns value of result end for end function
```

Its precondition (ACL2 syntax) looks like $(and\ (integer\text{-}listp\ a)\ (integerp\ n)$ $(integerp\ key)\ (<\ 0\ n)\ (<=\ n\ (length\ a)))$ whereas its postcondition is $(and\ (implies\ (=>\ \ entr\ (cnt\ 0\ (-\ n\ 1)\ key\ a))\ (equal\ result\ 1))\ (implies\ (<\ entr\ (cnt\ 0\ (-\ n\ 1)\ key\ a))\ (equal\ result\ 0)))$. The function cnt computes the number of elements equal to key in the sublist from the i-th up to the j-th element. Its definition can be found in repository [1]. The symbolic method introduces logical functions representing substitution operation for the mutable objects within loop body [11]. For the program under discussion function rep1 symbolically reflects changes of variable count:

```
(defun rep1(i key entr a) (if (zp i) 0
  (if (= entr (rep1 (- i 1) key entr a)) (rep1 (- i 1) key entr a)
   (if (= key (nth (- i 1) a)) (+ 1 (rep1 (- i 1) key entr a))
                     (rep1 (- i 1) key entr a)))))
```

while rep2 embodies the effect of assignments to result:

```
(defun rep2(i key entr a)
    (if (zp i) 0 (if (= entr (rep1 i key entr a)) 1
                (rep2 (- i 1) key entr a))))
```

However, ACL2 fails to prove such VC when it uses solely induction on n. This answer of ACL2 was analyzed automatically resulting in automatic application of the proof strategy from the following Section.

## 3   The Proof Strategy

What hints can be given to ACL2 in order to achieve the goal? The idea is as follows: for a given VC $\phi$ we construct a logically stronger formula $\theta$ (though inequivalent in general case). Strategy itself is based on a stepwise transformation of formula $\phi$. Every local rewriting gives a stronger (perhaps nonequivalent) formula. When we have a choice, we prefer rewritings allowing to avoid problems in ACL2. The arguments of the algorithm are formula $\phi$, the sub-array length $n$, functions $rep_i$ (let $k$ be their quantity), an underlying theory, initial values of program variables (at loop entry point) and loop exit condition. Underlying theory includes definitions of functions whose applications are sub-formulas in $\phi$ as well as theorems about these functions. The result of this algorithm can be "formula $\phi$ is valid" if ACL2 proves stronger formula $\theta$ or "unknown" otherwise.

Our algorithm consists of the following six steps:

1. Formula $\phi$ is being converted into equivalent clause conjunction.
2. For every clause we construct a graph of relations between variables and functional applications in the clause premise. So, variables and function applications are the nodes. As long as clause premise is a conjunction of hypotheses we analyze them to establish edges. Namely, the nodes $a$ and $b$ are joined by the edge $(a, b)$ with a label $R$ where $R \in \{=, \neq, <, >, \leq, \geq\}$ iff either $a$ or $b$ is variable and hypothesis $R(a, b)$ exists in clause premise.

For every clause, for every variable $v$ and for every relation $R \in \{=, \neq, <, >, \leq, \geq\}$ we define a special procedure which searches for the (nearest or corresponding) function application and a list of hypotheses validating that application. The returned value can either be message "corresponding function application not found" or a function application accompanied by hypotheses list. Depending on $R$ this procedure can be defined as follows:

(a) if $R$ is "=", then let $F$ be a set of nodes in $G$ which are reachable from $v$ by transitive closure $=^*$;

(b) if $R$ is $\leq$, then let $F$ be a set of nodes reachable from $v$ by $(= \cup < \cup \leq)^*$ (i.e. we traverse all edges labeled by either $=$ or $<$ or $\leq$);

(c) if $R$ is $\geq$ then $F$ combines all nodes reachable from $v$ by $(= \cup > \cup \geq)^*$;

(d) if $R$ is $<$ then $F$ is a set of all nodes reachable from $v$ by relation $(= \cup < \cup \leq)^* \circ (<) \circ (= \cup < \cup \leq)^*$ (we traverse all edges labeled by $=$, $<$ or $\leq$ and one of them must be labeled by $<$);

(e) if $R$ is $>$ then let $F$ be a set of nodes reachable from $v$ by $(= \cup > \cup \geq)^* \circ (>) \circ (= \cup > \cup \geq)^*$ (one of the edges in the path must be $>$);

(f) if $R$ is $\neq$ we define $F$ as all nodes reachable from $v$ by $(=)^* \circ (\neq \cup < \cup >) \circ (=)^*$ (again, there must be an edge labeled by $\neq$ or $<$ or $>$);

Finally, if $F$ contains at least one function application then procedure returns the nearest one (by amount of used hypotheses) as well as a list of equalities used along the corresponding path. Otherwise, procedure signals "corresponding function application not found".

Now that relation graph has been constructed for a clause, we begin to process the conclusion of clause. Conclusion is a disjunction of goals, each of them looks like $R(c, d)$ where $R \in \{=, \neq, <, >, \leq, \geq\}$, $c$ and $d$ are either constants, variables or function applications. For a given $R(c, d)$ we introduce auxiliary variables $v$ and $w$ assigning them values of $c$ and $d$ respectively. Another pair of auxiliary variables $q$ and $r$ is initialized with empty lists. In case that the first argument $c$ of relation $R$ is a variable, the searching procedure starts. If search is successful the discovered function application and list conjuncts are assigned to variables $v$ and $q$ respectively. Next we analyze the second argument $d$ of relation $R$. If $v$ is equal to $c$ or $R$ is not "$\neq$" and $d$ is a variable then the search procedure looks for corresponding function application:

- if relation $R$ is either "=" or "$\neq$" then $d$ and $R$ are passed to the procedure as its arguments;
- if relation $R$ is either $<$ or $\leq$ then $d$ and an "opposite" relation ($>$ or $\geq$ respectively) are passed to the procedure as its arguments;
- if relation $R$ is either $>$ or $\geq$ then $d$ and an "opposite" relation ($<$ or $\leq$ respectively) are passed to the procedure as its arguments.

In case of success the corresponding function application and conjunct list are assigned to variables $w$ and $r$ respectively.

If the initial value of either $v$ or $w$ was changed the goal $R(c, d)$ is replaced by goal $(= \quad v \quad w)$ within conclusion of the clause under consideration. In the meantime, if $R$ is $=$ the premise of the clause is being stripped of all hypotheses that occur in at least one of the lists $q$ or $r$.

3. All $rep_i$ that admit non-recursive redefinition are submitted to explicit substitution. It is sufficient to demonstrate that when the loop-exit condition is false $rep_i$ is equal to initial value of the corresponding program variable. For every such function we create a tree representing its body. The internal nodes of such tree are `if` statements and leaves are values returned by function. The left descendant of a statement is its value when condition is true. The corresponding edge is labeled by condition of the statement. Correspondingly, the right descendant becomes the value when condition does not hold. The edge is labeled by negation of condition then.

4. For every clause we process its conclusion which in effect is a disjunction of individual goals. Let $g$ be one of goals while $c$ is an application of a non-recursive function occurring in $g$. We replace $g$ by a conjunction of special implications. First, consider the set of interim implications. Every interim implication corresponds to a leaf in function tree. Its premise represents conjunction of all edge labels on the path from root to that leaf. Its conclusion is the goal $g$ in which every occurrence of $c$ is replaced by leaf-value. For every interim implication the replacement procedure substitutes the actual arguments from invocation of $c$ instead of variables within function body, thus transforming interim implication into the special one. After substitutions each conclusion needs to be transformed to fit the clause form. This step repeats as long as conclusions in clauses contain non-recursive functions.

5. If the steps (1)–(4) resulted in modification of the formula we repeat them.

6. Finally, ACL2 is applied to prove the formula. Depending on its verdict the answer of the whole algorithm is either "formula $\phi$ is valid" or "unknown".

We believe this algorithm can be generalized even further to be applied in SMT-solvers. The idea of the step (2) is replacement of variables by function applications. Thus we can use induction on arguments of these applications. So we also plan to generalize this strategy by using not only $=, \leq, \geq, <, >$ but also other transitive relations. Now we use the set of arithmetic relations because the Sisal environment is frequently applied to computational mathematics tasks [7].

In order to derive benefit from strategy we must prove it is sound. First, note that it always terminates. After each of the steps (2)–(4) the number of invocations of functions that can be redefined in a non-recursive way strictly decreases. Obviously, zero is the bottom element of this well-ordered chain of numbers. Finally, using induction on strategy steps we proved the following

**Theorem 1.** *The proof strategy is sound.*

## 4    Applying the Proof Strategy to Study Case

The initial underlying theory in this case is the definition of `cnt`, `rep1` and `rep2`.

Let $A$ stand for the formula $(and\ (integerp\ n)\ (integerp\ key)\ (integerp\ entr)$ $(integer\text{-}listp\ a))$. Let $B$ denote formula $(and\ (<\ 0\ n)\ (<=\ n\ (length\ a))\ (<\ 0\ entr))$. The formula $C$ stands for $(<=\ entr\ (cnt\ 0\ (-\ n\ 1)\ key\ a))$. Another abbreviation $D$ stands for $(=\ (rep2\ n\ key\ entr\ a)\ 1)$. The formula $E$ is negation

of $C$. The formula stands for $F\ (=\ (rep2\ n\ key\ entr\ a)\ 0)$. The formula $J$
stans for $(=\ entr\ (rep1\ n\ key\ entr\ a))$. The formula $K$ stands for $(zp\ n)$. Let
$L \equiv A \wedge B \wedge C$ and $M \equiv A \wedge B \wedge E$. Just before the step (1) of our algorithm the
VC $\phi$ corresponds to the pattern $A \Rightarrow (B \Rightarrow ((C \Rightarrow D) \wedge (E \Rightarrow F)))$. Let us omit
the detailed description [1] of results produced by each step (1)–(4). Enough to
say that after single iteration of those steps we obtain the formula $\phi'$:

$$(L \Rightarrow (\neg K \vee (0 = 1))) \wedge (L \Rightarrow ((K \vee \neg J) \vee (1 = 1))) \wedge$$
$$(L \Rightarrow ((K \vee J) \vee (0 = 1))) \wedge (M \Rightarrow (\neg K \vee (0 = 0))) \wedge$$
$$(M \Rightarrow ((K \vee \neg J) \vee (1 = 0))) \wedge (M \Rightarrow ((K \vee J) \vee (0 = 0)))$$

Note that until this very step equivalence to the original $\phi$ is being kept. Since $\phi$
has been changed we can repeat steps (1)–(4). The step (2) may transform the
following disjunct $S \equiv (M \Rightarrow ((K \vee \neg J) \vee (1 = 0)))$. The relation graph has been
produced for $S$. Let us consider its component that consists of vertices "$X$" and
"$Y$" and edge "$<$" that connects "$X$" and "$Y$".

The label $X$ stands for $(cnt\ 0\ (-\ n\ 1)\ key\ a)$ whereas $Y$ means $entr$. Remind
that this graph component is actually formula $E$. Which subgoal will lead to
modification of $\phi'$? In fact it is $\neg J$ corresponding to the pattern $g(c, d)$ where
$g$ is "$\neq$", $c$ is $entr$ and $d$ is $(rep1\ n\ key\ entr\ a)$. So, the searching procedure
begins to look for a function application corresponding to the variable $entr$.
The search begins at node $X$. During the search a subgraph of the relation
graph emerges. This subgraph is exactly the component demonstrated above.
The expression $(cnt\ 0\ (-\ n\ 1)\ key\ a)$ is the function application we were looking
for. The conjunct $E$ is the path we need. So, the expression $(cnt\ 0\ (-\ n\ 1)\ key\ a)$
must be assigned to variable $v$, and $E$ becomes the value of $q$. As a result we have
the new formula $T \equiv (=\ (cnt\ 0\ (-\ n\ 1)\ key\ a)\ (rep1\ n\ key\ entr\ a))$. Let $Z$ denote
the disjunct $S$ after replacement of the goal $\neg J$ by $T$: $(M \Rightarrow ((K \vee T) \vee (1 = 0)))$.
Note that $Z \not\sim S$ but the truth of $S$ follows from the truth of $Z$. So we may
replace $S$ by $Z$ in $\phi'$ which results in formula $\phi''$:

$$(L \Rightarrow (\neg K \vee (0 = 1))) \wedge (L \Rightarrow ((K \vee \neg J) \vee (1 = 1))) \wedge$$
$$(L \Rightarrow ((K \vee J) \vee (0 = 1))) \wedge (M \Rightarrow (\neg K \vee (0 = 0))) \wedge$$
$$(M \Rightarrow ((K \vee T) \vee (1 = 0))) \wedge (M \Rightarrow ((K \vee J) \vee (0 = 0)))$$

On the step (6) ACL2 is able to prove $\phi''$ by induction on $n$ thus validating $\phi$.

## 5    Conclusion

We described a new approach to verification of Sisal programs iterating over
data structures. The approach owes its success to integration of three projects.
First, question of the Sisal program soundness is reduced to soundness of a
corresponding C program. Second, C-lightVer is able to handle it. Finally, we
can facilitate verification of restricted loop cases by means of a symbolic method.

As a result of such integrating experiments we developed a proof strategy
for loops. This heuristic approach involves such formula rewritings that soundness of resulting formula provides soundness of the original one. However, the

total equivalence may be lost during application of a procedure related to equality/inequality. The study case in this paper illustrates successful application of the strategy. In general case our strategy does not guaranty success, even for a true VC. Perhaps, it will require some revisions based on the main principle: the truth of resulting formula implies validity of the original one.

Our future experiments will include less artificial study cases. The first goal is verification of Sisal programs for sorting and linear algebra. Such programs imply iterations over vectors and matrices, thus making them appropriate objects for the symbolic verification method. A more distant task consists of developing of axiomatic semantics for Sisal.

# References

1. Automated Sisal program verification using proof strategy for ACL2. https://bitbucket.org/Kondratyev/verify-sisal. Accessed 29 Apr 2019
2. De Angelis, E., Fioravanti, F., Pettorossi, A., Proietti, M.: Verification of imperative programs by constraint logic program transformation. In: Festschrift for Dave Schmidt, SAIRP 2013. Electronic Proceedings in Theoretical Computer Science, vol. 129, pp. 186–210 (2013)
3. Galeotti, J.P., Furia, C.A., May, E., Fraser, G., Zeller, A.: Inferring loop invariants by mutation, dynamic analysis, and static checking. IEEE Trans. Softw. Eng. **41**(10), 1019–1037 (2015)
4. Gotlieb, A.: Euclide: a constraint-based testing framework for critical C programs. In: ICST, pp. 151–160. IEEE Computer Society (2009)
5. Kalyanasundaram, K., Marché, C.: Automated generation of loop invariants using predicate abstraction. Research Report 7714, p. 32. INRIA (2011)
6. Kasyanov, V., Kasyanova, E.: A system of functional programming for supporting of cloud supercomputing. WSEAS Trans. Inf. Sci. Appl. **15**(9), 81–90 (2018)
7. Kasyanov, V., Kasyanova, E.: Methods and system for cloud parallel programming. In: Proceedings of the 21st International Conference on Enterprise Information Systems, vol. 1, pp. 623–629. SciTePress, INSTICC, Setubal (2019)
8. Kaufmann, M., Moore, J.S.: An industrial strength theorem prover for a logic based on common lisp. IEEE Trans. Softw. Eng. **23**(4), 203–213 (1997)
9. Kondratyev, D.: Implementing the symbolic method of verification in the C-light project. In: Petrenko, A.K., Voronkov, A. (eds.) PSI 2017. LNCS, vol. 10742, pp. 227–240. Springer, Cham (2018). https://doi.org/10.1007/978-3-319-74313-4_17
10. Kosmatov, N., Marché, C., Moy, Y., Signoles, J.: Static versus dynamic verification in Why3, Frama-C and SPARK 2014. In: Margaria, T., Steffen, B. (eds.) ISoLA 2016. LNCS, vol. 9952, pp. 461–478. Springer, Cham (2016). https://doi.org/10.1007/978-3-319-47166-2_32
11. Maryasov, I.V., Nepomniaschy, V.A., Kondratyev, D.A.: Invariant elimination of definite iterations over arrays in C programs verification. Model. Anal. Inf. Syst. **24**(6), 743–754 (2017)
12. Nepomniaschy, V.A.: Symbolic method of verification of definite iterations over altered data structures. Program. Comput. Softw. **31**(1), 1–9 (2005)
13. Nepomniaschy, V.A., Anureev, I.S., Mikhailov, I.N., Promsky, A.V.: Towards verification of C programs. C-light language and its formal semantics. Program. Comput. Softw. **28**(6), 314–323 (2002)

# Assessing Job Satisfaction of Software Engineers Using GQM Approach

Aleksandr Tarasov[✉]

Innopolis University, Innopolis, Russia
alxndrtarasov@gmail.com

**Abstract.** In this study, the Goals Questions Metrics (GQM) approach was utilized to analyze the relationship between lifestyle and software process-oriented factors and the job satisfaction level of Software Engineers. The author organized the questionnaire that included questions addressing all the metrics identified during GQM activities. Gathered metrics are analyzed on being correlated with workplace contentment of survived developers. The author found ten statistically significant factors on a confidence interval of 95%. Those are age, deadline pressure, personality, an average number of lines of code contributed to a project weekly, relationships with peer colleagues and management, an intensity of interaction with customers, sleep duration, quality of working environment, and prevalence of agile methods in the development process in a company. However, a number of factors, that are generally believed to influence job satisfaction, were found to be insignificant. Overtime working, project criticality were demonstrated to have no considerable effect on job satisfaction. Multivariate regression was employed to build the model to recognize what metrics are the most important to assess workplace contentment. The author shows that depending on included factors it is possible to achieve R-square of 59–89%.

**Keywords:** Job satisfaction · Correlation coefficient · GQM approach · Agile development

## 1 Introduction

When we talk about software project, people are usually seen as the primary factor defining success or a failure. According to DeMarco & Lister [1], "Most software development projects fail because of failures with the team running them". Software development productivity and efficiency of resource allocation are highly dependent on social and psychological factors [2]. In the research study [3], researchers found a positive connection between company climate factors and the overall level of job satisfaction in software development teams.

Psychological definition of job satisfaction is "present-oriented evaluation of the job involving a comparison of an employee's multiple values" [4]. The process of industrial software development is mostly teamwork. Consequently, comprehension of the metrics that influence or, at least, correlate with software engineers' level of job satisfaction is a pivotal concern in software development management.

© Springer Nature Switzerland AG 2019
M. Mazzara et al. (Eds.): TOOLS 2019, LNCS 11771, pp. 121–135, 2019.
https://doi.org/10.1007/978-3-030-29852-4_10

It is worth mentioning that it was shown in one of the recent studies that the level of job satisfaction strongly affects the turnover intention of software programmers [5]. Another important reason to pursue a higher level of job satisfaction for all of the team members is a dependency between it and professional burnout rate that was discovered in [6]. Professional burnout is a widely accepted stress outcome. Since software development is often strictly deadline-oriented process, the level of stress among software engineers tends to be high (especially, it is stated to be common for less experienced developers) which was found in [7]. Consequences of professional burnout [8], depersonalization and reduced personal accomplishment specifically correlate with SE sphere since the first one is decreasing communication efficiency, while the second one may affect effort estimation.

Inspired by the work [9], this study is focused on finding the main factors and metrics that influence the level of job satisfaction of software engineers. Data have been collected through an online questionnaire. The question formulations can be found in Sect. 3. This research contributes to a challenging open question on the effects of practices of agile methods in industrial settings [10].

The rest of the paper is organized as follows. Related works are reviewed in Sect. 2. In Sect. 3 the proposed approach is described in detail. Section 4 includes experimental results, comparison of multivariate regression models including different combinations of metrics to predict job satisfaction. Finally, in Sect. 5 the short summary and concluding remarks are given.

## 2  Related Works

The field of study of factors related to job satisfaction has brought considerable attention over the past three decades while the software development sphere was on the rise.

### 2.1  Balance Between Personal Treatment and the Working Environment Quality

Due to high demand, it is generally easier for software developers to change the job [11]. That is why companies are constantly trying to improve their level of job satisfaction to increase their loyalty. The most important conclusion was that general companies' effort to improve money-related welfare of employees and their working environment can lead to lower employees' job satisfaction and loyalty if personal treatment for them is insufficient. It can be interpreted in the way that developers are likely to think that an employer is trying to compensate for his poor personal treatment to "buy" their loyalty. Such perception leads to a decrease in their job satisfaction which makes a company's effort counterproductive.

### 2.2  Effect of Employing Agile Approaches on Job Satisfaction

Another research checking dependency of software developers job satisfaction on using agile approaches was conducted in 2015 [12]. Using data collected from 252 software-development professionals, "a model of job design that connects agile development practices to perceptions of job characteristics and, thereby, improve agile team members' job satisfaction" was tested. This model was representing agile project management (responsive to requirements changes and iterative) coupled with using special software development practices that are usually associated with agile development such as Test-Driven Development (TDD) [13], continuous integration [14], pair programming [15], etc. The described model was found to have a positive impact on employees' level of job satisfaction. Job autonomy was another factor tested and proven to be valuable for developers and consequently leading to higher satisfaction. However, the inference about job autonomy to be helpful for getting your employees happier should be taken very carefully. According to Maslach [8], those workers that are spending a lot of working time unproductively tend to have symptoms of professional burnout.

## 2.3 The Controversial Question of Schedule Flexibility

Decision-making on how to do job and schedule flexibility are usually associated with job autonomy and were tested on having a connection with job satisfaction in the research conducted in China in 2018 [16]. The study made the conclusion that applying work flexibility in a company is able to increase the employees' appreciation of organizational support. As a result, the employees will have better recognition to the working place and tasks, and their job satisfaction level will increase accordingly.

While for those departments flexible schedule can have a definite positive impact, software engineering companies have to adjust this model of a flexible schedule. Research on workplace flexibility in the software development sphere was conducted by Coenen in 2014 [17]. It was shown that face-to-face interaction cannot be completely replaced with virtual contact. Any form of interaction is enabling knowledge sharing, cross-functional cooperation, however, the productivity of the team and the quality of all these activities are higher when face-to-face contact is involved. Flexible working schedules were found to make virtual interaction more frequent.

## 2.4 Pair Programming Analysis Regarding a Collaborative Environment

The impact of pair programming on job satisfaction of developers was analyzed by professor Succi in 2002 [18]. Using the GQM approach [19], the questionnaire was prepared to get answers on using pair programming. 108 replies were gathered, 54 of developers using pair programming and 54 of developers not using pair programming. Given the nominal and ordinal nature of the data, non-parametric tests were used.

It was found that pair programming has a notable, positive influence on the level of job satisfaction of developers. It has identified a favorable side of pair programming. However, it does not support or defy other opinions on pair programming, such as the increased quality and reliability, the higher productivity, etc.

Another paper by the same authors [9] is also contributing to the theme of factors on which job satisfaction is dependent. A model of job satisfaction of developers working in the collaborative environment was suggested and analyzed. The study found two primary causes of job satisfaction. Those are communication and work sustainability. It was identified that the use of Pair Programming does not increase the level of job satisfaction by itself. The final conclusion is that the combination of high job satisfaction, well-organized meetings, good communication with the designers, and a sustainable amount of work is much likelier with the adoption of Pair Programming.

It can be seen that dependency between using agile techniques and the higher level of job satisfaction of software developers was identified in a substantial number of scientific studies [9, 10, 12, 18, 20–22].

## 3    The Design of the Study

### 3.1    Factors Related to Job Satisfaction

To find out what exact factors are usually associated with job satisfaction, related scientific studies were analyzed. The number of factors was extracted. In analyzed literature, the focus of the study was not always on software engineering sphere. In this proposed approach, the relation of those factors on job satisfaction level is studied with respect to software developers, which additionally highlights the novelty of the study.

First identified factor was sports exercise activity. According to a recent study [29], examined participants showed a higher level of job satisfaction and higher work performance score after the workplace exercise intervention.

Another study [30] showed a strong connection between doing hobby activity and a lower rate of professional burnout. Another theme of the study is that workers that perceive their job as a hobby tend to be more satisfied with the workplace. That is why, how often software developers are doing their hobbies and their attitude to programming as an activity was picked as factors to analyze in the current research.

Another factor is the sleep shortage. It was perceived as common sense to add it to analyzed components. Also, its connection with job satisfaction was confirmed by the contemporary study [31]. It was shown that the attitude of workers towards their workplace decreased as a result of sleep deprivation, which led to a lower overall level of job satisfaction.

Personality type in terms of introversion/extraversion was discovered to be a significant indirect predictor for turnover intention among IT specialists [32]. Another study [5] showed that turnover intention can be a result of low level of job satisfaction. Taking both findings into account, the chances of personality type to be one of the factors related to perceived job satisfaction were considered high enough.

Apart of already discussed paper [11] showing the importance of the proper working environment for business to have employees satisfied, there were a lot of studies showing the same significance of job condition when we speak about personnel's satisfaction [33–35]. Since the working environment is obviously a predicting factor of staff contentment, it was analyzed in this research and became a part of the analysis.

An agile development environment is a controversial theme when it comes to job satisfaction. The capability to make an impact on decisions that influence you, the chance to work on interesting projects and daily interaction with users were found to be statistically significant satisfiers [20]. While a high level of uncertainty (that is common for agile teams due to a commitment to welcome changing requirements [36]) is associated with decreasing of employees' job satisfaction [37]. Since the chance to contribute to open question was discovered, usage of agile approaches was picked as the factor to analyze in the survey.

Another disagreement is brought in the field of study of how job satisfaction is related to workload in software engineering sphere. There were found no modern scientific papers about it. However, the high workload is perceived to be a factor that leads to professional burnout by psychologists [6, 8]. While Maslach discovered in one of his contemporary studies [8] that those workers that are spending a lot of working time unproductively also tend to have symptoms of professional burnout.

It was found by one of the classic studies [38] that the relationship between job satisfaction and age is averagely U-shaped. Increase in job satisfaction level later during life is explained by the fact that workers after the age of 30 are usually moving to higher paying positions. Another suggestion is reduced aspiration, "due to a recognition that there are few alternative jobs available once a worker's career is established". Since the referenced study is investigating employees in general, additional research on how job satisfaction is related to the age of software engineers can provide new insights and contributions to the theme.

To make an important inference about how often low level of job satisfaction leads to employees' intention to quit their current workplace, the corresponding question was added to the survey.

### 3.2    GQM Design

Then the GQM approach [19] was used in order to come up with the way of measuring these factors metrics and formulating questions for the online survey. The common GQM template provides a sufficient definition of the overall goal, without any inconsistencies and ambiguities. The list of questions was prepared to address all the factors described in Sect. 3.1. The formulated overall goal is:

*Analyze* the lifestyle and working process-oriented factors
*For the purpose of* evaluating it
*With respect to* job satisfaction
*From the viewpoint of* software engineers
*In the context of* the development of software systems

In the proposed approach all the possible answers that examined developers can use were formulated in such a way, so the data collected from it would be on an ordinal scale [23]. To achieve it, most of the questions were formulated in a way to correspond Likert scale [24]. It naturally provides answers in the form of data on the ordinal scale since examined people have to show their level of agreement with the provided statement.

To avoid the well-known tendency of survey participants, when having odd number response variants, to choose medium one [25], the format of a typical five-level Likert item was replaced with six-level one. All the variants of answer formulation (sorted by level of agreement from low to high) are:

(1)  Strongly disagree
(2)  Disagree
(3)  Rather disagree
(4)  Rather agree
(5)  Agree
(6)  Strongly agree

Mapping for these answers to numbers was defined as from 1 (Strongly disagree) to 6 (Strongly agree). Ordinal scale usage allows employing Pearson's correlation coefficient computation for the means of measuring relations between factors and job satisfaction.

The problem of using Pearson's correlation coefficient for such form of studies was discussed quite broadly [26–28]. The final takeaway from the corresponding literature analysis is that the Pearson correlation coefficient is the most common to use. It shows how strong the linear relationship between variables that have a normal distribution.

Questionnaire was answered by 59 software engineers. Figure 1 below represents histogram obtained by analyzing collected answers about job satisfaction level. The x-axis corresponds to the intervals of answers. Y-axis - to a number of people that used the answer option from this interval. Since answers about job satisfaction level, as well as the most of the collected data, can be classified as being normally distributed (which is still an assumption to a certain extent, due to having not big enough dataset to make clear prediction about distribution of the population), the decision was to employ Pearson's correlation coefficient.

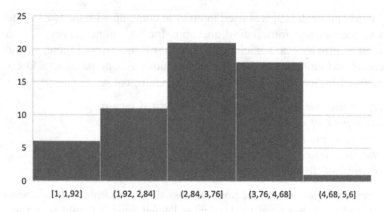

**Fig. 1.** Histogram of job satisfaction level on the ordinal scale.

The questions of GQM template associated with the corresponding questions in the survey are presented below in the following form:

GQM-question/{question-marker (to simplify understanding of comparison tables in result section of this study)} survey-question/with-respect-to-what-answer-options-in-the-survey-were-prepared (complete list of answer options is not presented because of space reasons).

Q1. How job satisfaction is dependent on sports exercise activity?/{sport} How often do you exercise (go to the gym, do running, workout, etc.)?/number of exercise activities per week

Q2. How job satisfaction is dependent on hobby activity?/{hobby} How much time do you spend doing your hobby?/hours per week

Q3. How job satisfaction is dependent on sleep shortage?/{sleep} How much hours do you usually sleep?/hours per day

Q4. How job satisfaction is dependent on personality?/{personality} What is your personality in terms of introversion/extroversion?/introversion-extroversion ordinal scale

Q5. How job satisfaction is dependent on interest in programming?/{interest} Do you agree with the following statement about yourself? "I love to code so much that I can't imagine my life without it"/Likert scale personal evaluation

Q6. How job satisfaction is dependent on the working environment?/{environment} Do you agree with the following statement about yourself? "I find the working environment in my previous (current) company very supportive"/Likert scale personal evaluation

Q7. How job satisfaction is dependent on Agile methods using?/{agile} Do you agree with the following statement? "My previous (current) company was using only Agile-oriented approaches to development"/Likert scale personal evaluation

Q8. How job satisfaction is dependent on communication activity while performing work?/To answer it the separate block in the survey is prepared with respect to differentiation between customer and colleagues communication and between communication by messaging and face-to-face, which is hypothesized to produce a different effect on job satisfaction. It consists of questions:

(1) {customers messaging} How often did you usually communicate with the customers by messaging during the development process?/times a week

(2) {customers face-to-face} How often did you usually communicate with the customers face-to-face?/times a week

(3) {colleagues messaging} How often did you usually communicate with your colleagues by messaging?/times a day

(4) {colleagues face-to-face} How often did you usually communicate with your colleagues face-to-face?/times a day

Q9. How job satisfaction is dependent on relationships with colleagues?/To answer it, the separate block in the survey is prepared with respect to differentiation between peers and management relationships which are hypothesized to have a different impact on job satisfaction. It consists of questions:

(1) {peers relationships} Do you agree with the following statement about your relationships with peer colleagues? "My relationships with peer colleagues were warm, respectful and enjoyable"/Likert scale personal evaluation

(2) {management relationships} Do you agree with the following statement about your relationships with management? "My relationships with the company management were warm, respectful and enjoyable"/Likert scale personal evaluation

Q10.  How job satisfaction is dependent on workload?/To answer it, the separate block in the survey is prepared. It consists of questions:
  (1)  {overtime} Do you tend to work overtime?/working hours per week
  (2)  {weekends work} How often do you work at the weekends?/times it happened in the last year
  (3)  {LOC} How many lines of code were you contributing to the project weekly? (If applicable, not required to answer)/a number of lines of code contributed to the project weekly
Q11.  How job satisfaction is dependent on deadline pressure?/{deadline pressure} Do you agree with the following statement about yourself? "I was working under constant unbearable deadline pressure"/Likert scale personal evaluation
Q12.  How job satisfaction is dependent on an amount of unproductive activity during the working process?/{unproductive activity} How many hours a day while working did you usually spend unproductively (watching YouTube, surfing the web, social networks, talking to peers about the themes not connected with your job, etc.)?/hours per working day
Q13.  How job satisfaction is dependent on project criticality?/{project criticality} Do you agree with the following statement about yourself? "The project I was doing was critical and meaningful for the company"/Likert scale personal evaluation
Q14.  How job satisfaction is dependent on the individual feeling of usefulness?/{usefulness} Do you agree with the following statement about yourself? "The project successfulness was highly dependent on my performance and decision making"/Likert scale personal evaluation
Q15.  How job satisfaction affects people's tendency to leave the company?/{quitting} Was job dissatisfaction the primary reason for you to quit any of your previous working places?/nominal scale (Yes/No, I didn't quit/No, I quitted because of another reason)
Q16.  How job satisfaction is dependent on age?/{age} What is your age?/age (number)

Associated metrics for each of the questions are Pearson's correlation coefficients of the collected values with the level of job satisfaction that is provided by survey participant while answering the question "How would you characterize your level of job satisfaction? Please, try not to take salary into account and think about the working process, everyday routine".

To shift the survey participants attention from money consideration while assessing their job satisfaction, an ordering effect was employed [41]. It was done by placing questions about job satisfaction at the end of the survey, after all the other questions that are supposed to bring to mind other (different from money) factors related to job satisfaction.

### 3.3  Data Collection and Analysis

For data collection, the prepared questionnaire was posted online. To avoid obvious typos, misinterpreting, or misunderstanding of the questions in it, a prototype of the survey was tested by 3 anonymous peer students.

Obtained results were used to calculate Pearson's correlation coefficients for each of the identified factors. Inferences regarding these values were made. To find out what factors, that are believed to be related to job satisfaction, but do not have a tangible impact on it, hypothesis testing on a confidence interval of 90% was used.

After this, the multivariate regression model was constructed to approximate what part of random errors while predicting job satisfaction can be explained by adding various combinations of identified factors in the model.

It allowed to come up with the list of factors for project managers and team leads to measure in order to effectively make indirect conclusions about the level of job satisfaction of developers.

# 4 Results and Discussion

## 4.1 Pearson's Correlation Coefficients Analysis and Inferences

Calculated Pearson's correlation coefficients, showing how strong the linear relationship between the identified factors and job satisfaction level of developers and their statistical significance levels, are presented in Table 1.

**Table 1.** Pearson's correlation coefficients showing how strong the linear relationship between the identified factors and job satisfaction level of developers

| Factor marker | Pearson's correlation coefficient | Statistical significance level |
|---|---|---|
| Environment | 0.79089902 | 0.99999999 |
| Peers relationships | 0.65290516 | 0.999999963 |
| Management relationships | 0.6309429 | 0.99999986 |
| Personality | 0.58344614 | 0.99999809 |
| Deadline pressure | −0.5749865 | 0.9999971 |
| Customers messaging | 0.44999241 | 0.99955524 |
| Age | −0.3617873 | 0.9943124 |
| LOC | 0.32160939 | 0.98529236 |
| Sleep | 0.31746041 | 0.98388409 |
| Agile | 0.29748849 | 0.97538408 |
| Sport | 0.24506287 | 0.93383743 |
| Customers face-to-face | 0.2340725 | 0.92031095 |
| Weekends work | −0.2216921 | 0.90255156 |
| Hobby | 0.15457963 | 0.74907764 |
| Unproductive activity | −0.0582444 | 0.33306561 |
| Colleagues messaging | 0.04403495 | 0.25500734 |
| Usefulness | 0.02953528 | 0.17264399 |
| Colleagues face-to-face | 0.01098636 | 0.06464551 |
| Project criticality | 0.00428355 | 0.02522786 |
| Overtime | 0.00264184 | 0.01556065 |
| Interest | −0.0014406 | 0.00848553 |

Statistical significance level (1-p) can be interpreted as the probability of not making a mistake about relationship direction. For example, having a factor with positive linear relationship calculated using the sample of the study answers, we have probability equals statistical significance level to have a positive relationship between this factor and job satisfaction in real life (generalized for the whole population).

In this research, the significance level $\alpha$ is set to be 0.05. Which means that only 10 of 21 identified factors are statistically significant.

It can be easily noticed that working environment quality in the proposed experiment showed by far the highest strength of the linear relationship with job satisfaction. Its Pearson's correlation coefficient was found to be 0.79. Moreover, it is hardly interpretable as a consequence of the job satisfaction level. That is why the inference is that working environment perception is the most powerful predictor of job satisfaction of software engineers. It confirms the findings of the studies [11, 33–35] analyzed in Sect. 3.

Relationships with both peers and management showed a high level of correlation coefficients (more than 0.62 for both) with job satisfaction. There was no contradiction with previous researches [9, 18] found at this point.

Inference about extroversive persons being more inclined to high turnover rate [32] was not confirmed. Extroversion was found to be one of the most significant predictors of a high level of job satisfaction with Pearson's correlation coefficient of 0.58.

Deadline pressure with a correlation coefficient of $-0.57$ was found to be negatively related to job satisfaction. It proves the inferences of previous studies [6, 8]. However, the amount of lines of code committed to a project has a positive relation to contentment. It can be explained by the assumed capability and desire of satisfied developers to produce more code. Which means that LOC factor is not a predictor for contentment, rather it is depending on the level of a developer's job satisfaction.

Another explanation may be that developers averagely tend to like to produce code more than to do other software engineering activities. This inference was mention in the classic study by Michael Jackson [39]. The inference could be that developers that are overloaded by tasks connected with coding are not that inclined to have decreased level of job satisfaction when compared to developers that are under the pressure of paperwork or requirements management. Moreover, this overload may be a predictor of higher contentment. However, this relation may be not linear but U-formed. Testing the linearity of relationships was not part of the proposed approach.

Interaction with customers by messages is another significant factor that is positively related to job satisfaction. This factor is a novelty of the current study. While a lot of attention was paid to a collaboration of developers inside the team [9, 10, 12, 18, 20–22], communication with customers was not specifically investigated in terms of its connection with job satisfaction in modern science works.

What is interesting, face-to-face communication with the customers was found to be insignificant on a confidence interval of 95%. It may be considered as evidence of one of the main agile principles, namely "The most efficient and effective method of conveying information to and within a development team is a face-to-face conversation." [36], being incapable to increase developers' level of job satisfaction. However, the factor of face-to-face communication with the customers is significant on a confidence interval of 90% and inference above may be a consequence of statistical error.

Age factor showed a significant negative relationship to job satisfaction. It confirms the findings of the research [38] described in Sect. 3. Even though in this study, the linear relationship between factors and job satisfaction is investigated, inferences about age can be reconsidered. More than 95% of the survey respondents were 22 to 34 years old. It is almost exactly that age when employees of any profession are experiencing a decrease in their job satisfaction [38]. It means that the lack of older examined developers did not let us observe the U-shaped relationship between age and workplace contentment. However, even linear analysis corresponds to the previous discoveries in this sphere.

Sleep duration was shown to be slightly positively related (0.32) to job satisfaction. The attitude of workers towards their workplace tend to decrease as sleep is deprived, which leads to a lower overall level of job satisfaction. This inference proves the validity of another study [31] checking the connection between sleep shortage and workers contentment. The same is true for the prevalence of agile approaches in development cycles. Its Pearson's correlation coefficient of 0.3 is significant on a confidence interval of 95%.

The frequency of working on the weekends and sport exercise activities are considered significant only on a 90% confidence interval. Its correlation coefficients of −0.22 and 0.25 respectively can be considered neither denials nor proofs for inferences of previous scientific works [6, 8, 29].

Such factors as frequency of doing hobby activity, unproductive behavior during working hours, project meaningfulness and criticality, and perception of the usefulness of own working contribution are shown to be insignificant in terms of having an impact on a level of job satisfaction of software engineers. These findings are pretty interesting since all those elements are believed to have an effect on developers' work contentment [8, 20, 30].

Another important finding is that developers that were not satisfied with workplace quitted the company in 74% of the cases. In 68% of cases, the primary reason for quitting was job discontent.

## 4.2 Multivariate Regression Model Design

Multivariate regression was built to estimate what part of random errors while predicting job satisfaction can be explained by including different combinations of identified factors in the model. It allows to come up with the list of factors for project managers and team leads to measure in order to make indirect conclusions about the level of job satisfaction of developers. To estimate this part of explained random errors the coefficient of determination (R squared) was used. In statistics, it is defined as the proportion of the variance in the dependent variable that is predictable from the independent variable(s).

The results demonstrated by different variants of the model are shown in Table 2.

Such metrics as age, deadline pressure (overtime hours a week before a deadline), regularity of working on weekends, personality (by single time personnel assessment), average number of lines of code contributed to a project weekly, can be obtained by management without regular assessment of the developers which would make

**Table 2.** R squared coefficients of different identified factors combinations

| Factors included in the model | R squared |
|---|---|
| All factors | 0,89346994 |
| Environment, deadline pressure, peers relationships, management relationships, LOC, age, weekends work, sleep, customer interaction | 0,84903521 |
| Environment, deadline pressure, peers relationships, management relationships, LOC, personality | 0,73057786 |
| age, deadline pressure, weekends work, personality, LOC | 0,58865875 |

employees less aware of the process of evaluation of their level of job satisfaction. It is helpful to avoid counterfeit developers' behavior.

It can be seen that only by observing the metrics described above, R squared of 59% was achieved. According to [40], any field that tries to predict human way of behaving, such as psychology (and our experiment can be also considered psychology-oriented), in most of the cases has R squared values lower than 60%. Humans are simply more difficult to predict than general physical processes. That is why even the simplest way of metrics collecting can be considered useful.

By adding to metrics described above other ones such as developer's evaluation of working environment, his relationships with peer colleagues and management, amount of sleep, the frequency of interaction with customers, quality of prediction of his job satisfaction can be increased. The coefficient of determination of the model combining those factors is 85% which is 12% higher than R squared of the model including 6 factors with the highest absolute values of Pearson's correlation coefficients. Moreover, the model combining all the identified factors achieves R squared value that is only about 4% higher, while it requires collecting 2.3 times more metrics.

The R squared score achieved by model allows considering obtained multivariate regression model successful. It exceeds a threshold of the success of 60% for R squared coefficients demonstrated in psychological sphere assessment by considerable 25–29% (depending on the combination of factors added to the model).

## 5    Conclusions

In this paper, correlation of lifestyle and working process-oriented factors with the job satisfaction level of Software Engineers is investigated. Statistically significant factors on a confidence interval of 95% are identified. Those are age, deadline pressure, personality, average number of lines of code contributed to a project weekly, relationships with peer colleagues and management, an intensity of interaction with customers, sleep duration, quality of working environment, the prevalence of agile methods in the development process in a company.

Other factors such as working overtime, criticality of the project on which developer is working, and being interested in programming as an activity, that are believed to correlate with job satisfaction, were shown to not be related to workplace contentment.

Multivariate regression model combining various combinations of factors was built to find out what metrics should be evaluated to predict a level of employees' job satisfaction.

In future research, the sample size can be extended in order to make inferences more robust. Special attention should be paid to calling developers older than 40 years of age to participate in the survey. It would allow to further investigate the U-shaped relationship between age and job satisfaction in software engineering sphere. Also, answer options for the questions about communication with colleagues should be revised. It may be worthwhile to conduct separate research on how job satisfaction is related to interaction with customers. This theme was not explicitly investigated in scientific works yet. Another topic of possible interest is the correlation between a number of lines of code contributed to a project and developer's contentment.

# References

1. DeMarco, Lister: Productive Projects and Teams. Dorset House (1987)
2. Boehm, B., et al.: Cost Estimation with COCOMO II. Prentice-Hall, Upper Saddle River (2000)
3. Acuña, S.T., Gómez, M.N., Hannay, J.E., Juristo, N., Pfahl, D.: Are team personality and climate related to satisfaction and software quality? Aggregating results from a twice replicated experiment. Inf. Softw. Technol. **57**, 141–156 (2015)
4. Locke, E.A.: Job satisfaction. In: Gruneberg, M., Wall, T. (eds.) Social Psychology and Organizational Behavior, pp. 93–117. Wiley, New York (1984)
5. Sukriket, P.: The relationship between job satisfaction and turnover intention of Thai software programmers in Bangkok, Thailand. AU J. Manag. **12**(2), 42–52 (2014)
6. Maudgalya, T., Wallace, S., Daraiseh, N., Salem, S.: Workplace stress factors and 'burnout' among information technology professionals: a systematic review. Theor. Issues Ergon. Sci. **7**(3), 285–297 (2006)
7. Bingulac, S.P.: On the compatibility of adaptive controllers. In: Proceedings of the Fourth Annual Allerton Conference on Circuit and System Theory, pp. 8–16 (1994). (Conference Proceedings)
8. Maslach, C.: Burnout: a multidimensional perspective. In: Professional Burnout, pp. 19–32. Routledge (2017)
9. Pedrycz, W., Russo, B., Succi, G.: A model of job satisfaction for collaborative development processes. J. Syst. Softw. **84**(5), 739–752 (2011)
10. Layman, L., Williams, L., Cunningham, L.: Exploring extreme programming in context: an industrial case study. In: Agile Development Conference 2004, pp. 32–41. IEEE, June 2004
11. Zhu, Q., Yin, H., Liu, J., Lai, K.H.: How is employee perception of organizational efforts in corporate social responsibility related to their satisfaction and loyalty towards developing harmonious society in Chinese enterprises? Corp. Soc. Responsib. Environ. Manag. **21**(1), 28–40 (2014)
12. Tripp, J.F., Riemenschneider, C., Thatcher, J.B.: Job satisfaction in agile development teams: agile development as work redesign. J. Assoc. Inf. Syst. **17**(4), 267 (2016)
13. Beck, K.: Test-Driven Development: By Example. Addison-Wesley Professional, Boston (2003)
14. Fowler, M., Foemmel, M.: Continuous integration. Thought-Works, vol. 122, p. 14 (2006). http://wwwthoughtworks.com/ContinuousIntegration.pdf

15. Beck, K.: Extreme Programming Explained – Embracing the Change. Addison Wesley, Boston (2000)
16. Ma, X.: The effect mechanism of work flexibility on employee job satisfaction. In: Journal of Physics: Conference Series, vol. 1053, no. 1, p. 012105. IOP Publishing, July 2018
17. Coenen, M., Kok, R.A.: Workplace flexibility and new product development performance: the role of telework and flexible work schedules. Eur. Manag. J. 32(4), 564–576 (2014)
18. Succi, G., Pedrycz, W., Marchesi, M., Williams, L.: Preliminary analysis of the effects of pair programming on job satisfaction. In: Proceedings of the 3rd International Conference on Extreme Programming (XP), pp. 212–215, May 2002
19. Basili, V.R.: Applying the Goal/Question/Metric paradigm in the experience factory. Softw. Qual. Assur. Meas.: Worldwide Perspect. 7(4), 21–44 (1993)
20. Melnik, G., Maurer, F.: Comparative analysis of job satisfaction in agile and non-agile software development teams. In: Abrahamsson, P., Marchesi, M., Succi, G. (eds.) XP 2006. LNCS, vol. 4044, pp. 32–42. Springer, Heidelberg (2006). https://doi.org/10.1007/11774129_4
21. Biddle, R., Meier, A., Kropp, M., Anslow, C.: Sources of satisfaction in agile software development. In: Proceedings of the 40th International Conference on Software Engineering: Companion Proceedings, pp. 333–334. ACM, May 2018
22. Tessem, B., Maurer, F.: Job satisfaction and motivation in a large agile team. In: Concas, G., Damiani, E., Scotto, M., Succi, G. (eds.) XP 2007. LNCS, vol. 4536, pp. 54–61. Springer, Heidelberg (2007). https://doi.org/10.1007/978-3-540-73101-6_8
23. Agresti, A.: A model for agreement between ratings on an ordinal scale. Biometrics 539–548 (1988)
24. Allen, I.E., Seaman, C.A.: Likert scales and data analyses. Qual. Progress 40(7), 64–65 (2007)
25. Cox III, E.P.: The optimal number of response alternatives for a scale: a review. J. Mark. Res. 407–422 (1980)
26. Norman, G.: Likert scales, levels of measurement and the "laws" of statistics. Adv. Health Sci. Educ. 15(5), 625–632 (2010)
27. Hauke, J., Kossowski, T.: Comparison of values of Pearson's and Spearman's correlation coefficients on the same sets of data. Quaestiones Geographicae 30(2), 87–93 (2011)
28. Newson, R.: Parameters behind "nonparametric" statistics: Kendall's tau, Somers' D and median differences (2002)
29. Lai, W.P.B.: A workplace exercise intervention in China: an outcome and process evaluation (Doctoral dissertation, University of Nottingham) (2018)
30. Rubino, C., Luksyte, A., Perry, S.J., Volpone, S.D.: How do stressors lead to burnout? The mediating role of motivation. J. Occup. Health Psychol. 14(3), 289 (2009)
31. Kumari, K., Usmani, S., Siddiqui, S.J., Husain, J.: The effects of sleep deprivation on the job performance of working mothers. J. Bus. Stud. 12(1), 95–120 (2016)
32. Eckhardt, A., Laumer, S., Maier, C., Weitzel, T.: The effect of personality on IT personnel's job-related attitudes: establishing a dispositional model of turnover intention across IT job types. J. Inf. Technol. 31(1), 48–66 (2016)
33. Raziq, A., Maulabakhsh, R.: Impact of working environment on job satisfaction. Procedia Econ. Finan. 23, 717–725 (2015)
34. Jain, R., Kaur, S.: Impact of work environment on job satisfaction. Int. J. Sci. Res. Publ. 4(1), 1–8 (2014)
35. Duffy, R.D., Autin, K.L., Bott, E.M.: Work volition and job satisfaction: examining the role of work meaning and person–environment fit. Career Dev. Q. 63(2), 126–140 (2015)
36. Beck, K., et al.: Manifesto for agile software development (2001)

37. Cullen, K.L., Edwards, B.D., Casper, W.C., Gue, K.R.: Employees' adaptability and perceptions of change-related uncertainty: implications for perceived organizational support, job satisfaction, and performance. J. Bus. Psychol. **29**(2), 269–280 (2014)
38. Clark, A., Oswald, A., Warr, P.: Is job satisfaction U-shaped in age? J. Occup. Organ. Psychol. **69**(1), 57–81 (1996)
39. Jackson, M.: The world and the machine. In: Proceedings of the 17th International Conference on Software Engineering, pp. 283–292. ACM, April 1995
40. Cheung, G.W., Rensvold, R.B.: Evaluating goodness-of-fit indexes for testing measurement invariance. Struct. Equ. Model. **9**(2), 233–255 (2002)
41. Fan, W., Yan, Z.: Factors affecting response rates of the web survey: a systematic review. Comput. Hum. Behav. **26**(2), 132–139 (2010)

# Software Development and Customer Satisfaction: A Systematic Literature Review

Rozaliya Amirova, Ilya Khomyakov, Ruzilya Mirgalimova,
and Alberto Sillitti[✉]

Innopolis University, Innopolis, Russian Federation
{r.amirova,i.khomyakov,r.mirgalimova,a.sillitti}@innopolis.ru

**Abstract.** *Background:* Customer satisfaction is one of the vital components of a successful software company. It is not possible to develop successful products with functional and/or non-functional properties that are not able to satisfy the customer's needs. To this end, it is important to identify factors that affect customer satisfaction and approaches to measure them also in relation with the adopted development methodology.

*Goals:* The purpose of this work is to provide an extensive investigation of the existing studies related to evaluation of customer satisfaction and analyze them.

*Method:* The Systematic Literature Review approach was applied. We have identified an initial set of 310 studies obtained from the three largest digital libraries that was reduced to 34 after the application of a number of filters. These studies were analyzed in depth in this paper.

*Results:* The analysis performed points out that in the majority of the identified studies, one of the main factor that affects customer satisfaction is related to the application of Agile Software Development approaches due to their deep involvement of the customer in the development process.

**Keywords:** Customer satisfaction · Agile ·
Systematic literature review

## 1 Introduction

Customer satisfaction is one of the most important aspects in any market since it is able to make the customers loyal and generate recurrent revenues. In the software domain, the development approaches have evolved over time centering the overall process on customers needs. Agile methods have developed this concept and made it common in almost any application domain [6,8–10].

Due to the increasing level of competition among software producers identifying approaches to attract more customers and improve their loyalty is of paramount importance. Customer satisfaction provides a leading indicator of

© Springer Nature Switzerland AG 2019
M. Mazzara et al. (Eds.): TOOLS 2019, LNCS 11771, pp. 136–149, 2019.
https://doi.org/10.1007/978-3-030-29852-4_11

consumer purchase intentions and loyalty [12]. When organizations attempt to create a more customer-focused environment, they need to consider strategies such as:

- Identifying the perceived role of customer.
- Collaborating with customer.
- Active involvement of customer in quality improvements.
- Customer integration in developing new products.
- Designing feedback loops between the customer and the engineering team.

These are just an example of possible strategies that can be implemented to improve customer involvement but they can also include an analysis of how developers approach the needs of the customer in the activities they perform every day [5,7].

The main goal of this systematic literature review is to understand whether there are common approaches to establish collaborations with customers, the main challenges, the main factors that affect the customer satisfaction, and whether the chosen software development methodology plays any role.

The paper is organized as follows: Sect. 2 and subsections describe the adopted approach and protocol; Sects. 3 and 4 present and analyze the results obtained; Sect. 5 discusses the threats to validity of the research; finally, Sect. 6 draws the conclusions and introduces future work.

## 2  Adopted Approach

### 2.1  Goals of the Research

Due to the increasing number of software producers, there is a need for them to measure the degree of customers satisfaction and find ways to improve. For this reason, it is important to understand the factors that affect customer satisfaction and methods for measuring it. Literature in this field is both fragmented and unvaried. In this paper, we look at how previous reviews within Agile Software Development (ASD) and other software development methodologies considered customer satisfaction and we use these insights to identify common aspects.

### 2.2  Research Questions

This study aims to answer two following questions:

- RQ1: Which are the factors that affect customer satisfaction?
- RQ2: How can we measure the factors that affect customer satisfaction?
- RQ3: How can we evaluate customer satisfaction for a project?

### 2.3  Search Process

This section describes the search process activities considering the resources and keywords used, and example of search queries.

**Resources.** In our research, we used three largest digital libraries available: ACM Digital Library, IEEE Xplore Digital Library, and Google Scholar. As many other studies pointed out, we have realized that Google Scholar includes all the publications listed in the other repositories considered here and in other smaller ones such as the ones of Elsevier, Wiley, etc.

**Keywords.** We used research questions RQ1, RQ2 also to identify the search keywords. Table 1 lists the keywords identified.

**Table 1.** Keywords identified.

| Area | Keywords |
|------|----------|
| Factors that affect customer satisfaction | Customer satisfaction |
| Customer satisfaction measurement | |
| Software development methodology | Software development, agile, scrum, extreme programming, xp, kanban, lean, plan based, traditional, waterfall, rup, spiral, iterative, v-shape |

**Queries.** Proper search queries have been defined for each digital library. As an example, one of the query defined for the ACM Digital Library is the following:

```
acmdlTitle:(software development) AND
acmdlTitle:(customer satisfaction) AND
acmdlTitle:(waterfall agile xp scrum extreme plan based
traditional kanban lean programming rup spiral iterartive
v-shape).
```

### 2.4   Selection Process

The following sections are used to determine which studies are included and excluded through the definition of inclusion and exclusion criteria, an implementation of data extraction strategy, and data synthesis method.

**Studies Selection Procedures.** The selection criteria are applied to the identified papers by one author and then verified by the other authors in accordance with the following criteria:

– Inclusion criteria
  • Available online to ensure paper accessibility
  • Focused on customer satisfaction factors to ensure its relevance

- Focused on software development process to ensure its compliance with the study
- Publication format of research paper (books, thesis, posts, videos, etc. are not included)
- Written in English
- Exclusion criteria
  - Any paper that does not satisfy any of the inclusion criteria.
  - Papers written by the same authors describing the same factors.

**Quality Assessment Procedures.** The following aspects where considered for assessing the quality of the individual studies:

- QA1: Is the study based on a focused question that is adequately formulated and described?
- QA2: Were inclusion and exclusion criteria for investigated studies predefined and specified?

The purpose of the quality assessment criteria is to develop a checklists to define the inclusion or exclusion of the identified studies.

**Data Extraction Strategy.** To avoid errors and bias of the results, data extraction forms are used. These forms include:

1. General information
   - A date of Data extraction
   - A title and authors
   - Name of publication, year and other publication details
2. Study characteristics
   - Study design
   - Outcomes and interventions (if applicable)
   - Comments on limitations and generalisability that reviewers can identity after reading the paper.

**Synthesis of the Extracted Data.** The narrative synthesis includes:

- Study type (e.g., intervention, observational)
- Number and characteristics of participants (e.g., age, specialization, etc.)
- Description of interventions and/or outcome measures
- Study quality
- Discussion of heterogeneity (differences across studies).

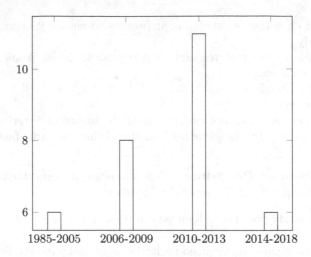

**Fig. 1.** Distribution of papers over the years

# 3   Results

This section presents the quantitative results of this study. It starts with an overview of the sources where the studies were found: 84% Google Scholar; 13% ACM Digital Library; 3% IEEE Xplore. Then, it provides an overview of the included studies according to the year of publication (Fig. 1). Finally, it discusses the results of studies classification, which show numerical results our SLR.

Search was executed in January 2019 and covered the years between 1985–2018. The final number of papers that were included for data analysis was 34 and a total of 276 papers were excluded (Table 2).

**Table 2.** Excluded papers.

| Exclusion criterion | Papers | % |
|---|---|---|
| Lack of focus on customer satisfaction | 99 | 34% |
| Lack of focus on software development | 92 | 31% |
| Paper format | 67 | 22% |
| **Total** | 310 | 100% |
| **Included** | 34 | 10% |

# 4   Discussion

This section focuses on reporting the results of the SLR research questions. It reports on factors that affect customer satisfaction and how customer satisfaction is measured and evaluated.

## 4.1   RQ1: Factors that Affect Customer Satisfaction

This section shows what factors affect the Customer Satisfaction in Agile, focusing on SCRUM, ACRUM, and XP, and in traditional software development processes.

**ASD.** One way to achieve a high level of customer satisfaction using Agile software development methodology is to increase the level of customer confidence. This can be done by:

- Clearly identifying the customer and their role [25].
- Characterising customers to enable the development team to manage better their expectations [25].
- Active client participation during the project [1,14,17] and active communication with customers and team members [3]. This increases the satisfaction, enhances the level of trust between the parties, and creates a feeling of "personal touch".
- Introduce practices such as on-site customer, planning, small release, customer usage test, etc. Where the customers can join the development process and identify problems and the product is modified or rebuilt iteratively to maximize its satisfaction with the final product [33].
- Ability to incorporate early and continuous customer feedback, thus better tailoring to features that are really used by customers and not to the features planned up-front [22].
- Ability to deliver meaningful functionality to the customer and get immediate feedback [28,30,31].
- Strong support after delivery [17].
- Understand how customer use a feature [17].
- Ability to deliver what customers want when they want [17].
- Establishing long lasting relationships between the development team and the customer [25]. [11] suggests also that a strong relationship has a long term economic value in terms of continuity of cash flows and saving in time and resources for starting new projects.

Several papers consider five characteristics of agile development (iteration, continuous integration, test-driven design, feedback and collective ownership) strictly linked to the customer satisfaction measuring satisfaction with the development process and with the development outcome (Table 3).

All the five characteristics have strong direct effects on both process and outcome customer satisfaction. According to [35], factors that affect customer satisfaction are:

- Increase
  - Focus on shortening overall project duration.
  - Good communication (e.g., no last minute surprises).
  - Collaboration.
- Decrease

**Table 3.** Development characteristics linked to customer satisfaction.

| Characteristic | Description | Correlation with process satisfaction | Correlation with outcome |
|---|---|---|---|
| Iterative development | Quick delivery of small working (and tested) software releases at regular intervals or cycles [2] | 0.75 | 0.81 |
| Continuous integration | New code is integrated into the production base code continuously, ideally after each task is completed [2,34] | 0.65 | 0.74 |
| Collective code ownership | Any developer has the right to add or maintain the code anywhere in the system at any time [2] | 0.75 | 0.81 |
| Test-driven development | Developers write tests before they code [2] | 0.66 | 0.67 |
| Feedback | Frequent feedback loop with customers allows developers to ascertain the accuracy of the functionality [15] | 0.60 | 0.66 |

- Late delivery and long project duration.
- Defects.
- Issues with testing and deployment.
- Unclear requirements.
- Bad documentation.
- Hidden business rules.
- Bad communication.

Notably, the project cost seems not an important issue for customers.

**SCRUM.** There are mixed findings in this area. In [26], authors found that daily SCRUM meetings and planning meetings are helpful since they keep customers up-to-date and reduce the confusion about what should be developed increasing customer satisfaction. However, [4] reports that it was not possible to establish any evidence that using SCRUM may help to improve customer satisfaction and, consequently, increase the success rates of software projects.

**XP.** All of the included papers dealing with XP show that introducing this technique makes a good impact on customer satisfaction.

- Factors that increase Customer Satisfaction
  - unit testing, refactoring, and feedback during the project [21].
  - acceptance tests and tracking [21].
- Factors that decrease Customer Satisfaction

- Attempting to increase customer satisfaction through marketing and incentives, rather than based on true satisfaction with the product can actually harm the organisation in the long term [13].
- The greater the customer involvement, the greater the potential for customer dissatisfaction [13].
- Close customer involvement cannot make up for the failings of a development team. Instead of the customer perceiving that the involvement is helping the team meet the customer's needs, the customer may feel obliged to exert authority over internal development decisions and may also feel mistreated by perceiving that the team is not delivering a valuable product [13].

As a separate factor, which negatively impact on customer satisfaction is changing requirements. However, [33], propose Agile practices such as positive work climate, final product adaptability, and willingness to change positively could mitigate this negative effect.

### 4.2 RQ2: Measurement of Customer Satisfaction

This section describes the approaches used to measure customer satisfaction in the included papers (Table 4).

**Table 4.** Measurement approaches for customer satisfaction.

| Approach | Description | Study |
|---|---|---|
| Rates | Evaluating the satisfaction on a Likert scale | [23, 29, 34] |
| Interviews | Semi-structured interviews with open-ended questions | [14, 17, 24] |
| Web analytic tools | Automatic mechanism for the evaluation of customer focus | [25, 30, 34] |
| Feedback reports | Acquired rapidly and at minimal cost | [25, 27, 29, 30, 35] |
| Meetings | Face-to-face discussion activities (often in a formal setting) | [14, 30] |
| Brainstorming | A group creativity activity to identify new features | [35] |
| Questionnaires and surveys | Set of questions with different formats | [18, 27, 29, 32, 34, 35] |
| Consultants, representatives | The most interested persons are chosen | [25, 29] |

Customer satisfaction measurement activities are impossible without consideration communication channels. [20] describes all common channels of communication and gives recommendations on their usage: Face-to-face communication is the default communication method in agile development. It has proven to be effective, so it should be applied whenever possible. Videoconferencing comes second in richness and the study suggests using videoconferencing in situations when effective customer communication and feedback is needed and the customer is not available on-site. Phone is not capable of transmitting visual cues, but it enables instant feedback. It can be useful for example for negotiating schedules with the customer. Emails are suitable for communicating well-understood issues.

### 4.3   RQ3: Evaluation of Customer Satisfaction

The most straightforward way for the evaluation of customer satisfaction is through interrogating them in a direct way through popular approaches such as interviews, questionnaires, meetings, and combinations of them. Within the 34 reviewed studies, we analyzed these approaches by the following criteria: the way of defining questions, collecting and analyzing information. This allowed us to define initial models for the evaluation of the customer satisfaction.

**Interviews.** [24] used subjective means – customer interviews and surveys – which were structured to reduce the effect of influencing factors beyond the XP practices as much as possible. [23] collected information based on on-site observations, a research diary, and interviews. [30] conducted semi-structured interviews with open-ended questions. During 24 interviews, an interview guide consisting of three predefined themes: an organisation and current way of working, a customer interaction mechanisms/models and strengths & weaknesses in ways of working. In [17], the authors interviewed the team leader, the system manager, the system designer, and the function tester. At each customer unit they interviewed the person with which the customer-specific teams interact, and who has direct contact with the customer. Finally, they conducted interviews with a program manager, a product manager and an integration leader at the main development site to capture the context in which the customer-specific teams operate. In [1], researchers collected information using interviews with representatives of two North-European software companies: one is relatively young company and the second one is plan-driven organization with a long business history. They interviewed the developers and the project manager from the first company and the lead architect and technical manager from the second company in separate interviews that lasted about 60 min each. During the interviews, they asked narrative-pointed questions related to client's involvement and its impact on it that both covered a longer period of time and focused on specific events. The collected data were analyzed by means of thematic analysis techniques, because of the flexibility it offers to researchers. In [23], in each company, the project managers were questioned about their last completed projects, which had to be as the complete system for an external client or another department inside the company. Data collection was carried out by phone interviews with a web-aided questionnaire. Study participants were asked to rate the level of satisfaction of the project's customer using a 7-point Likert scale. In addition to the quantitative research data, qualitative data was also used. In [29], the interviewees were selected by key contact persons from each company, who were asked to nominate experts from Product Management, R&D, Validation&Verification and Sales&Marketing. All interviewees had a lot of experience in working in companies for long periods of time and in multiple projects.

**Questionnaires.** In [11], to develop the survey instrument, the authors performed an extensive literature review to derive an initial pool of scale items. Then a structured questionnaire was constructed to capture information from an appropriate key informant within each organisation. The key informant was asked about the extent to which they agreed with a number of statements reflecting the use of the five agile characteristics in their most recently completed software development project, as well as the level of stakeholder satisfaction with that project. The instrument used was a five-point Likert type scale. The questionnaire, accompanied by a covering letter, was emailed to the listed contact in each organisation. A survey methodology to gather the information was used. The target population of this study consists of firms that use agile software development methodologies. The respondents was obtained from the social network Linkedin. Then authors interviewed three experienced professionals working in software development with agile methodologies and two experienced researchers. The interviewees critiqued the questionnaire with regard to its clarity, completeness and the appropriateness of its measures. Researchers collected 102 valid questionnaires and analyzed them through hierarchical multiple regression. They used two regression models. First model was created by entering five control variables: organization size, project size, agility, customer collaborative attitude, and customer active participation. In the second model, they included the predictor (control and independent) variables. The results of the regression analysis show that the active participation of the customer was the most important factor. In [27], a survey composed of rapid customer-focused iterations was used. This survey constituted a guideline on developing their application based on customers feedback. The authors got in contact with 15 potential customers to gain insights from their feedback. They used a questionnaire based survey on 204 respondents to investigate Greek consumers' familiarity with electronic food ordering and its applications. Their main goal was to understand customer's opinion on what features an application should have so to increase their satisfaction.

**Meetings.** In [33], customer collaboration improved by continuous meetings. In arranged meetings, customer represents or amends requirements. Also customers themselves decide whether they should submit some important changes. In [14], evolutionary project management is a highly scheduled process where weekly iterations follow a fixed schedule that defines responsibilities per day.

For example, "on Fridays there is a management design review meeting for iteration N, on Mondays stakeholders test the product of iteration N-1". In [25], the authors attended daily team meetings, iteration sessions and training sessions. Such observations showed that there were large discrepancies between the document the team were working on and the actual user stories being discussed at these meetings. To establish the reliability and validity of the case study, researchers followed the three principles of data collection: use multiple sources of evidence, create a case study database, maintain a chain of evidence.

**Combination of Methods.** In [25], data were collected through a variety of methods: unstructured and semi-structured interviewing, document review and observation. In [35], the authors used a formal and informal channels of communication. Formal: letters and documentation exchanges. According to this channel, everyone could communicate regularly. So that the organizational structure and management processes of the parties are well known to project developers. Project progress were reported weekly. Customer satisfaction surveys were carried out yearly. Then there is the informal communication way. The common ways are after-meals dinner, send birthday gifts, and group activities. In these ways, developers could understand customers situation, the progress of customer care, customer satisfaction processes, and to understand the customer's internal culture.

## 5    Threats to Validity

Customer satisfaction and customer relationships tend to be a sorely unexplored and largely misunderstood aspect of software engineering [13]. Here we list three major threats, which can affect to our findings:

1. **Papers sources:** although the applied guideline recommends to consider about seven digital libraries for performing an exhaustive search, in our case only three beginning ones have been chosen. The reason of it is that the rest sources contain quite few amount of unique papers, so majority of them is overlapping in ACM DL and IEEE. Nevertheless, to extend the set of publications, also Google Scholar was used.
2. **Handling query results:** a way of automatically merging the outcome lists from that libraries is risky, because even single differing symbol in title might affect a lot. For that reason, 310 repeating papers were identified and eliminated manually for obtaining a merged list.
3. **Keeping results up-to-date:** it may happen that some information has not been included in the final table concerning empirical studies either because it was accidentally skipped or new studies appeared.

## 6    Conclusions

This SLR aimed to identify factors that affect customer satisfaction in Agile Software Development and explore the ways to increase it. The SLR included a total of 34 papers and excluded 276 papers that were published from the year 1985 till 2018 (33 years). The findings were quantitatively classified. Industrial practitioners can use the obtained information for their work to improve the level of customer satisfaction and increase the demand for their products. This study pointed out that there are a number of ways for measuring the level of customer satisfaction (Table 4). However, there is a lack of a comprehensive framework for measuring the different aspects of the customer satisfaction focusing also on the practices and approaches that can be actually adopted by practitioners in real projects.

# References

1. Bakalova, Z., Daneva, M.: A comparative case study on clients participation in a 'traditional' and in an agile software company. In: 12th International Conference on Product Focused Software Development and Process Improvement (PROFES 2011), Torre Canne, Brindisi, Italy (2011)
2. Beck, K.: Embracing change with extreme programming. IEEE Comput. 32(10), 70–77 (1999)
3. Bhalerao, S., Ingle, M.: Analysing the modes of communication in agile practices. In: 3rd International Conference on Computer Science and Information Technology, Chengdu, China (2010)
4. Cartaxo, B., Araújo, A., Sá Barreto, A., Soares, S.: The impact of scrum on customer satisfaction: an empirical study. In: 27th Brazilian Symposium on Software Engineering, Brasilia, Brazil (2013)
5. Coman, I., Sillitti, A.: An empirical exploratory study on inferring developers' activities from low-level data. In: 19th International Conference on Software Engineering and Knowledge Engineering (SEKE 2007), Boston, MA, USA, 9–11 July 2007
6. Coman, I.D., Sillitti, A., Succi, G.: Investigating the usefulness of pair-programming in a mature agile team. In: Abrahamsson, P., Baskerville, R., Conboy, K., Fitzgerald, B., Morgan, L., Wang, X. (eds.) XP 2008. LNBIP, vol. 9, pp. 127–136. Springer, Heidelberg (2008). https://doi.org/10.1007/978-3-540-68255-4_13
7. Coman, I., Sillitti, A.: Automated identification of tasks in development sessions. In: 16th IEEE International Conference on Program Comprehension (ICPC 2008), Amsterdam, The Netherlands, 10–13 June 2008
8. Corral, L., Sillitti, A., Succi, G.: Software development processes for mobile systems: is agile really taking over the business? In: 1st International Workshop on Mobile-Enabled Systems (MOBS 2013) at ICSE 2013, San Francisco, CA, USA, 25 May 2013
9. Coman, I., Robillard, P.N., Sillitti, A., Succi, G.: Cooperation, collaboration and pair-programming: field studies on backup behavior. J. Syst. Softw. 91(5), 124–134 (2014)
10. Corral, L., Sillitti, A., Succi, G.: Software assurance practices for mobile applications. Computing 97(10), 1–22 (2014)
11. Corvello, V., Verteramo, S.: The role of the customer in the adoption of agile software development methodologies. In: 8th Mediterranean Conference on Information Systems, Verona, Italy (2014)

12. Farris, P.W., Bendle, N.T., Pfeifer, P.E., Reibstein, D.J.: Marketing Metrics: The Definitive Guide to Measuring Marketing Performance. Pearson Education, London (2010)
13. Grisham, P.S., Perry, D.E.: Customer relationships and extreme programming. In: 2005 Workshop on Human and Social Factors of Software Engineering, St. Louis, MO, USA (2005)
14. Hanssen, G.K., Faegri, T.E.: Agile customer engagement: a longitudinal qualitative case study. In: 2006 ACM/IEEE International Symposium on Empirical Software Engineering, Rio de Janeiro, Brazil (2006)
15. Highsmith, J., Cockburn, A.: Agile software development: the business of innovation. IEEE Comput. **34**(9), 120–122 (2001)
16. Hollender, M., Rudin, M.: Customer focus, TQM and usability engineering in the development of complex interactive software products. In: Conference TQM and Human Factors, Linkoeping, Sweden (1999)
17. Holmstrom Olsson, H., Bosch, J., Alahyari, H.: Customer-specific teams for agile evolution of large-scale embedded systems. In: 39th EUROMICRO Conference Software Engineering and Advanced Applications (SEAA), Santander, Spain (2013)
18. Huijgens, H., van Deursen, A., van Solingen, R.: The effects of perceived value and stakeholder satisfaction on software project impact. Inf. Softw. Technol. **89**, 18–36 (2017)
19. Jeon, S., Han, M., Lee, E., Lee, K.: Quality attribute driven agile development. In: 9th International Conference on Software Engineering Research, Management and Applications, Baltimore, MD, USA (2011)
20. Kautz, K.: Customer and user involvement in agile software development. In: Abrahamsson, P., Marchesi, M., Maurer, F. (eds.) XP 2009. LNBIP, vol. 31, pp. 168–173. Springer, Heidelberg (2009). https://doi.org/10.1007/978-3-642-01853-4_22
21. Khalaf, S.J., Maria, K.A.: An empirical study of XP: the case of Jordan. In: International Conference on Information and Multimedia Technology, Jeju Island, South Korea (2009)
22. Klein, H., Canditt, S.: Using opinion polls to help measure business impact in agile development. In: 1st International Workshop on Business Impact of Process Improvements, Leipzig, Germany (2008)
23. Kohlbacher, M., Stelzmann, E., Maierhofer, S.: Do agile software development practices increase customer satisfaction in Systems Engineering projects? In: IEEE International Systems Conference, Montreal, QC, Canada (2011)
24. Layman, L.: Empirical investigation of the impact of extreme programming practices on software projects. In: 19th Annual ACM SIGPLAN Conference on Object-Oriented Programming Systems, Languages, and Applications, Vancouver, BC, Canada (2004)
25. Lohan, G., Lang, M., Conboy, K.: Having a customer focus in agile software development. In: Pokorny, J., et al. (eds.) ISD2010, pp. 441–453. Springer, New York (2010). https://doi.org/10.1007/978-1-4419-9790-6_35
26. Mann, C., Maurer, F.: A case study on the impact of scrum on overtime and customer satisfaction. In: Agile Development Conference, Denver, CO, USA (2005)
27. Nikou, A., Chatzigiannakis, I.: Applying a customer centric development approach for web 2.0 applications. In: 19th Panhellenic Conference on Informatics, Athens, Greece (2015)

28. Pagrut, D.S.: Testing of changing requirement in an agile environment - a case study of telecom project. In: Testing: Academic and Industrial Conference Practice and Research Techniques - MUTATION (TAICPART-MUTATION 2007),, Windsor, UK (2007)
29. Rushinek, A., Rushinek, S.: Order processing and inventory control software related to computer user satisfaction: an interactive online evaluation system. ACM SIGS-MALL Symposium on Small Systems, Danvers, MA, USA (1985)
30. Sauvola, T., et al.: Towards customer-centric software development a multiple-case study. In: 41st Euromicro Conference on Software Engineering and Advanced Applications, Funchal, Portugal (2015)
31. Trimble, J., Webster, C.: From traditional, to lean, to agile development: finding the optimal software engineering cycle. In: 46th Hawaii International Conference on System Sciences, Wailea, Maui, HI, USA (2013)
32. Vanhanen, J., Lehtinen, T.O.A., Lassenius, C.: Software engineering problems and their relationship to perceived learning and customer satisfaction on a software capstone project. J. Syst. Softw. **137**, 50–66 (2018)
33. Wang, X., Wu, Z., Zhao, M.: The relationship between developers and customers in agile methodology. In: International Conference on Computer Science and Information Technology, Singapore (2008)
34. Welo, T., Ringen, G.: Customer-focused development practices in Systems Engineering companies: a case study across industry sectors. In: Annual IEEE Systems Conference (SysCon), Orlando, FL, USA (2016)
35. Xinhui, C., Zhanglin, Z.: On customer knowledge acquisition in agile development method of software project (2012)

# Object-Oriented Requirements:
# Reusable, Understandable, Verifiable

Alexandr Naumchev[1,2]([✉])

[1] Innopolis University, Innopolis 420500, Russian Federation
a.naumchev@innopolis.ru
[2] Paul Sabatier University, Toulouse, France

**Abstract.** Insufficient requirements reusability, understandability and verifiability jeopardize software projects. Empirical studies show little success in improving these qualities separately. Applying object-oriented thinking to requirements leads to their unified treatment. An online library of reusable requirement templates implements recurring requirement structures, offering a starting point for practicing the unified approach.

**Keywords:** Object-oriented requirements · Reusable requirements · Understandable requirements · Verifiable requirements

## 1  Introduction

The industry is not actively applying requirements reuse [11], which is regrettable: it might help, if practiced, not only to save resources in the requirements specification phase, but also to obtain documents of better quality both in content and syntax. It might also decrease the risk of writing low quality requirements and lead to the reuse of design, code, and tests.

Meyer in 1985 described seven understandability problems common to natural-language specifications [5] and proposed the process of passing them through a formal notation to produce their more understandable versions. He has more recently given a name to the approach – "The Formal Picnic Approach"[1]. The amount of requirements and their volatility have grown, and the seven problems remain valid. Formal picnics should be practiced more actively and should be reusable across projects.

The general problem of reuse finds itself in requirements' verifiability too. Requirements' verifiable semantics follows several recurring patterns in most of the cases [2]. If a pattern exists, it should be reused, and to be reused it should be encoded as a template. The template should also be connected to the main instruments of software verification – tests and contracts.

Applying object-oriented thinking to the problems of requirements reusability, understandability and verifiability draws a new roadmap towards addressing

---

[1] https://tinyurl.com/ycn526rm.

© Springer Nature Switzerland AG 2019
M. Mazzara et al. (Eds.): TOOLS 2019, LNCS 11771, pp. 150–162, 2019.
https://doi.org/10.1007/978-3-030-29852-4_12

them simultaneously. A reusable library of requirement templates, taking the familiar form of object-oriented classes, provides a starting point for practicing the approach. Each template encodes a formal semantics pattern [2] as a generic class reusable across projects and components, for verifying candidate solutions through either testing or program proving.

## 2 The Problem Explained

### 2.1 Reusability

Reusability has become a success story in the reuse of code [16] and tests [13], but not requirements. On that side too, many patterns recur again and again, causing undue repetition of effort and mistakes. The practice of industrial projects, however, involves little reuse of requirements. Textual copy and subsequent modification of requirements from previous projects are still the most commonly used requirements reuse techniques [11], which has already been long recognized as deficient in the world of code reuse.

The most critical factors inhibiting the industrial adoption of requirements reuse through software requirement patterns (SRP) catalogues are [11]:

- The lack of a well-defined reuse method.
- The lack of quality and incompleteness of requirements to reuse.
- The lack of convenient tools and access facilities with suitable requirements classification.

Scientific literature studying requirements reuse approaches pays little attention to these factors when measuring the studied approaches [4]. The degree of reuse is the most frequently measured variable, but it is measured under the assumption that the evaluated approach is fully practiced. This assumption does not meet the reality: most of the practitioners who declare to practice requirements reuse approaches, apply them very selectively [11]. Secondary studies, which study other studies, equally ignore the factors that matter to practitioners [4].

### 2.2 Understandability

Meyer, in his work "On Formalism in Specifications" [5], described "the seven sins of the specifier" – a classification of the frequently recurring flaws in requirements specifications. Analyzing a specification of a well-known text-processing problem illustrated that even a small and carefully written natural-language requirements document may suffer from the following problems:

- *Noise* – the presence in the text of an element that does not carry information relevant to any feature of the problem. Variants: redundancy; remorse.
- *Silence* – the existence of a feature of the problem that is not covered by any element of the text.

- *Overspecification* – the presence in the text of an element that corresponds not to a feature of the problem but to features of a possible solution.
- *Contradiction* – the presence in the text of two or more elements that define a feature of the system in an incompatible way.
- *Ambiguity* – the presence in the text of an element that makes it possible to interpret a feature of the problem in at least two different ways.
- *Forward reference* – the presence in the text of an element that uses features of the problem not defined until later in the text.
- *Wishful thinking* – the presence in the text of an element that defines a feature of the problem in such a way that a candidate solution cannot realistically be validated with respect to this feature.

Identified in the times when software processes were following the Waterfall model, which takes good care of every software development lifecycle phase, these problems remain. Nowadays processes pursue continuity, and requirements analysts have little time to process new requirements before passing them to the developers. The processes are iterative and collecting requirements for another iteration often starts before the current iteration finishes. The pace of work lowers availability of expert developers for evaluating the new requirements' verifiability. The pervasiveness of Internet technologies like Google Search brings problems too. Many sources of unclear origins now offer tons of potentially unchecked information, which is sometimes overly trusted.

Denying the progress makes no sense, however. Requirements engineering tools should help the practitioners to improve the quality of information they consume and rely on. The improved information should be reusable across projects.

### 2.3  Verifiability

The reusability concern applies to requirements' verifiability as well. Dwyer et al. analyzed 555 specifications for finite-state verification from different domains and successfully matched 511 of them against 23 known patterns [2]. The patterns were encoded in modeling notations without a guidance on how to reuse them across projects for verifying candidate solutions. The gap still exists, and the state-of-the-practice [11] and literature reviews [4] of requirements reuse approaches, as well as the studies they cite, do not evaluate requirements' verifiability in the studied approaches.

Requirements reuse approaches should properly address the verifiability aspect: reusing non-verifiable requirements makes little sense. The approaches should make it clear how to capture and reuse recurring verifiable semantics' structures.

## 3  Running Example

Wikipedia represents a notable example of an intensely used and trusted Internet resource. The rest of the discussion relies on a Wikipedia page describing a

24-h clock[2] as a requirements document example. The "24-h clock" document is prone to the seven requirements understandability problems [5]. It only has few statements relevant to clock behavior:

1. The 24-h clock is a way of telling the time in which the day runs from midnight to midnight and is divided into 24 h, numbered from 0 to 24.
2. A time in the 24-h clock is written in the form hours:minutes (for example, 01:23), or hours:minutes:seconds (01:23:45).
3. Numbers under 10 usually have a zero in front (called a leading zero); e.g. 09:07.
4. Under the 24-h clock system, the day begins at midnight, 00:00, and the last minute of the day begins at 23:59 and ends at 24:00, which is identical to 00:00 of the following day.
5. 12:00 can only be mid-day.
6. Midnight is called 24:00 and is used to mean the end of the day and 00:00 is used to mean the beginning of the day.

The rest of the text is *noise*. The "or" connective in Statement 2 results in *wishful thinking*: is it acceptable to decide between the two options for every clock object, or should the decision be taken once and uniformly applied to all objects? None of the requirements after Statement 2 talk about seconds, from which it follows that the author silently made the choice in favor of the "hours:minutes" format. This "sin" falls into the *silence* category. The "usually" qualification introduces the *wishful thinking* problem to Statement 3: how are the developers expected to check candidate solutions against this requirement? Statements 4 and 6 result in a *contradiction* each other: statement 4 says that midnight is 00:00, while statement 6 defines *24:00* as midnight and *00:00* as the beginning of the day. The contradiction may arise as a result of *forward referencing*: *24:00* and *00:00* are only defined in 6, while first used in 1 and 4. The last part of Statement 4 is a *remorse*: the author implicitly admits that the first part of the statement was not enough and adds the "which is..." part. Statement 5 introduces an *ambiguity*, since the document never defines the "mid-day". Moreover, terms like "mid-day", "midnight", "afternoon" should be defined through specific clock states; it is not clear then what the author means by saying that a specific state can only be mid-day/midnight/afternoon: it can be whatever, depending on the terminology.

The illustration of the object-oriented requirements approach handles a fragment of Statement 1.: "the day runs from midnight to midnight", referred to as "Statement 1.1". Understanding this requirement's treatment will suffice to understand the approach. A GitHub repository[3] hosts the complete treatment of the "24-h clock" example.

## 4   Reuse Methodology

Requirements reuse methodologies are essentially bidimensional [4]. The first dimension, known as *development for reuse*, describes the procedure of

---

[2] https://tinyurl.com/ybocy485.
[3] https://tinyurl.com/y6w7nlcs.

identifying and capturing new requirement patterns. The second dimension, known as *development with reuse,* describes the process of searching and reusing the captured patterns for specifying new requirements with lower efforts as compared to specifying them without the patterns.

### 4.1   Development for Reuse

Given a collection of requirements:

1. Perform the standard commonality and variability analysis on the collection.
2. Capture the identified commonality in an object-oriented class.
3. Capture the semantical commonality through a contracted routine [7,13] to support verification.
4. Capture the structural commonality through a string function to support formal picnics.
5. Parameterize the identified variability points through abstraction and genericity.

### 4.2   Development with Reuse

Given an informal requirement:

1. Analyze the requirement's meaning and structure.
2. Find the most appropriate requirement template class through the IDE's search facilities.
3. Inherit from the found template in a new class representing the requirement.
4. Refine the abstractions into domain definitions.
5. Replace the genericity with the specified types and domain definitions.
6. Perform a formal picnic to see if the new string representation of the requirement has a different meaning from the original one.
7. Verify candidate solutions through running [13] or proving [7] the contracted routine.

## 5   Technical Artifacts

Two major technical contributions support the method.

### 5.1   Library of Templates

A ready-to-use GitHub library[4] of template classes captures known requirement patterns [2]. The library represents a result of applying the *development for reuse* process to the patterns and provides basis for *development with reuse.* The library is written in Eiffel for readability, but the method scales to other object-oriented languages with support for genericity.

---

[4] https://tinyurl.com/ybd4b5un.

## 5.2   Library of Multirequirement Patterns

An online OneNote notebook[5] rearranges the original collection of patterns[6] in
the form of multirequirements [6] to support their understanding. Dwyer et al.
have initially developed the patterns in 5 notations: LTL, CTL, GIL, Inca, QRE.
Their online collection consists of 5 large pages corresponding to these notations.
The alternative collection consists of 23 pages making it possible to study individual patterns in all the 5 notations simultaneously. The representations are
clickable and lead to their sources in the original repository developed by Dwyer
et al. Each page includes a link leading to the corresponding template in the
GitHub library.

# 6   Applying a Template

The following illustration handles the "Statement 1.1" requirement by applying
a reusable template class from the GitHub library. The requirement fits into the
"Global Response" pattern [2]. The pattern reads: "S responds to P globally",
for events S and P. It is the most frequently used pattern: out of the 555 analyzed
requirements [2], 241 represented this pattern. For "Statement 1.1", both S and
P map to the midnight event: "midnight responds to midnight globally". This
new statement paraphrases the original one, "the day runs from midnight to
midnight".

Class *STATEMENT_1_1* (Fig. 1(a)) captures the requirement. The class
inherits from:

- A generic application of class *RESPONSE_GLOBAL* to classes *CLOCK* and
  *MIDNIGHT*, where *RESPONSE_GLOBAL* is a generic template encoding
  the "Global Response" pattern. The *RESPONSE_GLOBAL [CLOCK, MID-
  NIGHT, MIDNIGHT]* application reads: "for type *CLOCK, MIDNIGHT*
  response to *MIDNIGHT* globally".
- Class *CLOCK_REQUIREMENT* recording domain information common to
  all clock requirements: the fact that the *tick* routine advances a clock's state,
  and the *start* routine initializes a new clock.

The *CLOCK* class is a candidate solution implementing the "clock" concept,
and the *MIDNIGHT* class captures the definition of midnight through effecting
the deferred *holds* Boolean function inherited from generic class *CONDITION*
applied to the *CLOCK* class. The generic application emphasizes the fact that
the notion of midnight applies to the notion of clock.

The classes have something in common: the "note" section at the bottom
with Web links of two kinds. Links named "Source", when followed, highlight
the fragments in the original requirements documents from which the enclosing
requirement classes were derived. Links named "GitHub", when followed, lead

---

[5] https://1drv.ms/u/s!AsXOYPvbmuEyh4IsDdYj-i6V5yX0OA.
[6] http://patterns.projects.cs.ksu.edu.

(a) EiffelStudio with the *STATEMENT_1_1* class representing the "Statement 1.1" requirement.

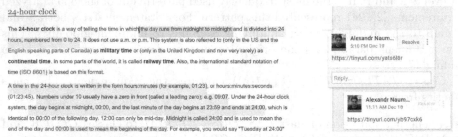

(b) Google document with the contents of the "24-hour clock" Wikipedia page.

**Fig. 1.** Requirement classes in EiffelStudio (a), and the contents of the "24-h clock" Wikipedia page copied to a Google document (b). The "Source" link in the *STATEMENT_1_1* class leads to the corresponding commented fragment in the Google document. The comment contains the GitHub location of the fragment's object-oriented version, equal to the location in the "GitHub" EIS link in *STATEMENT_1_1*.

to the enclosing classes' locations on GitHub. The "Source" link in *STATEMENT_1_1*, for example, highlights, when followed, the "the day runs from midnight to midnight" phrase in the Google document[7], and brings the comment on this phrase to the reader's attention (Fig. 1(b)). The comment contains the GitHub link leading back to the *STATEMENT_1_1* class on GitHub; this link is identical to the "GitHub" link in the *STATEMENT_1_1* class' "note" section.

---

[7] https://tinyurl.com/y96rj2v3.

# 7    Formal Picnic

The *RESPONSE_GLOBAL* class implements its string representation through redefining the standard *out* function present in all Eiffel classes. Any instruction that expects a string argument, such as *print*, automatically invokes this function to get the argument's string representation if the argument has a non-string type.

**Fig. 2.** The executable code (the upper window) outputs the automatically generated string representation of the requirement to the console (the lower window).

Routine *run* of class *TESTER* (Fig. 2) is a configurable entry point of the console application illustrating formal picnics and verification of object-oriented requirements.

Line 11 of *TESTER* outputs the structured string representation of the *STATEMENT_1_1* object-oriented requirement. The *.default* expression returns the default object of the *STATEMENT_1_1* class, and the *print* instruction puts the object's string representation to the "Output" window below the "TESTER" window. The requirement's name, "STATEMENT_1_1", goes before the colon and its string representation goes after.

The requirements analyst now has two comparable string representations of the requirement: the original and the generated one. Comparing them facilitates analysis and may result in asking clarifying questions to the customer and in additional communication.

## 8    Verification

The template classes, including *RESPONSE_GLOBAL*, contain instruments of their own verification in the form of a contracted routine called "verify". The *run* routine of the *TESTER* class may call *verify* to test a candidate solution.

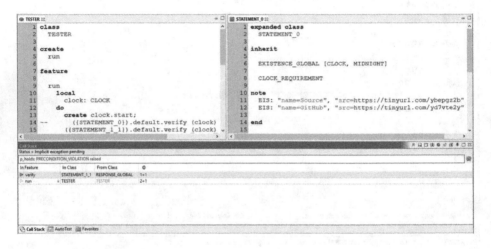

**Fig. 3.** An exception caused by violating the requirement's verification precondition.

Line 15 of the *TESTER* class (Fig. 3) tests class *CLOCK* as a candidate solution of the *STATEMENT_1_1* requirement. Line 13 instantiates a *CLOCK* variable, while lines 14 and 15 use the variable as test input. The following discussion explains the nature of line 14. The line is commented to illustrate the problem that the line fixes when uncommented.

The *verify* routine has a precondition. For the *STATEMENT_1_1* class, the precondition becomes the *holds* Boolean function from the *MIDNIGHT* class. This function returns *True* only for the *24:00* time, and the newly instantiated *clock* variable is set to time *00:00*. Line 14 fixes this mismatch, and its removal crashes the execution. The "Call Stack" window provides information related to the failure: a precondition tagged "p_holds" is violated in *STATEMENT_1_1*, inherited from the *RESPONSE_GLOBAL* template class. The testing code should set the *clock* variable's state to time *24:00* before testing *STATEMENT_1_1*; line 14 does exactly this. *STATEMENT_0* is a requirement class saying that the midnight state should be in principle achievable by *CLOCK*. The *EXISTENCE_GLOBAL* pattern [2] captures this semantics. Line 14 tests

*CLOCK* against *STATEMENT_0* by trying to reach the midnight state on the input variable. Uncommenting the line will remove the precondition violation.

The process of deriving *STATEMENT_0* is an example of how the verification process may help identify a new requirement and learn a new template.

Program proving and Design by Contract may be used instead of testing. The automatic prover (AutoProof [14] in the context of Eiffel) should be applied to the requirements classes, *STATEMENT_0* and *STATEMENT_1_1*. The prover will statically check the contracted *verify* routine according to the principles of Hoare logic [3]. The prover will only accept the routine if the *CLOCK* class has a strong enough and correct contract [7]. The illustration relies on testing because AutoProof, in its current state, requires a lot of additional annotations to check classes like *STATEMENT_1_1*, and explaining these annotations goes beyond the object-oriented requirements idea's essentials.

## 9   Assessment

The approach helps to fix the identified problems undermining the lack of requirements reuse:

- *The lack of a well-defined reuse method*: the reuse method is object-oriented software construction, which is a well-defined method.
- *The lack of quality and incompleteness of requirements to reuse*: the templates library implements the existing collection of specification patterns proven to cover most of the cases, which makes the library complete and quality in that sense.
- *The lack of convenient tools and access facilities with suitable requirements classification*: the tools and access facilities are object-oriented IDEs and GitHub, with all their powerful features. The classification is that of the Dwyer et al.'s collection, proven to be practically relevant.

The approach helps to fix the requirements understandability problems:

- *Noise*: only those requirements remain that fall into an existing verifiable requirement template.
- *Silence*: an attempt to verify existing object-oriented requirements may uncover missing requirements, as it was the case with *STATEMENT_0*.
- *Overspecification*: only those requirements remain that fall into an existing verifiable requirement template. Implementation details cannot map to a requirement template.
- *Contradiction*: one notion may be defined in only one way, otherwise the IDE will raise a compilation error. The contradiction caused by two inconsistent definitions of midnight was resolved by defining this notion in the form of the *MIDNIGHT* class.
- *Ambiguity*: little can be done to remove the possibility for different interpretations – the requirements interpretation process is performed by a cognitive agent anyway. If an interpretation is identified as erroneous, however, switching to another template will automatically update both the generated string

representation and the underlying verifiable semantics. In other words, the templates may help to reduce the effort spent on fixing the consequences of the misinterpretation.

- *Forward reference*: the approach removes this problem. There is no notion of requirements' order in the object-oriented approach, and meaningful statements are connected by the standard "client-supplier" relationship, extensively supported by the object-oriented IDEs.
- *Wishful thinking*: only those requirements remain that fall into an existing verifiable requirement template. The compiler will not accept a template's application in which the verifiable semantics is not fully defined.

The approach helps to fix the requirements verifiability problem. The GitHub library of classes fixes the lack of reusable templates covering the identified verifiable specification patterns. The approach makes it possible to capture and reuse newly identified patterns using the existing object-oriented techniques complemented with contracts.

Besides the benefits, the approach has some limitations:

- Requirements analysts' familiarity with the principles of object-oriented analysis and design.
- Software developers' familiarity with the principles of Hoare logic based reasoning.

## 10   Supporting Work

The idea to use a programming language as a requirements notation is not new [6,8–10] and is well justified. Many groups of stakeholders prefer descriptions of operational activity paths over declarative requirements specifications [12]. A demand exists for educating developers capable of both abstracting in a problem space and automating the transition to a solution space [15].

Other approaches to requirements reuse do not share the aspirations towards connecting the requirements and the solution spaces, as follows both from the state-of-the-practice [11] and the literature [4] studies. The studied approaches focus on reusing natural language, use cases, domain models and several other artifacts disjoint from the solution space.

The decision to express requirements in a programming language may bridge the gap. It may also be the only way to bring the developers closer to the requirements they implement: industry practitioners are generally not keen to switching their tools [1]. The advanced state of code reuse has all chances to skyrocket the state of requirements reuse if the requirements take the form of code.

## 11   Future Work

Intelligent tools should be embedded into existing text editors for:

- Detecting known patterns in what requirements analysts specify manually.
- Proposing reusable templates corresponding to the identified patterns.
- Identifying new patterns in requirements that do not map to existing patterns.

Natural language processing (NLP) would be an appropriate instrument for implementing these tools [1].

# References

1. Dalpiaz, F., Ferrari, A., Franch, X., Palomares, C.: Natural language processing for requirements engineering: the best is yet to come. IEEE Softw. (2018). https://doi.org/10.1109/MS.2018.3571242
2. Dwyer, M.B., Avrunin, G.S., Corbett, J.C.: Patterns in property specifications for finite-state verification. In: Proceedings of the 21st International Conference on Software Engineering, ICSE 1999 (1999). https://doi.org/10.1145/302405.302672
3. Hoare, C.A.R.: An axiomatic basis for computer programming. Commun. ACM **12**(10), 576–580 (1969)
4. Irshad, M., Petersen, K., Poulding, S.: A systematic literature review of software requirements reuse approaches. Inf. Softw. Technol. **93**, 223–245 (2018). https://doi.org/10.1016/j.infsof.2017.09.009
5. Meyer, B.: On formalism in specifications. In: Colburn, T.R., Fetzer, J.H., Rankin, T.L. (eds.) Program Verification. COGS, vol. 14, pp. 155–189. Springer, Dordrecht (1993). https://doi.org/10.1007/978-94-011-1793-7_8
6. Meyer, B.: Multirequirements. In: Seyff, N., Koziolek, A. (eds.) Modelling and Quality in Requirements Engineering (Martin Glinz Festscrhift). MV Wissenschaft (2013)
7. Naumchev, A., Meyer, B.: Complete contracts through specification drivers. In: Proceedings of the 10th International Symposium on Theoretical Aspects of Software Engineering, TASE 2016 (2016). https://doi.org/10.1109/TASE.2016.13
8. Naumchev, A., Meyer, B.: Seamless requirements. Comput. Lang. Syst. Struct. **49**, 119–132 (2017). https://doi.org/10.1016/j.cl.2017.04.001. http://linkinghub.elsevier.com/retrieve/pii/S1477842416301981
9. Naumchev, A., Meyer, B., Mazzara, M., Galinier, F., Bruel, J.M., Ebersold, S.: Expressing and verifying embedded software requirements. CoRR abs/1710.0 (2017). http://arxiv.org/abs/1710.02801
10. Naumchev, A., Meyer, B., Rivera, V.: Unifying requirements and code: an example. In: Mazzara, M., Voronkov, A. (eds.) PSI 2015. LNCS, vol. 9609, pp. 233–244. Springer, Cham (2016). https://doi.org/10.1007/978-3-319-41579-6_18
11. Palomares, C., Quer, C., Franch, X.: Requirements reuse and requirement patterns: a state of the practice survey. Empirical Softw. Eng. **22**, 2719–2762 (2017). https://doi.org/10.1007/s10664-016-9485-x
12. Sindre, G., Firesmith, D.G., Opdahl, A.L.: A reuse-based approach to determining security requirements. In: The 9th International Workshop on Requirements Engineering: Foundation for Software Quality, REFSQ 2003, vol. 8, pp. 127–136 (2003)
13. Tillmann, N., Schulte, W.: Parameterized unit tests. ACM SIGSOFT Softw. Eng. Notes **30**(5), 253 (2005). https://doi.org/10.1145/1095430.1081749. http://portal.acm.org/citation.cfm?doid=1095430.1081749

14. Tschannen, J., Furia, C.A., Nordio, M., Polikarpova, N.: AutoProof: auto-active functional verification of object-oriented programs. In: Baier, C., Tinelli, C. (eds.) TACAS 2015. LNCS, vol. 9035, pp. 566–580. Springer, Heidelberg (2015). https://doi.org/10.1007/978-3-662-46681-0_53
15. Whittle, J., Hutchinson, J., Rouncefield, M.: The state of practice in model-driven engineering. IEEE Softw. (2014). https://doi.org/10.1109/MS.2013.65
16. Zaimi, A., et al.: An empirical study on the reuse of third-party libraries in open-source software development. In: Proceedings of the 7th Balkan Conference on Informatics Conference, BCI 2015 (2015). https://doi.org/10.1145/2801081.2801087

# Measurements for Energy Efficient, Adaptable, Mobile Systems - A Research Agenda

Vladimir Ivanov(✉), Sergey Masyagin, Andrey Sadovykh, Alberto Sillitti, Giancarlo Succi, Alexander Tormasov, and Evgeny Zouev

Innopolis University, Innopolis, Russia
{v.ivanov,s.masyagin,a.sadovykh,a.sillitti,g.succi, a.tormasov,e.zouev}@innopolis.ru

**Abstract.** Software systems are the enabling technology for the development of sustainable systems. However, such devices consume power both from the client side and from the server side. This scenario poses to software engineering a new challenge that concerns the development of software for sustainable systems i.e. systems that explicitly characterize the resources under control, that dynamically evolve to maintain an acceptable consumption of resources making the best possible trade-off with user needs and that are opportunistic and proactive in taking actions that can optimize future resource consumption based on context and past experiences. This paper outlines a research agenda in this area.

**Keywords:** Energy-saving applications · Adaptable systems · Software metrics

## 1  Introduction

Software systems are the enabling technology for the development of sustainable systems. Systems that pervade our everyday life are inherently dynamic since they need to operate in a continuously changing environment and must be able to quickly react and adapt to different types of changes, even unanticipated while guaranteeing the efficient use of the available resources [23,26,41].

On one side, this need comes from the compelling necessity to use cautiously the decreasing natural resources and to reduce the overall impact on the environment. On the other side, these systems are more and more embedded in a digital society, thus moving the user from the role of a passive consumer to the role of active producer capable of changing the system itself by interacting with it with distributed, possibly mobile, devices [18].

Along with this, the tendency to reduce power consumption gradually penetrates into the server segment due to the large-scale spread of virtualization and the construction of cloud systems. This scenario poses to software engineering a new challenge that concerns the development of software for sustainable systems i.e. systems that explicitly characterize the resources under control, that

M. Mazzara et al. (Eds.): TOOLS 2019, LNCS 11771, pp. 163–175, 2019.
https://doi.org/10.1007/978-3-030-29852-4_13

dynamically evolve to maintain an acceptable consumption of resources making the best possible tradeoff with user needs and that are opportunistic and proactive in taking actions that can optimize future resource consumptions based on context and past experiences.

The proposed agenda aims at building and validating a quantitative framework to guide the development and the evolution of sustainable software systems using a variety of metrics collected throughout the life-cycle of software systems, from the initial concept to the deployment, execution, and maintenance, optimizing the performances of the systems under a variety of nowadays relevant factors, including quality, productivity, efficient use of resources.

This paper is organized as follows.

## 2    Background

Energy and mobility—power and movement—are essential for human society. However, the global economy faces unprecedented challenges in meeting growing energy and mobility demands, due to the clash between economic development and resource limitations [16,22]. Every year, mobile device manufacturers seek to expand the range of devices. The new devices require more energy, one of the most urgent problems is to increase the number of hours of operation. An important issue to reduce the energy consumption of mobile devices, the ability of software components to adapt to their specific needs in order to minimize energy consumption [16,17].

Mills, CEO of Digital Power Group and author of the report "The Cloud Begins With Coal" [29] claims, that to use one iPhone spent about 361 kW per year, taking into account the wireless connections, data transfer, and battery charging. By comparison, for a medium-sized refrigerator, compliance with international standards of energy efficiency of consumer goods Energy Star, require only about 322 kW per year.

Along with this, a great interest in energy efficiency arises in the development of data centers. Currently, a large amount of computation is performed on virtualized servers in the cloud. Which confirms the advisability of using energy-efficient server solutions. Thus, the main task in the design of modern processors has not achieved the highest possible productivity, but a high level of performance in providing energy consumption at an acceptable level. The need to use energy-saving technologies is dictated not only by the desire to save resources, but also the inability to provide an acceptable battery life of mobile devices. Today it is one of the driving forces behind the improvement architectures and technologies such as mobile processors and supercomputers and servers. Fully cope with the problem, using only hardware solutions (increase the battery capacity, optimization tools) is not possible, so it needs to use software solutions and tools to assess, monitor and predict the values of key parameters. Development of methods to address this problem is the main objective of the proposed research.

Attention to low-power system design has been increasing due to the widespread use of portable devices [20]. Excessive power consumption adversely impacts several key design metrics. First, the battery lifetime is shortened, thus reducing the usefulness of the portable device. Second, heat dissipation is increased proportionally to power consumption, thus packaging and cooling cost is also increased and the system speed up and reliability is limited by this factor. Third, the environmental impact is seriously raised due to the demand for more electricity.

Software optimization is the key issue in low-power design because most large-scale systems include processors and memories. These components are often responsible for a large fraction of system power dissipation [7]. The software running on a processor (and its memory system) determines, to a large degree, its power dissipation. Clearly, the power consumption due to software execution is tightly related to the target system architecture. For this reason, most of previous research for software optimization has focused on low-level code optimization, i.e. assembly or binary executable code, which is the most appropriate level to have the most accurate software analysis model with the consideration of the underlying hardware [7,20].

Optimization of energy consumption. Optimization of power consumption in mobile devices can be performed both in hardware and software level. Actively developed two main areas: Dynamic Power Management (DPM) [39] and Dynamic Voltage Scaling (DVS) [45]. The main idea of the first direction is that operations that do not require all the processing power of the CPU, performed in more energy-efficient CPU states. The CPU may pass to a state in which the performance is lowered, which in turn reduces power consumption. The main challenge is to correctly predict the moment of transition into power saving mode. Dynamic Voltage Scaling offers another approach, the idea is to dynamically change the power supplied to the various hardware components (such as CPU, RAM, and others.) depending on the requirements of the currently executing software. Based on DPM and DVS approaches are implemented P-state- and C-state-processor status. P- state-status - active modes of the processor, characterized by a combination of a clock signal and operating voltage. For different models of CPU, these modes may differ. If the computing load is reduced, the processor may adjust its clock signal and voltage. This process is not much impact on performance but gives a considerable gain in efficiency. In contrast, C-State indicates the degree of sleep processor during "idle" when it does not execute instructions. Each state has a number. The larger number corresponds to the lower power consumption of the processor, but the more time and energy required for the transition to an active state. An important role in the design of energy efficient systems takes the analysis of values of the basic parameters (metrics) of energy consumption. The use of a coherent system of metrics to evaluate the energy consumption has been studied extensively in the literature. To estimate the energy consumption can be used classical physical characteristics: Watts, Watt * hours and Joules. Weiser et al. proposed to use a new physical quantity: MIPJ (millions of instructions per joule) [44]. This value characterizes the energy efficiency of the computing system. For a long time, this metric is used to compare the energy efficiency of computing devices. Similarly to the Top500 most high- performance systems in the world has created a list of the most energy-efficient systems - Green5003. In 2010 was offered an alternative metric – FTTSE (f(timetosolution) *energy) [6]. Thus, the question of the definition and application of metrics to evaluate the energy consumption is the great practical interest.

## 3    Proposed Approach

Given the sharp growth of IT systems and their impact on worldwide energy consumption, energy efficiency is becoming a real concern. It is estimated that the energy consumption of the ICT sector will reach 433 GW in 2020, meaning more than 14.5% of worldwide power consumption. Of this, 57% will come from PCs, peripherals, and printers. This is because of the highly increasing number of machines used by individuals and businesses (4 billion PCs in the world by 2020). Therefore, it is essential to have precise figures of the current energy consumption of computer and mobile devices and how much of this is due to the software running on them, to understand how to reduce their power consumption and design future energy efficient equipment.

Software measurement will thus play a central role in the process of engineering sustainable software systems [10,15]. In this context, the measurements have to address the quantification (and the satisfaction) of the sustainability goals: the ability to measure and characterize the resources will play an important role. Literature focuses in particular on memory and power consumption. Existing static approaches address memory consumption in terms of both heap [1], and stack requirements [11]. Model-based approaches have been proposed for distributed systems to estimate the overall energy cost of each component [28]. Other pieces of work successfully adapt profiling techniques to measure the energy consumption of desktop [24] or mobile applications [9,25]. The experiments conducted by [43] assess the impact of software over power consumption.

Autili et al. [5] proposed the combination of static analysis and profiling to infer bounds on platform-dependent resource consumption, and used this information to adapt applications to the execution environment provided by mobile devices. In general, adaptive systems can use dynamic data collection mechanisms to detect unexpected situations and adapt autonomously [4]. Data gathering mechanisms can be grouped into three categories: logging, instrumentation and event-based mechanisms. Logging is extensively used in software development, to analyze data produced during system execution and support the identification of anomalies [40]. However, logging relies on dedicated code manually inserted by developers, which is typically error prone and may lead to low quality data [2,3]. Instrumentation techniques automatically insert probes at relevant code locations to collect data. If extensively applied with fine granularity, instrumentation determines monitoring infrastructures with high runtime overhead, which may reduce the effectiveness of the target system. Existing approaches attempt to reduce this overhead by crossing data recorded at different locations through different executions, adjusting the set of instrumented program points at runtime, or replacing complex monitoring infrastructures with simpler ones. Event-based mechanisms address observing the behaviour of distributed systems based on event-based middleware [8, 30].

The analysis at design-time of a software system is commonly based on the notion of software architecture [32]. Software architecture has emerged as an important field of software engineering for managing the realm of large-system development and maintenance [21]. The main intent of software architecture is to provide intellectual control over a sophisticated system of enormous complexity. Software architecture is developed during the early phases of the development process; it hugely constraints or facilitates the achievement of specific functional requirements, non-functional requirements, and business goals. Hence, reviewing the software architecture represents a valid means to check the conformance of the system and to reveal early any potentially missed objective including resource allocation and performances [21]. Moreover, architectural models have a wide spread use for supporting designers in providing recommendations based on the analysis of structural metrics like coupling and cohesion.

Finally, a problem to consider in the development of sustainable systems is that the software portfolio of many organizations consists mostly of legacy systems that cannot be simply replaced, but need to be reengineered to make their services available within new mobile and distributed infrastructures. This requires that a balance between issues related to energy efficiency, usability, and security, in addition to maintainability are taken into account within reengineering processes. Research on dynamically adaptable and evolvable software systems also became very active in recent years. The approach will exploit a model-centric approach to adaptation, where system models (defined at design-time) are kept alive at run time and used:

1. for reasoning about the application and,
2. for deciding when and how the application needs to adapt.

With respect to run-time self-adaptation problems, many approaches have been proposed but the most famous is the top-down approach proposed by IBM in which the system manages itself by using an external decision-making entity (IBM), while there are other emerging bottom-up approaches that are currently being investigated in the area. In bottom-up approaches the self-* properties emerge at a global level through the interactions of the individual components, similarly to what happens in biological social phenomena.

Adaptation refers to the actions taken at run time to react to the changing context in which these systems operate. User tastes and profile, external environmental factors, current trends and involved phenomena are today recognized as parts of the notion of context. Modern applications adopt a context-aware perspective to manage situation- awareness, like modelling location and environment aspects (physical situation) or the current user activity (personal situation). Because the applications are different, context should be modelled in terms of observable parameters that have a symbolic internal representation within a context schema. At run time, the context is "sensed", and then validated, when

the discovered combinations of values constituting the current context are verified against the context schema. This can be achieved through monitoring, i.e.,
collecting and storing state data of such dynamic systems.

When dealing with portable devices and wireless sensors to collect data, the
designer faces main technological issue related to power amount. In software
systems a lot of work has been done to achieve power reduction at the device
level to extend battery life of mobile devices. Nowadays, low power techniques
and energy savings mechanisms are progressively introduced in server environments. All major industrial players are taking a position in the green IT arena,
while autonomic techniques have been developed to determine optimal trade-offs
between performance and energy costs.

## 4    Concrete Plan

As the main approach allows to measure the software will approach the goal-
question-metric (GQM method). We will define a measurement model on three
levels:

- Conceptual level (Goal). At this stage, will be described the main goals to be
  achieved through the collection of metrics.
- Operational level (Question). We will use a set of questions to define models
  of the object of study and then focus on that object to characterize the
  assessment or achievement of a specific goal.
- Quantitative level (Metric) We will associate a set of metrics, based on the
  models, with every question in order to answer it in a measurable way. At
  this stage, on the basis of the issues, we will define metrics to describe, interpret and measure the value of resources software components of adaptive
  systems throughout their life cycle (design, implementation, operation). Will
  be developed methods for calculating the values of metrics, methods, and
  principles of integration of metrics in the development process software components of adaptive systems. These metrics will correlate with specific monitored resources, architectural elements and the behavior of the system as a
  whole.

Non-invasive technology for data collection and monitoring of the software
development process. For the data collection process, we will use non-invasive
tools for monitoring the process of software development. This technology allows
with minimal interference to track a lot of factors clearly affecting the efficiency
of software development. Technology provides for the collection and calculation
of values of the key metrics in real time during development [36]. Non-invasive
measurement techniques have the potentials of overcoming the limitations of
manual data collection. Their aim is to collect data and to deduce measures
from such data with the minimal possible user intervention. The advantages of
this approach are [Johnson et al. 2003] [37]:

- the processes can be analyzed continuously and not on a punctual basis;

- the level of detail can be increased compared to the manual data collection;
- the data collection process does not disturb or interrupt the users in their work;
- the data can be collected more reliably.

A set of metrics for measuring software (source code), and the development process can be adjusted [14, 31, 33]. The toolkit integrates with major software development environment and office applications, so developers are not distracted from the main workflow. This technology has been successfully tested for problem analysis methodologies pair programming on software quality [12, 13].

Overall, the idea is to organize the project in 5 phases:

1. development of the reference scenario,
2. metrics definition,
3. data gathering,
4. development support,
5. experimentation and validation.

### 4.1 Development of the Reference Scenario

The goal of this phase is to analyze the state of the art related to the topics addressed within the project and devise a set of scenarios guiding the work in the technical phases.

*State of the Art.* While evaluating the state of the art, the research units will perform a systematic literature review related to the main topics of the project: i.e., resource-and sustainable-wise metrics, pervasive and non-invasive data collection instruments, quality- oriented development support tools and methods, self-adaptation techniques and policies.

As far as possible and depending on the characteristics of the available literature, this activity will provide an organized body of empirical evidence w.r.t. to the main themes of concern for the project.

*Definition of Scenarios.* The technical tasks of the project, both theoretical and practical, cannot be conducted without considering specific contexts. The most evident example is the definition of metrics that typically involve a goal in its essence. For these reasons, this preliminary activity consists of the definition of a set of scenarios that will constitute the framework for guiding the work in the technical WPs.

In particular, it is important to identify a set of sample-specific technological infrastructure for which the resource awareness and sustainability can be exploited (e.g., mobile devices, cloud computing, wireless sensor networks for security and device control, etc.).

### 4.2 Metrics Definition

he second phase of the project provides a general framework of metrics and models characterizing software entities and resources and integrating it into the software production process.

*Definition of a Metrics Framework.* This activity provides the general framework, based on a GQM measurement plan, for definition and interpretation of the measures for characterizing software entities and resources during both design time evolution of systems and their run-time operation, e.g., code quality measures and those needed for the quantification of resource usage and QoS [42]. The measures are theoretically validated to make sure that they are solid and potentially useful in practice. The measures will be characterized in terms of their applicability in the identified scenarios and the technological context (e.g., cloud, mobile, embedded, etc.). Attention is paid to existing quality models and the integration in them of new measures for sustainability. In addition, it is necessary to introduce a resource modeling framework that includes the relations among resource-specific measures and both process and product specific measures. Finally, available tools are investigated for the computation of the metrics and the relations in the framework, if possible, with an Open Source license, and a suitable system is prototype on the basis of such tools [27,34,35,38], also promoting a suitable creation of a community around it [19].

*Integrating Metrics and Models in the Software Production Process.* This activity defines models and methods for relating the measures defined previously with specific resources, architectural elements, and the run-time behavior of systems. These models and methods will form the basis to enrich the current development and run-time processes from a practical point of view. This allow the results previously obtained to be integrated into development processes so to enable developers to perform practical resource- and QoS-aware design and programming, execution and validation. To this end, new methodologies are defined in support of developers during all the phases of the development process, from requirements elicitation to testing.

## 4.3   Data Gathering

This phase deals with the definition of techniques for collecting data during the lifecycle of a sustainable system. It is divided into two parts: one for data gathering in early life cycle phases (before design), and one for data gathering in late life cycle phases (from design onward).

*Early Life Cycle Phases.* This activity deals with collecting metrics during the early life cycle phases of software development, that is, before development, with the challenge of dealing with artifacts that are not always fully formalized in an unambiguous way. On the basis of the framework previously defined this activity leads to the definition of an approach to collect and provide the information required by the metrics identified.

*Late Life Cycle Phases.* This activity is similar to the previous, but it focuses on late lifecycle artifacts, from development onward. It starts on the same premises, and, in addition to focusing on data collection for design, development, testing, etc, tries to elaborate new analysis techniques that support, on the base of the work previously done, the inference of sustainability properties of the target systems. Moreover, it identifies design patterns that will support re-design and refactoring of software systems for increasing their sustainability.

## 4.4   Design and Development Support

The goal of this phase is to develop models and tools to support the evolution of systems based on measures collected as early in the software lifecycle as possible, with special emphasis on the design phase. This includes two major activities about profiling the components and developing the experience factory.

*Profiling Components.* This activity concerns the development of methods and tools to integrate metrics and models of software attributes (and specifically attributes related to the efficient use of resources) defined previously in early and late life cycles into a comprehensive view suitable for evaluation, monitoring, and prediction of the overall software development. Specific attention is paid to the definition of methods and tools for annotating analysis and design models with measures, context attributes and other information that cannot be directly derived through the data gathering processes defined in WP3. The annotations allow developers/engineers to manually express context attributes and constraints on the allocation of software components to resources and can be used to guide (and constrain) run-time adaptation. Annotations can also be used to suggest context-aware software composition and configuration and, when used to tag resources, can contribute to the calculation of the trade-off between the overall resource demand and the other nonfunctional aspects.

*Experience Factory.* Within this activity, the results of the data gathering processes is be used to develop methods and tools that enact an experience factory helping the software engineer during software design, development, and maintenance activities. Particular attention is paid to predicting and alerting the software engineer about potential problems related to the inefficient use of resources and to suggest possible alternative design and refactoring solutions. However, within the project, we will also consider other issues, such as predicting fault proneness, impact analysis of changes, and software vulnerabilities.

## 4.5   Experimentation and Validation

The goal of this phase is to integrate methods and tools developed within the previous phases inside software production and to evaluate them in empirical studies for the evaluation of the overall approach. This phase has two major activities, integration and empirical studies.

*Integration.* The goal of this task is to provide a coherent view of the results of the technical work packages to allow software engineers and researcher to effectively apply the techniques developed within the project. To this end the task will go into two directions:

1. exploiting the scenarios to identify complementary techniques working on different application scenarios and interchangeable techniques working on the same scenarios with different results
2. identification of software prototypes that can work in the same execution environment without integration problems to form complex toolsets targeting software sustainability

*Empirical Studies.* The case studies will start inside the different labs on "in vitro" experiments and will move on "in vivo" in suitable partner companies. For the analysis of the data coming form the case studies, statistical techniques are used together with methods coming from data mining and big data, supplemented by meta-analysis for generalization of the results

## 5    Conclusion

In this paper we have presented a detailed research agenda to develop sustainable and energy efficient software systems. Theoretical work and actual experimentation are outlined.

Our future plan is to move ahead with this research and be effective in its implementation.

**Acknowledgments.** The work presented in this paper was supported by the grant of Russian Science Foundation №19 − 19 − 00623.

## References

1. Albert, E., Arenas, P., Genaim, S., Puebla, G., Zanardini, D.: Cost analysis of object-oriented bytecode programs. Theor. Comput. Sci. **413**(1), 142–159 (2012)
2. Andrews, D., Criscuolo, C., Gal, P.: Frontier firms, technology diffusion and public policy: micro evidence from OECD countries. In: The Future of Productivity: Main Background Papers, pp. 1–50 (2016)
3. Andrews, D., Criscuolo, C., Gal, P.: The global productivity slowdown, technology divergence and public policy: a firm level perspective. In: The Future of Productivity: Main Background Papers, pp. 1–50 (2016)
4. Ardagna, D., et al.: MODAClouds: a model-driven approach for the design and execution of applications on multiple clouds. In: Proceedings of the 4th International Workshop on Modeling in Software Engineering, MiSE 2012, pp. 50–56. IEEE Press, Piscataway (2012)
5. Autili, M., Malavolta, I., Perucci, A., Scoccia, G.L.: Perspectives on static analysis of mobile apps. In: Proceedings of the 3rd International Workshop on Software Development Lifecycle for Mobile, DeMobile 2015, pp. 29–30. ACM, New York (2015)
6. Bekas, C., Curioni, A.: A new energy aware performance metric. Comput. Sci.-Res. Dev. **25**(3), 187–195 (2010)
7. Benini, L., Micheli, G.: System-level power optimization: Techniques and tools. ACM Trans. Des. Autom. Electron. Syst. **5**(2), 115–192 (2000)

8. Bertolino, A., Calabrò, A., Lonetti, F., Di Marco, A., Sabetta, A.: Towards a model-driven infrastructure for runtime monitoring. In: Troubitsyna, E.A. (ed.) SERENE 2011. LNCS, vol. 6968, pp. 130–144. Springer, Heidelberg (2011). https://doi.org/10.1007/978-3-642-24124-6_13

9. Bhattacharya, P., Srivastava, P.R., Prasad, B.: Software test effort estimation using particle swarm optimization. In: Satapathy, S.C., Avadhani, P.S., Abraham, A. (eds.) INDIA 2012. AINSC, vol. 132, pp. 827–835. Springer, Heidelberg (2012). https://doi.org/10.1007/978-3-642-27443-5_95

10. Briand, L.C., Melo, W.L., Wüst, J.: Assessing the applicability of fault-proneness models across object-oriented software projects. IEEE Trans. Softw. Eng. **28**(7), 706–720 (2002)

11. Chin, W.-N., David, C., Nguyen, H.H., Qin, S.: Enhancing modular OO verification with separation logic. ACM SIGPLAN Not. **43**(1), 87–99 (2008)

12. Coman, I.D., Sillitti, A., Succi, G.: Investigating the usefulness of pair-programming in a mature agile team. In: Abrahamsson, P., Baskerville, R., Conboy, K., Fitzgerald, B., Morgan, L., Wang, X. (eds.) XP 2008. LNBIP, vol. 9, pp. 127–136. Springer, Heidelberg (2008). https://doi.org/10.1007/978-3-540-68255-4_13

13. Coman, I.D., Sillitti, A., Succi, G.: A case-study on using an automated in-process software engineering measurement and analysis system in an industrial environment. In: Proceedings of the 31st International Conference on Software Engineering, ICSE 2009, Vancouver, Canada, pp. 89–99. IEEE Computer Society, May 2009

14. Coman, I.D., Sillitti, A., Succi, G.: Ensuring continuous data accuracy in AISEMA systems. In: Proceedings of the 23rd International Conference on Software Engineering & Knowledge Engineering, SEKE 2011, Eden Roc Renaissance, Miami Beach, USA, 7–9 July 2011, pp. 640–645. Knowledge Systems Institute Graduate School (2011)

15. Corral, L., Georgiev, A.B., Sillitti, A., Succi, G.: A method for characterizing energy consumption in Android smartphones. In: 2nd International Workshop on Green and Sustainable Software, GREENS 2013, pp. 38–45. IEEE, May 2013

16. Corral, L., Georgiev, A.B., Sillitti, A., Succi, G.: Can execution time describe accurately the energy consumption of mobile apps? An experiment in Android. In: Proceedings of the 3rd International Workshop on Green and Sustainable Software, pp. 31–37. ACM (2014)

17. Corral, L., Sillitti, A., Succi, G.: Software development processes for mobile systems: is agile really taking over the business? In: Engineering of Mobile-Enabled Systems (MOBS), pp. 19–24, May 2013

18. Corral, L., Sillitti, A., Succi, G., Garibbo, A., Ramella, P.: Evolution of mobile software development from platform-specific to web-based multiplatform paradigm. In: Proceedings of the 10th SIGPLAN Symposium on New Ideas, New Paradigms, and Reflections on Programming and Software, Onward! 2011, pp. 181–183. ACM, New York (2011)

19. Di Bella, E., Sillitti, A., Succi, G.: A multivariate classification of open source developers. Inf. Sci. **221**, 72–83 (2013)

20. Dürango, J., Dellkrantz, M., Maggio, M.: Control-theoretical load-balancing for cloud applications with brownout. In: 53rd IEEE Conference on Decision and Control, pp. 5320–5327. IEEE (2014)

21. Falessi, D., Cantone, G., Kazman, R., Kruchten, P.: Decision-making techniques for software architecture design: a comparative survey. ACM Comput. Surv. **43**(4), 33:1–33:28 (2011)

22. Fiksel, J.: A framework for sustainable materials management. JOM **58**(8), 15–22 (2006)

23. Fronza, I., Sillitti, A., Succi, G.: An interpretation of the results of the analysis of pair programming during novices integration in a team. In: Proceedings of the 2009 3rd International Symposium on Empirical Software Engineering and Measurement, ESEM 2009, pp. 225–235. IEEE Computer Society (2009)

24. Kansal, A., Saponas, S., Brush, A.J., McKinley, K.S., Mytkowicz, T., Ziola, R.: The latency, accuracy, and battery (lab) abstraction: programmer productivity and energy efficiency for continuous mobile context sensing. In: Proceedings of the 2013 ACM SIGPLAN International Conference on Object Oriented Programming Systems Languages & Applications, pp. 661–676. ACM (2013)

25. Kaur, A., Kaur, K.: Systematic literature review of mobile application development and testing effort estimation. J. King Saud Univ.-Comput. Inf. Sci., November 2018

26. Kivi, J., Haydon, D., Hayes, J., Schneider, R., Succi, G.: Extreme programming: a university team design experience. In: 2000 Canadian Conference on Electrical and Computer Engineering. Conference Proceedings. Navigating to a New Era (Cat. No.00TH8492), vol. 2, pp. 816–820, May 2000

27. Kovács, G.L., Drozdik, S., Zuliani, P., Succi, G.: Open source software for the public administration. In: Proceedings of the 6th International Workshop on Computer Science and Information Technologies, October 2004

28. Autili, P.I.M., Di Benedetto, P.: A hybrid approach for resource-based comparison of adaptable Java applications. Sci. Comput. Program. **78**, 987–1009 (2012)

29. Mills, M.P.: The cloud begins with coal. Technical report (2013). http://eduscol. education.fr/sti/sites/eduscol.education.fr.sti/files/ressources/techniques/1751/ 1751-cloud-begins-with-coal.pdf. Accessed 2 Apr 2019

30. Miranda, B., Bertolino, A.: An assessment of operational coverage as both an adequacy and a selection criterion for operational profile based testing. Softw. Qual. J. **26**(4), 1571–1594 (2018)

31. Pedrycz, W., Iljazi, J., Sillitti, A., Succi, G.: Predicting the fate of requirements in embedded domains. In: Ciancarini, P., Sillitti, A., Succi, G., Messina, A. (eds.) Proceedings of 4th International Conference in Software Engineering for Defence Applications. AISC, vol. 422, pp. 297–306. Springer, Cham (2016). https://doi. org/10.1007/978-3-319-27896-4_25

32. Pedrycz, W., Russo, B., Succi, G.: Knowledge transfer in system modeling and its realization through an optimal allocation of information granularity. Appl. Soft Comput. **12**(8), 1985–1995 (2012)

33. Pedrycz, W., Succi, G., Sillitti, A., Iljazi, J.: Data description: a general framework of information granules. Knowl.-Based Syst. **80**, 98–108 (2015)

34. Petrinja, E., Sillitti, A., Succi, G.: Comparing OpenBRR, QSOS, and OMM assessment models. In: Ågerfalk, P., Boldyreff, C., González-Barahona, J.M., Madey, G.R., Noll, J. (eds.) OSS 2010. IAICT, vol. 319, pp. 224–238. Springer, Heidelberg (2010). https://doi.org/10.1007/978-3-642-13244-5_18

35. Rossi, B., Russo, B., Succi, G.: Adoption of free/libre open source software in public organizations: factors of impact. Inf. Technol. People **25**(2), 156–187 (2012)

36. Scotto, M., Sillitti, A., Succi, G., Vernazza, T.: A non-invasive approach to product metrics collection. J. Syst. Archit. **52**(11), 668–675 (2006)

37. Sillitti, A., Janes, A., Succi, G., Vernazza, T.: Measures for mobile users: an architecture. J. Syst. Archit. **50**(7), 393–405 (2004)

38. Succi, G., Paulson, J., Eberlein, A.: Preliminary results from an empirical study on the growth of open source and commercial software products. In: EDSER-3 Workshop, pp. 14–15 (2001)

39. Triki, M., Wang, Y., Ammari, A.C., Pedram, M.: Dynamic power management of a computer with self power-managed components. In: Ayala, J.L., Shang, D., Yakovlev, A. (eds.) PATMOS 2012. LNCS, vol. 7606, pp. 215–224. Springer, Heidelberg (2013). https://doi.org/10.1007/978-3-642-36157-9_22
40. Vaarandi, R.: Methods for detecting important events and knowledge from data security logs. In: Proceedings of the 2011 European Conference on Information Warfare and Security (2011)
41. Valerio, A., Succi, G., Fenaroli, M.: Domain analysis and framework-based software development. SIGAPP Appl. Comput. Rev. 5(2), 4–15 (1997)
42. Vernazza, T., Granatella, G., Succi, G., Benedicenti, L., Mintchev, M.: Defining metrics for software components. In: Proceedings of the World Multiconference on Systemics, Cybernetics and Informatics, volume XI, pp. 16–23, July 2000
43. Vetrò, A., Ardito, L., Procaccianti, G., Morisio, M.: IT power consumption in a research center - seven facts. In: Proceedings of Energy 2011 (2011)
44. Weiser, M., Welch, B., Demers, A., Shenker, S.: Scheduling for reduced CPU energy. In: Proceedings of the 1st USENIX Conference on Operating Systems Design and Implementation, OSDI 1994. USENIX Association, Berkeley (1994)
45. Yun, H., Wu, P.-L., Arya, A., Kim, C., Abdelzaher, T., Sha, L.: System-wide energy optimization for multiple DVS components and real-time tasks. Real-Time Syst. 47(5), 489 (2011)

# Complex Systems: On Design and Architecture of Adaptable Dashboards

Dragos Strugar[✉]

Innopolis University, Innopolis, Russia
d.strugar@innopolis.ru

**Abstract.** Over the years dashboards have become an essential part of managers' toolkit. The recent developments in the field of IT allowed companies to build complex monitoring and metric-driven solutions for their business needs. The increasing amount of complexity in these dashboards resulted in the increased cost of maintenance and further development. In addition, large corporations have experienced concerns with designing dashboards that are suitable for multiple roles within the organization, i.e. showing the appropriate metrics to people at different positions. By having a self-adjusting, adaptable dashboard, businesses would not only increase the productivity of their workers but could benefit from a fully-fledged Adaptable System (AS) that requires little to no maintenance while performing better than a manually-built and maintained dashboard. Nevertheless, such a system would have a broader set of additional requirements that will be discussed later. This paper presents the design and the architecture of types of adaptable dashboards that address the above-mentioned concerns.

**Keywords:** Adaptable Systems · Complex Systems · Dashboards

## 1 Introduction

We start by claiming that by coming up with a self-adjusting metric analysis tool, organizations of all sizes would make more informed decisions in their own use cases. More specifically, our aim was to come up with a tool that displays only the relevant information to the person looking at it, taking into consideration one's position, the ongoing project that the dashboard is a part of, and much more. The goal of our ongoing research is to verify the above-stated claim, as well as to develop a solution that has the characteristics stated above, following a long trend of research in this area [26,32].

### 1.1 Notions from Complexity Theory

In order to truly overcome the limitations imposed by non-self-adjusting dashboards, we shifted our research into making dashboards more self-sustainable and

© Springer Nature Switzerland AG 2019
M. Mazzara et al. (Eds.): TOOLS 2019, LNCS 11771, pp. 176–186, 2019.
https://doi.org/10.1007/978-3-030-29852-4_14

more relevant to its users over time [8,9,15]. Advances in the field of Complex Systems [4,12] have shown that by applying the common concepts from Complexity Theory such as Non-linear Dynamics [30] and Dynamic Equilibrium [27] it would lead to a more self-sustainable system that requires less maintenance and is cost-effective.

## 1.2 Literature Review

As noted above, we have built an entire prototype featuring the ideas presented in the next few sections. However, our use case was Software Development team tracking, and thus the choices we made on the side should be covered, too [16,28].

Our work is primarily grounded on the works of Pishulin [13], Zorin and Ivanov [14], who did the seminal work for the system that we are currently developing. In addition, Sarikaya, Correll, Bartram, Tory, and Fisher in their [25], performed an extensive systematic literature review on the design of dashboards for different domains. Their idea was to classify dashboards according to their types, taking into account different criteria, and later went to explain the common features and patterns for each of these classes. Lastly, our work is based on the work of Yigitbasioglu and Velcu in their [33], who also reviewed an extensive amount of papers on dashboard design. In addition, they suggested the mechanism for decision-making in their functionality.

## 1.3 Structure Overview

We start by showcasing some of the important questions that helped us greatly in our research in Sect. 2, we introduce Complex Adaptive Systems (CAS) in Sect. 3 as potential solutions to metric relevance concerns. That section also includes the supporting claims to justify the selection of using techniques from Complexity Theory in our use case. To show that existing dashboards are not capable of delivering the same results, in Sect. 4 we discuss the running time of common operations on metrics inside the system. Section 5 applies the concepts from Evolutionary Algorithms to the concepts from CAS (Non-linear Dynamics and Dynamic Equilibrium). Section 6 gives the final thoughts and reflections. Lastly, Sect. 7 highlights the new research milestones.

## 2 Three Metric Relevance Questions

According to Ivanov [13], the main challenge that goes into planning the dashboard layout is to select the most appropriate metrics and to display them in a structured way. That is, every dashboard should "provide intuitive, actionable, flexible, and programmable visualization to support effective decision making" also in the context of mobile development [5–7].

Additionally, effective representation of selected metrics in Valiullin's previous work is also a great challenge that we were facing. By resolving this problem, we could allow users to easily notice and address the issues that may occur during the agile development process [11,17,21,23,31].

To solve these problems and choose the most appropriate visualization techniques for more effective representation, Brath and Peters in [2] argue that the following three questions could lead dashboard designers in the right direction:

1. What metrics does the user need to see?
2. What context does each metric require to make it meaningful?
3. What is the visual representation that best communicates the metric?

Throughout our research, we have been focusing on these three questions, and they have greatly helped us make strategic and long-term based decisions.

As a last point, we consider Open Source as a reference for our development effort, to promote a wide diffusion of our ideas and also to promote the growth of our platform, as widely discussed [10,18,20,22,24,29].

## 3   Complex Adaptive Systems (CAS)

The dynamic behavior that we want from our dashboard could be achieved by using the techniques and concepts from Complexity Theory. However, not all systems are complex, indeed. In literature, for a system to be complex, it needs to have components whose behavior is intrinsically difficult to model. The difficulty comes from the observation that components within the system may be interacting with each other in various ways, or the system as a whole may be interacting with its environment in an unstructured and stochastic manner.

### 3.1   Dashboards as CAS

We argue that dashboards, more and more, are becoming complex systems. Dashboards consist of numerous metrics that need to be displayed to the end user. If we represent each of these metrics as agents within the system, we can more closely look at their relationships. We immediately noticed that almost no agents are isolated, i.e. almost all agents are involved in complex relationships to produce much more complex structures.

In our use case, a perfect example is the Iteration Burndown Chart, depicted in Fig. 1. It is a graphical representation of work left (development) to do versus time. It combines several less-complex metrics, like the number of story points per developer, effort per developer, work done as a function of time, and software development iterations (sprints) among others. And none of these metrics are independent. A single metric such as the Iteration Burndown Chart we mentioned here is comprised of dozens of complex metrics. Practise has shown that this chart is very useful to managers as they can see how fast their team is getting the work done. One can notice that this gets drastically more complex as new agents enter the system, i.e. as new metrics get introduced. To manually come up with new metrics that may interest managers using the dashboard would take a lot of time, and would require developer intervention. Furthermore, it is only by managers getting an idea of what could be useful that new metrics get created. Our idea is to let the system decide which metrics are more relevant than others, and only show these options to the end user. This all is possible due to the feedback loop complex systems have - where end users would rate how useful a particular metric is, and evolving based on that feedback.

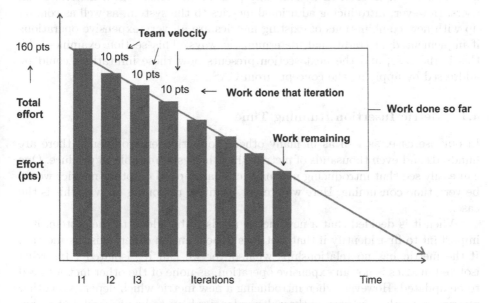

**Fig. 1.** Iteration Burndown Chart

By embracing adaptation and the feedback loop, these agents are able to synchronize their internal states with the other agents in the system. Additionally, the system should be able to recognize these changes and self-adjust with the emergence of globally coherent patterns of adjustment developing.

Then, the dashboard should be able to feed back this information to micro-level agents. Preserving the relevance of certain metrics based on users' feedback is crucial. Therefore, the system should naturally select metrics based on their fitness criteria, which we define in our use case as follows: "An agent has a higher contribution/fitness to the overall system if and only if a slight change in that specific metric would yield a significant change in the overall system fitness, the difference between the expected value and the actual value is above average, or a metric answers some custom questions that dashboard users may have". Contextualized to our use case, the metrics are more relevant if the current value greatly differs from the expected one, or a slight change in a specific metric may yield a substantial increase in the well-being of the entire system.

Such a system would embrace the complex dynamics between the micro-level components (metrics) and the overall system (the dashboard). Interaction between the differentiation of micro- and macro-level agents with different goals and agendas creates the core dynamic of complexity in our system.

# 4    Running Time Complexity Considerations

Intrinsic to the Complex Adaptive Systems is the concept of innovation; i.e. ability to come up with novel outcomes that we could not have predicted beforehand. We go on to argue that this is in fact, a decisive aspect of developing a dashboard engineered to dynamically present the most useful metrics to all users. However, introducing additional metrics to the system, as well as coming up with new combinations of existing metrics are all very expensive operations if implemented in traditional, deterministic ways. This section examines why this is the case, and the next section presents how these limitations could be addressed by applying the concepts from CAS.

## 4.1    Metric Insertion Running Time

In our use case, as well as in many other production environments, there are hundreds and even thousands of metrics that the system is able to produce. One can easily see that introducing new metrics that depend on other metrics would be very time-consuming. Here we present intuitive reasoning on why this is the case.

When it is decided that a new metric needs to be added to the system, it is important to first identify if that metric is dependent on other, existing metrics. If the metric has no relationships whatsoever we call it "isolated". Inserting isolated metrics is not an expensive operation, as none of the other metrics need to be updated. However, when introducing a metric which depends on other metrics, not only does each of these dependencies have to be updated, but rather all the composite structures including these dependencies have to be altered, too. This operation introduces a well-known dependency cascading effect, aka "avalanche", where one change in the system causes many more changes and is thus way more expensive than it should have been.

Thus, we observe the following: given a new metric $a$, the number of its dependencies $n$, and the maximum number of the composite structures that each of these dependencies make - $m$, the running time of the algorithm that inserts a new metric to the dashboard is $O(n * m)$.

If we are inserting a new metric named $a$ into the system, first we check if there are functional dependencies with other metrics. If not, the insertion operation runs in $O(1)$ time. In contrast, if there *are* dependencies, we denote them as $n_i$ and the total number of them as $n$. These metrics may have other composite structures, too, i.e. designate $n_k$ where $k \in N$ and $k \leq n$, as the metric with the maximum number of dependencies it is involved in. If we mark that number of additional dependencies as $m$, we obtain a total running time of the insertion algorithm which is $O(n * m)$.

In fact, such operations would have a running time of $O(n * m)$, where $n$ is the number of metrics the newly added metric depends on, and $m$ is the number of already existing dependencies.

## 4.2 Metric Combinations Running Time

As stated earlier, one of the most important metrics we decided to show to managers of Software Development teams is the Iteration Burndown Chart shown on Fig. 1. It is a very complex metric, as it encapsulates many smaller structures. However, it was first created because managers came up with that idea and communicated it to the developers who then made it work.

Our opinion is that new dashboard metrics should not only be created upon the request from users. Rather, the system should be able to produce new metrics periodically, and based on users' feedback, past data, and much more decide whether or not to keep the new metric for the next time period.

Such an approach has several benefits over the old-fashioned one:

1. system has the ability to come up with new metrics that dashboard users would have never thought of
2. dashboard embraces change and further development
3. costs less to maintain.

The first point has been already discussed. To support our claim that the dashboard embraces change, let us compare the non-adaptable dashboards to the adaptable ones. A dashboard that has been built with adaptability in mind increases its effectiveness when it receives more data. Whether the change is referred to as the process of insertion or deletion, the system will quickly adjust and evolve taking into account the new data that has been fed to the system. On the other hand, introducing changes in non-adjustable dashboards usually involves contacting the development team and handing them the requirements. Such a process is typically time-consuming and the business expenses increase over time.

Having discussed the benefits of combining metrics and coming up with novel metrics that one would have otherwise never thought of, we proceed to argue on the upper-bound of the running time of the brute-force algorithm that implements the combinations feature.

Therefore, we observe: given the number of existing metrics, $n$, and the number of composite structures these metrics make, $m$, the running time of the algorithm that produces all the combinations is given by $O(n * m)$.

As the system we are trying to model is evolving over time, it is crucial to note that this quadratic algorithm should be performed on each iteration of the system life-cycle. This is quite an expensive operation and is thus infeasible to implement the algorithm the brute force way. Therefore, to reduce the running time and let the system be independently making its choices, we suggest combining some of the techniques used in Evolutionary algorithms [1,3] with the notions like Non-linear Dynamics [30] and Dynamic Equilibrium [19] from the Complexity theory.

## 5   CAS and Evolutionary Algorithms

The last section examined how modern adaptable dashboards can benefit from having novel metrics introduced by the system, i.e. how complex systems embrace the idea of innovation. This section dives deeper into the details suggesting a way to implement these ideas using some of the concepts and techniques from CAS and Evolutionary Algorithms (EAs). First, we examine the EA part and then move on to Non-Linear Dynamics and Dynamic Equilibrium concepts. To see why we chose these aspects of CAS specifically, reference the Sect. 7.

### 5.1    Evolutionary Algorithms

In order to achieve the self-organization and autonomy we want from our dashboard, a mechanism that handles the selection of the fittest metrics is needed. Section 3.1 covered in greater detail what do we mean by "fittest" in our case. Fitness score is determined using the fitness function, and as it is a central concept we will repeat our fitness function once again:

> An agent has a higher contribution/fitness to the overall system if and only if a slight change in that specific metric would yield a significant change in the overall system fitness, the difference between the expected value and the actual value is above average, or a metric answers some custom questions that dashboard users may have.

By applying the fitness function from above to each of the metrics inside of our system we would obtain a numeric value that represents how important is it to show that particular metric to the user. Several key observations should be pointed out:

- metrics that deviate from the mean are more likely to be shown to the user.
- metrics whose improvement may result in other metrics' fitness are more likely to be shown to the user.
- metrics of all sizes that indicate less important information to the user will have a smaller chance of being shown to the user.

Taking these factors into consideration, the algorithm would run as follows:

1. assign a fitness score to each agent in the system
2. select members to act upon using some variation operators (crossover and mutations)
3. replace certain members of the population with these children from variation operators
4. keep some members from the previous population in the new population (Table 1).

The major problem now is how to perform the selection between the agents. We chose the technique often used in Genetic Algorithms that is based on natural selection. The members with higher fitness would undertake a tournament-like contest where the winner would continue to breed, and the loser would be eliminated, or considered for breeding later. Again, Sect. 7 showcases how we are planning to expand on these ideas.

**Table 1.** Definitions in our use case.

| | |
|---|---|
| Population | All metrics in the system |
| Sample | A proper subset of the population |
| Agent | A member of the population |
| Fitness score | A real number |
| Fitness function | Function from agent to fitness score |
| Crossover | Combination of parents' genetic information |
| Mutation | Change in agent's genetic information |
| Variation operators | Crossover and mutation |

In our concrete case, fitness is highly dependent on users' feedback. To really grasp which metrics are useful for dashboard users and which are not, we suggest using feedback loops. The user would rate the usefulness of a particular metric which would then allow us to assign fitness scores to each agent.

## 5.2 Non-linear Dynamics.

Due to the emergent complexity of CAS, managers, and stakeholders operating such systems would have difficulties making decisions on which agent (metric) is performing better than others. For example, a manager may spend a lot of time looking at one metric that is showing that his/her team is doing very well, albeit some of the other metrics indicate otherwise. This would result in a waste of resources and confusion. Non-linear dynamics in adaptive systems is necessary to constantly change the internal states of the agents within the system, resulting in the change the entire system's state.

It is the non-linear relationship between the agents that causes complexity. Some metrics are not only linear functions of others, they are much more advanced. Making manual decisions thus becomes infeasible, and states like Dynamic Equilibrium should be achieved.

## 5.3 Dynamic Equilibrium

Utilizing the concept of the Dynamic Equilibrium allowed us to expand on our previous research to come up with the state which has the following characteristics:

- the current state is never in complete chaos, where there is nothing to bind individual actors together
- the current state is never completely stable, which results in the full stagnation
- the current state is always in a so-called "Dynamic Equilibrium" where all actors are loosely bound to each other with the plethora of room to innovate and improve

Having such a system embraces innovation and allows for novel contributions to the range of possible metrics to be displayed to users with various roles.

# 6 Conclusions

As businesses grow, so does their need to effectively manage their products and services. Dashboards have greatly impacted the way corporations operate on a global scale. They have enabled managers to not only have a useful overview of the ongoing project but to make crucial decisions for their business. However, the increasing amount of data and metrics that need to be tracked introduced several challenges that need to be overcome to allow the normal dashboard functioning. These challenges include, but are not limited to: choosing the right metrics to display, handling the requirement changes, adapting the dashboard to users from various positions. This work suggests that dashboards are becoming Complex systems and that these challenges have become far more dangerous when dealt with on a larger scale - not only does the maintenance cost increase, but the whole operation process gets harder due to complex relationships between metrics in the dashboard. We then went into more detail by explaining the algorithm which would address the issues mentioned above.

Complex Adaptive Systems consist of many interacting entities. Some of these entities, in our case metrics that we used to monitor the performance of Software Development teams, may or may not be relevant to the user who is using the dashboard at a given time. By utilizing the constant improvement and self-adaptability based on users' feedback, the relevancy of metrics that get presented improves over time.

All this would not have been possible if there was no balance between the chaos and the state of stagnation. That trade-off is essential to CAS as it allows the system to be innovative while still performing well.

# 7 Future Work

The work presented here lays the ground to further research and development. It serves as the starting point, and theory described here is going to be the blueprint that we are going to follow. Concepts like Non-linear Dynamics and Dynamic Equilibrium have been mentioned, although not thoroughly contextualized in the use case of Software Development teams. Aspects of Complex systems and Evolutionary Algorithms that we have not touched on, such as Game Theory, Collective Behavior, and Pattern Formation among others are also a part of our research agenda. What also follows is a working prototype implementing the theoretical aspects presented here on a real-world use case of Software development team monitoring.

**Acknowledgments.** The work presented in this paper was supported by the grant of Russian Science Foundation №19 – 19 – 00623.

# References

1. Back, T.: Evolutionary Algorithms in Theory and Practice: Evolution Strategies, Evolutionary Programming, Genetic Algorithms. Oxford University Press, Oxford (1996)
2. Brath, R., Peters, M.: Dashboard design: why design is important. DM Direct **85** (2004)
3. Coello, C.A.C., Lamont, G.B., Van Veldhuizen, D.A., et al.: Evolutionary Algorithms for Solving Multi-objective Problems, vol. 5. Springer, Heidelberg (2007)
4. Corrado, A.J.: Dynamics of Complex Systems. CRC Press, Boca Raton (2019)
5. Corral, L., Georgiev, A.B., Sillitti, A., Succi, G.: A method for characterizing energy consumption in Android smartphones. In: 2nd International Workshop on Green and Sustainable Software (GREENS 2013), pp. 38–45. IEEE, May 2013
6. Corral, L., Sillitti, A., Succi, G.: Software development processes for mobile systems: is agile really taking over the business? In: 2013 1st International Workshop on the Engineering of Mobile-Enabled Systems (MOBS), pp. 19–24, May 2013
7. Corral, L., Sillitti, A., Succi, G., Garibbo, A., Ramella, P.: Evolution of mobile software development from platform-specific to web-based multiplatform paradigm. In: Proceedings of the 10th SIGPLAN Symposium on New Ideas, New Paradigms, and Reflections on Programming and Software, Onward! 2011, pp. 181–183. ACM, New York (2011)
8. Danovaro, E., Remencius, T., Sillitti, A., Succi, G.: PEM: experience management tool for software companies. In: Companion to the 23rd ACM SIGPLAN Conference on Object-oriented Programming Systems Languages and Applications, OOPSLA Companion 2008, pp. 733–734. ACM (2008)
9. Danovaro, E., Remencius, T., Sillitti, A., Succi, G.: PKM: knowledge management tool for environments centered on the concept of the experience factory. In: Companion of the 30th International Conference on Software Engineering, ICSE Companion 2008, pp. 937–938. ACM (2008)
10. Di Bella, E., Sillitti, A., Succi, G.: A multivariate classification of open source developers. Inf. Sci. **221**, 72–83 (2013)
11. Fronza, I., Sillitti, A., Succi, G.: An interpretation of the results of the analysis of pair programming during novices integration in a team. In: Proceedings of the 2009 3rd International Symposium on Empirical Software Engineering and Measurement, ESEM 2009, pp. 225–235. IEEE Computer Society (2009)
12. Harel, D.: Statecharts: a visual formalism for complex systems. Sci. Comput. Program. **8**(3), 231–274 (1987)
13. Ivanov, V., Pischulin, V., Rogers, A., Succi, G., Yi, J., Zorin, V.: Design and validation of precooked developer dashboards. In: Proceedings of the 2018 ACM Joint Meeting on European Software Engineering Conference and Symposium on the Foundations of Software Engineering, ESEC/SIGSOFT FSE 2018, Lake Buena Vista, FL, USA, 04–09 November 2018, pp. 821–826 (2018)
14. Ivanov, V., Rogers, A., Succi, G., Yi, J., Zorin, V.: Precooked developer dashboards: what to show and how to use - poster. In: Proceedings of the 40th International Conference on Software Engineering Companion, ICSE 2018, Gothenburg, Sweden, May-June 2018. ACM (2018)
15. Janes, A., Sillitti, A., Succi, G.: Effective dashboard design. Cutter IT J. **26**(1), 17–24 (2013)
16. Janes, A., Succi, G.: Lean Software Development in Action. Springer, Heidelberg (2014). https://doi.org/10.1007/978-3-642-00503-9

17. Kivi, J., Haydon, D., Hayes, J., Schneider, R., Succi, G.: Extreme programming: a university team design experience. In 2000 Canadian Conference on Electrical and Computer Engineering. Conference Proceedings. Navigating to a New Era (Cat. No. 00TH8492), vol. 2, pp. 816–820, May 2000
18. Kovács, G.L., Drozdik, S., Zuliani, P., Succi, G.: Open source software for the public administration. In: Proceedings of the 6th International Workshop on Computer Science and Information Technologies, October 2004
19. Lajoie, Y., Teasdale, N., Bard, C., Fleury, M.: Attentional demands for static and dynamic equilibrium. Exp. Brain Res. **97**(1), 139–144 (1993)
20. Paulson, J.W., Succi, G., Eberlein, A.: An empirical study of open-source and closed-source software products. IEEE Trans. Softw. Eng. **30**(4), 246–256 (2004)
21. Pedrycz, W., Russo, B., Succi, G.: Knowledge transfer in system modeling and its realization through an optimal allocation of information granularity. Appl. Soft Comput. **12**(8), 1985–1995 (2012)
22. Petrinja, E., Sillitti, A., Succi, G.: Comparing OpenBRR, QSOS, and OMM assessment models. In: Ågerfalk, P., Boldyreff, C., González-Barahona, J.M., Madey, G.R., Noll, J. (eds.) OSS 2010. IAICT, vol. 319, pp. 224–238. Springer, Heidelberg (2010). https://doi.org/10.1007/978-3-642-13244-5_18
23. Phaphoom, N., Succi, G., Vlasenko, J., di Bella, E., Fronza, I., Sillitti, A.: Pair programming and software defects-a large, industrial case study. IEEE Trans. Softw. Eng. **39**(7), 930–953 (2013)
24. Rossi, B., Russo, B., Succi, G.: Adoption of free/libre open source software in public organizations: factors of impact. Inf. Technol. People **25**(2), 156–187 (2012)
25. Sarikaya, A., Correll, M., Bartram, L., Tory, M., Fisher, D.: What do we talk about when we talk about dashboards? IEEE Trans. Vis. Comput. Graph. **25**, 682–692 (2018)
26. Sillitti, A., Janes, A., Succi, G., Vernazza, T.: Measures for mobile users: an architecture. J. Syst. Architect. **50**(7), 393–405 (2004)
27. Smith, W.K., Lewis, M.W.: Toward a theory of paradox: a dynamic equilibrium model of organizing. Acad. Manag. Rev. **36**(2), 381–403 (2011)
28. Succi, G., Benedicenti, L., Vernazza, T.: Analysis of the effects of software reuse on customer satisfaction in an RPG environment. IEEE Trans. Softw. Eng. **27**(5), 473–479 (2001)
29. Succi, G., Paulson, J., Eberlein, A.: Preliminary results from an empirical study on the growth of open source and commercial software products. In: EDSER-3 Workshop, pp. 14–15 (2001)
30. Thompson, J.M.T., Thompson, M., Stewart, H.B.: Nonlinear Dynamics and Chaos. Wiley, Hoboken (2002)
31. Valerio, A., Succi, G., Fenaroli, M.: Domain analysis and framework-based software development. SIGAPP Appl. Comput. Rev. **5**(2), 4–15 (1997)
32. Vernazza, T., Granatella, G., Succi, G., Benedicenti, L., Mintchev, M.: Defining Metrics for Software Components. In: Proceedings of the World Multiconference on Systemics, Cybernetics and Informatics, vol. XI, pp. 16–23, July 2000
33. Yigitbasioglu, O.M., Velcu, O.: A review of dashboards in performance management: Implications for design and research. Int. J. Account. Inf. Syst. **13**(1), 41–59 (2012)

# Machine Learning

# Human Activity Recognition Using Deep Models and Its Analysis from Domain Adaptation Perspective

Nikita Gurov[1]($\boxtimes$), Adil Khan[1], Rasheed Hussain[1], and Asad Khattak[2]

[1] Innopolis University, Innopolis, Russia
{n.gurov,a.khan,r.hussain}@innopolis.ru
[2] College of Technological Innovation, Zayed University,
Abu Dhabi, United Arab Emirates
asad.khattak@zu.ac.ae

**Abstract.** Human activity recognition (HAR) is a broad area of research which solves the problem of determining a user's activity from a set of observations recorded on video or low-level sensors (accelerometer, gyroscope, etc.) HAR has important applications in medical care and entertainment. In this paper, we address sensor-based HAR, because it could be deployed on a smartphone and eliminates the need to use additional equipment. Using machine learning methods for HAR is common. However, such, methods are vulnerable to changes in the domain of training and test data. More specifically, a model trained on data collected by one user loses accuracy when utilised by another user, because of the domain gap (differences in devices and movement pattern results in differences in sensors' readings.) Despite significant results achieved in HAR, it is not well-investigated from domain adaptation (DA) perspective. In this paper, we implement a CNN-LSTM based architecture along with several classical machine learning methods for HAR and conduct a series of cross-domain tests. The result of this work is a collection of statistics on the performance of our model under DA task. We believe that our findings will serve as a foundation for future research in solving DA problem for HAR.

**Keywords:** Human activity recognition · Domain adaptation

## 1 Introduction

Human activity recognition (HAR) is a problem of determining human activities (walking, running, etc.) from a set of observations recorded on video or low-level sensors. This issue is highly relevant to such real-world task as medical care (constant monitoring of patients with severe motor diseases). That is why much work exists on HAR which addresses the problem from different perspectives: video [1–4], audio signal [5] and low-level sensors [6,7] based activity recognition.

© Springer Nature Switzerland AG 2019
M. Mazzara et al. (Eds.): TOOLS 2019, LNCS 11771, pp. 189–202, 2019.
https://doi.org/10.1007/978-3-030-29852-4_15

Unfortunately, most of the proposed methodology needs additional equipment for data collection (video recording, wearable sensors). This greatly complicates the possibility of their use in the real world. Works [8,9] use smartphones as a framework for HAR task. These devices have all the necessary sensors (gyroscope, accelerometer and magnetometer) and they have become an inseparable part of modern life.

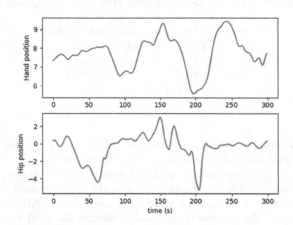

**Fig. 1.** Accelerometer sensor readings for "walking" activity of the same person. Signals were recorded simultaneously for 3 s from two positions: hand and hip. Though two signals have some common patterns, there are many differences (for example different mean values).

However, different devices have different sensors and as a consequence - specific data representations. People also have different behavioural patterns. The result is that the model trained for one person or a particular position on the body will lose performance when a user or position changes. Figure 1 illustrates this situation. This difference in the source (train) and target (test) domains is called domain gap. Despite the significant results in HAR, the problem of domain adaptation (DA) in the context of activity recognition is not studied thoroughly. There are few works on this problem: [10–13] which mainly exploit deep learning techniques. However, the number of existing research studies is too small to build a global understanding of what methodologies are suitable for that problem.

In our work, we conduct a set of tests on the performance of different machine learning (ML) methodologies in DA task. These approaches are divided into two main groups: deep learning and classical ML. Most of the recent works use deep learning, defining classical methods as less effective. However, such conclusions for the DA problem are not supported by any specific tests.

The contributions of our work are the following.

- We employ a variety of models for HAR: deep network and such models from classical ML as Random Forest, multi-layer perceptron (MLP), logistic regression and k nearest-neighbours (KNN).
- We conduct a set of tests for cross-domain and cross-position evaluation of these models.
- The main contribution is a comprehensive, structured collection of performance statistics for most of the traditional approaches to HAR.

We believe that the results of our work will provide a reliable foundation for future research in this field. It will be a starting point for planning new studies and designing novel architectures for HAR.

## 2   Related Work

In this work we address sensor based HAR because it is one of the most frequently used and general HAR approaches. Sensor-based HAR is proposed in numerous works: [6–9,14].

Activity recognition pipeline for time series sensor data involves sliding window segmentation, feature extraction, and activity classification [15]. There are two main approaches to feature extraction. First is hand-craft feature extraction when data is preprocessed manually, representing the signal as its mean, variance, deviation and many other statistical and wavelet features [16–18]. Classical models such as SVM [19], Decision Trees [20] or KNN [21] are trained to make predictions based on extracted features. This methodology is extensively explored as the traditional approach to HAR. However, it is a challenging task and it requires a deep understanding of signal processing to design good features.

The second approach is based on deep learning. Deep neural networks (DNNs) have had revolutionary impact on all kinds of ML problems: [22–24]. DNNs also provided good results in HAR task [25–27]. When applied to sensor-based HAR, deep learning allows for automated feature extraction and thus, eliminates the need for manual feature extraction. However, the traditional DNNs fail to consider the order of time series signals. To solve this problem long short-term memory (LSTM) proposed by Hochreiter and Schmidhuber [28] is successfully applied in [29–31]. [29] Combine convolutional and LSTM layers to provide good results in recognition performance.

Research in this area achieved impressive results, but most of the experiments are provided on a single dataset, thus generalization is not guaranteed. These models provide high accuracy classification only on a single domain and could lose efficiency if tested on another domain because of the domain gap.

Cross-domain activity recognition is a real problem that prevents using proposed methods in real life. A few works address this problem in HAR context. [11–13] achieve DA with several deep learning techniques. For example, [12] propose a method of adversarial knowledge transfer named SA-GAN (Subject Adaptor GAN which utilizes Generative Adversarial Network) and [11] provides Stratified Transfer Learning which uses major-voting for partial labelling of the target data and trains the initial model with provided latent labels. [13] combine the supervised convolutional neural network (CNN) and CNN-Encoder-Decoder to perform semi-supervised learning for HAR.

## 3   Methods

We consider traditional approaches to a classification problem in HAR domain. This includes such models as DNN, MLP, decision trees, KNN and logistic regression. We skip the support vector machine (SVM) in the context of our research because of its high complexity, which makes it difficult to use in our experiments.

### 3.1   Deep Model

We propose a deep model, shown in Fig. 2, which is a pipeline of convolutional, LSTM and dense layers. This is a general architecture which we use to provide an evaluation of the basic deep learning approach to HAR. Deep model is assumed to extract features from signal automatically, and CNN have been used to address this. Convolution through input with different kernels is a powerful pattern detection technique, illustrated in Fig. 3.

The convolutional layer is followed by LSTM layers. Use of LSTM [32] is due to the fact that sensor signal is a continuous stream of measurements and it is important for the time-series classification method to have access to past data in order to recognize long-time patterns. It is a recurrent network which is capable of learning long-term dependencies. The detail algorithm description is depicted in Fig. 4.

$$forget_t = \sigma(W_f\Delta[h_{t-1}, x_t] + b_f) \tag{1}$$

$$input_t = \sigma(W_i\Delta[h_{t-1,x_t}] + b_i) \tag{2}$$

$$\hat{cell}_t = \tanh(W_C\Delta[h_{t-1}, x_t] + b_C) \tag{3}$$

$$Cell_t = forget_t * Cell_{t-1} + input_t * \hat{cell}_t \tag{4}$$

$$output_t = \sigma(W_o\Delta[h_{t-1}, x_t] + b_o) * \tanh(Cell_t) \tag{5}$$

$W$ and $b$ are weights and biases learned during training. Last layers of the model are standard fully-connected Dense layers for mapping results provided by the deep model into output vector.

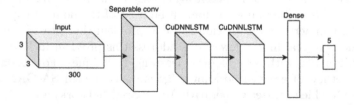

**Fig. 2.** Deep model architecture.

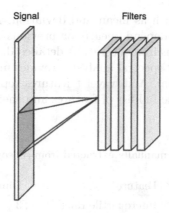

**Fig. 3.** Convolution layer has a set of kernels (filters). Each kernel convolves through the data with some window size and stride. In other words kernel calculates how different data sections reflects its feature.

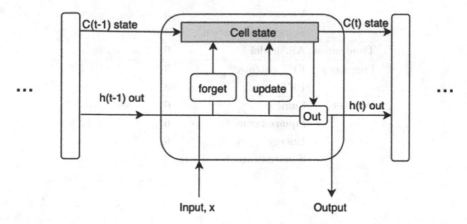

**Fig. 4.** LSTM structure. The key to this model is a cell state. It is a buffer which stores data from previous iterations. It is used for generating an output of the layer. LSTM can add (update) and remove (forget) information from it. Equation (1) is a mathematical description of *forget* function. Equations (2–4) calculate updated *Cell* state. Finally, Eq. (5) provides an output based on the relevant information.

## 3.2   Classical Methods

Classical methods and deep models are different in extracting features. While a deep model extracts them automatically, the classical model requires manual feature extraction before the classification step. That is why we first address the feature extraction process.

**Feature Extraction.** We take 4 feature types described in [16–18]: Statistical, Time series, Frequency, and Wavelet. Statistical features extract general parameters of the series such as mean and deviation. An autoregressive (AR) model specifies how values depend linearly on previous values and on a stochastic term, which model learns from a series. A detailed description of this method is presented in [33]. Fourier spectral analysis provides measurements for the frequency domain of the signal. And wavelet features represent basic parameters of a wavelet oscillation. The full list of features and their dimensions is given in Table 1.

**Table 1.** Features manually extracted from sensory data [16–18]

| Type | Feature | Dimensions |
| --- | --- | --- |
| Statistical | Interquartile range | 3 |
| | Partial auto-correlation | 3 |
| | Mean | 3 |
| | Median | 3 |
| | Variance | 3 |
| | Standard deviation | 3 |
| Time series | AR model | 9 |
| Frequency | FFT entropy | 3 |
| | FFT energy | 3 |
| Wavelet | Sum | 6 |
| | Squared sum | 6 |
| | Energy | 6 |
| | Squared ratio | 3 |

**Dense Network Classifier.** We provide a fully connected Dense network architecture in Fig. 5. Dense layers are traditionally used as last layers of deep models to provide decision making step based on extracted features. We use it because separate Dense model, trained with hand-crafted features will allow us to compare the hand-crafted features with ones provided by the deep model.

**Random Forest.** Decision tree algorithms are successfully applied to various classification tasks [34, 35], including HAR [20]. However, if the dataset has a lot of features, the decision tree algorithm usually overfits and makes the learning process more complicated. We solve this issue by utilizing Random Forest classifier which is an improved version of the decision tree approach. The key idea is to split feature set on random batches of features and apply decision trees for each batch. Figure 6 illustrates this strategy. The ensemble of decision trees makes the model more robust to noise and overfitting.

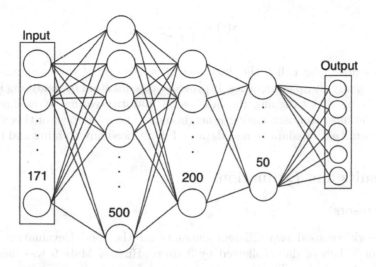

**Fig. 5.** MLP with 3 hidden Dense (fully-connected) layers. Last output layer is a categorical vector (one-hot encoding of labels).

**Logistic Regression.** Regression techniques are frequently exploited in the classification task [36, 37]. We are interested in getting prediction accompanied by its probability because some existing methodologies to HAR DA use majority-voting for providing latent labels [11]. The performance of such unsupervised methods could be increased if we support our decisions with probabilities and skip candidates with low confidence. The logistic function is a sigmoid function, which takes any real input, and outputs a value between zero and one, so it could be used as a probabilistic measure for the confidence of the predicted label. The logistic function $\sigma(t)$ is defined as follows:

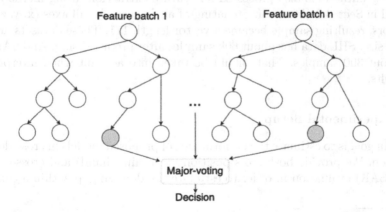

**Fig. 6.** Representation of the Random Forest model. Each decision tree provides its candidate label. After majority-voting, model defines its final decision.

$$\sigma(t) = \frac{1}{1 + e^{-t}} \qquad (6)$$

**KNN** classifier, also called the 'lazy algorithm', is one of the most naive and computationally cheap approaches. It provides classification by analysing k nearest neighbours and assigning the label with majority-voting. It assigns label which is the most frequent among k neighbours. The advantage of this method is that it could easily adapt to new data and don't need any training and tuning.

## 4     Results and Evaluation

### 4.1     Datasets

In this work we used two different datasets for the model evaluation: SHL[1] consists of 9 days of data collected by 3 users. Huawei Mate 9 was used as a data collection device. The data was collected from 4 phone positions: Hips, Bag, Torso and Hand. Dataset consists of 3 sensors' readings (accelerometer, gyroscope and magnetometer). It has 19 types of activities overall.

Sensors Activity Recognition DataSet (SAR) [38][2] is a collection of 3–4 min recordings made by ten participants. The data was collected by the same set of sensors (accelerometer, gyroscope and magnetometer) which are built in Samsung Galaxy SII (i9100). The data was collected from 5 phone positions: right/left hip pocket, belt, right upper arm and right wrist. This dataset provides seven types of activities.

For our evaluation purposes, we take two SHL subsets - SHL hip and hand for one user. Dataset for right hip device position for one user is also taken from SAR. In order to bring datasets to the same label domain, we left only five activities, which they share: sitting, standing, walking, running and biking. We also segmented datasets on 3 s windows with 50% overlap. Each sample from these datasets is also processed for feature extraction, using methodology provided in Sect. 3.2. After concatenating of all features for all axes (x, y, z) and all sensors, resulting sample became a vector length 171. These datasets are not of equal size. SHL data has about 60k samples after preprocessing. And SAR has only about 300 samples. That should be taken into account when interpreting the results.

### 4.2     Experimental Setup

Our main goal is to estimate the performance of proposed models in cross-domain evaluation. We provide both cross-position (SHL hip - hand) and cross-domain (SHL - SAR) evaluation in order to estimate the domain gap within a common

---

[1] Sussex-Huawei Locomotion Dataset, http://www.shl-dataset.org/dataset/.

[2] Sensors Activity Recognition Dataset, https://www.researchgate.net/publication/ 266384007_Sensors_Activity_Recognition_DataSet.

environment (user, device) and within totally different domains. Cross-validation accuracy was used as an evaluation metric for all tests.

In the first test, we train all the models on source data and evaluate it on target. The idea is to collect the statistics of the models' performance when the training set is a composition of the source domain and of different amount of data from target domain: source + target*(0, 0.001, 0.01, 0.1, 1). The hypothesis is that if the training domain contains some portion of the target domain, performance will be improved. We also suppose, that there is a threshold for ratio, when the amount of target data added to the training set, raises the performance to the maximum available values for the target domain.

The second test is a support to the first one. The logic is the same, we train all models with different ratio of the target data, but without source at all. It is important for making the right conclusions from the first test. There is no way to figure out whether the source domain increases overall performance or vice-versa decreases it only by first test results. Because of the small size of SAR dataset, some ratios used in tests return an empty set of samples for it.

### 4.3 Implementation Details

Deep model is implemented using Python keras framework. In order to reduce the model size and complexity, we replace the first convolutional layer with Depth wise Separable Convolution [39]. A convolutional layer is followed by two CuDNNLSTM layers with a number of units equal to 64. The model ends with two Dense layers of 32 and 5 neurons respectively. After hyperparameter tuning, the optimal parameters were defined as binary-cross-entropy loss, Rmsprop optimizer and sigmoid activation.

Dense model is also implemented with keras. After iterating through a different number of layers and the number of neurons in each, we came to the architecture proposed in Fig. 2 as an optimal one. The same hyperparameter tuning algorithm as used for the deep model was applied to this network. The set of optimal hyperparameters remains the same: binary-cross-entropy loss, Rmsprop optimizer and sigmoid activation. All the other classifiers (KNN, Logistic regression, Random Forest) are implemented using the sklearn framework. Random Forest has 50 estimators. That is the optimal time/performance value. Logistic regression was used out of the box without any additional options. The KNN algorithm work with 5 nearest-neighbours for classification. In order to provide train/test sets, all datasets are shuffled and split as 1/4 for test/train. In this work, we use only one fold for cross-validation. The reason is the small size of SAR which makes several folds splitting meaningless. In order to remain the same approach to each dataset, we left only one fold.

### 4.4 Results

Following figures represent the performance of the chosen methods. Each figure contains results of three combinations of datasets used for cross-domain evaluation: Figs. 7, 8, 9, 10 and 11(a) is when source data is full SHL hand dataset and target domain is SHL hip. Figures 7, 8, 9, 10 and 11(b) is where Source is SHL hip, and target is SHL hand. Finally, in Figs. 7, 8, 9, 10 and 11(c) source is SHL hip, whereas target is SAR. The horizontal axis represents the ratio of target data used in the experiment. For example, in the experiment represented by Fig. 7a SHL hand data is the source and SHL hip is the target. Lines on the chart represent results of two tests.

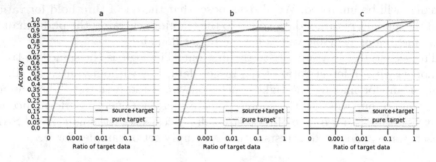

**Fig. 7.** Results for deep model.

**Discussion.** The results of the provided tests show that deep model is the most resistant model from DA perspective. Its performance remains high even when no target data was added to the training set. For example Fig. 7a: 89% out of maximum 95% for that dataset. We also conclude that domains could be of different complexity.

Dense network from Fig. 8 has a gap of 5–6% from the deep model. It means that deep learning approach to feature extraction is more accurate. Despite this, dense model's performance under DA task is not inferior to the deep model. We can conclude that network-based classification methods are better at learning general information than other proposed approaches.

Logistic regression, Fig. 9, provides impressive results in activity classification (up to 99%), however, it's performance degrades when the amount of training

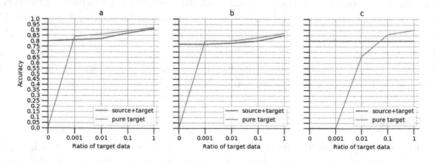

**Fig. 8.** Results for MLP model.

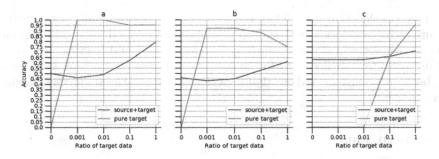

**Fig. 9.** Results for Logistics regression.

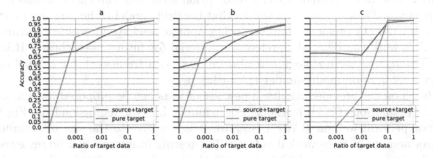

**Fig. 10.** Results for Random Forest.

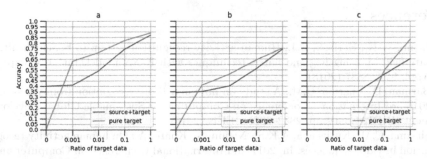

**Fig. 11.** Results for KNN.

data increases. That may be also the reason for poor performance in DA, as this test assumes having one of SHL sets in full size. Random Forest, Fig. 10, also provide good performance in classification, but accuracy on DA is low. KNN Fig. 11, fails to perform high results in both classification and domain adaptation. That is probably because of data is high dimensional (the curse of dimensionality).

Deep model's feature extraction is really more accurate than hand-crafted features. Network-based architectures also show better resistance to domain gap, than classical approaches. But, some classical approaches outperform deep model in simple classification task. They are also more computationally inexpensive. An interesting conclusion is that deep models could be used for creation latent variables while classical models such as Random Forest and Logistic regression will use provided labelled data for classification. Logistic regression is suitable here because we have figured out that it performs better if the amount of training data is not big.

## 5    Conclusion

In this work, we have provided detailed statistics on the performance of traditional approaches to human activity recognition both from classification and DA perspectives. These results have shown that the deep model is the best approach to solving the DA problem. However, other approaches have interesting features too. This work can be used as reference material for future researches in HAR DA. The testing methodology can also be used as a framework for evaluation activity recognition models under DA task.

Based on the provided results, a new set of tests can be proposed for a more specific evaluation of HAR methods. For example, Logistic regression from Fig. 9 did not perform well on DA test because it is sensitive to the size of training dataset and in our framework it is large. The testing framework can be reviewed and changed in order to take into account the specifics of every model.

## References

1. Jasim, W.N., Harfash, E.J.: Human activity recognition system to benefit health-care field by using hog and harris techniques with K-NN model. Int. J. Comput. Appl. **975**, 8887 (2018)
2. Barman, D., Sharma, U.M.: A study on human activity recognition from video. In: 2016 3rd International Conference on Computing for Sustainable Global Development (INDIACom), pp. 2832–2835. IEEE (2016)
3. Sharma, C.M., Kushwaha, A.K.S., Nigam, S., Khare, A.: On human activity recognition in video sequences. In: 2011 2nd International Conference on Computer and Communication Technology, ICCCT 2011, pp. 152–158. IEEE (2011)
4. Wang, Y., Huang, K., Tan, T.: Human activity recognition based on r transform. In: 2007 IEEE Conference on Computer Vision and Pattern Recognition, pp. 1–8. IEEE (2007)
5. Giannakopoulos, T., Siantikos, G.: A ROS framework for audio-based activity recognition. In: Proceedings of the 9th ACM International Conference on PErvasive Technologies Related to Assistive Environments, p. 41. ACM (2016)
6. Asghari, P., Nazerfard, E.: Activity recognition using hierarchical hidden Markov models on streaming sensor data. In: 2018 9th International Symposium on Telecommunications (IST), pp. 416–420. IEEE (2018)
7. Chereshnev, R., Kertész-Farkas, A.: RapidHARe: a computationally inexpensive method for real-time human activity recognition from wearable sensors. J. Ambient Intell. Smart Environ. **10**(5), 377–391 (2018)

8. Khan, A.M., Tufail, A., Khattak, A.M., Laine, T.H.: Activity recognition on smartphones via sensor-fusion and KDA-based SVMs. Int. J. Distrib. Sens. Netw. **10**(5), 503291 (2014)
9. Khan, A.M., Lee, Y.-K., Lee, S.-Y., Kim, T.-S.: Human activity recognition via an accelerometer-enabled-smartphone using Kernel discriminant analysis. In: 2010 5th International Conference on Future Information Technology, pp. 1–6. IEEE (2010)
10. Saputri, T.R.D., Khan, A.M., Lee, S.-W.: User-independent activity recognition via three-stage GA-based feature selection. Int. J. Distrib. Sens. Netw. **10**(3), 706287 (2014)
11. Wang, J., Chen, Y., Hu, L., Peng, X., Philip, S.Yu.: Stratified transfer learning for cross-domain activity recognition. In: 2018 IEEE International Conference on Pervasive Computing and Communications (PerCom), pp. 1–10. IEEE (2018)
12. Soleimani, E., Nazerfard, E.: Cross-subject transfer learning in human activity recognition systems using generative adversarial networks. arXiv preprint arXiv:1903.12489 (2019)
13. Zeng, M., Yu, T., Wang, X., Nguyen, L.T., Mengshoel, O.J., Lane, I.: Semi-supervised convolutional neural networks for human activity recognition. In: 2017 IEEE International Conference on Big Data (Big Data), pp. 522–529. IEEE (2017)
14. Wang, J., Chen, Y., Hao, S., Peng, X., Lisha, H.: Deep learning for sensor-based activity recognition: a survey. Pattern Recogn. Lett. **119**, 3–11 (2019)
15. Bulling, A., Blanke, U., Schiele, B.: A tutorial on human activity recognition using body-worn inertial sensors. ACM Comput. Surv. (CSUR) **46**(3), 33 (2014)
16. Khan, A.M., Lee, Y.-K., Lee, S.Y., Kim, T.-S.: A triaxial accelerometer-based physical-activity recognition via augmented-signal features and a hierarchical recognizer. IEEE Trans. Inf. Technol. Biomed. **14**(5), 1166–1172 (2010)
17. Khan, A., Siddiqi, M., Lee, S.-W.: Exploratory data analysis of acceleration signals to select light-weight and accurate features for real-time activity recognition on smartphones. Sensors **13**(10), 13099–13122 (2013)
18. Preece, S.J., Goulermas, J.Y., Kenney, L.P.J., Howard, D.: A comparison of feature extraction methods for the classification of dynamic activities from accelerometer data. IEEE Trans. Biomed. Eng. **56**(3), 871–879 (2008)
19. Chathuramali, K.G.M., Rodrigo, R.: Faster human activity recognition with SVM. In: International Conference on Advances in ICT for Emerging Regions (ICTer2012), pp. 197–203. IEEE (2012)
20. Fan, L., Wang, Z., Wang, H.: Human activity recognition model based on decision tree. In: 2013 International Conference on Advanced Cloud and Big Data, pp. 64–68. IEEE (2013)
21. Paul, P., George, T.: An effective approach for human activity recognition on smartphone. In: 2015 IEEE International Conference on Engineering and Technology (Icetech), pp. 1–3. IEEE (2015)
22. Chorowski, J.K., Bahdanau, D., Serdyuk, D., Cho, K., Bengio, Y.: Attention-based models for speech recognition. In: Advances in Neural Information Processing Systems, pp. 577–585 (2015)
23. Pandey, H.M., Windridge, D.: A comprehensive classification of deep learning libraries. In: Yang, X.-S., Sherratt, S., Dey, N., Joshi, A. (eds.) Third International Congress on Information and Communication Technology. AISC, vol. 797, pp. 427–435. Springer, Singapore (2019). https://doi.org/10.1007/978-981-13-1165-9_40
24. Szegedy, C., et al.: Going deeper with convolutions. In: Proceedings of the IEEE Conference on Computer Vision and Pattern Recognition, pp. 1–9 (2015)

25. Plötz, T., Hammerla, N.Y., Olivier, P.L.: Feature learning for activity recognition in ubiquitous computing. In: Twenty-Second International Joint Conference on Artificial Intelligence (2011)
26. Ronao, C.A., Cho, S.-B.: Deep convolutional neural networks for human activity recognition with smartphone sensors. In: Arik, S., Huang, T., Lai, W.K., Liu, Q. (eds.) ICONIP 2015. LNCS, vol. 9492, pp. 46–53. Springer, Cham (2015). https:// doi.org/10.1007/978-3-319-26561-2_6
27. Xue, L., et al.: Understanding and improving deep neural network for activity recognition. arXiv preprint arXiv:1805.07020 (2018)
28. Hochreiter, S., Schmidhuber, J.: Long short-term memory. Neural Comput. **9**(8), 1735–1780 (1997)
29. Ordóñez, F., Roggen, D.: Deep convolutional and lstm recurrent neural networks for multimodal wearable activity recognition. Sensors **16**(1), 115 (2016)
30. Hammerla, N.Y., Halloran, S., Plötz, T.: Deep, convolutional, and recurrent models for human activity recognition using wearables. arXiv preprint arXiv:1604.08880 (2016)
31. Guan, Y., Plötz, T.: Ensembles of deep LSTM learners for activity recognition using wearables. Proc. ACM Interact. Mob. Wear. Ubiquit. Technol. **1**(2), 11 (2017)
32. Zeng, M., et al.: Understanding and improving recurrent networks for human activity recognition by continuous attention. In: Proceedings of the 2018 ACM International Symposium on Wearable Computers, pp. 56–63. ACM, (2018)
33. Khan, A.M., Lee, Y.-K., Kim, T.-S.: Accelerometer signal-based human activity recognition using augmented autoregressive model coefficients and artificial neural nets. In: 2008 30th Annual International Conference of the IEEE Engineering in Medicine and Biology Society, pp. 5172–5175. IEEE (2008)
34. Chatterjee, S.K., et al.: Comparison of decision tree based classification strategies to detect external chemical stimuli from raw and filtered plant electrical response. Sens. Actuators B: Chem. **249**, 278–295 (2017)
35. Xiaowei, L.: Application of decision tree classification method based on information entropy to web marketing. In: 2014 Sixth International Conference on Measuring Technology and Mechatronics Automation, pp. 121–127. IEEE (2014)
36. Brzezinski, J.R., Knafl, G.J.: Logistic regression modeling for context-based classification. In: Proceedings of Tenth International Workshop on Database and Expert Systems Applications, DEXA 1999, pp. 755–759. IEEE (1999)
37. Kang, K., Gao, F., Feng, J.: A new multi-layer classification method based on logistic regression. In: 2018 13th International Conference on Computer Science & Education (ICCSE), pp. 1–4. IEEE (2018)
38. Shoaib, M., Bosch, S., Incel, O., Scholten, H., Havinga, P.: Fusion of smartphone motion sensors for physical activity recognition. Sensors **14**(6), 10146–10176 (2014)
39. Howard, A.G., et al.: MobileNets: efficient convolutional neural networks for mobile vision applications. arXiv preprint arXiv:1704.04861 (2017)

# Spontaneous Emotion Recognition in Response to Videos

Alisa Gazizullina[(✉)] and Manuel Mazzara

Institute of Software Development and Engineering,
Innopolis University, Innopolis, Russia
{a.gazizullina,m.mazzara}@innopolis.ru

**Abstract.** In order to understand human emotions correctly taking into account only facial expressions, we are conducting the experiments on the spontaneous emotional facial videos of people watching musical video clips from *DEAP* open source dataset. We are reporting the comparative results of emotion recognition done in two ways: sequential extraction of spatial and temporal features done by CNN-RNN, simultaneous extraction of both types of features performed by 3D convolutions in our C3D networks architecture. In order to study the contribution of microexpressions to emotion recognition we are augmenting videos in two ways: reducing to 1 fps, thus losing a significant amount of temporal information, reducing to 10 fps, thus preserving most of the muscle movement information.

**Keywords:** Emotion detection · Emotion detection from videos · DEAP dataset · Emotion prediction from DEAP dataset

## 1 Introduction

Emotion recognition research goes back to 1872 when Charles Darwin in his work The Expression of the Emotions in Man and Animals [5] through the discovery of the fact that humans and animals follow a similar pattern when expressing emotions has suggested that emotions are universal. His ideas gave rise to the emotion recognition research that seeks for a way for the machines to estimate the psychological and physiological state of the person in order to provide a better user experience. Besides its long history, there is still no 100% accurate model determining exact emotions correctly. The reason is that the emotion recognition experiment involves a lot of free variable: emotional theory used, discrete or dimensional [2]; modalities studied [4], facial expressions, electroencephalogram [18], galvanic skin response [6], voice [1], etc.; number of modalities analyzed, unimodal, multimodal [12]; nature of emotions, spontaneous [19] or acted [7]; emotion elicitation techniques used to gather the data [3].

In the early research, emotion recognition frameworks were making their focus on a single modality/measure. The tolerable prediction results, performance and rather simple complexity of such an approach keeps uni-modal emotion recognition relevant up to today. Facial expressions are generally assumed to

© Springer Nature Switzerland AG 2019
M. Mazzara et al. (Eds.): TOOLS 2019, LNCS 11771, pp. 203–209, 2019.
https://doi.org/10.1007/978-3-030-29852-4_16

be the base modality for the emotion recognition system. Tomkins has reported in his work [14] that emotional affects are closely linked to the face and motivation. He was the first to demonstrate that facial expressions were associated with certain emotional states [15]. Thus, we are aimed to analyze a single frame dimension of multimodal video data, focusing on facial expressions to more broadly investigate the role of human's facial expressions to read the emotions.

We are also aimed to analyze the spontaneously expressed emotions as a model trained on videos of people acting spontaneously will generalize with stronger confidence for the real-life data. The data for spontaneous emotions is specific, as it contains microexpressions. Microexpressions are conscious actions of suppressing the facial expressions when they occur on the face inappropriately. Paul Ekman in late 19's discovered the importance of the ability to be able to detect microexpressions from videos. He was analyzing a video of a patient suffering from depression, who attempted to commit a suicide [17]. Ekman recognized brief and intense sadness of a patient that has quickly changed to the smile. This was the starting point in microexpression recognition from facial expressions research. Microexpressions contain a significant amount of information about the true emotions. They are difficult to analyze due to the short duration and brief nature of movements. Modern methods based on deep models achieve good results analyzing microexpressions from facial videos. These models mostly rely on the representative power features extracted by deep 3-dimensional convolutional network (C3D) or by the hybrid of convolutional neural network and recurrent neural network (CNN-RNN), as well as on the effectiveness of video preprocessing steps, such as temporal and spatial frame normalization and rich features extraction (optical flow, frame patching).

This research is aimed to construct a framework being able to map humans' facial expressions to valence, arousal and dominance values responsible to represent a particular emotional state. Our networks designed to solve multitask binary classification recognition task (i.e. prediction of valence, arousal, and dominance as separate tasks). We base our experiments on two types of models: CNN-LSTM and C3D network. Also, provide performance results of two models on video data preprocessed spatially in two ways: either by aligning detected faces and then cropping them or by just cropping faces with no alignment. We also apply and report the affect of the use of different ways to do temporal normalization: keyframe extraction to shorten original videos to 1 fps, frame skipping to shorten videos to 10 fps.

## 2   The Dataset

In this research, we use a multimodal database for Emotion Analysis using Physiological Signals *DEAP* [9]. The database consists of electroencephalogram (EEG), galvanic skin response (GSR), electrooculography (EOG) and peripheral physiological signals of 32 participants. Also for the 22 participants, frontal face videos were also recorded during the experiment session. The experiment was constructed in such a way that while each of the participants was watching

40-min long excerpts of music video clip physiological signals, EEG, facial videos were recorded and each participant also rated the videos. For this research, we restrict ourselves to the facial videos only, as we want to asses the power of facial expressions to represent humans emotions. For that purpose, we took the subset of the DEAP dataset which consisted of facial videos for 22 participants labeled their physiological and psychological states measured during the experimental session. Each person took part in 40 trials, so in the dataset there are 40 videos for each of 22 people, in total, we get about $22 \times 40 = 880$ videos in total. Each video is labeled in terms of valence, arousal, dominance and liking with each taking values in the 1–9 range.

## 3    Data Preprocessing

Videos on our dataset are converted to frame sequences and then undergo one of the two types of preprocessing: normalization and alignment or go only through normalization. Normalization is done in spatial as well as in temporal domains [11]. For the spacial normalization we crop all the frames by contours of the bounding boxes of detected faces to the sizes special for different types of networks (i.e. ResNet-LSTM pre-trained on ImageNet2012 supports image sizes of $224 \times 224$, C3D networks pre-trained on Sports1M support images of size $112 \times 112$, and $95 \times 95$ is the size of the images typical for face recognition pipeline that reduces the computation time and memory load). Faces are detected by the Dlib's DNN model. We have stopped on the two types of temporal augmentations for the training videos: reduced to 1 fps using ffmpeg's keyframe extractor, reduced to 10 fps using frame skipping approach. We have constructed two sets of videos *DEAP_CROPPED* and *DEAP_ALIGNED* that are different by the spatial normalization applied. The last step of the video normalization - face cropping, requires bounding box coordinates smoothing across time, we have used approaches similar to SGD with momentum and Mean Average Smoothing.

All the images are converted to grayscale, after that standard normalization method using training dataset statistics (mean, standard deviation) are applied to each frame in the resulting dataset.

## 4    The Proposed Methods

In this section we are going to describe the two architectures we constructed for emotion recognition from videos: CNN-RNN, C3D network. Both networks are trained end-to-end for the emotion recognition in the Valence-Arousal-Dominance space and are optimized for multitask binary classification, predicting classes for 3 categories: *high* or *low* for *valence*, *arousal* and *dominance* (reconstructing original labels from 1–9 range to 1–0 range, using the $\geq 6$ thresholding).

**CNN-RNN Network.** Previous research shows that RNN models can achieve good results in emotion recognition tasks [8,13],

In our CNN-RNN hybrid model, we use CNN as a feature extractors which act on videos at the frame level, learning features for each frame separately, thus not taking into account temporal relationships between frames. ResNet-18 architecture is used as a backbone for the CNN part of our network. Prior to using CNN model as a part of hybrid model we have pre-trained it on large emotional datasets VGGFace2 and Facial Expression Recognition database (Fer2013+). CNN receives as input images with a batch size equal the length of the sequence (55 frames or 600 frames), then as all these features are extracted from one video we stack them and pass to the LSTM for later classification.

**C3D Network.** Deep 3-dimensional convolutional networks are commonly adopted for video classification tasks. C3D networks, unlike CNN-RNN models, can model appearance and motion information simultaneously.

1. **C3D+Sport1M architecture.** For the model used in our research, we took the C3D network consisting of 8 convolutions, 5 max-pooling layers, and 3 Fully connected layers, followed by sigmoid for multitask binary classification. As we use model pretrained on Sports1M, that contain videos of length 16 and $112 \times 112$ of width and height, we are randomly sampling 16 frames from our training videos and cropping them to the corresponding spatial sizes.
2. **C3D+1 fps / C3D+10 fps architecture.** For the 3D CNN network trained on longer sequences of images, we are using a slight modification of the C3D network architecture described above. We resize images to $95 \times 95$ in order to ensure adequate learning time. A number of convolutional, pooling layers their configurations, structure, and kernel sizes are the same as in the C3D+Sport1M model. The only thing we have changed is that we replaced the last three Fully connected layers to the global average pooling. Fully connected layers end up having a very large number of weights. Thus, they require a large amount of computational power, may cause overfitting by memorizing the training examples rather than generalizing from them. The use of global average pooling serves as a regularization as well as allows to save the computation. It completely replaces fully connected layers in the top of the network by computing the mean value for each feature map and supplies it to a softmax layer.

## 5    Evaluation and Discussion

In this section, we are going to describe the performance of our models on the emotion recognition task. We train CNN-LSTM and C3D network models for the multitask binary classification tasks separately to compare the performance of two different deep architectures on the spontaneous emotion prediction when dealing with microexpressions.

**Experimental Setting.** Our models were implemented on Pytorch [10] and we used a GPU Server with NVIDIA Tesla V100 (16 GB) graphics processor for training and testing our models. Both CNN-LSTM and C3D networks are trained using Binary Cross Entropy (BCE) for the multi-label

Table 1. Comparative results of C3D and CNN-RNN models

| Model | F1 arousal | F1 valence | F1 dominance | ROC-AUC |
|---|---|---|---|---|
| CNN-LSTM + 1 fps + *DEAP_ALIGN* | 0.557 | 0.4 | 0.3 | 0.5 |
| CNN-LSTM + 10 fps + *DEAP_CROPPED* | 0.59 | 0.51 | 0.45 | 0.62 |
| C3D + Sport1M + *DEAP_CROPPED* | 0.609 | 0.5 | 0.54 | 0.56 |
| C3D + 1 fps + *DEAP_ALIGN* | 0.618 | 0.577 | 0.597 | 0.576 |
| C3D + 10 fps + *DEAP_ALIGN* | 0.75 | 0.69 | 0.7 | 0.8 |
| Tripathi, Samarth, et al. | 0.57 | 0.66 | - | - |

**Tripathi, Samarth, et al.** refers to the model described in [16] based on the deep convolutional neural network fitted on the same *DEAP* database videos. However, it has to be noted that f1-score of the given model has to be even lower as we have put to the current table the accuracy score measured by authors instead of f1-score which is more accurate (authors did not report the results on f1-score).

multi-output classification. For the optimization technique, we use Stochastic Gradient Descent (SGD) with the learning rate of $1e - 3$, weight decay $5e - 4$, momentum 0.9. In order to ensure that while optimizing the network we did not miss local optimum and to make the model generalize better to unseen data, we are using Cyclic learning rate scheduler. Training is done in 100 epochs with batch sizes of 1 and 4 for the datasets of 10 fps and 1 fps videos respectively. The input dimensions for LSTM-CNN network are either $4 \times 1 \times 224 \times 224 \times 55$ (1 fps) or $4 \times 1 \times 224 \times 224 \times 600$ (10 fps), and for the C3D networks either $1 \times 1 \times 112 \times 112 \times 16$ or $1 \times 1 \times 95 \times 95 \times 55$ or $1 \times 1 \times 95 \times 95 \times 600$. Both of our models are trained on two versions of the same DEAP dataset: DEAP_ALIGN and DEAP_CROPPED. The first one was constructed by applying face cropping and alignment, while the other constructed to preserve the head rotations with no alignment applied.

**Experimental Results.** Table 1 makes come to the conclusion that C3D networks that perform temporal and sequential modeling subsequently are able to learn more rich features compared to CNN-RNN models first operating on the spatial level and then capturing the sequential nature of the data. While training the network with the videos reduced to 1 fps (i.e. sequences of 55 frames) by keyframe extraction we have discovered that the network is not learning much and nearly overfits. This happens as microexpressions are of short duration and they might be lost with the interpolated or skipped frames. This leads us to give up speed and stick to 10 fps.

## 6 Conclusion

In this paper, we have designed two deep models for the task of spontaneous emotion recognition. First one is based on the frame level features extraction prior to extraction of video level features, while the second one extracts spatial and temporal features simultaneously with the use of 3D convolutions over the frame sequence. We have reported and compared the measures of the ability of both approaches to recognize in the 3D Valence-Arousal-Dominance space emotions from facial videos. We have discovered that C3D networks are better suited for the micro-emotional nature of the DEAP dataset. Also, we have conducted the experiments on different temporal and spatial augmentations of videos varying the length, receptive field size and interest object's orientation to determine whether the microexpressions captured in a video augmented to a longer duration or head movements affected by alignment are critical for the emotion recognition from facial expressions. The conclusion we made is that microexpressions and head rotations when preserved lead to better recognition results.

## References

1. Alu, D., Zoltan, E., Stoica, I.C.: Voice based emotion recognition with convolutional neural networks for companion robots. Sci. Technol. **20**(3), 222–240 (2017)
2. Barrett, L.F., Robin, L., Pietromonaco, P.R., Eyssell, K.M.: Are women the "more emotional" sex? Evidence from emotional experiences in social context. Cogn. Emot. **12**(4), 555–578 (1998)
3. Braun, M., Weiser, S., Pfleging, B., Alt, F.: A comparison of emotion elicitation methods for affective driving studies, pp. 77–81 September 2018. https://doi.org/10.1145/3239092.3265945
4. Castellano, G., Kessous, L., Caridakis, G.: Emotion recognition through multiple modalities: face, body gesture, speech. In: Peter, C., Beale, R. (eds.) Affect and Emotion in Human-Computer Interaction. LNCS, vol. 4868, pp. 92–103. Springer, Heidelberg (2008). https://doi.org/10.1007/978-3-540-85099-1_8
5. Darwin, C.: The Expression of the Emotions in Man and Animals (1872). The original was published 1898 by Appleton, New York. Reprinted 1965 by the University of Chicago Press, Chicago and London
6. Das, P., Khasnobish, A., Tibarewala, D.: Emotion recognition employing ECG and GSR signals as markers of ANS. In: 2016 Conference on Advances in Signal Processing (CASP), pp. 37–42. IEEE (2016)
7. Dhall, A., Goecke, R., Lucey, S., Gedeon, T., et al.: Collecting large, richly annotated facial-expression databases from movies. IEEE multimedia **19**(3), 34–41 (2012)
8. Fan, Y., Lu, X., Li, D., Liu, Y.: Video-based emotion recognition using CNN-RNN and C3D hybrid networks. In: Proceedings of the 18th ACM International Conference on Multimodal Interaction ICMI 2016, pp. 445–450. ACM, New York (2016). https://doi.org/10.1145/2993148.2997632
9. Koelstra, S., et al.: Deap: a database for emotion analysis; using physiological signals. IEEE Trans. Affect. Comput. **3**(1), 18–31 (2012). https://doi.org/10.1109/T-AFFC.2011.15

10. Paszke, A., et al.: Automatic differentiation in pytorch (2017)
11. Peng, M., Wang, C., Chen, T., Liu, G., Fu, X.: Dual temporal scale convolutional neural network for micro-expression recognition. Front. psychol. **8**, 1745 (2017)
12. Soleymani, M., Pantic, M., Pun, T.: Multimodal emotion recognition in response to videos. IEEE Trans. Affect. Comput. **3**(2), 211–223 (2011)
13. Sun, M.C., Hsu, S.H., Yang, M.C., Chien, J.H.: Context-aware cascade attention-based RNN for video emotion recognition. In: 2018 First Asian Conference on Affective Computing and Intelligent Interaction (ACII Asia), pp. 1–6. IEEE (2018)
14. Tomkins, S.S.: Affect, Imagery, Consciousness. Springer, Heidelberg (1962)
15. Tomkins, S.S., McCarter, R.: What and where are the primary affects? Some evidence for a theory. Percept. Mot. Skills **18**(1), 119–158 (1964). https://doi.org/10.2466/pms.1964.18.1.119
16. Tripathi, S., Acharya, S., Sharma, R.D., Mittal, S., Bhattacharya, S.: Using deep and convolutional neural networks for accurate emotion classification on DEAP dataset. In: Twenty-Ninth IAAI Conference (2017)
17. Vrij, A.: Book review - 'Telling lies: clues to deceit in the marketplace, politics, and marriage' by Paul Ekman. Int. J. Police Sci. Manag. **5**, 209–210 (2003). https://doi.org/10.1350/ijps.5.3.209.16063
18. Wu, S., Xu, X., Shu, L., Hu, B.: Estimation of valence of emotion using two frontal EEG channels. In: 2017 IEEE International Conference on Bioinformatics and Biomedicine (BIBM), pp. 1127–1130. IEEE (2017)
19. Zeng, Z., Hu, Y., Roisman, G.I., Wen, Z., Fu, Y., Huang, T.S.: Audio-visual spontaneous emotion recognition. In: Huang, T.S., Nijholt, A., Pantic, M., Pentland, A. (eds.) Artifical Intelligence for Human Computing. LNCS (LNAI), vol. 4451, pp. 72–90. Springer, Heidelberg (2007). https://doi.org/10.1007/978-3-540-72348-6_4

# CNN LSTM Network Architecture
# for Modeling Software Reliability

Kamill Gusmanov[(✉)]

Innopolis University, Innopolis, Russian Federation
k.gusmanov@innopolis.ru

**Abstract.** In this work, Convolutional Neural Network Long Short-Term Memory (CNN LSTM) architecture is proposed for modelling software reliability with time-series data. Evaluation of the model coming from 2 open source datasets that describe the development and testing of modern mobile operating systems - "Tizen" and "CyanogenMod". The results of the proposed model are compared with four parametric Software Reliability Growth Models and simple Convolutional Neural Network model using the Root Mean Squared Error (RMSE) metric.

**Keywords:** Neural Networks · CNN · LSTM ·
Software reliability modeling · Software Reliability Growth Models ·
Time-series forecasting

## 1 Introduction

Software reliability is directly connected to software failures because if a software is not correctly functioning there is the assumption that a software failure has occurred [1]. Typically, the reliability of software is measured with the number of defects that exist in the source code of the released software or with failures that happen during its execution [2]. Ability to model and predict software reliability of the systems provides more effective management of the overall development process [3–8]. This becomes even more important in nowadays environments, characterised by agile processes [9,10] and other forms of structuring the development process, like code reuse [11], and targeting a wide set of potentials users, as it happens in mobile applications [12,13], where also energy efficiency becomes of paramount importance [14].

In the previous work [15] software reliability approaches were classified as: (a) software reliability growth models, (b) multiple linear regression models, (c) Bayesian models, and (d) neural network models.

This work is based on the application of Convolutional Neural Network Long Short-Term Memory architecture for software reliability modelling, due to ability of CNN models for good feature extraction technique and LSTM models to ability "of learning long-term dependencies" [16].

We thank Innopolis University for generously supporting this research.

M. Mazzara et al. (Eds.): TOOLS 2019, LNCS 11771, pp. 210–217, 2019.
https://doi.org/10.1007/978-3-030-29852-4_17

This paper is organized as follows. Section 2 discusses the related work. Section 3 details our approach and our experiments. Section 4 presents the results that we have obtained so far and discusses them. Section 5 draws some conclusions and outlines the lines of future research.

## 2    Related Works

Neural networks can be used to perform various tasks, as discussed extensively by Gamboa [17] and evidenced in several other works [18–20].

Selvin et al. [21] compares Recurrent Neural Networks (RNN), Long Short-Term Memory (LSTM) Networks and Convolutional Neural Networks (CNN) in time-series forecasting using a sliding window method for creating training data. Comparison of RNN and CNN for multivariate time-series data was made in the work of Groß et al. [22].

Paper of Borovykh et al. [23] proposed application of WaveNet architecture [24] for conditional time-series forecasting. The WaveNet architecture is based on the dilated causal convolution layer, "which allows it to properly treat temporal order and handle long-term dependencies without an explosion in model complexity" [25].

CNN-LSTM architecture for time-series forecasting was proposed in works of Wang et al. [26], Liu et al. [27], Lin et al. [28], Karim et al. [29], He [30]. There CNN model was used for feature extraction from the input data. The results of this model were fed to the LSTM model. Wang et al. [26] proposed CNN model with 5 layers: an input layer, convolution layer, sampling layer, fully connected layer and output layer. A paper of Liu et al. [27] based on the stock data and proposed CNN model feature extraction and judging stock trends.

## 3    Experimentation

Proposed CNN LSTM architecture and simple CNN model were developed using Keras Deep Learning Library [31].

### 3.1    Parametric SRGMs

Software reliability models can be classified into two types: (1) models that predict from data configurations and (2) models that predict from provided datasets of failures. One of the most frequently mentioned models is parametric Software Reliability Growth Models. The performance of parametric SRGMs strongly depends on prior assumptions about the data, i.e. software reliability depends on the type of the dataset [32]. Thus, to apply parametric SRGMs engineers have to manually select multiple software reliability models and apply them in parallel. Although some of the models can give good results, no single parametric SRGM can equally well perform on the different data [33].

We considered four well-known traditional parametric SRGMs: Goel-Okumoto concave model, Goel-Okumoto S-shaped model, Logistic model and Weibull model. We used 80% of every dataset to train our models and looked how well the remaining part of the cumulative curve has been fitted.

## 3.2 CNN Model

As CNN model a one-dimensional CNN was used. This model has a convolutional hidden layer that operates over a 1D sequence and pooling hidden layer. These layers are followed by a flatten layer to reduce the feature maps to a single one-dimensional vector, which is feeding to a dense fully connected layer that interprets the features extracted by the convolutional part of the model.

Mean Squared Error (MSE) metric was used as a loss function of the model and Adam algorithm [34] as an optimizer.

## 3.3 CNN LSTM Model

LSTM is a recurrent neural network architecture that has been adopted for time-series forecasting. Adding a convolutional layer at the top of LSTM layers can be extremely helpful to capture local, temporal patterns. Convolutional part of the model contains: a convolutional hidden layer, a pooling hidden layer, and a flatten layer as a simple CNN model. The output of the flatten layer was fed to the two stacked hidden LSTM models that followed by a dense layer to provide the output.

## 3.4 Datasets

In this work, two open source datasets were extracted from open online resources that describe the development and testing of modern mobile operating systems, Tizen and CyanogenMod. For **Tizen** the data was collected from the corresponding issue tracking system of the project. It based on 5590 bugs during 1327 days of development (Fig. 1). For **CyanogenMod** the data was collected from the project's issue tracking system. It based on 10674 bugs during 1040 days of development (Fig. 2).

The use of Open Source data is particularly important, as it promote the comparison of these results, the replication of the experiments, and the creation of a community around this area of science [35–39].

This work face with supervised learning for univariate time series data, where only a single variable is observed at each time (in our case it is the number of found bugs for every timestep). Thus, data transformation is needed. The most common approach for time-series data is a sliding window method. For the training set we do the following:

1. Take first N values (from 1 to N) of the cumulative number of failures as input (X).
2. Take value with index $N + 1$ as the output (Y).
3. Move window of size N and take new input values from 2 to $N + 1$ index and output from $N + 2$ index.
4. Repeat these steps and create two input and output vectors.

After fitting the model we need to make predictions of the future number of bugs based on the previous data. For this the following steps are made:

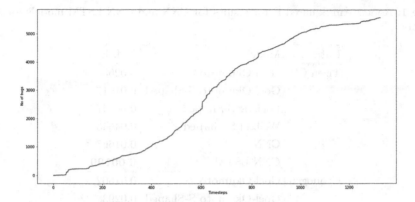

**Fig. 1.** Data from issue tracking system of the "Tizen OS" project

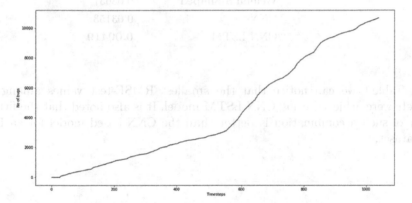

**Fig. 2.** Data from issue tracking system of the "Cyanogen" project

1. Feed the vector with last N values from the training data to the model as input.
2. Take predicted value and add it to the end of the input vector (now vector contains N + 1 values).
3. Remove the first value from the input vector and feed a new vector of size N as input to the model.
4. Repeat this process for generating predictions of the remaining 20% of the original data.

## 4   Results and Discussion

In the previous section, we described models and datasets of this work. To compare the fitting and predictive power of described models, meaningful performance criteria is needed. In this experiment, we utilize the Root Mean Squared Error (RMSE) metric.

**Table 1.** Root Mean Squared Error results for CNN and CNN LSTM models for two datasets.

| Dataset | Model | RMSE |
|---|---|---|
| Tizen OS | Goel-Okumoto | 0.0265 |
| | Goel-Okumoto S-Shaped | 0.01917 |
| | Logistic S-Shaped | 0.00647 |
| | Weibull S-Shaped | 0.04645 |
| | CNN | 0.01667 |
| | CNN LSTM | **0.00199** |
| Cyanogen | Goel-Okumoto | 0.01502 |
| | Goel-Okumoto S-Shaped | 0.02938 |
| | Logistic S-Shaped | 0.0812 |
| | Weibull S-Shaped | 0.03631 |
| | CNN | 0.03153 |
| | CNN LSTM | **0.00419** |

In Table 1 we can notice that the smallest RMSE-test values among all datasets were achieved using CNN LSTM model. It is also noted that the fitting power of such a combination is better than the CNN-based model for each of the dataset.

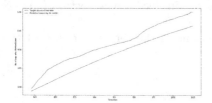

(a) CNN model for "Tizen OS" project.

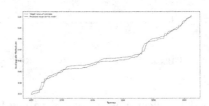

(b) CNN LSTM model for "Tizen OS" project.

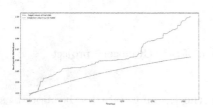

(c) CNN model for "Cyanogen" project.

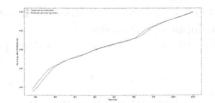

(d) CNN LSTM model for "Cyanogen" project.

**Fig. 3.** Comparisons of the real test data and predicted by models

Figure 3a and b show plots of the real test data compared to the predicted by CNN and CNN LSTM data of "Tizen OS" project. Figure 3c and d show the same for the "Cyanogen" project.

## 5    Conclusion

In modern software engineering, reliability issues are very important. This paper has proposed a Convolutional Neural Network Long Short-Term Memory architecture to modelling software reliability. Results show that that proposed model works better with low RMSE values that simple Convolutional Neural Network model. Next steps will update the neural network model by applying autoencoder networks and extend the results considering also additional data coming from software metrics [40,41].

## References

1. Kumar, A.: Software reliability growth models, tools and data sets-a review. In: Proceedings of the 9th India Software Engineering Conference, pp. 80–88. ACM (2016)
2. Wood, A.: Software reliability growth models. Tandem technical report, vol. 96, no. 130056 (1996)
3. Succi, G., Pedrycz, W., Stefanovic, M., Russo, B.: An investigation on the occurrence of service requests in commercial software applications. Empir. Softw. Eng. 8(2), 197–215 (2003)
4. Rossi, B., Russo, B., Succi, G.: Modelling failures occurrences of open source software with reliability growth. In: Ågerfalk, P., Boldyreff, C., González-Barahona, J.M., Madey, G.R., Noll, J. (eds.) OSS 2010. IAICT, vol. 319, pp. 268–280. Springer, Heidelberg (2010). https://doi.org/10.1007/978-3-642-13244-5_21
5. Ivanov, V., Mazzara, M., Pedrycz, W., Sillitti, A., Succi, G.: Assessing the process of an Eastern European software SME using systemic analysis, GQM, and reliability growth models: a case study. In: Proceedings of the 38th International Conference on Software Engineering Companion (ICSE 2016), Austin, Texas, pp. 251–259. ACM, May 2016
6. Ivanov, V., Reznik, A., Succi, G.: Comparing the reliability of software systems: a case study on mobile operating systems. Inf. Sci. 423, 398–411 (2018)
7. Succi, G., Ivanov, V.: Comparison of mobile operating systems based on models of growth reliability of the software. Comput. Res. Model. 10(3), 325–334 (2018)
8. Moser, R., Pedrycz, W., Succi G.: Analysis of the reliability of a subset of change metrics for defect prediction. In: Proceedings of the Second ACM-IEEE International Symposium on Empirical Software Engineering and Measurement, pp. 309–311. ACM (2008)
9. Kivi, J., Haydon, D., Hayes, J., Schneider, R., Succi, G.: Extreme programming: a university team design experience. In: 2000 Canadian Conference on Electrical and Computer Engineering, Conference Proceedings, Navigating to a New Era (Cat. No.00TH8492), vol. 2, pp. 816–820, May 2000
10. Fronza, I., Sillitti, A., Succi, G.: An interpretation of the results of the analysis of pair programming during novices integration in a team. In: Proceedings of the 2009 3rd International Symposium on Empirical Software Engineering and Measurement, ESEM 2009, pp. 225–235. IEEE Computer Society (2009)

11. Valerio, A., Succi, G., Fenaroli, M.: Domain analysis and framework-based software development. SIGAPP Appl. Comput. Rev. **5**, 4–15 (1997)
12. Corral, L., Sillitti, A., Succi, G., Garibbo, A., Ramella, P.: Evolution of mobile software development from platform-specific to web-based multiplatform paradigm. In: Proceedings of the 10th SIGPLAN Symposium on New Ideas, New Paradigms, and Reflections on Programming and Software, Onward! 2011, (New York, NY, USA), pp. 181–183. ACM (2011)
13. Corral, L., Sillitti, A., Succi, G.: Software development processes for mobile systems: is agile really taking over the business? In: 2013 1st International Workshop on the Engineering of Mobile-Enabled Systems (MOBS), pp. 19–24, May 2013
14. Corral, L., Georgiev, A. B., Sillitti, A., Succi, G.: A method for characterizing energy consumption in Android smartphones. In: Green and Sustainable Software (GREENS 2013), pp. 38–45. IEEE, May 2013
15. Gusmanov, K.: On the adoption of neural networks in modeling software reliability. In: Proceedings of the 2018 26th ACM Joint Meeting on European Software Engineering Conference and Symposium on the Foundations of Software Engineering, pp. 962–964. ACM (2018)
16. Understanding LSTM networks. https://colah.github.io/posts/2015-08-Understanding-LSTMs. Accessed 01 May 2019
17. Gamboa, J.C.B.: Deep learning for time-series analysis. arXiv preprint arXiv:1701.01887 (2017)
18. Pedrycz, W., Chun, M.-G., Succi, G.: N4: computing with neural receptive fields. Neurocomputing **55**(1), 383–401 (2003)
19. Pedrycz, W., Russo, B., Succi, G.: Knowledge transfer in system modeling and its realization through an optimal allocation of information granularity. Appl. Soft Comput. **12**, 1985–1995 (2012)
20. Pedrycz, W., Succi, G., Sillitti, A. (eds.): Computational Intelligence and Quantitative Software Engineering. Springer, Heidelberg (2016). https://doi.org/10.1007/978-3-319-25964-2
21. Selvin, S., Vinayakumar, R., Gopalakrishnan, E., Menon, V. K., Soman, K.: Stock price prediction using LSTM, RNN and CNN-sliding window model. In: 2017 International Conference on Advances in Computing, Communications and Informatics (ICACCI), pp. 1643–1647. IEEE (2017)
22. Groß, W., Lange, S., Bödecker, J., Blum, M.: Predicting time series with space-time convolutional and recurrent neural networks. In: Proceeding of European Symposium on Artificial Neural Networks, Computational Intelligence and Machine Learning, pp. 71–76 (2017)
23. Borovykh, A., Bohte, S., Oosterlee, C. W.: Conditional time series forecasting with convolutional neural networks. arXiv preprint arXiv:1703.04691 (2017)
24. Van Den Oord, A., et al.: WaveNet: a generative model for raw audio. In: SSW, vol. 125 (2016)
25. Joseph eddy blog. https://jeddy92.github.io/JEddy92.github.io/ts_seq2seq_conv. Accessed 01 May 2019
26. Wang, H., Yang, Z., Yu, Q., Hong, T., Lin, X.: Online reliability time series prediction via convolutional neural network and long short term memory for service-oriented systems. Knowl.-Based Syst. **159**, 132–147 (2018)
27. Liu, S., Zhang, C., Ma, J.: CNN-LSTM neural network model for quantitative strategy analysis in stock markets. In: Liu, D., Xie, S., Li, Y., Zhao, D., El-Alfy, E.S. (eds.) ICONIP 2017. LNCS, vol. 10635, pp. 198–206. Springer, Cham (2017). https://doi.org/10.1007/978-3-319-70096-0_21

28. Lin, T., Guo, T., Aberer, K.: Hybrid neural networks for learning the trend in time series. Technical report (2017)
29. Karim, F., Majumdar, S., Darabi, H., Chen, S.: Lstm fully convolutional networks for time series classification. IEEE Access **6**, 1662–1669 (2017)
30. He, W.: Load forecasting via deep neural networks. Procedia Comput. Sci. **122**, 308–314 (2017)
31. Keras homepage. https://keras.io. Accessed 01 May 2019
32. Lyu, M.R., et al.: Handbook of Software Reliability Engineering, vol. 222. IEEE Computer Society Press, Los Alamitos (1996)
33. Su, Y.-S., Huang, C.-Y.: Neural-network-based approaches for software reliability estimation using dynamic weighted combinational models. J. Syst. Softw. **80**(4), 606–615 (2007)
34. Kingma, D.P., Ba, J.: Adam: a method for stochastic optimization, arXiv preprint arXiv:1412.6980 (2014)
35. Succi, G., Paulson, J., Eberlein, A.: Preliminary results from an empirical study on the growth of open source and commercial software products. In: EDSER-3 Workshop, pp. 14–15 (2001)
36. Kovács, G. L., Drozdik, S., Zuliani, P., Succi, G.: Open source software for the public administration. In: Proceedings of the 6th International Workshop on Computer Science and Information Technologies, October 2004
37. Petrinja, E., Sillitti, A., Succi, G.: Comparing OpenBRR, QSOS, and OMM assessment models. In: Ågerfalk, P., Boldyreff, C., González-Barahona, J.M., Madey, G.R., Noll, J. (eds.) OSS 2010. IAICT, vol. 319, pp. 224–238. Springer, Heidelberg (2010). https://doi.org/10.1007/978-3-642-13244-5_18
38. Rossi, B., Russo, B., Succi, G.: Adoption of free/libre open source software in public organizations: factors of impact. Inf. Technol. People **25**(2), 156–187 (2012)
39. Di Bella, E., Sillitti, A., Succi, G.: A multivariate classification of open source developers. Inf. Sci. **221**, 72–83 (2013)
40. Vernazza, T., Granatella, G., Succi, G., Benedicenti, L., Mintchev, M.: Defining metrics for software components. In: Proceedings of the World Multiconference on Systemics, Cybernetics and Informatics, vol. XI, pp. 16–23, July 2000
41. Sillitti, A., Janes, A., Succi, G., Vernazza, T.: Measures for mobile users: an architecture. J. Syst. Architect. **50**(7), 393–405 (2004)

# An Intelligent Tutoring System Tool Combining Machine Learning and Gamification in Education

Riccardo Di Pietro[1(✉)] and Salvatore Distefano[2]

[1] Centro Informatico Ateneo di Messina - CIAM, University of Messina,
Piazza Pugliatti, 1, 98100 Messina, Italy
rdipietro@unime.it
[2] MIFT Department, University of Messina,
Viale F.S. d'Alcontres, 31, 98166 S. Agata, Messina, Italy
sdistefano@unime.it,
http://mdslab.unime.it/rdipietro

**Abstract.** Technological development has brought about a profound transformation of modern society. New technologies and media have completely redefined the way we communicate, inform, study, work, create and disseminate knowledge, weaving social relationships, with significant benefits in our daily lives. However, from an educational point of view, the availability of unlimited knowledge did not correspond to an improvement in school productivity of the new generation of learners. The *Intelligent Tutoring Systems* (ITSs) promised the dream of definitive learning experience almost 30 years ago but, nevertheless, promising student learning results have not improved as expected. In this paper, we briefly introduce the idea behind the *"Virtual Study Buddy"* tool that represents our ITS project, and we discuss the reasons that led us to its design and implementation. The solution integrates machine learning and gamification concepts with Cloud technologies by exploiting personal and mobile devices in a smart way.

**Keywords:** Intelligent Tutoring Systems · Gamification ·
Cloud computing · Machine learning · Virtual Study Buddy

## 1 Introduction

The spread of Information and Communication Technologies (ICT) has significantly impacted our day life: on the one hand, new opportunities have been created, on the other, the relationships have changed. This phenomenon has certainly led to benefits and improvements in the way of communicating, allowing to overcome time and space barriers, for example giving access to almost infinite information sources. E-learning, webinars and online educational institutions are now becoming increasingly common, indeed. Today it is possible to learn almost everything thanks to online courses and MOOC, everything is just a *"click"*

© Springer Nature Switzerland AG 2019
M. Mazzara et al. (Eds.): TOOLS 2019, LNCS 11771, pp. 218–226, 2019.
https://doi.org/10.1007/978-3-030-29852-4_18

away. The current trend in online learning of different disciplines can naturally lead to better educational opportunities and consequently to work. With regard to textbooks, on the other hand, e-books are becoming increasingly common, leading to faster and easier availability of texts and a reduction in the production of printed paper. Furthermore, the very way we think about textbooks is now completely different. No longer just words and images, but specific websites, evaluations, animations, additional materials and whatever else allows the assimilation of new contents are offered alongside the more traditional reading methods. No less important is the speed with which today we can find information in a few seconds: up to a decade ago it was necessary to spend hours in the library to find what we were looking for. Given these premises, it seems that technological development has created a perfect world within the reach of learners. The *Intelligent Tutoring System (ITS)* term refers to a computer system used to support the student by a learning system that performs functions similar to those of a human tutor. These technologies are designed to interact with human learners in a natural adaptable way. The final goal of an ITS is to analyze the competencies and behaviour of the student framed within a digital learning system that is linked to a specific field of knowledge. The ITS is able to assess the difference between the learner's educational situation and the educational goals to be achieved. Normally, during the training activity, the ITS gives learners proper comments and suggestions by selecting the most appropriate contents and types of activities to help them correct themselves. Doing so, it fills learner gaps and allows them to progress in the scheduled training process. Despite literature show us that the ITSs have improved the learner achievement and enhance learning, there are problems in their systemic use. On the one hand, ITSs still have problems of a technical and organizational nature, of which we will give some consideration in Sect. 2; on the other hand, ITSs have shown problems of *"longevity"* in their use. These problems can be summarized both in the lack of interest and in the boredom of performing repetitive actions by learners. For this reason, the research is going in the direction of studying how to use and integrate gamification concepts and mechanisms together with traditional ITSs. The *Gamification* term consists of the use of game mechanics to influence performance and create accountability. These game mechanics satisfy some basic human psychological needs like a sense of competence, autonomy and relatedness. Gamification uses the *"intrinsic motivation"* which is the strongest driver of long term engagement. Gamification uses sophisticated game mechanics and takes a long term approach to behavioural changes and students work-habit creation. Through its power to communicate goals and give real-time feedback about learners achievement, gamification is an ideal *tool* for the creation of a new identity of being a study participant, enabling smooth structural change. In this paper, we briefly introduce our idea on an ITS that acts as a *cognitive tool*, that is able to help learners in the development of the correct study method by interacting with a digital virtual study partner that can assess and suggest them how to improve their performance, also learning by such interactions.

The remainder of this paper is organized as follows. Section 2 describes motivations, some choices and theoretical and technological considerations of our proposal. Section 3 gives a brief overview of existing works in ITS and gamification. The *"Virtual Study Buddy"* system, its features and usage scenario are introduced in Sect. 4.1. Section 5 concludes this paper with some considerations on planned improvements as future work.

## 2    Motivation

As stated in [8], ICT technologies can help create an education system based on the principles that help teachers, students and administration to be effective in what they do, improving the quality and relevance of teaching-learning process. With this goal in mind, we started the design and development of our idea of ITS, we called it *"Virtual Study Buddy"* or simply *"VSB"*. Initially, we focused on *digital native* [10] needs, namely the generation of people who grew up in the digital age, comfortable with technology and computers at an early age. Digital natives who, from an educational point of view, have nevertheless shown difficulties navigating this new world. As the first milestone of this research, we have released a prototype that is freely available in beta version [14]. This prototype is able to detect and process data obtained from a user's teaching activity during the learning of a theoretical concept taken from a written text and, therefore, to return assessments on acquired skills and predictive analysis. Currently, *VSB* is experimentally used in a class of a primary school in the province of Messina (Italy). In this phase, we are collecting user experience feedback in order to improve the system setup, the gamification process elements we adopted, and the self-provisioning mechanism of the educational contents we implemented.

### 2.1    Choices and Theoretical/Technological Considerations

**Is it worth using ITS? Why didn't they prospered? Does it still make sense to talk about it in 2019?** Although in the last 30 years there has been a great research activity related to the development of ITS, with a large number of projects funded, a lot of money spent, experiments well underway, the use of these systems has never been started concretely, it never became systemic. Why? The lack of use of ITS systems in the real world outside the university research labs certainly does not depend on the lack of results obtained in the various experimentation experiences described in the literature. All research suggests that ITSs can achieve remarkable increases in student learning over traditional education community. From a historical point of view, research on ITS has the main aim to provide an advanced tutoring experience comparable with that obtainable with a human tutor rather than the one achieved by conventional computer-aided instruction (simple check on the correctness of the answer given). From a strictly operational point of view, many ITSs were not adopted by the education system in a definitive way because it was difficult to manage them from an educational point of view. Often it was not so simple and fast for instructors to create new teaching materials or updating the existing ones. In most systems, the *"knowledge maintenance"* had to be done by skilled programmers at great expense. In our opinion, this fact has led to an increase in costs and time to be taken into account by the instructors and by the educational institutions, effectively blocking their diffusion and actual use. Reducing the costs of all aspects of implementation and management of ITSs is the only way to make them systemic. In our proposal, we decided to automate the phase of the *"knowledge maintenance"* by using artificial intelligence techniques. *VSB* accepts input teaching materials in digital format that does not require prior processing (e.g. the normal textbooks recommended in class). This makes our *"knowledge maintenance"* economically sustainable. Furthermore, considering this automatism together with those provided for return assessments on acquired skills and predictive analysis, it appears clear how *VSB* is easy to manage even for non-technical personnel.

**Why Gamification?** According to [6], good videogames are *"machines for learning"* since they incorporate some of the most important learning principles postulated by today's cognitive science. In [15] the authors explain how a good gamification process needs the presence of two essential components: the application of effective dynamics and the use of the right technologies. Moreover, they declare that *"gamification is 75% Psychology and 25% Technology"*.

From the psychological point of view, thanks to the model proposed in [5], it is possible to identify three fundamental phases to effectively involve the participants in the game:

*Provide a Motivation.* The starting point of each gamification activity is to give people a reason to participate. The mechanism of the game and the challenge is deeply rooted in the human mind and is a powerful stimulus but for it to work at its best it is essential that the players have a prize in front of them, a goal, an objective that attracts attention and increases determination. The choice of benefits and prizes is very important because the more accurate it is, the greater the drive to compete that will be generated in the group.

*Provide Tools to Participate.* In order for the gamification to work, it is necessary that all the subjects involved have, at least at the outset, the same possibilities and the same tools to scale the rankings. In order to adopt gamification to get positive results, it is necessary to include one or more training and preparation moments to avoid the possibility of insinuating among the participants that someone could have been favoured by the organizer.

*Offer a Starting Point.* Every gamification activity needs a start-up moment (also called Kickoff) that acts as a zero moment from which to start the challenge. This means, for example, in creating a dedicated event, a team building activity, an official communication, and so on. In the case of long-term competitions, intermediate stages must be planned in which to check the progress of the activity, deliver special prizes, celebrate who is achieving results and motivate participants in difficulty.

But the most important thing in gamification activity is the *timing*: if all the mechanics of the game are not activated simultaneously and in a coordinated manner the risk is that the participants quickly lose interest in what they are doing. In Sect. 3 we give an overview of some experimental gamification tools and technology which have positively contributed to learning and achievements. In Sect. 4.2 we describe techniques and strategies discussed in [5] that we are using in *VSB* experimentation with the aim to involve our participants.

## 3    Related Work

Some work in literature adopted gamification techniques to ITS solutions. In [7] the authors present some empirical results on teaching basic Mandarin as a second language to college students using a gamification approach. This study shows some evidence that gamification outperforms non-gamification teaching method in related to learning concentration, skills, feedback, and immersion. In [4] the authors examine the benefit of an RPG (Role-Playing Game) to learn other language and their complicated letters, in this case, Japanese kanji. Moreover, the paper provides some suggestions with particular reference to how gamification can bridge learning outcomes as well as a game-play experience. In [13] the authors define the concept of gamification and introduce its elements. They describe how the gamification model and how the connection between motivation and gamification works. They give some examples of applied gamification in the focus of smartphone applications. In [1] the authors describe and analyze some gamification methods used by Zagreb School of Economics and Management (ZSEM) in different courses related to technologies and to legal discipline. The results showed students' satisfaction and an increase in their motivations in their studies. In [11] the authors analyze how the application of gamification strategies in MOOCs on energy sustainability affects participants' engagement and motivation in students. The results show the achievement of high levels both of engagement and student motivation. In [3] the authors present the integration 'Gamification' instructional strategy along with traditional teaching modes for the final year of Computer Science and Engineering students for the course of Information and Cyber Security. The results show that problem-solving among students increased significantly. In [12] the authors applied gamification in mobile learning for memorizing Alquran in order to increase the fun factor. The test results showed that there were significant differences in learning outcomes between the experimental group and the traditional group. In [9] the authors carried out an exploratory study assessing the effect of using the gamification of interactive digital storytelling on classroom dynamics and students' interaction. The results showed an increase in classroom discussions and in students' engagement.

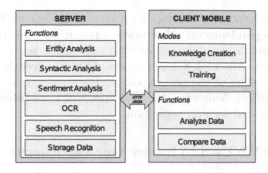

**Fig. 1.** *"Virtual Study Buddy"* architecture general scheme.

# 4  The Virtual Study Buddy Tool

## 4.1  Scenario

Figure 1 shows the general architectural scheme of the *Virtual Study Buddy* scenario. It consists of a client-server architecture that communicates via HTTP through JSON files. In [2] we detailed the technological choices behind *VSB*. The system offers two main ways to interact, one in which it is possible to create knowledge and another one in which it is possible to exercise a particular knowledge previously initialized in the system itself. As already mentioned, *VSB* accepts input educational materials in digital format, labelled in topic and subtopic, which does not require previous processing. In particular, the educational contents can be inserted using the keyboard, capturing it from an image (or from a photo), or extracting it from a PDF file. After entering new knowledge into the system, in a completely automatic and transparent way to the user, the system proceeds with the extraction of the text and some "metrics" using machine learning services. Texts and metrics will be stored in the system and used for future comparisons during the users' learning actions. As detailed in [2], the metrics that the system is able to extract come from the following types of analysis: Sentiment Analysis, Entity Analysis, Syntactic Analysis and Content Classification. The user can decide at any time to exercise his knowledge on a topic simply by selecting one of those available from the system and starting a training session. During a training session, thanks to the features provided by his own mobile device, the user records his speech on the topic he wants to train and then sends it and to the system. Thanks the machine learning, the system is able to understand the natural language of man. This means that the users can present the topic orally in a very personal way and not strictly identical to the text stored in the system. Once the speech is acquired, the system extracts text and metrics in the same way as it does in the knowledge creation process. The final step is to examine the equivalence, the conformity, the oral exposition and the equal meaning between the text inserted during the knowledge creation and the text coming from the transcription of the received vowel during the training session. The two texts are compared and analyzed structurally, syntactically and semantically. The system analyzes each part of the speech by detecting the morphology, the dependence on other words present and the taxonomy of the text, in order to match arguments, concepts, and words present in both texts. The training session ends with a *score* expressed in hundredths and in relative percentages which refers to the oral exposure, the equivalence of the texts, the similarity of the subject dealt with, the percentage of knowledge of the acquired text, the time dedicated for oral repetition.

### 4.2  Techniques We Used to Involve Our Participants

*VSB* was designed to use gamification dynamics and mechanics in different mixes and modes depending on the goal you want to achieve. Each user is associated with a profile in which it is possible to view its "carrier" in the system, for example, points, levels, badges, rankings, missions, achievements, and so on. *VSB* offers three learning methods: *autonomous*, *cooperative* and *guided*. The autonomous one was explained in Sect. 4.1. The cooperative and guided ones are based on the same operating principle as the autonomous one, it only changes learners organization and educational goals. In the cooperative method, the learners are grouped in open peer groups and all the participants can share educational materials, goals to reach and results. All the learning activities are public. In the guided method, there is a user who has the privilege of a "teacher" that can create closed groups, invite learners, associate different educational material and goals to learners of the same group, evaluate and reward progress achieved by the learners with the possibility or not publish the results.

## 5   Conclusion

This work briefly introduces *Virtual Study Buddy*, our idea of ITS which uses machine learning and gamification concepts with Cloud technologies using personal and mobile devices. We focused our initial efforts on *digital natives* because they represent the weak link in this constantly changing world. Furthermore, because they're living the ICT technologies as an integral and necessary part of their lives, digital natives represent a fertile and unexplored field of experimentation for cognitive tools. *VSB* is currently used experimentally in a class of a primary school in the province of Messina (Italy), and right now we are collecting feedback and data on both learning and usage activities. As future work, we planned to make changes and improvements. The data we will get at the end of the experimentation will guide us in the direction of making *VSB* more user-friendly, economically sustainable, easy to maintain even by non-technical personnel, to encourage its adoption on a larger scale.

**Acknowledgements.** The work presented in this paper was partially supported by the ERASMUS+ Key Action 2 (Strategic Partnership) project IOT-OPEN.EU (Innovative Open Education on IoT: improving higher education for European digital global competitiveness), reference no. 2016-1-PL01-KA203-026471. The European Commission support for the production of this publication does not constitute the endorsement of the contents which reflects the views only of the authors, and the Commission cannot be held responsible for any use which may be made of the information contained therein.

## References

1. Aleksić-Maslać, K., Rašić, M., Vranešić, P.: Influence of gamification on student motivation in the educational process in courses of different fields. In: 2018 41st International Convention on Information and Communication Technology, Electronics and Microelectronics (MIPRO), pp. 0783–0787, May 2018. https://doi.org/10.23919/MIPRO.2018.8400145
2. Di Pietro, R., Campanile, D.G., Distefano, S.: Virtual study partner: a cognitive training tool in education. In: 2019 IEEE International Conference on Smart Computing (SMARTCOMP), June 2019
3. Dixit, R., Nirgude, M., Yalagi, P.: Gamification: an instructional strategy to engage learner. In: 2018 IEEE Tenth International Conference on Technology for Education (T4E), pp. 138–141, December 2018. https://doi.org/10.1109/T4E.2018.00037
4. Fathoni, A.F.C.A., Delima, D.: Gamification of learning kanji with "Musou Roman" game. In: 2016 1st International Conference on Game, Game Art, and Gamification (ICGGAG), pp. 1–3, December 2016. https://doi.org/10.1109/ICGGAG.2016.8052664
5. Fogg, B.: Persuasive technology. In: Fogg, B. (ed.) Persuasive Technology. Interactive Technologies, Morgan Kaufmann, San Francisco (2003). https://doi.org/10.1016/B978-155860643-2/50001-9
6. Gee, J.: What video games have to teach us about learning and literacy. Comput. Entertain. **1**, 20 (2003). https://doi.org/10.1145/950566.950595
7. Heryadi, Y., Muliamin, K.: Gamification of M-learning mandarin as second language. In: 2016 1st International Conference on Game, Game Art, and Gamification (ICGGAG), pp. 1–4, December 2016. https://doi.org/10.1109/ICGGAG.2016.8052645
8. Keswani, B., Banerjee, D., Patni, P.: Role of technology in education: a 21st century approach. J. Commer. Inf. Technol. **8**, 53–59 (2008)
9. Molnar, A.: The effect of interactive digital storytelling gamification on microbiology classroom interactions. In: 2018 IEEE Integrated STEM Education Conference (ISEC), pp. 243–246, March 2018. https://doi.org/10.1109/ISECon.2018.8340493
10. Prensky, M.: Digital natives, digital immigrants part 1. On Horiz. **9**(5), 1–6 (2001). https://doi.org/10.1108/10748120110424816
11. Romero-Rodríguez, L.M., Ramírez-Montoya, M.S., Gonzàlez, J.R.V.: Gamification in MOOCs: engagement application test in energy sustainability courses. IEEE Access **7**, 32093–32101 (2019). https://doi.org/10.1109/ACCESS.2019.2903230
12. Rosmansyah, Y., Rosyid, M.R.: Mobile learning with gamification for Alquran memorization. In: 2017 International Conference on Information Technology Systems and Innovation (ICITSI), pp. 378–383, October 2017. https://doi.org/10.1109/ICITSI.2017.8267974
13. Tóth, Tóvölgyi, S.: The introduction of gamification: a review paper about the applied gamification in the smartphone applications. In: 2016 7th IEEE International Conference on Cognitive Infocommunications (CogInfoCom), pp. 000213–000218, October 2016. https://doi.org/10.1109/CogInfoCom.2016.7804551

14. Virtual-Study-Partner: Virtual Study Partner - Istruzione (2019). https://play.
google.com/store/apps/details?id=com.knowledgepkg.domenicogiacomocampanile
.knowledgeapp
15. Zichermann, G., Cunningham, C.: Gamification by Design: Implementing Game
Mechanics in Web and Mobile Apps. O'Reilly Media, Inc., Sebastopol (2011)

# Early Within-Season Yield Prediction and Disease Detection Using Sentinel Satellite Imageries and Machine Learning Technologies in Biomass Sorghum

Ephrem Habyarimana[1]([⊠]), Isabelle Piccard[2],
Christian Zinke-Wehlmann[3], Paolo De Franceschi[1],
Marcello Catellani[1,4], and Michela Dall'Agata[1]

[1] CREA Research Center for Cereal and Industrial Crops, Foggia, Italy
ephrem.habyarimana@crea.gov.it
[2] Vlaamse Instelling voor Technologisch Onderzoek N.V., Mol, Belgium
[3] Institute for Applied Informatics, Leipzig, Germany
[4] Italian National Agency for New Technologies, Energy and Sustainable
Economic Development, Rome, Italy

**Abstract.** Sorghum is grown for several purposes including biomass for producing energy and fodder, and grain for producing health-promoting foods. Sorghum is a drought resistant cereal with low input requirements, making it one of the most promising crops under the world's tropics and higher latitudes. Crop monitoring, one of the leading activities in smart farming, can help cut production costs and more so under climate change. In this study, Sentinel 2A and 2B-derived fAPAR and NDVI data were used to monitor sorghum phenology, foliar diseases, and to predict aboveground biomass yields months before harvest, using machine learning approaches including Bayesian methods and region-convolutional neural network. The results obtained in this work were encouraging. We were able to predict biomass yields up to 6 months before harvest with mean absolute percentage error (MAPE) < 0.2, while diseases were detected with accuracy up to 90%. The best machine learning algorithm was Bayesian additive regression trees (bartMachine method), while the best biomass yields prediction regressors were the days of year 150 and 165. These results were achieved at a Pilot level and the technologies showed industrial scale implementation potentials with tremendous benefits for the farmer, extension services, policy makers, and other parties at interest.

**Keywords:** Sorghum biomass · Sorghum diseases · Prediction modeling · Machine learning · Bayesian learning · NDVI and fAPAR · Satellite imagery · Sentinel-2

# 1 Introduction

Sorghum crop (*Sorghum bicolor* (L.) Moench) is cultivated worldwide mainly for cost-effectively producing feed, forage, fuel, and health promoting foods [1–3]. Crop yield and disease forecasting is one of the most important strategies in agriculture which

© Springer Nature Switzerland AG 2019
M. Mazzara et al. (Eds.): TOOLS 2019, LNCS 11771, pp. 227–234, 2019.
https://doi.org/10.1007/978-3-030-29852-4_19

enables sustainable development and helps avoid famines and shortages in several commodities. Many studies have shown that forecasting models based on remote sensing satellite data can give similar or better performance compared to the more sophisticated crop growth models [4]. The use of remote sensing parameters as proxies for grain and biomass yields was documented in previous works, but their use in biomass sorghum is very limited [5–12]. In addition, several machine learning techniques were implemented in previous remote sensing predictive analytics [13], but, no Bayesian inference approach was deployed, and this paper is therefore aimed at addressing this gap. On the other hand, this work aims to make the Sentinel data usable for the agricultural domain to support large-scale crop disease detection relying upon chlorophyll dynamics [14, 15]. The specific objectives of this entire work are therefore to develop machine learning models for within-season prediction of sorghum foliar disease development based on Sentinel-derived NDVI (normalized difference vegetation index) and biomass yields before harvest based on fAPAR (fraction of absorbed photosynthetically active radiation) measurements from Sentinel 2A and Sentinel 2B satellite constellation images.

## 2    Materials and Methods

### 2.1    Open-Field Trials and Biomass Data Collection

Forty-three demonstration trials were run in this work 24 and 19 of which were evaluated in 2017 and 2018, respectively. The field trial management was fully described in Habyarimana et al. [1, 13]. The experimental fields were established in commercial farmers' fields in Mirandola, Nonantola, and Conselice, and in CREA's research station of Anzola. The fields areas ranged from 0.06 ha to 50 ha, with a mean and median of 5.56 ha and 1.00 ha, respectively. The Biomass from Anzola was spread over the producing fields, while for the other trials, chopped and baled biomasses were supplied to private biogas and combustion bioreactors, respectively. Standard operating procedures [13] were followed to derive dry mass fraction of the fresh materials and dry mass yields of the trials.

### 2.2    Satellite Data Acquisition

The fields were geolocalized, geolocation data saved as kml files before they were integrated into watchITgrow application (www.watchitgrow.be). Sentinel-2A and Sentinel-2B images from tile 32TQQ (pilots in Conselice) and 32TPQ (pilots in Anzola, Mirandola and Nonantola) were downloaded from ESA and processed through atmospheric correction with iCOR [16], cloud and shadow detection using Sen2COR v2.5.5 (ESA-STEP) and calculation of biophysical parameters using BV-NET (Biophysical Variable Neural Network) methodology [13, 17]. The fAPAR estimates were generated at decametric spatial resolution (10 m pixel size), and a temporal resolution of 5 days up to 2–3 days in those areas where the different satellite overpasses overlapped. Spatial resolution was represented by an individual pixel.

## 2.3    Modelling Total Aboveground Biomass Yields

Four models assessed in this study included simple linear model (LM), Bayesian additive regression trees (bartMachine method), Bayesian generalized linear model (bayesglm method), and eXtreme Gradient boosting (xgbTree method). The simple linear model was used as a benchmark to gauge the performance of the models implemented. The models evaluated in this work were selected based on their robustness as reported in previous studies [13, 18]. Fortnightly fAPAR values acquired from late April to late August were used in this work, resulting in nine days of year (DOY) that is, from DOY 120 in April to DOY 240 in August. These days of year were used as explanatory (regressors) variables in successive predictive modelling of sorghum biomass yields.

During data preparation, zero-variance predictors were removed and, those remaining were centered and scaled in order to avoid predictors with zero or near-zero variance which often constitute a problem and behave as second intercepts in predictive models [18]. The dataset was randomly partitioned into training (80% of the entire dataset) and testing set (20% of the entire dataset). The training set was used to run a cross-validation experiment to train and assess the models using a 10x repeated 5-random fold cross-validation (CV), rendering a total of 50 estimates of accuracy and prediction error. Models were validated on the testing set which was an external test (validation) sample. The models were evaluated based on the coefficient of determination ($R^2$), mean absolute error (MAE), mean absolute percentage error (MAPE), and symmetrical mean absolute percentage error (SMAPE). The MAPE makes it possible to compare the prediction of different dependent variables that were evaluated using different scales. The MAE measured the average magnitude of the errors in the set of predicted values without considering their direction. The MAE provides an unambiguous measure of the magnitude of the average error and is therefore more appropriate than the Root Mean Square Error (RMSE) for dimensioned evaluations of average model performance error. The symmetrical MAPE (SMAPE) was used to deal with some of the limitations of the MAPE. As in MAPE, SMAPE averages the absolute percentage errors but these errors are computed using a denominator representing the average of the forecast and observed values. SMAPE has an upper limit of 200%, that is a 0 to 2 range that is useful to judge the level of accuracy and that should be influenced less by extreme values. Furthermore, SMAPE corrects for the computation asymmetry of the percentage error. The MAE built within the repeated cross validation procedure was used to assess the dependability of the model performance. On the other hand, all the above metrics as obtained on the testing set were used to assess the model predictive ability. The importance of the explanatory variables (useful prediction times) was determined using a 0 to 100 index, with 0 no effect and 100 the highest magnitude of the regressor's importance. All statistical analyses were carried out using R software [19]; the predictive modeling was implemented using the caret R package.

## 2.4  Disease Detection

The large-scale sorghum disease monitoring experiments were carried out in Anzola, Italy. The overall process proceeded with annotating and setting the regions of interests (ROIs) before Sentinel data were downloaded and prepared to create a training set. The Region-convolutional neural network (R-CNN) was trained and tested; R-CNN was mainly used for object detection purposes, and a total of five training and test fields for crop disease detection were identified. Within the diseased field, the most diseased area of about 1000 m$^2$ ($\sim$232 m of perimeter) was delimited within which leaf disease occurred in about 60 to 70% of the plants. Two foliar diseases were observed, i.e., Anthracnose (Colletotrichum sublineolum, most prevalent) and Bacterial stripe (Robbsia andropogonis). The results obtained on Anthracnose are presented in this work. The primary hypotheses are that most crop diseases highly correlate with the chlorophyll content of the crop, and that the content of this pigment can be measured by multispectral images.

# 3  Results

## 3.1  Assessment and Validation of the Predictive Models

Four models implemented in this work were assessed using SMAPE, MAPE, MAE, and the coefficient of determination ($R^2$). MAE was used both on the testing and the training set, while SMAPE, MAPE, and $R^2$ were used on the testing set. During the cross-validated training, MAE was used to assess model reliability (Fig. 1). A repeated cross-validation was run resulting in MAE resample vectors, each with 50 elements, for each model. The MAE dispersion during training was increasingly narrower in the order LM > bayesglm > xgbTree > bartMachine methods. Over the months evaluated, the prediction errors in the testing set were mostly higher with the linear model which also displayed the least value of the coefficient of determination (Table 1). Overall, the bartMachine method showed relatively high $R^2$ values and least values of prediction errors. The best regressors were D.150 (second half of May) and D.165 (first half of June) (Fig. 1). D.240, D.195, D.210, and D.120 showed minor effects, while D.135, D.180, and D.225 showed no prediction importance.

## 3.2  Foliar Disease

In the global monitoring of sorghum diseases, we were able to process the results for Anthracnose that were presented in the below Fig. 2. The network worked as it should and detected the fields of interest. The network was even able to detect the disease and distinguished it from surrounding areas.

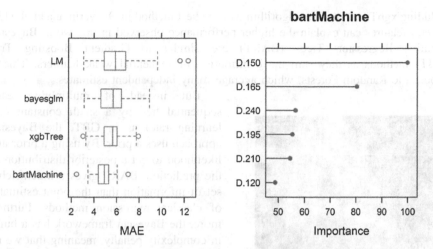

**Fig. 1.** Left: visualization of models cross-validation MAE (t ha$^{-1}$) dispersion using boxplot approach and fAPAR acquired from April to August. LM, bartMachine, bayesglm, xgbTree, respectively, simple linear model, Bayesian additive regression trees (bartMachine method), Bayesian generalized linear model (bayesglm method), and eXtreme Gradient boosting (xgbTree method). Right: Relative importance of regressors (day of year, D) on sorghum biomass yields using bartMachine method.

**Table 1.** Model performance metrics.

| Model | SMAPE (%) | MAPE (%) | MAE (t ha$^{-1}$) | R$^2$ |
|---|---|---|---|---|
| LM | 0.74 | 0.99 | 10.47 | 0.47 |
| bartMachine | 0.18 | 0.16 | 2.32 | 0.51 |
| Bayesglm | 0.74 | 0.98 | 10.34 | 0.48 |
| xgbTree | 0.44 | 0.36 | 4.07 | 0.62 |

SMAPE, MAPE, MAE, R$^2$, respectively, symmetrical mean absolute percentage error, mean absolute percentage error, mean absolute error, and coefficient of determination. LM, bartMachine, bayesglm, xgbTree, respectively, simple linear model, Bayesian additive regression trees (bartMachine method), Bayesian generalized linear model (bayesglm method), and eXtreme Gradient boosting (xgbTree method).

## 4 Discussion

In this work, high levels of model prediction performance (e.g., SMAPE < 0.2, MAE ~ 2 t ha$^{-1}$, R$^2$ ~ 51%) were obtained from the best model. One of the motivations for undertaking this work was to compare the performance of the recently implemented machine learning techniques [13] with the Bayesian machine learning methods. On account of the error metrics used in this work, the Bayesian additive regression trees (bartMachine method) approach outperformed the other methods including xgbTree. The later algorithm was the best method in Habyarimana et al. [13]. Several features can explain the higher performance observed in this work. Bayesian Additive Regression Trees (BART) are similar to Gradient Boosting Tree (GBT) methods as they sum the contribution of sequential weak learners. This is opposed to Random Forests, which average many independent estimates.

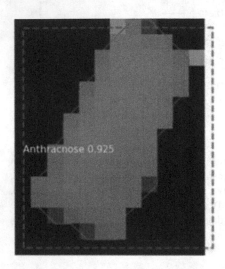

**Fig. 2.** Sorghum foliar diseases detected area with reliability of 0.925.

But instead of multiplying each sequential tree by a small constant (the learning rate) as in GBT, the Bayesian approach uses a prior. By using a prior and likelihood to get a posterior distribution of the prediction, BART gives a much richer set of information than the point estimates of classical regression methods. Furthermore, the Bayesian framework has a built-in complexity penalty, meaning that we no longer have to make empirical choices about regularization, max tree-depth and the plethora of other options we normally tune via cross-validation. The performance of bartMachine in this work is supported by recent findings in scientific literature. As Jost [20] put it, BART method outperformed all the others that were compared, including gradient boosting machine and Random Forests, on the 42 different datasets evaluated. The most important prediction regressors were the DOYs 150 and 165, which supports the previous findings [13]. The months of May and July can therefore be recommended as the best time to predict sorghum biomass yields in the Mediterranean region, which is in agreement with Habyarimana et al. [13]. These favorable prediction times coincide with the fast growth stage in sorghum grown in the Mediterranean region. In this region, sorghum is sown mid-to-late April. Therefore, being able to perform accurate sorghum biomass yields prediction in May-June, i.e., up to six months ahead of harvesting is a remarkable opportunity for the farmer and farming cooperatives that can use this information for several business-related purposes. The models developed in this work will also help the extension services and other policy makers for strategic planning purposes including assessing alternative means for energy supply and ways to avoid energy crises. As for crop diseases, they not only reduce yields but also reduce the quality of the produce. The encouraging results on disease modelling present therefore sorghum stakeholders with interesting opportunity as they can be harnessed globally for crop protection purposes.

# 5  Conclusions

The importance of sorghum cannot be overemphasized. It is used for food, feed, and biofuel and in other socioeconomic sectors. Biomass sorghum demonstrated higher yields with better energy balance relative to major crops of agroindustrial interest. Harnessing satellite technology is well poised to help sorghum biomass growers add more value and stay longer in the business. Sentinel-2-derived fraction of absorbed photosynthetically active radiation was found to explain primary productivity and was used in this study as biophysical variable in the predictive modelling of aboveground biomass yields in annual and perennial sorghums. Bayesian additive regression trees (bartMachine method), a Bayesian machine learning approach, was found more promising than recently implemented artificial intelligence approaches, and predicting sorghum biomass yields using as regressors days of year 150 and 165 offered much modelling performance.

**Acknowledgments.** Part of this work was supported (beneficiary: first author) by the project Data-driven Bioeconomy (www.databio.eu), GA number: 732064 (H2020-ICT-2016-1—innovation action), and the project Risorse GeneticheVegetali (RGV/FAO) 2014e2016 of the Ministero delle PoliticheAgricole, Alimentari e Forestali, Rome.

# References

1. Habyarimana, E., Lorenzoni, C., Redaelli, R., Alfieri, M., Amaducci, S., Cox, S.: Towards a perennial biomass sorghum crop: a comparative investigation of biomass yields and overwintering of Sorghum bicolorx S. halepense lines relative to long term S. bicolor trials in northern Italy. Biomass Bioenergy **111**, 187–195 (2018)
2. El Bassam, N.: Handbook of Bioenergy Crops: A Complete Reference to Species, Development and Applications. Earthscan Ltd., London (2010)
3. Stefaniak, T.R., Dahlberg, J.A., Bean, B.W., Dighe, N., Wolfrum, E.J., Rooney, W.L.: Variation in biomass composition components among forage, biomass, sorghum-sudangrass, and sweet sorghum types. Crop Sci. **52**, 1949–1954 (2012)
4. Gallego, J., Kravchenko, A.N., Kussul, N.N., Skakun, S.V., Shelestov, A.Y., Grypych, Y.A.: Efficiency assessment of different approaches to crop classification based on satellite and ground observations. J. Autom. Inf. Sci. **44**, 67–80 (2012)
5. Diouf, A.A., et al.: Fodder biomass monitoring in Sahelian rangelands using phenological metrics from FAPAR time series. Remote Sens. **7**, 9122–9148 (2015). https://doi.org/10.3390/rs70709122
6. Shafian, S., et al.: Unmanned aerial systems-based remote sensing for monitoring sorghum growth and development. PLoS ONE **13**, e0196605 (2018)
7. Kross, A., McNairn, H., Lapen, D., Sunohara, M., Champagne, C.: Assessment of RapidEye vegetation indices for estimation of leaf area index and biomass in corn and soybean crops. Int. J. Appl. Earth Obs. Geoinf. **34**, 235–248 (2015)
8. Panda, S.S., Ames, D.P., Panigrahi, S.: Application of vegetation indices for agricultural crop yield prediction using neural network techniques. Remote Sens. **2**, 673–696 (2010)
9. López-Lozano, R., Duveiller, G., Seguini, L., Meroni, M., García-Condado, S., Hooker, J.: Towards regional grain yield forecasting with 1 km-resolution EO biophysical products: strengths and limitations at pan-European level. Agric. For. Meteorol. **206**, 12–32 (2015)

10. Kussul, N., Kolotii, A., Skakun, S., Shelestov, A., Kussul, O., Oliynuk, T.: Efficiency estimation of different satellite data usage for winter wheat yield forecasting in Ukraine. In: Proceedings of the 2014 IEEE International Geoscience and Remote Sensing Symposium (IGARSS), Quebec City, Canada (2014)
11. Duveiller, G., López-Lozano, R., Baruth, B.: Enhanced processing of 1-km spatial resolution fAPAR time series for sugarcane yield forecasting and monitoring. Remote Sens. **5**(3), 1091–1116 (2013)
12. Yang, C., Everitt, J.H., Bradford, J.M., Escobar, D.E.: Mapping grain sorghum growth and yield variations using airborne multispectral digital imagery. Trans. ASAE **43**, 1927–1938 (2000)
13. Habyarimana, E., Piccard, I., Catellani, M., De Franceschi, P., Dall'Agata, M.: Towards predictive modeling of sorghum biomass yields using fraction of absorbed photosynthetically active radiation derived from Sentinel-2 satellite imagery and supervised machine learning techniques. Agronomy **9**, 203 (2019)
14. Rumpf, T., Mahlein, A.-K., Steiner, U., Oerke, E.-C., Dehne, H.-W., Plümer, L.: Early detection and classification of plant diseases with Support Vector Machines based on hyperspectral reflectance. Comput. Electron. Agric. **74**(1), 91–99 (2010). https://doi.org/10.1016/j.compag.2010.12.012
15. Yang, C., Everitt, J.H., Murde, D.: Evaluating high resolution SPOT 5 satellite imagery for crop identification. Comput. Electron. Agric. **75**(2), 347–354 (2011). https://doi.org/10.1016/j.compag.2010.12.012
16. De Keukelaere, L., et al.: Atmospheric correction of Landsat-8/OLI and Sentinel-2/MSI data using iCOR algorithm: validation for coastal and inland waters. Eur. J. Remote Sens. **51**, 525–542 (2018)
17. Weiss, M., Baret, F.: ATBD S2ToolBox Level 2 Products: LAI, FAPAR, FCOVER (Version 1.1). http://step.esa.int/docs/extra/ATBD_S2ToolBox_L2B_V1.1.pdf. Accessed 04 May 2019
18. Kuhn, M.: Building predictive models in R using the caret package. J. Stat. Softw. **28**, 1–26 (2008)
19. R Core Team: R: A Language and Environment for Statistical Computing; R Foundation for Statistical Computing, Vienna, Austria (2013)
20. Jost, Z.: "Bayesian Additive Regression Trees" paper summary. https://towardsdatascience.com/bayesian-additive-regression-trees-paper-summary-9da19708fa71. Accessed 04 May 2019

# Internet of Things

# UniquID: A Quest to Reconcile Identity Access Management and the IoT

Alberto Giaretta[1]([✉]), Stefano Pepe[2], and Nicola Dragoni[1,3]

[1] Centre for Applied Autonomous Sensor Systems (AASS), Örebro University,
Örebro, Sweden
**alberto.giaretta@oru.se**
[2] UniquID Inc., San Francisco, USA
**pepe@uniquid.com**
[3] DTU Compute, Technical University of Denmark, Kongens Lyngby, Denmark
**ndra@dtu.dk**

**Abstract.** The Internet of Things (IoT) has caused a revolutionary paradigm shift in computer networking. After decades of human-centered routines, where devices were merely tools that enabled human beings to authenticate themselves and perform activities, we are now dealing with a device-centered paradigm: the devices themselves are actors, not just tools for people. Conventional identity access management (IAM) frameworks were not designed to handle the challenges of IoT. Trying to use traditional IAM systems to reconcile heterogeneous devices and complex federations of online services (e.g., IoT sensors and cloud computing solutions) adds a cumbersome architectural layer that can become hard to maintain and act as a single point of failure. In this paper, we propose UniquID, a blockchain-based solution that overcomes the need for centralized IAM architectures while providing scalability and robustness. We also present the experimental results of a proof-of-concept UniquID enrolment network, and we discuss two different use-cases that show the considerable value of a blockchain-based IAM.

**Keywords:** IAM · Identity management systems · Blockchain · Internet of Things · IoT · Machine-to-machine · M2M

## 1 Introduction

Information Technology (IT) has radically changed throughout history. In just a few decades, with the advent of the Internet, computers evolved from standalone machines to powerful devices capable of sharing information with other devices. This explosion of capabilities has led to a concomitant expansion of complexity in a variety of areas, including identity access management (IAM).

Conventional IAM systems are essential for traditional local networks and businesses, but not well-suited for large networks of complex, highly distributed devices, such as the combination of Internet of Things (IoT) and machine to

© Springer Nature Switzerland AG 2019
M. Mazzara et al. (Eds.): TOOLS 2019, LNCS 11771, pp. 237–251, 2019.
https://doi.org/10.1007/978-3-030-29852-4_20

machine (M2M) communication. The main reason is that IAM systems were designed for human beings, not devices. Until a decade ago, a typical scenario involved a known number of terminals and a comparable number of human users with well-defined roles. Accounts were issued for each person and access rights stored on a central server, making access control (AC) relatively easy to manage. Today, IT is much more complex than it once was.

The Internet of Things is causing the old user-centered paradigm to shift toward a device-centered one. Previously, accounts were tied to human beings and devices were just a means to the end of accomplishing all the tasks those humans performed. Today, devices are increasingly becoming the actors themselves, with the tasks narrowed down from general purpose functions to very specific operations. With this in mind, traditional IAM solutions are expensive, make maintaining cross-domain consistency challenging, and represent a critical single point of failure in organizations due to their centralized nature.

## 1.1 Contribution of the Paper

This paper describes UniquID[1], a solution based on an infrastructure that takes advantage of certificates and blockchain technology to overcome the difficulties in reconciling IoT credentials and cross-domain IAM.

As we discuss in Sect. 2, UniquID delivers both agnosticism (with respect to the underlying blockchain chosen) and full decentralization, characteristics that other solutions cannot provide despite being blockchain-based. Indeed, we would like to highlight that using the blockchain as part of an architecture does not entail that the whole architecture is fully decentralized. We will show in the next section a few examples of this concept.

Summing up, the goals of this paper include the following:

- Describing a cheaper and simpler alternative to traditional IAM systems.
- Illustrating the implementation of cross-domain identities for IoT devices to circumvent account reconciliation.
- Showing how the proposed design removes single points of failure from the trust structure.
- Demonstrating direct peer-to-peer (P2P) authentication and authorization among IoT devices.
- Showing how an IoT device, empowered to locally confirm a smart transaction, deals with partitioning issues as defined by the CAP Theorem.

## 1.2 Paper Outline

The paper is organized as follows. Section 2 briefly presents the main players in the blockchain-based IAM landscape, how UniquID addresses some of the distributed IoT challenges, and how it is linked to the CAP Theorem. Section 3 describes the general concepts behind UniquID, and Sect. 4 shows the experimental evaluation of an enrolment proof-of-concept. Section 5 describes two example case studies, and Sect. 6 lays out the paper conclusions and discusses future work.

---

[1] http://www.uniquid.com.

## 2   Related Work

In the past, blockchain has already been advocated for more secure IAM systems. For example, Kshetri [10] suggests that blockchain can help in strengthen the IoT in different ways, such as preventing DDoS and IP spoofing attacks. Furthermore, Gartner estimates that by 2020 the IoT will require up to 1000 times the 2016 network capacity [12]. This entails that the centralized IAM paradigm might not scale enough to tolerate such requirements, and this is where the decentralized IAM can provide both more security and scalability.

In Roman et al. [16], the authors lay out the main challenges of distributed IoT. They argue that identity and authentication are primary concerns due to the inherent dynamism introduced by device mobility, unstable connections, and related problems. Throughout this paper, we show how UniquID provides direct identification and authentication, which in turn enables efficient M2M resource negotiation. Another issue raised is security, which UniquID ensures through asymmetric encryption, adding symmetric cipher-based encryption for larger data streams. Furthermore, depending on the chosen backbone, privacy can be partially or even totally lost. In cases where privacy is needed, it can be enforced through non-interactive zero-knowledge proofs such as zk-SNARKs [17] and Bulletproofs [4], but this involves considerable overhead that may not be appropriate for resource-constrained devices.

Several parallel projects have been proposed to address the problem of identity management over blockchain, yet most of them do not address the access management part. For example, IBM Hyperledger Indy aims to provide an SDK solution to manage identities over distributed ledgers [6]. Even though UniquID similarly provides an SDK, our proposal addresses both the identity and the access management parts of the equation, whereas Indy addresses only identity.

Scholars proposed some solutions as well. Le and Mutka propose CapChain [11], a blockchain-based access control framework that enables IAM on public blockchains, ensuring at the same time privacy. The authors built a proof-of-concept over Monero source code and ran processing time local benchmarks. However, as shown by the authors, CapChain takes Monero 13 KB transactions and modifies them, obtaining 30 KB transactions. Therefore, their solution is tied to a particular blockchain specification, meaning that a dedicated blockchain should be deployed.

Ouaddah et al. [15] propose a blockchain-based access control named FairAccess, and implemented a proof-of-concept which uses Bitcoin OP_RETURN as a storage field. However, their solution is not completely decentralized, since that their architecture supposes that every local network has a dedicated centralized point called authorization management point (AMP). Similarly, Novo [14] proposes a blockchain-based access management that utilizes a management hub (e.g., an edge node) as a middlepoint between IoT devices and the blockchain.

Even though all the aforementioned papers prove that blockchain-based IAM is possible, none of them delivers a solution which is, at the same time, data-storage agnostic and totally decentralized. Furthermore, none of such works envisage a way to autonomously verify a policy without Internet connection, failing to take full advantage of the M2M paradigm. In particular, no one highlights the strong relationship between Brewer's CAP Theorem and IAM solutions, nor motivations and implications of choosing consistency over availability (or vice-versa) in their proposals.

### 2.1   Consistency, Availability, and Partition Tolerance (CAP)

According to Brewer's CAP Theorem [3], one cannot ensure all three of the following in a system at any given time: *consistency (C)*, *availability (A)* and *partition tolerance (P)*. CAP is often misunderstood, with people thinking that a distributed system is always unable to assure all three requirements. In reality, the choice is only between consistency and availability when a partition or a failure occurs; under normal circumstances, all three can be assured simultaneously. Another misunderstanding is about consistent-available (CA) systems, which are simply not possible in a distributed scenario. According to CAP, a system could be designed to be CA, but it would require a network that ensures no packet is ever dropped at any moment in time. For a fixed partition tolerance requirement, the only real choice is between consistency and availability.

Consistency, which is a property related to read operation, can be either strong or eventual. In a consistent-partition-tolerant (CP) scenario typical of a relational database management system (RDBMS), the system ensures that every commit to the database is propagated and kept consistent throughout all database replicas, so that every read operation returns the most recently updated result. In an available-partition-tolerant (AP) scenario typical of NoSQL, the read operation does not ensure that the user receives the most up-to-date result. But even though AP sounds problematic, consistency is eventually achieved, and this approach is common in many non-critical applications due to its strong support for partition tolerance and availability.

It is important to keep in mind that partitions and latency are strongly related, to the point that we can define a partition as a function of latency: the developer can decide the latency threshold beyond which partitioning occurs. By indefinitely retrying communications, one is essentially choosing a CP solution over an AP one, whereas replying right away to a user request means choosing AP over CP, as the data might be stale (inconsistent with the current state). The idea of selecting either CP or AP is a false dichotomy, however, as tuning the time threshold makes it possible to switch from a CP solution to an AP one after a chosen amount of time.

UniquID aims to provide similar flexibility depending on the application domain. This can be easily done by deciding for how long an IoT device will try to download an up-to-date smart contract from the blockchain (i.e., CP behavior) before conceding the resources to the client based on the locally stored smart contract (i.e., AP behavior). In this particular case, the IoT device is a UniquID node that can locally read a smart contract even though it does not store the whole blockchain. The ability to locally read a smart contract means that any network failure happening between the node and the rest of the UniquID network is a partition. Therefore, the CAP theorem applies and a thoughtful decision must be made between consistency and availability.

## 3   UniquID Overall Architecture

Figure 1 shows how different networks interact with each other in a traditional IAM infrastructure. An IoT device in Network A must go through the IAM platform to authenticate on a different IoT network, such as Network B. In the event of network unavailability, a device cannot authenticate, showing that this solution does not provide good availability.

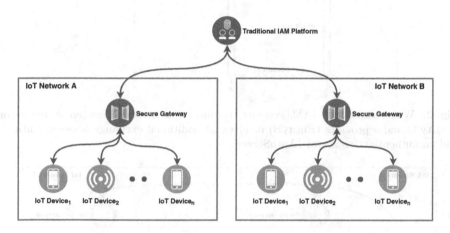

**Fig. 1.** Traditional IAM systems impose a hierarchical structure over managed devices. This introduces potential single points of failure in the architecture and strongly impedes direct M2M communications.

Furthermore, as shown in Fig. 2, this kind of architecture involves a considerable number of message exchanges. This overhead decreases the overall responsiveness of the system and means that it cannot ensure availability in the event of network partitioning. Indeed, we can classify a traditional IAM architecture as CP-compliant without any possibility of choosing an AP solution. This system was acceptable in the old days of fixed and stable architectures, but IoT networks require greater flexibility and interoperability.

A primary goal of UniquID is to replace traditional IAM structures with a less expensive architecture that is more flexible and easier to manage. As shown in Fig. 3, the system uses an infrastructure where devices can directly authenticate each other without a trusted third party IAM platform, as envisioned by the PGP Web of Trust [5, 7].

Figure 4 shows the UniquID workflow, illustrating two main differences from the IAM setup depicted in Fig. 2. First of all, fewer messages are required than

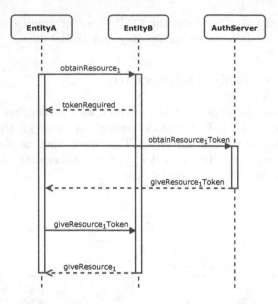

**Fig. 2.** With traditional IAM systems, resource negotiation between a requestor (EntityA) and a provider (EntityB) involves an additional exchange between EntityA and an authentication server (AuthServer).

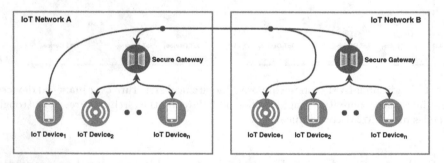

**Fig. 3.** UniquID removes the authentication server, which has two important implications. First, the potential single point of failure disappears from the network. Second, scalability greatly improves, as M2M communication is possible and a central authority is no longer essential for negotiation.

in a traditional approach, which entails that UniquID provides better performances than a centralized IAM, assuming that AuthServer and Blockchain have comparable response times. Second, and more important, the entities use smart contracts stored in a tamper-proof public blockchain instead of tokens. This not only ensures higher security but also enables Entity B to store the contract so it can still authenticate Entity A in the event of a network failure.

This might pose some security issues. Suppose a malicious person M steals Entity A, the laptop of an important CEO. The network administrator imme-

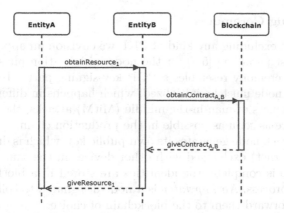

**Fig. 4.** UniquID communication is more straightforward than in traditional IAM. EntityA can negotiate for resources directly with EntityB, which can interrogate the blockchain to confirm that the request is valid. But this interrogation is not mandatory, since EntityB can store hash trees and locally confirm certificate validity thanks to the Merkle tree data structure.

diately revokes all Entity A permissions by issuing a blockchain transaction. If Entity B is instructed to allow authentication without double-checking the currentness of the permission, M might try to gain as much time as possible to cause damage by initiating a network fault that isolates Entity B from the blockchain. This would enable M to authenticate despite the staleness of the Entity A permissions stored within Entity B.

At the same time, the ability to verify a smart contract offline might be invaluable for some other applications. Take as an example a public transportation service. Assume that user U pays for a one-hour ride ticket that allows him to take any city bus line he likes. Assume that the city buses pull this ticket from the blockchain, and temporarily store it locally. After U has done all his errands, he goes to the bus stop and tries to get on the bus, but a network fault occurs. If the buses have been configured to authenticate him without double-checking the current status of the ticket on the blockchain, U will be able to board the bus. If, on the other hand, the buses need to perform a double-check, U will be left waiting until the network fault is resolved, which might take a long time. Again, a malicious user M might isolate the bus he is boarding and extend his ticket for some time. However, this is a small economic risk that the company would be willing to take given the more serious consequences that a network fault would have on all of its transportation infrastructure.

Each scenario has different requirements. One of the strengths of UniquID is that the end users can decide whether a CP system or an AP system is best suited to their needs.

## 3.1   Imprinting Ceremony

With the goal of excluding any kind of PKI, we envision an approach similar to the Web of Trust paradigm [5,7] for the node initialization phase. In UniquID, the imprinting ceremony resembles a PGP key-signing party. To be enrolled in UniquID, every node must be initialized, which happens in different phases. To minimize the chances of man-in-the-middle (MitM) attacks, the following steps should take place as soon as possible in the production chain.

First of all, each node generates its own public key, which is directly (i.e., not through the Internet) exchanged with other devices in the same local network. After this phase is complete, the identities are stored in a blockchain through the imprinting process. An *imprinter* is a node designated to collect all the new identities, and forward them to the blockchain of choice.

In details, the imprinter is appointed to perform some critical tasks. First, the imprinter generates a special smart contract, the imprinting contract (IC), which links the device to the public key of its administrator. Once the generation is done, the imprinter collects the ICs and announces them to the blockchain, in order to ensure data immutability. From this moment on, these enrolled devices are able to interact with the UniquID infrastructure. If the device is transferred to another entity (e.g., sold to a customer), the administrator (e.g., the manufacturer) signs a contract and transfers the administrative rights by replacing its public key with that of the new owner. Ideally, due to the critical role of the imprinter, the manufacturer deploys a number of different imprinting nodes, to both speed up the imprinting process, and to avoid single point of failures in the architecture.

In Fig. 5, we show the main tasks performed during the imprinting phase. After that a node has created its identity (i.e., the public key), it announces such identity to the imprinter which is appointed to create the IC and to communicate it to the blockchain. At that point, the IC will go under the underlying blockchain processes, until it will be included in a new block and become almost immutable.

## 4   Experimental Evaluation

In this section, we present the experimental results of a UniquID enrolment instance, executed on a cloud service. Even though we measured the performance of the identity generation phase, as well as the imprinting phase, our goal is not to assess the performance of such instance. Indeed, the system scalability is tightly tied to the utilized resources, and the small setup we used for our experiments cannot represent a fully operating UniquID network. The aim of these experiments is to show that our solution is feasible, and that it successfully stores immutable identities on a public blockchain. On a larger scale, this would be enough to make PKIs, passwords, and certificates unnecessary.

To perform our experiments, we created 7 parallel clients, designated to generate 1000 virtual IoT identities and communicate such identities to 1 imprinting node. Every identity is announced as soon as it is created, and the receiving imprinting node is appointed both to create the IC transactions and forward

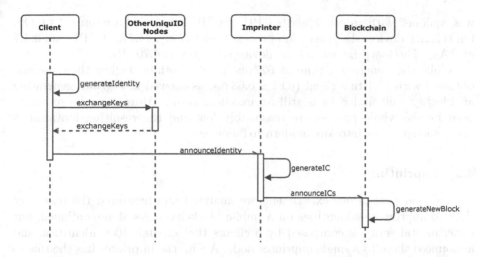

**Fig. 5.** Sequence diagram that depicts a standard imprinting ceremony.

them to the Litecoin Testnet blockchain (arbitrarily chosen for experimental purposes). Imprinter and clients ran over AWS T2. Micro instances, burstable performance instances equipped with 1 Gb of RAM. As a communication protocol between the imprinter and the clients, we used MQTT (Message Queue Telemetry Transport), an ISO standard (ISO/IEC PRF 20922) publish-subscribe-based messaging protocol [9], designed for lightweight communications.

As aforementioned, we chose Litecoin as a storing public blockchain, which ensures one mined block every 2.5 min. Considering that a Litecoin block is 1 Mb and that a UniquID transaction is 400 byte, this design choice entails a theoretical upper bound of 2500 enrolled devices per 2.5 min, or 1000 devices per minute. More in general, we can define the theoretical upper bound of enrolments per minute as follows:

$$\frac{Block\ Size\ (bytes)}{400\ (bytes)\ \cdot\ Average\ Mining\ Time\ (m)}, \tag{1}$$

where 400 bytes are the size of a UniquID transaction, and the other parameters depend on the underlying blockchain.

## 4.1   Identity Generation

In the first evaluation phase, we measured the time required to generate an identity on a virtual client. As shown in Fig. 6a, on average it took $6.61 \pm 0.03$ ms to generate an identity.

As stated before, in our experiments we delegated the generation task to the virtual clients. In an ideal scenario, the IoT devices would create and announce their identity themselves, therefore we performed an additional experiment, in order to evaluate the generation time on a low power device. The device we used was equipped with an *arm926ejste* CPU, 256 MB RAM, and a *mlinux 3.3.6* OS. On this IoT device, the generation process took 627 ms, 44.7% of CPU and 0.4% of RAM. The footprint left on the device storage was 6.70 MB.

While the generation time of 627 ms is substantially higher than the one obtained with a virtual client (6.61 ± 0.03 ms, as showed in Fig. 6a), generating an identity well under 1 s is still an excellent result. Moreover, the resources used by the whole process are reasonably low and the resulting footprint is small enough to fit into any modern IoT device.

## 4.2   Imprinting

As a second part of our experiment, we analysed and measured the necessary time to imprint new identities on a public blockchain. As aforementioned, our experimental setup is composed by 6 clients that created 1000 identities, and announced them to a single imprinter node. Again, the imprinter has the role to create an IC transaction for each identity and submit all the transactions to the blockchain. In Fig. 6b, we show that the average time to imprint one identity is 9.06 ± 0.35 min.

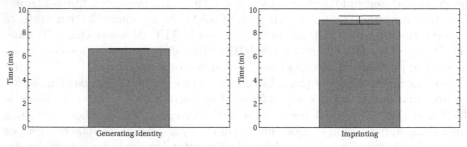

(a) Time is in *milliseconds*, error bar shows the Standard Error (SE).

(b) Time is in *minutes*, error bar shows the Standard Error (SE).

**Fig. 6.** Average times for generating and imprinting identities, respectively.

Our experiments clearly show that the imprinting phase took longer than identity generation phase: the former took minutes, whereas the latter took milliseconds. However, when we consider the imprinting time, we have to take into consideration that a public blockchain has inherent delays. As an example, Litecoin takes 2.5 min for generating a new block, and there is no guarantee that every transaction is going to be included in the next block, since many others might be waiting in the mining pool. Moreover, writing on the blockchain happens only when an identity has to be imprinted, or when its access policy has to be modified. Therefore, an average imprinting time of 9.06 ± 0.35 min is a reasonable result.

### 4.3  Summing Up: Enrolment

Our experiments show that, in total, it took around 4.5 h to automatically enrol (i.e., create, announce, and imprint) 1000 identities, without any human intervention. We tried to isolate the issue and find the reason why this practical result is considerably under the theoretical upper bound of 1000 enrolments per minute. Identity generation and imprinting processes took, altogether, less than 10 min per device, therefore we focused on the time that it took the IoT devices to announce their identity to the imprinter.

As we show in Fig. 7, we found out that generated identities were communicated to the imprinter with considerable delays. As a matter of fact it took an average time of $115.86 \pm 2.19$ min to announce a single identity, which is significantly larger than the time for identity generation ($6.61 \pm 0.03$ ms) and imprinting ($9.06 \pm 0.35$ min). We investigated the problem and we found out that, due to limitations in the Amazon AWS solution we used for the experiment, our virtual clients could not open more than 5 concurrent sockets, per each. This is a huge bottleneck that would not happen under normal conditions, as we show in the next paragraph.

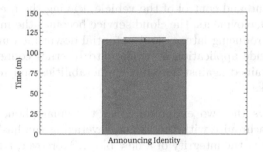

**Fig. 7.** Average time to announce one identity. Announce time is in minutes, error bar shows the Standard Error (SE).

**Internal Experiment.** In order to further investigate this communication bottleneck, we ran some internal tests with exactly the same network setup. These tests showed that we can easily run up to 50 concurrent threads per MQTT client, overcoming the communication bottleneck and increasing our capacity to 400 enrolments per minute. Still, at the present stage UniquID does not enable us to get near the theoretical upper bound, but this is purely due to software limitations that are currently being addressed.

To sum up, our experiments successfully show that is possible to automatically enrol IoT devices in a blockchain-based IAM. In practice, this means that enrolled devices no longer need to rely upon PKIs, centralized CA authorities, certificates, nor passwords. Moreover, our experiments lead to immutable identities, publicly verifiable by anyone on the Litecoin Testnet[2]. Once showed that our approach works in practice, the next step will be to optimise the performance to get as close as possible to the theoretical upper bound.

# 5   Case Studies

In this section, we present a couple of case studies to highlight UniquID strengths and variety of applications.

## 5.1   Smart Vehicle

Let us assume a connected vehicle with 3G cellular capability and a mobile app designed to unlock the doors or start the engine. In a typical scenario, the smartphone app connects to a RESTful cloud service responsible for authenticating the user and forwarding the command to the vehicle, leveraging an encrypted session pushed through an available 3G connection. This architecture presents three main issues:

- In the absence of 3G signal coverage, the cloud service cannot perform any remote command and control of the vehicle, leaving the user locked out [2].
- In large-scale deployments, the cloud service becomes the main bottleneck of the system, introducing latency and potential downtime during peak hours.
- Every vehicle-side application is exposed to Internet connectivity and thus must be maintained against zero-day vulnerabilities and malware and ransomware attacks [8].

UniquID allows the two endpoints (i.e., the smartphone and vehicle) to independently synchronize with the ledger, leveraging the hashcash PoW cost-function [1] to verify the integrity of a new block. Moreover, transactions stored as Merkle tree leaves allow efficient verification of the veracity of a new authorization [13]. Once this information is locally stored on both ends, handshake and authorization are performed through low-energy and proximity protocols (e.g., BLE) without relying on Internet connectivity or remote command-and-control services, as previously shown in Fig. 4. Figure 8 shows the resulting architecture.

## 5.2   Industrial Sensor Network

Consider an industrial Internet application where a large network of remotely installed, battery-operated sensors collect time series data in a low-connectivity environment. These sensors do not have cellular signal coverage, and satellite uplink is not a feasible option. The data from these sensors is periodically "harvested" by human operators through a portable device, such as a laptop or rugged tablet, using an ad-hoc Wi-Fi connection to the sensors. This architecture presents two main challenges:

---

[2] For instance, the first enrolment is verifiable at: https://testnet.litecore.io/tx/feac5a1dc645c701ea17ceb1657541d7094fbb43f18749cd9bd8a54014bd0197.

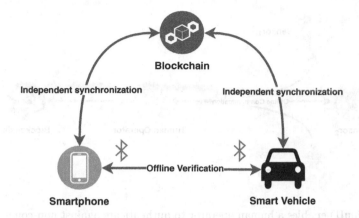

**Fig. 8.** UniquID enables M2M offline verification of smart contracts, which makes possible to start a loaned smart vehicle even in case of network failure.

- IAM for the sensors is achieved through Wi-Fi passwords, which require complex maintenance and periodic rotation (e.g., in case of operator change).
- Multi-tenancy scenarios require an additional layer of authentication at the application level, which needs to manage passwords stored on the sensor itself.

UniquID approach pushes the storage of these credentials onto the distributed ledger, enabling a remotely controlled, asynchronous IAM solution. A typical implementation leverages a central orchestration interface that sends microtransactions containing the ACL between one sensor and its authorized users on the distributed ledger. As a result, no passwords are needed: combining the ledger pseudonymous identity from the wallets (installed on the operator's device and the sensor), and blockchain-stored transactions that contain the ACLs, a sensor can recognize the operator's device and provide the data that the user is authorized to collect.

Furthermore, the operator acts as the dispatcher of the most recent blocks on the ledger. PoW is sufficient to verify the integrity of any received block, reducing the risk of forged blocks (which would require network consensus) and removing the need for a trusted session between peers. In this way, even if always disconnected from the Internet, sensors can be kept up to date with the latest authorizations stored on the ledger. Figure 9 shows the resulting architecture.

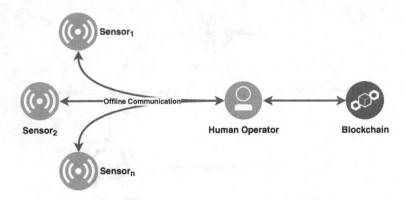

**Fig. 9.** UniquID enables a human operator to authenticate against non-connected sensors. Furthermore, the user dispatches to the sensors the latest blocks of the shared ledger.

# 6    Conclusion

In this paper, we first briefly covered why current IAM systems and PKIs are too cumbersome for the challenges posed by the IoT paradigm. We also showed how the CAP theorem strongly applies to blockchain-based IAMs, and how developers can independently decide how their applications react to network partitions.

We illustrated the overall UniquID architecture and how its SDK aims to simplify both the trust architecture as a whole and resource negotiation flows. We also discussed in detail how the backbone architecture of a blockchain-based IAM can be designed, as well as the benefits and drawbacks of each solution.

We provided an overview of the essential features that devices need to implement to participate in UniquID, as well as how the initial imprinting ceremony of such devices happens. We performed a proof-of-concept experiment which led to generating and imprinting 1000 identities on the Litecoin Testnet, virtually immutable and publicly verifiable by anyone. Last, but not least, we provided two relevant case studies that showed how UniquID could help unlock the potential of IoT. In future works we will conduct extensive experiments to assess the robustness and responsiveness of UniquID under a number of adverse conditions, such as man-in-the-middle and denial-of-service attacks.

Having shown the feasibility of our approach through practical experiments, future work will focus on optimising the performance of the system to get as close as possible to the theoretical upper bound of 1000 enrolled devices per minute.

**Acknowledgements.** We would like to thank Charles Kozierok for his help to proofread the manuscript.

# References

1. Back, A., et al.: Hashcash-a denial of service counter-measure (2002). http://www. hashcash.org/papers/hashcash.pdf
2. Boyle, D.: Tesla driver gets stranded in the desert after leaving his keys behind (2017). http://www.dailymail.co.uk/news/article-4128220/Tesla-driver-stranded-desert-forgot-keys.html
3. Brewer, E.: Cap twelve years later: How the "rules" have changed. Computer **45**(2), 23–29 (2012). https://doi.org/10.1109/MC.2012.37
4. Bünz, B., Bootle, J., Boneh, D., Poelstra, A., Wuille, P., Maxwell, G.: Bulletproofs: short proofs for confidential transactions and more. In: 2018 IEEE Symposium on Security and Privacy (SP), pp. 319–338 (2018). https://doi.org/10.1109/SP.2018. 00020
5. Caronni, G.: Walking the web of trust. In: IEEE 9th International Workshops on Enabling Technologies: Infrastructure for Collaborative Enterprises 2000, WET ICE 2000, pp. 153–158. IEEE (2000)
6. Dhillon, V., Metcalf, D., Hooper, M.: The hyperledger project. In: Dhillon, V., Metcalf, D., Hooper, M. (eds.) Blockchain Enabled Applications, pp. 139–149. Apress, Berkeley (2017). https://doi.org/10.1007/978-1-4842-3081-7_10
7. Grandison, T., Sloman, M.: A survey of trust in internet applications. IEEE Commun. Surv. Tutor. **3**(4), 2–16 (2000). https://doi.org/10.1109/COMST.2000. 5340804
8. Greenberg, A.: Hackers remotely kill a jeep on the highway with me in it (2015). https://www.wired.com/2015/07/hackers-remotely-kill-jeep-highway/
9. ISO/IEC: Iso/iec 20922:2016 - information technology - message queuing telemetry transport (mqtt) v3.1.1 (2016). https://www.iso.org/standard/69466.html
10. Kshetri, N.: Can blockchain strengthen the internet of things? IT Prof. **19**(4), 68–72 (2017). https://doi.org/10.1109/MITP.2017.3051335
11. Le, T., Mutka, M.W.: Capchain: a privacy preserving access control framework based on blockchain for pervasive environments. In: 2018 IEEE International Conference on Smart Computing (SMARTCOMP), pp. 57–64, June 2018. https://doi. org/10.1109/SMARTCOMP.2018.00074
12. van der Meulen, R.: Gartner says 6.4 billion connected "things" will be in use in 2016, up 30 percent from 2015 (2015). www.gartner.com/newsroom/id/3165317
13. Nakamoto, S.: Bitcoin: A peer-to-peer electronic cash system (2008). https:// bitcoin.org/bitcoin.pdf
14. Novo, O.: Blockchain meets IoT: an architecture for scalable access management in IoT. IEEE Internet Things J. **5**(2), 1184–1195 (2018). https://doi.org/10.1109/ JIOT.2018.2812239
15. Ouaddah, A., Abou Elkalam, A., Ait Ouahman, A.: Fairaccess: a new blockchain-based access control framework for the internet of things. Secur. Commun. Netw. **9**(18), 5943–5964 (2017). https://doi.org/10.1002/sec.1748
16. Roman, R., Zhou, J., Lopez, J.: On the features and challenges of security and privacy in distributed internet of things. Comput. Netw. **57**(10), 2266–2279 (2013). https://doi.org/10.1016/j.comnet.2012.12.018. http://www.sciencedirect. com/science/article/pii/S1389128613000054
17. Sasson, E.B., et al.: Decentralized anonymous payments from bitcoin. In: 2014 IEEE Symposium on Security and Privacy, pp. 459–474, May 2014. https://doi. org/10.1109/SP.2014.36

# Automated Composition, Analysis and Deployment of IoT Applications

Francisco Durán[1], Gwen Salaün[2(✉)], and Ajay Krishna[2]

[1] University of Málaga, Málaga, Spain
[2] Univ. Grenoble Alpes, CNRS, Grenoble INP, Inria, LIG, 38000 Grenoble, France
`Gwen.Salaun@inria.fr`

**Abstract.** Building IoT applications of added-value from a set of available devices with minimal human intervention is one of the main challenges facing the IoT. This is a difficult task that requires models for specifying objects, in addition to user-friendly and reliable composition techniques which in turn prevent the design of erroneous applications. In this work, we tackle this problem by first describing IoT applications using abstract models obtained from existing models of concrete devices. Then, we propose automated techniques for building compositions of devices using a repository of available devices, and an abstract goal of what the user expects from such compositions. Since the number of possible solutions can be quite high, we use both filtering and ranking techniques to provide the most pertinent solutions to users. The provided solutions satisfy the given goal and may be analysed with respect to properties such as deadlock-freeness or unmatched send messages. Finally, the application can be deployed using existing execution engines.

## 1 Introduction

The Internet of Things (IoT) is a network of physical devices and software entities that interact together for fulfilling an overall objective. Although the devices are already available and omnipresent in our daily lives, the software allowing us to easily connect and manipulate those objects is still under development. Composition of devices and objects is a difficult and error-prone task for several reasons. First, there is a need for languages and models for describing (heterogeneous) objects or object interfaces. Several levels of expressiveness can be considered depending on the characteristics of the object (signature, behaviour, semantics, quality of service). Once a model of objects is properly defined, one can design a composition by specifying how these objects interact. This composition process should be as automated as possible to make it usable in practice by any end-user. Moreover, when building such a composition, several kinds of mismatch can arise resulting in an erroneous application. Finally, the goal is to deploy and run IoT applications with minimal human intervention.

In this paper, we propose techniques for supporting end-users during the composition and deployment tasks. We have a specific focus in this work on behavioural models for objects, that is, each object must exhibit the actions or messages it can execute as well as the order in which these actions must be triggered. Given such models, our

© Springer Nature Switzerland AG 2019
M. Mazzara et al. (Eds.): TOOLS 2019, LNCS 11771, pp. 252–268, 2019.
https://doi.org/10.1007/978-3-030-29852-4_21

techniques aim at automatically building satisfactory compositions given a repository of available objects and a description of the result that we call *goal*. The goal is an abstract specification of what the user expects from the resulting composition. A composition is satisfactory if it conforms to the goal requirements. Moreover, a composition can be analysed to check whether some additional correctness properties are verified. For example, such a property can state that each reachable send message has a matching receive message in another object. Finally, when a satisfactory composition is obtained, it is deployed by relying on existing execution engines.

Our solution consists of several consecutive steps for computing satisfactory compositions. First, we extract from the repository relevant objects wrt. the goal of the composition. For those objects, we compute all combinations and apply filtering techniques for keeping only objects exhibiting expected interactions according to the goal. We then check whether the remaining candidate compositions respect a defined compatibility notion. In this paper, we use a notion based on the equivalence of the intended goal with a candidate composition of objects. Additional properties can be verified on the resulting compositions, such as, e.g., the absence of deadlocks. If there are several compositions that satisfy the goal, we use ranking techniques for presenting the results in a specific order according to several possible relevance criteria.

The whole composition process is automated by an implementation in Maude [11]. We also propose full automation of the deployment of the designed application, which allows our approach to support the development of IoT applications from the selection of a subset of satisfactory objects to their final deployment. In this work, we rely on Mozilla Project Things as execution and deployment platform, although other IoT platforms could have been used (Home Assistant, IFTTT, OpenHAB, etc.). We assume that objects are described using the Web Thing Description format by Mozilla. We also assume that the objects available in a given context (room, house, building, etc.) can be discovered using a *search* service, resulting in what we call a repository of objects. The goal provided by the end-user is described using a set of rules *IF event THEN action* representing what is expected from the generated composition.

Our prototype tool was applied to several examples for validation purposes. Since we target in this work applications at the level of a building (private house, office, nurse home, etc.), we made experiments with repositories consisting of about one hundred objects, for which the approach was able to compute compositions satisfying a given goal within a reasonable amount of time.

The rest of this paper is organized as follows. Section 2 introduces the model we use for objects and other notions (repository, goal, environment). Section 3 first presents the different steps that constitute our approach for automated composition of objects, and then describes our implementation and some experiments we carried out on several examples. Section 4 presents how IoT applications can be deployed in practice. Section 5 compares our approach to related work and Sect. 6 concludes the paper.

## 2   Models

In this section, we first introduce the model we use for describing devices and objects. Note that in the paper, for the sake of simplicity, we mainly use *object* as a common term for both devices and software elements. A repository is a set of objects, each object belonging to a family (TV, camera, light bulb, software app, window, etc.). We then present our notion of composition, which relies on implicit bindings. Finally, we define the notion of goal that is used in this work for guiding the composition process and the notion of environment for modelling open systems.

```
{ "name": "Hue temp sensor",
  "type": "",
  "@context": "https://iot.mozilla.org/schemas",
  "@type": [ "TemperatureSensor" ],
  "href": "/things/hue-2",
  "properties": { "temperature": {
       "title": "Temperature",
       "type": "number",
       "@type": "TemperatureProperty",
       "unit": "degree celsius",
       "readOnly": true,
       "links": [ { "rel": "property",
       "href": "/things/hue-2/properties/temperature" } ] } } }
```

**Listing 1.** An excerpt from the JSON Thing Description of Hue temperature sensor

In this work, we assume that objects are described using Mozilla's Web Thing Description format,[1] which provides a vocabulary for describing objects in a machine readable format with a JSON encoding. The description is complementary to the current W3C Web of Things (WoT) Working Group's abstract data model. WoT architectural style uses foundations of Web technology to build IoT in a decentralised, inter-operable, and scalable fashion [15]. Our choice of WoT-based description is guided by the fact that *things* in WoT are backed by a standard data model and APIs which help in real-world deployment of objects. However, for designing the composition, we prefer to rely on an abstract model for objects, where we just keep the two most important attributes from a composition perspective, namely Event and Action. An *event* is emitted by a device (e.g., a room becomes too dark) whereas an *action* can be carried out on a device (e.g., turn on a light). The *properties* attribute in a Thing Description provides information on the type of event or action the device supports. Listing 1 shows an excerpt of the Hue temperature sensor description which describes a temperature sensor property. Since an order is possible between several events/actions (e.g., turn on a light and then turn off the light), we also keep this order in the model. To sum up, we describe an object using a Labelled Transition System (LTS) where labels either correspond to events or actions.

**Definition 1.** *An object is an LTS* $(S, s^0, \Sigma, T)$ *where* $S$ *is a finite set of states,* $s^0 \in S$ *is the initial state,* $\Sigma = \Sigma^! \cup \Sigma^? \cup \{\tau\}$ *is a finite alphabet partitioned into a set of events, a set of actions, and the internal action* $\tau$, *and* $T \subseteq S \times \Sigma \times S$ *is a transition relation.*

We write $m!$ for an action $m \in \Sigma^!$ and $m?$ for an event $m \in \Sigma^?$. We also call them as send and receive messages, respectively, for homogeneity reasons. We use the symbol $\tau$ for representing internal activities (variable assignment, internal computation, local decision, etc.). A transition is represented as $s \xrightarrow{l} s' \in T$ where $l \in \Sigma$.

---

[1] Project Things by Mozilla: https://iot.mozilla.org/wot/.

This abstract model presents two advantages. First, it allows us to support any concrete model for a Thing Description in a uniform way. Second, it is simple and expressive enough for designing a composition consisting of several objects.

We assume that each object comes with a defined model that can be automatically obtained from its JSON description. As far as the behavioural part is concerned (LTS), this can be defined by an expert who has the knowledge of the device (i.e., device manufacturers can provide the model along with the datasheet) or they can be built by learning the behaviour of these devices [23].

We call *repository* a set of objects available, for example, in a room, a house or a building, depending on the context of the application. In practice, these objects are discovered using a *search* functionality that allows to identify all objects available on a given network. Search can be implemented using the mDNS protocol on the network or via Bluetooth Eddystone beacon for devices in close physical proximity. Each object is defined by its concrete model in JSON format. As far as composition is concerned, abstract models introduced before are enough, and therefore we assume that each object is defined by its abstract model (LTS) and is associated to a family.

**Definition 2.** *A repository is a set of couples $(F, O)$ where $F$ is a family name and $O$ is a set of objects defined by their abstract model.*

A *composition* is defined as a set of objects described by their abstract models. We assume the objects involved in a composition interact using binary communication. This means that one interaction occurs between one send message (action) and one receive message (event) of two different objects on the same message name. Additionally, we consider a synchronous communication model, that is, two objects involved in an interaction evolve at the same time when communicating (a.k.a. handshake communication). Considering asynchronous communication (communication via message buffers or publish-subscribe) is part of the perspectives of this work.

A *goal* is an abstract description of what the end-user expects from the composition-to-be. To define this goal, we take inspiration into recent languages proposed for connecting devices and software (IFTTT) or for smart home software automation (Open-HAB). A goal is thus defined as a set of rules *IF x THEN y*, where $x$ and $y$ correspond to interactions between two objects. A goal is also defined by a set of family names, which gives an information about the objects to participate in the composition. E.g., the user can write that she wants three objects in the composition: a TV, a camera and a motion sensor. Family names can be derived from the @*type* member annotation of the Web Thing Description model. This annotation describes the device capabilities and required properties which is the basis for defining families. E.g., the Hue temperature sensor description in Listing 1 belongs to the TemperatureSensor family of devices.

**Definition 3.** *A goal is a couple $(R, FS)$ where $R$ is a set of rules and $FS$ is a set of family names.*

Since a set of rules directly translates to an LTS (each rule transforms to a sequence of two transitions outgoing from the initial state and coming back to it), goals can also be designed as LTSs (as shown in the running example at the end of this section).

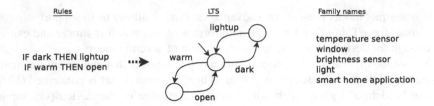

**Fig. 1.** Running example: goal

Last, it is worth observing that, given the dynamicity of IoT applications, we cannot assume that compositions of objects are built once and for all. They can evolve over time and objects can be added/removed for several reasons (replacement, loss of connectivity, upgrade, failure, etc.). Therefore, an IoT application can be seen like an open system where all messages are not necessarily bound and can be kept open for further addition of objects. Unbound messages can also correspond to external behaviours (a motion or an action of a human being). In our approach, we consider these actions to be part of the *environment*. The environment can be initially empty and enriched throughout the composition process, if necessary.

**Definition 4.** *An environment is a set of send and receive messages.*

*Example.* As a running example, we use a smart home application, which aims at automatically regulating the temperature and brightness in a house. To do so, we require five objects, namely a temperature sensor, a connected window, a brightness sensor, a light, as well as a piece of software, namely a smart home application running on a smartphone and acting like an orchestrator. We now define the goal of the composition using the rules (and corresponding LTS) given in Fig. 1. As described in this figure, the end-user expects two behaviours from the composition-to-be: (i) when a temperature sensor detects a too-high temperature with respect to human standards (say 20 °C), a window should be opened; (ii) when a brightness sensor detects a too low level of luminosity, a light should be turned on. We will present in the next section the techniques we propose for automatically computing compositions satisfying the goal from a set of objects available in the repository.

## 3    Composition and Analysis

In this section, we present our techniques for automatically computing IoT applications by composition of available objects. Figure 2 presents an overview of the different steps of our approach, which takes as input a repository of objects, a goal and an environment. As output, we generate a list of resulting compositions satisfying the goal (also called compatible compositions) and possibly satisfying additional properties of interest such as deadlock freeness. This list can be empty if there is no solution. If there is more than a solution, the solutions are ranked with respect to some quality criterion. Note that human intervention is required only at the beginning of the composition process to define the goal and if necessary, the environment. Each step of our approach refines the number of candidate compositions ($C' \subseteq C$ and $C'' \subseteq C'$), but for the last step (ranking) that only orders the compositions taken as input without discarding any of them.

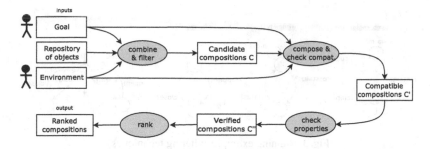

**Fig. 2.** Overview of the approach

In the rest of this section, we first present with more details each step of the approach. Then, we introduce the implementation of these techniques using Maude. Finally, we describe some experiments we carried out for validating our approach.

### 3.1   Steps of Our Approach

**Combine and Filter.** The first step of our approach takes as input the part of the goal corresponding to the set of family names and the repository, and generates all possible combinations. For example, if the composition needs a temperature sensor and a connected window, and there are two different temperature sensors and three windows in the repository, we generate all possible combinations (six possible couples in that specific case). For each combination, we apply some filtering techniques to discard it if we know beforehand that this composition will not be able to satisfy the given goal. To do so, we rely on static analysis of the alphabets of the objects involved in a candidate composition. We do not want to build the result of the composition (the LTS corresponding to all possible executions of a set of interacting objects) because this would be too costly computationally speaking. This composition LTS will be built in the next step only for candidate compositions that are not discarded by the filtering process.

The filtering process aims at traversing the alphabet of the goal and at checking whether, for each element of the goal alphabet, there are two objects in the composition with matching messages on that message, that is, one send message and one receive message with that label in two different objects. This is mandatory, otherwise no interaction would be possible on that message, resulting in a deadlock. This approach is purely syntactic, so it is very efficient, but we may still have unsatisfactory candidate compositions. The next step builds the behavioural composition for this set of candidate objects and explores all possible executions to verify that the aforementioned interactions can effectively occur according to the behavioural models of the involved objects.

**Definition 5.** *Given a goal $(G, FS)$ with $G = (S_G, s_G^0, \Sigma_G, T_G)$ and a set of n object LTSs $(S_i, s_i^0, \Sigma_i, T_i)$ corresponding to a candidate composition according to the family names*

*given in FS, this composition is not filtered out iff for each $m \in \Sigma_G$, $\exists i, j \in \{1, \ldots, n\}$,
such that $m \in \Sigma_i^!$ and $m \in \Sigma_j^?$.*

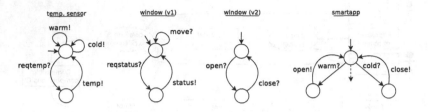

**Fig. 3.** Running example: filtering techniques

*Example.* Let us illustrate filtering techniques on the running example, and more particularly on the bottom half of the goal given in Fig. 1, which focuses on temperature and
windows. In this part of the goal, we need one temperature sensor, one window and one
smart app. The smart app acts like an orchestrator and is usually defined by end-users
or reused from existing applications proposing common scenarios for them. The smart
app may provide many functionalities, but we focus on those of interest with respect
to the current goal. Figure 3 gives four possible objects that match the required family
names. Consider successively the two following combinations (temp. sensor, window
(v1), smartapp) and (temp. sensor, window (v2), smartapp). The first composition is
discarded by our filtering techniques, because there is one interaction appearing in the
goal ('open') that is not possible in the composition (missing 'open?' message). The
second composition is preserved by our filtering techniques because both 'warm' and
'open' interactions are possible.

**Compose and Check Compatibility.** This step takes as input all combinations of
objects obtained using the family names defined in the goal and the repository, which
have been kept after application of the filtering techniques. For each combination, we
first build the resulting LTS corresponding to the composition a.k.a. synchronous product [2] in the automata-based terminology. This LTS is built independently of the goal.
It considers the objects involved in the combination and the environment. All synchronize on the intersection of their alphabets (no independent evolution of observable messages). We recall that the communication model is synchronous, binary, and matches
two transitions with the same label and opposite directions (sender and receiver).

**Definition 6.** *Given a set of n object LTSs $(S_i, s_i^0, \Sigma_i, T_i)$, the synchronous composition
is the labelled transition system $CLTS = (S_c, s_c^0, \Sigma_c, T_c)$ where:*

- $S_c = S_1 \times \ldots \times S_n$
- $s_c^0 \in S_c$ *such that* $s_c^0 = (s_1^0, \ldots, s_n^0)$
- $\Sigma_c = \cup_i \Sigma_i$
- $T_c \subseteq S_c \times \Sigma_c \times S_c$, *and for* $s = (s_1, \ldots, s_n) \in S_c$ *and* $s' = (s_1', \ldots, s_n') \in S_c$:

*(interact)* $s \xrightarrow{m} s' \in T_c$ *if* $\exists i, j \in \{1, \dots, n\}$ *where* $i \neq j : m \in \Sigma_i^! \cap \Sigma_j^?$ *where* $\exists$
$s_i \xrightarrow{m!} s_i' \in T_i,$ *and* $s_j \xrightarrow{m?} s_j' \in T_j$ *such that* $\forall k \in \{1, \dots, n\}, k \neq i \wedge k \neq$
$j \Rightarrow s_k' = s_k$

*(internal)* $s \xrightarrow{\tau} s' \in T_c$ *if* $\exists i \in \{1, \dots, n\}, \exists s_i \xrightarrow{\tau} s_i' \in T_i$ *such that* $\forall k \in \{1, \dots, n\}, k \neq$
$i \Rightarrow s_k' = s_k$

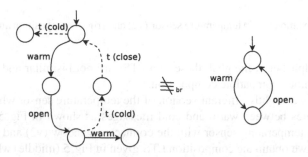

**Fig. 4.** Running example: composition and compatibility

Once the composition LTS is built, we first hide all interactions in the composition LTS that do not belong to the alphabet of the goal. Then, we need to compare both LTSs (goal LTS and composition LTS) to check if they produce the same observational behaviours. Since there are possibly hidden (or $\tau$) transitions in the composition LTS, we need to use a comparison notion that takes these specific transitions into account. This is the case of the branching bisimulation [25] ($\equiv_{br}$), which is one of the finest bisimulation notions to compare LTSs in presence of hidden actions.

**Definition 7.** *Given a goal LTS G and a composition LTS CLTS build from a set of object LTSs, these objects satisfy the goal iff:* $hide_{\Sigma_G}(CLTS) \equiv_{br} G$.

These two steps are applied to all candidate compositions issued from the combine and filter step. Each composition respecting the above criterion is part of the resulting set of compatible compositions.

*Example.* Going back to the running example and particularly to the result obtained in the previous step to compose objects temp. sensor, window (v2), and smartapp (Fig. 3), we first build the composition of those three objects. We assume the environment is empty in that case. Figure 4 shows the resulting composition LTS where we can see that there are four possible interactions in a loop. Note that this loop exists because the window can alternatively be opened and closed in sequence. Moreover, there are two other interactions ('cold' and 'warm') corresponding to messages exchanged between the temperature sensor and the smart application. Therefore, as far as compatibility is concerned, when we compare the goal (half of it to be precise) with the composition LTS where we hide interactions 'cold' and 'close' (dashed transitions) that do not

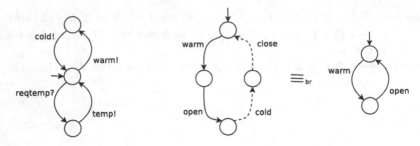

**Fig. 5.** Running example: (left) temperature sensor (v2) and (right) composition and compatibility

belong to the alphabet of the goal, these two LTSs are not bisimilar and the candidate composition is not a compatible composition.

Assume now a slightly different version of the temperature sensor where the model actually alternates between warm and cold messages as shown in Fig. 5 (left). When composing this temperature sensor with the connected window (v2) and the smart app given in Fig. 3, we obtain the composition LTS given in Fig. 5 (middle) where only four possible interactions in a loop are maintained. This LTS turns out to be bisimilar then compatible when focusing on the goal alphabet only.

**Check Properties.** After compatibility checking, we keep only compositions that satisfy the goal as explained beforehand. However, these compositions may not satisfy additional properties. In this paper, we focus on properties that are independent of the application. Properties that depend on the application (e.g., a specific message never occurs after another one) can be specified using temporal logic and verified using model checking techniques [4] for instance. As far as independent properties are concerned, we present two examples of such properties in this paper, namely deadlock freeness and unmatched send messages.

In our context, a deadlock occurs when there is a (global) state in the composition LTS without outgoing transition and there is one object that could evolve independently from its (local) state because in its own model there is an outgoing transition. If we put it in another way, this object has a possible behaviour to move on in its model but this transition cannot be executed in the context of the composition.

**Definition 8.** *Given a set of object LTSs $(S_i, s_i^0, \Sigma_i, T_i)$ and the corresponding composition LTS CLTS = $(S_c, s_c^0, \Sigma_c, T_c)$, the composition is deadlocking if there is a global state $s = (s_1, \ldots, s_n) \in S_c$ such that $\nexists s \xrightarrow{l} s' \in T_c$ but $\exists j \in \{1, \ldots, n\}, s_j \in S_j$ and $s_j \xrightarrow{l'} s_j' \in T_j$ where $l'$ is either a send or receive message.*

This notion of deadlock is quite strong, because we focus on global states without outgoing transitions. There is another similar case in which there is a global state with at least one outgoing transition, and there is one object with a local transition outgoing from that state labelled with a send message that does not appear in the composition LTS. This property allows one to detect unmatched send messages.

**Definition 9.** *Given a set of object LTSs $(S_i, s_i^0, \Sigma_i, T_i)$ and the corresponding composition LTS CLTS = $(S_c, s_c^0, \Sigma_c, T_c)$, there is unmatched send messages if $\exists s =$*

$(s_1, \ldots, s_n) \in S_c$, such that $\exists s \xrightarrow{l} s' \in T_c$ and $\exists j \in \{1, \ldots, n\}, s_j \in S_j$ and $s_j \xrightarrow{m!} s'_j \in T_j$ and $\forall s \xrightarrow{l} s' \in T_c, l \neq m$.

*Example.* For illustration purposes, let us focus on the part of the running example that aims at lighting up/down the room depending on the level of brightness. To do so, we present three objects in Fig. 6 (left) resulting in a compatible composition: the composition LTS (middle) and the goal (right) are bisimilar. The resulting composition (middle) is free of deadlocks, but is not free of unmatched send messages because in both global states in the composition, the brightness sensor can always send a 'bright!' message, which is not caught in the composition because there is no counterpart ('bright?') in any other object. In such a situation, the user can either decide to move on because this is not a problem (can be amended, for example, by adding 'bright?' to the environment) or to choose another compatible composition satisfying this property.

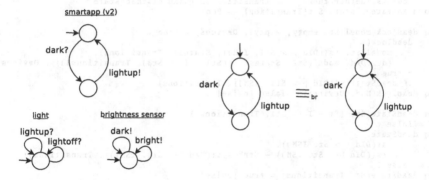

**Fig. 6.** Running example: (left) objects, (middle) composition and (right) goal

**Rank.** In its current version, we rank satisfactory compositions according to their *complexity*. As complexity criterion, we consider the size of the composition LTS in terms of number of transitions. The composition ranked first corresponds to the solution that can satisfy the expected goal with the lowest number of interactions.

## 3.2    Implementation

We have developed the techniques presented in the former section using Maude's rewriting logic framework [11]. We chose Maude for implementing the composition techniques because its declarative style facilitates program writing, and specifically, it is quite simple to implement filtering techniques, composition or compatibility analysis. Moreover, Maude is adequate to specify concurrent systems and is equipped with a large variety of analysis tools.

Maude is a high-level language and a high-performance system that supports membership equational logic, and rewriting logic specification and programming of systems. Rewriting logic [20] is a logic of change that can naturally deal with state and with highly nondeterministic concurrent computations. Rewriting logic is parameterised by an equational logic, and therefore, Maude integrates an equational style of functional programming with rewriting logic computation. In the Maude implementation of rewriting logic, the equational logic is membership equational logic [7]. Membership equational logic is a Horn logic whose atomic sentences are equalities $t = t'$ and membership assertions of the form $t : S$, stating that a term $t$ has sort $S$. Such a logic extends order-sorted equational logic, and supports sorts, subsort relations, subsort polymorphic overloading of operators, and the definition of partial functions with equationally defined domains. Further details may be found in [11].

The Maude's implementation consists of different modules. Unfortunately, for the sake of space, we cannot present in detail the contents of these modules. The interested reader should look at the Maude specification, together with a set of examples, which is available online [13].

```
1  ---- seeks a global state corresponding to a deadlock
2  op deadlock : LTS Set{Device} -> Bool .
3  ---- checks whether there is a transition outgoing of that state
4  op deadState : State Set{Transition} -> Bool .
5
6  eq deadlock(model(St, empty, empty), Devices) = true .
7  ceq deadlock(
8          model(St, (s((DId |-> St1, ISM)), States), Transitions),
9          (dev(DId, model(St2, States1, ((St1 - I -> St3), Transitions1))), Devices))
10     = true
11     if deadState(s((DId |-> St1, ISM)), Transitions) .
12  eq deadlock(Mod, Devices) = false [owise] .
13
14  eq deadState(St, (St - I -> St1, Transitions))
15     = false .
16  eq deadState(
17          s((DId |-> St, ISM)),
18          (s((DId |-> St, ISM)) - Str -> s((DId |-> St1, ISM1)), Transitions))
19     = false .
20  eq deadState(St, Transitions) = true [owise] .
```

**Listing 2.** Equations for deadlock checking in the Maude implementation

A first module defines all necessary data types presented in Sect. 2 (object model, repository, goal, environment). Then, we have one module for each step of the approach presented in Sect. 3.1 and summarized in Fig. 2. Finally, we use a couple of additional modules for defining concrete objects grouped in a repository and several examples of goals for making experiments that we will present in Sect. 3.3.

Let us illustrate our Maude implementation with the verification of compositions. Listing 2 gives the equations used for identifying that a (global) state corresponds to a deadlock state. The deadlock operation takes as input the composition LTS and the set of device models. The first equation (line 6) applies when the composition LTS does not contain any state. The second equation is the most interesting. It says that if there is one global state (line 8) in the composition LTS corresponding to a deadlock state (line 11) that is a state without outgoing transition, and if there is one device with one possible transition from that local state (line 9), then this means that this behaviour cannot be executed in the context of this composition, and the equation returns true (line 10). The deadState operation (lines 14–20) takes a state and an LTS as input and checks whether from that state there is an outgoing transition. The first equation (lines 14–15) applies to simple devices. The second equation (line 16–19) applies to composition LTSs. Both

**Table 1.** Experimental results (~0 for values smaller than 0.1 s)

| Goal | | | \|Repo.\| | \|Combinations\| | | | Time (s) | | | |
|---|---|---|---|---|---|---|---|---|---|---|
| Ident. | \|O\| | \|T\| | | Combine | Filter | Compo/check | Combine | Filter | Compo | Check |
| G1 | 3 | 6 | 30 | 160 | 1 | 1 | ~0 | ~0 | ~0 | ~0 |
| G1 | 3 | 6 | 80 | 220 | 1 | 1 | ~0 | ~0 | ~0 | ~0 |
| G1 | 3 | 6 | 150 | 5,544 | 13 | 12 | ~0 | ~0 | ~0 | ~0 |
| G2 | 5 | 4 | 30 | 288 | 18 | 1 | ~0 | ~0 | ~0 | ~0 |
| G2 | 5 | 4 | 80 | 217,800 | 5,760 | 2 | 1.7 | 3.8 | 3.1 | 5.9 |
| G2 | 5 | 4 | 150 | 401,544 | 11,000 | 2 | 3.3 | 8.3 | 14.8 | 10.9 |
| G3 | 5 | 8 | 30 | 7 | 0 | 0 | ~0 | ~0 | ~0 | ~0 |
| G3 | 5 | 8 | 80 | 119 | 0 | 0 | ~0 | ~0 | ~0 | ~0 |
| G3 | 5 | 8 | 150 | 218 | 1 | 1 | ~0 | ~0 | ~0 | ~0 |
| G4 | 8 | 10 | 30 | 336 | 0 | 0 | ~0 | ~0 | ~0 | ~0 |
| G4 | 8 | 10 | 80 | 143,990 | 220 | 0 | 19.9 | 22.1 | ~0 | ~0 |
| G4 | 8 | 10 | 150 | 374,088 | 220 | 0 | 54.5 | 49.1 | ~0 | ~0 |
| G5 | 10 | 10 | 150 | 1,800 | 1 | 1 | ~0 | 0.1 | ~0 | ~0 |
| G6 | 15 | 10 | 150 | 57,600 | 2 | 2 | 1.1 | 4.7 | 0.3 | 1.6 |
| G7 | 20 | 20 | 150 | 225,792 | 1 | 1 | 5.9 | 28.5 | 0.1 | 12.6 |

equations correspond to the case in which there is such a transition and return false. The final equation (line 20) applies otherwise and returns true.

## 3.3 Experiments

The final part of this section presents some experiments we carried out to see how our approach scales with respect to the number of objects available in the repository and with respect to the size of the goal. The experiments were run on a macOS Mojave machine with a 2.8 GHz Intel Core i7 processor, 16 GB of DDR3 RAM and 256 GB PCIe-based flash storage. We recall that our approach targets small to medium-size applications, corresponding to a number of objects available in a smart home or building.

Table 1 presents the results obtained for seven different goals. G2 corresponds to the goal of the running example given in Fig. 1. For the first four goals, we vary the size of the repository, that is, the number of objects available in the repository. More specifically, we use three repositories of different sizes (30 objects, 80 objects, and 150 objects). As for the three last goals (G5 to G7), we only use the largest one (150 objects). Table 1 then gives the number of possible combinations according to the list of family names given in the goal (combine), the number of compositions selected after application of the filtering techniques (filter), the number of compatible compositions satisfying the goal (compose and check compatibility), and the time it takes to compute all these steps. When a time is smaller than 0.1 s, we use ~0.

First of all, it is worth noting that for all these small and medium size (yet realistic) compositions, the results are computed in a reasonable time (about a total of four minutes for all the examples given in Table 1).

The increase in terms of computational time mainly comes from the number of possible combinations. It takes more time to compute and explore all possible combinations to see whether they are possible candidates (kept after filtering) and finally solutions wrt. the expected goal. The number of combinations augments for three reasons. The first factor is the number of objects in the repository. When looking at G2 in the table for instance, one can see that the number of combinations and the computation times increase when considering a repository with 30, 80 or 150 objects. The second factor is the number of objects involved in the composition. Goals G5, G6 and G7 show compositions involving 10, 15 and 20 objects. Here again, the number of objects induces a larger number of combinations and an increase in computation time. The third reason is not obvious because it concerns the number of objects in each family. If we look at goals G2 or G4 in the table with a repository of 150 objects, we can see that even for a limited number of objects (5 and 8), the number of combinations is rather high. This is because in both cases, the families of objects specified in the goal have many instances of objects in the repository (more than 10 concrete objects for each family), resulting in many combinations. In contrast, if the goal has many objects, but families with fewer instances, as it is the case for goal G5 for example, there are not so many combinations.

Once all combinations are computed, filtering is applied on all those combinations. Obviously, the more combinations, the costlier is filtering. This is why these two numbers (time for generating combinations and for applying filtering) are related and usually quite close. The final step computes the synchronous composition of all objects for each remaining combination and checks whether the resulting composition LTS matches the goal. This step is definitely the costliest. As an example, for G2 (150 objects), after filtering there still are 11,000 possible candidates, and it takes about 25 s to generate the compositions and analyse them, whereas it takes less than 10 s to generate all combinations (about 400,000) and apply filtering on them.

As a conclusion, it is worth noting the importance of the filtering techniques that can avoid the unnecessary and costly computation of some candidate compositions as well as their compatibility analysis. All the times given in the table are reasonable because the filtering techniques return a low number of candidate compositions.

## 4    Deployment

This section details the real-world deployment of IoT devices using an execution platform. We use the Mozilla Project Things as it is open-source and one of the feature-rich implementations of WoT. However, any standard IoT platform, such as OpenHAB or Home Assistant, can also be used for deployment. Specifically from our point of interest, Things Gateway from Mozilla has a unified Web interface to monitor and control devices. It also provides REST APIs to create and deploy rules.

Given a set of available objects (repository) and a set of abstract rules (goal), after the application of the process presented in Sect. 3, we obtain a subset of these objects satisfying the rules. This section explains how this application can be deployed on the platform. Recall that the events and actions in the abstract rules are associated with the *properties* attribute of the Thing Description. Therefore, in order to deploy each abstract rule, we first map the events and actions of the abstract rules to its corresponding *properties* in the JSON Thing Description. An action or an event relates to a change in property values. Using this idea, we generate a rule in JSON format for each abstract rule. Further, we use the gateway API provided by the platform, which takes a JSON rule as input, to deploy each newly created rule.

*Example.* We have deployed our running example using the following devices: Philips Hue Play Light, Philips Motion Sensor which has a built-in ambient light sensor and a temperature sensor. As our device repository did not have smart window, we created virtual Things adapters to emulate the smart window. We use the *TemperatureProperty* of the Philips Hue temperature sensor as shown in Fig. 1 to build the concrete rule "IF warm THEN open". The deployable rule is shown in Listing 3, where we notice that warm translates to temperature greater than 20 °C (*value* attribute set to 20). Users can configure such constants or keywords to make the rules closer to the natural language. The action in the rule is described in the *effect* attribute, where a boolean property is set to *on* in the virtual environment thing.

```
{ "enabled": true,
  "trigger": { "type": "MultiTrigger",
    "op": "AND",
    "triggers": [ { "type": "LevelTrigger",
      "label": "Temperature",
      "property": { "type": "number", "thing": "hue-2", "id": "temperature", "unit
        ": "degree celsius" },
      "value": 20,
      "levelType": "GREATER"} ] },
  "effect": { "type": "MultiEffect",
    "effects": [ { "type": "SetEffect", "label": "On/Off",
      "property": { "type": "boolean", "thing": "virtual-env-1", "id": "on" },
      "value": true } ] } }
```

**Listing 3.** WoT rule JSON corresponding to abstract rule IF warm THEN open

# 5   Related Work

We discuss in this section some relate work on automated composition of Web services, compatibility of behavioural models, and (automated) composition of IoT objects.

Automated composition was mainly studied in the Web services area. Several papers have been published on that problem, see, e.g., [5,6,18,21]. Most of these techniques rely on Web service languages, namely WSDL and BPEL, whereas we preferred to rely on generic behavioural models to make our solution more easily reusable in other application areas. These papers make use of existing planning techniques and tools. We preferred a different solution since we choose rule-based programming and rewriting logic for computing the resulting compositions. Our approach also provides (automated) verification techniques to check for compatibility and other properties of interest.

As far as compatibility checking is concerned, several works have focused on this problem assuming that entities are described using behavioural models, see, e.g. [3,8,10,12,17,19,26]. [10] proposes the $\pi$-calculus as modelling language and defines a compatibility relation taking inspiration into Milner's bisimulation notion.

[19] presents a framework for modelling Web service with Petri nets and for analysing several properties on these models, the most important being the usability property, which is verified using the soundness criterion for workflow modules. In [3], the authors address the composability of components. They assume that two software components are composable if their respective services are pairwise compatible, where service compatibility is understood as deadlock-freeness. [17] proposes an approach based on Symbolic Observation Graphs (SOG) allowing one to decide whether two services can cooperate safely. The compatibility between two services is defined by the well-known soundness property on open workflow nets. Our approach proposes a notion of goal-based compatibility for IoT applications obtained by composition of available devices and its verification using rewriting logic and Maude's framework.

We finally introduce recent results and tools for the composition and configuration of IoT applications. From an industrial perspective, Node-RED [16] and IFTTT [22] are two tools that provide graphical support for visually and manually building applications consisting of connected objects. We chose full automation and synthesis of the object composition in our approach. [14] shows how to use Answer Set Programming (ASP) techniques to represent configuration scenarios for basic applications in the IoT. [1] proposes an approach that makes a set of things connect and cooperate temporarily to achieve a user goal. [24] presents a formal approach for the decomposition of process-aware applications to be deployed in IoT environments. These applications are modelled using Petri nets and correctness of the decomposition is proved with respect to language preservation. In [9], the authors present a solution to the dynamic composition of services. To do so, they rely on stateful models of services, contextual information, a goal description and planning techniques in order to generate automatically a resulting composition of services. Similarly to [9,24], we rely on behavioural models of objects with a specific focus here on the automated composition of objects. We provide additional techniques for facing the large number of solutions (filtering and ranking) as well as automated verification techniques for ensuring compatibility and additional properties. Last but not least, we also support the deployment of concrete applications.

## 6   Concluding Remarks

We have presented some automated techniques for generating and deploying satisfactory compositions given an abstract goal of the composition-to-be and a set of object families. Our approach works applying successively different steps. First, from a repository of available objects, we generate a set of candidate compositions statically filtering those that cannot satisfy the goal. Then, we check if these candidates satisfy the given goal and are therefore compatible compositions. The user can also decide to verify additional properties that are independent of the application such as deadlock freeness or the absence of unmatched send messages. If there is more than one solution, we rank them according to some complexity criterion. Finally, the resulting composition is deployed using an existing execution engine. The composition and analysis process are supported by an implementation in Maude. The deployment process is carried out using Mozilla's Project Things platform. We applied the whole approach on several case studies for validation purposes.

The first perspective of this work is to consider location of objects in the object model and composition goal. We believe that this information would allow us to make our approach scalable in order to target larger applications (at the level of a campus or a city for example). More precisely, this information would be used during the composition process for improving our filtering techniques and for finding the best combinations without exhaustively producing and analysing all of them. Considering asynchronous communication (communication via message buffers or publish-subscribe) is another perspective of this work.

# References

1. Alkhabbas, F., De Sanctis, M., Spalazzese, R., Bucchiarone, A., Davidsson, P., Marconi, A.: Enacting emergent configurations in the IoT through domain objects. In: Pahl, C., Vukovic, M., Yin, J., Yu, Q. (eds.) ICSOC 2018. LNCS, vol. 11236, pp. 279–294. Springer, Cham (2018). https://doi.org/10.1007/978-3-030-03596-9_19
2. Arnold, A.: Finite Transition Systems - Semantics of Communicating Systems. Prentice Hall, Upper Saddle River (1994)
3. Attiogbé, C., André, P., Ardourel, G.: Checking component composability. In: Löwe, W., Südholt, M. (eds.) SC 2006. LNCS, vol. 4089, pp. 18–33. Springer, Heidelberg (2006). https://doi.org/10.1007/11821946_2
4. Baier, C., Katoen, J.: Principles of Model Checking. MIT Press, Cambridge (2008)
5. Berardi, D., Calvanese, D., De Giacomo, G., Lenzerini, M., Mecella, M.: Automatic composition of $E$-services that export their behavior. In: Orlowska, M.E., Weerawarana, S., Papazoglou, M.P., Yang, J. (eds.) ICSOC 2003. LNCS, vol. 2910, pp. 43–58. Springer, Heidelberg (2003). https://doi.org/10.1007/978-3-540-24593-3_4
6. Bertoli, P., Pistore, M., Traverso, P.: Automated composition of web services via planning in asynchronous domains. Artif. Intell. **174**(3–4), 316–361 (2010)
7. Bouhoula, A., Jouannaud, J.-P., Meseguer, J.: Specification and proof in membership equational logic. Theore. Comput. Sci. **236**(1), 35–132 (2000)
8. Brand, D., Zafiropulo, P.: On communicating finite-state machines. J. ACM **30**(2), 323–342 (1983)
9. Bucchiarone, A., Marconi, A., Pistore, M., et al.: A context-aware framework for dynamic composition of process fragments in the internet of services. J. Internet Serv. Appl. **8**(1), 6:1–6:23 (2017)
10. Canal, C., Pimentel, E., Troya, J.M.: Compatibility and inheritance in software architectures. Sci. Comput. Program. **41**(2), 105–138 (2001)
11. Clavel, M., et al.: All About Maude - A High-Performance Logical Framework. LNCS, vol. 4350. Springer, Heidelberg (2007). https://doi.org/10.1007/978-3-540-71999-1
12. Durán, F., Ouederni, M., Salaün, G.: A generic framework for N-protocol compatibility checking. Sci. Comput. Program. **77**(7–8), 870–886 (2012)
13. Durán, F., Salaün, G.: A note on automated composition, analysis and deployment of IoT applications, April 2019. http://maude.lcc.uma.es/iotcompo
14. Felfernig, A., Falkner, A., Müslüm, A. et al.: ASP-based Knowledge Representations for IoT Configuration Scenarios. In: Proceedings of the ICW 2017, p. 62 (2017)
15. Guinard, D., Trifa, V., Mattern, F., Wilde, E.: From the internet of things to the web of things: resource-oriented architecture and best practices. In: Uckelmann, D., Harrison, M., Michahelles, F. (eds.) Architecting the Internet of Things, pp. 97–129. Springer, Heidelberg (2011). https://doi.org/10.1007/978-3-642-19157-2_5

16. JS-Foundation. Node-RED: Flow-based Programming for the IoT (2018)
17. Klai, K., Ochi, H.: Checking compatibility of web services behaviorally. In: Arbab, F., Sirjani, M. (eds.) FSEN 2013. LNCS, vol. 8161, pp. 267–282. Springer, Heidelberg (2013). https://doi.org/10.1007/978-3-642-40213-5_17
18. Marconi, A., Pistore, M., Traverso, P.: Automated composition of web services: the ASTRO approach. IEEE Data Eng. Bull. **31**(3), 23–26 (2008)
19. Martens, A.: Analyzing web service based business processes. In: Cerioli, M. (ed.) FASE 2005. LNCS, vol. 3442, pp. 19–33. Springer, Heidelberg (2005). https://doi.org/10.1007/978-3-540-31984-9_3
20. Meseguer, J.: Conditional rewriting logic as a unified model of concurrency. Theor. Comput. Sci. **96**(1), 73–155 (1992)
21. Narayanan, S., McIlraith, S.A.: Simulation, verification and automated composition of web services. In: Proceedings of the WWW 2012, pp. 77–88. ACM (2002)
22. Ovadia, S.: Automate the internet with "This Then That". Behav. Soc. Sci. Libr. **33**(4), 208–211 (2014)
23. Raffelt, H., Steffen, B., Berg, T., Margaria, T.: LearnLib: a framework for extrapolating behavioral models. STTT **11**(5), 393 (2009)
24. Tata, S., Klai, K., Jain, R.: Formal model and method to decompose process-aware IoT applications. In: Panetto, H., et al. (eds.) OTM 2017. LNCS, vol. 10573, pp. 663–680. Springer, Cham (2017). https://doi.org/10.1007/978-3-319-69462-7_42
25. van Glabbeek, R.J., Weijland, W.P.: Branching time and abstraction in bisimulation semantics. J. ACM **43**(3), 555–600 (1996)
26. Yellin, D.M., Strom, R.E.: Protocol specifications and component adaptors. ACM Trans. Program. Lang. Syst. **19**(2), 292–333 (1997)

# Security

# Applying Face Recognition in Video Surveillance Security Systems

Bauyrzhan Omarov[1], Batyrkhan Omarov[2,3(✉)],
Shirinkyz Shekerbekova[4], Farida Gusmanova[1],
Nurzhamal Oshanova[4], Alua Sarbasova[1], Zhanna Yessengaliyeva[1],
Agyn Bedelbayev[1], Akmarzhan Maikhanova[1], Nurzhan Omarov[5],
and Daniyar Sultan[1]

[1] Al-Farabi Kazakh National University, Almaty, Kazakhstan
[2] International Information Technology University, Almaty, Kazakhstan
batyahan@gmail.com
[3] Kazakhstan Innovations Lab Supported by UNICEF, Almaty, Kazakhstan
[4] Abay Kazakh National Pedagogical University, Almaty, Kazakhstan
[5] Kazakh University of Railways and Communications, Almaty, Kazakhstan

**Abstract.** Face Detection and Recognition is an important surveillance problem to provide citizens' security. Nowadays, many citizen service areas as airports, railways, security services are starting to use face detection and recognition services because of their practicality and reliability. In our research, we explored face recognition algorithms and described facial recognition process applying Fisherface face recognition algorithm. This process is theoretically justified and tested with real-world outdoor video. The experimental results demonstrate practically applying of face detection from several foreshortenings and recognition results. The given system can be used in building a smart city as a smart city application, also in different organization to ensure security of people.

**Keywords:** Smart city · Video surveillance · Face recognition · Face detection

## 1 Introduction

If we talk about the concept of "smart city", first and foremost, it is improving the quality of life and creating comfortable living conditions for citizens. This is the combination of various technologies, management of communications, infrastructure, in the near future IOT.

The goal is the optimal use of modern technologies in each of the spheres of city life for more rational use of resources and improving the quality of life, doing business, etc. So, "Safe City" is the most important component of the "smart city" concept, besides video surveillance as part of a safe city, the state is becoming "the eyes" of a smart city.

Smart cities often intersect with a digital city, a wireless city, a safe city, an eco-city, a city with low carbon monoxide emissions, architectural perfection and other regional development concepts. This should be confused with the concepts of the

© Springer Nature Switzerland AG 2019
M. Mazzara et al. (Eds.): TOOLS 2019, LNCS 11771, pp. 271–280, 2019.
https://doi.org/10.1007/978-3-030-29852-4_22

industry of information technologies, electronic document management, electronic reporting, intellectual transport and an intelligent urban water/gas/power supply network. Smart City is sharing data over the Internet, cloud services, geospatial infrastructure, dedicated telecommunication channels and other new generations of information technology. CCTV cameras, included in open or protected monitoring and control systems, ensure broadband cross-border interaction of all municipal structures, and facilitate the intellectual integration of applications into user innovations, open innovations, public innovations, and joint innovations. The process of transition to a smart city is characterized by a steady interest of both local enterprises and foreign investors. In this process, there are no templates for the use of video surveillance and network technologies. The main thing is an intelligent and cost-effective result. In addition, of course, there are increased requirements to the processing of video data streams, the quality of video surveillance equipment.

## 2 Literature Review

There are several approaches to create a face recognition algorithm.

The empirical approach was used at the very beginning of the development of computer vision. It is based on some of the rules that a person uses to detect a face. For example, the forehead is usually brighter than the central part of the face, which, in turn, is uniform in brightness and color. Another important feature is the presence of parts of the face in the image - the nose, mouth, eyes. To determine the faces, we did a significant reduction of the image area, where the presence of a face was assumed, or perpendicular histograms are constructed. These methods are easy to implement, but they are practically unsuitable in the presence of a large number of foreign objects in the background, several persons in the frame or when changing the angle.

The following approach uses invariant features characteristic of a face image. At its core, as in the previous method, lies the empiricist, that is, the attempt of the system to "think" as a person. The method reveals the characteristic parts of the face, its boundary, change in shape, contrast, etc., combines all these signs and verifies. This method can be used even when turning the head, but with the presence of other faces or a heterogeneous background, recognition becomes impossible.

The following algorithm is the detection of faces using patterns that are specified by the developer. A person appears to be a kind of template or standard, the purpose of the algorithm is to check each segment for the presence of this pattern, and the check can be made for different angles and scales. Such a system requires many time-consuming calculations.

All modern facial recognition technologies use systems that learn through test images. For training, bases with images containing faces and not containing faces are used. Each fragment of the investigated image is characterized as a feature vector, with which the classifiers (algorithms for determining an object in a frame) determine whether this part of the image is a face or not.

Currently, several dozens of computer methods for face recognition are actively used: methods based on neural networks [1]; the main components (own persons) [2, 3, 4]; based on linear discriminant analysis [5, 6]; elastic graph method [7]; a method based on hidden Markov models [8–12]; method based on flexible contour models of the face; method of comparison of standards; optical flux method; methods based on lines of the same intensity; algebraic moments; Karunen-Loeve decomposition; fuzzy logic; Gabor filters, etc. A good overview of these methods can be found in [13].

One of the first developed methods of facial recognition is the method of main components (own faces). Its distinguishing feature is that the main components carry information about the signs of a certain generalized face. Face recognition using linear discriminant analysis is based on the assumption of linear separability of classes (persons) in image space. Neural network methods have a good generalizing ability.

# 3 Facial Recognition Problem

Recognition of objects is an easy task for people, the experiments conducted in [14] showed that even children aged one to three days are able to distinguish between remembered faces. Since a person sees the world not as a set of separate parts, our brain must somehow combine various sources of information into useful patterns. The task of automatic face recognition is to isolate these significant features from an image, transforming them into a useful presentation and producing some kind of classification.

The process of face recognition, which is based on geometrical features of the face, is probably the most intuitive approach to the problem of face recognition [14, 15]. Experiments on a large data set have shown that, alone, geometric features cannot provide enough information for face recognition.

In this work, we explore face detection and recognition process, describe their mathematical representation and do experiments with facial recognition using Fisher-face algorithm.

## 3.1 Development Overview

The solution as proposed in this research work consists of two parts as recovering low resolution image and the identity of object using the recovered high resolution image.

Image restoration part consists of three subtasks as

1. Converting the low resolution image to digital form
2. Image enhancement and recovery
3. Converting to graphical image from digits.

## 3.2 Face Detection

At the first stage, the face is detected and localized in the image. At the recognition stage, the image of the face is aligned (geometric and luminance), the calculation of the signs and the direct recognition - the comparison of the calculated signs with the standards embedded in the database. The main difference of all the algorithms presented will be the calculation of signs and the comparison of their aggregates among themselves. Such face detection system types shown in Fig. 1.

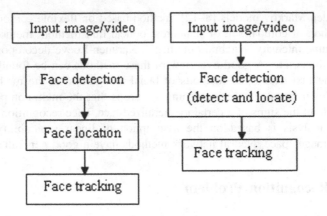

**Fig. 1.** Face detection architecture.

### 3.3 Face Recognition

There are several different face recognition algorithms as correlation, eigenfaces, linear subspaces and fisherfaces. There were several experiments on identification the effectiveness of those algorithms where the FisherFaces algorithm was chosen as the best one with the lowest error rate in human face recognition. In accordance with experiment results made before we decided to choose the FisherFaces algorithm for face identification and recognition processes due to its fast and guaranteed recognition of the human. Figure 2 shows the plot that illustrates the error rate depending on the number of principal components.

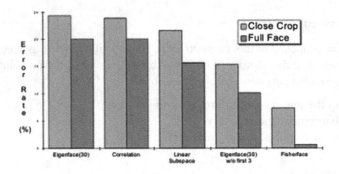

**Fig. 2.** Face detection architecture.

As can be seen from the above graph, the FisherFace method learns the set of projections which perform well over a range of lighting variation, facial expression and even presence of glasses. Below, we explain the algorithmic description of the Fisherfaces method:

Let there be a random vector with samples drawn from classes: $X = \{X_1, X_2, \ldots, X_n\}$

$$X_i = \{X_1, X_2, \ldots, X_n\} \tag{1}$$

The scatter matrices $S_B$ and S_{W} are calculated as:

$$S_b = \sum_{i=1}^{c} N_i(\mu_i - \mu)(\mu_i - \mu)^T \tag{2}$$

$\sum_{i=1}^{c} \sum_{x_i \in X_i} (x_i - \mu_i)(x_j - \mu_j)^T$, where $\mu$ is the total mean:

$$\mu = \frac{1}{N} \sum_{i=1}^{N} x_i \tag{3}$$

And $\mu_i$ is the mean of class $i \in \{1, \ldots, c\}$:

$$\mu_i = \frac{1}{|x_i|} \sum_{x_j \in X_j} x_j \tag{4}$$

Fisher's classic algorithm now looks for a projection that maximizes the class separability criterion:

$$W_{opt} = \arg\max_W \frac{|W^T S_B W|}{|W^T S_W W|} \tag{5}$$

Following the method of Belhumer, Hespanha and Kriegman, a solution for this optimization problem is given by solving the General Eigenvalue Problem:

$$S_W^{-1} S_B v_i = \lambda_i v_i \tag{6}$$

There's one problem left to solve: The rank of $S_W$ is at most (N-c), with N samples and classes. In pattern recognition problems the number of samples N is almost always smaller than the dimension of the input data (the number of pixels), so the scatter matrix $S_W$ becomes singular. In [BHK97] this was solved by performing a Principal Component Analysis on the data and projecting the samples into the (N-c)-dimensional space. A Linear Discriminate Analysis was then performed on the reduced data, because $S_W$ isn't singular anymore. The optimization problem can then be rewritten as:

$$W_{fld} = \arg\max_W \frac{\left|W^T W_{pca}^T S_B W_{pca} W\right|}{\left|W^T W_{pca}^T S_W W_{pca} W\right|} \tag{7}$$

The transformation matrix that projects a sample into the (c-1) dimensional space is then given by:

$$W = W_{fld}^T W_{pca}^T \qquad (8)$$

Face detection, recognition and gender classification experiments carried out on the basis of facial images database [16]. Sample images are shown in Fig. 3. In the formation of the database size of the images and the shooting conditions were the same. They used a 24-bit JPEG format. The base [16] contains pictures of people, male and female, of different nationalities and ages. It reflects changes in a person's appearance: different hairstyles, beards and glasses presence. In preparation for the experiment, two training samples have been created. The first of them contains five images of each person (only 5 × 395 = 1975 images). Second, 10 images of each person's individual learning (10 × 395 = 3950 images). In addition, the dataset has several datasets as Face94, Face95, Face96, and Grimace that the characteristics are listed, below.

**Fig. 3.** Sample images of faces.

The approach that is used in this method finds out the facial features to discriminate between the persons. The performance of the system that uses the FisherFaces algorithm is highly depends on the input data. The FisherFaces provides a total reconstruction of the projected image by normalizing processing of the image [5, 17–19]. The total set of procedures is given in the Fig. 4.

As can be seen from the Fig. 4, the process of face verification starts with the detection stage, where the image is taken from the camera and is considered as an input data. Then, there goes the normalization process in order to construct the proper image that can be used in FisherFace algorithm. Face normalization actually consists of geometry normalization, background removal and lighting normalization. The images of the face are normalized to a fixed size. If the face was in a wrong angle this angle is determined then is corrected in accordance with rules.

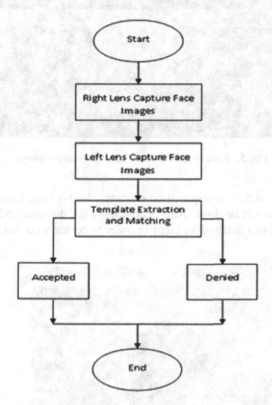

**Fig. 4.** Face detection architecture.

## 4 Facial Recognition Problem

Face recognition system generally involves two main stages as "Face Detection" and "Face Identification". First one is face detection, where the system is searching for any faces then takes the image of this face. Following this, image processing cleans up the facial image into black-white colors. In our research, face can be detected from several foreshortenings. Implemented results are given in Fig. 5.

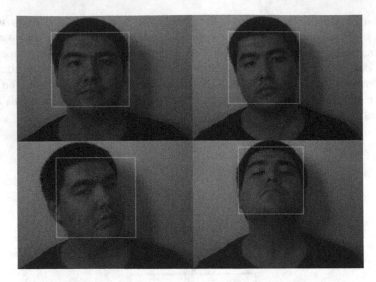

**Fig. 5.** Face detection from several foreshortenings.

After detecting face, next step will be executed. In this step, feature extraction and verification process will be done. After recognizing the detected and processed facial image is compared to a database of faces in order to decide who that person is, Fig. 6.

**Fig. 6.** Face recognition. Identification of personal id

# 5  Conclusion

In this work, we applied Fisherface face recognition algorithm for facial recognition problem as a video surveillance system of Smart City application. We used Fisherface algorithm because of its practicality and high recognition rate. The mathematical representation of facial recognition problem and Fisherface algorithm was investigated. Experiment results demonstrate face detection and recognition results. Further, we are going to use the proposed system as an application of a Smart City Platform and for schools to identify pupils by faces.

# References

1. Collins, R., et al.: A system for video surveillance and monitoring. Technical report. CMU-RI-TR-00-12VSAM, Final Report. Carnegie Mellon University, Pittsburgh, May 2000
2. Haritaoglu, I., David, H., Larry, S.D.: W4: real time surveillance of People and their Activities. IEEE Trans. Pattern Anal. Mach. Intell. 22(8), 809–830 (2000)
3. Remagnino, P., Jones, G.A., Paragios, N., Regazzoni, C.S.: Video Based Surveillance Systems Computer Vision and Distributed Processing. Kluwer, Norwell (2002). https://doi.org/10.1007/978-1-4615-0913-4
4. Stauffer, G.: Learning patterns of activity using real-time tracking. IEEE Trans. Pattern Anal. Mach. Intell. 22(8), 747–757 (2000)
5. VACE: Video analysis and content exploitation. http://www.ic-arda.org/InfoExploit/vace/
6. Jain, A.K., Bolle, R., Pankanti, S. (eds.): Biometrics: Personal Identification in Networked Security. Kluwer Academic Publishers, Norwell (1999)
7. Wan, Q., et al.: Face description using anisotropic gradient: thermal infrared to visible face recognition. In: Proceedings of Mobile Multimedia/Image Processing, Security, and Applications 2018, SPIE, vol. 10668, p. 106680V, 14 May 2018. https://doi.org/10.1117/12.2304898
8. Wolf, M.: Image and video analysis. Smart Camera Design, pp. 163–197. Springer, Cham (2018). https://doi.org/10.1007/978-3-319-69523-5_5
9. Kumar, S., Pandey, A., Satwik, K.S.R.: Deep learning framework for recognition of cattle using muzzle point image pattern. Measurement 116, 1–17 (2018)
10. Kumar, S., Tiwari, S., Singh, S.K: Face recognition for cattle. In: Proceedings of 3rd IEEE International Conference on Image Information Processing (ICIIP), pp. 65–72 (2015)
11. Turk, M.A., Pentland, A.P.: Face recognition using eigenfaces. In: Proceedings of IEEE Computer Society Conference on Computer Vision and Pattern Recognition (CVPR 1991), pp. 586–591 (1991)
12. Belhumeur, P.N., Hespanha, J.P., Kriegman, D.J.: Eigenfaces vs. fisherfaces: recognition using class specific linear projection. IEEE Trans. Pattern Anal. Mach. Intell. 19(7), 711–720 (1997)
13. Baudat, G., Anouar, F.: Generalized discriminant analysis using a kernel approach. Neural Comput. 12(10), 2385–2424 (2000)
14. Muller, K.R., Mika, S., Ratsch, G., Tsuda, K., Scholkopf, B.: An introduction to kernel-based learning algorithms. IEEE Trans. Neural Netw. 12(2), 181–201 (2001)
15. Kang, M.G., Park, S.C., Park, M.K.: Super-resolution image reconstruction: a technical overview. IEEE Signal Process. Mag. 20, 21–36 (2013)

16. Suliman, A., Omarov, B.S.: Applying Bayesian regularization for acceleration of Levenberg-Marquardt based neural network training. Int. J. Interact. Multimedia Artif. Intell. 5(1), 68–72 (2018)
17. Omarov, B., Altayeva, A., Cho, Y.I.: Smart building climate control considering indoor and outdoor parameters. In: Saeed, K., Homenda, W., Chaki, R. (eds.) CISIM 2017. LNCS, vol. 10244, pp. 412–422. Springer, Cham (2017). https://doi.org/10.1007/978-3-319-59105-6_35
18. Altayeva, A., Omarov, B., Cho, I.Y.: Towards smart city platform intelligence: PI decoupling math model for temperature and humidity control. In: 2018 IEEE International Conference on Big Data and Smart Computing (BigComp), pp. 693–696. IEEE January 2018
19. Altayeva, A., Omarov, B., Cho, I.Y.: Multi-objective optimization for smart building energy and comfort management as a case study of smart city platform. In: 2017 IEEE 19th International Conference on High Performance Computing and Communications; IEEE 15th International Conference on Smart City; IEEE 3rd International Conference on Data Science and Systems (HPCC/SmartCity/DSS), pp. 627–628. IEEE December 2017

# Cyber-Resilience Concept for Industry 4.0 Digital Platforms in the Face of Growing Cybersecurity Threats

Sergei Petrenko$^{(\boxtimes)}$ (ID) and Elvira Khismatullina (ID)

Innopolis University, Universitetskaya 1, Innopolis 420500, Russia
s.petrenko@rambler.ru

**Abstract.** Modern cyber systems acquire the more emergent system properties, as far as their complexity is being increased: cyber resilience, controllability, self-organization, proactive cyber security and adaptability. Each of the listed properties is the subject of the cybernetics research (comes from Greek κυβερνητική (kybernētikḗ) - the art of the governance) and each subsequent feature makes sense only if there is a previous one.

This article presents a valuable experience and the exploratory study practical results of the Innopolis University Information Security Center on the scientific problem of the cyber-resilient critical information infrastructure organization under the conditions of previously unknown heterogeneous mass cyber attacks of intruders, based on similarity invariants. It is essential that the obtained results significantly complement the well-known practices and recommendations of ISO 22301 (https://www.iso.org), MITRE PR 15-1334 (www.mitre.org) and NIST SP 800-160 (www.nist.gov) in terms of developing the quantitative metrics and cyber resistance measures. This makes it possible for the first time to discover and formally present the ultimate efficiency law of the cyber resilience of modern Industry 4.0 systems under increasing security threats.

**Keywords:** Digital transformation · Digital economy · Cyber stability · Manageability capability · Self-organization · Proactive cyber security and adaptability · Models and methods of artificial intelligence · Cognitive computing · Big data · Robotics · Internet of things IIoT/IoT

## 1 Introduction

Firstly, we regard a number of so-called primary concepts: the cyber system, the behavior of the cyber system, the intended purpose of the cyber system, the disturbance of the behavior of the cyber system, and the state of the cyber system (Figs. 1 and 2).

A *cyber system* is understood as a certain set of hardware and software components of a critically important information infrastructure with communications on control and data between them, designed to perform the required functions. Therefore the cyber system behaviour is understood as some algorithm introduction and implementation for the system functioning in time. At the same time, the targeted corrective actions are allowed ensuring the system behaviour cyber resilience. The cyber system mission is

© Springer Nature Switzerland AG 2019
M. Mazzara et al. (Eds.): TOOLS 2019, LNCS 11771, pp. 281–294, 2019.
https://doi.org/10.1007/978-3-030-29852-4_23

**Fig. 1.** Relationship of cyber resistance, cyber security and business sustainability concepts.

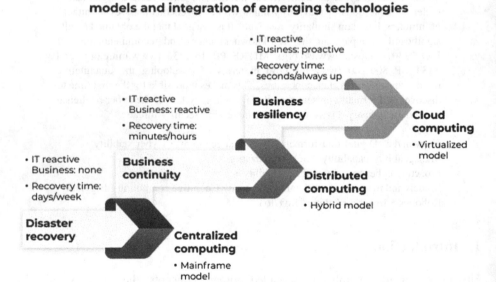

**Fig. 2.** Cybersecurity concept evolution

called the *mission*; corrective measures are the cyber disturbance *detection and neutralization*. In other words, a cyber system is designed for a specific purpose and may have some protective mechanism, customizable or adjustable means to ensure cyber resilience.

A *cyber system behaviour disturbance* is a single or multiple acts of an external or internal destructive impact of the internal and/or external environment on the system. The disturbance leads to a change in the cyber system functioning parameters, prevents or makes the system purpose difficult. A disturbance combination forms a *disturbance set*. *The cyber system state* is a certain set of numerical parameter characteristics of the system functioning in space. The numerical process characteristics depend on the functioning conditions of the cyber system, disturbances and corrective actions to detect and neutralize the disturbances and, in general, from time. The set of all corrective actions for detecting and neutralizing the disturbances is called the *corrective action set*; the set of all digital platform behaviour system states is called the *state set*. Thus, we will assume that without disturbances, as well as the corrective measures for the disturbance detection and neutralization, the cyber system is in an operational state, and meets some intended purpose. As a disturbance result, the cyber system transits into a new state, which may not meet its intended purpose.

In the conditions of the destructive disturbances, the two main tasks appear [1–5]:

(1) *Detection of the disturbance fact* and, possibly, changes made to the normal cyber system functioning process;
(2) *Setting the optimal (cyber-resilient)* in a certain sense (based on a given priority functional) *organization of the cyber-system behaviour* to bring the cyber system to an operating state (including redesigning and/or restarting the system, if this solution is considered the best).

## 2 Cyber Resilience Management

Now let us we reveal the content of the elementary, complex, and perturbed calculations in R.E. Kalman' terms of the dynamic interrelationships [6–9].

Further, we will use the term *"elementary cyber system behaviour"*, considering the structure, which input receives some input value at certain points in time and from which some output value is derived at certain time points. The above concept of the elementary cyber system behavior as a system $\Sigma$ includes an auxiliary time point set $T$. At each time point $t \in T$, the system $\Sigma$ receives some input value $u(t)$ and generates some output value $y$ $(t)$. In this case, the input variable values are selected from some fixed set U, i.e. at any time moment t, the symbol u(t) belongs to $U$. The system input value segment is a function of the form $\omega: (t1, t2) \rightarrow U$ and belongs to some class $\Omega$. The output variable value $y(t)$ belongs to some fixed set $Y$. The output values segment represents a function of the form $\gamma: (t2, t3) \rightarrow Y$.

The *complex cyber system behaviour* is understood as a generalized structure, the components of which are elementary given system behaviours with communications on control and data among themselves.

Now let us define the concept of the *immunity pre history (memory)* of the cyber system behaviour to destructive influences. We assume that under group and mass cyber-attacks, the output variable value of the system $\Sigma$ depends both on the source data and the system behavior algorithm and on the *immunity pre history (memory)* destructive influences. In other words, the *disturbed cyber system behavior* is a structure in which the current output variable value of the $\Sigma$ system depends on the $\Sigma$ system state with an accumulated *immunity pre history (memory)* to destructive disturbances. In this case, we will assume that the internal $\Sigma$ system state set allows containing information about the $\Sigma$ system immunity history (memory).

Let us note that the considered content of the disturbed cyber system behaviour allows describing some "dynamic" self-recovery behaviour system of the above system under disturbances, if knowledge of the $x(t1)$ state and the restored computation segment $\omega = \omega^{(t_1 t_2]}$ is a necessary and sufficient condition to determine the state $x$ $(t_2) = \varphi(t_2; t_1, x(t_1), \omega)$, where $t_1 < t_2$. Here the time point set $T$ is orderly, i.e. it defines the time direction.

Let us reveal the characteristic features of *single, group* and *mass* Industry 4.0 cyber system disturbances using the following definitions.

Now we define the concept of the immunity prehistory (memory) of the cyber system behaviour to destructive influences. We assume that under group and mass cyber-attacks, the output variable value of the system $\Sigma$ depends both on the source data and the system behavior algorithm and on the immunity prehistory (memory) destructive influences. In other words, the disturbed cyber system behavior is a structure in which the current output variable value of the $\Sigma$ system depends on the $\Sigma$ system state with an accumulated immunity prehistory (memory) to destructive disturbances. In this case, we will assume that the internal $\Sigma$ system state set allows containing information about the $\Sigma$ system immunity history (memory).

Let us note that the considered content of the disturbed cyber system behaviour allows describing some "dynamic" self-recovery behaviour system of the above system under disturbances, if the knowledge of the $x(t1)$ state and the restored computation segment $\omega = \omega$ is a necessary and sufficient condition to determine the state of $x$ $(t2) = \varphi(t2; t1, x(t1), \omega)$, where $t1 < t2$. Here the time point set $T$ is in order, i.e. it defines the time direction.

Let us reveal the characteristic features of single, group and mass Industry 4.0 cyber system disturbances applying the following definitions.

**Definition 1.1.** The dynamic self-recovery cyber system behavior system under group and mass cyber attacks $\Sigma$ is called *stationary (constant)* if and only if:

(a) $T$ is an additive group (according to the usual operation of adding real numbers);
(b) $\Omega$ is closed according to the shift operator $z^\tau$: $\omega \to \omega'$, defined by the relation: $\omega'$ $(t) = \omega(t + \tau)$ for all $\tau, t \in T$;
(c) $\varphi(t; \tau, x, \omega) = \varphi(t + s; \tau + s, x, z^s\omega)$ for all $s \in T$;
(d) the mapping $\eta(t, \cdot): X \to Y$ does not depend on $t$.

**Definition 1.2.** A dynamic system of self-recovery cyber-system behavior under group and mass cyber-attacks $\Sigma$ is called a system with continuous time, if and only if $T$ coincides with a set of real numbers, and is called a system with discrete time, if and only if $T$ is an integer set. Here, the difference between systems with continuous and discrete time is insignificant and, mainly, the mathematical convenience of the development of the appropriate behavior models of the cyber systems under group and mass disturbances, determines the choice between them. The systems of self-recovery cyber system behavior under group and mass cyber-attacks with continuous time correspond to classical continuous models, and the mentioned systems with discrete time correspond to discrete behavior models. An important cyber system complexity measure in group and mass cyber-attacks is its state space structure.

**Definition 1.3.** The dynamic system of cyber system behavior in group and mass cyber-attacks $\Sigma$ is called the finite-dimensional if and only if $X$ is a finite-dimensional linear space. Moreover, $dim \, \Sigma = dimX_\Sigma$. A system $\Sigma$ is called finite if and only if the set $X$ is finite. Finally, a system $\Sigma$ is called a *finite automaton* if and only if all the sets $X$, $U$, and $Y$ are finite and, in addition, the system is stationary and with discrete time. The finite dimensionality assumption of the given system is essential to obtain specific numerical results.

**Definition 1.4.** A dynamic system of cyber system behavior in group and mass cyber-attacks $\Sigma$ is called *linear*, if and only if:

(a) Spaces $X$, $U$, $\Omega$, $Y$, and $G$ are vector spaces (over a given arbitrary field $K$);
(b) Mapping $\varphi$ (t; $\tau$, $\cdot$, $\cdot$): $X \times \Omega \to X$ is K-linear for all t and $\tau$;
(c) Mapping $\eta$ (t, $\cdot$): $X \to Y$ is K-linear for any t.

If it is necessary to use the mathematical apparatus of differential and integral calculus, it is required that some assumptions about continuity are included in the system $\Sigma$ definition. For this, it is necessary to assume that the various ($T$, $X$, $U$, $\Omega$, $Y$, $G$) sets are the topological spaces and that the mappings $\varphi$ and $\eta$ are continuous with respect to the corresponding (*Tikhonov*) topology.

**Definition 1.5.** The dynamic system of cyber system behavior in group and mass cyber-attacks $\Sigma$ is called smooth if and only if:

(a) $T = R$ is a set of real numbers (with the usual topology);
(b) $X$ and $\Omega$ are topological spaces;
(c) Transition mapping $\varphi$ has the property that $(\tau, x, \omega) \to \varphi(\cdot; \tau, x, \omega)$ defines a continuous mapping $T \times X \times \Omega \to C^l(T \to X)$.

For any given initial state ($\tau$, x) and an input action segment $\omega^{(\tau,t_2]}$ of system $\Sigma$, the system $\gamma^{(\tau,t_2]}$ reaction is specified, i.e. the mapping is given: $f_{\tau,x}: \omega^{(\tau,t_2]} \to \gamma^{(\tau,t_2]}$.

Here, the output variable value at time $t^c \in (\tau, t_1]$ is determined from the relation: $f_{\tau,x}\left(\omega^{(\tau,t_2]}\right)(t) = \eta(t, \varphi(t; \tau, x, \omega))$.

**Definition 1.6.** The dynamic system of cyber system behavior under group and mass cyber-attacks $\Sigma$ (in terms of its external behavior) is the following mathematical concept:

(a) Sets $T$, $U$, $\Omega$, $Y$, and $G$ that satisfy the properties discussed above are given.
(b) A set that indexes a function family: $F = \{f_\alpha: T \times \Omega \to Y, \alpha \in A\}$, is defined, where each family $F$ element is written explicitly as $f_\alpha(t, \omega) = y(t)$, i.e. it is the output value for the input effect $\omega$ obtained in the $\alpha$ experiment. Each $f_\alpha$ is called an input-output mapping and has the following properties:
  (1) (The time direction.) There is a mapping $\iota: A \to T$, that $f_\alpha(t, \omega)$ such that $f_\alpha(t, \omega)$ is defined for all $t \geq \iota(\alpha)$.

(2) (Causality.) Let, $t \in T$ and $\tau < t$. If $\omega$, $\omega' \in \Omega$ and $\omega_{(\tau, t]} = \omega'_{(\tau, t]}$, then $f_\alpha(t, \omega) = f_\alpha(t, \omega')$, for all $\alpha$ for which $\tau = \iota(\alpha)$.

## 3  Cyber Resilient System Design

Let us define a hypervisor model (an abstract converter) of the cyber system behavior under the group and mass cyber-attacks as follows.

**Definition 1.7.** The abstract mapping of the cyber system behavior under group and mass cyber-attacks $\Sigma$ is a complex mathematical concept defined by the following axioms.

(a) $T$ time points set, $X$ computation states set, the instantaneous values set of $U$ input variables, $\Omega = \{\omega: T \to U\}$ set of acceptable input variables, the instantaneous values set of output variables Y and $G = \{\gamma: T \to Y\}$ set of acceptable output values are given.

(b) (Time direction) set $Y$ is some ordered subset of the real number set.

(c) The input variable set $\Omega$ satisfies the following conditions:

  (1) (Nontrivial) The set $\Omega$ is not empty.

  (2) (Input variable articulation) Let us call the segment of input action $\omega = \omega^{(\tau, t_2]}$ for $\omega \in \Omega$, the restriction $\omega$ to $(t_1, t_2] \cap T$. Then if $\omega$, $\omega' \in \Omega$ and $t_1 < t_2 < t_3$, then there $\omega'' \in \Omega$, that $\omega''^{(\tau, t_2]} = \omega^{(\tau, t_2]}$ and $\omega''^{(\tau, t_2]} = \omega'^{(\tau, t_2]}$.

(d) There is a state transition function $\varphi: T \times T \times X \times \Omega \to X$, the values of which are the states $x(t) = \varphi(t; \tau, x, \omega) \in X$, in which the system turns out to be at time $\tau \in T$ if at the initial time $\tau \in T$ it was in the initial state $x = x(\tau) \in X$ and if its input received the input value $\omega \in \Omega$. The function $\varphi$ has the following properties:

  (1) (Time direction) The function $\varphi$ is defined for all $t \geq \tau$ and is not necessarily defined for all $t < \tau$.

  (2) (Consistency) The equality $\varphi(t; t, x, \omega) = x$ holds for any $t \in T$, any $x \in X$, and any $\omega \in \Omega$.

  (3) (Semigroup property) For any $t_1 < t_2 < t_3$ and any $x \in X$ and $\omega \in \Omega$, we have $\varphi(t_3; t_1, x, \omega) = \varphi(t_3; t_2, \varphi(t_2; t_1, x, \omega), \omega)$.

  (4) (Causality) If $\omega$, $\omega'' \in \Omega$ and $\omega_{(\tau, t]} = \omega'_{(\tau, t]}$, then $\varphi(t; \tau, x, \omega) = \varphi(t; \tau, x, \omega')$.

(e) The output mapping $\eta: T \times X \to Y$ is given, that defines the output values $y(t) = \eta(t, x(t))$. The mapping $(\tau, t] \to Y$, defined by the relation $\sigma \mapsto \eta(\sigma, \varphi(\sigma; \tau, x, \omega))$, $\sigma \in (\tau, t]$, is called an *input variable segment*, i.e. the restriction $\gamma_{(\tau, t]}$ of some $\gamma \in G$ on $(\tau, t]$.

Additionally, the pair $(\tau, x)$, where $\tau \in T$ and $x \in X$, is called *the event (or phase) of the system $\Sigma$*, and the set $T \in X$ is called the system $\Sigma$ event space (or phase space). The transition function of the states $\varphi$ (or its graph in the event space) is called a trajectory or a solution curve, etc. Here, the input action, or control $\omega$, transfers, translates, changes, converts the state $x$ (or the event $(\tau, x)$) to the state $\varphi(t; \tau, x, \omega)$ (or the event *(t, φ (t; τ, x, ω)))*. The cyber system behavior motion is understood as the function of states φ.

**Definition 1.8.** *In a more general form, the abstract converter model of the cyber system behavior under disturbances* $\Re$ *with discrete time, m inputs and p outputs over the field of integers K is a complex object* ($\aleph$, $\wp$, $\emptyset$), *where the mappings* $\aleph$: $l \to l$, $\wp$: $K^m \to l$, $\emptyset$: $l \to K^p$ *are core abstract K - homomorphisms, l is some abstract vector space is above K. The space dimension l(diml) determines the system dimension* $\Re(\dim\Re)$.

It is significant that the chosen representation allows formulating and proving the statements, confirming the fundamental existence of the desired solution.

**Definition 1.9.** The cyber system behavior with memory is called the complex mathematical concept of the dynamical system $\Sigma$, defined by the following axioms.

(a)  A time point set $T$, a set of computational states $X$ under intruder cyber-attacks, an instantaneous value set of standard and destructive input actions $U$, a set of acceptable input effects $\Omega = \{\omega: T \to U\}$, an instantaneous value set of output values $Y$ and a set output values of the reconstructed calculations $G = \{\gamma: T \to Y\}$.

(b)  (Time direction) set $Y$ is some ordered subset of the real number set.

(c)  The set of the acceptable input actions $\Omega$ satisfies the following conditions:

(1)  (Nontrivial) The set $\Omega$ is not empty.

(2)  (Input variable articulation) Let us call the segment of input action $\omega = \omega^{(t_1, t_2]}$ for $\omega \in \Omega$, the restriction $\omega$ on $(t_1, t_2] \cap T$. Then if $\omega$, $\omega' \in \Omega$ and $t_1 < t_2 < t_3$, then there $\omega'' \in \Omega$, that $\omega''^{(t_1, t_2]} = \omega^{(t_1, t_2]}$ and $\omega''^{(t_2, t_3]} = \omega'^{(t_{21}, t_3]}$.

(d)  There is a state transition function $\varphi: T \times T \times X \times \Omega \to X$, the values of which are the states $x(t) = \varphi(t; \tau, x, \omega) \in X$, in which the system is at time $t \in T$, if at the initial time $\tau \in T$ it was in the initial state $X = X(\tau) \in X$ and if it was influenced by the input action $\omega \in \Omega$. The function $\varphi$ has the following properties:

(1)  (Time direction) The function $\varphi$ is defined for all $t \geq \tau$ and is not necessarily defined for all $t < \tau^4$.

(2)  (Consistency) The equality $\varphi(t; t, x, \omega) = x$ holds for any $t \in T$, any $x \in X$, and any $\omega \in \Omega$.

(3)  (Semigroup property) For any $t_1 < t_2 < t_3$ and any $x \in X$ and $\omega \in \Omega$, we have $\varphi(t_3; t_1, x, \omega) = \varphi(t_3; t_2, \varphi(t_2; t_1, x, \omega), \omega)$.

(4)  (Causality) If $\omega$, $\omega'' \in \Omega$ and $\omega_{(\tau, t]} = \omega'_{(\tau, t]}$, then $\varphi(t; \tau, x, \omega) = \varphi(t; \tau, x, \omega')$.

(e)  An output mapping $\eta: T \times X \to Y$ is specified, which defines the output values $y$ $(t) = \eta(t, x(t))$ as a self-recovery result. The mapping $(\tau, t] \to Y$, defined by the relation $\sigma \mapsto \eta(\sigma, \varphi(\sigma; \tau, x, \omega))$, $\sigma \in (\tau, t])$, is called a segment of the input variable, i.e. the restriction $\gamma_{(\tau, t]}$ of some $\gamma \in G$ on $(\tau, t]$.

Additionally, we introduce the following terms. A pair $(\tau, x)$, where $\tau \in T$ and $x \in X$, is called the system $\Sigma$ event, and the set $T \in X$ is called the system $\Sigma$ event space (or phase space). The transition function of states $\varphi$ (or its graph in the event space) is called the trajectory of the cyber system self-recovery behavior. We assume that the input action, or the self-recovery control $\omega$, transforms the state $x$ (or the event $(\tau, x)$) into the state $\varphi(t; \tau, x, \omega)$ or in the event.

The above concept definition of the cyber *system self-recovery behavior* is still quite general and is caused by the need to develop common terminology, explore and clarify basic concepts. The further definition specification is presented below.

## 4  Behaviour Models

Imagine the cyber system behavior under the disturbances as the vector field in the phase space. Here the phase space point defines the above system state. The vector attached at this point indicates the system state change rate. The points at which this vector is zero reflect equilibrium states, i.e. at these points; the system state does not change in time. The steady-state modes are represented by a closed curve, the so-called limit cycle on the phase plane (Fig. 3).

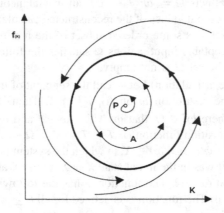

**Fig. 3.** Phase behavior of the cyber systems.

Earlier V.I. Arnold [9] showed that only two main options of restructuring the phase portrait on the plane are possible (Fig. 4).

(1)  When a parameter is changed from an equilibrium position, a limit cycle is born. *Equilibrium stability* goes to the cycle; the very same equilibrium becomes unstable.

(2)  In the equilibrium position, an unstable limit cycle dies; the equilibrium position attraction domain decreases to zero with it, after which the cycle disappears, and its instability is transferred to the equilibrium state.

The catastrophe theory begins with the works of R. Tom and V.I. Arnold [9] and allows analyzing the jump transitions, discontinuities and sudden qualitative changes in the cyber system behavior in response to a smooth change in external conditions that have some common features. It applies the "bifurcation" concept, which is defined as forking and is used in a broad sense to denote the possible changes in the system

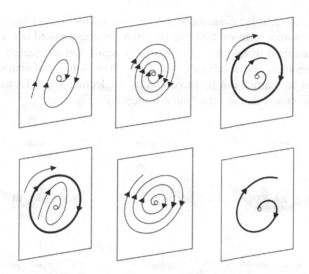

**Fig. 4.** Cycle generation bifurcation.

functioning when the parameters on which they depend change. A bifurcation set is a boundary separating the space domains of control parameters with a qualitatively different system behavior under study.

In order to study the jump transitions in the cyber system behavior, we study the critical points $u \in R^n$ of smooth real functions $f: R^n \to R$, where the derivative vanishes: $\partial f / \partial x_i|_u = 0$, $i = 1, n$. The importance of such a study is explained by the following statement: if some system properties are described by a function $f$ that has the potential energy meaning, then of all possible displacements, there will be real ones for which $f$ has a minimum (the *Lagrange fundamental theorem* says that the minimum of the full potential system energy is sufficient for stability).

The most common types of critical points for a smooth function are local maxima, minima and inflexion points (Fig. 5).

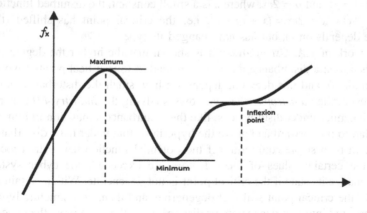

**Fig. 5.** Critical points representation if $n = 1$.

In a general case, in the catastrophe theory, the following technique is applied to study the cyber system features: first, the function $f$ is decomposed into a Taylor series and then it is required to find a segment of this series that adequately describes the system properties close to the critical point for a given number of control parameters. The calculations are carried out by the correctly neglecting some Taylor series members and leaving others that are the "most important" (Fig. 6).

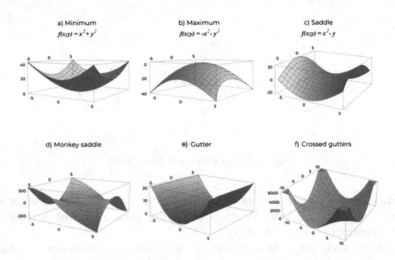

**Fig. 6.** Critical points representation, if $n = 2$.

Rene Tom, in his works, pointed out the importance of the structural stability requirements or insensitivity to small disturbances. The "structural stability" concept was first introduced into the differential equation theory by *A.A. Andronov* and *L.S. Pontryagin* in 1937 under the name "*system robustness*" [9].

A function $f$ is considered structurally stable, if for all sufficiently small smooth functions $p$ the critical points $f$ and $(f + p)$ are of the same type. For example, for the function $f(x) = x^2$ and $p = 2\varepsilon x$, where $\varepsilon$ is a small constant, the disturbed function takes the form: $f(x) = x^2 + 2\varepsilon x = (x + \varepsilon) - \varepsilon^2$, i.e. the critical point has shifted (the shift magnitude depends on $\varepsilon$), but has not changed its type.

In the work of *V.A. Ostreykovsky* it is shown that the higher the degree of $n$, the worse $x^n$ behaves: a disturbance $f(x) = x^5$ can lead to four critical points (two maxima and two minima), and this does not depend on how small the disturbance is (Fig. 7).

As a result, the *catastrophe theory* allows studying the *Industry 4.0* cyber system behavior dynamics under disturbances, like the disturbance simulation in living nature. In particular, to put forward and prove the hypothesis that under mass disturbances, the cyber system is in stable equilibrium if the potential function has a strict local minimum. If the certain values of these factors are exceeded, the cyber system will smoothly change its state if the critical point is not degenerate. With a certain increase in the load, the critical point will first degenerate, and then, as a structurally unstable, will be separated into non-degenerate or disappear. At the same time, the cyber system

A) $f(x) = x^3$ function behavior under disturbance

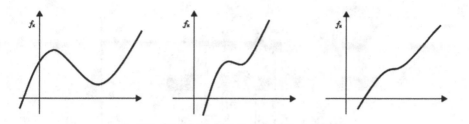

B) $f(x) = x^4$ function behavior under disturbance

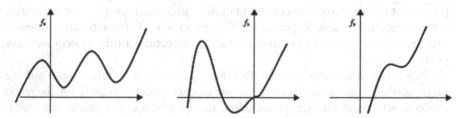

C) $f(x) = x^5$ function behavior under disturbance

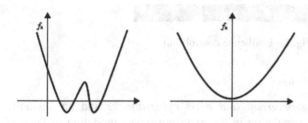

**Fig. 7.** Function behavior under disturbance.

behavior program will jump into a new state (abrupt stability, destruction, critical changes in structure and behavior).

## 5 Cyber Resilience Management System Design

In order to design a cyber resilience control system, we use the theory of the multilevel hierarchical systems (M. Mesarovic, D. Mako, Y. Takahara) [7–9]. In this case, we will distinguish the following hierarchy types: "echelon", "layer", "stratum" (Fig. 8).

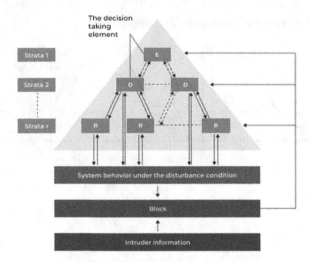

**Fig. 8.** Resilience control unit

The main strata are listed below:

- *Stratum 1* is a *monitoring of group and mass cyber-attacks* and an *immunity accumulation*: the intruder simulation in the exposure types; modeling of the disturbance dynamics representation and the scenario definition to return the cyber system behavior to the equilibrium (stable) state; macro model (program) development of the system self-recovery under disturbances (E),
- *Stratum 2* is a *development and verification* of the cyber system self-recovery program at the micro level: development of the micromodel (program) of the system self-recovery under disturbances; modeling by means of *denotational, axiomatic and operational semantics* to prove the partial correctness of the system recovery plans (D),
- *Stratum 3* is a *self-recovery of the disturbed cyber-system behavior when solving target problems at the micro level*: output of operational standards for recovery; model development for their presentation; recovery plan development and execution. Here (R) corresponds to the hierarchy levels of the given organization system.

Let us note that a certain step of some micro- and macro-program *self-usable translator* (or intellectual controller, or hypervisor) to recover the cyber system behavior under disturbances is consistently implemented here.

A possible algorithm fragment of the named system recovery is shown in Fig. 9.

Here, $S^k = \left( S^k_1, S^k_2, \ldots, S^k_p; t \right)$ is a state vector of the cyber system behavior; $Z(t) = (z_1, z_2, \ldots, z_m; t)$ are the parameters of the intruder actions; $X(t) = (x_1, x_2, \ldots, x_n; t)$ are the controlled parameters; $V(R, C)$ are the control actions, where $R$ is a set of accumulated immunities to exposure; $C$ is a variety of cyber behavior purposes.

The decision on the cyber system behavior self-recovery under disturbances is based on the information *(S)* on the system state, the immunity presence to disturbances ®, taking into account the system functioning purposes ®. The indicators *S* are formed

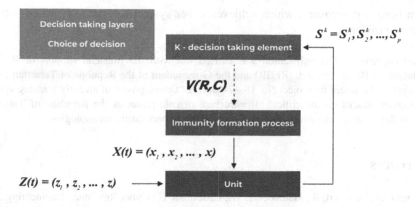

**Fig. 9.** Cyber system self-recovery algorithm fragment

based on the parameters $X$, which is input, intermediate and output data. The attacker influence parameters $Z$ are understood as values that are weakly dependent (not dependent) on the system, ensuring the required cyber resilience. The *Industry 4.0 cyber system* behavior analysis under growing threats to cybersecurity makes it possible to present the above systems as a dynamic system, provided that knowledge of the previous system state and the recovered system operation segment is a necessary and sufficient condition to determine the next observed state. It also implies that the time point set is ordered, i.e. it defines the time direction.

# 6 Conclusion

The selected *abstract translator representation of the cyber system behavior* with memory based on the identified dynamic interrelations allows formulating and proving statements, confirming the *fundamental solution existence* to self-recovery programs of the Industry 4.0 cyber systems behavior under group and mass perturbations

The analysis shows the possibility of the *catastrophe theory* application to analyze the *Industry 4.0 cyber-system behavior* dynamics under disturbances by analogy with the disturbance simulation in wildlife. It is shown that under mass disturbances, the cyber system is in stable equilibrium if the potential function has a strict local minimum. If certain values of these factors are exceeded, the system will smoothly change its state if the critical point is not degenerate. With a certain increase in the load, the critical point will first degenerate, and then, as a structurally unstable, will decay into nondegenerate or disappear. At the same time, the observed cyber system will abruptly move into a new state (*loss of cyber-resilience, destruction, critical changes in structure and behavior, irreversible critical state*).

The results of the cyber-resilience memory control system design allowed identifying the following strata: monitoring of group and mass cyber-attacks and immunity accumulation; self-recovery program development and verification of the disturbed system behavior; recovery, which achieves cyber system self-recovery when solving the target problems.

**Acknowledgement.** The publication was carried out with the financial support of Russian Foundation for Basic Research (RFBR) and the Government of the Republic of Tatarstan in the framework of the scientific project No. 18-47-160011 "Development of an early warning system for computer attacks on the critical infrastructure of enterprises of the Republic of Tatarstan based on the creation and development of new NBIC cybersecurity technologies".

# References

1. Bodeau, D., Graubart, R., Heinbockel, W., Laderman, E.: Cyber Resiliency Engineering Aid-The Updated Cyber Resiliency Engineering Framework and Guidance on Applying Cyber Resiliency Techniques, MTR140499R1, PR 15-1334, May 2015
2. Ross, R.S.: Risk Management Framework for Information Systems and Organizations: A System Life Cycle Approach for Security and Privacy, 20 December 2018
3. ISO/TS 22318:2015: Societal security – Business continuity management systems – Guidelines for supply chain continuity, ISO/TC 292 (2015)
4. ISO/IEC 27005:2018: Information technology – Security techniques, ISO/TC 292 (2018)
5. Kott, A., Linkov, I.: Cyber Resilience of Systems and Networks (Risk, Systems and Decisions), p. 475. Springer, Cham (2019). https://doi.org/10.1007/978-3-319-77492-3
6. Mailloux, L.O.: Engineering Secure and Resilient Cyber-Physical Systems, Systems Engineering Cyber Center for Research, US Air Force (2018)
7. NIST Special Publication 800-160 Volume 2: Systems Security Engineering. Cyber Resiliency Considerations for the Engineering of Trustworthy Secure Systems (2018)
8. Petrenko, S.: Big Data Technologies for Monitoring of Computer Security: A Case Study of the Russian Federation, 1st edn, p. XXVII, 249. Springer, Cham (2018). https://doi.org/10.1007/978-3-319-79036-7
9. Petrenko, S.: Cyber Security Innovation for the Digital Economy: A Case Study of the Russian Federation, River Publishers Series in Security and Digital Forensics, 1st edn, p. 490. River Publishers, Gistrup (2018)

# Method of Improving the Cyber Resilience for Industry 4.0. Digital Platforms

Sergei Petrenko[(⊠)] and Khismatullina Elvira

Innopolis University, Universitetskaya 7, Innopolis 420500, Russia
s.petrenko@rambler.ru

**Abstract.** Cyber resilience is the most important feature of any cyber system, especially during the transition to the sixth technological stage, and related Industry 4.0 technologies: Artificial Intelligence (AI), Cloud and foggy computing, 5G +, IoT/IIoT, Big Data and ETL, Q-computing, Block chain, VR/AR, etc. We should even consider the cyber resilience as primary one, because the mentioned systems cannot exist without it. Indeed, without the sustainable formation, made of the interconnected components of the critical information infrastructure, it does not make sense to discuss the existence of 4.0 Industry cyber-systems. In case when the cyber security of these systems is mainly focused on assessment of the incidents' probability and prevention of possible security threats, the cyber security is mainly aimed at preserving the targeted behavior and cyber systems' performance under the conditions of known (about 45%) as well as unknown (the remaining 55%) cyber-attacks.

**Keywords:** Digital transformation · Digital economy · Cyber resilience · Manageability capability · Self-organization · Proactive cyber security and adaptability · Models and methods of artificial intelligence · Cognitive computing · Big data · Robotics · Internet of Things IIoT / IoT

## 1 Introduction

It should be noted that the modern cyber systems do not have the required cyber resilience for targeted operation under conditions of heterogeneous mass cyber-attacks, due to the high structural and functional complexity of these systems, the potential danger of the existing vulnerabilities and "dormant" hardware and software tabs, the so-called "digital bombs" [1–3]. Moreover, the modern cyber security tools, including anti-virus protection, vulnerability scanners, as well as systems for detecting, preventing and neutralizing computer attacks [4–8], are still not sufficiently effective. The applied classical methods and means of ensuring reliability, response and recovery, using the capabilities of structural and functional redundancy, N - multiple reservation, standardization and reconfiguration, are no longer suitable for providing the required cyber resilience and prevent catastrophic consequences [9–12].

© Springer Nature Switzerland AG 2019
M. Mazzara et al. (Eds.): TOOLS 2019, LNCS 11771, pp. 295–302, 2019.
https://doi.org/10.1007/978-3-030-29852-4_24

The results of the Ernst & Young (EY) international research on information security[1] evidence that the second year in a row 87% of World leading companies executive board and management representatives are uncertain about the adequacy of the taken cyber security measures. At the same time, the most part of managers seek to increase the speed of rapid response to the emergence of new challenges and threats in cyberspace. In particular, the public investments are made for the creation and development of SOCs of the second and next generations. However, the main question is: does the company have the required cyber resilience? Does it have enough capacity to minimize the risks of business interruption? Apparently, high cyber resilience of critical business information infrastructure is not solely limited to the prompt response to new challenges and cyber threats. We need the fundamentally new ideas and new approaches of ensuring the business sustainability.

Also, the results of the aforementioned research indicate the need for a paradigm shift - from response and recovery to cyber resilience. Indeed, recently the issues of building response and recovery corporate systems that can effectively withstand the typical failures under normal operating conditions were among the top priorities. However, it is no longer enough to limit ourselves to ensuring the response and recovery under the conditions of an unprecedented increase in security threats. It requires a new paradigm for building a corporate cyber-resilient system that will be able to timely detect and prevent cyber-attacks, and in the case of cyber-attacks, it will "soften" the blow, reduce the strength and nature of destructive impact, and minimize the consequences [9, 10, 13–18]. Moreover, such a "smart" protection organization, if necessary, should allow sacrificing some of the functions and components of the protected infrastructure for the business resumption.

According to the CSIRT[2] of Innopolis University, the average flow of cyber security events in 2018 was 57 million events per day. The share of critical security incidents exceeded 18.7%, i.e. every fifth incident had become critical. This dynamic correlates with the results of cyberspace control and monitoring the cybersecurity threats of leading international CERT/CSIRT in the United States and the European Union, and also confirms the investigation results of the well-known cyber-attacks: "STUXNET" (2010), "Duqu" (2011), Flame (2012), "Wanna Cry" (2017), "Industroyer" and "TRITON / TRISIS / HATMAN" (2018), etc. At the same time, the increasing concern has the number of unknown and, accordingly, undetectable cyber-attacks is between 60% and 40% out of a possible. Collectively, this all suggests that the known methods for ensuring cybersecurity, response and recovery are no longer enough to provide the required cyber resilience and preventing the transfer of critical information infrastructure to irreversible catastrophic states [4, 6, 7, 11, 12, 19–21].

The above mentioned poses a problematic situation that lies in the contradiction between the ever-increasing need to ensure the cyber resilience of critical information infrastructure under the conditions of destructive software impacts and the imperfection of methods and means of timely detection, prevention and neutralization of cyber-attacks. The removal of this contradiction requires the resolution of an urgent scientific

---

[1] https://www.ey.com/en_gl/cybersecurity/global-information-security-survey.

[2] https://university.innopolis.ru/research/tib/csirt-iu.

and technical problem - the organization of the cyber resilience of information infrastructure in terms of heterogeneous mass cyber-attacks, based on new models and methods of similarity theory, Big data collection and processing and stream data extract, transfer, load (ETL), deep learning, semantic and cognitive analysis.

## 2 Cyber Resilience Concept

The cyber resilience characteristic is a fundamental feature of any cyber system created on the *Industry 4.0* breakthrough technologies (*Society 5.0–SuperSmart Society*). The characteristic can intuitively be defined as a certain constancy, the permanence of a certain structure (*static resilience*) and behaviour (*dynamic resilience*) of the named systems. As applied to technical systems, the resilience definition was given by an outstanding Russian mathematician, Academician of the St. Petersburg Academy of Sciences A. M. Lyapunov (1857–1918): *"Resilience is a system's ability to function in conditions close to equilibrium, under constant external and internal disturbing influences"*.

It is proposed to clarify the above definition, since the cyber resilience of *Industry 4.0* systems does not always mean the ability to maintain an equilibrium state. Initially, the resilience feature was interpreted in this way, since it was noticed as a real phenomenon, when studying homeostasis (returning to an equilibrium state when unbalancing) of biological systems. The system analysis apparatus use implies a certain adaptation of the term "resilience" to the characteristic features of the studied cyber systems under information and technical influences, one of which is the operation purpose existence. Therefore, the following resilience definition is proposed: *"Cyber Resilience is an ability of the cyber-system functioning, according to a certain algorithm, in order to achieve the operation purpose under the intruder information and technical influences"*.

Indeed, according to *Fleishman B.S.*, it is necessary to distinguish the active and passive resilience forms. The active resilience form (*reliability, response and recovery, survivability, and etc.*) is inherent in the complex systems, which behaviour is based on the *decision act*. Here the decisive act is defined as the alternative choice, the system desire to achieve its preferred state that is purposeful behaviour, and this state is its goal. The passive form (strength, balance, homeostasis) is inherent in the *simple* systems that are not capable of the *decision act*.

Additionally, in contrast to the classical equilibrium approach, the central element here is the concept of *structural and functional resilience*. The fact is that the normal cyber system functioning is usually far from an equilibrium. At the same time, the intruder external and internal information and technical influences constantly change the equilibrium state itself. Accordingly, the proximity measure that allows deciding whether the cyber system behaviour changes significantly under the disturbances, here, is the performed function set.

After the work of *Academician Glushkov V.M.* (1923–1982), the researches of *V. Lipaev.* (1928–2015), *Dodonova A. G, Lande D. V, Kuznetsova M. G, Gorbachik E.S., Ignatieva M. B, Katermina T. S* and other scientists were devoted to the resilience theory development. However, the resilience theory in these works was developed only in regards to the structure vulnerability of the computing system without taking into account explicitly the system behaviour vulnerability under a priori uncertainty of the intruder information and technical influences. As a result, in most cases, such a system is an example of a predetermined change and relationships and connection preservation. This preservation is intended to maintain the system integrity for a certain time period under normal operating conditions. This predetermination has a dual character: on the one hand, the system provides the best response to the normal operating disturbance conditions, and on the other hand, the system is not able to withstand another, a priori unknown information and technical intruder influences, changing its structure and behaviour.

## 3   Problem Solution

The design and development practice of Industry 4.0 cyber system indicates the following. The modern confrontation conditions in cyberspace assign these systems features that exclude the possibility of designing cyber-resilient systems in traditional ways. The following Table 1 gives the complexity factors arising at the same time, and the generated difficulties.

**Table 1.** Complexity factors in ensuring cyber resilience

| # | Complexity factors | Generated difficulties |
|---|---|---|
| 1 | Complex structure and behaviour of the automated systems of critically important in objects (AS CIO) | Solved problem awkwardness and multidimensionality |
| 2 | AS CIO behaviour randomness | System behaviour description uncertainty, complexity in the task formulation |
| 3 | AS CIO activity | Limiting law definition complexity of the potential system efficiency |
| 4 | Mutual impact of the AS CIO data structures | Cannot be considered by the known type models |
| 5 | Failure and denial influence on the AS CIO hardware behaviour | System behaviour parameter uncertainty, complexity in the task formulation |
| 6 | Deviations from the standard AS CIO operation conditions | Cannot be considered by the known type models |
| 7 | Intruder information and technical impacts on AS CIO | System behaviour parameter uncertainty, complexity in the task formulation |

Here the factors 1, 4 and 7 are determinant ones. They exclude the possibility to be limited by the generally valid features of Industry 4.0 cyber systems in group and mass cyber-attacks. However, traditional cyber security and resilience methods are based on the following approaches:

- Simplifying the behaviour of cyber systems before deriving generally valid algorithmic features;
- Generalization of the empirically established specific behaviour laws of the named systems.

The use of these approaches does not only cause a significant error in the results but also has fundamental flaws. The lack of the analytical modelling of cyber system behaviour, under group and mass cyber-attacks, is the difficulty of the transitioning from the system behaviour class, characterized by the derivation of general algorithmic features, to a single behaviour, which is additionally characterized by the operating conditions under growing cyber threats. The empirical simulation disadvantage of the cyber system behaviour is an inability to extend the results to other system behaviour that differs from the studied one in the functioning parameters.

Therefore, in practice, the traditional cyber security and fault tolerance approaches can only be used to develop systems for approximate forecasting of system cyber resilience in group and mass cyber-attacks.

In order to resolve these contradictions, there is a proposed approach, based on the dimension and similarity theory methods, which lacks these drawbacks and allows the implementation of the so-called cyber-system behaviour decomposition principle under group and mass cyber-attacks, according to the structural and functional characteristics. In the dimension and similarity theory, it is proved that the relation set between the parameters that are essential for the considered system behaviour is not the natural studied problem property. In fact, the individual factor influences of the cyber system external and internal environment, represented by various quantities, appear not separately, but jointly. Therefore, it is proposed to consider not individual quantities, but their total (the so-called similarity invariants), which have a definite meaning for the certain cyber system functioning.

Thus, an application of the method of the dimensions and similarity theory allows formulating the necessary and sufficient conditions for the two-model isomorphism of the allowed cyber system behaviour under group and mass cyber-attacks, formally described by systems of homogeneous power polynomials (polynomials).

As a consequence, the following actions become possible:

- Producing an analytical verification of the cyber system behavior and check the isomorphism conditions;
- Numerical determination of the certain model representation coefficients of the system behavior to achieve isomorphism conditions.

This, in turn, allows the following actions:

- Controlling the semantic correctness of the cyber system behavior under exposure by comparing the observed similarity invariants with the invariants of the reference, isomorphic behavior representation;
- Detection (including in real time) the anomalies of system behavior resulting from the destructive software intruder actions;
- Restoring the behavior parameters that significantly affect the system cyber resilience.

# 4  Method of Improving the Cyber Resilience

A new Method of improving the Cyber Resilience consist of the following four stages.

*The first stage* is the $\pi$-analysis of the cyber system behavior models. The main stage goal is to separate the semantic system behavior correctness standards, based on similarity invariants.

The step procedure includes the following steps:

(1) Structural and functional standard separation;
(2) Time standard separation;
(3) Control relation development, necessary to determine the semantic system behavior correctness.

*The second stage* is the *algorithm development* of the obtaining semantic cyber system behavior correctness standards. Its main purpose is to obtain the system behavior probabilistic algorithms of standards or similarity invariants in a matrix and a graphical form.

The step procedure includes the following steps:

(1) Construction of the standard algorithm in the tree form;
(2) Algorithm implementations listing;
(3) Weighting of algorithm implementations (a probabilistic algorithm construction);
(4) Algorithm tree rationing.

*The third stage* is the standard synthesis of the semantic cyber-system behavior correctness, adequate to the application goals and objectives. Its main goal is to synthesize algorithmic structures formed by a set of sequentially executed standard algorithms.

This procedure is carried out in the following steps:

(1) Structural and functional standard synthesis;
(2) Time standard synthesis;
(3) Symmetrization and ranking of matrices describing standards.

*The fourth stage* is the simulation of the stochastically defined algorithmic structures of the semantic cyber system behavior correctness standards. The step procedure includes the following steps:

(1) Analysis of the empirical semantic correctness;
(2) Determining the type of the empirical functional dependence;
(3) Control ratio development sufficient to determine the semantic system behavior correctness and to ensure the required cyber resilience.

As a result, the method applicability of dimensions and similarity theory to decompose *Industry 4.0 cyber-systems behavior algorithms*, according to functional characteristics and the necessary invariants formation of semantically correct systems operation, was shown. The self-similarity property presence of similarity invariants allowed forming static and dynamic standards of the semantically correct system behavior and uses them for engineering problem solution *of control, detection, and neutralization* of intruder information and technical influences.

# 5 Conclusion

It is significant that the proposed approach significantly complements the well-known MITRE[3] [8, 13, 14] and NIST SP 800-160[4] [3, 23, 24] approaches and allows developing cyber resilience metrics and measures. Including engineering techniques for modelling, observing, measuring and comparing cyber- resilience based on similarity invariants.

**Acknowledgement.** The publication was carried out with the financial support of Russian Foundation for Basic Research (RFBR) and the Government of the Republic of Tatarstan in the framework of the scientific project No. 18-47-160011 "Development of an early warning system for computer attacks on the critical infrastructure of enterprises of the Republic of Tatarstan based on the creation and development of new NBIC cybersecurity technologies".

# References

1. Bodeau, D., Graubart, R., Heinbockel, W., Laderman, E.: Cyber Resiliency Engineering Aid-The Updated Cyber Resiliency Engineering Framework and Guidance on Applying Cyber Resiliency Techniques (MTR140499R1PR 15-1334), May 2015
2. Bodeau, D., Brtis, J., Graubart, R., Salwen, J.: Resiliency Techniques for System of Systems: Extending and Applying the Cyber Resiliency Engineering Framework to the Space Domain (MTR 130515, PR 13-3513), September 2013
3. Ross, R.S.: Risk Management Framework for Information Systems and Organizations: A System Life Cycle Approach for Security and Privacy, 20 December 2018
4. NIST Special Publication 800-160 VOLUME 4. Systems Security Engineering. Hardware Assurance Considerations for the Engineering of Trustworthy Secure Systems – (Draft), 20 December 2020
5. NIST SP 800-34. Rev. 1: Contingency Planning Guide for Federal Information Systems Paperback, 18 February 2014
6. NIST, Framework for improving critical infrastructure cybersecurity, version 1.1, draft 2, 16 April 2018
7. Petrenko, S.: Big Data Technologies for Monitoring of Computer Security: A Case Study of the Russian Federation. Springer, Cham (2018). https://doi.org/10.1007/978-3-319-79036-7
8. Petrenko, S.: Cyber Security Innovation for the Digital Economy: A Case Study of the Russian Federation. River Publishers, Huddesfield (2018)
9. ISO/IEC 27002:2013, Information technology – Security techniques – Code of practice for information security controls. https://www.iso.org/standard/54533.html
10. ISO/IEC 27005:2018, Information technology – Security techniques
11. Kott, A., Linkov, I. (eds.): Cyber Resilience of Systems and Networks. RSD. Springer, Cham (2019). https://doi.org/10.1007/978-3-319-77492-3
12. Mailloux, L.O.: Engineering Secure and Resilient Cyber-Physical Systems (2018)
13. ISO 22301:2012. Societal security – Business continuity management systems – Requirements
14. ISO 22313:2012. Societal security – Business continuity management systems – Guidance

---

[3] www.mitre.org.
[4] www.nist.gov.

15. ISO/TS 22317:2015. Societal security – Business continuity management systems – Guidelines for business impact analysis (BIA)
16. ISO/TS 22318:2015, Societal security – Business continuity management systems – Guidelines for supply chain continuity
17. ISO/TS 22330:2018, Security and resilience – Business continuity management systems – Guidelines for people aspects of business continuity
18. ISO/TS 22331:2018, Security and resilience – Business continuity management systems – Guidelines for business continuity strategy
19. NIST Special Publication 800-160 VOLUME 2. Systems Security Engineering. Cyber Resiliency Considerations for the Engineering of Trustworthy Secure Systems, March 2018
20. NIST Special Publication 800-160 VOLUME 3. Systems Security Engineering. Software Assurance Considerations for the Engineering of Trustworthy Secure Systems, 20 December 2019
21. NIST Special Publication 800-160 VOLUME 4. Systems Security Engineering. Hardware Assurance Considerations for the Engineering of Trustworthy Secure Systems, 20 December 2020
22. Graubart, R.: The MITRE corporation, cyber resiliency engineering framework. In: The Secure and Resilient Cyber Ecosystem (SRCE) Industry Workshop Tuesday, 17 November 2015
23. Ross, R.S., McEvilley, M., Oren, J.C.: Systems Security Engineering: Considerations for a Multidisciplinary Approach in the Engineering of Trustworthy Secure Systems, 21 March 2018
24. The BCI Cyber Resilience Report, Business Continuity Institute (2018)

# Computer Architectures and Robotics

# Can We Rely on Smartphone Applications?

Sonia Meskini[1], Ali Bou Nassif[2], and Luiz Fernando Capretz[3(✉)]

[1] Prophix Software, Mississauga, ON L5B 3J1, Canada
sonya.meskini@gmail.com
[2] Department of Electrical and Computer Engineering, University of Sharjah,
27272 Sharjah, UAE
anassif@sharjah.ac.ae
[3] Department of Electrical and Computer Engineering, Western University,
London, ON N6A 5B9, Canada
lcapretz@uwo.ca

**Abstract.** Smartphones are becoming necessary tools in the daily lives of millions of users who rely on these devices and their applications. There are thousands of applications for smartphone devices such as the iPhone, Blackberry, and Android, thus their reliability has become paramount for their users. This work aims to answer two related questions: (1) Can we assess the reliability of mobile applications by using the traditional reliability models? (2) Can we model adequately the failure data collected from many users? Firstly, it has been proved that the three most used software reliability models have fallen short of the mark when applied to smartphone applications; their failures were traced back to specific features of mobile applications. Secondly, it has been demonstrated that the Weibull and Gamma distribution models can adequately fit the observed failure data, thus providing better means to predict the reliability of smartphone applications.

**Keywords:** Smartphone applications · Software reliability · NHPP model · Software Reliability Growth Models · SRGM

## 1 Introduction

Smartphones are now so useful that many people prefer them over desktop or laptop computers. Hundreds of applications, usually suited to desktop or laptop computers, have been adapted to and carried out by these smartphones. The high usage and trust placed in these devices and their applications make their reliability a critically important goal to achieve [1]. Thus, owing to their highly integrated software, smartphones are far more advanced devices and their functionalities far exceed those of the classic mobile phones. Therefore, increased attention is now being paid to the reliability and security of these devices. Software Reliability Growth Models (SRGMs) are among the tools that deal with the reliability of software applications; they have been constructed and successfully applied to desktop (classic/standard) applications. In recent work [2], we thoroughly investigated the applicability of these SRGMs to the mobile area. We applied three of the most used SRGMs to the collected failure data of three smartphone applications; our main conclusion was that none of the selected

© Springer Nature Switzerland AG 2019
M. Mazzara et al. (Eds.): TOOLS 2019, LNCS 11771, pp. 305–312, 2019.
https://doi.org/10.1007/978-3-030-29852-4_25

models was able to account for the observed failure data satisfactorily. Basically, we addressed the following research questions:

(1) How do the existing successful reliability models, used to assess the desktop/laptop applications, perform when applied to the mobile area?
(2) What are the best non-linear distributions that fit smartphone application failure data?
(3) What useful information can be gained from this approach?

The rest of the paper is organized as follows: in Sect. 2 we provide a short list of the existing models that we will use, we describe our dataset collection, and we test the applicability of existing software reliability models. Finally, in Sect. 3, we carry out an analysis of the failure data with model distributions followed by a discussion in Sect. 4. We present our conclusions in Sect. 5 and outline future work possibilities.

## 2 SRGMs Applied to Smartphone Applications

The SRGMs used later in our experiments are: the NHPP – Crow – AMSAA model (also termed the NHPP-Power Law model), the Musa-Basic execution time model (or the exponential model), and the Musa-Okumoto model (or the Logarithmic Poisson model). The applications that have been chosen are Skype, Vtok, and a private Windows phone application. The relevant equations of these models are given in [3].

We present the procedure devised to collect the failure data for each application followed by the results of the application of the chosen SRGM to failure data for each application, and, finally, an analysis of the observed results.

### 2.1 Datasets and Experiments

We used Apple devices (iPhone, iPad and iPod Touch) crash files as well as a Windows Phone crash file as our "experimental" data. These crash files are not public, but are confidential.

The reliability demonstration of smartphone applications was carried out through traditional testing, failure data collection, and the application of the most used SRGMs for standard applications to observe and check the adequacy of these models in the mobile area.

The first iPhone application studied was Skype, which had been tested and used for one year (from November 1, 2011 to November 11, 2012). Hence, the data has been collected during this year with some missing values due to the occasional non-use of the application. We were, however, able to collect 39 data points for the Skype application.

The second application studied was Vtok (an application for Google talk). This application was used continuously every day for two months (from September 19, 2012 to November 25, 2012). Hence, we were able to collect failures every day (81 data points).

During these periods, both the Skype and the Vtok applications were upgraded when new versions were released.

On the other hand, the Windows phone application was used and tested continuously for six months (from March 2012 to August 2012) by different users located in different parts of the world (more than 100 users).

We used two Software Reliability tools for this application to double check the results. The first tool is RGA 7 from ReliaSoft [4] and the second one is Statistical Modeling and Estimation of Reliability Functions for Software (SMERFS).

## 2.2 Evaluation

Figure 1 presents the cumulative number of failures per time for the Skype application when applying the NHPP model. The RGA tool indicates an evident failure. Moreover, we tested the Vtok application and we found that the NHPP model also failed.

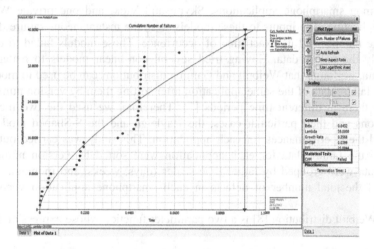

**Fig. 1.** Cumulative number of failures per Time (Skype).

In order to confirm our results, we used a second tool, SMERFS, and we applied the NHPP model to the same data points. The result was the same – the failure of the model each time. This failure can be traced back to the main differences between the desktop area and smartphones. One of the mobile application failure characteristics is that they are application dependent, in the sense that they are dynamic and non-homogenously spread in time. Moreover, they are unpredictable; sometimes they decrease and sometimes they increase. One possible explanation is that reliability depends on how the application is used, where it is used, and when it is used. The usage may differ from one person to another, from one country to another, from one condition and time to another, etc.; this explains the uncertainty of usage of the application in the execution and release time because all these factors play an important role in the reliability of the application.

Another reason is that the DLC (Development Life Cycle) of a mobile application is short (up to 90 days) and the programmer aims to develop the application as fast as possible to satisfy the time to market constraint, which leads to skip phases from the

DLC. The phase most often skipped is the design phase, which is the most important phase in the DLC of the application [5]. Thus, it would be difficult to identify the causes of errors during the execution time and to find a convenient solution to fix them. Besides that, the failure or unreliability of the application may be caused by the technology used during the development process. The skills of the developer and the tester also play a huge role in the reliability of the application. Moreover, the device itself and its hardware characteristics – such as the size of the screen, the performance, the keyboard, etc. – can have a direct effect on the reliability of the application [6].

## 3 Failure Data Analysis Using Model Distributions

The preceding section was devoted to the application of the three most used SRGMs to two common smartphone applications, Skype and Vtok, and one private Windows phone application. The inputs to these models were the instantaneous failure data, i.e, the failure number and its exact time of occurrence. Those models failed to describe adequately the failure data. Having tried several non-linear models to better fit the failure data, we found that Weibull and Gamma distributions can be used to model new collected failure data of the same application after sorting them by version number and grouping them in different time periods [7]. Therefore, we used the two mentioned distributions and their particular cases, the Rayleigh and the S-Shaped models, and compared their performances for each application. This study was carried out in two steps: (1) the failure data for each application were sorted by version number and (2) the data were grouped by larger time scales (days, weeks, and months). An estimation of the total number of defects in each smartphone application version was obtained.

The Weibull distribution [8] is a two parameter function whose expression is given by:

$$f(t) = \text{wblpdf}(t, a, b) = \frac{b}{a} * \left(\frac{t}{a}\right)^{b-1} \exp\left(-\left(\frac{t}{a}\right)^{b}\right). \tag{1}$$

The parameters $a$ and $b$ take positive values as well as the variable $t$. If we define $A = 1/a^{b}$ and $B = b$, the expression simplifies to:

$$f(t) = B\, A\, t^{B-1} \exp\left(-A\, t^{B}\right). \tag{2}$$

A maximum for this function occurs at time $t = T_{max}$, such that

$$T_{max}^{b} = \frac{B - 1}{A\, B}. \tag{3}$$

The Gamma distribution is a two parameter function whose expression is given by:

$$f(t) = \text{gampdf}(t, a, b) = \frac{1}{b^a \Gamma(a)} (t)^{a-1} \exp\left(-\frac{t}{b}\right). \tag{4}$$

for $a$, $b$ and $t$ taking positive values. The maximum of this function occurs at $t = T_{max}$, such that:

$$T_{max} = b\,(a - 1). \tag{5}$$

## 3.1 Results

This section presents a comparison and an evaluation of the use of the above mentioned distributions to model the failure data of the Skype application, based on the usual evaluation criteria: RMSE, Ad-R-Square, and MRE. Due to space limitation, only Skype V1 will be presented from the versions we studied. The full and detailed results are found in [3].

For each application, the four distributions used were compared on the basis of their Root-Mean-Squared-Error (RMSE) and their Adjusted R-Square. The results of the estimated total number of defects were evaluated using the Magnitude of Relative Error (MRE). These statistical indicators are defined in [3].

Table 1 gives a compilation of all model parameters (a, b) along with the predicted or estimated $T_{max}$ (time of maximum failure rate) and the expected proportion ($Y(t = T_{max})/C$) of encountered failures by $T_{max}$. It also gives results of RMSE, As-R-Square, the estimated cumulative number of failures $C$, and the MRE shown by each model. Only the best and the second best model distributions are given for each application version.

**Table 1.** Skype version 1 – error evaluation and model comparison.

| Skype V1 | Weibull | Gamma |
| --- | --- | --- |
| Model parameters and deduced estimated values | a = 6.17 (5.26, 7.09)<br>b = 2.82 (1.81, 3.84)<br>Observed $T_{max}$ = 6<br>Estimated $T_{max}$ = 5.98<br>Estimated ($Y(t = T_{max})/$ $C$) = 47% | a = 6.14 (1.84, 10.44)<br>b = 0.97 (0.21, 1.73)<br>Observed $T_{max}$ = 6<br>Estimated $T_{max}$ = 5.01<br>Estimated ($Y(t = T_{max})/$ $C$) = 38.5% |
| RMSE | 2.1966 | 2.2305 |
| Ad-R-Square | 0.6374 | 0.6262 |
| C: Estimated cumulative number of failures or defects | 50.54 (34.51, 66.58) | 51.81 (34.32, 69.31) |
| MRE(%) | 6.4 | 4 |

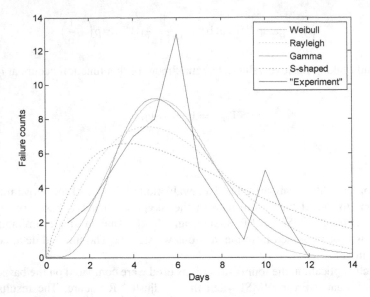

**Fig. 2.** Skype version 1 – model comparison.

Figure 2 portrays the results reported in Table 1. It can be noted from the figure that the Weibull distribution is the closest to the actual behavior curve of the application followed by the Gamma distribution.

## 4  Discussion and Answers to Research Questions

According to the preceding section, and as an answer to the first research question raised in the abstract, it can be concluded that the most successful reliability models [9] failed to account for the failure data and to predict the reliability of mobile applications. This failure can be traced back to the following main reasons: (1) Operational Environment and Usage Profiles of Smartphones Applications, (2) Hardware and Software Limitations [10].

Assuming all of these uncertainties, at a second stage, and in order to answer the second research question, we collected data from many users in different regions of the world, sorted them by application versions, and grouped them in different time periods (days, weeks, and months). Each application version failure data, when plotted in time periods, shows the same pattern: an early "burst of failures", due probably to the most evident defects, followed by a steep decrease in failure rate. After trying several non-linear models to fit the failure data, we found that the observed behavior is better modeled by the Weibull or Gamma distributions.

To answer the third research question the main features of this approach can be summarized as follows:

- For each application version, the model distributions are in fact distinguished by tiny differences in the calculated errors RMSE and Ad-R-Squared. Nevertheless, it can be concluded that no one single distribution can fit the data of all applications or even the different versions of the same application.

- As the parameters are given along with their 95% confidence intervals, it is to be noted that parameter $b$ of the Weibull distribution, which is fixed to the value $b = 2$ for the particular case of Rayleigh distribution, has confidence intervals that include the value $b = 2$. The same can be noted for parameter $a$ of the Gamma distribution, which is fixed to the value $a = 2$ in the particular case of the S-shaped model distribution. But most of the time, the general distribution models fit the failure data better than the particular cases.
- Similar to the famous 40% rule of the Rayleigh distribution, and independent of any application, the S-shaped distribution has a 26.4% rule. This means that by $T_{max}$, only 26.4% of the defects in a smartphone application will be uncovered. This can be tested on larger datasets and across many applications.

# 5  Conclusions

Our work is a step toward the application and evaluation of traditional Software Reliability models in the mobile area. We selected three of the most used models that are known for their efficiency in the desktop area: the NHPP, Musa-Basic, and Musa-Okumoto models. We examined two iPhone applications, Skype and Vtok, which were used and tested differently to evaluate the models under different conditions, and one Windows phone application. It turned out that none of the selected SRGMs was able to account for the failure data satisfactorily.

Our study also highlighted the causes of the failure of the models and the need for a meticulous SRGM for Smartphone applications, because the existing software reliability approaches were developed for traditional desktop software applications that are static and stable during their execution. This is not the case for smartphone applications, which have an unknown operational profile, a highly dynamic configuration, and changing execution conditions. On a continuous background, the smartphone failures come in relatively short bursts from time to time, which explain the abrupt in the observed cumulative failure number curves. This particular feature cannot be accommodated by the SRGMs that were used. Thus, in order to evaluate the reliability of smartphone applications, new models, principles, and tools are needed to incorporate the underlying uncertainties of such applications [11–14].

Our investigation of smartphone application reliability through the use of well-known available growth models suited primarily to desktop applications is twofold: (1) highlight the versatile nature of mobile applications, their dynamic configuration, unknown operational profile, and varying execution conditions in contrast to the static and stable desktop ones, and (2) stress the need for the design of new reliability models suited for mobile applications that take into account the inherent versatility of such applications [15]. Our future work will focus on analyzing these selected SRGMs in more depth and trying to modify the closest one to the data and adapt in to smartphone applications. Moreover, we will check to find out if we need to have a specific model for each type of applications or if one model is applicable to all the categories, of Smartphone applications, taking into consideration the severity of the failure.

# References

1. Verkasalo, H., Lopez-Nicolas, C., Molina-Castillo, F.J., Bouwman, H.: Analysis of users and non-users of smartphone applications. Telematics Inform. 27(3), 242–255 (2010)
2. Meskini, S., Nassif, A.B., Capretz, L.F.: Reliability models applied to mobile applications. In: Proceedings of 7th IEEE International Conference on Software Security and Reliability Companion, Washington, DC, USA, pp. 155–162 (2013)
3. Meskini, S.: Reliability Models Applied to Smartphone Applications, Master Thesis, Western University, London, Ontario, Canada (2013)
4. ReliaSoft: Reliability Growth & Repairable System Data Analysis Reference (2010). http:// rga.reliasoft.com/
5. Wasserman, A.I.: Software engineering issues for mobile application development. In: Proceedings of FSE/SDP Workshop on the Future of Software Engineering Research, FoSER 2010, Santa Fe, NM, USA, pp. 397–400 (2010)
6. Jang, S., Lee, E.: Reliable mobile application modeling based on open API. In: Ślęzak, D., Kim, T.-h., Kiumi, A., Jiang, T., Verner, J., Abrahão, S. (eds.) ASEA 2009. CCIS, vol. 59, pp. 168–175. Springer, Heidelberg (2009). https://doi.org/10.1007/978-3-642-10619-4_21
7. Meskini, S., Nassif, A.B., Capretz, L.F.: Reliability prediction of smartphone Applications through failure data analysis. In: Proceedings of 19th IEEE Pacific Rim International Symposium on Dependable Computing, Vancouver, BC, Canada, pp. 124–125 (2013)
8. Murthy, D.N.P., Xie, M., Jiang, R.: Weibull Models. Wiley, Hoboken (2004)
9. Xu, J., Ho, D., Capretz, L.F.: An empirical validation of object-oriented design metrics for fault prediction. J. Comput. Sci. 4(7), 571–577 (2008)
10. Mirvat, P., Marin, I., Ortin, F., Rodriguez, J.: Framework for the declarative implementation of native mobile applications. IET Softw. J. 8(1), 19–32 (2014)
11. Capretz, L.F., Capretz, M.A.M.: Object-Oriented Software: Design and Maintenance, p. 263. World Scientific, Singapore (1996). ISBN 981-02-2731-0
12. Raza, A., Capretz, L.F., Ahmed, F.: Users' perception of open source usability: an empirical study. Eng. Comput. 28(2), 109–121 (2012)
13. Nassif, A.B., Azzeh, M., Capretz, L.F., Ho, D.: Neural network models for software development effort estimation: a comparative study. Neural Comput. Appl. 27(8), 2369–2381 (2016)
14. Ahmed, F., Capretz, L.F., Babar, M.A.: A model of open source software-based product line development. In: 32nd IEEE International Computer Software and Applications Conference (COMPSAC), Turku, Finland, pp. 1215–1220 (2008)
15. Malek, S., Roshandel, R., Kilgore, D., Elhag, I.: Improving the reliability of mobile software systems through continuous analysis and proactive reconfiguration. In: Proceedings of 31st IEEE International Conference in Software Engineering, ICSE-Companion 2009, Vancouver, BC, Canada, pp. 275–278 (2009)

# Distributed Computing System
# on a Smartphones-Based Network

Hamza Salem[✉]

Innopolis University, Innopolis, Russia
h.salem@innopolis.university

**Abstract.** The number of Smartphone users in the world is expected to
pass the five billion in 2019. The major credit for this exponential growth
is the competition between Smartphones manufacturing companies and
increasing Internet availability in the world. Processing power considered
to be one of the most important features in Smartphones and it is evolving year by year. Until now, building a distributed computing system
done exclusively using PCs and other server infrastructure. In this paper
we will propose a new architecture for a distributed computing system
consists of a network of Smartphones and use their computation power to
execute machine learning models on each Smartphone. As proof of concept, our solution will provide a stable layer to execute large data-sets
using common machine learning algorithms such as Linear Regression.

**Keywords:** Distributed system · Computation power · JS-Regression

## 1 Introduction

Latest industry forecasts indicate that the annual worldwide IP traffic consumption will reach 3.3 Zetta-bytes (1015 MB) by 2021, S Smartphone traffic
exceeding PC traffic by the same year [1,2]. Smartphones companies compete
with each other by improving features such as processing power, memory, and
capacity. These features are improving exponentially every year. In the near
future, Smartphones will have better performance to compete with PCs and
other devices such as PlayStation and Xbox. Overall, the expansion of the network scale and the diversification of services in the 5G [3,4] era will experience
an explosive growth, which can help these devices to be more powerful.

Machine learning is a computational process and machine learning algorithm
needs data-sets to train models. However, When the data-sets are big more computational power is needed. In order to increase the accuracy of any machine
learning model, we need to provide more data. Also, in general data-sets are
constantly increasing in size and complexity. The main challenge is that computational power will increase when the data-sets are increasing. One of the
main solutions is Distributed Computation [5]. It is a universal approach to deal
with large data-sets. When data-sets are partitioned across several machines (or
nodes), the machines perform computations locally and communicate only small

M. Mazzara et al. (Eds.): TOOLS 2019, LNCS 11771, pp. 313–325, 2019.
https://doi.org/10.1007/978-3-030-29852-4_26

bits of information with each other and they coordinate to compute the desired quantity. This is the standard approach taken at large technology companies, which routinely deal with huge data-sets spread over computer clusters.

Computer Cluster defined by Bader [6] as a set of loosely or tightly connected computers that work together so that, in many respects, they can be viewed as a single system. Additionally, according to Bakery and Buyya [7] computing industry is one of the fastest growing industries and it is fueled by the rapid technological developments. For example, chip development, fabrication technologies, fast and cheap microprocessors, as well as high bandwidth and low latency interconnection networks. On one hand, creating a distributed system cannot depend only on the hardware, the software is the other key for the process. For example, in personal computers and servers, we have Apache Spark [23] as a popular open-source platform for large-scale data processing that is well-suited for iterative machine learning tasks. Mengy [8] defined Spark as a fault-tolerant and general-purpose cluster computing system providing APIs in Java, Scala, Python, and R, along with an optimized engine that supports general execution graphs. As mentioned by Xiangrui, Spark can be efficient at iterative computations and well-suited for the development of large-scale machine learning applications. On the other hand, software in Smartphones or (Applications) has been improved to deal with complex computation too. From the beginning of Smartphones era, we have seen a lot of operating systems like Android, iOS, Blackberry can deal with complex computation processes. Nowadays, as mentioned by Bala et al. [9]. Smartphones provide a wide range of services such as sending or receiving SMS, music, online shopping, playing games, web browsing, messaging using different apps like Whats-App, Facebook or Telegram. However, all these applications still did not use computation power inside the Smartphone with machine learning processes.

Currently, every software in the world is a kind of distributed system. For example, when we have a website connected to APIs, the source code can be hosted on a static server, the database hosted on a different server and the APIs also in a different server too. In this paper, we will focus on distributed computing system only [21], and the implementation will be on a network of Smartphones.

In order to understand how can machine learning processes work on Smartphones, we will divide it into three main parts. The first part is when machine learning processes such as, training and predicting happen on Cloud and the application access these models using APIs. For example, Snap-chat filters [10] its combination of augmented reality and machine learning algorithms for computer vision used in mobile devices. However, the main part of the process happens on Cloud so when the devices are connected to the Internet the application will not work. The second part is when the prediction happens on the device and the training on Cloud. For example, in Talos App [11] the authors developed On-Device machine learning using Tensor Flow [24] to detect Android Malware. The app aims to solve the problem of malware detection using "Requested Permissions" as the input parameters. And they declared that the entire detection process takes place on the mobile device, and it does not require an Internet connection to work. The third part when both of the training and the prediction running on the device as partial tasks from a distributed system with a network. In this paper we will propose a new architecture for a distrusted system consists network of Smartphones working together to train and predicate with a specific type of machine learning algorithm. The aim of this paper implement and validate the new architecture and examines which machine learning algorithm can fit with such a system. Also, what is the main conditions and circumstances should be provided in the data to make sure the accuracy of the results.

## 2   Related Work

Distributed Computing is increasingly becoming one of the main hot topics to researchers especially using mobile devices. Few researchers have addressed the idea of converting cloud computing in the large environment into a mobile computing environment. For example, in [30] the authors proposed Hyrax a platform like Hadoop, but it supports cloud computing on Android Smartphones. Users can conveniently utilize data and execute computing jobs on networks of Smartphones. However, in [31] the authors proposed a new architecture to accessing and processing of data distributed across mobile devices without an external communication infrastructure, all communication uses a local wireless network. Both papers identified Mobile devices as resources for computing power on local network and deal with regular jobs in computing. In our paper, we will discuss three different perspectives as follows: Smartphones, Statistical Analysis, and Networks perspective. The first paper is a case study presented the prediction process for machine learning models from Smartphones perspective. In the second paper, Dobriban and Sheng [5] demonstrates the concept of "distributed linear regression by averaging" and how the algorithm will work on a distributed system. The third part focuses on the aspects of improving communication efficiency and speeds up the federated learning system using the local network and other devices that will have the processing power.

### 2.1   On-Device Machine Learning Using Tensor-Flow to Detect Android Malware

The paper proposing a lightweight method of malware analysis. Talos application [11] uses on-device machine learning and Tensor-Flow. It aims to solve the problem of malware detection using 'Requested Permissions' as the input parameters. The entire detection process takes place on the mobile device, and it does not require an Internet connection to work. Talos has demonstrated an accuracy of 93.2%. The authors claimed [11] that the app analyzes apps within a second, even on low-end Android devices. Talos use Tensor-Flow for creating the machine learning model but the training part is done on computers because this process is very computed intensive. The authors described Smartphones as "very low powered" for accomplishing this task. In the end, when the model is trained then the weights and biases are frozen and the frozen model is exported on to the device. It is then used on the Smartphone to deliver predictions [11]. From Smartphones perceptive Talos [11] is one of the apps that integrated machine learning model on a production product. However, the training part still is done by computers. In order to take a further step in this field, Smartphones have to develop more power in computing. Having said that, Smartphones becoming more and more powerful in computing and the future of Smartphones computing power still in the beginning.

## 2.2    Distributed Linear Regression by Averaging

Dobriban and Sheng [5] discuss one-step parameter averaging in statistical linear models under data parallelism. By doing linear regression on each machine, and take a weighted average of the parameters and studying the performance loss in estimation error, test error, and confidence interval length in high dimensions, where the number of parameters is comparable to the training data size. They introduced several key phenomena. First, averaging is not optimal, but the results are simple to use in practice and compare. Second, different problems area affected differently by the distributed framework. Estimation error and confidence interval length increases a lot, while the prediction error increases much less. From Statistical perspective, averaging is one of the ways to distribute the load on different nodes in a system. However, using such as algorithms have some restrictions and limitations. For example, you should work with normalized data before distributing it because without normalization the results will be biased depend on the data distributions. To put it another way, each node has to present as a mini copy of the system from the perspective of the data-set. Despite that, averaging is still one of the best practice to work with large data-sets especially with linear regression algorithms.

## 2.3    Federated Learning via Over-the-Air Computation

Typical machine learning processes including the training and prediction done on Cloud. For example, a centralized cloud data center with the broad accessibility of computation, storage, and the whole data-set provide APIs for other devices to use machine learning models. However, the emerging intelligent mobile devices and high-stake applications such as drones, smart vehicles and augmented reality, call for the critical requirements of low-latency and privacy. This makes cloud computing based machine learning methodologies inapplicable [11]. Therefore, it becomes increasingly attractive to possess data locally at the edge devices and then performing training and prediction directly at the edge, instead of sending data to the cloud or networks. In [12] the authors focus on designing the fast model aggregation approach for the Federation Average algorithm to improve communication efficiency and speed up the federated learning system. Global model aggregation procedure consists of the transmission of locally predicted values from each device, followed by the computation of their weighted average at a central node. From the Network perspective, this paper split machine learning processes into two different components working together on the same network. For example, the central node is like the computers on Talos [3] or the Cloud on regular systems. In conclusion, this architecture focus on working with a wireless local network only and the interpretation between it and our proposed system is implemented the same system using the Internet as network and do the training process for machine learning models on edge device through the network.

## 3  System Design and Development

### 3.1  System Design

In order to understand the system design for a distributed computing system to execute machine learning models, we will demonstrate the architecture for a typical centralized web application has the same functionality and after it, we will compare with the proposed architecture. Figure 1 shows the 4-tier system architecture and the connection between the components.

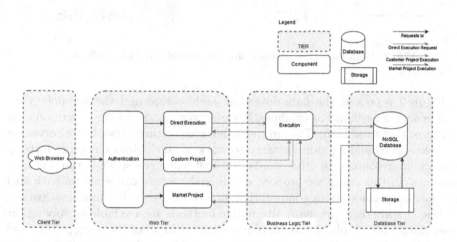

**Fig. 1.** 4-tier system architecture for centralized web application

Figure 1 represent a centralized web application working as a platform between companies and data scientists. The system provides an environment to execute machine learning models and provide predictions. One of the main issues in this architecture is scalability. For example, in Business Logic Tier the execution component is the main components for training machine learning models and as mentioned in [11] training process is very computed intensive and need a computation power. In other words, more users will join more computation power will be required. In order to mitigate this risk, the system should increase the computation power per each user or limit the usage of the system resources for all users.

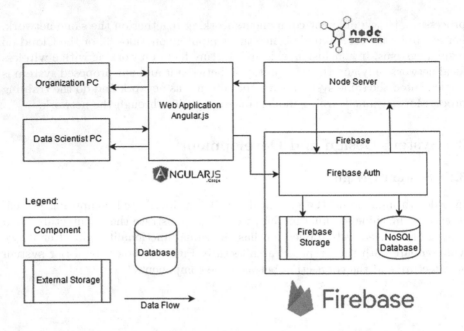

**Fig. 2.** Data flow view architecture for centralized web application

Figure 2 represent the data-flow view architecture and the technology are used in such a system. For example, Node Server represents the execution component or (Business Logic Tier) in the 4-tier architecture. Also, Node Server can be scaled-up by adding more instance to work parallel. However, every instance means more resources. In other words, the cost will increase when you add more resources. In this paper we propose a new architecture can scale up with such system and provide more computation power for executing machine learning models. Despite there are many alternative methods are available for solving this issue, the proposed solution has only investigated to proof the concept that such a system can be applied and implemented. To put it another way, will not discuss the feasibility of the system or compare it to other centralized systems. The proposed solution suggested replacing the execution component (Node Server) with Smartphones connected together using Cloud Functions to organize the distribution of the data-sets between all nodes on the network. Figure 3 show details of data-flow view architecture and how the interaction between all components.

In this paper, we will focus on the execution component only. So, all the other components in the system will stay the same from the centralized web application architecture as seen in Fig. 3. For example, we have used Firebase services (Authentication, Storage, NO-SQL Database) and in the proposed solution we add new service (Cloud Functions). Figure 4 represent layered view architecture, our goal form using this view is to describe the relationship between layers. For example, Richards [25] described each layer in closed layered view architecture can use the under-layer and not the opposite.

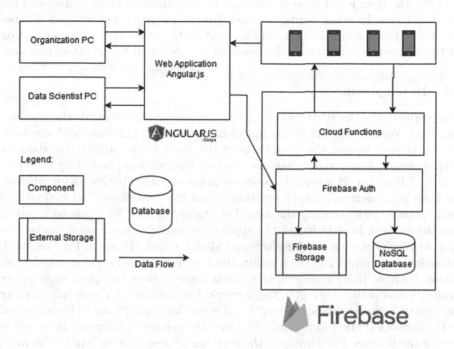

**Fig. 3.** Proposed data flow view architecture for distributed web application

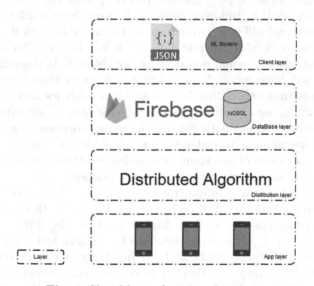

**Fig. 4.** Closed layered view architecture

Likewise, from Fig. 4 we conclude that the Distribution layer control and use the App Layer. In other words, the Distributed Algorithm use all Smartphones to execute the machine learning models and do the training and the prediction on the device and send the results again to be calculated for all nodes together.

## 3.2   Development

As described, the Distribution layer is the component that controls the Application layer. We have split the main functionality into two functions with one task. As can be seen before, the main task for this layer is distributing the data-set over all Smartphones and collect the results. This process covered by the "Distributor" function. However, in order to make the distribution more efficient, we have implemented another function called the "Evaluator" to evaluate all Smartphones before sending the data. For example, every Smartphone wants to join the network have to install the application and give permission to evaluate all characteristics such as Manufacturer, Model, Cores, Threads, Process (nm), Graphics Card, and CPU. As a result, the function returns a value called Evaluation Number (EV) represent how much Smartphones has processing power (min = 0, max = 10) to invest in the network. Furthermore, EV depends on other two dynamic characteristics. First, the time for the Smartphone to be connected to the network (Period in Seconds). Second, the percentage of usage in resources during the process. For Example, the user can choose time to join in the night during the sleeping hours and select the percentage of the resources used during that period. Also, EV is always changing its value before the user joining the network depending on these characteristics. For example, we can have two nodes with Smartphone type (Samsung NOTE8) with the same features and same characteristics [13]. However, both of the users have a different period to join the network and different percentage of the usage of each device. Both of the Smartphones will have different EV and it will be more for the user who approves to put more time and resources for the network. In the same way, some Smartphones will have fewer characteristics or features than others. However, EV can be more than others that have more characteristics and best features.

In our solution, we are aiming to validate the idea of implementing a distributed system to execute both machine learning processes (training and predicting) on Smartphones. In order to implement the system, we have chosen linear regression as one of the simplest algorithms in machine learning. Linear Regression [26] is an approach to show the relationship between some dependent variables and in our solution, we used a library that works on a mobile device and web application called JS-Regression [27] to use this algorithm. Also, we have used two main services from Google Firebase [28]. First, we have used NO-SQL database [14] as the main database for all data inside the application. Second, "Cloud Functions" to build both functions in the Distribution layer (Evaluator and Distributor function). The main reason to choose NO-SQL Firebase database is the real-time database feature that achieves the synchronization between Smartphones. However, there a lot of provider to this service, but we have chosen Google because they have a full platform integrated together and Firebase working with cross-platform web or mobile easily.

On the application layer, we have worked with Smartphones that have Android operating system only. The extension for the application file is APK and it is containing all the libraries such as Dex files, manifest file, assets, and resources for the application [11]. We have chosen the Android operating system to deploy our solution because Android provides the freedom of using the features on the Smartphones and there is no restriction on the permissions of using it. In addition, at the bottom of the Software stack in Android, there is a Linux kernel [11]. It acts as the heart of the whole system. It provides various functionalities like memory management, process management, and device management. Linux kernel as open source project provides more flexibility to control the resources on Smartphones for developers. For the application Framework, we have used Cross-Platform called ionic framework [15]. It's a framework build on the top of the Web-View [16] in Android and it is not a good option for processing based apps. However, ionic provide plugins called "ionic native" to access all native libraries. That can enough to build our solution to achieve the goal of the study.

The basic functionality for our solution is to execute and train the data and provide results and send it to the Database. As a result, in this stage, we did not use any new special kind of permission to access more features in the device. We have used the requires permission to access the internet and Web-View components only. JS-Regression library represents the core functionality in the application, it is used to train and predicate results from the data that comes from the distributor function. Also, the data type is JSON [29], because Google Firebase Database is NO-SQL written using JSON schema and the result will be written directly to the database when it is ready. We have used Cross-Platform like Ionic to make the solution testable in all type of Smartphones. In addition, we need to with web-based framework working with JavaScript support JS-Regression too.

## 3.3   Proof of Concept

As mentioned before, JSON is the data type structure in our solution, because it is compatible with the database base platform. For Example, ["height": 181, "weight": 80, "shoesize": 44, "Gender": male] as JSON object is easy to read and write and provide more control on data-sets instance. Every Smartphone will receive data-set contains a number of JSON objects. This value will be calculated from EV for each device. The process will start after the distributor function send all data to all Smartphones that are connected to the network. The training process will be held on every device separated. Inside every device, the data will be split to (X, Y). X represents height, weight, shoe size and Y represent Gender. When the process will finish Y-Predicate will be sent to the database and the distributor function will calculate the result by taking the average of Y-predicate for all results from all devices.

## 4   Discussion and Limitations

Our solution has tended to focus on implementing a distributed system to execute machine learning models on Smartphones rather than the efficacy and the capacity of the process. We are aware that our solution has three main limitations: Data Limitation, Study Design Limitation and Impact Limitation. These limitations highlight some of the threats and requirements have to been achieved during the process or it can be future work. In Data Limitation, for such system deals with machine learning models on distributed system data normalization can be the main threats for the prediction accuracy. Data Normalization [17] is the technique applied as part of data preparation for machine learning and the goal is changing the values of numeric columns in the data-set to a common scale, without distorting differences in the ranges of values. So, to have an accurate prediction on each Smartphone, every data-set must be sample or small copy from the main data-set. Without normalization, we could have the wrong prediction depend on these de-normalized biased data-sets.

In Study Design Limitation, different operating systems for Smartphones means different rules and permission on the usage of resources and features. For example, IOS operation system in iPhone or iPod has a lot of restrictions on using the device resources such as the processor or the memory. Also, Apple has restrictions on their store to submit an application use some features such as threads on background mode. However, if we will publish the application on the Google store for Android only, the application will lose user-base that uses only an iPhone. In 2018, 44.6% of smartphone users in the United States used an iPhone, this share was expected to stay at around 45.2% in 2019 [18].

In Impact limitations, machine learning algorithms are very different. In our solution, we have to choose one of the simplest algorithms to validate the proposed solution. However, linear regression provides flexibility to support distribution and collecting predictions using averaging between all nodes, but other algorithms in machine learning need instance feedback inside the processing unit itself. As a result, implementing other algorithms can be challenging in the future of our solution. To sum up, data normalization can be suppressed by providing normalized data from the beginning of the experiment. On Design Study Limitations, Apple restrictions cannot be overcome easily, but as a mitigation strategy, in the beginning, we can use only Android. Likewise, choosing the algorithm can be overcome by working with machine learning algorithms that support distributed systems and parallel processes.

## 5   Conclusion and Future Scope

Smartphones will be improved year after year and the competitions between companies are focused on how to improve the features more and more. As a smartphone user, in the next ten years, we will have in our pocket a device with a huge amount of features. However, we will use less than 30% of such machine during the period of owning it. This paper purposes a new architecture that allows users to monetizes their own Smartphones by providing their processing power to a huge network that contains other Smartphones to share their processing power and using it in execution and training machine learning model on the device and provide the results for a central server. The paper aims to validate the implementation for such a system using Ionic framework, JS-Regression and NO-SQL database (Firebase). Future work will concentrate to extend the proposed implementation to work with IOT system. For example, in regular IOT system, sensors generate huge amounts of data and transfer that data to the cloud for further processing. These data include structured data, such as temperature, vibration or multimedia information, such as video, images, and sounds. By using the processing power for the closest node on the network, IOT devices can get the result fast and without any connection to the main server on the cloud. However, there is research that proposed a new concept called "Edge computing" by moving computing ability from centralized cloud servers to edge nodes near the user end [19]. Also, another research talking about the same concept in machine learning specific "Edge Learning" by deploying machine-learning algorithms at the network edge [22]. Both of these research provides the same idea of using the processing power for each node on the network and reduce the usage of the centralized cloud server. For example, our proposed solution can reduce a huge amount of processing power in the main server and let the participant in the network (Smartphones) share their execution power inside the network. In addition, the process can be improved by adding payment form Machine to Machine using IOTA [20]. IOTA is an emerging technology being developed by the open source community based on a new distributed ledger technology called the Tangle. So, Smartphones can receive payment using cryptocurrency from the IOT component(sensors) direct after finishing the process of data training. The main server will provide permission for the Smartphones to take the data through WIFI from IOT components and the process will be organized on the local network only. Our future tasks include the implementation of the proposed architecture and create other use cases using IOTA and improve the performance for the execution layer and build a stable solution.

# References

1. Zhang, C., Patras, P., Haddadi, H.: Deep learning in mobile and wireless networking: a survey. IEEE Commun. Surv. Tutorials. arXiv:1803.04311, March 2018
2. Cisco: Cisco visual networking index: forecast and methodology, June (2017). https://www.cisco.com/c/en/us/solutions/collateral/service-provider/visual-networking-index-vni/white-paper-c11-741490.html
3. Sun, Y., Peng, M., Zhou, Y., Huang, Y., Mao, S.: Application of machine learning in wireless networks: key techniques and open issues. arXiv:1809.08707, September 2018
4. Han, S., Chih-Lon, I., Li, G., Wang, S., Sun, Q.: Big data enabled mobile network design for 5G and beyond. IEEE Commun. Mag. **55**(9), 150–157 (2017)
5. Dobriban, E., Shengy, Y.: Distributed linear regression by averaging. arXiv:1810.00412, October 2018

6. Bader, D.A., Pennington, R.: Applications. Int. J. High Perform. Comput. Appl. **15**(2), 181–185 (2001)
7. Bakery, M., Buyya, R.: Cluster computing at a glance, Chapter One, p. 4, September (2000)
8. Mengy, X.: Machine learning in apache spark. J. Mach. Learn. Res. **17**(34), 17 (2016)
9. Bala, K., Sharma, S., Kaur, G.: A study on smartphone based operating system. Int. J. Comput. Appl. (0975–8887) **121**(1) (2015)
10. Top machine learning mobile apps • appy pie. https://www.appypie.com/top-machine-learning-mobile-apps. Accessed 16 Apr 2019
11. Takawale, H., Thakur, A.: Talos App: on-device machine learning using tensor flow to detect android malware. In: MCSMS (2018)
12. Yang, K., Jiang, T., Shi, Y., Ding, Z.: Federated learning via over-the-air computation. arXiv 1812(11750) (2018)
13. Galaxy note features; Samsung phones. https://www.samsung.com/ph/Smart phones/gal-axy-note8/. Accessed 16 Apr 2019
14. Burd, G.: NoSQL (2011)
15. What is ionic framework? http://ionicframework.com/. Accessed 16 Apr 2019
16. Ionic framework angular JS on the rise. https://blog.codecentric.de/en/2014/11/ionic-angularjs-framework-on-the-rise/. Accessed 16 Apr 2019
17. Jin, J., Li, M., Jin, L.: Data normalization to accelerate training for linear neural net to predict tropical cyclone tracks. Math. Probl. Eng. **2015**, 8 (2014). Hindawi Publishing Corporation
18. Percentage of US population that own an iPhone smartphone. https://www.statista.com/statistics/236550/percentage-of-us-population-that-own-a-iphone-smartphone. Accessed 16 Apr 2019
19. Sureddy, S., Rashmi, K., Gayathri, R., Nadhan, A.S.: Flexible deep learning in edge computing for IoT. Int. J. Pure Appl. Math. **119**(10), 531–543 (2018)
20. Strugar, D., Hussain, R., Mazzara, M., Rivera, V., Afanasyev, I., Lee, J.Y.: An architecture for distributed ledger-based M2M auditing for electric autonomous vehicles. In: Barolli, L., Takizawa, M., Xhafa, F., Enokido, T. (eds.) WAINA 2019. AISC, vol. 927, pp. 116–128. Springer, Cham (2019). https://doi.org/10.1007/978-3-030-15035-8_11
21. Burns, B.: Designing Distributed Systems, pp. 80–81. O'Reilly Media Inc., Sebastopol (2018). ISBN: 9781491983638
22. Zhu, G., Liu, D., Du, Y., You, C., Zhang, J., Huang, K.: Towards an intelligent edge: wireless communication meets machine learning. arXiv preprint 1809.00343 (2018)
23. Unified analytics engine for big data. https://spark.apache.org/. Accessed 6 June 2019
24. Guide to Tenserflow. https://www.tensorflow.org/guide/. Accessed 6 June 2019
25. Richards, M.: Software Architecture Patterns, pp. 54–55. O'Reilly Media Inc., Sebastopol (2015). ISBN: 9781491971437
26. Lunt, M.: Introduction to statistical modelling: linear regression. Rheumatology **54**(7), 1137–1140 (2015)
27. Js-Regression. https://github.com/chen0040/js-regression. Accessed 6 June 2019
28. Firebase. https://firebase.google.com. Accessed 6 June 2019

29. JavaScript Object Notation (JSON). https://json.org. Accessed 6 June 2019
30. Marinelli, E.: Hyrax: cloud computing on mobile devices using mapreduce. Master's thesis, CMU, USA (2009)
31. Remédios, Diogo, Teófilo, António, Paulino, Hervé, Lourenço, João: Mobile Device-to-Device Distributed Computing Using Data Sets. 12th EAI International Conference on Mobile and Ubiquitous Systems: Computing, Networking and Services (2015)

# Above the Clouds: A Brief Study

Subham Chakraborty and Ananga Thapaliya[✉]

Innopolis University, 1 Universitetskaya, Innopolis 420500, Russia
{s.chakraborty,a.thapaliya}@innopolis.ru

**Abstract.** Cloud Computing is a versatile technology that can support a broad-spectrum of applications. The low cost of cloud computing and its dynamic scaling renders it an innovation driver for small companies, particularly in the developing world. Cloud deployed enterprise resource planning (ERP), supply chain management applications (SCM), customer relationship management (CRM) applications, medical applications, business applications and mobile applications have potential to reach millions of users. In this paper, we explore the different concepts involved in cloud computing and we also examine clouds from technical aspects. We highlight some of the opportunities in cloud computing underlining the importance of clouds showing why that technology must succeed and we have provided additional cloud computing problems that businesses may need to address. Finally, we discuss some of the issues that this area should deal with.

**Keywords:** Cloud computing · IoT

## 1 Introduction

Cloud computing is a recently developing paradigm of distributed computing though it is not a new idea that emerged just recently. In 1969 L. Kleinrock anticipated that, "As of now, computer networks are still in their infancy" [24]. But as they grow up and become more sophisticated, we will probably see the spread of 'computer utilities' which, like present electric and telephone utilities, will service individual homes and oces across the country." His vision was the true indication of today's utility based computing paradigm. One of the giant steps towards this world was taken in mid 1990s when grid computing was rst coined to allow consumers to obtain computing power on demand. The origin of cloud computing can be seen as an evolution of grid computing technologies. The term Cloud computing was given prominence rst by Google's CEO Eric Schmidt in late 2006 (maybe he coined the term). So the birth of cloud computing is very recent phenomena although its root belongs to some old ideas with new business, technical, social and architectural perspectives.

© Springer Nature Switzerland AG 2019
M. Mazzara et al. (Eds.): TOOLS 2019, LNCS 11771, pp. 326–333, 2019.
https://doi.org/10.1007/978-3-030-29852-4_27

# 2   Essential Characteristics

In this section we describe the essential characteristics that a cloud must possess. Any cloud is expected to have these five characteristics that are being described below.

## 2.1   On-Demand Self-service

A consumer can unilaterally provision computing capabilities, such as server time and network storage, as needed automatically without requiring human interaction.

## 2.2   Broad Network Access

A consumer can unilaterally provision computing capabilities, such as server time and network storage, as needed automatically without requiring human interaction.

## 2.3   Resource Pooling

The provider's computing resources are pooled to serve multiple consumers using a multitenant model, with different physical and virtual resources dynamically as-signed and reassigned according to consumer demand. There is a sense of location independence in that the subscriber generally has no control or knowledge over the exact location of the provided resources but may be able to specify location at a higher level of abstraction (e.g., country, state, or data center). Examples of resources include storage, processing, memory, network bandwidth, and virtual machines.

## 2.4   Rapid Elasticity

Capabilities can be rapidly and elastically provisioned, in some cases automatically, to quickly scale out and rapidly released to quickly scale in. To the consumer, the capabilities available for provisioning often appear to be unlimited and can be purchased in any quantity at any time.

## 2.5   Measured Service

Cloud systems automatically control and optimize resource use by leveraging a metering capability at some level of abstraction appropriate to the type of service (e.g., storage, processing, bandwidth, and active user accounts). Resource usage can be monitored, controlled, and reported providing transparency for both the provider and consumer of the utilized service.

# 3   Cloud Deployment Strategies

## 3.1   Public Cloud

In simple terms, public cloud services are characterized as being available to clients from a third party service provider via the Internet. The term "public" does not always mean free, even though it can be free or fairly inexpensive to use. A public cloud does not mean that a user's data is publicly visible; public cloud vendors typically provide an access control mechanism for their users. Public clouds provide an elastic, cost effective means to deploy solutions.

## 3.2   Private Cloud

A private cloud offers many of the benefits of a public cloud computing environment, such as being elastic and service based. The difference between a private cloud and a public cloud is that in a private cloud-based service, data and processes are managed within the organization without the restrictions of net-work bandwidth, security exposures and legal requirements that using public cloud services might entail.

## 3.3   Community Cloud

A community cloud is controlled and used by a group of Organizations that have shared interests, such as specific security requirements or a common mission. The members of the community share access to the data and applications in the cloud.

## 3.4   Hybrid Cloud

A hybrid cloud is a combination of a public and private cloud that inter-operates. In this model users typically outsource non business-critical information and processing to the public cloud, while keeping business-critical services and data in their control.

# 4   Cloud Delivery Models

This section of the paper describes the various cloud delivery models. Cloud can be delivered in 3 models namely SaaS, PaaS, and IaaS.

## 4.1   Software as a Service (SaaS)

In a cloud-computing environment. SaaS is software that is owned, delivered and managed remotely by one or more providers and that is offered in a pay-per-use manner [8]. SaaS in simple terms can be defined as "Software deployed as a hosted service and accessed over the Internet" [9]. SaaS clouds provide scalability and also shifts significant burdens from subscribers to providers, resulting in a number of opportunities for greater efficiency and, in some cases, performance. The typical user of a SaaS offering usually has neither knowledge nor control about the underlying infra-structure [10].

## 4.2 Platform as a Service (PaaS)

This kind of cloud computing provides development environment as a service. The consumer can use the middleman's equipment to develop his own program and deliver it to the users through Internet and servers. The consumer controls the applications that run in the environment, but does not control the operating system, hardware or network infrastructure on which they are running. The platform is typically an application framework 4.3.

## 4.3 Infrastructure as a Service (IaaS)

Infrastructure as a service delivers a platform virtualization outsourced service [15]. The consumer can control the environment as a service. Rather than purchasing servers, software, data center space or network equipment, consumers instead buy those resources as a fully operating system, storage, deployed applications and possibly networking components such as firewalls and load balancers, but not the cloud infra-structure beneath them.

# 5  Opportunities

In this section we explain the vast opportunities the cloud computing field offers to IT industry. Cloud Computing is concerned with the delivery of IT capabilities as a service on three levels: infrastructure (IaaS), platforms (PaaS), and software (SaaS). By providing interfaces on all three levels, clouds address different types of customers [11]:

## 5.1 End Consumers

These consumers mainly use the services of the SaaS layer over a Web browser and basic offerings of the IaaS layer as for example storage for data resulting from the usage of the SaaS layer.

## 5.2 Business Costumers

These consumers access all three layers - the IaaS layer in order to enhance the own infrastructure with additional resources on demand, the PaaS layer in order to be able to run own applications in a Cloud and eventually the SaaS layer in order to take advantage of available applications offered as a service [16].

## 5.3 Developers and Independent Software Vendors

Independent Software Vendors that develop applications that are supposed to be offered over the SaaS layer of a Cloud. Typically, they directly access the PaaS layer, and through the PaaS layer indirectly access the IaaS layer, and are present on the SaaS layer with their application. From the perspective of the user, the utility-based payment model is considered as one of the main benefits of Cloud Computing. There is no need for up-front infrastructure investment: investment in software licenses and no risk of unused but paid software [8]. Thus, capital expenditure is turned licenses, and investment in hardware infrastructure and related maintenance and staff into operational expenditure.

# 6    Challenges and Issues

In this section we explain the challenges and issues cloud computing has to face. As a lot of economics is tied to this field it will be better that these issues are resolved as early as possible. The following are the issues that a cloud computing environment has to still resolve:

## 6.1    Security

When using cloud-based services, one is entrusting their data to a third-party for storage and security. Cloud-sourcing involves the use of many services, and many cloud based services provide services to each other, and thus cloud-based products may have to share your information with third parties if they are involved in processing or transferring of your information [12]. They may share your information with advertisers as well. Security presents a real threat to the cloud and some security concerns are such as lost in control of physical security, damaged rules and regulations because of organizations, capacity inconsistency between various cloud and administrations merchants [13] and no basic standard to guarantee the information [14].

## 6.2    Performance

At the point when a business moves to the cloud it ends up depending on the service providers. The following conspicuous difficulties of moving to cloud computing develop this partnership. In any case, this partnership frequently gives organizations inventive innovations they wouldn't generally have the capacity to get to. The cloud provider must ensure that the performance of the service being provided re-mains the same all through [20].

## 6.3    Cost Management and Containment

The following part of our cloud computing challenge list includes costs. Generally cloud computing can spare organizations money. In the cloud, an association can undoubtedly increase its preparing abilities without making substantial interests in new equipment. Cloud computing can have high costs due to its requirements for both using a large amounts of data back in-house [21].

## 6.4    Regulatory Requirements

What legislative, judicial, regulatory and policy environments are cloud-based information subject to? This question is hard to ascertain due to the decentralized and global structure of the internet, as well as of cloud computing [22]. This is complicated by the fact that some data in transit may also be regulated.

## 6.5    Bandwidth, Quality of Service and Data Limits

Cloud computing requires "b speed" Whilst many websites-broadband connections or slow broadband connections; cloud-based applications are often not usable. Connection speed in kilobyte per second (or MB/s and GB/s) is important for use of cloud computing services. Also important are Quality of Service (QoS); indicators for which include the amount of time the connections are dropped, response time (ping), and the extent of the delays in the processing of network data (latency) and loss of data (packet loss) [18].

## 6.6    Lack of Resources/Suppliers

One of the cloud difficulties organizations and endeavours are confronting today is absence of assets or potentially mastery. Associations are progressively setting more workload in the cloud while cloud technologies continue to quickly advance. Because of these components, associations are having an extreme time staying aware of the instruments [17].

## 6.7    Integration with Internet of Things Security (IoT)

Each and every gadget and sensor in the IoT speaks to a potential hazard. How certain can an association be that every one of these gadgets have the controls set up to protect the privacy of the information gathered and the respectability of the information sent [25]. Corporate frameworks will be bombarded by information from all way of associated sensors in the IoT [7]. The information gathered will enable us to settle on more brilliant choices. Yet, this will likewise affect security desires [19]. We are as of now observing consumers place higher desires on organizations and governments to defend their own data [23]. Subsequently, a few difficulties about the security issue in the integration of IoT and cloud computing are listed below:

- Heterogeneity: A major challenge in integration of cloud computing and IoT is concerned with the wide heterogeneity of gadgets, working frameworks, stages and administrations accessible and perhaps utilized for new and improved applications [1].
- Performance: Frequently Cloud Computing and IoT mix's applications present explicit execution and quality of service prerequisites at a few dimensions (for example for correspondence, calculation, and capacity angles) and in some specific situations meeting prerequisites may not be effectively feasible [2,3].

- Reliability: At the point when Cloud Computing and IoT reconciliation is embraced for mission-basic applications, unwavering quality concerns normally emerge e.g., with regards to keen versatility, vehicles are regularly progressing and the vehicular systems administration and correspondence is frequently discontinuous or temperamental [4].
- Big Data: With an expected number of 50 billion gadgets that will be arranged by 2020, explicit consideration must be paid to transportation, stockpiling, access, and preparing of the gigantic measure of information they will create [5].
- Monitoring: As to a great extent archived in the writing, checking is a basic movement in Cloud conditions for scope quantification, for overseeing assets, service level agreements, execution and security, and for investigating [6].

## 7    Conclusion

We have a brief look at the basics of cloud. There are interests and concerns in the cloud. From a technology point of view, there are interesting technical problems to solve. From a service or consumer point of view, there are essential usability, stability, and reliability problems to solve. We are at a crossroads with cloud technology. On one hand, there are many stories of problems with clouds, from data loss, to service interruption, to compromised sensitive data. To stay relevant, to remain meaningful, to grow in the service space, the cloud providers must step up their game and produce robust cloud implementations. On the other hand, the world is poised to explode with a billion new devices that will be desperate for the very technology that clouds almost offer today. It is possible that the wave of users, applications and demand will just wash over the cloud landscape, regardless of how robust they are. If the cloud providers are too slow to provide safe, secure, reliable data storage and application services, they "always on" connection, as well may miss one of the greatest opportunities of this century.

## References

1. Grozev, N., Buyya, R.: Inter-cloud architectures and application brokering: taxonomy and survey. Softw. Pract. Exp. **44**(3), 369–390 (2014)
2. Jeffery, K.: Keynote: CLOUDs: a large virtualisation of small things. In: 2nd International Conference on Future Internet of Things and Cloud, FiCloud-2014 (2014)
3. Rao, B.P., Saluia, P., Sharma, N., Mittal, A., Sharma, S.V.: Cloud computing for Internet of Things & sensing based applications. In: 2012 Sixth International Conference on Sensing Technology (ICST), pp. 374–380. IEEE, December 2012
4. He, W., Yan, G., Da Xu, L.: Developing vehicular data cloud services in the IoT environment. IEEE Transact. Industr. Inf. **10**(2), 1587–1595 (2014)
5. Dobre, C., Xhafa, F.: Intelligent services for big data science. Future Gener. Comput. Syst. **37**, 267–281 (2014)
6. Aceto, G., Botta, A., De Donato, W., Pescapè, A.: Cloud monitoring: a survey. Comput. Netw. **57**(9), 2093–2115 (2013)

7. Stergiou, C., Psannis, K.E., Kim, B.G., Gupta, B.: Secure integration of IoT and cloud computing. Future Gener. Comput. Syst. **78**, 964–975 (2018)
8. Aoun, R., Gagnaire, M.: Towards a fairer benefit distribution in grid environments. In: 2009 IEEE/ACS International Conference on Computer Systems and Applications, pp. 21–26. IEEE, May 2009
9. Mertz, S.A., Eschinger, C., Eid, T., Pring, B.: Dataquest insight: SaaS demand set to outpace enterprise application software market growth. Gartner RAS Core Research Note, 3 (2007)
10. Moixe, M.: New tricks for defeating SSL in practice. In: BlackHat Conference, USA, February 2009
11. Chong, F., Carraro, G.: Architecture Strategies for Catching the Long Tail, pp. 9–10. MSDN Library, Microsoft Corporation (2006)
12. Eymann, T.: Cloud Computing-Enzyklopaedie der Wirtschaftsinformatik (2008)
13. Patidar, S., Rane, D., Jain, P.: A survey paper on cloud computing. In: 2012 Second International Conference on Advanced Computing & Communication Technologies, pp. 394–398. IEEE, January 2012
14. Mell, P., Grance, T.: The NIST definition of cloud computing (2011)
15. Garbacki, P., Naik, V.K.: Efficient resource virtualization and sharing strategies for heterogeneous grid environments. In: 2007 10th IFIP/IEEE International Symposium on Integrated Network Management, pp. 40–49. IEEE, May 2007
16. Buyya, R., Yeo, C.S., Venugopal, S.: Market-oriented cloud computing: Vision, hype, and reality for delivering it services as computing utilities. In: 2008 10th IEEE international conference on high performance computing and communications, pp. 5–13. IEEE, September 2008
17. Aoun, R., Doumith, E.A., Gagnaire, M.: Resource provisioning for enriched services in cloud environment. In: 2010 IEEE Second International Conference on Cloud Computing Technology and Science, pp. 296–303. IEEE, November 2010
18. Roy, S., Bose, R., Sarddar, D.: A fog-based dss model for driving rule violation monitoring framework on the internet of things. Int. J. Adv. Sci. Technol. **82**, 23–32 (2015)
19. Kryftis, Y., Mastorakis, G., Mavromoustakis, C.X., Batalla, J.M., Pallis, E., Kormentzas, G.: Efficient entertainment services provision over a novel network architecture. IEEE Wirel. Commun. **23**(1), 14–21 (2016)
20. Rouse, M.: IoT security (Internet of Things security). IoT Agenda **1**(11) (2015)
21. Gupta, B.B., Badve, O.P.: Taxonomy of DoS and DDoS attacks and desirable defense mechanism in a cloud computing environment. Neural Comput. Appl. **28**(12), 3655–3682 (2017)
22. Skourletopoulos, G., Mavromoustakis, C.X., Mastorakis, G., Batalla, J.M., Sahalos, J.N.: An evaluation of cloud-based mobile services with limited capacity: a linear approach. Soft. Comput. **21**(16), 4523–4530 (2017)
23. Salikhov, D., Khanda, K., Gusmanov, K., Mazzara, M., Mavridis, N.: Microservice-based IOT for smart buildings. arXiv preprint arXiv:1610.09480 (2016)
24. Kleinrock, L.: A vision for the Internet. ST J. Res. **2**(1), 4–5 (2005)
25. Dragoni, N., Giaretta, A., Mazzara, M.: The internet of hackable things. In: Ciancarini, P., Litvinov, S., Messina, A., Sillitti, A., Succi, G. (eds.) SEDA 2016. AISC, vol. 717, pp. 129–140. Springer, Cham (2018). https://doi.org/10.1007/978-3-319-70578-1_13

# Exploring IA-32: Lessons from Analysis and Experience

Yauhen Klimiankou(✉)

Belarusian State University of Informatics and Radioelectronics,
6 P. Brovki Street, 220013 Minsk, Belarus
klimenkov@bsuir.by

**Abstract.** IA-32 is ISA on which market of high-end computing, including personal computers, laptops, workstation, and servers, had grown up at the last three decades. This ISA, along with IBM PC architecture, was one of the main drivers of the personal computer revolution and still is one of the principal ISA on the microprocessor market. The long history of the development of IA-32 and its widespread use in computing devices makes it interesting to analyze and to extract lessons about ISA design based on its current usage. This paper provides an analysis of such sort and highlights conclusions made.

We have explored IA-32 ISA using statistical analysis of the compiler-generated code of real-world application of industrial quality and level of optimization. We demonstrate the presence of useless complexity burden born by backward compatibility and speculating about the idea of the design of a simplified version of IA-32 ISA.

**Keywords:** IA-32 · ISA · Code analysis · Statistical analysis

## 1 Introduction

x86 instruction set architecture originally was introduced in 1978 in the form of 16-bit ISA. Over the years, three variants of x86 with many additions and extensions have been provided: original 16-bit version of x86, IA-32 and x86-64. Each of them came with a burden of almost complete backward compatibility with all previously existing predecessors. History of the development of x86 is tightly coupled with the history of IBM PC compatible personal computers and with computer revolution that they had performed [11]. Today, x86 processors are ubiquitous in stationary and portable personal computers, workstations, servers, and supercomputers. They also can be found in embedded devices and even cell phones. In general, x86 is monopolist on markets that require intensive computations, while ARM dominates on markets where low power consumption is preferable to high performance. A large amount of software, including the long list of operating systems and compilers, exist for x86 ISA.

This ISA is commonly considered a canonical example of CISC architecture with variable instruction length from 1 and up to 15 bytes. In contrast to

© Springer Nature Switzerland AG 2019
M. Mazzara et al. (Eds.): TOOLS 2019, LNCS 11771, pp. 334–341, 2019.
https://doi.org/10.1007/978-3-030-29852-4_28

load/store architecture widely adopted by RISC processors, most of the IA-32 instructions are capable directly address in-memory operands, as well as accept immediate arguments encoded into instruction body. Like typical CISC, IA-32 benefits from more dense code. The same program compiled for IA-32 will contain fewer code bytes than program compiled for ARM. Current implementations of IA-32 represent one of the most complex processors which exploit many computation acceleration features including complex CISC-to-RISC design with pipelining, multilevel caches, extensive internal buffering, superscalar, out-of-order and speculative execution, and $\mu$-op fusion [10].

When initially programs for IA-32 were writing mostly directly by hands in assembly language, currently a vast majority of IA-32 applications are writing in high-level programming languages, and their machine code is generated by compilers automatically. In this paper, we perform an attempt to analyze the usage of the IA-32 ISA in the compiler-generated machine code and reevaluate assumptions and design decisions made by IA-32 designers. Our goal is to obtain simplified both execution- and interpretation-friendly high-performance version of IA-32 free of backward compatibility burden and without all unused or rarely used features, as well as to gain knowledge's about ISA design principles came from actual usage practice in modern applications.

In this paper, we provide the results of analysis about the intensity of use of different features of IA-32 ISA in the code generated by current compilers including but not limiting by the use frequencies of particular kinds of instructions, addressing modes and immediate arguments. The aim of the analysis is understanding of how the IA-32 ISA used in the era of machine-generated programs. In other words, we want to understand how the current compilers use IA-32 ISA.

## 2   Analysis of IA-32 Usage in the Code of Modern Applications

IA-32 has more than 35 years of history and has been advanced many times during that period. Furthermore, its actual usage could be changed over time too. The analysis of IA-32 were done in past [2,12]. However, in contrast to previous works, we are trying to understand how the IA-32 instruction set is using by current industrial-quality software. To achieve some insight in that field we have unpacked, parsed and analyzed the Linux kernel [1] binary of version 3.13.0-37-generic extracted from Linux Mint 7.1 Rebecca distributive. We have chosen this binary because it represents real-world complicated industrial-quality software. Linux kernel is built using the widespread toolchain and therefore represents code generation patterns of modern compilers. Finally, it has tremendous size and thus provides a good source for statistics collection. We have collected statistical data about IA-32 instruction set over code sections of kernel binary. We have also considered Windows XP kernel binary to exclude the impact of a particular compiler from the statistical data, but have obtained results similar to the data captured for the Linux kernel.

Linux kernel binary contains 2141376 instructions in total in the 7082752 bytes of code. As was mentioned earlier IA-32 is an ISA with variable length instructions starting from 1 byte and up to 15 bytes. At the same time, the analysis demonstrates that the actual average instruction length is 3.31 bytes per instruction.

IA-32 supports three types of instructions depending on the number of arguments:

- Commands – instructions without arguments (*nop, retn*)
- Predicates – instructions accepting only one argument (*call, pop*)
- Operations – instruction accepting two arguments (*mov, test*)

Results of analysis demonstrate that almost every two out of three instructions are operations (64.14%). Thirty percent of code are predicates (30.44%). Finally, every twentieth instruction is a command (5.41%). We should note that more than half of them (55.44%) is *nop* instructions which compilers usually insert into the binary for code alignment purposes. Nevertheless, all three types of instructions are in relatively extensive use.

IA-32 is a 32-bit architecture. However, in addition to the 32-bit data type, it supports two auxiliary data types: 8-bit and 16-bit. Analysis results show that most of the instructions found in program code are 32-bit instructions (71.8%), while 16-bit and 8-bit instructions are rare (0.73% and 2.84% respectively). Data type agnostic instructions like *jmp imm* occupy rest of code (24.64%). Thus, instructions supporting not a native data type takes only 3.57% of the code. Due to this, we can hypothesize that ISA supporting single data type can be quite reasonable for industrial use.

IA-32 contains 8 general purpose registers, 6 segment registers, *EFLAGS* register, Instruction Pointer (*EIP*) register and registers of ISA extensions like FPU, SSE etc. *EIP* and *EFLAGS* are hidden and can be accessed only using dedicated set of instructions. At the same time, the analysis shows that extension registers are extremely rare in the real programs. That does not necessarily mean that such registers are valueless in general because ISA extensions are usually used only in special purpose software such as math applications, video decoders, and others, where they boost calculations. Furthermore, floating point calculations are slow comparing to the integer calculations [3] and thus minimized in high-performance kernel code. Because of this kernel developers tries to reduce the number of floating point calculations to a minimum. Segment registers are rarely used too, because of the flat memory model used by the Linux kernel. The analysis shows that less than 2.5% of registers referenced in machine code are not 32-bit registers. Furthermore, 16-bit and 8-bit registers used are limited mostly by three pairs: *AX/AL*, *CX/CL* and *DX/DL*. 32-bit registers in its turn can be split into two groups: primary (*EDX/EBX/EBP/ESI*) and secondary (*ECX/ESP/EDI*) with an exception of *EAX* register which is referenced more than two times frequently than any primary register.

IA-32 instruction set extensively uses immediate arguments. Such arguments are constant integer numbers embedded into instruction body. We found that more than half of the instructions in machine code (60.12%) uses them. IA-32 has instructions which have two immediate (for example *mov [eax+0x1234], 0x5678*). Due to this, the density of immediate arguments is even higher than 60% – 0.6473 immediate per instruction. 55.55% of such immediate arguments are pure immediate (*mov eax, 4*), while the rest 44.45% of them are parts of complex addressing modes (*mov eax, [ecx+4]*).

There are multiple addressing modes supported by IA-32 [8]. This feature distinguishes IA-32 from the variety of RISC processors based on load/store architecture [5] and significantly complicates its design and implementation. We can see that despite a rich set of addressing modes available, only a few of them are found extensive use in practice. Results of the analysis show that some types of addressing mode are used more frequently than others. For example, the raw register argument (*inc eax*) is the dominating type which covers more than half of use cases. Raw immediate integer argument (*call 0x1234*) and register-offset in-memory argument (*inc [eax+0x1234]*) form a second group of frequently used types of arguments and together cover another 39% use cases. Therefore, all these three argument types cover about 94.5% of use cases in total. Finally, raw immediate address of in-memory variable (*call [0x1234]*) and in-register address of in-memory variable (*inc [eax]*) form a third group of relatively frequently used types of arguments and together cover additional 5.93% use cases. Thus, in total, five most frequently used argument types cover more than 99.25% of use cases. Thus, all other addressing modes are not used intensively in modern industrial-quality machine-generated code. The analysis shows that all complex addressing modes with the scale factor, which were introduced by Intel, specially for high-level languages support, are not in demand in current compilers.

Modern variants of IA-32 ISA supports more than 330 types of instructions. We have analyzed frequency of their usage in the code generated by nowadays compilers. This analysis has shown that every third instruction facing in the code is *mov* operation. At the same time, every second instruction in the code is from group *add, call, mov, test*. In general, the 25 most frequently used instructions cover more than 95% of the code while the rest instructions are rare and each of them covers less than 0.25% of the code (less than 1 "rare" instruction per 400 instructions of code). 7% of available instructions (20 from more than 330 [9]) covers more than 93% of the industrial quality code.

Instructions supported by IA-32 can be grouped into families according to their purpose. From the analysis results, we can see that almost 80% of them in the IA-32 code is used for data management, control flow management, and stack management, while less than 20% of them perform calculations.

At the same time, we found that machine-generated code of modern programs does not use many kinds of instructions and even instruction families which were the part of initial 8086 instruction set [7] and which has added to the IA-32 ISA with the introduction of different generations of x86 processors. For instance, we found that decimal arithmetic instructions (*aaa, aad, aam, aas, daa* and *das*) are untapped by compilers. The same is true for segment register instructions (*lss, les, lds, lfs* and *lgs*), which is not surprising due to the complete abandonment of the segmentation memory model in favor of the flat memory model. Far jumps and far returns are ignored by compilers too.

There is also a set of instructions which ISA designers have added to the IA-32 intentionally for specific use cases. Their assumptions were wrong. Due to this, both assembler programmers and compilers ignore these instructions. Such instructions as *rcr/rcl, jcxz/jecxz, lahf/sahf, bound, enter, xlat* and entire family of *LOOPcc* instructions represent this case.

IA-32 ISA includes the especial register *EFLAGS* which contains multiple bits which are modified and tested as a side effect by a bunch of arithmetic and control transfer instructions. However, we can see that modern code completely excludes from usage two bits: *Parity Flag* (*PF*) and *Auxiliary Carry Flag* (*AF*). The compiler-generated code excludes all instructions using them including those from families *CMOVcc, SETcc* and *Jcc*. As for the flags *Overflow Flag* (*OF*) and *Sign Flag* (*SF*), although machine-generated code extensively uses them, instructions which explicitly test them are not found in the code (except *cmovs/cmovns* and *js/jns*). In addition, instructions for direct manipulation of *Carry Flag* (*CF*) are also out of use (*cmc, clc* and *stc*).

IA-32 is a 32-bit ISA based on the original 16-bit 8086 architecture. Many of its instructions are 8086 instructions with extended operand size (from 16-bits up to 32-bits). However original 16-bit instructions are staying a part of 32-bit ISA. Nevertheless, the analysis shows that some of such original 8086 instructions, while being a part of ISA, drops out of actual use. For instance *pushf/popf* instructions become unsafe in 32-bit environment. Instructions *cwd, cbw* and *cwde* in their turn lose all their benefits in 32-bit environment.

Interestingly, but compilers intensively use string instructions from families *stos* and *movs*. The compilers typically use first ones in automatically generated default constructors, while the second ones they use for automatically generated copy constructor implementations. Meantime, compilers do not employ other string instructions (*cmps, lods* and *scas*), and they appear mostly in runtime library implementations.

The *nop* instruction represents an interesting case in IA-32 ISA. The *nop* is an auxiliary one-byte instruction which has distinct opcode and which execution has no effect. Compilers typically use *nop* for two purposes: the creation of code stubs for self-modifying code and the code alignment. IA-32 maintains multiple variants of *nop* instructions which differ in size (starting by 1 byte and up to 15 bytes long) while there is no any significant reason to maintain multiple variants of the instruction because each of them can be built using original one-byte 8086 *nop*. Moreover, there are many instructions like *mov eax, eax, xchg ecx, ecx, lea edx, [edx+0]* which reproduces exactly the same behavior as an original *nop*. Finally, *mov eax, eax* instruction has the same one-byte size. Due to this, keeping the separate *nop* instruction in the ISA does not provide any benefits but provides additional redundancy and complexity to the ISA.

Furthermore, the in-depth analysis focused on the use patterns of each particular instruction brings to light the extra insight. For example, some instructions are used mostly with the same register used for both arguments. We found that *test r32, r32* instruction in 99.6% of cases accepts the same register for both operands. Similarly, *xor r32, r32* instruction demonstrates the same use pattern – in the 95% of use cases, *xor* receives the same register in both operands. Some other instructions do not accept some registers for their parameters. For example, we found that *mov* instructions which load *esp* and *ebp* registers are extremely rarely faced in code, less than 0.01% of register load cases. The only exception is *mov ebp, esp* and *mov esp, ebp* which are used by compilers for stack frame creation and destruction. Many other instructions demonstrate the same behavior of elimination of specific registers usage.

Finally, the detailed analysis of use cases of particular instructions reveals the presence of ordering patterns. For example, there are patterns of an ordered set of instructions used by the compiler to create function prolog and function epilog. In the case of function prolog, the compiler issues a series of instructions which stores on the stack the values of registers modified by function body and creates the stack frame by preserving the value of stack pointer in register *ebp*. Similarly, at the function end compiler restores the state of preempted function by series of *pop* instructions, restoring the *esp* state from *ebp* register and *ret* instruction. The prolog and epilog of function is very often faced patterns in the compiled code. Another very constantly faced example of ordered instruction pairs are pairs of *test r32, r32/jz imm* and *test r32, r32/jnz imm* where *r32* represents the same 32-bit register. Indeed, these pairs represents the classical programming language construction *if value is null/false* and *if value not null/true*.

As can be seen from the analysis, the industrial-quality machine-generated code uses different features of IA-32 with unequal intensity. Furthermore, it is evident that a significant part of the ISA is out of use but still maintained by processor designers for backward compatibility with legacy hand-written programs. It is easy to note that the easy-distinguishable core of extensively used features presents in nearly every set of captured statistical data. IA-32 has an intensely used ISA core while there is a broad set of instructions that are used rarely or even not used at all in the actual machine-generated industrial code. This observation makes valuable the idea about the radically simplified version of IA-32, on which most of the original IA-32 programs could be migrated by in a fairly straightforward way, but which will have lost the complexity introduced by backward compatibility burden. Such redesigned IA-32 version, due to the lower level of complexity, will make the processor design and implementation cheaper, simplify the bunch of system software tools like assemblers, compilers, binary code analyzers, and others while will be able to run IA-32 programs.

## 3   Lessons Learned

IA-32 is a canonical example of CISC architecture with a large number of two-address instructions, the absence of limitations of load/store architecture and the low number of general purpose registers [4]. As a result, a principal part of the IA-32 application's code devotes on data flow management, control flow management, and stack management. While IA-32 has proved that CISC is an appropriate architecture for performance-oriented computer markets, the IA-32 itself is over-complicated.

For example, the concept of variable length instructions based on 8-bit atomic blocks leads to significant complexities in instruction decoding [6]. Furthermore, instruction length cannot be determined based only on its first block. Special complex state-machine based circuits with byte stream feeding become required in the superscalar CISC processors with pipelines for the instruction length evaluation purposes. Reduction of instruction length variability level by rebasing ISA on new strict instruction format could be beneficial. The new instruction format can split instruction into two strictly separated blocks: fixed-size opcode and variable length immediate arguments block, where opcode defines the size of the second block. In this case, the decoder will be able to fetch each instruction in two steps.

The concept of prefixes was the wrong design decision. Rejection of rarely used features of ISA painlessly eliminates most of them. The only reasonable and commonly used instruction prefix is *lock*.

Compilers tend to ignore a part of addressing modes supported by IA-32 and introduced especially for the support of high-level programming languages. Hence, the simplified version of ISA can exclude them without significant losses.

Finally, decimal arithmetic instructions, segment register instructions, *into*, *bound* and *xlat* and a lot of others are not used by modern software and could be deprecated and removed from IA-32 ISA as well as *nop* instruction, which has the same effect as a *mov eax, eax*. Some of them can be replaced (for example *xor eax, eax* by *null eax*) and even compounded into new instructions (for example *test eax, eax; jz label;* into *jmpifnull eax, label*). The distinguishable ISA core, found in the statistical data collected over the industrial-quality machine-generated code of real applications, provides an opportunity of deep RISCification of IA-32. Such RISCified IA-32 could lead to reduced cost of processor development and verification as well as significantly reduce the cost of development and maintenance of its software infrastructure.

Backward compatibility is a painful point of x86. While compatibility provides significant benefits in the short term perspective, at the same time, it over-complicates ISA on the long-term run. After 35 years of development, IA-32 pulls heavy baggage of useless features caused by backward compatibility. We can suggest that periodical dramatic refreshes of ISA with the depreciation of rarely used features can maintain the ISA complexity on a constant acceptable level. At the same time, we can suggest that reasonably useful ISA can be designed based on IA-32 using a radical simplification approach. Such ISA can lead to reduced power consumption, silicon size, and maintenance cost while benefit from the large code base collected in and inherited from IA-32 ecosystem. In particular, the new ISA can be designed in such a way, which will allow it to inherit not only existing software packages but also existing program development toolchains. The benefits of reduced complexity gained through rejection of rarely used features can outweigh the drawbacks of the partially broken backward compatibility. The simplified version of IA-32 which will be able to run 99%

of currently used x86 applications and, which is more important, will be able to use existing toolchains for development of new software, can be attractive at least for some applications and markets.

# 4 Conclusion

IA-32 is one of fundamental ISA in the computer industry that has made an invaluable contribution to its development. Nevertheless, for more than 34 years of development, it has accumulated tremendous baggage of complexity that currently does not carry any significant value. Based on its usage analysis in the current applications, we came to the three main conclusions. Firstly, not all assumptions made by ISA developers were right in strategic perspective. Secondly, IA-32 could be revised to produce straightforward and efficient ISA of the second generation of IA-32. Finally, we can hypothesize that any big and complicated architecture should experience revision every 10–20 years to validate assumptions and design decisions made, to perform clean up of the design from the useless features and complexity, and to identify right directions for future development and advancement.

# References

1. The Linux Kernel Archives. https://www.kernel.org/. Accessed 26 Feb 2019
2. Adams, T.L., Zimmerman, R.E.: An analysis of 8086 instruction set usage in MS DOS programs. SIGARCH Comput. Archit. News **17**(2), 152–160 (1989)
3. Bovet, D.P., Cesati, M.: Understanding the Linux Kernel - From I/O Ports to Process Management: Covers Version 2.6, 3rd edn. O'Reilly, Sebastopol (2005)
4. Dandamudi, S.P.: Fundamentals of Computer Organization and Design. Springer, Berlin (2002). https://doi.org/10.1007/b97279
5. Flynn, M.J.: Computer Architecture: Pipelined and Parallel Processor Design, 1st edn. Jones and Bartlett Publishers Inc., USA (1995)
6. González, A., Latorre, F., Magklis, G.: Processor Microarchitecture: An Implementation Perspective. Synthesis Lectures on Computer Architecture. Morgan & Claypool Publishers, San Rafael (2010)
7. Intel Corporation: The 8086 Family User's Manual. Intel Corporation (1979)
8. Intel Corporation: IA-32 Intel® Architecture Software Developer's Manual. Volume 1: Basic Architecture. Intel Corporation (2003). 245470–012
9. Intel Corporation: IA-32 Intel® Architecture Software Developer's Manual. Volume 2: Instruction Set Reference. Intel Corporation (2003). 245471–012
10. Intel Corporation: Intel® 64 and IA-32 Architectures Optimization Reference Manual. Intel Corporation, June 2016. 248966–033
11. Thome, A.: 25 years of PC history at BECKHOFF. PC-Control: New Autom. Technol. Mag. (3), 6–9 (2011)
12. Wiecek, C.A.: A case study of VAX-11 instruction set usage for compiler execution. In: Proceedings of the First International Symposium on Architectural Support for Programming Languages and Operating Systems, pp. 177–184. ASPLOS I, ACM, New York (1982)

# Continuous Integration and Continuous Delivery in the Process of Developing Robotic Systems

Vadim Rashitov$^{(\boxtimes)}$ and Mikhail Ivanou

Robotics Institute, Innopolis University, Innopolis, Russia
{v.rashitov,m.ivanov}@innopolis.ru

**Abstract.** There are hundreds of companies out there that are bringing new solutions in the field of robotics and trying to get rid of a thousand problems they face. Nevertheless, most of their results do not leave the doors of the lab and remain without any decent attention from society. Institutions and companies require highly qualified personnel to accelerate the development of new solutions and products. High expenses deter broad masses from participating in this activity. It is not only the high price that keeps people away from being a part of the community but also a high entry level to the field. In our paper we consider an approach that makes the process of developing and integration of robotic systems faster and more accessible to the others. At first, the idea implies removing a technical barrier between science labs and other individuals. Secondly, all processes must be automatized by different tools to the greatest possible extent. As a result, we get a cloud web application where anyone can add or edit robotic systems algorithms. There are open technologies that can help us to implement this solution: virtualization, dockerization, web 3d simulator Gazebo, robot operation system (ROS).

**Keywords:** Docker · Virtualization · Cloud · CI/CD ·
Web application · Robot system

## 1 Introduction

The last decade has been marked by the rapid development of various fields of robotics. As a result, many human activities have undergone robotization, from heavy industry to households [2]. On the one hand, the process of development and implementation of robotic systems is not going to stop, but its pace does not meet the challenges of modernity in the form of economic and social problems that need to be addressed as soon as possible. The current situation is characterized by the weak involvement of society in this process. Due to high expenses, the development of robotic systems is carried out by a narrow circle of scientific laboratories and companies. In such a situation, highly qualified staff is required. People that can quickly solve problems they face during development. But not everyone can afford it for all sorts of reasons. As a result, it takes a long time

© Springer Nature Switzerland AG 2019
M. Mazzara et al. (Eds.): TOOLS 2019, LNCS 11771, pp. 342–348, 2019.
https://doi.org/10.1007/978-3-030-29852-4_29

from prototype development to implementation of the final product and related software.

The next point is that the introduction of robots into human life doesn't take a widespread character. There are several reasons here, but the main ones are high price and insufficient development of the final product. In other words, the quality of software and algorithms for robots. One of the solutions that can change the current situation is a continuous process [5] of robotic systems development. The process with the following characteristics: continuity, accessibility, scalability.

Continuity means a continuous process of code writing, with automated functional and security testing.

The accessibility of the system is determined by the guarantee that anyone can join the robots development at any time. Development of robots requires high-performance hardware and other equipment, which unaffordable for many people. Also plays a role in a high entry level to the field. In some case, software preparation takes an enormous amount of time. Eventually, the process becomes more complicated.

The solution to the problem of the availability of necessary resources is to rent them. It is not only hardware renting but also about using a pre-configured robots software. It is the best way to achieve economic balance and reduce the requirement for initial user skills.

Scalability means the ability to add a large number of new robot models to the development process.

According to the trends, cloud technologies [1] fit well all these criteria. The idea is to move the robot development of robot applications and algorithms to a cloud platform. Virtual robot models are planned to be loaded to the simulator Gazebo. ROS is used as a virtual robot control bus [4].

## 2   Application

For the current day, our standard process of robotic applications development looks as follows:

1. Purchase of expensive hardware
2. Installation and configuration of the software
3. Robot modeling
4. Code development
5. Install additional packages
6. Recompile

In some cases, it is necessary to buy a physical robot.

These steps can be divided into two stages: preparation and application development. There is a 4-level scheme of workplace preparation for the developer below on the Fig. 1.

Hardware layer. As a rule, it is necessary to have high-performance hardware for considerable computations volume. The price of the hardware can reach several thousand dollars. The next layer is the operating system layer. Currently,

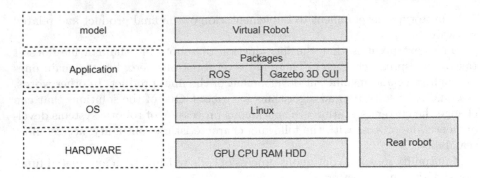

**Fig. 1.** A 4-level scheme of workplace preparation

the main operating system in robotic development is the Linux. On the one hand, open source software support has a positive influence on the development of the industry as a whole. But in this case, users of other operating systems such as Windows, Mac OS are ignored. The third layer is an application layer. At this level, the process of preparing the working environment can take a long time and a lot of efforts for a developer starting with various packages installation. The last layer is a model layer. A real physical robot is not always available, so a virtual robot model needs to be prepared. It can take a long time to make a 3D robot model and create virtual environment in a simulator.

The next stage is application development. The first challenge to be met is the development team expansion. Each team member should have hardware and software with the same characteristics, settings, and packages. As the result from above we have low amount of human resources and a chaotic development process. There is a block diagram of robot software development process below on the Fig. 2.

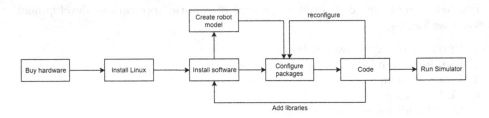

**Fig. 2.** A robot software development process

Cloud technology simplifies the development process. There is no need to prepare the work environment and buy expensive hardware. It is possible to start algorithm development at any time from anywhere in the world [8]. There are a block diagrams of robot software development process in a cloud below on the Figs. 3 and 4.

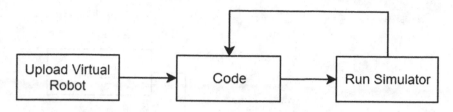

**Fig. 3.** A robot software development process in a cloud.

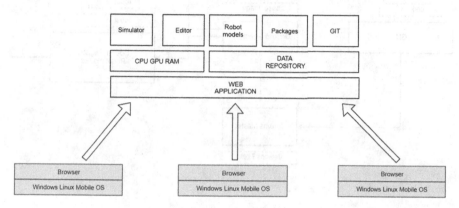

**Fig. 4.** A robot software development process in a cloud.

The cloud application has two main components: a data repository and Web interface to work with robots. The data repository includes a GIT repository, a packages repository, and a repository for robot virtual images. A separate GIT repository is provided for each robot model. The web interface has a graphical simulator with a code editor.

There are two types of users in the application, a provider of robotic systems in the form of scientific laboratories or companies, and a developer of applications and algorithms for robots. Users can easily access the application from any computer connected to the Internet using a standard browser. An user creates a project using service or connects to an existing one. The next thing the user can do is to start his work, upload virtual robot, download necessary packages and run algorithms. The developer focuses on his work on the robot application as much as possible.

## 3 Architecture and Process Development

As mentioned in the previous section, the key components of the application are the web interface and data repository.

Basically, the cloud application is server cluster. Resources of the cluster are managed by XEN hypervisor. Based on the primary purpose of the application, it needs a tool to virtualize robots model. Docker is used for this task [7]. The

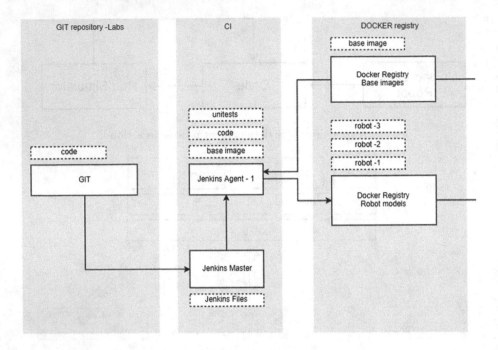

**Fig. 5.** A development process of a provider.

virtual Robot model is packed inside a docker image and uploaded to Docker-registry. Docker-registry is a part of the data repository. Besides a robot's code and ROS packages inside an image, there are also Gazebo server and Gazebo Web client. Docker-registry consists of two parts. The first part is a repository for basic images. These images are used to build virtual robot models. They have Gazebo, ROS and additional libraries that are needed to build new images. The second part is a repository for virtual robot models. The build and test code process is performed on the Jenkins cluster (Jenkins Master and Jenkins Agents). Jenkins Master transfers ready-made images from Jenkins Agent to the second section of docker registry. To manage containers, there is a docker-compose tool. Also, there are additional services such as GIT repository, package repository. All elements of the system communicate with each other via Application Programming Interface (API).

Depending on the type of user (developer or provider), different development processes are possible. The provider builds a virtual robot model and the developer works on the robot application. Jenkins master checks updates in GIT repository Fig. 5, if there is a new pull request in the master branch it starts building process on the Jenkins agent. Jenkins agent downloads a base image from docker-registry and builds code inside the image. It runs unit tests on the correctness of the code afterwards. If all tests are successful, the image is marked as the latest and uploaded to the Docker-regisrty. Application checks data repository for updates Fig. 6. If there is a new image with a virtual robot, the image

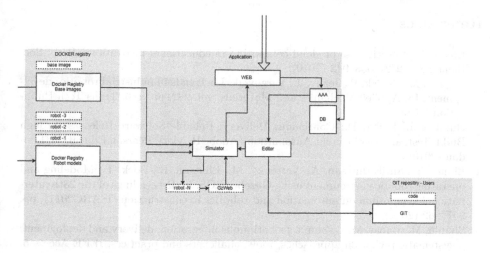

**Fig. 6.** A development process of a developer.

becomes available to developers in the web user interface [3]. When a developer runs a robot, two containers are used. One container from the base GZweb image acts as the Gazebo Client, the second container is the Gazebo Server with the robot [6]. The developer's code is loaded into the GZweb container. Communication between containers is carried out through ROS and Gazebo sockets.

## 4 Conclusion and Suggestion for Further Work

In the current version of the platform, a full cycle of robot application development is implemented. The application allows to launch simulation, write an algorithm and immediately test it. It is possible to work simultaneously with several users on a single project. However, the development process is realized only in one lab. In the future, it is planned to create a universal pipeline and add integration with other laboratories and companies. Upcoming work will describe the implementation of container orchestration and system monitoring. It is also necessary to solve the issues with platform scalability and security.

**Acknowledgments.** This work has been supported by the Ministry of Science and Higher Education of the Russian Federation with the project "Development of anthropomorphic robotic complexes with variable stiffness actuators for movement on the flat and the rugged terrains" (agreement: 075-10-2018-010 (14.606.21.0007), ID: RFMEFI60617X0007).

# References

1. Ercan, T.: Effective use of cloud computing in educational institutions. Proc. Soc. Behav. Sci. **2**(2), 938–942 (2010)
2. Hajduk, M., Jenčík, P., Jezný, J., Vargovčík, L.: Trends in industrial robotics development. In: Applied Mechanics and Materials, vol. 282, pp. 1–6. Trans Tech Publication (2013)
3. Humble, J., Farley, D.: Continuous Delivery: Reliable Software Releases through Build, Test, and Deployment Automation (Adobe Reader). Pearson Education, London (2010)
4. Linner, T., Shrikathiresan, A., Vetrenko, M., Ellmann, B., Bock, T.: Modeling and operating robotic environment using Gazebo/ROS. In: Proceedings of the 28th international symposium on automation and robotics in construction (ISARC2011), pp. 957–962 (2011)
5. Shahin, M., Babar, M.A., Zhu, L.: Continuous integration, delivery and deployment: a systematic review on approaches, tools, challenges and practices. IEEE Access **5**, 3909–3943 (2017)
6. Sokolov, M., Lavrenov, R., Gabdullin, A., Afanasyev, I., Magid, E.: 3D modelling and simulation of a crawler robot in ROS/Gazebo. In: Proceedings of the 4th International Conference on Control, Mechatronics and Automation, pp. 61–65. ACM (2016)
7. Turnbull, J.: The Docker Book: Containerization is the New Virtualization. James Turnbull (2014)
8. Zhang, S., Zhang, S., Chen, X., Huo, X.: Cloud computing research and development trend. In: 2010 Second International Conference on Future Networks, pp. 93–97. IEEE (2010)

# Projects

# VERCORS: Hardware and Software Complex for Intelligent Round-Trip Formalized Verification of Dependable Cyber-Physical Systems in a Digital Twin Environment (Position Paper)

Alexandr Naumchev[1,2]([✉]), Andrey Sadovykh[1], and Vladimir Ivanov[1]

[1] Innopolis University, Innopolis 420500, Russian Federation
a.naumchev@innopolis.ru
[2] Paul Sabatier University, Toulouse, France

**Abstract.** Formal specification, model checking and model-based testing are recommended techniques for engineering of mission-critical systems. In the meantime, those techniques struggle to obtain wide adoption due to inherent learning barrier, i.e. it is considered difficult to use those methods. There is also a common difficulty in translating the specifications in natural language, a common practice nowadays, to formal specifications. In this position paper we discuss the concept of an end-to-end methodology that helps identify specifications from various sources, automatically create formal specifications and apply them to verification of cyber-physical systems. Thus, we intent to address the challenges of creation of formal specifications in an efficient automated and tool-supported manner. The novelty of the approach is analyzed through a survey of state of the art. It is currently planned to implement this concept and evaluate it with industrial case studies.

**Keywords:** Cyber-physical systems (CPS) · Digital twin ·
Verification · Model-based testing · Natural · Language processing ·
Formal specification · Traceability · Multi-modelling · Co-simulation

## 1 Motivation

Unmanned vehicles, drones and robots became mission-critical for many industries and society in general. These Cyber-Physical System (CPS) become more and more complex, since they represent interconnection of thousands of software and hardware components coming from multiple vendors and must work in harmony with an uncertain physical environment to provide dependability guarantees. Digital twin technologies help to accelerate the development and start verification earlier in the development cycle using multi-models combined with hardware-in-the-loop and software-in-the-loop co-simulations to reap most of the cost reduction benefits. In the meantime, the verification of mission critical systems is still very expensive and labor intensive.

© Springer Nature Switzerland AG 2019
M. Mazzara et al. (Eds.): TOOLS 2019, LNCS 11771, pp. 351–363, 2019.
https://doi.org/10.1007/978-3-030-29852-4_30

The efforts may reach 80% of project costs. The automated verification with test generation can dramatically accelerate the specification of test input. However, there is still a fundamental problem of the test oracle that should assess results of test cases. Formal specification techniques have long been studied for test input generation and as a remedy for the oracle problem. Nevertheless, they could not gain a massive uptake due to overall complexity of the formalization process. The modern methods for natural language processing and paraphrasing provide opportunities to automate specification extraction and formalization. It is thus becoming possible to enable digital twin platforms with automated verification methods based on formal specifications in a cost effective manner and address the dependability problem of the modern CPSs. The decision makers may have the dependability properties expressed in different forms starting from informal ones in natural language collected during face-to-face meetings. The challenge that the current work addresses is facilitating the translation of these properties to the form understandable by the multi-model verification environment through (1) extracting natural language specifications from available sources, (2) formalizing the extracted natural languages specifications, (3) automatically generating test input and outputs from the generated oracles, (4) tests execution in a co-simulation environment interplaying logical/cyber and physical models.

## 2   The Solution

In this section we present the conceptual view of the solution that we think will simplify the CPSs' verification process.

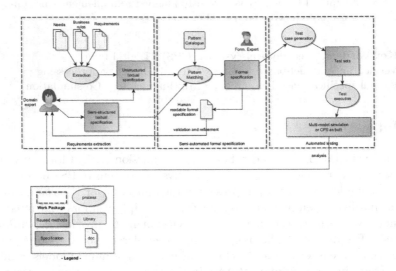

**Fig. 1.** Top level view of the system. (Color figure online)

The resulting process will execute the following major activities (the boxes with the blue dotted frames in Fig. 1):

1. Requirements extraction.
2. Requirements formalization.
3. Automated testing and co-simulation.

Each of these activities consumes on input the previous activity's output. The following human agents control execution of these activities:

- Domain expert controls requirements extraction and confirms the results of requirements formalization.
- Formalization expert maintains the requirement patterns catalogue (RPC) and supports instantiation of the patterns into requirements.

The agents will oversee producing the following artifacts (the green rectangles in Fig. 1):

- Unstructured and semi-structured textual specifications.
- Formal specification.
- Test sets.

The VERCORS project has the objective to automate some of the human agents' tasks (the light green ellipses in Fig. 1):

- Extracting natural language requirements from available sources.
- Matching the extracted requirements against known patterns.
- Automatically generating test input and test oracles based on the formal semantics encoded inside the patterns.
- Running the generated tests in a co-simulation environment, interplaying logical/cyber and physical models.

Requirements extraction will analyze available information sources and propose candidate natural-language requirements. The proposed candidate requirements will be reviews by the domain expert Semi-automated requirements formalization will consume the extracted informal requirements and produce their formalized versions along with more structured natural-language representations. The domain expert will evaluate the two natural-language representations of the same requirement and decide whether to accept the formalization or make the initial requirement more precise. As soon as the domain expert confirms the formalization, it is submitted to automated testing; the domain expert will then analyze failures and either correct the input requirements or file bug reports to the development team.

## 3   State of the Art

As Sect. 2 states, the project will tool-support three major activities: (1) requirements extraction, (2) requirements formalization and (3) automated testing and co-simulation. The present section describes the state of the art in these areas.

## 3.1   Natural Language Processing for Requirements Extraction

As stated in [51], natural language processing (NLP) is a promising approach to support the requirements engineering process due to the increasing complexity of the systems to develop and hence of the requirements to manage. Some studies have adopted NLP to transform requirements into analysis models [45,66]. Others have analyzed requirements to identify textual ambiguity [27,63,64]. In the current article we focus on and review the following directions of research:

– NLP techniques for extraction and/or recovery of requirements from unstructured texts.
– NLP techniques for requirements analysis with respect to ambiguity and/or complexity.

**NLP Techniques for Extraction and/or Recovery of Requirements from Unstructured Texts.** The problem of extraction or recovery of requirements has to be distinguished from the requirement elicitation problem. In requirements extraction or recovery, we expect that a software system is already developed (or at least the requirement elicitation process finished). Thus, there is some textual corpus that has been collected. The text corpus contains unstructured text files that should be processed using NLP techniques in order to extract a set of text segments (prototype requirements). It is also possible to use existing specifications to facilitate the process.

In this research direction there are two main classes of techniques: rule-based methods and statistical methods (or machine learning) techniques. Ferrari et al. [16] collected and published online a public dataset of 79 software requirements documents (47 pages of text per document). In [54] authors describe an NLP pipeline to transform a set of heterogeneous natural language requirements into a knowledge representation graph. Key steps of the pipeline are tokenizing, POS-tagging and semantic role labeling. This article illustrates typical rule-based approach [10]. Another approach is based on machine learning techniques that have shown good performance in the past decade. A wide range of models are applied in this direction to categorize requirements [29], to extract relevant text segments and to assess quality of textual requirements [14,15,30].

**NLP Techniques for Requirements Analysis with Respect to Ambiguity and/or Complexity.** Most of the software complexity measures are based on code, but when we use the code for computing software complexity it is too late. In [57] a method for measurement of The Requirement Based Complexity based on text analysis of software requirements specifications. The authors conclude that the proposed measure follows the trend of all the other established measures (code based and cognitive information complexity based) in a comprehensive manner. However, their measure applicable on the textual requirements that comply to the IEEE standard (IEEE830:1993).

In [5] Antinyan et al. define a complexity measure for textual requirements. They found that there is a significant agreement between the manual assessors which means that the manual assessors significantly agree on the criteria of requirements understandability.

## 3.2 Specification Formalization

Specification formalization can be broken into the following work packages:

- Matching the input specifications against known specification patterns to reuse these patterns.
- Producing paraphrased requirements from the patterns for checking with the human agent.
- Generating the formalization from the patterns marked by the human agent as valid.

We expect the biggest amount of work in the first package – pattern matching. A recent literature review by Irshad et al. [24] provides a comprehensive survey of the existing body of knowledge in this field. Blok and Cybulski [9] used lexical and semantic matching to identify and reuse the requirements represented in UML. Paydar et al. [46] proposed to use matching of UMLs to identify the reuse potential and this matching was done by using a metric for measuring the similarity of UML-based use-cases. Niu et al. proposed requirements reuse approach based on the lexical affinity to retrieve the reusable requirements [43]. Castano et al. [11] describe requirements as conceptual components that facilitate the requirements reuse by matching these conceptual components. Perednikas proposed requirements reuse approach that works by forecasting of user needs [48]. Ryan et al. used conceptual graphs to develop a matching mechanism to identify the similar cases for reuse [52]. Sutcliffe transforms the use-case scenarios into a model and then compares the model with the library of existing models; the requirements from the matching model are reused to develop new requirements [58]. Biddle et al. derive scenarios from the use-cases and suggest the reuse cases by matching with existing scenarios [8]. Periyasamy and Chidambaram compare signatures of the requirements' Z representations to identify reuse cases [49]. The "Requirements Reuse Model for Software Requirements Catalogue" [44] approach suggests the activities and a method that enable requirements to reuse in requirements catalogue. Another approach [6] extracts high-frequency words from the documents describing the natural language requirements and identifies features for reuse based on the words' frequencies. Bakar et al. [7] demonstrated a reuse approach based on extracting frequently occurring words in documents and used the statistical analysis, based on the distance measure, to identify similar requirements.

## 3.3 Automated Testing for Multi-model Simulation Environments

Testing techniques relying on automated tests generation fit into the following major categories:

- Model-based testing.
- Search-based testing.
- Uncertainty-wise testing.

Model-based Testing (MBT) is a technique for performing software system testing using models [56]. In MBT, models can be used to express the expected behavior of the system under test, and/or its environment to be tested. The feasibility and cost-effectiveness of MBT have been demonstrated by the intensive research work and industrial practices [25,60]. The typical process of MBT includes five steps: (1) construct models with respect to the system under testing and/or its environment; (2) generate a set of abstract test cases based on the constructed models according to the defined test selection criteria; (3) concretize the abstract test cases to executable ones; (4) execute the test cases on test infrastructures and assign verdicts; and (5) analyze execution results of the test cases.

Search-based Software Testing (SBST) applies meta-heuristic optimizing search techniques to tackle automatic generation of test data and other challenges of automated testing [19,21,22,31,32]. In SBST, these challenges are normally reformulated as search problems for seeking optimal or near-optimal solutions in a search space. The process is guided by fitness functions that are defined to evaluate the sought solution for seeking the better ones. The applicability and effectiveness of SBST can be demonstrated by many successful works and related surveys [3,4,20,26,65]. Multi-objective approaches are increasingly applied for optimizing the testing process, such as test set selection, minimization and prioritization [19,26].

Uncertainty is inherent in CPSs due to various reasons such as unpredictable environment under which the CPSs are operated. It is crucial to identify uncertainties in CPSs and test CPSs under the uncertainties. This process is called uncertainty-wise testing. Walkinshaw and Fraser [62] proposed a black-box testing framework to select test cases for execution to decrease uncertainty about the correctness of a software system. Another work [18] focuses exclusively on time-related uncertainty. David et al. [12] presented test generation principles and algorithms (e.g., the online testing tool UPPAAL-TRON [23]) and discussed the feasibility of applying them for testing timed systems under uncertainty, at a high level of abstraction. In [50], the authors presented a solution to transform UML use case diagrams and state diagrams into usage graphs appended with probability information about the expected use of the software. Zhang et al. [67] combined the benefits of model-based, search-based and uncertainty-wise testing inside the UncerTest framework for testing CPSs under uncertainty.

Simulation on virtual models is the most cost, effort and time effective method for verifying the correctness of complex embedded systems such as CPSs. Moreover, the simulation environments often concentrate one type only of the simulations: discrete-event or continuous. Furthermore, the available simulators often require the complete set of binaries to be executed on each node. In addition, simulations are an important Intellectual Property, that many vendors strive to preserve. The current trend is multi-model co-simulations based on the

Functional Mock-up Interface (FMI) technology. This technology allows packaging simulators as binaries and run them in parallel on distributed nodes with an orchestration engine [47] and [53]. Thus, the interplay of simulators of different types are provided, while preserving the Intellectual Property of vendors. The whole set of simulators may represent a digital twin of the developed system.

## 4  Expected Contributions to the State of the Art

We plan to make the following conceptual contributions to the state of the art:

1. In requirements extraction and classification task we will add a new value by developing a system that combines the knowledge-based approaches to information extraction with modern machine learning techniques to easily transfer results to new domains.
2. In the specification formalization task, we will add value by embedding the paraphrasing and formalization algorithms directly into the requirement patterns. As the main consequence of this contribution, matching requirements against the patterns will automatically imply choosing the most appropriate paraphrasing and formalization.
3. For the automated testing and multi-model simulation, we want to combine the cutting edge techniques of testing CPSs and model-based simulation inside our requirement patterns-based framework. More precisely, the patterns should include the mechanisms of their own automated testing in automatically simulated environments.

The following technical artifacts will support the conceptual contributions:

1. Experimental environment for specification extraction from text.
2. Training and test sets for training and evaluation of the engine for requirements specification extraction, including analysis of specifications granularity
3. Templates catalogue for specification formalization.
4. Natural language pattern recognition engine for specification formalization.
5. formal specification generation engine.
6. Round-trip mechanism based on paraphrasing for validation of the formal specification by the user and continuous adaptation.
7. Engine for generation of test input from formal specifications applying a set of strategies such as automated random testing and boundary value analysis.
8. Engine for oracles generation for prediction of test outcomes from the formal specifications.
9. Multi-model co-simulation engine for execution of generated test sets in Hardware-In-The-Loop, Software-In-The-Loop modes for the digital twin environment.
10. Traceability engine that collects the test verdicts, links them to the formal specifications and enables the root cause analysis by the user.
11. Seamless framework applicable in several domains of cyber-physical systems.
12. End-to-end demonstrator to showcase the results of the project.

# 5 Discussion

Developing high quality software amounts to the following major tasks:

- Implement correct requirements.
- Implement requirements correctly.

Checking that requirements are implemented correctly assumes their formal verification against the implementation, which assumes that the requirements are formalized. Requirements, however, start their life cycle in the form of notes recorded during early requirements elicitation sessions. When the informal-to-formal transition happens, a mechanism should be in place to make sure that the formalization does not alter the original meaning. The formalization process, on the other hand, may reveal additional insights [33]; a mechanism should be in place to "de-formalize" requirements for comparing them with their original informal versions. The process of checking implementations against formalized requirements should correctly reflect the requirements' semantics. The VERCORS project will address these concerns in a unified fashion.

As the Sect. 3 suggests, a big corpus of knowledge covers the three major separate activities that constitute VERCORS. The project will unify these activities inside a single framework with the help of seamless development [35,61]. More specifically, through the notion of multirequirements – requirements expressed in several notations, one of which is a programming language with contracts [36]. Mutlirequirements seamlessly connect requirements and their implementations in the same programming language [42]. Automated program proving [59] adds the possibility to formally reason about requirements' completeness and consistency [37,39]. Combining multirequirements with program proving and development through Design by Contract (DbC) [34] makes it possible to incrementally, in an agile fashion, develop formally verified software [40]. The approach scales to specifying and verifying temporal and timing requirements for control software, which is at heart of any cyber-physical system [17,41]. Trying to make multirequirements reusable across software projects results in seamless object-oriented requirements (SOOR) and their templates (SOORT) [38]. SOORTs capture recurring requirement patterns in the form of object-oriented classes. The VERCORS process will rely on an existing catalogue of SOORTs that encode known patterns [13,28]. It maps to the "Pattern Catalogue" component in Fig. 1). The catalogue will evolve during the framework's operation. It will support the VERCORS activities in the following way, given a requirement provided by the extraction engine from the "Requirement extraction" package:

1. The pattern matching engine will identify SOORTs that are likely to cover the provided requirement.
2. For each identified SOORT, the formalization expert will refine it into a SOOR based on the expert's understanding of the input requirement.
3. The SOOR will automatically generate a structured natural language version of the requirement; it inherits the generation logic from the parent SOORT.

4. The domain expert will look at the structured version and either use it instead of the input requirement or reject it.
5. If the domain expert rejects the structured version, the formalization expert will continue with the next identified SOORT.
6. If the domain expert accepts the structured version, the formalization expert will pass the SOOR to the "Automated testing" package.
7. The test case generation engine analyzes the predicates characterizing valid test inputs; the SOOR inherits these predicates from the parent SOORT.
8. The test case generation engine generates test inputs that cover every disjunct in the predicate's disjunctive normal form.
9. The test execution engine runs the test for checking the requirement's semantics, providing the generated test inputs; the SOOR inherits the test from the parent SOORT.

Seamless object-oriented requirements and their templates will become the junction point of the whole process. Their multi-faceted project-agnostic nature will support the various agents in their activities.

# References

1. Proceedings of IEEE International Symposium on Requirements Engineering, RE 1993, San Diego, California, USA, 4–6 January 1993. IEEE Computer Society (1993)
2. 25th IEEE International Requirements Engineering Conference, RE 2017, Lisbon, Portugal, 4–8 September 2017. IEEE Computer Society (2017)
3. Afzal, W., Torkar, R., Feldt, R.: A systematic review of search-based testing for non-functional system properties. Inf. Softw. Technol. **51**(6), 957–976 (2009)
4. Ali, S., Briand, L.C., Hemmati, H., Panesar-Walawege, R.K.: A systematic review of the application and empirical investigation of search-based test case generation. IEEE Trans. Softw. Eng. **36**(6), 742–762 (2010)
5. Antinyan, V., Staron, M., Sandberg, A., Hansson, J.: A complexity measure for textual requirements. In: Heidrich, J., Vogelezang, F.W. (eds.) 2016 Joint Conference of the International Workshop on Software Measurement and the International Conference on Software Process and Product Measurement, IWSM-MENSURA 2016, Berlin, Germany, 5–7 October 2016, pp. 148–158. IEEE Computer Society (2016)
6. Bakar, N.H., Kasirun, Z.M., Salleh, N.: Terms extractions: an approach for requirements reuse. In: 2015 2nd International Conference on Information Science and Security (ICISS), pp. 1–4, December 2015. https://doi.org/10.1109/ICISSEC.2015.7371034
7. Bakar, N.H., Kasirun, Z.M., Jalab, H.A.: Towards requirements reuse: identifying similar requirements with latent semantic analysis and clustering algorithms. In: Proceedings of the Second International Conference on Advances In Computing, Communication and Information Technology-CCIT 2014, pp. 19–24 (2014)
8. Biddle, R., Noble, J., Tempero, E.: Supporting reusable use cases. In: Gacek, C. (ed.) ICSR 2002. LNCS, vol. 2319, pp. 210–226. Springer, Heidelberg (2002). https://doi.org/10.1007/3-540-46020-9_15

9. Blok, M.C., Cybulski, J.L.: Reusing UML specifications in a constrained application domain. In: 5th Asia-Pacific Software Engineering Conference (APSEC 1998), Taipei, Taiwan, ROC, 2–4 December 1998, pp. 196–202. IEEE Computer Society (1998)

10. Caron, M., Bäumer, F.S., Geierhos, M.: Back to basics: extracting software requirements with a syntactic approach. In: Schmid et al. [55]

11. Castano, S., Antonellis, V.D.: Reuse of conceptual requirement specifications. In: Proceedings of IEEE International Symposium on Requirements Engineering, RE 1993, San Diego, California, USA, 4–6 January 1993 [1], pp. 121–124 (1993)

12. David, A., Larsen, K.G., Li, S., Mikucionis, M., Nielsen, B.: Testing real-time systems under uncertainty. In: Aichernig, B.K., de Boer, F.S., Bonsangue, M.M. (eds.) FMCO 2010. LNCS, vol. 6957, pp. 352–371. Springer, Heidelberg (2011). https://doi.org/10.1007/978-3-642-25271-6_19

13. Dwyer, M.B., Avrunin, G.S., Corbett, J.C.: Patterns in property specifications for finite-state verification. In: Boehm, B.W., Garlan, D., Kramer, J. (eds.) Proceedings of the 1999 International Conference on Software Engineering, ICSE 1999, Los Angeles, CA, USA, 16–22 May 1999, pp. 411–420. ACM (1999)

14. Ferrari, A., dell'Orletta, F., Spagnolo, G.O., Gnesi, S.: Measuring and improving the completeness of natural language requirements. In: Salinesi, C., van de Weerd, I. (eds.) REFSQ 2014. LNCS, vol. 8396, pp. 23–38. Springer, Cham (2014). https://doi.org/10.1007/978-3-319-05843-6_3

15. Ferrari, A., Gnesi, S.: Using collective intelligence to detect pragmatic ambiguities. In: Heimdahl, M.P.E., Sawyer, P. (eds.) 2012 20th IEEE International Requirements Engineering Conference (RE), Chicago, IL, USA, 24–28 September 2012, pp. 191–200. IEEE Computer Society (2012)

16. Ferrari, A., Spagnolo, G.O., Gnesi, S.: PURE: a dataset of public requirements documents. In: 25th IEEE International Requirements Engineering Conference, RE 2017, Lisbon, Portugal, 4–8 September 2017 [12], pp. 502–505 (2017)

17. Galinier, F., Bruel, J., Ebersold, S., Meyer, B.: Seamless integration of multirequirements in complex systems. In: IEEE 25th International Requirements Engineering Conference Workshops, RE 2017 Workshops, Lisbon, Portugal, 4–8 September 2017, pp. 21–25 (2017)

18. Garousi, V.: Traffic-aware stress testing of distributed real-time systems based on UML models in the presence of time uncertainty. In: First International Conference on Software Testing, Verification, and Validation, ICST 2008, Lillehammer, Norway, 9–11 April 2008, pp. 92–101. IEEE Computer Society (2008)

19. Harman, M., Jia, Y., Zhang, Y.: Achievements, open problems and challenges for search based software testing. In: 8th IEEE International Conference on Software Testing, Verification and Validation, ICST 2015, Graz, Austria, 13–17 April 2015, pp. 1–12. IEEE Computer Society (2015)

20. Harman, M., Mansouri, S.A., Zhang, Y.: Search based software engineering: a comprehensive analysis and review of trends techniques and applications. Department of Computer Science, King's College London, Technical report TR-09-03, p. 23 (2009)

21. Harman, M., Mansouri, S.A., Zhang, Y.: Search-based software engineering: trends, techniques and applications. ACM Comput. Surv. 45(1), 11:1–11:61 (2012)

22. Harman, M., McMinn, P., de Souza, J.T., Yoo, S.: Search based software engineering: techniques, taxonomy, tutorial. In: Meyer, B., Nordio, M. (eds.) LASER 2008–2010. LNCS, vol. 7007, pp. 1–59. Springer, Heidelberg (2012). https://doi.org/10.1007/978-3-642-25231-0_1

23. Hessel, A., Larsen, K.G., Mikucionis, M., Nielsen, B., Pettersson, P., Skou, A.: Testing real-time systems using UPPAAL. In: Hierons, R.M., Bowen, J.P., Harman, M. (eds.) Formal Methods and Testing. LNCS, vol. 4949, pp. 77–117. Springer, Heidelberg (2008). https://doi.org/10.1007/978-3-540-78917-8_3
24. Irshad, M., Petersen, K., Poulding, S.M.: A systematic literature review of software requirements reuse approaches. Inf. Softw. Technol. **93**, 223–245 (2018)
25. Jorgensen, P.C.: The Craft of Model-Based Testing. Auerbach Publications (2017)
26. Khatibsyarbini, M., Isa, M.A., Jawawi, D.N.A., Tumeng, R.: Test case prioritization approaches in regression testing: a systematic literature review. Inf. Softw. Technol. **93**, 74–93 (2018)
27. Kiyavitskaya, N., Zeni, N., Mich, L., Berry, D.M.: Requirements for tools for ambiguity identification and measurement in natural language requirements specifications. Requir. Eng. **13**(3), 207–239 (2008)
28. Konrad, S., Cheng, B.H.C.: Real-time specification patterns. In: Roman, G., Griswold, W.G., Nuseibeh, B. (eds.) 27th International Conference on Software Engineering (ICSE 2005), St. Louis, Missouri, USA, 15–21 May 2005, pp. 372–381. ACM (2005)
29. Kurtanovic, Z., Maalej, W.: Automatically classifying functional and nonfunctional requirements using supervised machine learning. In: 25th IEEE International Requirements Engineering Conference, RE 2017, Lisbon, Portugal, 4–8 September 2017 [2], pp. 490–495 (2017)
30. Maalej, W., Nayebi, M., Johann, T., Ruhe, G.: Toward data-driven requirements engineering. IEEE Softw. **33**(1), 48–54 (2016)
31. McMinn, P.: Search-based software test data generation: a survey. Softw. Test. Verif. Reliab. **14**(2), 105–156 (2004)
32. McMinn, P.: Search-based software testing: past, present and future. In: Fourth IEEE International Conference on Software Testing, Verification and Validation, ICST 2012, Berlin, Germany, 21–25 March, 2011, Workshop Proceedings, pp. 153–163. IEEE Computer Society (2011)
33. Meyer, B.: On formalism in specifications. IEEE Softw. **2**(1), 6–26 (1985)
34. Meyer, B.: Applying "design by contract". IEEE Comput. **25**(10), 40–51 (1992)
35. Meyer, B.: Object-Oriented Software Construction, 2nd edn. Prentice-Hall, Upper Saddle River (1997)
36. Meyer, B.: Multirequirements. In: Modelling and Quality in Requirements Engineering: Essays dedicated to Martin Glinz on the occasion of his 60th birthday. Verl.-Haus Monsenstein u. Vannerdat (2013)
37. Naumchev, A.: Detection of inconsistent contracts through modular verification. In: Ciancarini, P., Mazzara, M., Messina, A., Sillitti, A., Succi, G. (eds.) SEDA 2018. AISC, vol. 925, pp. 206–220. Springer, Cham (2020). https://doi.org/10.1007/978-3-030-14687-0_19
38. Naumchev, A.: Object-oriented requirements: reusable, understandable, verifiable. CoRR abs/1903.04165 (2019)
39. Naumchev, A., Meyer, B.: Complete contracts through specification drivers. In: 10th International Symposium on Theoretical Aspects of Software Engineering, TASE 2016, Shanghai, China, 17–19 July 2016, pp. 160–167. IEEE Computer Society (2016)
40. Naumchev, A., Meyer, B.: Seamless requirements. Comput. Lang. Syst. Struct. **49**, 119–132 (2017)
41. Naumchev, A., Meyer, B., Mazzara, M., Galinier, F., Bruel, J.M., Ebersold, S.: Autoreq: expressing and verifying requirements for control systems. J. Comput. Lang. **51**, 131–142 (2019)

42. Naumchev, A., Meyer, B., Rivera, V.: Unifying requirements and code: an example. In: Mazzara, M., Voronkov, A. (eds.) PSI 2015. LNCS, vol. 9609, pp. 233–244. Springer, Cham (2016). https://doi.org/10.1007/978-3-319-41579-6_18
43. Niu, N., Savolainen, J., Niu, Z., Jin, M., Cheng, J.C.: A systems approach to product line requirements reuse. IEEE Syst. J. **8**(3), 827–836 (2014)
44. Pacheco, C.L., Garcia, I.A., Calvo-Manzano, J.A., Arcilla-Cobián, M.: Reusing functional software requirements in small-sized software enterprises: a model oriented to the catalog of requirements. Requir. Eng. **22**(2), 275–287 (2017)
45. Paech, B., Martell, C. (eds.): Monterey Workshop 2007. LNCS, vol. 5320. Springer, Heidelberg (2008). https://doi.org/10.1007/978-3-540-89778-1
46. Paydar, S., Kahani, M.: A semantic web enabled approach to reuse functional requirements models in web engineering. Autom. Softw. Eng. **22**(2), 241–288 (2015)
47. Pedersen, N., Lausdahl, K., Sanchez, E.V., Thule, C., Larsen, P.G., Madsen, J.: Distributed co-simulation of embedded control software using INTO-CPS. In: Obaidat, M.S., Ören, T., Rango, F.D. (eds.) SIMULTECH 2017. AISC, vol. 873, pp. 33–54. Springer, Cham (2019). https://doi.org/10.1007/978-3-030-01470-4_3
48. Perednikas, E.: Requirements reuse based on forecast of user needs. In: Proceedings of the 20th EURO Mini Conference on Continuous Optimization and Knowledge-Based Technologies, Neringa, Lithuania, pp. 450–455 (2008)
49. Periyasamy, K., Chidambaram, J.: Software reuse using formal specification of requirements. In: Bauer, M.A., Bennet, K., Gentleman, W.M., Johnson, J.H., Lyons, K.A., Slonim, J. (eds.) Proceedings of the 1996 conference of the Centre for Advanced Studies on Collaborative Research, Toronto, Ontario, Canada, 12–14 November 1996, p. 31. IBM (1996)
50. Riebisch, M., Philippow, I., Götze, M.: UML-based statistical test case generation. In: Aksit, M., Mezini, M., Unland, R. (eds.) NODe 2002. LNCS, vol. 2591, pp. 394–411. Springer, Heidelberg (2003). https://doi.org/10.1007/3-540-36557-5_28
51. Ryan, K.: The role of natural language in requirements engineering. In: Proceedings of IEEE International Symposium on Requirements Engineering, RE 1993, San Diego, California, USA, 4–6 January 1993 [1], pp. 240–242 (1993)
52. Ryan, K., Mathews, B.: Matching conceptual graphs as an aid to requirements re-use. In: Proceedings of IEEE International Symposium on Requirements Engineering, RE 1993, San Diego, California, USA, 4–6 January 1993 [1], pp. 112–120 (1993)
53. Sadovykh, A., et al.: SysML as a common integration platform for co-simulations: example of a cyber physical system design methodology in green heating ventilation and air conditioning systems. In: Proceedings of the 12th Central and Eastern European Software Engineering Conference in Russia, CEE-SECR 2016, pp. 1:1–1:5. ACM, New York (2016)
54. Schlutter, A., Vogelsang, A.: Knowledge representation of requirements documents using natural language processing. In: Schmid et al. [55]
55. Schmid, K., et al. (eds.): Joint Proceedings of REFSQ-2018 Workshops, Doctoral Symposium, Live Studies Track, and Poster Track co-located with the 23rd International Conference on Requirements Engineering: Foundation for Software Quality (REFSQ 2018), Utrecht, The Netherlands, 19 March 2018. CEUR Workshop Proceedings, vol. 2075. CEUR-WS.org (2018)
56. Shafique, M., Labiche, Y.: A systematic review of model based testing tool support (2010)
57. Sharma, A., Kushwaha, D.S.: Complexity measure based on requirement engineering document and its validation. In: 2010 International Conference on Computer and Communication Technology (ICCCT), pp. 608–615, September 2010

58. Sutcliffe, A.G., Maiden, N.A.M., Minocha, S., Manuel, D.: Supporting scenario-based requirements engineering. IEEE Trans. Softw. Eng. **24**(12), 1072–1088 (1998)
59. Tschannen, J., Furia, C.A., Nordio, M., Polikarpova, N.: AutoProof: auto-active functional verification of object-oriented programs. In: Baier, C., Tinelli, C. (eds.) TACAS 2015. LNCS, vol. 9035, pp. 566–580. Springer, Heidelberg (2015). https://doi.org/10.1007/978-3-662-46681-0_53
60. Utting, M., Legeard, B.: Practical Model-Based Testing - A Tools Approach. Morgan Kaufmann, Burlington (2007)
61. Walden, K., Nerson, J.: Seamless Object-Oriented Software Architecture - Analysis and Design of Reliable Systems. Prentice-Hall, Upper Saddle River (1994)
62. Walkinshaw, N., Fraser, G.: Uncertainty-driven black-box test data generation. In: 2017 IEEE International Conference on Software Testing, Verification and Validation, ICST 2017, Tokyo, Japan, 13–17 March 2017, pp. 253–263. IEEE Computer Society (2017)
63. Weber-Jahnke, J.H., Onabajo, A.: Finding defects in natural language confidentiality requirements. In: RE 2009, 17th IEEE International Requirements Engineering Conference, Atlanta, Georgia, USA, 31 August–4 September 2009, pp. 213–222. IEEE Computer Society (2009)
64. Yang, H., Willis, A., Roeck, A.N.D., Nuseibeh, B.: Automatic detection of nocuous coordination ambiguities in natural language requirements. In: Pecheur, C., Andrews, J., Nitto, E.D. (eds.) ASE 2010, 25th IEEE/ACM International Conference on Automated Software Engineering, Antwerp, Belgium, 20–24 September 2010, pp. 53–62. ACM (2010)
65. Yoo, S., Harman, M.: Regression testing minimization, selection and prioritization: a survey. Softw. Test. Verif. Reliab. **22**(2), 67–120 (2012)
66. Yue, T., Briand, L.C., Labiche, Y.: A systematic review of transformation approaches between user requirements and analysis models. Requir. Eng. **16**(2), 75–99 (2011)
67. Zhang, M., Ali, S., Yue, T.: Uncertainty-wise test case generation and minimization for cyber-physical systems. J. Syst. Softw. **153**, 1–21 (2019). https://doi.org/10.1016/j.jss.2019.03.011. http://www.sciencedirect.com/science/article/pii/S0164121219300561

# MELODIC: Selection and Integration of Open Source to Build an Autonomic Cross-Cloud Deployment Platform

Geir Horn[1]([⊠]), Paweł Skrzypek[2], Marcin Prusiński[2], Katarzyna Materka[2], Vassilis Stefanidis[3], and Yiannis Verginadis[3]

[1] University of Oslo, P.O. Box 1080, Blindern, 0316 Oslo, Norway
`Geir.Horn@mn.uio.no`
[2] 7Bulls.com, Al. Szucha 8, 00-582 Warsaw, Poland
`{pskrzypek,mprusinski,kmaterka}@7bulls.com`
[3] Institute of Communication and Computer Systems (ICCS), Athens, Greece
`{stefanidis,jverg}@mail.ntua.gr`

**Abstract.** MELODIC is and open source platform for autonomic deployment and optimized management of Cross-Cloud applications. The MELODIC platform is a complete, enterprise ready solution using *only* open source software. The contribution of this paper is the discussion of approaches to integration and various options for large scale open source projects and their evaluation showing that only a combination of an Enterprise Service Bus (ESB) with Business Process Management (BPM) for platform integration and control, and the use of a distributed Event Management Services (EMS) for monitoring state and creating context awareness, will provide the required stability and reliability. Consequently, the selection, the evaluation, and the design process of these three crucial components of the MELODIC platform are described.

**Keywords:** Open source · Integration · Cloud computing

## 1 The Challenge

Open source software is no longer an exotic activity or hobby for the passionate. Open source software has become mainstream. Most of the advanced software in big companies and organizations is already open source, using open source, or it is based on open source components and frameworks. This trend continues. Thus, the open source software ecosystem continuously expands by providing building blocks for other, advanced open source software systems and platforms. In this paper, we consider the case of a platform called Multi-cloud Execution

This work has received funding from the European Union's Horizon 2020 research and innovation programme under grant agreement No 731664 MELODIC: Multi-cloud Execution-ware for Large-scale Optimised Data-Intensive Computing.

ware for Large scale Optimised Data Intensive Computing (MELODIC)[1] doing optimised deployment and management of Cross-Cloud applications. We have used two categories of software for building the MELODIC platform:

1. Tools and frameworks: applications, components, tools, libraries and frameworks that are commonly available and have significant groups of users.
2. Cloud computing open source components: These are related functionally to the MELODIC platform, of which some are developed in other European Union research projects that are predecessors of MELODIC and some are developed within the MELODIC project, and some are existing open source solutions developed and maintained by the MELODIC team members.

Each of the categories has a different set of challenges which should be addressed within the project. For the first category, commonly used tools and frameworks, the key challenges to address within an integration project are:

1. To choose the right tool or framework. The process of choosing the right software should be systematic and based on precisely defined requirements.
2. The design of an architecture using the chosen tools or frameworks where the software capabilities, limitations, and specific functions must be properly handled during the design phase since different frameworks use different integration methods, both in tools used and types of communication, *i.e.* synchronous or asynchronous.
3. To integrate the tools or frameworks into the platform. The technical integration of the selected components is a very demanding process, which makes it necessary to acquire deeper knowledge about the given tool or framework and how to use it properly. The various modules of MELODIC could be implemented in different languages and again include other open source libraries. Choosing the proper license for the platform is therefore very important. The compatibility of licenses is consequently a crucial element when selecting the tools and frameworks.
4. To maintain the future development of the MELODIC platform and independent upgrades of the third-party tools and frameworks. Maintainability is the one of key aspects for the continued development of the MELODIC platform in conjunction with the development of the tools and frameworks. It must be properly planned and managed.
5. To identify bugs in the tools and frameworks, and to manage bug fixing and workaround implementation. It is crucial for the maintainability to have a plan for handling bugs discovered in the platform and in the underlying tools and frameworks, especially with focus on preparing workarounds until the bugs have been fixed by the third-party tool or framework developers.

Properly addressing the above challenges within the effort available is fundamental to the success of any large scale integration project. The architecture of the MELODIC is provided in Sect. 2 to provide an understanding of the integration challenge and scope. The essential technologies for the integration in

---

[1] https://www.melodic.cloud/.

MELODIC are described in Sect. 3 dealing with the requirements and the selection of an ESB for exchanging control data among components, and the BPM for orchestrating the component composition using the control plane. Section 4 describes the EMS to support the monitoring of both the platform and the application deployed through the MELODIC platform, which is necessary to create the needed execution context awareness enabling the autonomic management of the deployed application.

Furthermore, Sect. 2 describes the second software category, *i.e.* the specific MELODIC Cloud computing open source components. Also for this integration there are essential challenges that all large integration projects must manage:

1. To select the most appropriate components to be integrated with the platform based on the requirements, capabilities, and technical limitations of both the components and the MELODIC platform. It should also take into consideration legal aspects like licensing.
2. To assess the quality of each component, its technical limitations, and potential compatibility issues.
3. To carefully design the integrated architecture of the platform including the selected components based on the previous steps of selection and assessments.
4. To integrate and adapt the selected components into the platform. In some cases the components should not only be integrated but *included* into the MELODIC platform. In the latter case, the work then entails both adaptation and customisation of the desired components. Hence, this challenge could be the most demanding task that requires most of the integration effort.
5. Finally, one needs to maintain the further development of the MELODIC platform in parallel to the continuous development of the selected and integrated components.

## 2    MELODIC Architecture

### 2.1    Main Features

The MELODIC platform is an advanced autonomous middleware that acts as an automatic DevOps [12] for one, managed Cloud application, and make the necessary adaptations to the deployment configuration as the application's running context changes.

The fundamental MELODIC architecture is inherited from the PaaSage[2] project [10]. The idea is that the application architecture, its components, the data sets processed, and the available monitoring sensors can all be described in a Domain Specific Language (DSL) [3]. The application architecture description will be coupled with the goals for the deployment, the given deployment constraints, and monitoring information to allow the MELODIC platform to optimise the deployment. MELODIC can therefore be seen as a particular implementation of the models@run.time [8] part of a Cloud Modelling Framework [15].

---

[2] https://paasage.ercim.eu/.

The MELODIC architecture has three main layers: The application modeling based on The Cloud Application Modelling and Execution Language (CAMEL) [2]; the *upperware* solving the optimization problem and adapting the deployment model; and the *executionware* based on the Cloudiator[3] Cross-Cloud orchestration tool responsible for the deployment of the solution prepared by the upperware to the chosen Cloud providers. The MELODIC architecture is presented in Fig. 1.

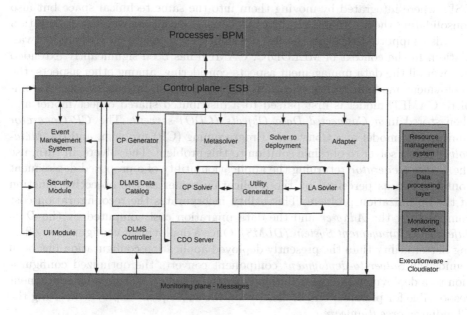

**Fig. 1.** High-level overview of the MELODIC platform architecture with blue elements ensuring the integration, the red elements are the components of the *upperware* and the yellow components belong to the *executionware* (Color figure online)

## 2.2 Upperware

The Upperware part of the MELODIC platform is responsible for modeling, profiling, reasoning, and orchestrating the application deployment. CAMEL[4] is considered a super-DSL which includes multiple DSLs, each focusing on a particular aspect of application modeling. CAMEL has been designed based on the Eclipse Modeling Framework (EMF) [4] and the Object Constraint Language (OCL)[5]. EMF Ecore enables the specification of meta-models based on the Unified Modeling Language (UML), while OCL constraints accompany these meta-model specifications by introducing additional domain semantics. CAMEL has been derived from several preexisting languages, including:

---

[3] http://cloudiator.org/.

[4] http://camel-dsl.org/.

[5] https://www.omg.org/spec/OCL/About-OCL/.

1. CloudML [15] for supporting the application deployment aspects;
2. Saloon feature meta-model [17], for the coverage of provider modelling; and
3. Common European Research Information Format (CERIF) [9], for supporting the organization modeling aspects.

Other sub-DSLs, like the Scalability Rule Language (SRL) [11], were developed during the PaaSage project to cover aspects about the desired reconfiguration of the deployment topologies according to the incoming workload. All these sub-DSLs where integrated by moving them into the same technical space but also consolidating them to diminish their respective conceptual overlaps. Integration was also supported through the use of OCL rules focusing on cross-model validation. In the context of MELODIC, CAMEL has been significantly extended to cover all the data management aspects considering, among other aspects, the deployment modelling of applications based on big data frameworks. A complete CAMEL model is first parsed to a distributed shared object model and then stored in *a Connected Data Objects (CDO) server*[6]. The *CP-Generator* converts the model to a Constraint Programming (CP) problem, and the *Meta-solver* uses a solver to obtain a solution to this problem. The solvers, in turn, use the *Utility Generator* returning the application utility of a proposed deployment configuration as perceived by the application owner as the objective function of the optimization problem. This utility incorporates the reconfiguration cost computed by the *Adapter* and the data migration cost computed by the *Data Life-cycle Management System (DLMS)*. Once a deployment configuration offering better utility than the presently deployed application configuration has been found, the *Solver-to-deployment* component converts the optimized configuration to a deployment model maintained by the *Adapter*, which is the component responsible for planning and orchestrating the subsequent deployment using the Cloudiator *executionware*.

All components, except the DLMS and the Utility Generator, were prototyped in the PaaSage project. However, they have been significantly re-factored by the MELODIC team, and each of them is maintained as a separate open source project that can be reused in other applications, and each component may further reuse other open source projects. Most components are written in Java, but that is not a necessity. As an example, consider the LA-Solver [7] written in C++ based on the Learning Automata (LA) framework[7] and the Theron++ actor framework[8], and using the Nonlinear Optimization (NLopt) library[9]. The developers of the LA-Solver must ensure that it remains compatible with any changes in the underlying frameworks and libraries, and ensure the compatibility of the involved licenses.

---

[6] https://www.eclipse.org/cdo/.

[7] https://bitbucket.org/GeirHo/la-framework/.

[8] https://github.com/GeirHo/TheronPlusPlus/.

[9] https://nlopt.readthedocs.io/en/latest/.

## 2.3  Executionware

The executionware consists of three main modules: The *resource management system* to enact the reconfiguration commands planned by the adapter to create and move components among Cloud providers and ensuring that the components are correctly connected after the application reconfiguration. Application data is managed, and potentially migrated, by the DLMS exploiting the features of Alluxio[10]. The *data processing layer* is responsible for managing the computing resources for big data processing frameworks like Hadoop[11] and Spark[12], and scheduling processing jobs on these resources. Finally, the *monitoring services* are collecting the measurements of the current execution context using a hierarchical and distributed Esper[13] Complex Event Processing (CEP) installation for gathering and aggregating the context metric values. The latter is further discussed in Sect. 4.

# 3  Integration and Control

Integrating components from different development teams into an easy to deploy platform makes it mandatory to have high availability and reliability to ensure a consistent flow of the invoked operations, with full control over an operation's execution and the results it returns. The integration framework must therefore provide unified exception handling and retries of operations. This requires the ability to monitor all operations invoked on the integration layer, with a configurable level of detail, and configurable and easy use of a single logging mechanism for all the invoked operations.

The integration framework must also support flexible orchestration method invocations of underlying components, with the ability to reconfigure this method if needed. It should be possible to configure the orchestration without the need to code and recompile the whole code base. This implies that the integration framework must have support for the most commonly used integration protocols; at least the Simple Object Access Protocol (SOAP), the Representational State Transfer (REST) and the Java Messaging Service (JMS)[14]. It must also support both synchronous and asynchronous communication methods with an easy way to switch from one to the other. Ideally, it should also have the ability to perform complex data model transformations. In general there are three ways to support communication:

---

[10] https://www.alluxio.org/.
[11] http://hadoop.apache.org/.
[12] https://spark.apache.org/.
[13] http://www.espertech.com/esper/.
[14] https://www.techopedia.com/definition/4298/java-message-service-jms.

1. Point to point integration provides the fastest and most resilient scalable communication among the components, especially for large data volumes or low latency applications. However, the effort to maintain the consistency of the connection graph increases exponentially with the number of components in the architecture, and it is impossible to monitor globally the transactions to verify the correct sequence of interaction among the components.
2. Queue based integration requires a central *message broker* receiving messages from *publishers* on a queue and pushing the messages to the *subscribers* of the queue. The broker is a single point of failure and could be a performance bottleneck, but it also provides functionality for persisting messages for dynamically arriving subscribers, and monitor and log transactions on the queues.
3. Using an ESB, which is a common integration method used to integrate enterprise grade systems. The bus provides support for both synchronous and asynchronous communication, and support for most of the integration protocols in use. Furthermore it provides a reliable and easy way to configure the components with high availability support for the bus itself. It also has the ability to integrate with other enterprise applications due to use Enterprise Application Integration (EAI) standards.

For the *Control Plane* of Fig. 1, performance is not a critical issue as long as the integration layer has sufficient performance for the needed orchestration. It is more important that the it is possible to scale the integration layer both horizontally and vertically, and the integration layer must support security mechanisms with support for both authentication and authorization, as well as definition of the access rights to invoke a given operation. Finally, integration layer should be light weight and easy to use as the integration framework will be running with the MELODIC platform for each deployed application. For the selection of the most appropriate integration and adaptation strategy for MELODIC, the following methodology has been used. This methodology has been devised according to our experience and the actual objectives that must be fulfilled, and the methodology consists of the following steps:

1. The first step is to identify the objectives and general requirements for the integration and the adaptation strategy of the project, as well as the purpose of the integration and the alignment of the components.
2. The second step is to research, review, and evaluate typical integration methods used. There are plenty of such methods but – based on our professional experience and knowledge – the most typical and most suitable methods were chosen. This second step is further broken down into the following sub-steps:
   - A state-of-the-art analysis of available integration methods must be conducted. A small set of the most suitable integration methods is then selected for the shortlist.
   - Each of the shortlisted integration methods is compared against the fulfillment of the integration requirements for MELODIC identified in the first step of the methodology. For each method of integration an assessment of the level of fulfillment for each requirement was conducted and

the results are presented in Table 1. The summary results calculated in points are presented in Table 2.

**Table 1.** Summary of the fulfillment of integration requirements

| Requirement | Point-to-Point | Queue | ESB | ESB + BPM |
|---|---|---|---|---|
| Reliability | Not OK | Partially | OK | OK |
| Performance | Partially | OK | OK | OK |
| Scalability | Not OK | Partially | OK | OK |
| High availability | Not OK | Partially | OK | OK |
| Flexible orchestration | Not OK | Not OK | Not OK | OK |
| Synchronous + asynchronous | Not OK | Not OK | OK | OK |
| Security | Not OK | OK | OK | OK |
| Monitoring | Partially | Partially | OK | OK |
| Logging | Partially | Partially | OK | OK |
| Different integration protocols | Not OK | Not OK | OK | OK |
| Data model transformation | Not OK | Not OK | Partially | OK |
| Exceptions + retries | Partially | Partially | Partially | OK |
| Low resource usage | OK | OK | Partially | Partially |
| Easy to use | OK | OK | Partially | Partially |

Based on the results presented in Table 2, the ESB with BPM method has been chosen as integration method for the MELODIC platform as only an ESB is able to satisfy all the requirements. Three possible open source solutions have been evaluated as the framework to implement the ESB:

1. ServiceMix[15] is a high performance and available integration solution, and considered the most mature and stable.
2. MuleESB[16] is the most innovative solution, especially in the Cloud computing area, with an easy to use Graphical User Interface (GUI) and optional paid support from the developer team at MuleSoft.
3. WSO2[17] ESB is a dynamically developed integration solution, supported by the WSO2 technology provider, but is still not fully matured. Paid support is offered.

After carefully evaluating each of these framework, the MuleESB was chosen as the most suitable ESB implementation for the MELODIC platform. The methodology and details of ranking calculations for the various options are provided in [21], and summarised in Table 3.

---

[15] http://servicemix.apache.org/.

[16] https://www.mulesoft.com/platform/soa/mule-esb-open-source-esb.

[17] https://wso2.com/products/enterprise-service-bus.

**Table 2.** Ease of use ranking of the different integration methods

| Requirement | Point-to-point | Queue | ESB | ESB + BPM |
|---|---|---|---|---|
| Reliability | 0 | 3 | 5 | 5 |
| Performance | 3 | 5 | 5 | 5 |
| Scalability | 0 | 3 | 5 | 5 |
| High availability | 0 | 3 | 5 | 5 |
| Flexible orchestration | 0 | 0 | 0 | 5 |
| Synchronous + asynchronous | 0 | 0 | 5 | 5 |
| Security | 0 | 5 | 5 | 5 |
| Monitoring | 3 | 3 | 5 | 5 |
| Logging | 3 | 3 | 5 | 5 |
| Different integration protocols | 0 | 0 | 5 | 5 |
| Data model transformation | 0 | 0 | 3 | 5 |
| Exceptions + retries | 3 | 3 | 3 | 5 |
| Low resource usage | 5 | 5 | 3 | 3 |
| Easy to use | 5 | 5 | 3 | 3 |
| Sum of points | 25 | 42 | 59 | 67 |

**Table 3.** Choosing the Enterprise Service Bus (ESB) platform

| Criteria | ServiceMix | Mule ESB | WSO ESB |
|---|---|---|---|
| Stable and reliable solution | Yes | Yes | Yes |
| Cloud computing support | No | Yes | Yes |
| Easy user interface | Yes | Yes | Yes |
| Support of different integration patterns | No | Yes | Yes |

Integration goes beyond just enabling communication among the components and surveillance of their operation. Orchestration of the components means that one must start the components in certain orders, establish the right connections once the components have started, and take corrective actions if something goes wrong to ensure the high availability of the orchestrated components. Thus, this goes beyond a simple work flow as a flexible logic implementation is needed that supports most of the integration protocols and integration with other enterprise applications using EAI. It is better to regard the orchestration as a *process*, and hence use a BPM, which is a standard approach for describing and executing business processes. For the BPM implementation, four possible solutions were evaluated:

1. Activiti[18] is one of the oldest and most mature open source BPM implementations.

---

[18] https://www.activiti.org/.

**Table 4.** Choosing the Business Process Management (BPM) platform

| Criteria | Activiti | jBPM | Camunda | Flowable |
|---|---|---|---|---|
| Easy maintenance and deployment | Yes | No | Yes | Yes |
| REST support | Yes | Yes | Yes | Yes |
| Docker images availability | No | Yes | Yes | No |
| Easy upgrade and maintainability | No | No | Yes | No |

2. jBPM[19] is also a mature and stable BPM implementation, developed by Jboss[20], with integration support for the business rule server Drools[21]. However, it requires the whole Jboss technology stack, which makes the MELODIC platform unnecessary complicated.
3. Camunda[22] is a mature and robust implementation of BPM. It does not require the whole Jboss stack to work.
4. Flowable[23] is the newest solution, and it is a fork developed by a team of former Activiti developers. However, the Flowable project is not yet mature, and so it fails to satisfy the reliability requirements of the MELODIC platform.

The result of the evaluation was to use Camunda as the BPM implementation for the MELODIC platform [21]. The summary evaluation is given in Table 4.

In PaaSage the actual deployment of the management platform was done directly on server or Virtual Machine (VM) using shell scripts and the configuration tool Chef[24], but alternatively, one could have used Ansible[25]. The advantages of deploying directly on the server or VM using configuration tools are that they do not require creating additional artefacts during the build process, and that they do not introduce additional virtualization layers. However, one often faces a very complex configuration process with many dependencies, and this leads to a *fragile* deployment process where one requires a certain version of the operating system and the libraries used, and the deployed components are not configured separately, but are dependent. In addition, direct deployment requires knowledge about the specific configuration tool used in the process.

In contrast, the development and integration process can be significantly simplified by the use of a container based technology like Docker[26]. The use of containers allows the separation of components and run-time environments created during the build process as there are no dependencies on the underlying operating system and libraries since the complete run-time environment is

---

[19] https://www.jbpm.org/.
[20] https://www.jboss.org/.
[21] https://www.drools.org/.
[22] https://camunda.com/.
[23] https://www.flowable.org/.
[24] https://www.chef.io/chef/.
[25] https://www.ansible.com/.
[26] https://www.docker.com/.

included in the container image. This enables each component developer to be responsible for his or her own component with minimal dependencies between components at run-time level. Hence, the deployment, management and configuration processes are simplified, and the management and distribution of the containers are facilitated by Docker Swarm[27]. The only disadvantage of using containers is the introduction of an additional virtualization layer. It is not a full virtualization like for a VM but light virtualisation, so the impact on performance is minimal [6]. However, there may be a price to pay in terms of total memory required or storage space as it will be additive with containers, whereas resources could be shared under a direct deployment.

If particular components are not designed to run within containers, Docker images can effectively be prepared even for these components. Also the ESB and the BPM frameworks are prepared to run within containers. Finally, owing to the use of Docker Swarm, it is possible to ensure high availability and resource management for the MELODIC platform as it is possible to run MELODIC platform components on separate servers or VMs. Consequently, all MELODIC platform components are running in Docker containers, and we are currently investigating how to make a *lean* integration using Docker containers.

## 4   Monitoring

A flexible monitoring mechanism is needed for the deployment and reconfiguration of the modern, distributed IT systems [14]. The number of monitoring events and the ability to process them efficiently is a critical issue for such systems, since it can reach more than 10 000 events per second for large scale, big data, distributed systems [18]. The use of a central metric collection and processing point may result in a high network bandwidth used just for monitoring purposes. Last, but not least, the existence of only one event processing engine represents a single point of failure [13].

On the other hand, the design and implementation of a Distributed Complex Event Processing (DCEP) [20] approach provides concrete benefits such as avoiding bottlenecks [19], and message flooding and information overloading scenarios that can lead to significant delays in the processing of monitoring data [16]. Consequently, as an initial approach, the DCEP mechanism of the MELODIC platform is deployed in a three-layer architecture [20]:

1. Raw sensor values from the application or the computing platform are processed first at the VM level;
2. Then there is another CEP layer performing event processing at the Cloud Provider level; and Finally, there is a top-level CEP integrated with the MELODIC platform providing the complete view of all events for a cross-Cloud application deployment. Each level will gather, filter, and aggregate sensor value messages and thereby effectively limit the number of messages passed to higher layers.

---

[27] https://docs.docker.com/engine/swarm/themanagement.

In the future, the number of layers may be configured according to the requirements of the particular system at hand, *e.g.* additional layers could be added per Cloud availability zone or even region.

It is therefore paramount that the CEP engine is able to scale in order to cope with a potential huge number of events generated by hundreds of sources; to apply complex formulas for the aggregation of the metrics; and to detect and publish complex events based on event algebra operators over the current global or local application execution context, identified by the all or a subsets of the metric values. Furthermore, the monitoring system must be flexible enough to be able to efficiently handle metrics from a single application component up to huge deployments with hundreds of VMs. Using a DCEP platform facilitates the *Monitoring Plane* and the distribution of metric values to all the other MELODIC components allowing them to create a situation awareness for the application's execution context and decide on necessary application and deployment adaptations. However, at the same time the CEP engine must have low resource usage since one instance will be deployed in each VM to realize the first level of the layered DCEP architecture.

The Esper CEP engine was chosen because it offers a high availability option in comparison to other CEP products, and its basic version can even cope with 500 000 events per second, and it supports a rich set of configurable data windows that can be placed into intersection or union set-logic relationships, while other engines provide a basic set of very simple rolling, sliding, or hopping windows [5]. Esper also supports the expression of complex event patterns that allow us to perform nested queries over a monitored data stream by using the Event Processing Language (EPL) [1], which is an important advantage over even more performance-oriented engines like Siddhi [5]. Finally, Esper supports all aspects of object-oriented design as well as dynamic typing and it can therefore handle schema evolution for adapting event processing rules[28], and it is widely accepted in the event processing community and well-known for its commercial use.

The distributed Esper CEP engines of MELODIC are currently connected by a federation of ActiveMQ[29] brokers with one instance per VM and one central instance in the MELODIC platform. This architecture is easier to integrate and control than a point-to-point communication; it presents sufficient performance as each broker can efficiently cope with up to 22 000 messages per sec and per topic[30]; and in addition it provides a lightweight, open-source JMS compliant solution that offers high availability, high performance, and fault tolerance. In fact, our decision to federate a number of ActiveMQ brokers present some additional advantages over other prominent, open-source distributed streaming platforms like the Apache Kafka[31]. Specifically, using Kafka's features for achieving the required capabilities of our platform would lead to much more complicated communication topologies. In particular, the need to interconnect and manage

---

[28] http://www.espertech.com/esper/esper-faq/#comparison.
[29] http://activemq.apache.org.
[30] http://activemq.apache.org/performance.html.
[31] https://kafka.apache.org/.

several Zookepers, and thus adding further network communication overhead. In addition, since ActiveMQ is JMS compliant, the support and maintenance of a distributed network of brokers together with several Esper engines become efficient and feasible. On the other hand, using Kafka for achieving the same integration would imply the use of dedicated Kafka adapters that have been developed, so far, only for the commercial Enterprise Edition of Esper, which is conflicting with our ambition to build MELODIC using *only* open source technologies.

## 5   Conclusion

The MELODIC platform is based entirely on open source components, as this is the only way to ensure further development and maintenance of the platform. This paper has shown that it is possible to build complex, enterprise grade solutions based on only open source, and it presented the work done for the MELODIC platform and its open source components, frameworks and tools. We hope that our considerations in this respect may enlighten the processes of making similar selections and large scale integration, and that the overall results of MELODIC may inspire the combination and reuse of open source solutions to expand the offerings of high quality open source tools and infrastructures.

## References

1. Albek, E., Bax, E., Billock, G., Chandy, K.M., Swett, I.: An event processing language (EPL) for building sense and respond applications. In: 19th IEEE International Parallel and Distributed Processing Symposium, pp. 5 pp.-, April 2005. https://doi.org/10.1109/IPDPS.2005.97
2. Rossini, A., et al.: The cloud application modelling and execution language (CAMEL), p. 39. Open Access Repositorium der Universität Ulm (2017). https://doi.org/10.18725/OPARU-4339
3. Bergmayr, A., et al.: The evolution of CloudML and its applications. In: Paige, R., Cabot, J., Brambilla, M., Hill, J.H. (eds.) Proceedings of the 3rd International Workshop on Model-Driven Engineering on and for the Cloud and 18th International Conference on Model Driven Engineering Languages and Systems (MoDELS 2015), vol. 1563, pp. 13–18. CEUR Workshop Proceedings (2015). http://ceur-ws.org/Vol-1563/
4. Steinberg, D., Budinsky, F., Paternostro, M., Merks, E.: EMF: Eclipse Modeling Framework. Part of the Eclipse Series series, 2nd edn. Addison-Wesley Professional, Boston (2008)
5. Dayarathna, M., Perera, S.: Recent advancements in event processing. ACM Comput. Surv. (CSUR) 51(2), 33 (2018)
6. Felter, W., Ferreira, A., Rajamony, R., Rubio, J.: An updated performance comparison of virtual machines and Linux containers. In: 2015 IEEE International Symposium on Performance Analysis of Systems and Software (ISPASS), pp. 171–172, March 2015. https://doi.org/10.1109/ISPASS.2015.7095802

7. Horn, G.: A vision for a stochastic reasoner for autonomic cloud deployment. In: Babar, M.A., Dumas, M., Solberg, A. (eds.) Proceedings of the Second Nordic Symposium on Cloud Computing & Internet Technologies (NordiCloud 2013), pp. 46–53. ACM, Oslo, September 2013. https://doi.org/10.1145/2513534.2513543

8. Blair, G., Bencomo, N., France, R.B.: Models@run.time. Computer **42**(10), 22–27 (2009). https://doi.org/10.1109/MC.2009.326

9. Jeffery, K., Houssos, N., Jörg, B., Asserson, A.: Research information management: the CERIF approach. Int. J. Metadata Semant. Ontol. **9**(1), 5–14 (2014). https://doi.org/10.1504/IJMSO.2014.059142

10. Jeffery, K., Horn, G., Schubert, L.: A vision for better cloud applications. In: Ardagna, D., Schubert, L. (eds.) Proceedings of the 2013 International Workshop on Multi-Cloud Applications and Federated Clouds, MultiCloud 2013, pp. 7–12. ACM, Prague, April 2013. https://doi.org/10.1145/2462326.2462329

11. Kritikos, K., Domaschka, J., Rossini, A.: SRL: a scalability rule language for multi-cloud environments. In: 2014 IEEE 6th International Conference on Cloud Computing Technology and Science, pp. 1–9, December 2014. https://doi.org/10.1109/CloudCom.2014.170

12. Bass, L., Weber, I., Zhu, L.: DevOps: A Software Architect's Perspective. SEI Series in Software Engineering, 1st edn. Addison Wesley, Boston (2015)

13. Mdhaffar, A., Halima, R.B., Jmaiel, M., Freisleben, B.: A dynamic complex event processing architecture for cloud monitoring and analysis. In: 2013 IEEE 5th International Conference on Cloud Computing Technology and Science, vol. 2, pp. 270–275. IEEE (2013)

14. Munawar, M.A., Ward, P.A.: Adaptive monitoring in enterprise software systems. SysML, June 2006

15. Ferry, N., Chauvel, F., Song, H., Rossini, A., Lushpenko, M., Solberg, A.: CloudMF: model-driven management of multi-cloud applications. ACM Trans. Internet Technol. (TOIT) **18**(2), 16:1–16:24 (2018). https://doi.org/10.1145/3125621

16. Paraiso, F., Hermosillo, G., Rouvoy, R., Merle, P., Seinturier, L.: A middleware platform to federate complex event processing. In: 2012 IEEE 16th International Enterprise Distributed Object Computing Conference (EDOC), pp. 113–122. IEEE (2012)

17. Quinton, C., Haderer, N., Rouvoy, R., Duchien, L.: Towards multi-cloud configurations using feature models and ontologies. In: Proceedings of the 2013 International Workshop on Multi-Cloud Applications and Federated Clouds, MultiCloud 2013, Prague, Czech Republic, pp. 21–26. ACM, New York (2013). https://doi.org/10.1145/2462326.2462332

18. Reidemeister, T.: Fault diagnosis in enterprise software systems using discrete monitoring data. Ph.D. thesis, University of Waterloo, Waterloo, Ontario, Canada (2012)

19. Schultz-Møller, N.P., Migliavacca, M., Pietzuch, P.: Distributed complex event processing with query rewriting. In: Proceedings of the Third ACM International Conference on Distributed Event-Based Systems, p. 4. ACM (2009)

20. Stefanidis, V., Verginadis, Y., Patiniotakis, I., Mentzas, G.: Distributed complex event processing in multiclouds. In: Kritikos, K., Plebani, P., de Paoli, F. (eds.) ESOCC 2018. LNCS, vol. 11116, pp. 105–119. Springer, Cham (2018). https://doi.org/10.1007/978-3-319-99819-0_8

21. Verginadis, Y., et al.: D5.1 integration and adaptation strategy. Technical report, The MELODIC project, February 2018. https://melodic.cloud/, http://www.melodic.cloud/deliverables/D5.1

# Quality-Aware Rapid Software Development Project: The Q-Rapids Project

Xavier Franch[1], Lidia Lopez[1], Silverio Martínez-Fernández[2],
Marc Oriol[1(✉)], Pilar Rodríguez[3], and Adam Trendowicz[2]

[1] Universitat Politècnica de Catalunya, Barcelona, Spain
{franch,llopez,moriol}@essi.upc.edu
[2] Fraunhofer IESE, Kaiserslautern, Germany
{silverio.martinez,
adam.trendowicz}@iese.fraunhofer.de
[3] University of Oulu, Oulu, Finland
pilar.rodriguez@oulu.fi

**Abstract.** Software quality poses continuously new challenges in software development, including aspects related to both software development and system usage, which significantly impact the success of software systems. The Q-Rapids H2020 project defines an evidence-based, data-driven quality-aware rapid software development methodology. Quality requirements (QRs) are incrementally elicited, refined and improved based on data gathered from software repositories, project management tools, system usage and quality of service. This data is analysed and aggregated into quality-related key strategic indicators (e.g., development effort required to include a given QR in the next development cycle) which are presented to decision makers using a highly informative dashboard. The Q-Rapids platform is being evaluated in-premises by the four companies participating in the consortium, reporting useful lessons learned and directions for new development.

**Keywords:** Software quality · Data-driven requirements engineering ·
Software analytic tools · Software repositories · Quality models ·
Agile software development · Rapid software development ·
Quality requirements · Non-functional requirements

## 1 Introduction

The Q-Rapids project proposes a data-driven approach to the elicitation, prioritization and management of quality requirements (QRs), see Fig. 1. Data comes from: the organization, through software development repositories and project management tools; the users, through explicit feedback and usage logs. This basic data is elaborated into strategic indicators (e.g., team productivity, product quality) and presented to decision-makers through a dashboard that also offers techniques as what-if analysis and prediction. Expert-defined alerts inform about violations on quality thresholds, and QR patterns are suggested to remedy them. The decision-maker can explore the effects of applying them and eventually decide to include a QR in the backlog, closing the cycle.

M. Mazzara et al. (Eds.): TOOLS 2019, LNCS 11771, pp. 378–392, 2019.
https://doi.org/10.1007/978-3-030-29852-4_32

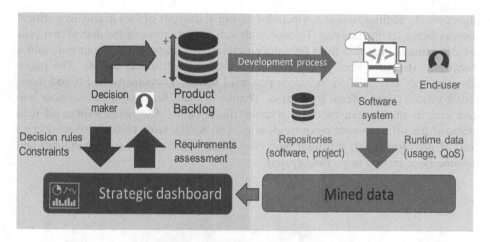

**Fig. 1.** The Q-Rapids framework

The project started in November 2016 and finishes in October 2019. The consortium is composed of 3 research partners (UPC, U. Oulu and Fraunhofer-IESE) and 4 companies (Bittium, ITTI, Softeam and Nokia). The project URL is https://www.q-rapids.eu/ and the software may be found at https://github.com/q-rapids.

The rest of the paper is organized as follows. Section 2 explains the first part of the Q-Rapids cycle, namely data gathering and analysis. Section 3 introduces Q-Rapids process related aspects, remarkably process metrics. Section 4 provides details on the strategic dashboard fed by the result of the analysis. Section 5 presents the results of the evaluation conducted so far. Then, Sect. 6 summarizes some lessons learned and Sect. 7 finalizes the paper with the conclusions and related work.

## 2 Data Gathering and Analysis

The ultimate goal of data gathering and analysis is to gain relevant knowledge about software quality (in particular at runtime) from the available software data, including development and runtime data. To achieve this goal, several tasks must be accomplished. Figure 2 presents the Cross Industry Standard Process for Data Mining, CRISP-DM [1], which Q-Rapids applied to guide analysis of software quality.

In the *business understanding* phase, the research goals of the project and business expectations of the project partners were translated into the specific objectives of data analysis. One of the analysis goals was to explore dependency between quality of software during development and its runtime quality. The development quality was represented by properties of software artifacts and development environment, in particular code, whereas runtime quality was represented by software misbehavior during testing and operation (in particular user crash reports).

The *data understanding* phase aimed at identifying sources of relevant software quality data available at application project partners and gaining first insights into the data to better understand its meaning and potential usefulness for achieving project objectives. In addition, this phase included an initial analysis of data quality as a critical success factor for the analysis. To cope with various structures of the data at involved project partners, that data from the source systems was imported as documents into a distributed storage system supported by ElasticSearch (ES) and Kibana. The major advantages of this solution include a powerful search functionality of ES and interactive visualizations offered by Kibana. Thanks to these features, initial insights into data and its quality can be made without much effort. The main sources of data included the software code repositories (e.g., Git, SVN), issue tracking systems (e.g., Jira, Mantis, Redmine), structural properties of software code (e.g., SonarQube) and runtime issue reports (e.g., Hockeyapp).

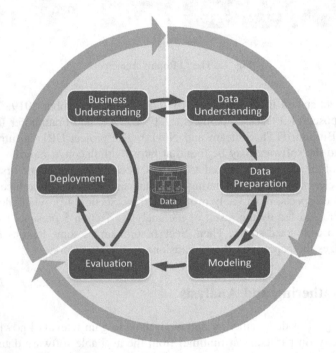

**Fig. 2.** CRISP-DM model used in Q-Rapids to guide the analysis of software quality

The *data preparation* phase focused on handling data quality deficits and preparing the data for specific data analyses. Data preparation tasks included: (1) integrating data stored in different source systems and structures, (2) handling data quality deficits, such as incomplete, inconsistent, and incorrect data, and (3) transforming data into the format acceptable for specific methods and tools used during the analysis. The data preparation phase is in practice the most challenging and the most expensive phase of the entire data analysis cycle; Q-Rapids was not different in this matter. Table 1 summarizes the most relevant challenges and the associated lessons we learned in the context of Q-Rapids. Summarizing, Q-Rapids replicates the experiences gained in several other projects regarding relatively low usefulness of software engineering data for quantitative analysis of software quality. Analysis of dependencies between development- and runtime-quality of software requires, on the one hand, complete and consistent data on potentially relevant quality factors (product-, process- and context characteristics); on the other hand, analysis of quality dependencies requires the data from different sources can be connected to each other, i.e., be integrated. Unfortunately, primary objectives of data collection do typically not include quality analysis and modeling. For example, the primary objective of issue tracking is to record and monitor progress of software issues, not to learn from issues, especially in connection with other software development aspects such as properties of software artifacts issues refer to or properties of the environment in which an issue occurred. In other words, quantitative cause-effect analysis does typically not belong to primary objectives of data collection.

**Table 1.** Example challenges of data preparation and analysis in Q-Rapids

| Challenge | Recommendation |
|---|---|
| **Availability/Accessibility:** The required quality data is not available because appropriate data collection tools or/and processes are missing or systems were data is stored cannot be accessed. E.g., available code measurement tool does not cover all important base code metrics. For instance, although SonarQube provides data on violations of rules that are based upon specific base metrics it does not provide raw data for these metrics | Select and set up data collection tool based on the explicitly defined business and analysis objectives, and potentially relevant data required for achieving these objectives. Data analysis should always start with business and data understanding (first two phases of the CRISP-DM model) |
| **Completeness:** Issue and change tracking data are incomplete, e.g., documented code changes are not associated to any issue | Predefine orthogonal issue categories; use them consistently to classify issues; ensure every change can be associated to an issue |
| **Correctness:** Actual type (nature) of change is not documented and cannot be recognized automatically. In particular, file rename or movement is recognized as deletion and addition of an entire file | Label actual amount of change (e.g., in terms of its labor cost) to distinguish between changes that are or are not significant from the perspective of their potential impact on software quality |
| **Consistency:** Summary changes for multiple issues of different type are documented in single change tracking entry. So, the exact amount of change per issue type is unknown | Collection of already aggregated data should be avoided. Raw data on possibly atomic level should be supported by data collection tools (e.g., issue and change records) |
| **Consistency:** Inconsistent temporal granularity of different data sets, e.g., code changes and measurement data are recorded per commit (e.g., several times per day) but test and usage issues are recorded once a week or on an irregularly basis | Associated data should be collected on a consistent granularity level, i.e., one entry per issue or issue type (e.g., new feature development, bug fix) to support data integration and cause-effect quality analyses |

*(continued)*

**Table 1.** (*continued*)

| Challenge | Recommendation |
|---|---|
| **Precision:** Data is collected on a granularity level inappropriate for accomplishing analysis objectives. An example are source code measurements, collected on a file level. In such case, fine-granular changes on class- and function-level can compensate each other within a file and be thus not visible in the corresponding measurement data | Based on explicitly defined business and analysis goals, specify precision (granularity) requirements for the necessary data. Set up tools that support collecting data with the required precision |
| **Redundancy:** Issue tracking data contain duplicated entries | Data collection and reporting tool should support real-time checks for duplicated, incorrect and inconsistent data entries |

The *modeling* phase various analysis and visualization techniques are applied on the prepared data to explore and model software quality dependencies represented by the data. Example analysis may investigate the probability (or frequency) of software bugs of runtime issues (user issue reports) in association with structural properties of software code and amount and type of software changes along its evolution. Figure 3 illustrates example quality analysis. Input data are gathered from multiple sources and include software code quality metrics, which represent specific product factors, and product quality data in terms of bug issues found in the software. The analysis provides two outcomes: relevancy of individual metrics as predictors of product quality and a quality model that captures quantitatively dependencies between the most relevant metrics and the product quality.

In the *evaluation* phase the outcomes of the data analysis phases, incl. data understanding, preparation, and modeling, are assessed from the perspective of business expectations defined in the very first business understanding phase. In our case these where to overall Q-Rapids research objectives and the specific business objectives of project partners whose software project data were analyzed in the project.

Finally, during the *deployment* phase, models (e.g., quality forecasting) will be integrated into the Q-Rapids tool to provide information to the strategies dashboard (e.g., predicted evolution of software quality or indication of the most relevant factors influencing software quality). For example, prediction models created in Python might be deployed as REST API service. As soon as new project data are available in ElasticSearch, Q-Rapids dashboard will call the Quality Model API with the required input data (metrics) and receive the answer regarding the predicted quality (forecasted number of bug issues to be found).

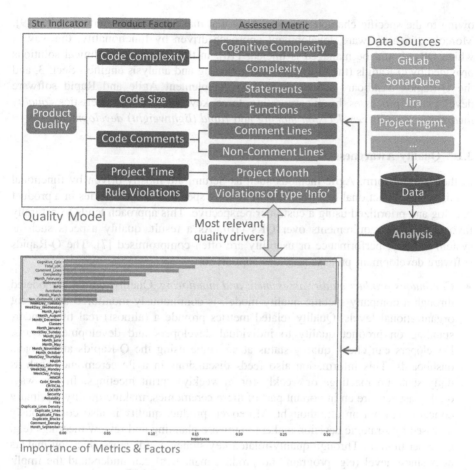

**Fig. 3.** Example of data-driven quality model

# 3 The Q-Rapids Software Development Process

Q-Rapids provides solutions for quality management in the context of Agile and Rapid Software Development. Under the umbrella of the Agile Manifesto, agile software development methods, such as Scrum and XP, are already the most popular software development approaches in industry [2]. Indeed, the tendency is towards reducing development cycles more and more to achieve a continuous software development flow, using principles from Lean thinking (e.g. lean software development [3]) and methods such as Kanban [4]. This is commonly known as Rapid software development [5, 6]. However, faster and more frequent release cycles should not compromise software quality [7, 8]. Indeed, quality is essential to be able to satisfy customers, which is, certainly, the ultimate goal of Agile and Rapid Software Development processes.

The literature evidences that this is not often the case, though. For example, technical debt (TD) has become a popular concept in Agile software development owing to the specific characteristics of ASD that make it prone to incurring TD [9]. Moreover, in a software development approach driven by functionality, the way in which QRs should be managed is unclear [10]. In this sense, the technical solutions provided by Q-Rapids (the Q-Rapids data gathering and analysis engine - Sect. 3, and the Q-Rapids dashboard - Sect. 5) aim to complement Agile and Rapid software development processes by incorporating three key process characteristics: *quality awareness, data-driven decision making* and *rapid (lightweight) development*.

## 3.1  Quality Awareness

In their current form, Agile methods such as Scrum, are mostly driven by functional requirements. Functional requirements are usually specified as user stories in a product backlog and prioritized using a customer perspective. This approach tends to naturally favor functional requirements over QRs [10]. As a result, quality aspects such as system security, performance or usability are often compromised [7]. The Q-Rapids software development process provides support for:

- *Continuous product quality assessment and monitoring.* Quality, which is modeled through a company specific quality model, is continuously monitored at different organizational levels. Quality related metrics provide a (almost) real time understanding on product quality to individual developers and development teams. Developers can check quality status at any time using the Q-Rapids and Kibana dashboards. This information also feeds discussions in agile ceremonies such as daily stand-up meetings or weekly (or bi-weekly) sprint meetings. In this way, quality aspects are an important part of these ceremonies, making quality a primary concern, and not an afterthought. Moreover, product quality is also continuously assessed by strategic decision makers in release planning and review meetings (e.g. once per month). Through quality-related key strategic indicators, decision makers at business level (e.g. program and product managers) can understand the implications that their decisions will have upon product and process quality.
- *Incremental elicitation of QRs*: the Q-Rapids software development process provides incremental and semi-automatic elicitation of QRs based on the continuous analysis of quality data [11]. Thus, product owners and development teams get support when defining and prioritizing quality related backlog items. QRs are explicitly included in product backlogs, decreasing the risk to overlook them during sprint planning meetings. Moreover, Q-Rapids supports the tasks of refining and improving QRs as the development progresses, using practices such as backlog grooming and sprint planning.
- *Continuous process quality assessment and monitoring*: besides product quality, Q-Rapids also offers support to continuously monitor the status of the process. Through a complete set of process metrics, Q-Rapids supports ceremonies such as Agile retrospectives, in which the way of working is discussed. Development teams can use Q-Rapids to analyze trends and process metrics values. The hard evidence reported by Q-Rapids motivates the team to find problems in order to resolve them and improve their way of working. For example, Q-Rapids can be used to identify process bottlenecks or improve estimation capabilities. Indeed, the Q-Rapids

solutions and visualization of process metrics fill the current gap on tools related to processes in Agile and Rapid software development. Most existing tools focus on product quality or on continuous integration, without measures for the process (e.g. SonarQube). Basically, GitLab Time Tracker is one of the few competing solutions that could be used to analyze the process. However, Q-Rapids proposes a wider set of calculated process metrics, better visualization as well as enhanced analysis capabilities.

## 3.2 Evidence-Based, Data-Driven Software Development Process

Agile methods, such as Scrum, are founded on an evidence-based management style. Instead of making long-term predictions, Agile methods embrace a learning culture in which evidence drives decisions. However, to make accurate decisions, evidence must be reliable as well. Software analytics play a key role in this context. Agile's incremental development and extensive use of automation produce enormous amount of data that, properly used, can guide more accurate decisions. Quality related decisions in the Q-Rapids software development process are based on the insights provided by the Q-Rapids data gathering and analysis engine, which collects data from different systems such as software code repositories (e.g., Git, SVN), issue tracking systems (e.g., Jira, Mantis, Redmine), structural properties of software code (e.g., SonarQube) and runtime issue reports (e.g., Hockeyapp).

## 3.3 Rapid Software Development Process

A key aspect of the Q-Rapids software development process is that it supports quality management in a light-weight manner. Deploying the solution may be heavy at the beginning (e.g. defining the quality model, searching for data sources, customizing/defining connectors, etc.). However, once installed, quality support is smoothly integrated into existing agile practices such as sprint planning and review meetings, daily-stand up meetings and sprint retrospectives. Still, some extra practices and roles are needed to maintain the system up and running and to ensure that data is reliable and properly collected and analysed (e.g. data engineer).

The Q-Rapids software development process is being developed in close collaboration with the four companies participating in the consortium. It includes the use of Q-Rapids solutions in software development practices, such as coding and testing, and product management practices, such as sprint planning. It also includes the related supporting processes needed to make sure that the Q-Rapids machinery is up and running.

# 4   Strategic Decision Making Dashboard

The main goal of the strategic dashboard is twofold: (a) aggregating the gathered and analysed data into strategic indicators (SIs) and (b) providing extra analysis techniques that support decision-makers in their decisions.

Based on the quality factors resulting from the analysed data (see Sect. 2), the process metrics (see Sect. 3), and in collaboration with the use cases, we defined the following strategic indicators: *Blocking* (assessing when there is some problem that can alter the regular process flow, identifying potential blocking situations) [12], *Product Quality* (assessing the source code quality), *Process Performance* (assessing the fulfillment of the development process efficiently) [13], and *On-Time Delivery* (assessing the capability of fulfilling the issues planned for a specific release meeting internal and external delivery schedules) [14]. Although there is a generic definition for these strategic indicators, they must be customised in each use case to adapt them to the specific needs. For instance, for *Process Performance*, we have definitions from using two quality factors (*Testing Performance* and *Issues Velocity*) to five (*Testing Performance, Issues Velocity, Development Speed*, and *Realized Requirements*). Figure 4 includes the generic definition for the strategic indicators.

The list of strategic indicators has been extended by some use cases to support their specific scenarios. E.g., Softeam defined *Product Readiness* and *Quality Feedback Loop*, and Nokia defined *Operational Quality* and *Hardware Reliability*. In the case of Softeam, it is worth mentioning that the *Quality Feedback Loop* is a strategic indicator devoted to monitor the QRs generated by the dashboard (see below).

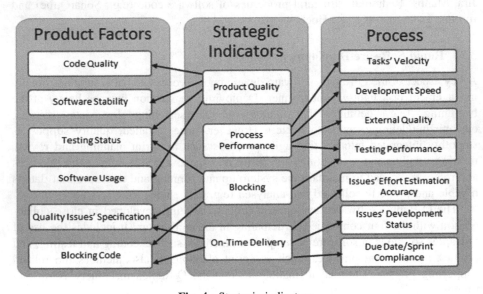

**Fig. 4.** Strategic indicators

A brief description of the main features of the dashboard are as follows.

*Quality Assessment Visualization.* The dashboard includes several views to analyse the status of the SIs, i.e. indicators meant to support decision-makers to analyse the achievement of their strategic goals, such as product quality, customer satisfaction, or process performance. These SIs are defined as an aggregation of quality factors resulting from the data analysis, and these factors as an aggregation of quality metrics. The dashboard allows the decision-maker to navigate through these aggregations to have a deeper understanding of the assessment. Figure 5 depicts the different kinds of charts and the navigational path.

*SI Assessment.* The dashboard provides two strategies to compute SIs: a quantitative approach based on computing the average of the quality factors, and a qualitative approach involving experts and historical data to define a Bayesian Network model [15]. Figure 5 shows the BN model for the *Product Quality* strategic indicator, impacted by *Code Quality*, *Stability*, and *Testing Status* quality factors. The probabilities for quality factors are computed using historical data, and for the strategic indicators we use domain experts.

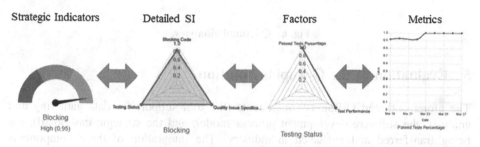

**Fig. 5.** Quality assessment navigation

*Prediction.* The dashboard provides several forecasting techniques that, applied over the SIs, allow decision-makers to analyse trends and behavioral patterns. Among others, it supports PROPHET, ARIMA, ETS, and THETA forecasting techniques [16, 17].

*What-if Analysis.* Decision-makers can simulate some scenarios in order to see how different simulated values on metrics and factors would affect the assessment of their strategic indicators.

*QR Candidates.* When the assessment values are below a given threshold, an alert is automatically raised and the dashboard identifies QR candidates from a QR patterns catalogue that, when implemented, would solve the alert [11]. For instance, if the dashboard receive an alert because the *testing performance* factor (impacting the *process performance* strategic indicator) assessment is below the defined threshold, the dashboard would suggest to consider the following QRs: (QR1) *the commit response time should be at least X%,* and (QR2) *the error correction should be at least X%.* The decision-maker can simulate the impact of each QR on the strategic indicators (see Fig. 6 for QR2). Then, the decision-maker can export the QR to the tool managing the backlog (e.g. Jira, OpenProject).

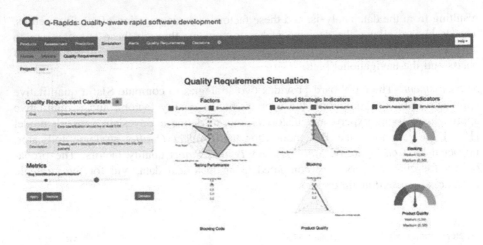

**Fig. 6.** QR simulation view

## 5   Evaluation of the Q-Rapids Solution

The aforementioned Q-Rapids components (the tool support for data gathering and analysis, the software development process model, and the strategic dashboard), are being transferred and evaluated in industry. The integration of these components comprise the Q-Rapids solution, which consists of both tool support and its corresponding process model. During the technology transfer of Q-Rapids, three releases have been deployed by the four industry partners in the Q-Rapids project (Bittium, ITTI, Nokia, and Softeam[1]) within their specific development environment, where practitioners have given feedback of the Q-Rapids solution, and used it within pilot projects for several months (since November 2018). It is worth mentioning that these companies have different profiles (one large corporation, two large/medium companies, one SME) and produce different types of systems (e.g., from modeling tools to telecommunication software).

The technology transfer and evaluation of the Q-Rapids solution follows a multi-staged process aligned with and supporting the iterative development process of the Q-Rapids components and integrated solution (see Table 2). The multi-stage evaluation process comprises two phases: formative and summative. First, the formative stage focused on supporting the evolution of concepts and ideas mainly of research work. Thus, we evaluated the first prototype and the intermediate version focusing on single components and functionalities of the Q-Rapids solution in controlled environments. We finished the formative stage with a static validation (i.e., presentation to prospective users) [18]. After the formative stage, the ongoing summative stage consists of the real use of the integrated Q-Rapids solution in under real settings of four pilot projects (i.e., dynamic validation with practitioners on-site).

---

[1] https://www.q-rapids.eu/consortium.

- *Formative evaluation on component level.* These components have been the incremental outputs of the scientific work packages, such as components implementing an expert-based or data-driven quality model for actionable analytics, company specific software development process models, and a strategic dashboard for supporting decision-making. This formative evaluation took place at developer sites for the first release of the Q-Rapids solution, and ended with a static validation presenting the component's capabilities to prospective users. The formative evaluation focused on technical aspects (e.g., general feasibility, scalability, and appropriateness of the gathered and visualized data). It was helpful to identify interweaved improvements of the components being developed for next releases. Examples of identified and addressed suggestions for improvement from the industrial context have been: explicitly linking the strategic indicators, quality factors, and metrics with other information sources (e.g., source code, user stories, and list of issues) in order to better support the decision making process with the help of the strategic dashboard [19], include visualization of the raw data in the quality model to facilitate decision-making [20], give a practitioner attractive support to follow of the software development process model (e.g., available on an interactive website rather than long documents[2]), and simplify the Q-Rapids solution installation and configuration process with easy deployment options such dockers [21]. Despite these suggestions for improvement, initial results have been promising in pilot projects, since participants agree on the understandability and usefulness of the Q-Rapids solution components.
- *Summative evaluation of the third and final release of the integrated Q-Rapids solution.* The summative evaluation is focusing on the application of the integrated Q-Rapids solution under the realistic circumstances of four selected projects in which the integrated Q-Rapids solution is being used. The Q-Rapids solution is being evaluated by its impact on the selected projects where it is being used. Preliminary results helped to characterize the value provided by the solution, since Q-Rapids users have experienced benefits such as including the semi-automated functionality of creating QRs, the improvement of product quality and process performance, and an increased awareness of product readiness. Furthermore, another goal is considering suggestions for the successful commercialisation of the solution, such as looking for bilateral collaborations with industrial partners out of the Q-Rapids consortium interested in the capabilities of the Q-Rapids solution, and making effective the installation process (which currently it is one of the main barriers for adoption).

---

[2] https://www.oulu.fi/q-rapids/.

**Table 2.** Phases of the evaluation and technology transfer of Q-Rapids.

| Characteristic | Iteration 1 | Iteration 2 | Iteration 3 |
|---|---|---|---|
| Q-Rapids solution release | Proof-of-concept | Consolidated version | Final |
| Evaluation phase | Formative evaluation | Formative evaluation | Summative evaluation |
| Object of study | Components of the Q-Rapids solution release | Components of the Q-Rapids solution release | Integrated Q-Rapids solution as a whole |
| Months within the project | From month 7 to month 15 | From month 16 to month 24 | From month 25 to month 33 |
| Environment | Controlled environment | Static validation (i.e., presentation to prospective users) | Dynamic validation (i.e.,. pilot project using the tool) |

## 6 Lessons Learned

In [21], we have presented the most relevant lessons learned during the project on the potential adoption of Q-Rapids by practitioners, based on the experiences of the companies in the consortium. Some of them follow:

- Incremental adoption approach. Companies are advised to start using Q-Rapids in a small product first in order to understand the solution and start to grow a base of tailored connectors and a quality model fit for purpose.
- Transparency in the organizational culture. The visibility of all quality-related issues managed in Q-Rapids provides confidence to decision-makers and other involved stakeholders.
- Single access point to quality assessment. One advantage that was not really foreseen in the conception of the project is the possibility to put together lots of indicators that are normally managed through several tools.
- Tailoring to product and projects. Quality is an elusive concept that may change in every single project, even in the same organization. It is important to tailor the quality model and strategic indicators to the needs in each context.
- Expert involvement. The Q-Rapids solution requires the participation of several experts in order to get the most, from developers to implement connectors up to data scientists to analyse the collected data.

## 7 Conclusions

In this paper we have presented the highlights of the Q-Rapids project. We have described the three major parts of the delivered solution (data gathering and analysis; software development process with Q-Rapids; strategic dashboard) and shown the evaluation done, as well as some lessons learned. More information is available in the project website, www.q-rapids.edu. Software components are available at https://github.com/q-rapids.

At this point of time, very close to the completion of the project, we can say that we have delivered a solution that fulfils most of the original objectives of the project. However, there are many improvements that we plan to address in the near future. The implementation of machine learning approaches to fine-tune and improve the strategic indicators definition in every organization is one of the most challenging extensions. Another important topic is the better definition of cost functions for the QR patterns, which would allow to make decisions in a more informed manner.

**Acknowledgements.** This work is a result of the Q-Rapids project, which has received funding from the European Union's Horizon 2020 research and innovation programme under grant agreement No. 732253.

# References

1. Shearer, C.: The CRISP-DM model: the new blueprint for data mining. J. Data Warehouse 5 (4), 13–22 (2000)
2. Rodríguez, P., Markkula, J., Oivo, M., Turula, K.: Survey on agile and lean usage in finnish software industry. In: Proceedings of the ACM-IEEE International Symposium on Empirical Software Engineering and Measurement (ESEM) (2012)
3. Poppendieck, M., Poppendieck, T.: Lean Software Development: An Agile Toolkit. Addison-Wesley, Boston (2003)
4. Anderson, D.J.: Kanban: Successful Evolutionary Change for Your Technology Business. Blue Hole Press, Sequim (2010)
5. Fitzgerald, B., Stol, K.J.: Continuous software engineering: a roadmap and agenda. J. Syst. Softw. **123**, 176–189 (2017)
6. Rodríguez, P., et al.: Continuous deployment of software intensive products and services: a systematic mapping study. J. Syst. Softw. **123**, 263–291 (2017)
7. Ramesh, B., Cao, L., Baskerville, R.: Agile requirements engineering practices and challenges: an empirical study. Inf. Syst. J. **20**(5), 449–480 (2010)
8. Guzmán, L., Oriol, M., Rodríguez, P., Franch, X., Jedlitschka, A., Oivo, M.: How can quality awareness support rapid software development? – A research preview. In: Grünbacher, P., Perini, A. (eds.) REFSQ 2017. LNCS, vol. 10153, pp. 167–173. Springer, Cham (2017). https://doi.org/10.1007/978-3-319-54045-0_12
9. Behutiye, W.N., Rodríguez, P., Oivo, M., Tosun, A.: Analyzing the concept of technical debt in the context of agile software development: a systematic literature review. Inf. Softw. Technol. **82**, 139–158 (2017)
10. Behutiye, W., et al.: Management of quality requirements in agile and rapid software development: a systematic mapping study. Submitted to IST
11. Franch, X., et al.: Data-driven elicitation, assessment and documentation of quality requirements in agile software development. In: Krogstie, J., Reijers, H. (eds.) CAiSE 2018. LNCS, vol. 10816, pp. 587–602. Springer, Cham (2018). https://doi.org/10.1007/978-3-319-91563-0_36
12. Franch, X., et al.: Data-driven Requirements engineering in agile projects: the Q-rapids approach. In: Proceedings of the International Workshop on Just-In-Time Requirements (JIT-RE) (2017)

13. Ram, P., Rodriguez, P., Oivo, M.: Software process measurement and related challenges in agile software development: a multiple case study. In: Kuhrmann, M., et al. (eds.) PROFES 2018. LNCS, vol. 11271, pp. 272–287. Springer, Cham (2018). https://doi.org/10.1007/978-3-030-03673-7_20

14. Manzano, M., et al.: Definition of the on-time delivery indicator in rapid software development. In: International Workshop on Quality Requirements in Agile Projects (QuaRAP@RE) (2018)

15. Manzano, M., Mendes, E., Gómez, C., Ayala, C., Franch, X.: Using Bayesian networks to estimate strategic indicators in the context of rapid software development. In: Proceedings of the International Conference on Predictive Models and Data Analytics in Software Engineering (PROMISE) (2018)

16. Taylor, S.J., Letham, B.: Forecasting at scale. Am. Stat. **72**(1), 37–45 (2006)

17. Hyndman, R.J., Khandakar, Y.: Automatic time series forecasting: the forecast package for R. J. Stat. Softw. **27**(3), 1–22 (2008)

18. Gorschek, T., Garre, P., Larsson, S., Wohlin, C.: A model for technology transfer in practice. IEEE Softw. **23**(6), 88–95 (2006)

19. López, L., et al.: Q-rapids tool prototype: supporting decision-makers in managing quality in rapid software development. In: Mendling, J., Mouratidis, H. (eds.) CAiSE 2018. LNBIP, vol. 317, pp. 200–208. Springer, Cham (2018). https://doi.org/10.1007/978-3-319-92901-9_17

20. Martínez-Fernández, S., Jedlitschka, A., Guzmán, L., Vollmer, A.M.: A quality model for actionable analytics in rapid software development. In: Proceedings of the Euromicro Conference on Software Engineering and Advanced Applications (SEAA) (2018)

21. Martínez-Fernández, S., et al.: Continuously assessing and improving software quality with software analytics tools: a case study. IEEE Access **7**, 68219–68239 (2019)

# MegaM@Rt² Project: Mega-Modelling at Runtime - Intermediate Results and Research Challenges

Andrey Sadovykh[1,3]([⊠]), Dragos Truscan[2], Wasif Afzal[4],
Hugo Bruneliere[5], Adnan Ashraf[2], Abel Gómez[6],
Alexandra Espinosa[4], Gunnar Widforss[4], Pierluigi Pierini[7],
Elizabeta Fourneret[8], and Alessandra Bagnato[1]

[1] Research and Development Department, Softeam, Paris, France
{andrey.sadovykh,alessandra.bagnato}@softeam.fr
[2] Åbo Akademi University, 20520 Turku, Finland
{dragos.truscan,adnan.ashraf}@abo.fi
[3] Innopolis University, Innopolis, Russia
a.sadovykh@innopolis.ru
[4] Mälardalen University, Västerås, Sweden
{wasif.afzal,alexandra.espinosa.hortelano,
gunnar.widforss}@mdh.se
[5] IMT Atlantique, LS2N (CNRS) & ARMINES, Nantes, France
hugo.bruneliere@imt-atlantique.fr
[6] Internet Interdisciplinary Institute, Universitat Oberta de Catalunya,
Barcelona, Spain
agomezlla@uoc.edu
[7] Intecs Solutions S.p.A., Rome, Italy
pierluigi.pierini@intecs.it
[8] Smartesting, Paris, France
elizabeta.fourneret@smartesting.com

**Abstract.** MegaM@Rt² Project is a major European effort towards the model-driven engineering of complex Cyber-Physical systems combined with runtime analysis. Both areas are dealt within the same methodology to enjoy the mutual benefits through sharing and tracking various engineering artifacts. The project involves 27 partners that contribute with diverse research and industrial practices addressing real-life case study challenges stemming from 9 application domains. These partners jointly progress towards a common framework to support those application domains with model-driven engineering, verification, and runtime analysis methods. In this paper, we present the motivation for the project, the current approach and the intermediate results in terms of tools, research work and practical evaluation on use cases from the project. We also discuss outstanding challenges and proposed approaches to address them.

**Keywords:** Cyber-Physical systems · Model-Driven Engineering ·
Runtime Analysis · Tools · Mega-Modelling · Traceability · ECSEL

M. Mazzara et al. (Eds.): TOOLS 2019, LNCS 11771, pp. 393–405, 2019.
https://doi.org/10.1007/978-3-030-29852-4_33

# 1 Introduction

Electronic systems are becoming more and more complex and software intensive. This situation calls for modern software and systems engineering practices in order to keep high productivity and quality levels. In the last decade, the ecosystem around Model-Driven Engineering (MDE) has flourished, providing developers with a plethora of tools. However, these tools need to be further developed to scale up for real-world industrial applications. They also need to be enhanced in order to provide advantages at runtime as well. This represents a real opportunity for achieving a complete continuous systems engineering lifecycle, thus connecting together the design and runtime phases [1, 2].

The MegaM@Rt$^2$ project's main goal is to create a framework incorporating methods and tools for the continuous development and runtime support of complex software-intensive systems. Our current architecture vision and development over the MegaM@Rt$^2$ framework integrate three main complementary big capabilities: systems design engineering, runtime analysis, and global model & traceability management. The project is organized around the research work and related technical developments concerning the tool sets supporting those capabilities.

The research topics include holistic Systems Engineering covering design, verification and validation; Runtime Analysis dealing with monitoring, online testing and verification as well as models@runtime techniques; and so-called Mega-Modelling, i.e. large-scale model and traceability management. The framework is under evaluation by 9 industrial case studies ranging from transportation - avionics, railway, automotive, traffic monitoring; and telecommunications - short range communications, base transceiver stations; to logistics - indoor positioning, smart warehouses domains. Among the partners providing use cases in the project, we can cite Thales, Volvo Construction Equipment, Bombardier Transportation and Nokia. These organizations have different product management and engineering practices, as well as regulatory and legal constraints. This results in a large and complex catalog of requirements to be realized by the architecture building blocks at different levels of abstraction. Thus, the development of the MegaM@Rt$^2$ framework is based on a feature-intensive architecture and on a related implementation roadmap that is kept up-to-date. A comprehensive set of the project information, as well as the published deliverables, are all publicly available from the project web site [3].

In this paper, we present the main project research and technological results after two years, and outline the outstanding challenges and further work. To this intent, the rest of the paper is structured as follows. Section 2 briefly describes the MegaM@Rt$^2$ overall approach. Then Sect. 3 focuses on the three complementary tools sets that are designed and developed in the project to support this MegaM@Rt$^2$ approach in practice. We notably insist on the main related research achievements we obtained so far, as well as on still open research and technical challenges. Finally, Sect. 4 concludes by summarizing the main results from this first phase of MegaM@Rt$^2$ and by opening on some future work to come during the second phase of the project.

## 2 Description of the Overall Approach

As stated in the Electronic Components and Systems for European Leadership program's Multi-Annual Strategic Plan [4], design methods and related technologies should fully support the constant technology push and corresponding new user/society demands of products/services based on more and more complex Electronic Components and Systems (ECS). This is particularly true in the context of the involved software components relying on hardware configurations and their interactions e.g. with their underlying environment, being very often numerous, complex, heterogeneous and strongly interrelated. In the past, Model-Based Engineering principles and techniques have already shown promising capabilities that have been experimented in such context. However, they have generally failed in terms of (1) scalability to support real-world scenarios implied by the full deployment and use of complex ECS and (2) efficient traceability, integration and communication between two fundamental system levels which are design time and runtime, notably as far as non-functional properties and their verification & validation aspects are concerned.

As a consequence, the overall idea of MegaM@Rt$^2$ is to scale up the use of model-based techniques by offering scalable methods and related tools interacting between both design time and runtime, as well as to validate the designed and developed approach in concrete industrial cases involving complex ECS. To this intent, MegaM@Rt$^2$ proposes an overall model-based approach combining existing techniques to be enhanced when relevant, and novel ones to be developed when needed. A fundamental challenge notably resides in providing efficient traceability support between the two levels i.e. from design models to runtime ones and back. In parallel to these, modern large-scale industrial software engineering processes require thorough configuration and model governance to provide the promised productivity gains. Thus, a scalable mega-modelling approach is being designed and will be deployed to manage all the involved artifacts e.g. the many different models, corresponding workflows, configurations, etc. and to better tackle their large diversity in terms of nature, number, size, complexity, etc.

To cover all these topics and deal with the complete value chain, MegaM@Rt$^2$ brings together prominent tool developers and vendors and research organisations with state-of-the-art methods and tools that are validated in highly relevant European industry case studies. The end users from the space, naval, railway, smart grid, smart warehouse and telecom industry domains are driving the project by providing real-world requirements and case studies as well as by validating and endorsing the MegaM@Rt$^2$ results.

Figure 1 provides an overview of the MegaM@Rt$^2$ global approach and emphasizes its key principles and concepts. Industries apply a set of current engineering practices based on SysML, AADL, EAST_ADL, but also Matlab/Simulink, and Method B, each one producing specific design models, requirement specifications and resulting software and hardware artefacts. MegaM@Rt$^2$ suggests to integrate those artefacts into a global system model providing a complete view of the Cyber-Physical System (CPS), and detailing the component, behaviour and desired quality properties of the system. These properties are then an object of exhaustive continuous testing and monitoring in the runtime environment to detect deviations in real-time, thanks to the configuration of the target platform and the injection of probes in the software. The detected deviations plus all the traces information collected in the process are analyzed to detect the impacted components in the integrated view of system models. When possible, automatic repairing suggestions are provided to correct the issue and reconfigure or redeploy the system to start the next iteration of the continuous integration process. This approach was further developed in [5] where we defined the specific tool sets - their requirements and features as well as outlined integration means.

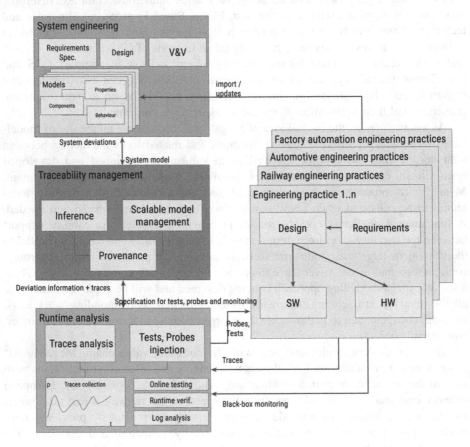

**Fig. 1.** Overall conceptual architecture of the MegaM@Rt project.

The methods and tools provided by MegaM@Rt$^2$ are evaluated and applied in several industrial case studies. Each individual case study defines a set of key performance indicators (KPIs) that are used to evaluate the improvement that the new technologies provide. The case study specific KPIs are aggregated into project level KPIs which provide a quantitative evaluation of the project goals.

The project has set challenging goals in terms of KPIs such as:

- Reduction of design time/design effort in the range of 10%–50% by design artefacts reuse.
- Reduction of validation effort in the range of 10%–30% by automated trace collection and analysis.
- Reduction 10%–50% in time/effort required for managing and handling all the involved models (e.g. time for model retrieval and access).
- Reduction 10%–50% in time/effort required for tracing and handling all the involved models at design and runtime levels (e.g. creation of and access to relations between system and traces models).

The above-mentioned KPIs are measured through out the project industrial case studies. At the current stage the first evaluation phase has finished. The next sections present the preliminary results.

## 3  Results of the First Evaluation Phase and Outstanding Research Challenges

At the time of writing this paper, the MegaM@Rt² project has entered its second half. In the following sections, we provide an overview of the current achievements of the project by focusing on research work and the corresponding results that we have already obtained.

### 3.1  The MegaM@Rt² System Engineering Tool Set

This tool set aims to support system design activities. It has been architected around three main topics: (i) requirements analysis & specification, (ii) system modeling and (iii) model verification & validation. The approach integrates up to 20 different open source tools, mainly Eclipse-based, such as Modelio, developed by the consortium research partners. These tools support a variety of current engineering practices based on standard modelling languages, profiles and extensions like: UML, SysML, MARTE, AADL, EAST_ADL, etc. The framework is designed to integrate additional "external" tools like Matlab/Simulink, AUTOSAR, Modelica and others, based on specific needs of the industrial partners.

Different techniques have been adopted to ensure the correctness of system models, either in terms of verification of languages syntactic paradigms (e.g. using SAT- and CP-solver technologies) and in terms of functional and non-functional validation of system artefacts with respect of given requirements (e.g. through model simulation, model testing, machine learning technique, etc.). For example, [6] proposes a framework to reason about the satisfiability of class models described using the Unified Modeling Language (UML). It allows to identify possible design flaws as early as possible in the software development cycle, by annotating UML Class Diagrams with Object Constraint Language (OCL) invariants. Then, the Constraint Logic Programming (CLP) paradigm allows to reason about UML Class Diagrams modeling foundations thanks to a translation to Formula.

Several other research areas have been investigating. For instance, the current trend on Internet-of-Things Systems of Systems (IoT-SoS) implies significant evolution of modeling, analysis and design approaches [7].

Separation of concerns is one of the fundamental principles allowing to build well-structured software and improving its maintainability/evolutivity. Executable models are good candidates to capture the behavior of a software-intensive system using separation of concerns approach. In [8], Domains Specific Languages (DSL) have been exploited to create executable models when business operations are tied to specific technological platforms. This method is applied both at design-time for creation of executable models with EMF and at run-time by monitoring operation calls from the deployed execution engine.

Another aspect investigated in [9, 10] is the availability of platform-independent SW models and HW synthesis tools able to automatically produce efficient implementations based on performance predictions of the system model and this on many different distributed and parallel computing resources.

Safety critical systems, e.g. as proposed by Bombardier Transportation and ClearSy in the project, require specific support for safety analysis, assessment and certification. The contract-based approach is adopted by some of the framework tools and is presented and discussed in [11]. It is based on finding static schedules relying on contracts and using this information in the verification process to reduce the number of invariant annotations needed. Moreover, contracts can be used to make compile-time scheduling decisions, improving runtime performance.

A complementary research area is related to the application of the Aspect-Oriented Methodologies focusing on the reduction of the modeling and verification effort by applying aspect-oriented principles in model construction [12]. The industrial partners have a preference for more classical and consolidated methodologies. However, such capabilities are still available for possible future applications in case needed.

In the general case, a main achievement is the ongoing contribution to the MARTE standard, as presented in [13] and responding to the Request for Information issued by the OMG for a new MARTE 2.0. Partners proposals have been collected in an initial survey, then an answer to the RFI has been prepared and sent back.

Finally, the last project period will focus on the exploitation, at design time, of the runtime trace collection and analysis capability, in order to address possible model refinements in the context of feedback loops. To this intent, the most promising approach is the one provided by PADRE tool on performance anti-pattern detection and model refactoring [14, 15]. Finally, as a part of an effort to automate system engineering, [16] provides a systematic mapping study on published tools and approaches that can be used for generating API documentation, or for assisting in the API documentation process. the paper presents an overview of what kind of tools have been developed, what kind of documentation they generate, and what sources the documentation approaches require.

## 3.2   The MegaM@Rt$^2$ Runtime (Trace) Analysis Tool Set

This tool set aims to define new methods and tools for creating and managing models at runtime verification and testing, including automated runtime testing and monitoring as well as a model-based log collection and analysis infrastructure supported by tools such as PauWare or CertifyIt. This runtime tool set integrates 24 tools that further propose automated code generation, model execution as a part of a system, runtime verification and online testing, such as CompleteTest, JTL, PauWare, Smartesting tools, AIPHS, Comformiq Designer, Modelio, etc. These tools within the MegaM@Rt$^2$ approach integrate with the analysis tools. The main ongoing activity is related to establishing a smooth connection with the analysis tools, that will allow user-friendly and simple inclusion within the continuous development process, addressed in MegaM@Rt$^2$.

Several results have been published. In the context of testing and test generation several papers address test generation using UPPAAL model checker and its extensions. For instance, [17] outlines a method for testing energy consumption in embedded systems using energy-related mutants for EAST-ADL architectural models, which are converted to UPPAAL Timed Automata and used for test generation UPPAAL Statistical Model Checker (SMC). A complementary approach is presented in [18], where we show how architectural models described in the EAST-ADL architectural language can also be used for testing the energy consumption of embedded systems, after transforming them into networks of formal models called priced timed automata. A mutation testing approach for UPPAAL TA has been proposed in [19] to mutate UPPAAL-TA models and use them for generating tests used for evaluating security vulnerabilities of web services. Last but not least, in order to enable the analysis of failed traces and quick fault localization, [20] proposes an approach that converts concrete test sequences generated and executed by Uppaal Tron against the system under test into symbolic traces that can be imported in the Uppaal tool and visualized in the Uppaal simulator.

In the same context of testing, [21] presents an approach for testing of software intensive safety-critical products to validate the hardware-in-the-loop simulation of a safety-critical system, by executing test cases both in the control setting (lab) and on the real product (train). The process is intended to be used when certifying the simulation which is a necessary step in order to certify the complete system. In addition, in [22], the authors propose an extension of base-choice criterion used for testing software-based on its nominal choice of input parameters, which takes into account time as another parameter when generating and executing tests by defining the timed base-choice coverage criterion. In [23], the authors conducted a comparative study on the cost and effectiveness of tests that are manually written versus those that are automatically generated in the field of industrial control software, where strict requirements on both specification-based testing and code coverage typically are met with rigorous manual testing.

In order to explore the performance of deployed systems at runtime, [24] suggests a performance space exploration approach for inferring the worst-case user scenario in a given workload model. The goal of this work is to detect which configuration of the load model has the potential to create the highest resource utilization on the system under test with respect to a given resource so that performance tests can be run with that configuration. An exact and an approximate method are suggested and compared.

Finally, in [25] we propose a marker design and an algorithm to detect the markers under different ambient conditions, with a long range to be executed on embedded systems with low computational requirements. The proposed method reduces the existing problems in the state-of-the-art related to the use of different environments and conditions such as different distances or different illumination.

### 3.3 The MegaM@Rt$^2$ Model and Traceability Management (MTM) Tool Set

The Model and Traceability Management (MTM) tool set aims at providing generic global model management and traceability capabilities, with a focus on the dedicated support for creating and using feedback loops between design-time and runtime models in the context of complex CPSs engineering. To this intent, the MTM tool set is composed of 5 different complementary tools supporting the Eclipse [26] and Modelio [27] technical modeling environments. These tools provide support for storing and handling large EMF models (NeoEMF) [28], building and handling views integrating different EMF models (EMF Views) [29], keeping consistency and traceability between different EMF models (JTL) [30], detecting and refactoring performance antipatterns (PADRE) [14] or organizing and managing Modelio-based models and their relationships (Modelio Constellation) [31]. In all cases, their main objective is notably to leverage the different kinds of models resulting from the System Engineering and Runtime Analysis tool sets, in order to handle and reuse these models altogether in a coherent way as part of the continuous CPS engineering approach promoted by MegaM@Rt$^2$. During the first phase of the MegaM@Rt$^2$ project, a significant research effort has been conducted by the involved partners in order to provide these fundamental capabilities via the various tools of the MTM tool set. We summarize significant related research achievements in what follows.

On one hand, we have worked on improving the general support for backward traceability and change propagation between different kinds of models thanks to the JTL tool [32]. We then used such a support in order to provide change propagation capabilities at architectural (design) model-level, and illustrated it in a software availability context [33]. We also used this same support in order to automate performance improvements via the detection of architectural antipatterns using PADRE and thanks to traceability with corresponding runtime data [15] (cf. also Sect. 3.1).

On the other hand, we have obtained interesting results in the model view area [34]. Notably, we have worked on supporting the creation and handling of scalable model views combining different large-scale models together (including design and runtime ones) via traceability links [35]. To this intent, we worked on providing the required infrastructure to store, handle and trace efficiently very large models. This has been implemented in practice by leveraging the EMF Views and NeoEMF tools from the MTM tool set. This was a required achievement in order to be able to implement runtime-to-design time feedback loops, which is one of the longer-term objectives of MegaM@Rt$^2$.

Interestingly, based on the two complementary efforts above-mentioned, we have then been able to apply our model view approach - EMF Views, in combination with our traceability capabilities in JTL, in order to provide a first concrete instantiation of the MegaM@Rt$^2$ runtime-to-design feedback loop in the context of a safety-critical system from our partner ClearSy [36]. In the second phase of the project, we plan to work on more practical instantiations of such a feedback loop by relying on tools from the MTM tool set.

Nevertheless, there are still open challenges in these promising research areas. We have already been able to discuss that within the Modeling community when organizing and running the first edition of the International Workshop on Model-Driven Engineering for Design-Runtime Interaction in Complex Systems (MDE@DeRun 2018), co-located with STAF 2018 in Toulouse, France [37]. Notably, we identified challenges related to the particularities of design-runtime traceability: e.g. which semantics has to be given to the traceability information, in which contexts and how? We also identified questions related to the analysis of the traced runtime information: e.g. what kind of runtime data is actually needed, in which contexts and how to collect it properly? Finally, we identified issues related to the overall objectives of such a design-runtime traceability: e.g. which engineering purposes or activities do we intend to address or cover thanks to such feedback loops?

### 3.4   Case Study Evaluation

A total of nine industrial case studies are used in the project in order to evaluate the MegaM@Rt$^2$ framework in practice. To provide measurable evidence on the extent to which the framework fits and provides benefits to the industrial development process, each case study defined a set of Key Performance Indicators (KPIs) that have been measured at baseline (i.e. when the project started) and have been/will be measured again after each of the two development phases of the project (i.e. at month 24 and month 36 respectively). At the time of writing this paper, the first evaluation phase has recently finished (at month 24).

During Phase 1, the case study providers have evaluated different scenarios using the tools and technologies offered by the different tool sets previously presented in this Sect. 3. The evaluation in terms of scenarios has put the focus on the benefits that MegaM@Rt$^2$ is expected to bring: (1) They allow to better understand the aspects that the case study providers found most important for their industrial activities and (2) They structure and organize the tools' verification and validation, which are based on the requirements and the KPIs defined by MegaM@Rt$^2$. The case study providers made some changes in the choice of the best scenario to validate a tool/technology and, conversely, in the judgement of the best way for using a tool in a certain scenario; many problems were encountered but solved thanks to the collaboration that the tool providers fully offered.

The details on the case study results are provided in deliverable D5.5 as available from the project website [38]. It is important to mention that case studies measure differently the KPIs depending on their respective contexts and designed experiments. Nevertheless, it is noteworthy to point out that the case studies succeeded to demonstrate improvements significantly above targets, in particular, in:

- Time required for identification of design problems;
- Time/effort for requirements validation;
- Productivity improvements;
- Cost savings for development and maintenance of large complex systems.

The project has also already demonstrated values close to the targets for the following set of KPIs:

- Reduction of validation effort by automated trace collection and analysis;
- Reduction in time/effort required for tracing and handling all involved models at design and runtime levels;
- Quality improvement by improving predictability and conformance to specifications.

# 4 Conclusions and Future Work

With a total of 40 deliverables and multiple tools provided via three complementary tool sets [39], MegaM@Rt$^2$ aims at improving the productivity and quality of the system development and at reducing the time-to-market for complex systems, as well as to reinforce the European scientific and technological leadership and competitiveness of the European market.

The project has already delivered a significant number of research approaches, technical tools and methods spanning from system-level modeling to runtime analysis and global traceability and model management. While the results are globally evaluated as substantial, we face several open challenges towards our goal for scalable and traceable model-driven engineering applicable to a variety of industrial domains. The first phase of the project put in place the baseline methods that were assessed in the industrial settings. We demonstrated the opportunities brought by the global traceability and model management technologies resulting from research activities. In the meantime, we identified several further challenges. One of them is the need for a common runtime trace format, i.e. a shared representation for different types of runtime (meta)data. Another challenge is the need for more automated inference methods that could systematically relate these runtime traces (uniformly represented/modeled) to the corresponding system design artifacts.

Therefore, during its last period, the project plans to concentrate on those open areas by scheduling dedicated activities such as hackathons, demonstration session and workshops. We would like to engage the project community, both case study providers and technology providers to focus on a common agenda that would push the state-of-the-art further (in these areas, but also in others of interest to the project). Moreover, we plan activities to create awareness about the approaches and technologies developed in the project, which have already been adopted and endorsed by the industrial partners. Finally, an important aspect is about planning and preparing for the sustainability of the project results by creating an ecosystem for all the tools and methods composing the MegaM@Rt$^2$ framework.

**Acknowledgement.** This project has received funding from the Electronic Component Systems for European Leadership Joint Undertaking under grant agreement No. 737494. This Joint Undertaking receives support from the European Union's Horizon 2020 research and innovation program and from Sweden, France, Spain, Italy, Finland and Czech Republic.

# References

1. Afzal, W., et al.: The MegaM@Rt2 ECSEL project: MegaModelling at runtime – scalable model-based framework for continuous development and runtime validation of complex systems. Microprocess. Microsyst. **61**, 86–95 (2018)
2. Sadovykh, A., et al.: Model-based system engineering in practice: document generation-MegaM@Rt2 project experience. In: Proceedings of the 14th Central and Eastern European Software Engineering Conference, pp. 9:1–9:6 (2018)
3. MegaMart2 - MegaModelling at runtime: MegaMart2 - MegaModelling at runtime. https://megamart2-ecsel.eu/. Accessed 25 June 2019
4. ECSEL's multi-annual strategic plan 2016. http://ec.europa.eu/research/participants/data/ref/h2020/other/legal/jtis/ecsel-multi-stratplan-2016_en.pdf. Accessed 25 June 2019
5. Sadovykh, A., et al.: A tool-supported approach for building the architecture and roadmap in MegaM@Rt2 project. In: Ciancarini, P., Mazzara, M., Messina, A., Sillitti, A., Succi, G. (eds.) SEDA 2018. AISC, vol. 925, pp. 265–274. Springer, Cham (2020). https://doi.org/10.1007/978-3-030-14687-0_24
6. Pérez, B., Porres, I.: Reasoning about UML/OCL class diagrams using constraint logic programming and formula. Inf. Syst. **81**, 152–177 (2019)
7. Villar, E.: Model-driven analysis and design of IoT systems. In: 1st International Workshop on Embedded Software for Industrial IoT, Dresden, Germany (2018)
8. Cariou, E., Le Goaer, O., Brunschwig, L., Barbier, F.: A generic solution for weaving business code into executable models. In MODELS 2018 ACM/IEEE 21th International Conference on Model Driven Engineering Languages and Systems, Copenhagen, Denmark (2018)
9. Muttillo, V., Valente, G., Pomante, L.: Design space exploration for mixed-criticality embedded systems considering hypervisor-based SW partitions. In: 2018 21st Euromicro Conference on Digital System Design (DSD) (2018)
10. Ciambrone, D., Muttillo, V., Pomante, L., Valente, G.: HEPSIM: an ESL HW/SW co-simulator/analysis tool for heterogeneous parallel embedded systems. In: 2018 7th Mediterranean Conference on Embedded Computing (MECO) (2018)
11. Wiik, J., Ersfolk, J., Walden, M.: A contract-based approach to scheduling and verification of dynamic dataflow networks. In: 2018 16th ACM/IEEE International Conference on Formal Methods and Models for System Design (MEMOCODE) (2018)
12. Vain, J., Truscan, D., Iqbal, J., Tsiopoulos, L.: On the benefits of using aspect-orientation in UPPAAL timed automata. In: 2017 International Conference on Infocom Technologies and Unmanned Systems (Trends and Future Directions) (ICTUS) (2017)
13. Medina, J.L., Villar, E.: Towards MARTE ++: an enhanced UML-based language to Model and Analyse Real-Time and Embedded Systems for the IoT age. Presented at the Forum on specification & Design Languages (FDL 2017), Verona, Italy (2017)
14. Arcelli, D., Cortellessa, V., Di Pompeo, D.: Automating performance antipattern detection and software refactoring in UML models. In: 2019 IEEE 26th International Conference on Software Analysis, Evolution and Reengineering (SANER) (2019)
15. Arcelli, D., Cortellessa, V., Di Pompeo, D., Eramo, R., Tucci, M.: Exploiting architecture/runtime model-driven traceability for performance improvement. In: 2019 IEEE International Conference on Software Architecture (ICSA) (2019)
16. Nybom, K., Ashraf, A., Porres, I.: A systematic mapping study on API documentation generation approaches. In: 2018 44th Euromicro Conference on Software Engineering and Advanced Applications (SEAA) (2018)

17. Marinescu, R., Filipovikj, P., Enoiu, E.P., Larsson, J., Seceleanu, C.: An energy-aware mutation testing framework for EAST-ADL architectural models. In: 29th Nordic Workshop on Programming Theory, Turku, Finland (2018)

18. Marinescu, R., Enoiu, E., Seceleanu, C., Sundmark, D.: Automatic test generation for energy consumption of embedded systems modeled in EAST-ADL. In: 2017 IEEE International Conference on Software Testing, Verification and Validation Workshops (ICSTW) (2017)

19. Siavashi, F., Truscan, D., Vain, J.: Vulnerability assessment of web services with model-based mutation testing. In: 2018 IEEE International Conference on Software Quality, Reliability and Security (QRS) (2018)

20. Iqbal, J., Truscan, D., Vain, J., Porres, I.: Reconstructing timed symbolic traces from rtioco-based timed test sequences using backward-induction. In: Proceedings of the Fifth European Conference on the Engineering of Computer-Based Systems – ECBS 2017 (2017)

21. Stratis, A., Causevic, A.: A practical approach towards validating HIL simulation of a safety-critical system. In: 2017 IEEE International Symposium on Software Reliability Engineering Workshops (ISSREW) (2017)

22. Bergstrom, H., Enoiu, E.P.: Using timed base-choice coverage criterion for testing industrial control software. In: 2017 IEEE International Conference on Software Testing, Verification and Validation Workshops (ICSTW) (2017)

23. Enoiu, E., Sundmark, D., Causevic, A., Pettersson, P.: A comparative study of manual and automated testing for industrial control software. In: 2017 IEEE International Conference on Software Testing, Verification and Validation (ICST) (2017)

24. Ahmad, T., Truscan, D., Porres, I.: Identifying worst-case user scenarios for performance testing of web applications using Markov-chain workload models. Future Gener. Comput. Syst. **87**, 910–920 (2018)

25. Diaz, A., Pena, D., Villar, E.: Short and long distance marker detection technique in outdoor and indoor environments for embedded systems. In: 2017 32nd Conference on Design of Circuits and Integrated Systems (DCIS) (2017)

26. Gronback, R.: Eclipse modeling project | the eclipse foundation. https://www.eclipse.org/modeling/emf/. Accessed 25 June 2019

27. Modelio open source - UML and BPMN modeling tool. https://www.modelio.org/. Accessed 25 June 2019

28. Daniel, G., et al.: NeoEMF: a multi-database model persistence framework for very large models. Sci. Comput. Programm. **149**, 9–14 (2017)

29. Bruneliere, H., Perez, J.G., Wimmer, M., Cabot, J.: EMF views: a view mechanism for integrating heterogeneous models. In: Johannesson, P., Lee, M.L., Liddle, S.W., Opdahl, A. L., López, Ó.P. (eds.) ER 2015. LNCS, vol. 9381, pp. 317–325. Springer, Cham (2015). https://doi.org/10.1007/978-3-319-25264-3_23

30. Cicchetti, A., Di Ruscio, D., Eramo, R., Pierantonio, A.: JTL: a bidirectional and change propagating transformation language. In: Malloy, B., Staab, S., van den Brand, M. (eds.) SLE 2010. LNCS, vol. 6563, pp. 183–202. Springer, Heidelberg (2011). https://doi.org/10.1007/978-3-642-19440-5_11

31. Desfray, P.: Model repositories at the enterprises and systems scale: the Modelio Constellation solution. In: 2015 International Conference on Information Systems Security and Privacy (ICISSP) (2015)

32. Eramo, R., Pierantonio, A., Tucci, M.: Enhancing the JTL tool for bidirectional transformations. In: Conference Companion of the 2nd International Conference on Art, Science, and Engineering of Programming – Programming 2018 Companion (2018)

33. Cortellessa, V., Eramo, R., Tucci, M.: Availability-driven architectural change propagation through bidirectional model transformations between UML and petri net models. In: 2018 IEEE International Conference on Software Architecture (ICSA) (2018)

34. Bruneliere, H., Burger, E., Cabot, J., Wimmer, M.: A feature-based survey of model view approaches. Softw. Syst. Model. **18**(3), 1931–1952 (2019)
35. Bruneliere, H., Marchand, F., Daniel, G., Cabot, J.: Towards scalable model views on heterogeneous model resources. In: ACM/IEEE 21th International Conference on Model Driven Engineering Languages and Systems (MODELS 2018), Copenhagen, Denmark, pp. 334–344 (2018)
36. Eramo, R., et al.: Model-driven design-runtime interaction in safety critical system development: an experience report. In: 15th European Conference on Modelling Foundations and Applications (ECMFA), Co-located with STAF 2019, Eindhoven, The Netherlands (2019)
37. Bruneliere, H., et al.: Model-driven engineering for design-runtime interaction in complex systems: scientific challenges and roadmap. In: Mazzara, M., Ober, I., Salaün, G. (eds.) STAF 2018. LNCS, vol. 11176, pp. 536–543. Springer, Cham (2018). https://doi.org/10.1007/978-3-030-04771-9_40
38. Deliverables - MegaMart2 - MegaModelling at Runtime. https://megamart2-ecsel.eu/deliverables/. Accessed 25 June 2019
39. MegaM@Rt2 tool box. http://toolbox.megamart2-ecsel.eu/. Accessed 25 June 2019

# REVaMP² Project: Towards Round-Trip Engineering of Software Product Lines - Approach, Intermediate Results and Challenges

Andrey Sadovykh[1,3]([✉]), Tewfik Ziadi[2], Alessandra Bagnato[1],
Thorsten Berger[4], Jan-Philipp Steghöfer[5], Jacques Robin[6],
Raul Mazo[6,7], and Elena Gallego[8]

[1] Research and Development Department, Softeam, Paris, France
{andrey.sadovykh,alessandra.bagnato}@softeam.fr
[2] Sorbonne University, Paris, France
tewfik.ziadi@lip6.fr
[3] Innopolis University, Innopolis, Russia
a.sadovykh@innopolis.ru
[4] Chalmers University of Technology, Gothenburg, Sweden
thorsten.berger@chalmers.se
[5] University of Gothenburg, Gothenburg, Sweden
jan-philipp.steghofer@gu.se
[6] University Paris 1, Panthéon-Sorbonne, Paris, France
{jacques.robin,raul.mazo}@univ-paris1.fr
[7] GIDITIC, Universidad Eafit, Medellin, Colombia
rimazop@eafit.edu.co
[8] The REUSE Company, Leganés, Spain
elena.gallego@reusecompany.com

**Abstract.** The REVaMP² Project is a major European effort towards Round-Trip Engineering of Software Product Lines for software intensive systems. Indeed, software is predominant in almost every modern industry. The importance of time-to-market has grown tremendously in many business domains. Organizations are in a constant search for approaches for mass production of highly customizable systems. The software product lines engineering approach promises to provide up to $10\times$ speed increase benefits in time-to-market. Traditionally, automated tools proposed a top-down approach, i.e., variants were generated from a model of the product line. However, the industry used a bottom-up approach that helped to re-create a product line out of various clones of a system. This operation is very costly and error prone. The goal of REVaMP² is to automate the process of extracting a product line from various system artifacts and help with verification and the co-evolution of the product line. The project involves 27 partners that contribute with diverse research and industrial practices to address case study challenges stemming from 11 application domains. In this paper, we would like to present the motivation for the project, the current approach, the intermediate results and challenges.

© Springer Nature Switzerland AG 2019
M. Mazzara et al. (Eds.): TOOLS 2019, LNCS 11771, pp. 406–417, 2019.
https://doi.org/10.1007/978-3-030-29852-4_34

**Keywords:** Software product lines engineering · Round-trip engineering · Model-driven engineering · Extraction · Co-evolution · Verification · Tools · ITEA3

# 1   Introduction

An ever-higher proportion of B2B and B2C products and services acquire leading market positions by becoming more software-intensive. This trend is illustrated by buildings and vehicles evolving from electro-mechanical systems into Cyber-Physical Systems (CPS) and by services such as utilities and transportation evolving towards personalized, adaptive offers based on analytics of data generated by the Internet of Things (IoT). This technological trend reinforces with the shift away from traditional product sales towards service subscription packages, which include leasing a product as one item in a customized turn-key service offer. These Software-Intensive Systems and Services (SIS) create and adapt to innovative market disruptions and customers' whims far quicker and at a lower cost than their less software based competitors. However, they also raise new engineering challenges. In particular, they require more agile, round-trip engineering processes that better leverage legacy assets, as well as a more systematic and automated variability management. An engineering process is called round-trip when it combines top-down steps that refine abstract assets such as requirement specifications and high-level architectural patterns into more concrete ones such as executable simulation models and source code, with bottom-up steps that abstract such these more concrete assets into the more abstract ones. Variability management refers to a method to systematically (a) reuse common assets shared by a whole family (or line) of system (or product or service) variants on a common theme and (b) organize and relate distinct assets proper to each variant along commercially and technologically relevant characteristics and constraints.

In this paper, we first summarize the main variability management challenges that SIS engineering companies face today, given the current State-of-the-Art (SotA thereafter), when they attempt to round-trip engineer SIS families at optimal cost by reusing legacy artifacts from past assets from their product or service portfolio. We then overview the current status and different outstanding challenges of the REVaMP² - Round-trip Engineering for VAriability Management Platform and Process project [1]. This is a collaborative research and innovation project labeled by the Eureka program ITEA-3 in a consortium of 27 partners in 5 European countries.

# 2   Motivation, Concept and Approach

Product Line Engineering (PLE) is a mature paradigm for variability management. It enables defining a family of product configurations to satisfy different customer needs and to later systematically generate the associated product variants by combining predefined reusable components. Benefits of PLE include achieving large-scale productivity gains and improving time-to-market and product quality. Reports describe gains following PLE adoption by as much as tenfold in productivity and quality, cost reduction by as much as 60%, decrease labour needs by as much as 87%, and decrease time to market (new variants) by as much as 98% [2]. As all sorts of devices, systems and services become more software intensive, the more they can benefit from PLE adoption. Commercially successful implementations of the PLE paradigm can be found in companies from domains ranging from avionics and automotive software, to printers, mobile phones or web applications.

However, adopting a PLE approach is still a major challenge and represents a risk for a company [3–6]. First, compared to single-system development, PLE variability management implies a methodology that highly impacts the life cycle of the products as well as the processes and roles inside the company. Second, adopting PLE from the beginning, an approach called proactive PLE [5], is a subject to two main assumptions: (1) the company must have, in advance, a complete understanding of the variability to anticipate all possible variations; (2) the company should start from scratch to specify the variability and implement the reusable assets.

Berger et al. showed in a survey with industrial companies that participated in industrial PLE, that around 50% of them cannot adopt proactive PLE [7]. On the one hand, the variability in these companies is discovered as customer needs emerge over time; so, it is very difficult if not impossible, to anticipate all the variations from the beginning. On the other hand, companies already have existing product variants that were implemented using an opportunistic reuse in an ad-hoc way to quickly respond to different customer needs. As mentioned by Dubinsky et al. [8], instead of adopting PLE, many companies clone an existing product and modify it to fit the new customer needs. This approach, called clone-and-own, is widely used because it is initially faster to start with an already developed and tested set of assets [8].

Figure 1 illustrates, the three main PLE processes: proactive, extractive and round-trip. Proactive PLE is shown on the left of the figure. It must start with the inception of the project in a high-cost upfront investment step t0 called domain modelling. During this phase, the requirements for the entire product line must be simultaneously elicited. From the resulting PL, all product variants satisfying the variability model constraints can then be automatically generated in a second step t1. In Fig. 1, the domain model mandatory features are grey squares, the variant-specific features are coloured squares, and constraints on features mutual exclusivity are annotated with the XOR operator. An extractive PLE is illustrated on the right of Fig. 1. It starts by the rapid development of a Minimal Viable Product (MVP). If this MVP fits its market, it is then followed by sequentially and opportunistically cloning-and-owning variants to quickly target other niches for which many common features from the initial product can be reused (steps t1 to t4). When these variants and the constraints among them become too numerous to be efficiently managed without an explicit and systematic variability model, they are then refactored and consolidated in bottom-up fashion into a PL (t5). Round-trip PLE combine both approaches.

However, the industrial SotA in variability management is restricted to tools that automate top-down product variant generation from a variability model and reusable product assets, i.e. step t1 on the left of Fig. 1. No tool is currently available to automate the bottom-up extraction of a variability model and reusable PL assets, i.e. step t5 on the right of Fig. 1.

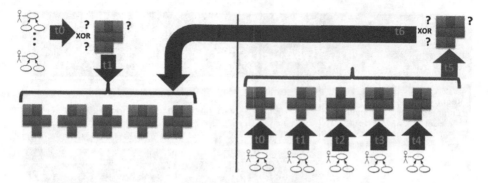

**Fig. 1.** Round-trip PLE adoption process

Companies thus face the software PL adoption dilemma: on the one hand, they are aware that PL can enable them to achieve large-scale productivity gains, improve time-to-market and product quality. On the other hand, however, these same companies already have existing variants created using the clone-and-own approach. This dilemma makes them practically unable to adopt PL. One solution to deal with this issue is to use round-trip engineering approach for PL adoption that consists in migrating, automatically or semi-automatically, the existing variants into a PL.

To conclude, innovative companies thus face the PLE adoption dilemma: the Return on Investment (ROI) of the proactive PLE adoption process is too uncertain, while the cost of late manual PLE is prohibitive. This dilemma considerably hinders PLE adoption. Many organizations eschew it, missing out on the massive long-term cost, robustness, customization, and competitiveness benefits that it would bring about for maintaining and developing their product portfolio. The REVaMP² project aims to provide the first solution to this dilemma by developing and validating on diverse industrial case studies, the first comprehensive round-trip engineering automation platform and process to support extractive, bottom-up PLE adoption and maximize reuse of legacy assets.

## 3   REVaMP² Tool Chain

The REVaMP² project develops a number of tool sets for Round-Trip Product Line Engineering as shown in Fig. 2, including innovative tools and services for Legacy and PL Asset Visualization, PL Asset Extraction Automation, PL Asset Verification Automation and PL Asset Co-Evolution Automation.

The first and second classes address the need to automate the extraction and visualization of product lines from legacy assets. This is needed because the extraction, verification and refactoring tools will not simultaneously reach 100% automation and quality. Human expertise will always be needed to adjust their parameters to trade-off automation for quality, evaluate their results and manually edit them. The realistic goal of REVaMP² is to minimize such manual edition steps, not to entirely eliminate them. The third class addresses the need to automate the formal verification of constraints on

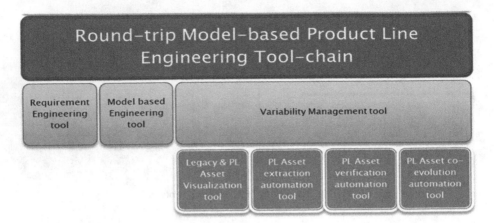

Fig. 2. REVaMP² tool sets for round-trip product line engineering.

product line variability models and assets. These constraints can be for example, inter-feature consistency constraints, safety and real-time constraints that must hold for the whole configuration space or the existence of a nonempty intersection of this space with some business configuration goal. The fourth class addresses the need for PL refactoring automation. Next paragraphs summarize the current stage of the tools and services related to extraction and visualization and verification.

**PL Asset Extraction and Visualization Automation.** The tool sets related to extraction and visualization take as inputs the legacy assets as illustrated in Fig. 3. Input legacy assets refer to any artefact needed to create a product and which are implemented without an explicit management of variability. For instance, systems that are implemented using the clone-and-own ad hoc reuse technique. The objective of the extraction and visualization tool sets is to analyse these legacy assets to extract the common and variable parts. The extraction process provide as output an explicit description of the variability in what is referred to as variability model eirshed with constraints that describe dependencies between variations points. It can also refactor the input asset to create reusable assets. Many challenges are identified in the context including the need to analyse and compare legacy assets. In addition, the extraction tools should support a variety of assets types ranging from textual requirements to the source code assets (in many different languages). Another identified challenge is to propose solutions to help and assist domain experts in the extraction process. REVaMP² aims implementing a tool chain including different tools to support the different asset types and including visualization supports to assist domain experts in this process (cf. Fig. 3).

At the current stage, many tools are implemented by the REVaMP² partners. This includes the following tool sets implemented by academics as well as industrial companies participating to the REVaMP² project: *BUT4Reuse* [9] framework from partner Sorbonne University, *VEXA* from partner ForschungsZentrum Informatik - FZI, *KernalHaven* [10] from partner University of Hildesheim, *Jittac Feature Filter* by Karlstad University [11], Tom Sawyer Visualization from partner Scopeset [12],

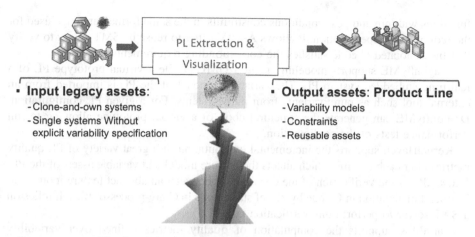

**Input legacy assets:**
- Clone-and-own systems
- Single systems Without
  explicit variability specification

PL Extraction & Visualization

**Output assets: Product Line**
- Variability models
- Constraints
- Reusable assets

**Fig. 3.** PL asset extraction and visualization automation

*FLiMEA* from partner University San Jorge, *pure::variants variability framework* from partner pure::systems [13], *M-XRAY Architectural* analysis from partner MES [14]. In addition, to the variety and richness of the implemented tools, special attention is now devoted to the integration aspect where the objective is to create a tool chain including all the individual tools.

The **PL Asset Verification** team works on developing tools assisting the PL engineering team verifying various kinds of PL artefacts using a variety of techniques. The current tool set includes the following tools: *Verification Studio* from partner Knowledge Centric Solutions, The Reuse Company [15], *AssetVerifier* from partner Kungliga Tekniska Högskolan - KTH, *KernelHaven* from partner Stiftung Universität Hildesheim - SUH [10], *DragonflyME* from partner ForschungsZentrum Informatik - FZI and *VariaMos* from partner Université Paris 1 Panthéon-Sorbonne - UP1PS [16].

Verification Studio supports the verification of the individual correctness, global consistency and completeness of requirement artefacts. It is part of KCS-TRC's *Systems Engineering Suite (SES)* that also includes complementary tools allowing the engineering team to specify an ontology of the PL domain model and associate with each concept and relation of the ontology a set of natural language templates, each one corresponding to a way to express it in a textual requirement specification. SES also includes a requirement editor that leverages these templates to auto-complete requirement specification sentence fragments thus insuring that the requirement text only contains phrases which semantics is defined in the ontology. Verification Studio provides as built-in the requirements quality metrics defined by the INCOSE Guide for Writing Requirements.

AssetVerifier includes an editor for the formal specification in first-order logic of individual requirements of an automotive system PL together with their dependencies, variability model and required *Automotive Safety Integrity Level (ASIL)*. AssetVerifier relies on a *Satisfiability Modulo Theory (SMT)* solver to scalably verify for given target PL configuration (a) the consistency of the requirement dependencies an (b) that the ASIL are assigned in accordance with the rules mandated by the automotive industry safety standard ISO26262. AssetVerifier also includes an editor to annotate C code functions with pre and post-conditions constraints in the same formal language used for the requirements specification. It allows AssetVerifier to reuse its SMT solver to verify that the annotated C code satisfies the corresponding requirements.

DragonflyME supports modeling using a UML profile a virtual prototype PL of a real-time embedded system PL. The variability model of the PL is imported from an external tool such as pure::variants from pure-systems. For a given PL configuration, DragonflyME can generate the structural code of a virtual prototype allowing to run performance tests of the configuration.

KernelHaven supports the incremental computation of a great variety of PL quality metrics after each commit which affects the feature model and variable assets of the PL. It also allows the verification of the consistency between an abstract feature model and its operationalization in C code by #ifdef statements in C pre-processor files. It relies on a SAT solver to perform this verification task.

VariaMos supports the computation of quality metrics defined over variability models following an arbitrary meta-model. It also supports the detection of feature model defects such as dead features, redundant features, false optional feature and false and void feature models. For this task, it relies on a finite domain constraint solver.

The overall approach is supported modeling tools such as Modelio, requirements tools including REUSE tool set, and commercial product line engineering tool - pure::variants.

## 4 Results of the First Evaluation Phase and Outstanding Challenges

The REVaMP$^2$ project has provided the first set of results that were evaluated by the industrial partners providing the Use Cases (UCs). The primary goal for this initial evaluation was to depict the relationships between the different Use Case providers and Technology providers to enhance the SIS PL methods and tools as we know them today and to identify the gaps.

One of the main advantages that we could identify from the beginning of the project is the variety of industrial contributors providing the needs of different industries such as Aerospace, Automotive, Electronics. Those needs are addressed by a number of service, technology providers from academia and industry. This variety provides additional value to the solution that is to be applicable to any interested organization outside the project.

The analysis performed during the project illustrates a solution addressing the most common needs identified by the industry. The key assets that have been considered to evaluate the framework status are two, firstly Use Case Software Demonstrators, in which industry providers showcase the industrial challenges for PLE and possible solutions implemented with the help of one or several REVaMP$^2$ technology providers.

Use Case providers categorised their requirements into different typologies, so that the requirements could be mapped to a related technology to address the PLE challenges. We have identified more than 150 requirements from the first evaluation of the use cases, which has been continuously evolving to ensure the feasibility of the needs established at first in each of the UC. In Fig. 4 the distribution of these requirements among the most relevant typologies is illustrated.

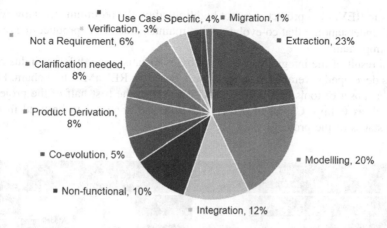

**Fig. 4.** Distribution of the main type of requirements from Use Cases satisfied by the technology demonstrators.

The abovementioned distribution of requirements among the different types is the starting point for the allocation of requirements from the UC into the different capabilities covered by the technology providers. The results of this analysis is illustrated in Fig. 5.

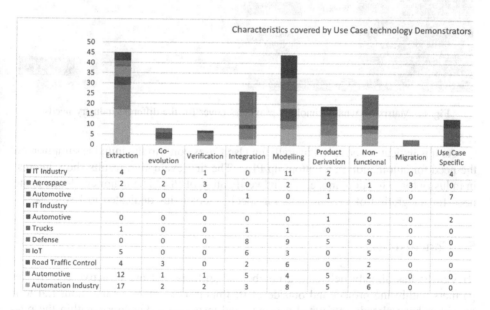

| | Extraction | Co-evolution | Verification | Integration | Modelling | Product Derivation | Non-functional | Migration | Use Case Specific |
|---|---|---|---|---|---|---|---|---|---|
| ■ IT Industry | 4 | 0 | 1 | 0 | 11 | 2 | 0 | 0 | 4 |
| ■ Aerospace | 2 | 2 | 3 | 0 | 2 | 0 | 1 | 3 | 0 |
| ■ Automotive | 0 | 0 | 0 | 1 | 0 | 1 | 0 | 0 | 7 |
| ■ IT Industry | | | | | | | | | |
| ■ Automotive | 0 | 0 | 0 | 0 | 0 | 1 | 0 | 0 | 2 |
| ■ Trucks | 1 | 0 | 0 | 1 | 1 | 0 | 0 | 0 | 0 |
| ■ Defense | 0 | 0 | 0 | 8 | 9 | 5 | 9 | 0 | 0 |
| ▩ IoT | 5 | 0 | 0 | 6 | 3 | 0 | 5 | 0 | 0 |
| ■ Road Traffic Control | 4 | 3 | 0 | 2 | 6 | 0 | 2 | 0 | 0 |
| ■ Automotive | 12 | 1 | 1 | 5 | 4 | 5 | 2 | 0 | 0 |
| ▩ Automation Industry | 17 | 2 | 2 | 3 | 8 | 5 | 6 | 0 | 0 |

**Fig. 5.** Distribution of the main characteristics covered by Use Case technology demonstrators.

The requirements distribution clearly indicates the focus on challenges in extraction of the PL. In addition, the modelling is second large category. The co-evolution, one of the axes in REVaMP² project, was not highlighted by the requirements. However, it is a global understanding that co-evolution, i.e. maintenance of the product line over time is very important.

As a result of the integration of technologies to satisfy the different industry need, partners developed several UC Demonstrators based on REVaMP² tool chain. Figure 6 depicts a subset of tools used in several Use Cases in the first half of the project. The tools such as Eclipse Capra, FLIMEA and Jittac are analysed to be used in the following stages of the project.

| USE CASE provider → / TECHNOLOGY provider | Automation Industry | Automotive | Road Traffic Control | IoT | Trucks | IT Industry |
|---|---|---|---|---|---|---|
| BUT4Reuse (Sorbonne University) | Extraction | | Extraction | | | Extraction |
| C Code Verifier (Scania and KTH) | | | Modelling and/or Visualiz | | Modelling and/or Visualization | |
| Crystal Bulb (Magillem) | | | | Extraction / Verification | | |
| Eclipse Capra (Univ. of Gothenburg) | TBD | | TBD | TBD | | |
| FeDeV-TS (ScopeSET) | Modelling and/or Visualiz | | | | | |
| FLIMEA (USJ) | TBD | | | | | |
| FINALIsT2 (ABB) | Extraction | | | | | |
| Jittac (Karlstad University) | TBD | | | | | |
| KernelHaven (SUH) | Verification | Extraction | | | | |
| M-XRAY (MES) | | | | | | |
| pure::variants-OMACC Exporter (Bosch) | | Modelling and/or Visualization | | | | |
| ReVaMP2 Plugin (TRC) | | | Verification | | | Extraction / Verification |
| VEXA (FZI) | Extraction | TBD | | | | |

**Fig. 6.** Matrix on what technology providers cover for the different industry needs.

As it is indicated above, on overall, the Use Cases confirm the initial assumption on the need for automation in a bottom-up PLE. The first evaluation results show interest in industry for extraction, modelling and verification of PLs. The major challenge is the need for integration of various tools for specific toolchains dedicated to Use Cases.

## 5   Conclusions

REVaMP² has already delivered a number of artifacts that are in active use by the partners within the project and outside of it. Importantly, many of the industrial tool providers have already integrated concepts and technology developed within the project into their offerings. Model Engineering Solutions MX-RAY [14] has, e.g., been extended to automatically extract architectural assets from the analysed models. Likewise, Siemens Industry Software has increased the technology readiness level of the product line support in LMS Imagine.Lab [17] for mechatronic system simulation.

The partners within the project are also working on new offerings for their customers or for internal use. ScopeSet is working on providing state-of-the-art feature and feature dependency visualisation capabilities based on technology developed in REVaMP². Automotive and Industrial control partners have developed specialised internal tools during the project that support engineers with constructing safety arguments for a product line and with feature location in C/C++ codebases respectively.

Furthermore, work has been conducted on several open source projects that provide reverse engineering capabilities or supporting functionality. One notable example is *BUT4Reuse* [9] which provides commonality and variability analysis, feature identification, feature location, feature constraints discovery, feature model synthesis and other functionality. *KernelHaven* [10] is a powerful tool suite for analysing product lines that, among many other things, can identify unused code and configuration mismatches. *VariaMos* [16] supports its users in the modeling of product lines and the analysis of these models. *Eclipse Capra* [18] supports traceability between the assets of a product line and thus ties feature, source code, models, and test together, thus enabling change impact analysis and improved program comprehension. *Revamp2Plug-in* [15] provides wide functionalities from identifying variability and commonality in requirements to measuring Consistency and completeness quality of the assets involved in the product.

REVaMP² has also produced a number of notable project deliverables [19], for instance an overview of the state of the art of practices and tools for product line reengineering. Of course, the project partners are also very active in the scientific community. With more than 50 publications, the project has had a significant impact on the state of the art, with notable publications at ASE [20], Isola [21], MODELS [22] as well as in IST [22, 23], TSE [24] and many others. Members of the project have also organised the main scientific event of the product line engineering community, SPLC in Gothenburg in 2018, with well over 100 participants and workshops and tutorials geared directly towards the topics of the projects.

Finally, the REVaMP² partners pure-systems, Thales, KTH, and Siemens are driving the standardisation of the *Variability Exchange Language* (VEL) in the context of OASIS [25]. They are joined by Dassault Systems, Intel, Accenture and PTC in the preparation of a standardised way to exchange variability information between different tools. This illustrates the relevance and impact of the results of REVaMP² beyond the project consortium and serves as an example of how the project results are disseminated to other interested parties.

**Acknowledgement.** This work was partially supported by the ITEA3 15010 REVaMP² project: FUI the Ile-de-France region and BPI in France, by Vinnova Sweden, and CDTI in Spain.

# References

1. Sadovykh, A., Bagnato, A., Robin, J., Viehl, A., Ziadi, T., Martinez, J.: REVAMP: challenges and innovation roadmap for variability management in round-trip engineering of software-intensive systems. Revue Genie Logiciel **120**, 32–36 (2017)

2. Martinez, J., Ziadi, T., Bissyandé, T.F., Klein, J., Le Traon, Y.: Bottom-up adoption of software product lines. In: Proceedings of the 19th International Conference on Software Product Line - SPLC 2015 (2015)
3. Apel, S., Batory, D., Kästner, C., Saake, G.: Feature-Oriented Software Product Lines: Concepts and Implementation. Springer, Heidelberg (2013). https://doi.org/10.1007/978-3-642-37521-7
4. Krueger, C.W.: Easing the transition to software mass customization. In: van der Linden, F. (ed.) PFE 2001. LNCS, vol. 2290, pp. 282–293. Springer, Heidelberg (2002). https://doi.org/10.1007/3-540-47833-7_25
5. van der Linden, F. (ed.): PFE 2001. LNCS, vol. 2290. Springer, Heidelberg (2002). https://doi.org/10.1007/3-540-47833-7
6. Kastner, C., Dreiling, A., Ostermann, K.: Variability mining: consistent semi-automatic detection of product-line features. IEEE Trans. Softw. Eng. 40(1), 67–82 (2014)
7. Berger, T., et al.: A survey of variability modeling in industrial practice. In: Proceedings of the Seventh International Workshop on Variability Modelling of Software-intensive Systems - VaMoS 2013 (2013)
8. Dubinsky, Y., Rubin, J., Berger, T., Duszynski, S., Becker, M., Czarnecki, K.: An exploratory study of cloning in industrial software product lines. In: 2013 17th European Conference on Software Maintenance and Reengineering (2013)
9. BUT4Reuse. https://but4reuse.github.io/. Accessed 26 June 2019
10. KernelHaven. https://github.com/KernelHaven/KernelHaven. Accessed 26 June 2019
11. Buckley, J., Mooney, S., Rosik, J., Ali, N.: JITTAC: a just-in-time tool for architectural consistency. In: 2013 35th International Conference on Software Engineering (ICSE) (2013)
12. Tom Sawyer Visualization. https://www.tomsawyer.com/products/visualization/. Accessed 26 June 2019
13. Pure-systems - product line and variant management tools. https://www.pure-systems.com/products/pure-variants-9.html. Accessed 26 June 2019
14. MES M-XRAY: consistent metrics of models - MES. https://model-engineers.com/en/quality-tools/mxray/. Accessed 26 June 2019
15. The REUSE company. https://www.reusecompany.com/
16. SPLA. https://github.com/SPLA/VARIAMOS. Accessed 26 June 2019
17. Simcenter system simulation. https://www.plm.automation.siemens.com/global/fr/products/simcenter/simcenter-system-simulation.html. Accessed 26 June 2019
18. Swart, S.: Eclipse capra, 28 July 2016. https://projects.eclipse.org/projects/modeling.capra. Accessed 26 June 2019
19. REVAMP2 projects public deliverables. http://www.revamp2-project.eu/publications/public-project-results
20. Mukelabai, M., Nešić, D., Maro, S., Berger, T., Steghöfer, J.-P.: Tackling combinatorial explosion: a study of industrial needs and practices for analyzing highly configurable systems. In: Proceedings of the 33rd ACM/IEEE International Conference on Automated Software Engineering - ASE 2018 (2018)
21. Nyberg, M., Gurov, D., Lidström, C., Rasmusson, A., Westman, J.: Formal verification in automotive industry: enablers and obstacles. In: Margaria, T., Steffen, B. (eds.) ISoLA 2018. LNCS, vol. 11247, pp. 139–158. Springer, Cham (2018). https://doi.org/10.1007/978-3-030-03427-6_14
22. Ballarín, M., Marcén, A.C., Pelechano, V., Cetina, C.: Measures to report the location problem of model fragment location. In: Proceedings of the 21th ACM/IEEE International Conference on Model Driven Engineering Languages and Systems – MODELS 2018 (2018)

23. El-Sharkawy, S., Yamagishi-Eichler, N., Schmid, K.: Metrics for analyzing variability and its implementation in software product lines: a systematic literature review. Inf. Softw. Technol. **106**, 1–30 (2019)
24. Passos, L., et al.: A study of feature scattering in the Linux Kernel. IEEE Trans. Softw. Eng. 1 (2018)
25. OASIS Variability Exchange Language (VEL) TC | OASIS. https://www.oasis-open.org/committees/tc_home.php?wg_abbrev=vel. Accessed 26 June 2019

# Author Index

Printed in the United States
By Bookmasters